ENGLISH BUSINESS
DICTIONARY

ENGLISH
BUSINESS
DICTIONARY

P. H. Collin

PETER COLLIN PUBLISHING

First published in Great Britain 1986
by Peter Collin Publishing Ltd
31 Teddington Park, Teddington, Middlesex

ISBN 0 948549 00 9

Computer Typeset in Helvetica, Times and Typewriter by SB Datagraphics,
Colchester

Printed by William Clowes, Beccles

PREFACE

This dictionary gives the user the basic business vocabulary used in both British and American English. The dictionary contains 4,500 words and phrases which cover all aspects of business life from the office to the Stock Exchange and the international trade fair. Each word is clearly defined in very simple English (only 470 words are used in the definitions which do not appear in the dictionary as main words); many examples are given to show how the words are used in normal contexts, and the examples themselves are "translated" into simple English. Some entries have simple grammar notes to remind the user of irregular word forms, constructions used with particular words, differences between American and British usage and other useful points. Because English is a world language of business, we have included short quotations to show how it is used in various countries round the world. These quotations are from newspapers and magazines published in England, the United States, Canada, Australia, Hong Kong and Nigeria.

At the back of the book, the user will find a supplement giving useful information about numbers (how to write and speak them), telephoning, writing business letters, understanding financial documents, together with a list of important world currencies.

I would like to thank the many people who have helped in the editing of this dictionary, in particular Derek Beattie and Françoise Collin, who read the early drafts and made a great many helpful suggestions; Lucy McCullagh who read the final version and added the grammatical notes; Tony Thorne, who wrote the supplement; and Peter Cartwright who was responsible for the design.

Aa

AAA letters indicating that a share *or* bond *or* bank is very reliable; **these bonds have an AAA rating**
NOTE: you say 'triple A'

"A" shares *plural noun* ordinary shares with limited voting rights

A1 *adjective* **(a)** best; **we sell only goods in A1 condition (b) ship which is A1 at Lloyd's** = ship which is in best condition according to Lloyd's Register
◇ **A1, A2, A3, A4, A5** *noun* standard international sizes of paper; **you must photocopy the spreadsheet on A3 paper; we must order some more A4 headed notepaper**

abandon *verb* **(a)** to give up *or* not to continue; **we abandoned the idea of setting up a New York office; the development programme had to be abandoned when the company ran out of cash; to abandon an action** = to give up a court case **(b)** to leave (something); **the crew abandoned the sinking ship**
◇ **abandonment** *noun* act of giving something up; **abandonment of a ship** = giving up a ship and cargo to the underwriters against payment for total loss

abatement *noun* act of reducing; **tax abatement** = reduction of tax

abroad *adverb* to or in another country; **the consignment of cars was shipped abroad last week; the chairman is abroad on business; half of our profit comes from sales abroad**

absence *noun* not being at work *or* at a meeting; **in the absence of** = when someone is not there; **in the absence of the chairman, his deputy took the chair; leave of absence** = being allowed to be absent from work; **he asked for leave of absence to visit his mother in hospital**
NOTE: no plural
◇ **absent** *adjective* not at work *or* not at a meeting; **ten of the workers are absent with flu; the chairman is absent in Holland on business**
◇ **absentee** *noun* worker who stays away from work for no good reason
◇ **absenteeism** *noun* staying away from work for no good reason; **absenteeism is high in the week before Christmas; the rate of absenteeism *or* the absenteeism rate always increases in fine weather**
NOTE: no plural

absolute *adjective* complete *or* total; **absolute monopoly** = situation where only one producer or supplier produces or supplies something; **the company has an absolute monopoly of imports of French wine**
◇ **absolutely** *adverb* completely; **we are absolutely tied to our suppliers' schedules**

absorb *verb* **(a)** to take in a small item so as to form part of a larger one; **to absorb a surplus** = to take back surplus stock so that it does not affect a business; **overheads have absorbed all our profits** = all our profits have gone in paying overhead expenses; **to absorb a loss by a subsidiary** = to write a subsidiary company's loss into the main accounts **(b) business which has been absorbed by a competitor** = a small business which has been made part of a larger one

◇ **absorption** *noun* making a smaller business part of a larger one
NOTE: no plural

abstract *noun* short form of a report *or* document; **to make an abstract of the company accounts**

a/c *or* **acc** = ACCOUNT

accelerated *adjective* made faster; **accelerated depreciation** = system of depreciation which reduces the value of assets at a high rate in the early years to encourage companies, because of tax advantages, to invest in new equipment

accept *verb* **(a)** to take something which is being offered; **to accept a bill** = to sign a bill of exchange to indicate that you promise to pay it; **to accept delivery of a shipment** = to take goods into the warehouse officially when they are delivered **(b)** to say "yes" *or* to agree to something; **she accepted the offer of a job in Australia; he accepted £200 for the car**

◇ **acceptable** *adjective* which can be accepted; **the offer is not acceptable to both parties**

◇ **acceptance** *noun* **(a)** signing a bill of exchange to show that you agree to pay it; **to present a bill for acceptance** = for payment by the person who has accepted it; **acceptance house** *or* US **acceptance bank** = ACCEPTING HOUSE **(b) acceptance of an offer** = agreeing to an offer; **to give an offer a conditional acceptance** = to accept provided that certain things happen *or* that certain terms apply; **we have his letter of acceptance** = we have received a letter from him accepting the offer; **acceptance sampling** = testing a small part of a batch to see if the whole batch is good enough

◇ **accepting house** *noun* firm which accepts bills of exchange (i.e. promises to pay them) and is paid a commission for this

access 1 *noun* **to have access to something** = to be able to obtain *or* reach something; **he has access to large amounts of venture capital; access time** = time taken by a computer to find data stored in it
NOTE: no plural
2 *verb* to call up (data) which is stored in a computer; **she accessed the address file on the computer**

accident *noun* something unpleasant which happens by chance (such as the crash of a plane); **industrial accident** = accident which takes place at work; **accident insurance** = insurance which will pay when an accident takes place

accommodation *noun* **(a)** money lent for a short time **(b) to reach an accommodation with creditors** = to agree terms for settlement **(c) accommodation bill** = bill of exchange where the person signing is helping someone to raise a loan **(d)** place to live; **visitors have difficulty in finding hotel accommodation during the summer; they are living in furnished accommodation; accommodation address** = address used for receiving messages but which is not the real address of the company
NOTE: no plural in GB English, but US English can have **accommodations** for meaning (d)

QUOTE: an airline ruling requires airlines to provide a free night's hotel accommodation for full fare passengers in transit
Business Traveller
QUOTE: any non-resident private landlord can let furnished or unfurnished accommodation to a tenant
Times
QUOTE: the airline providing roomy accommodations at below-average fares
Dun's Business Month

accompany *verb* to go with; **the chairman came to the meeting accompanied by the finance director; they sent a formal letter of complaint, accompanied by an invoice for damage**
NOTE: accompanied **by** something

accordance *noun* **in accordance with** = in agreement with *or* according to; **in accordance with your instructions we have deposited the money in your current account; I am submitting the claim for damages in accordance with the advice of our legal advisers**

◇ **according to** *preposition* as someone says or writes; **the computer was installed according to the manufacturer's instructions**

◇ **accordingly** *adverb* in agreement with what has been decided; **we have received your letter and have altered the contract accordingly**

> QUOTE: the budget targets for employment and growth are within reach according to the latest figures *Australian Financial Review*

account 1 *noun* (a) record of money paid *or* owed; **please send me your account** *or* **a detailed** *or* **an itemized account**; **expense account** = money which a businessman is allowed by his company to spend on travelling and entertaining clients in connection with his business; **he charged his hotel bill to his expense account** (b) (*in a shop*) arrangement which a customer has to buy goods and pay for them at a later date (usually the end of the month); **to have an account** *or* **a charge account** *or* **a credit account with Harrods**; **put it on my account** *or* **charge it to my account**; (*of a customer*) **to open an account** = to ask a shop to supply goods which you will pay at a later date; (*of a shop*) **to open an account** *or* **to close an account** = to start *or* to stop supplying a customer on credit; **to settle an account** = to pay all the money owed on an account; **to stop an account** = to stop supplying a customer until he has paid what he owes; **on account** = as part of a total bill; **to pay money on account** = to pay to settle part of a bill; **advance on account** = money paid as a part payment (c) customer who does a large amount of business with a firm and has an account; **he is one of our largest accounts; our salesmen call on their best accounts twice a month; account executive** = employee who looks after certain customers *or* who is the link between certain customers and his company (d) **the accounts of a business** *or* **a company's accounts** = detailed record of a company's financial affairs; **to keep the accounts** = to write each sum of money in the account book; **the accountant's job is to enter all the money received in the accounts; annual accounts** = accounts prepared at the end of a financial year; **management accounts** = financial information (sales, expenditure, credit, and profitability) prepared

for a manager so that he can take decisions; **profit and loss account** = accounts for a company with expenditure and income balanced to show a final profit or loss; **accounts department** = department in a company which deals with money paid, received, borrowed or owed; **accounts manager** = manager of an accounts department; **accounts payable** = money owed by a company; **accounts receivable** = money owed to a company (e) **bank account** *or* **US banking account** = arrangement to keep money in a bank; **building society account; savings bank account; Girobank account; Lloyds account; he has an account with Lloyds; I have an account with the Halifax Building Society; to put money in(to) your account; to take money out of your account** *or* **to withdraw money from your account; budget account** = bank account where you plan income and expenditure to allow for periods when expenditure is high; **current account** *or* **cheque account** *or* **US checking account** = account which pays no interest but from which the customer can withdraw money when he wants by writing cheques; **deposit account** = account which pays interest but on which notice usually has to be given to withdraw money; **external account** = account in a British bank of someone who is living in another country; **frozen account** = account where the money cannot by used or moved because of a court order; **joint account** = account for two people; **most married people have joint accounts so that they can each take money out when they want it; overdrawn account** = account where you have taken out more money than you have put in (i.e. where the bank is lending you money); **savings account** = account where you put money in regularly and which pays interest, often at a higher rate than a deposit account; **to open an account** = to start an account by putting money in; **she opened an account with the Halifax Building Society; to close an account** = to take all money out of a bank account and stop the account; **he closed his account with Lloyds** (f) (*Stock Exchange*) period of credit (usually fourteen days) at the end of which you must pay for shares bought; **account day** = day on which shares which have been bought must be paid for; **share prices rose at the** end of the account *or* the account end **(g)** notice; **to take account of inflation** *or* **to take inflation into account** = to assume that there will be a certain percentage inflation when making calculations **2** *verb* **to account for** = to explain and record a money deal; **to account for a loss** *or* a discrepancy; **the reps have to account for all their expenses to the sales manager**

◇ **accountancy** *noun* work of an accountant; **he is studying accountancy** *or* **he is an accountancy student**
NOTE: no plural

◇ **accountant** *noun* person who keeps a company's accounts *or* person who advises a company on its finances *or* person who examines accounts; **the chief accountant of a manufacturing group; I send all my income tax queries to my accountant; certified accountant** = accountant who has passed the professional examinations and is a member of the Association of Certified Accountants; *US* **certified public accountant** = accountant who has passed professional examinations; **chartered accountant** = accountant who has passed the professional examinations and is a member of the Institute of Chartered Accountants; **cost accountant** = accountant who gives managers information about their business costs; **management accountant** = accountant who prepares financial information for managers so that they can take decisions

◇ **accounting** *noun* work of recording money paid, received, borrowed or owed; **accounting machine; accounting methods** *or* **accounting procedures; accounting system; accounting period** = period usually covered by a firm's accounts; **cost accounting** = preparing special accounts of manufacturing and sales costs; **current cost accounting** = method of accounting which notes the cost of replacing assets at current prices, rather than valuing assets at their original cost
NOTE: no plural

accredited *adjective* (agent) who is appointed by a company to act on its behalf

accrual *noun* gradual increase by addition; **accrual of interest** = automatic addition of interest to capital
◇ **accrue** *verb* to increase and be due for payment at a later date; **interest accrues from the beginning of the month; accrued interest is added quarterly; accrued dividend** = dividend earned since the last dividend was paid

acct = ACCOUNT

accumulate *verb* to grow larger by adding; **to allow dividends to accumulate; accumulated profit** = profit which is not paid as dividend but is taken over into the accounts of the following year

accurate *adjective* correct; **the sales department made an accurate forecast of sales; the designers produced an accurate copy of the plan**
◇ **accurately** *adverb* correctly; **the second quarter's drop in sales was accurately forecast by the computer**

accuse *verb* to say that someone has committed a crime; **she was accused of stealing from the petty cash box; he was accused of industrial espionage**
NOTE: you accuse someone **of** a crime or **of** doing something

achieve *verb* to succeed in doing something *or* to do something successfully; **the company has achieved great success in the Far East; we achieved all our objectives in 1985**

acknowledge *verb* to tell a sender that a letter *or* package *or* shipment has arrived; **he has still not acknowledged my letter of the 24th; we acknowledge receipt of your letter of June 14th**
◇ **acknowledgement** *noun* act of acknowledging; **she sent an acknowledgement of receipt; they sent a letter of acknowledgement**

acquire *verb* to buy; **to acquire a company**

◇ **acquirer** *noun* person *or* company which buys something

◇ **acquisition** *noun* thing bought; act of getting *or* buying something; **the chocolate factory is his latest acquisition; data acquisition** *or* **acquisition of data** = obtaining and classifying data

acre *noun* measure of the area of land (= 0.45 hectares)
NOTE: the plural is used with figures, except before a noun: **he has bought a farm of 250 acres** *or* **he has bought a 250 acre farm**

across-the-board *adjective* applying to everything *or* everyone; **an across-the-board price increase**

act 1 *noun* **(a)** law passed by a parliament which must be obeyed by the people; *GB* **Companies Act** = Act which rules how companies should do their business; **Health and Safety at Work Act** = Act which rules how the health of workers should be protected by the companies they work for; **Finance Act** = annual Act of Parliament which gives the government power to raise taxes as proposed in the budget **(b) act of God** = something you do not expect to happen, and which cannot be avoided (such as storms *or* floods) 2 *verb* **(a)** to work; **to act as an agent for an American company; to act for someone** *or* **to act on someone's behalf (b)** to do something; **the board will have to act quickly if the company's losses are going to be reduced; the lawyers are acting on our instructions; to act on a letter** = to do what a letter asks to be done

◇ **acting** *adjective* working in place of someone for a short time; **acting manager; the Acting Chairman**

◇ **action** *noun* **(a)** thing which has been done; **to take action** = to do something; **you must take action if you want to stop people cheating you (b) direct action** = strike or go-slow by the workforce; **to take industrial action** = to do something (usually to go on strike) to show that you are not happy with conditions at work **(c)** case in a law court where a person or company sues another person or company; **to take legal action** = to sue someone; **action for damages; action for libel** *or* **libel action; to bring an action for damages against someone; civil action** = case

brought by a person *or* company against someone who has done them wrong; **criminal action** = case brought by the state against someone who is charged with a crime

◇ **active** *adjective* busy; **active partner** = partner who works in the company; **an active demand for oil shares; oil shares are very active; an active day on the Stock Exchange; business is active**

◇ **actively** *adverb* in a busy way; **the company is actively recruiting new personnel**

◇ **activity** *noun* being active *or* busy; **a low level of business activity; there was a lot of activity on the Stock Exchange; activity chart** = plan showing work which has been done so that it can be compared to the plan of work to be done; **monthly activity report** = report by a department on what has been done during the past month
NOTE: no plural

QUOTE: preliminary indications of the level of business investment and activity during the March quarter will provide a good picture of economic activity in 1985 *Australian Financial Review*

actual 1 *adjective* real *or* correct; **what is the actual cost of one unit? the actual figures for directors' expenses are not shown to the shareholders** 2 *plural noun* real figures; **these figures are the actuals for 1984**

actuary *noun* person employed by an insurance company to calculate premiums

◇ **actuarial** *adjective* calculated by an actuary; **the premiums are worked out according to actuarial calculations; actuarial tables** = lists showing how long people of certain ages are likely to live, used to calculate life assurance premiums

ad *noun* = ADVERTISEMENT

add *verb* **(a)** to put figures together to make a total; **to add interest to the capital; interest is added monthly (b)** to put things together to make a large group; **we are adding to the sales force; they have added two new products to their range; this all adds to the company's costs** = this makes the company's costs higher

◇ **add up** *verb* to put several figures together to make a total; **to add up a column of figures; the figures do not add up** = the total given is not correct

◇ **add up to** *verb* to make a total; **the total expenditure adds up to more than £1,000**

◇ **adding** *noun* which adds *or* which makes additions; **an adding machine**

◇ **addition** *noun* **(a)** thing or person added; **the management has stopped all additions to the staff; we are exhibiting several additions to our product line; the marketing director is the latest addition to the board (b) in addition to** = added to *or* as well as; **there are twelve registered letters to be sent in addition to this packet (c)** putting numbers together; **you don't need a calculator to do simple addition**

◇ **additional** *adjective* extra which is added; **additional costs; additional charges; additional clauses to a contract; additional duty will have to be paid**

address 1 *noun* details of number, street and town where an office is or a person lives; **my business address and phone number are printed on the card; accommodation address** = address used for receiving messages but which is not the real address of the company; **cable address** = short address for sending cables; **forwarding address** = address to which a person's mail can be sent on; **home address** = address of a house or flat where someone lives; **please send the documents to my home address; address list** = list of addresses; **we keep an address list of two thousand addresses in Europe 2** *verb* **(a)** to write the details of an address on an envelope, etc.; **to address a letter** *or* **a parcel; please address your enquiries to the manager; a letter addressed to the managing director; an incorrectly addressed package (b)** to speak; **to address a meeting**

◇ **addressee** *noun* person to whom a letter *or* package is addressed

◇ **addressing machine** *noun* machine which puts addresses on envelopes automatically

adequate *adjective* large enough; **to operate without adequate cover** = to act without being completely protected by insurance

adjourn *verb* to stop a meeting for a period; **to adjourn a meeting; the chairman adjourned the meeting until three o'clock; the meeting adjourned at midday**

◇ **adjournment** *noun* act of adjourning; **he proposed the adjournment of the meeting**

adjudicate *verb* to give a judgement between two parties in law; to decide a legal problem; **to adjudicate a claim; to adjudicate in a dispute; he was adjudicated bankrupt** = he was declared legally bankrupt

◇ **adjudication** *noun* act of giving a judgement *or* of deciding a legal problem; **adjudication order** *or* **adjudication of bankruptcy** = order by a court making someone bankrupt; **adjudication tribunal** = group which adjudicates in industrial disputes

◇ **adjudicator** *noun* person who gives a decision on a problem; **an adjudicator in an industrial dispute**

adjust *verb* to change something to fit new conditions; **to adjust prices to take account of inflation; prices are adjusted for inflation**

◇ **adjuster** *noun* person who calculates losses for an insurance company; **average adjuster** = person who calculates how much of an insurance is to be paid

◇ **adjustment** *noun* act of adjusting; slight change; **tax adjustment; wage adjustment; to make an adjustment to salaries; adjustment of prices to take account of rising costs; average adjustment** = calculation of the share of cost of damage or loss of a ship

◇ **adjustor** *noun* = ADJUSTER

QUOTE: inflation-adjusted GNP moved up at a 1.3% annual rate   *Fortune*
QUOTE: Saudi Arabia will no longer adjust its production to match short-term supply with demand   *Economist*

adman *noun informal* man who works in advertising; **the admen are using balloons as promotional material**

admin *noun informal* **(a)** work of administration, especially paperwork; **all this admin work takes a lot of my time; there is too much admin in this job; admin costs**

seem to be rising each quarter; the admin people have sent the report back (b) administration staff; **admin say they need the report immediately**
NOTE: no plural; as a group of people it can have a plural verb

◊ **administer** *verb* to organize *or* to manage; **he administers a large pension fund**; *US* **administered price** = price fixed by a manufacturer which cannot be varied by a retailer

◊ **administration** *noun* organization *or* control *or* management of a company; **the expenses of the administration** *or* **administration expenses** = costs of management, not including production, marketing or distribution costs; **letters of administration** = letter given by a court to allow someone to deal with the estate of a person who has died

◊ **administrative** *adjective* referring to administration; **administrative details**; **administrative expenses**

◊ **administrator** *noun* (a) person who directs the work of other employees in a business (b) person appointed by a court to manage the affairs of someone who dies without leaving a will

admission *noun* (a) allowing someone to go in; **there is a £1 admission charge**; **admission is free on presentation of this card**; **free admission on Sundays** (b) saying that something really happened; **he had to resign after his admission that he had passed information to the rival company**

admit *verb* (a) to allow someone to go in; **children are not admitted to the bank**; **old age pensioners are admitted at half price** (b) to say that something is correct *or* to say that something really happened; **the chairman admitted he had taken the cash from the company's safe**
NOTE: admitting - admitted

◊ **admittance** *noun* allowing someone to go in; **no admittance except on business**
NOTE: no plural

adopt *verb* to agree to (something) *or* to accept (something); **to adopt a resolution**; **the proposals were adopted unanimously**

ad valorem *phrase* showing that a tax is calculated according to the value of the goods taxed; **ad valorem duty; ad valorem tax**

advance 1 *noun* (a) money paid as a loan or as a part of a payment to be made later; **bank advance; a cash advance; to receive an advance from the bank; an advance on account; to make an advance of £100 to someone; to pay someone an advance against a security; can I have an advance of £50 against next month's salary?** (b) **in advance** = early *or* before something happens; **to pay in advance; freight payable in advance; price fixed in advance** (c) early; **advance booking; advance payment; you must give seven days' advance notice of withdrawals from the account** (d) increase; **advance in trade; advance in prices** 2 *verb* (a) to lend; **the bank advanced him £10,000 against the security of his house** (b) to increase; **prices generally advanced on the stock market** (c) to make something happen earlier; **the date of the AGM has been advanced to May 10th; the meeting with the German distributors has been advanced from 11.00 to 09.30**

advantage *noun* something useful which may help you to be successful; **fast typing is an advantage in a secretary; knowledge of two foreign languages is an advantage; there is no advantage in arriving at the exhibition before it opens**; **to take advantage of something** = to use something which helps you

adverse *adjective* bad *or* not helpful; **adverse balance of trade** = situation when a country imports more than it exports; **adverse trading conditions** = bad conditions for trade

advertise *verb* to announce that something is for sale *or* that a job is vacant *or* that a service is offered; **to advertise a vacancy; to advertise for a secretary; to advertise a new product**

◊ **ad** *noun informal* = ADVERTISEMENT **we put an ad in the paper; she answered an ad in the paper; he found his job through an ad in the paper; classified ads** *or* **small ads** *or* **want ads** = advertisements listed in a newspaper under special headings (like "property for sale","jobs wanted"); **look** in the small ads to see if anyone has a computer for sale; **coupon ad** = advertisement with a form attached, which is to be cut out and returned to the advertiser with your name and address for further information; **display ad** = advertisement which is well designed to attract attention

◇ **advert** *noun* *GB* *informal* = ADVERTISEMENT **to put an advert in the paper; to answer an advert in the paper; classified adverts; display advert**

◇ **advertisement** *noun* notice which shows that something is for sale *or* that a service is offered *or* that someone wants something *or* that a job is vacant, etc.; **to put an advertisement in the paper; to answer an advertisement in the paper; classified advertisements** = advertisements listed in a newspaper under special headings (such as "property for sale" or "jobs wanted"); **display advertisement** = advertisement which is well designed to attract attention; **advertisement manager** = manager in charge of the advertisement section of a newspaper

◇ **advertiser** *noun* person *or* company which advertises; **the catalogue gives a list of advertisers**

◇ **advertising** *noun* business of announcing that something is for sale *or* of trying to persuade customers to buy a product or service; **she works in advertising; he has a job in advertising; advertising agent; advertising budget; advertising campaign; advertising agency** = office which plans, designs and manages advertising for other companies; **advertising manager** = manager in charge of advertising a company's products; **advertising rates** = amount of money charged for advertising space in a newspaper *or* advertising time on TV; **advertising space** = space in a newspaper set aside for advertisements; **to take advertising space in a paper** = to put an advertisement in a newspaper
NOTE: no plural

advice *noun* (a) **advice note** = written notice to a customer giving details of goods ordered and shipped but not yet delivered; **as per advice** = according to what is written on the advice note (b) opinion as to what action to take; **to take legal advice** = to ask a lawyer to say what should be

done; **the accountant's advice was to send the documents to the police; we sent the documents to the police on the advice of the accountant** *or* **we took the accountant's advice and sent the documents to the police**
NOTE: no plural

advise *verb* (a) to tell someone what has happened; **we are advised that the shipment will arrive next week** (b) to suggest to someone what should be done; **we are advised to take the shipping company to court; the accountant advised us to send the documents to the police**

◇ **advise against** *verb* to suggest that something should not be done; **the bank manager advised against closing the account; my stockbroker has advised against buying those shares**

◇ **adviser** *or* **advisor** *noun* person who suggests what should be done; **he is consulting the company's legal adviser; financial adviser** = person *or* company which gives advice on financial problems for a fee

◇ **advisory** *adjective* as an adviser; **he is acting in an advisory capacity; an advisory board** = a group of advisers

affair *noun* business *or* dealings; **are you involved in the copyright affair? his affairs were so difficult to understand that the lawyers had to ask accountants for advice**

affect *verb* to change *or* to have a bad effect on (something); **the new government regulations do not affect us; the company's sales in the Far East were seriously affected by the embargo**

QUOTE: the dollar depreciation has yet to affect the underlying inflation rate
Australian Financial Review

affiliated *adjective* connected with *or* owned by another company; **one of our affiliated companies**

affirmative *adjective* meaning "yes"; **the answer was in the affirmative** = the answer was yes; *US* **affirmative action program** = programme to avoid discrimination in employment
NOTE: the GB equivalent is "equal opportunities"

affluent *adjective* very rich; **we live in an affluent society**

afford *verb* to be able to pay *or* buy; **we could not afford the cost of two telephones; the company cannot afford the time to train new staff**
NOTE: only used after **can, cannot, could, could not, able to**

AFL-CIO = AMERICAN FEDERATION OF LABOR - CONGRESS OF INDUSTRIAL ORGANIZATIONS an organization linking US trade unions

afraid *adjective* sorry, because something has happened; **I am afraid there are no seats left on the flight to Amsterdam; we are afraid your order has been lost in the post**
NOTE: only used after **to be**

after-hours *adjective* **after-hours buying** *or* **selling** *or* **dealing** = buying *or* selling *or* dealing in shares after the Stock Exchange has officially closed for the day
◊ **after-sales service** *noun* service of a machine carried out by the seller for some time after the machine has been bought
◊ **after-tax profit** *noun* profit after tax has been deducted

against *preposition* relating to *or* part of; **to pay an advance against a security; can I have an advance against next month's salary? the bank advanced him £10,000 against the security of his house**

QUOTE: investment can be written off against the marginal rate of tax *Investors Chronicle*
QUOTE: the index for the first half of 1985 shows that the rate of inflation went down by about 12.9 per cent against the rate as at December last year *Business Times (Lagos)*

agency *noun* **(a)** office *or* job of representing another company in an area; **they signed an agency agreement** *or* **an agency contract; sole agency** = agreement to be the only person to represent a company *or* to sell a product in a certain area; **he has the sole agency for Ford cars (b)** office *or* business which arranges things for other companies; **advertising agency** = office which plans *or* designs and manages advertising for companies; **employment**

agency = office which finds jobs for staff; **estate agency** = office which arranges for the sale of properties; **news agency** = office which distributes news to newspapers and television stations; **travel agency** = office which arranges travel for customers
NOTE: plural is **agencies**

agenda *noun* list of things to be discussed at a meeting; **the conference agenda** *or* **the agenda of the conference; after two hours we were still discussing the first item on the agenda; the secretary put finance at the top of the agenda; the chairman wants two items removed from** *or* **taken off the agenda**

agent *noun* **(a)** person who represents a company *or* another person in an area; **to be the agent for IBM; sole agent** = person who has the sole agency for a company in an area; **he is the sole agent for Ford cars; agent's commission** = money (often a percentage of sales) paid to an agent **(b)** person in charge of an agency; **advertising agent; estate agent; travel agent; commission agent** = agent who is paid by commission, not by fee; **forwarding agent** = person *or* company which arranges shipping and customs documents; **insurance agent** = person who arranges insurance for clients; **land agent** = person who runs a farm *or* a large area of land for the owner **(c)** *US* **(business) agent** = chief local official of a trade union

aggregate *adjective* total *or* with everything added together; **aggregate output**

agio *noun* charge made for changing money of one currency into another

AGM *noun* = ANNUAL GENERAL MEETING

agree *verb* **(a)** to approve; **the auditors have agreed the accounts; the figures were agreed between the two parties; we have agreed the budgets for next year; terms of the contract are still to be agreed; he has agreed your prices (b)** to say yes *or* to accept; **it has been agreed that the lease will run for 25 years; after some discussion he agreed to our plan; the bank will never**

agree to lend the company £250,000; we all agreed on the plan NOTE: to agree **to** *or* **on** a plan **(c) to agree to do something** = to say that you will do something; **she agreed to be chairman; will the finance director agree to resign?**

◇ **agree with** *verb* **(a)** to say that your opinions are the same as someone else's; **I agree with the chairman that the figures are lower than normal (b)** to be the same as; **the auditors' figures do not agree with those of the accounts department**

◇ **agreed** *adjective* which has been accepted by everyone; **an agreed amount; on agreed terms**

◇ **agreement** *noun* contract between two parties which explains how they will act; **written agreement; unwritten** *or* **verbal agreement; to draw up** *or* **to draft an agreement; to break an agreement; to sign an agreement; to witness an agreement; an agreement has been reached** *or* **concluded** *or* come to; **to reach an agreement** *or* **to come to an agreement on prices** *or* **salaries; an international agreement on trade; collective wage agreement; an agency agreement; a marketing agreement; blanket agreement** = agreement which covers many different items; **exclusive agreement** = agreement where a company is appointed sole agent for a product in a market; **gentleman's agreement** = verbal agreement between two parties who trust each other

QUOTE: after three days of tough negotiations the company has reached agreement with its 1,200 unionized workers *Toronto Star*

agribusiness *noun* farming, and making products used by farmers
NOTE: no plural

agriculture *noun* use of land for growing crops *or* raising animals
NOTE: no plural

◇ **agricultural** *adjective* referring to agriculture *or* referring to farms; **agricultural co-operative** = farm run by groups of workers who are the owners and share the profits; **agricultural economist** = person who specializes in the study of finance and investment in agriculture; **Common Agricultural Policy** = agreement between members of the EEC to protect farmers by paying subsidies to fix prices of farm produce

ahead *adverb* in front of *or* better than; **we are already ahead of our sales forecast; the company has a lot of work ahead of it if it wants to increase its market share**

aim 1 *noun* something which you try to do; **one of our aims is to increase the quality of our products; the company has achieved all its aims** = the company has done all the things it had hoped to do **2** *verb* to try to do something; **we aim to be No. 1 in the market in two years' time; each salesman must aim to double his previous year's sales**

air 1 *noun* method of travelling *or* sending goods using aircraft; **to send a letter** *or* **a shipment by air; air carrier** = company which send cargo *or* passengers by air; **air forwarding** = arranging for goods to be shipped by air; **air letter** = special sheet of thin blue paper which when folded can be sent by air mail without an envelope **2** *verb* **to air a grievance** = to talk about *or* to discuss a grievance; **the management committee is useful because it allows the workers' representatives to air their grievances**

◇ **air cargo** *noun* goods sent by air

◇ **aircraft** *noun* machine which flies in the air, carrying passengers or cargo; **the airline has a fleet of ten commercial aircraft; the company is one of the most important American aircraft manufacturers; to charter an aircraft** = to hire an aircraft for a special purpose
NOTE: no plural: **one aircraft, two aircraft**

◇ **air freight** *noun* method of shipping goods in an aircraft; **to send a shipment by air freight; air freight charges** *or* **rates**

◇ **airfreight** *verb* to send goods by air; **to airfreight a consignment to Mexico; we airfreighted the shipment because our agent ran out of stock**

◇ **airline** *noun* company which carries passengers or cargo by air

◇ **airmail 1** *noun* way of sending letters *or* parcels by air; **to send a package by airmail; airmail charges have risen by 15%; airmail envelope** = very light envelope for sending airmail letters; **airmail sticker** = blue sticker with the words "by air mail" which can be stuck to an envelope or

packet to show it is being sent by air
NOTE: no plural
2 *verb* to send letters *or* parcels by air; **to airmail a document to New York**

◇ **airport** *noun* place where planes land and take off; **we leave from London Airport at 10.00; O'Hare Airport is the main airport for Chicago; airport bus =** bus which takes passenger to and from an airport; **airport tax =** tax added to the price of the air ticket to cover the cost of running an airport; **airport terminal =** main building at an airport where passengers arrive and depart

◇ **air terminal** *noun* building in a town where passengers meet to be taken by bus to an airport outside the town

◇ **airtight** *adjective* which does not allow air to get in; **the goods are packed in airtight containers**

◇ **airworthiness** *noun* being able and safe to fly; **certificate of airworthiness =** certificate to show that an aircraft is safe to fly
NOTE: no plural

all *adjective & pronoun* everything *or* everyone; **all (of) the managers attended the meeting; the salesman should know the prices of all the products he is selling**

◇ **all-in** *adjective* including everything; **all-in price** *or* **rate =** price which covers all items in a purchase (goods, delivery, tax, insurance)

allocate *verb* to divide (a sum of money) in various ways and share it out; **we allocate 10% of revenue to publicity; $2,500 was allocated to office furniture**

◇ **allocation** *noun* **(a)** dividing a sum of money in various ways; **allocation of capital; allocation of funds to a project (b) share allocation** *or* **allocation of shares =** spreading a small number of shares among a large number of people who have applied for them

allot *verb* to share out; **to allot shares =** to give a certain number of shares to people who have applied for them
NOTE: **allotting - allotted**

◇ **allotment** *noun* **(a)** sharing out funds by giving money to various departments; **allotment of funds to a project (b)** giving some shares in a new company to people

who have applied for them; **share allotment; payment in full on allotment; letter of allotment** *or* **allotment letter =** letter which tells someone who has applied for shares in a new company how many shares he has been allotted

all-out *adjective* complete *or* very serious; **the union called for an all-out strike; the personnel manager has launched an all-out campaign to get the staff to work on Friday afternoons**

allow *verb* **(a)** to say that someone can do something; **junior members of staff are not allowed to use the chairman's lift; the company allows all members of staff to take six days' holiday at Christmas (b)** to give; **to allow someone a discount; to allow 5% discount to members of staff; to allow 10% interest on large sums of money (c)** to agree *or* to accept legally; **to allow a claim** *or* **an appeal**

◇ **allow for** *verb* to give a discount for *or* to add an extra sum to cover something; **to allow for money paid in advance; to allow 10% for packing; delivery is not allowed for =** delivery charges are not included; **allow 28 days for delivery =** calculate that delivery will take at least 28 days

◇ **allowable** *adjective* legally accepted; **allowable expenses =** expenses which can be claimed against tax

◇ **allowance** *noun* **(a)** money which is given for a special reason; **travel allowance** *or* **travelling allowance; foreign currency allowance; cost-of-living allowance =** addition to normal salary to cover increases in the cost of living; **entertainment allowance =** money which a manager is allowed to spend each month on meals with visitors **(b)** part of an income which is not taxed; **allowances against tax** *or* **tax allowances; personal allowances; wife's earned income allowance =** tax allowance to be set against money earned by the wife of the main taxpayer **(c)** money removed in the form of a discount; **allowance for depreciation; allowance for exchange loss**

◇ **allowed time** *noun* paid time which the management agrees a worker can spend on rest *or* cleaning *or* meals, not working

---

QUOTE: most airlines give business class the same baggage allowance as first class
Business Traveller
QUOTE: the compensation plan includes base, incentive and car allowance totalling $50,000+
Globe and Mail (Toronto)

---

all-risks policy *noun* insurance policy which covers risks of any kind, with no exclusions

all-time *adjective* **all-time high** *or* **all-time low** = highest or lowest point ever reached; **sales have fallen from their all-time high of last year**

alphabet *noun* the 26 letters used to make words
◇ **alphabetical order** *noun* arrangement of records (such as files, index cards) in the order of the letters of the alphabet (A,B,C,D, etc.)

alter *verb* to change; **to alter the terms of a contract**
◇ **alteration** *noun* change which has been made; **he made some alterations to the terms of a contract; the agreement was signed without any alterations**

alternative 1 *noun* thing which can be done instead of another; **what is the alternative to firing half the staff?; we have no alternative** = there is nothing else we can do 2 *adjective* other *or* which can take the place of something; **to find someone alternative employment** = to find someone another job

altogether *adverb* putting everything together; **the staff of the three companies in the group come to 2,500 altogether; the company lost £2m last year and £4m this year, making £6m altogether for the two years**

a.m. *adverb* in the morning *or* before 12 midday; **the flight leaves at 9.20 a.m.; telephone calls before 6 a.m. are charged at the cheap rate**

amend *verb* to change and make more correct *or* acceptable; **please amend your copy of the contract accordingly**
◇ **amendment** *noun* change to a document; **to propose an amendment to the constitution; to make amendments to a contract**

Amex *noun* *informal* = AMERICAN STOCK EXCHANGE; AMERICAN EXPRESS

amortize *verb* to pay off (a debt) by putting money aside regularly over a period of time; **the capital cost is amortized over five years**
◇ **amortizable** *adjective* which can be amortized; **the capital cost is amortizable over a period of ten years**
◇ **amortization** *noun* act of amortizing; **amortization of a debt**

amount 1 *noun* quantity of money; **amount paid; amount deducted; amount owing; amount written off; what is the amount outstanding? a small amount invested in gilt-edged stock** 2 *verb* **to amount to** = to make a total of; **their debts amount to over £1m**

analog computer *noun* computer which works on the basis of electrical impulses representing numbers

analyse *or* **analyze** *verb* to examine in detail; **to analyse a statement of account; to analyse the market potential**
◇ **analysis** *noun* detailed examination and report; **job analysis; market analysis; sales analysis; to carry out an analysis of the market potential; to write an analysis of the sales position; cost analysis** = examination in advance of the costs of a new product; **systems analysis** = using a computer to suggest how a company can work more efficiently by analysing the way in which it works at present
NOTE: plural is **analyses**
◇ **analyst** *noun* person who analyses; **market analyst; systems analyst**

announce *verb* to tell something to the public; **to announce the results for 1984; to announce a programme of investment**

◇ **announcement** *noun* telling something in public; **announcement of a cutback in expenditure; announcement of the appointment of a new managing director; the managing director made an announcement to the staff**

annual *adjective* for one year; **annual statement of income; he has six weeks' annual leave; the annual accounts; annual growth of 5%; annual report** = report of a company's financial situation at the end of a year, sent to all the shareholders; **on an annual basis** = each year; **the figures are revised on an annual basis**

◇ **annual general meeting** *noun* meeting of all the shareholders, when the company's financial situation is discussed with the directors

◇ **annualized** *adjective* shown on an annual basis; **annualized percentage rate** = rate of interest (such as on a hire-purchase agreement) shown on an annual compound basis

◇ **annually** *adverb* each year; **the figures are updated annually**

QUOTE: real wages have risen at an annual rate of only 1% in the last two years *Sunday Times*
QUOTE: the remuneration package will include an attractive salary, profit sharing and a company car together with four weeks annual holiday *Times*

annuity *noun* money paid each year to a retired person, usually in return for a lump-sum payment; **he has a government annuity** *or* **an annuity from the government; to buy** *or* **to take out an annuity; annuity for life** *or* **life annuity** = annual payments made to someone as long as he is alive; **reversionary annuity** = annuity paid to someone on the death of another person NOTE: plural is **annuities**

◇ **annuitant** *noun* person who receives an annuity

annul *verb* to cancel *or* to stop something being legal; **the contract was annulled by the court** NOTE: **annulling - annulled**

◇ **annullable** *adjective* which can be cancelled

◇ **annulling 1** *adjective* which cancels; **annulling clause 2** *noun* act of cancelling; **the annulling of a contract**

◇ **annulment** *noun* act of cancelling; **annulment of a contract**

answer 1 *noun* reply *or* letter or conversation coming after someone has written or spoken; **I am writing in answer to your letter of October 6th; my letter got no answer** *or* **there was no answer to my letter; I tried to phone his office but there was no answer 2** *verb* to speak or write after someone has spoken or written to you; **to answer a letter** = to write a letter in reply to a letter which you have received; **to answer the telephone** = to lift the telephone when it rings and listen to what the caller is saying

◇ **answering** *noun* **answering machine** = machine which answers the telephone automatically when someone is not in the office; **answering service** = office which answers the telephone and takes messages for someone *or* for a company

antedate *verb* to put an earlier date on a document; **the invoice was antedated to January 1st**

anti- *prefix* against

◇ **anti-dumping** *adjective* which protects a country against dumping; **anti-dumping legislation**

◇ **anti-inflationary** *adjective* which tries to restrict inflation; **anti-inflationary measures**

◇ **anti-trust** *adjective* which attacks monopolies and encourages competition; **anti-trust laws** *or* **legislation**

AOB = ANY OTHER BUSINESS item at the end of an agenda, where any matter can be raised

aperture *noun* hole; **aperture envelope** = envelope with a hole in it so that the address on the letter inside can be seen

apologize *verb* to say you are sorry; **to apologize for the delay in answering; she apologized for being late**

◇ **apology** *noun* saying you are sorry; **to write a letter of apology; I enclose a cheque for £10 with apologies for the delay in answering your letter**

appeal 1. *noun* **(a)** being attractive; **customer appeal** = being attractive to customers; **sales appeal** = quality which makes customers want to buy **(b)** asking a court *or* a government department to change its decision; **the appeal against the planning decision will be heard next month; he lost his appeal for damages against the company; she won her case on appeal** = her case was lost in the first court, but the appeal court said that she was right NOTE: no plural for (a)
2 *verb* **(a)** to attract; **this record appeals to the under-25 market; the idea of working in Australia for six months appealed to her (b)** to ask a government department *or* a law court to alter its decision; **the company appealed against the decision of the planning officers** NOTE: you appeal **to** a court or a person **against** a decision

appear *verb* to seem; **the company appeared to be doing well; the managing director appears to be in control**

apply *verb* **(a)** to ask for something, usually in writing; **to apply for a job; to apply for shares; to apply in writing; to apply in person (b)** to affect *or* to touch; **this clause applies only to deals outside the EEC**
◇ **applicant** *noun* person who applies for something; **applicant for a job** *or* **job applicant; there were thousands of applicants for shares in the new company**
◇ **application** *noun* asking for something, usually in writing; **application for shares; shares payable on application; attach the cheque to the share application form; application for a job** *or* **job application; application form** = form to be filled in when applying; **to fill in an application (form) for a job** *or* **a job application (form); letter of application** = letter in which someone applies for a job

appoint *verb* to choose someone for a job; **to appoint James Smith (to the post of) manager; we have appointed a new distribution manager** NOTE: you appoint a person **to** a job
◇ **appointee** *noun* person who is appointed to a job

◇ **appointment** *noun* **(a)** arrangement to meet; **to make** *or* **to fix an appointment for two o'clock; to make an appointment with someone for two o'clock; he was late for his appointment; she had to cancel her appointment; appointments book** = desk diary in which appointments are noted **(b)** being appointed to a job; **on his appointment as manager** = when he was made manager; **letter of appointment** = letter in which someone is appointed to a job **(c)** job; **staff appointment** = job on the staff; **appointments vacant** = list (in a newspaper) of jobs which are available

apportion *verb* to share out (costs); **costs are apportioned according to projected revenue**
◇ **apportionment** *noun* sharing out of (costs)

appraise *verb* to assess *or* to calculate the value of something
◇ **appraisal** *noun* calculation of the value of someone *or* something; **staff appraisals** = reports on how well each member of staff is working

appreciate *verb* **(a)** to notice how good something is; **the customer always appreciates efficient service; tourists do not appreciate long delays at banks (b)** to increase in value; **the dollar has appreciated in terms of the yen; these shares have appreciated by 5%**
◇ **appreciation** *noun* **(a)** increase in value; **these shares show an appreciation of 10%; the appreciation of the dollar against the peseta (b)** valuing something highly; **he was given a rise in appreciation of his excellent work** NOTE: no plural

apprentice 1 *noun* young person who works under contract with a skilled workman to learn from him 2 *verb* **to be apprenticed to someone** = to work with a skilled workman to learn from him
◇ **apprenticeship** *noun* time spent learning a skilled trade; **he served a six-year apprenticeship in the steel works**

appro *noun* = APPROVAL **to buy something on appro** = to buy something which you will only pay for if it is satisfactory

approach 1 *noun* getting in touch with someone with a proposal; **the company made an approach to the supermarket chain; the board turned down all approaches on the subject of mergers; we have had an approach from a Japanese company to buy our car division** 2 *verb* to get in touch with someone with a proposal; **he approached the bank with a request for a loan; the company was approached by an American publisher with the suggestion of a merger; we have been approached several times but have turned down all offers**

appropriate *verb* to put a sum of money aside for a special purpose; **to appropriate a sum of money for a capital project**
◊ **appropriation** *noun* act of putting money aside for a special purpose; **appropriation of funds to the reserve; appropriation account** = part of a profit and loss account which shows how the profit has been dealt with (i.e. how much has been given to the shareholders as dividends, how much is being put into the reserves, etc.)
NOTE: no plural

approve *verb* (a) **to approve of** = to think something is good; **the chairman approves of the new company letter heading; the sales staff do not approve of interference from the accounts division** (b) to agree to something officially; **to approve the terms of a contract; the proposal was approved by the board**
◊ **approval** *noun* (a) agreement; **to submit a budget for approval; certificate of approval** = document showing that an item has been approved officially (b) **on approval** = sale where the buyer only pays for goods if they are satisfactory; **to buy a photocopier on approval**
NOTE: no plural

approximate *adjective* not exact, but almost correct; **the sales division has made an approximate forecast of expenditure**
◊ **approximately** *adverb* almost correctly; **expenditure is approximately 10% down on the previous quarter**
◊ **approximation** *noun* rough calculation; **approximation of expenditure; the final figure is only an approximation**

APR = ANNUALIZED PERCENTAGE RATE

arbitrage *noun* selling on one market and buying on another at almost the same time to profit from different exchange rates; buying shares in companies which are likely to be taken over and so rise in price; **arbitrage syndicate** = group of people formed to raise the capital to invest in arbitrage deals
◊ **arbitrager** *or* **arbitrageur** *noun* person whose business is arbitrage

arbitrate *verb* (*of an outside party*) to be chosen by both sides to try to settle an industrial dispute; **to arbitrate in a dispute**
◊ **arbitration** *noun* settling of a dispute by an outside person, chosen by both sides; **to submit a dispute to arbitration; to refer a question to arbitration; to take a dispute to arbitration; to go to arbitration; arbitration board** *or* **arbitration tribunal** = group which arbitrates; **industrial arbitration tribunal** = court which decides in industrial disputes; **to accept the ruling of the arbitration board**
NOTE: no plural
◊ **arbitrator** *noun* person not concerned with a dispute who is chosen by both sides to try to settle it; **industrial arbitrator; to accept** *or* **to reject the arbitrator's ruling**

area *noun* (a) measurement of the space taken up by something (calculated by multiplying the length by the width); **the area of this office is 3,400 square feet; we are looking for a shop with a sales area of about 100 square metres** (b) region of the world; **free trade area** = group of countries practising free trade; **dollar area** *or* **sterling area** = areas of the world where the dollar *or* the pound is the main trading currency (c) subject; **a problem area** *or* **an area for concern** (d) district *or* part of a town; **the office is in the commercial area of the town; their factory is in a very good area for getting to the motorways and airports** (e) part of a country, a division for commercial purposes; **his sales area is the North-West; he finds it difficult to cover all his area in a week**
◊ **area code** *noun* special telephone number which is given to a particular area; **the area code for London is 01**

◇ **area manager** *noun* manager who is responsible for a part of the country

argue *verb* to discuss something about which you do not agree; **they argued over** *or* **about the price; we spent hours arguing with the managing director about the site for the new factory; the union officials argued among themselves over the best way to deal with the ultimatum from the management** NOTE: you argue **with** someone **about** *or* **over** something

◇ **argument** *noun* discussing something without agreeing; **they got into an argument with the customs officials over the documents; he was sacked after an argument with the managing director**

around *preposition* approximately; **the office costs around £2,000 a year to heat; his salary is around $85,000**

arrange *verb* **(a)** to put in order; **the office is arranged as an open-plan area with small separate rooms for meetings; the files are arranged in alphabetical order; arrange the invoices in order of their dates (b)** to organize; **we arranged to have the meeting in their offices; she arranged for a car to meet him at the airport** NOTE: you arrange **for** someone to do something; you arrange **for** something to be done; or you arrange **to** do something

◇ **arrangement** *noun* **(a)** way in which something is organized; **the company secretary is making all the arrangements for the AGM (b)** settling of a financial dispute; **to come to an arrangement with the creditors**

arrears *plural noun* money which is owed, but which has not been paid at the right time; **arrears of interest; to allow the payments to fall into arrears; salary with arrears effective from January 1st; in arrears** = owing money which should have been paid earlier; **the payments are six months in arrears; he is six weeks in arrears with his rent**

arrive *noun* **(a)** to reach a place; **the consignment has still not arrived; the shipment arrived without any documentation; the plane arrives in Sydney at 04.00; the**

train leaves Paris at 09.20 and arrives at Bordeaux two hours later NOTE: you arrive **at** *or* **in** a place or town, but only **in** a country **(b) to arrive at** = to calculate and agree; **to arrive at a price; after some discussion we arrived at a compromise**

◇ **arrival** *noun* reaching a place; **we are waiting for the arrival of a consignment of spare parts; "to await arrival"** = note written on an envelope to ask for it to be kept safe until the person it is addressed to arrives; **arrivals** = part of an airport dealing with passengers who are arriving

article *noun* **(a)** product *or* thing for sale; **to launch a new article on the market; a black market in luxury articles (b)** section of a legal agreement; **see article 8 of the contract (c) articles of association** *or* *US* **articles of incorporation** = document which sets up a company and says what work it will do; **director appointed under the articles of the company; this procedure is not allowed under the articles of association of the company**

◇ **articled** *adjective* **articled clerk** = clerk who is bound by contract to work in a lawyer's office for some years to learn the law

articulated lorry *or* **articulated vehicle** *noun* large lorry formed of two parts, the second pulled by the first

asap = AS SOON AS POSSIBLE

aside *adverb* to one side *or* out of the way; **to put aside** *or* **to set aside** = to save (money); **he is putting £50 aside each week to pay for his car**

ask *verb* **(a)** to put a question to someone; **he asked the information office for details of companies exhibiting at the motor show; ask the salesgirl if the bill includes VAT (b)** to tell someone to do something; **he asked the switchboard operator to get him a number in Germany; she asked her secretary to fetch a file from the managing director's office; the customs officials asked him to open his case**

◇ **ask for** *verb* **(a)** to say that you want *or* need something; **he asked for the file on 1984 debtors; they asked for more time to repay the loan; there is a man in reception**

asking for Mr Smith **(b)** to put a price on something for sale; **they are asking £24,000 for the car**
◇ **asking price** *noun* price which the seller asks for the goods being sold; **the asking price is £24,000**

assay mark *noun* mark put on gold or silver items to show that the metal is of the correct quality

assemble *verb* to put a product together from various parts; **the engines are made in Japan and the bodies in Scotland, and the cars are assembled in France**
◇ **assembly** *noun* **(a)** putting an item together from various parts; **there are no assembly instructions to show you how to put the computer together; car assembly plant** = factory where cars are put together from parts made in other factories NOTE: no plural **(b)** meeting NOTE: plural is **assemblies**
◇ **assembly line** *noun* production system where the product (such as a car) moves slowly through the factory with new sections added to it as it goes along; **he works on an assembly line** *or* **he is an assembly line worker**

assess *verb* to calculate the value of something; **to assess damages at £1,000; to assess a property for the purposes of insurance**
◇ **assessment** *noun* calculation of value; **assessment of damages; assessment of property; tax assessment; staff assessments** = reports on how well members of staff are working

asset *noun* thing which belongs to company or person, and which has a value; **he has an excess of assets over liabilities; her assets are only £640 as against liabilities of £24,000; capital assets** *or* **fixed assets** = property *or* machinery which a company owns and uses; **current assets** = assets used by a company in its ordinary work (such as materials, finished goods, cash); **frozen assets** = assets of a company which cannot be sold because someone has a claim against them; **intangible assets** = assets which have a value, but which cannot be seen (such as goodwill. or a patent, or a trademark);

liquid assets = cash, or bills which can be quickly converted into cash; **personal assets** = moveable assets which belong to a person; **tangible assets** = assets which are solid (such as furniture or jewels or cash); **asset value** = value of a company calculated by adding together all its assets; **asset stripper** = person who buys a company to sell its assets; **asset stripping** = buying a company to sell its assets

QUOTE: many companies are discovering that a well-recognised brand name can be a priceless asset that lessens the risk of introducing a new product *Duns Business Month*

assign *verb* **(a)** to give legally; **to assign a right to someone; to assign shares to someone** **(b)** to give someone a job of work; **he was assigned the job of checking the sales figures**
◇ **assignation** *noun* legal transfer; **assignation of shares to someone; assignation of a patent**
◇ **assignee** *noun* person who receives something which has been assigned
◇ **assignment** *noun* **(a)** legal transfer of a property *or* of a right; **assignment of a patent** *or* **of a copyright; to sign a deed of assignment** **(b)** particular job of work; **he was appointed managing director with the assignment to improve the company's profits; the oil team is on an assignment in the North Sea**
◇ **assignor** *noun* person who assigns something to someone

assist *verb* to help; **can you assist the stock controller in counting the stock? he assists me with my income tax returns** NOTE: you assist someone **in** doing something or **with** something
◇ **assistance** *noun* help; **financial assistance** = help in the form of money NOTE: no plural
◇ **assistant** *noun* person who helps *or* a clerical employee; **personal assistant** = secretary who also helps the boss in various ways; **shop assistant** = person who serves the customers in a shop; **assistant manager** = person who helps a manager

associate 1 *adjective* linked; **associate company** = company which is partly owned by another; **associate director =** director who attends board meetings, but has not been elected by the shareholders **2** *noun* person who works in the same business as someone; **she is a business associate of mine**

◇ **associated** *adjective* linked; **Smith Ltd and its associated company, Jones Brothers**

◇ **association** *noun* **(a)** group of people *or* of companies with the same interest; **trade association; employers' association; manufacturers' association (b) articles of association =** document which sets up a company and says what work it will do

assume *verb* to take; **to assume all risks; he has assumed responsibility for marketing**

◇ **assumption** *noun* taking; **assumption of risks**

assure *verb* to insure *or* to have a contract with a company where if regular payments are made, the company will pay compensation if you die; **to assure someone's life; he has paid the premiums to have his wife's life assured; the life assured =** the person whose life has been covered by the life assurance

◇ **assurance** *noun* insurance *or* agreement that in return for regular payments, a company will pay compensation for loss of life; **assurance company; assurance policy; life assurance =** insurance which pays a sum of money when someone dies

◇ **assurer** *or* **assuror** *noun* insurer *or* company which insures

NOTE: **assure** and **assurance** are used in Britain for insurance policies relating to something which will certainly happen (such as death); for other types of policy use **insure** and **insurance**

at best *phrase* **sell at best =** instruction to stockbroker to sell shares at the best price possible

at par *phrase* **share at par =** share whose value on the stock market is the same as its face value

ATM *noun* = AUTOMATIC TELLING MACHINE

attach *verb* to fasten *or* to link; **I am attaching a copy of my previous letter;**

please find attached a copy of my letter of June 24th; the machine is attached to the floor so it cannot be moved; the bank attaches great importance to the deal

◇ **attaché** *noun* junior diplomat who does special work; **commercial attaché =** diplomat whose job is to promote the commercial interests of his country; **attaché case =** small case for carrying papers and documents

◇ **attachment** *noun* holding a debtor's property to prevent it being sold until debts are paid

attempt 1 *noun* trying to do something; **the company made an attempt to break into the American market; the takeover attempt was turned down by the board; all his attempts to get a job have failed 2** *verb* to try; **the company is attempting to get into the tourist market; we are attempting the takeover of a manufacturing company; he attempted to have the sales director sacked**

attend *verb* to be present at; **the chairman has asked all managers to attend the meeting; none of the shareholders attended the AGM**

◇ **attend to** *verb* to give careful thought to (something) and deal with it; **the managing director will attend to your complaint personally; we have brought in experts to attend to the problem of installing the new computer**

◇ **attention** *noun* giving careful thought; **for the attention of the Managing Director; your orders will have our best attention**

attorney *noun* **(a)** person who is legally allowed to act on behalf of someone else; **power of attorney =** legal document giving someone the right to act on someone's behalf in legal matters; **his solicitor was granted power of attorney (b)** *US* lawyer

attract *verb* to make something or someone join *or* come in; **the company is offering free holidays in Spain to attract buyers; we have difficulty in attracting skilled staff to this part of the country**

◇ **attractive** *adjective* which attracts; **attractive prices =** prices which are cheap enough to make buyers want to buy;

attractive salary = good salary to make high-quality applicants apply for the job

QUOTE: airlines offer special stopover rates and hotel packages to attract customers and to encourage customer loyalty *Business Traveller*

attributable *adjective* **attributable profits** = profits which can be shown to come from a particular area

auction 1 *noun* selling of goods where people offer bids, and the item is sold to the person who makes the highest offer; **sale by auction; auction rooms; to sell goods by auction** *or US* **at auction; to put something up for auction** = to offer an item for sale at an auction; **Dutch auction** = auction where the auctioneer offers an item for sale at a high price and gradually reduces the price until someone makes a bid **2** *verb* to sell at an auction; **the factory was closed and the machinery was auctioned off**
◊ **auctioneer** *noun* person who conducts an auction

audio-typing *noun* typing to dictation from a recording
NOTE: no plural
◊ **audio-typist** *noun* typist who types to dictation from a recording on a dictating machine

audit 1 *noun* examination of the books and accounts of a company; **to carry out the annual audit; external audit** *or* **independent audit** = audit carried out by an independent auditor; **internal audit** = audit carried out by a department inside the company; **he is the manager of the internal audit department 2** *verb* to examine the books and accounts of a company; **to audit the accounts; the books have not yet been audited**
◊ **auditing** *noun* action of examining the books and accounts
◊ **auditor** *noun* person who audits; **the AGM appoints the company's auditors; external auditor** = independent person who audits the company's accounts; **internal auditor** = member of staff who audits a company's accounts

authenticate *verb* to say that something is true

authority *noun* **(a)** power to do something; **he has no authority to act on our behalf (b) local authority** = elected section of government which runs a small area of a country; **the authorities** = the government *or* the people in control
NOTE: no plural for (a)

authorize *verb* **(a)** to give permission for something to be done; **to authorize payment of £10,000 (b)** to give someone the authority to do something; **to authorize someone to act on the company's behalf**
◊ **authorization** *noun* permission *or* power to do something; **do you have authorization for this expenditure?; he has no authorization to act on our behalf**
NOTE: no plural
◊ **authorized** *adjective* permitted; **authorized capital** = amount of capital which a company is allowed to have, as stated in the articles of association; **authorized dealer** = person *or* company (such as a bank) which is allowed to buy and sell foreign currency

QUOTE: in 1934 Congress authorized President Franklin D. Roosevelt to seek lower tariffs with any country willing to reciprocate
Duns Business Month

automated *adjective* worked automatically by machines; **fully automated car assembly plant**
◊ **automation** *noun* use of machines to do work with very little supervision by people
NOTE: no plural

automatic *adjective* which works *or* takes place without any person making it happen; **there is an automatic increase in salaries on January 1st; automatic data processing** = data processing done by a computer; **automatic telling machine** *or US* **automatic teller machine** = machine which gives out money when a special card is inserted and special instructions given; **automatic vending machine** = machine which provides drinks, cigarettes, etc. when a coin is put in
◊ **automatically** *adverb* working without a person giving instructions; **the**

invoices are sent out automatically; addresses are typed in automatically; a demand note is sent automatically when the invoice is overdue

available *adjective* which can be obtained *or* bought; **available in all branches; item no longer available; items available to order only; funds which are made available for investment in small businesses; available capital** = capital which is ready to be used

◇ **availability** *noun* being easily obtained; **offer subject to availability** = the offer is valid only if the goods are available
NOTE: no plural

average 1 *noun* **(a)** number calculated by adding together several figures and dividing by the number of figures added; **the average for the last three months** *or* **the last three months' average; sales average** *or* **average of sales; weighted average** = average which is calculated taking several factors into account, giving some more value than others; **on an average** = in general; **on an average, £15 worth of goods are stolen every day (b)** sharing of the cost of damage or loss of a ship between the insurers and the owners; **average adjuster** = person who calculates how much of an insurance is to be paid; **general average** = sharing of the cost of the lost goods by all parties to an insurance; **particular average** = situation where part of a shipment is lost or damaged and the insurance costs are borne by the owner of the lost goods and not shared among all the owners of the shipment **2** *adjective* **(a)** middle (figure); **average cost per unit; average price; average sales per representative; the average figures for the last three months; the average increase in prices (b)** not very good; **the company's performance has been only average; he is an average worker 3** *verb* to produce as an average figure; **price increases have averaged 10% per annum; days lost through sickness have averaged twenty-two over the last four years**

◇ **average due date** *noun* date when several payments (due at different dates) are settled in one payment

◇ **average out** *verb* to come to a figure as an average; **it averages out at 10% per annum; sales increases have averaged out at 15%**

◇ **averager** *noun* person who buys the same share at various times and at various prices to give an average price

◇ **average-sized** *adjective* not large or small; **they are an average-sized company; he has an average-sized office**

◇ **averaging** *noun* buying shares at different times and at different prices to give an average price
NOTE: no plural

QUOTE: a share with an average rating might yield 5 per cent and have a PER of about 10
Investors Chronicle
QUOTE: the average price per kilogram for this season to the end of April has been 300 cents
Australian Financial Review

avoid *verb* to try not to do something; **the company is trying to avoid bankruptcy; my aim is to avoid paying too much tax; we want to avoid direct competition with Smith Ltd**
NOTE: you avoid something or avoid **doing** something

◇ **avoidance** *noun* trying not to do something; **avoidance of an agreement** *or* **of a contract; tax avoidance** = trying (legally) to pay as little tax as possible
NOTE: no plural

avoirdupois *noun* old system of weights used in Britain, shown in pounds, ounces, etc.; **one ounce avoirdupois**

await *verb* to wait for; **we are awaiting the decision of the planning department; they are awaiting a decision of the court; the agent is awaiting our instructions**

award 1 *noun* decision which settles a dispute; **an award by an industrial tribunal; the arbitrator's award was set aside on appeal 2** *verb* to decide the amount of money to be given to someone; **to award someone a salary increase; to award damages; the judge awarded costs to the defendant; to award a contract to someone** = to decide that someone will have the contract to do work

away *adverb* not here *or* somewhere else; **the managing director is away on business; my secretary is away sick; the company is moving away from its down-market image**

awkward *adjective* difficult to deal with; **the board is trying to solve the awkward problem of the managing director's son; when he asked for the loan the bank started to ask some very awkward questions; he is being very awkward about giving us further credit**

axe 1 *noun* **the project got the axe** = the project was stopped **2** *verb* to cut *or* to stop; **to axe expenditure; several thousand jobs are to be axed**

Bb

"B" shares *plural noun* ordinary shares with special voting rights (often owned by the founder of a company and his family)

baby bonds *plural noun US* bonds in small denominations (i.e. $100) which the small investor can afford to buy

back 1 *noun* opposite side to the front; **write your address on the back of the envelope; the conditions of sale are printed on the back of the invoice; please endorse the cheque on the back 2** *adjective* referring to the past; **back interest** = interest not yet paid; **back orders** = orders received in the past and not fulfilled (usually because the item is out of stock); **after the strike it took the factory six weeks to clear all the accumulated back orders; back pay** = salary which has not been paid; **I am owed £500 in back pay; back payment** = paying money which is owed; **the salesmen are claiming for back payment of unpaid commission; back payments** = payments which are due; **back rent** = rent owed; **the company owes £100,000 in back rent 3** *adverb* as things were before; **he will pay back the money in monthly instalments; the store sent back the cheque because the date was wrong; the company went back on its agreement to supply at £1.50 a unit 4** *verb* **(a) to back someone** = to help someone financially; **the bank is backing him to the tune of £10,000; he is looking for someone to back his project (b) to back a bill** = to sign a bill promising to pay it if the person it is addressed to is not able to do so

◊ **backdate** *verb* to put an earlier date on a cheque *or* an invoice; **backdate your invoice to April 1st; the pay increase is backdated to January 1st**

◊ **backer** *noun* **(a)** person who backs someone; **he has an Australian backer; one of the company's backers has withdrawn (b) backer of a bill** = person who backs a bill

◊ **background** *noun* **(a)** past work *or* experience; **his background is in the steel industry; the company is looking for someone with a background of success in the electronics industry; she has a publishing background; what is his background *or* do you know anything about his background? (b)** past details; **he explained the background of the claim; I know the contractual situation as it stands now, but can you fill in the background details?**

◊ **backhander** *noun* *informal* bribe *or* money given to someone to get him to help you

◊ **backing** *noun* **(a)** financial support; **he has the backing of an Australian bank; the company will succeed only if it has sufficient backing; who is providing the backing for the project *or* where does the backing for the project come from? (b) currency backing** = gold or government securities which maintain the strength of a currency
NOTE: no plural

◊ **backlog** *noun* work (such as orders *or* letters) which has piled up waiting to be done; **the warehouse is trying to cope with a backlog of orders; my secretary can't cope with the backlog of paperwork**
NOTE: no plural

◊ **back out** *verb* to stop being part of a deal *or* an agreement; **the bank backed out of the contract; we had to cancel the project when our German partners backed out**

◊ **back up** *verb* to support *or* to help; **he brought along a file of documents to back up his claim; the finance director said the managing director had refused to back him up in his argument with the VAT office**

◊ **backup** *adjective* supporting *or* helping; **we offer a free backup service to customers; after a series of sales tours by representatives, the sales director sends backup letters to all the contacts; backup copy** = copy of a computer disk to be kept in case the original disk is damaged

◇ **backwardation** *noun* penalty paid by the seller when postponing delivery of shares to the buyer

QUOTE: the businesses we back range from start-up ventures to established companies in need of further capital for expansion *Times*
QUOTE: the company has received the backing of a number of oil companies who are willing to pay for the results of the survey *Lloyd's List*

bad *adjective* not good; **bad bargain** = item which is not worth the price asked; **bad buy** = thing bought which was not worth the money paid for it; **bad debt** = debt which will not be paid; **the company has written off £30,000 in bad debts**

bag *noun* thing made of paper, cloth, or plastic for carrying items; **he brought his files in a Harrods bag; we gave away 5,000 plastic bags at the exhibition; shopping bag** = bag used for carrying shopping

baggage *noun* suitcases *or* bags for carrying clothes when travelling; **free baggage allowance** = amount of baggage which a passenger can take with him free on a plane; *US* **baggage room** = room where cases can be left while passengers are waiting for a plane or train
NOTE: no plural; to show one suitcase, etc., you can say **a piece of baggage**

bail *noun* payment made to a court as guarantee that a prisoner will return after being released; **to stand bail of £3,000 for someone; he was released on bail of $3,000** *or* **he was released on payment of $3,000 bail; to jump bail** = not to appear in court after having been released on bail
NOTE: no plural
◇ **bail out** *verb* **(a)** to rescue a company which is in financial difficulties **(b) to bail someone out** = to pay money to a court as a guarantee that someone will return to face charges; **she paid $3,000 to bail him out**
◇ **bail-out** *noun* rescue of a company in financial difficulties

QUOTE: the government has decided to bail out the bank which has suffered losses to the extent that its capital has been wiped out
South China Morning Post

balance 1 *noun* **(a)** amount in an account which makes the total debits and credits equal; **credit balance** = balance in an account showing that more money has been received than is owed; **debit balance** = balance in an account showing that more money is owed than has been received; **the account has a credit balance of £100; because of large payments to suppliers, the account has a debit balance of £1,000; balance in hand** = cash held to pay small debts; **balance brought down** = amount entered in an account at the end of a period to balance income and expenditure; **balance brought forward** *or* **balance carried forward** = amount entered in an account at the end of a period to balance the expenditure and income which is then taken forward to start the new period **(b)** rest of an amount owed; **you can pay £100 deposit and the balance within 60 days; balance due to us** = amount owed to us which is due to be paid **(c) balance of payments** = the international financial position of a country, including invisible as well as visible trade; **balance of trade** *or* **trade balance** = international trading position of a country, excluding invisible trade; **adverse** *or* **unfavourable balance of trade** = situation where a country imports more than it exports; **favourable trade balance** = situation where a country exports more than it imports; **the country has had an adverse balance of trade for the second month running (d) bank balance** = state of an account at a bank at a particular time
NOTE: no plural
2 *verb* **(a)** to calculate the amount needed to make the two sides of an account equal; **I have finished balancing the accounts for March; the February accounts do not balance** = the two sides are not equal **(b)** to plan a budget so that expenditure and income are equal; **the president is planning for a balanced budget**
◇ **balance sheet** *noun* statement of the financial position of a company at a particular time, such as the end of the financial year or the end of a quarter; **the company balance sheet for 1984 shows a substantial loss; the accountant has prepared the balance sheet for the first half-year**

bale 1 *noun* large pack of wool *or* paper *or* cotton,etc.; **a bale of cotton; 2,520 bales of wool were destroyed in the fire** 2 *verb* to tie wool *or* paper *or* cotton to make a bale

ballot 1 *noun* **(a)** election where people vote for someone by marking a cross on a paper with a list of names; **ballot paper =** paper on which the voter marks a cross to show who he wants to vote for; **ballot box =** sealed box into which ballot papers are put; **postal ballot =** election where the voters send their ballot papers by post; **secret ballot =** election where the voters vote in secret **(b)** selecting by taking papers at random out of a box; **the share issue was oversubscribed, so there was a ballot for the shares** 2 *verb* to take a vote by ballot; **the union is balloting for the post of president**

◊ **ballot-rigging** *noun* illegal arranging of the votes in a ballot, so that a particular candidate or party wins
NOTE: no plural

ban 1 *noun* order which forbids someone from doing something; **a government ban on the import of weapons; a ban on the export of computer software; overtime ban =** order by a trade union which forbids overtime work by its members; **to impose a ban on smoking =** to make an order which forbids smoking; **to lift the ban on smoking =** to allow people to smoke; **to beat the ban on something =** to do something which is forbidden - usually by doing it rapidly before a ban is imposed, or by finding a legal way to avoid a ban 2 *verb* to forbid something *or* to make something illegal; **the government has banned the sale of alcohol**
NOTE: banning - banned

band *noun* **rubber band =** thin ring of rubber for attaching things together; **put a band round the filing cards to stop them falling on the floor**

bank 1 *noun* **(a)** business which holds money for its clients, which lends money at interest, and trades generally in money; **Lloyds Bank; The First National Bank; The Royal Bank of Scotland; he put all his earnings into his bank; I have had a letter from my bank telling me my account is overdrawn; bank loan** *or* **bank advance =** loan from a bank; **he asked for a bank loan to start his business; bank borrowing =** money borrowed from a bank; **the new factory was financed by bank borrowing; bank borrowings have increased =** loans

given by banks have increased; **bank deposits =** all money placed in banks **(b)** **central bank =** main government-controlled bank in a country, which controls the financial affairs of the country by fixing main interest rates, issuing currency and controlling the foreign exchange rate; **the Bank of England =** central British bank, owned by the state, which, together with the Treasury, regulates the nation's finances; **the Federal Reserve Banks =** central banks in the USA which are owned by the state, and directed by the Federal Reserve Board; **the World Bank =** central bank, controlled by the United Nations, whose funds come from the member states of the UN and which lends money to member states **(c)** **savings bank =** bank where you can deposit money and receive interest on it; **merchant bank =** bank which lends money to companies and deals in international finance; **the High Street banks =** main British banks which accept deposits from and allow withdrawals by individuals **(d)** **data bank =** store of information in a computer 2 *verb* to deposit money into a bank or to have an account with a bank; **he banked the cheque as soon as he received it; where do you bank? =** where do you have a bank account?; **I bank at** *or* **with Barclays**

◊ **bankable** *adjective* which a bank will accept as security for a loan; **a bankable paper**

◊ **bank account** *noun* account which a customer has with a bank, where the customer can deposit and withdraw money; **to open a bank account; to close a bank account; how much money do you have in your bank account? she has £100 in her savings bank account; if you let the balance in your bank account fall below £100, you have to pay bank charges**

◊ **bank balance** *noun* state of a bank account at any particular time; **our bank balance went into the red last month**

◊ **bank bill** *noun* **(a)** *GB* order by one bank telling another bank (usually in another country) to pay money to someone **(b)** *US* piece of printed paper money

◊ **bank book** *noun* book, given by a bank, which shows money which you deposit or withdraw from your savings account

◊ **bank charges** *plural noun* charges which a bank makes for carrying out work for a customer

◊ **bank clerk** *noun* person who works in a bank, but not a manager

◊ **bank draft** *noun* order by one bank telling another bank (usually in another country) to pay money to someone

◊ **banker** *noun* **(a)** person who is in an important position in a bank; **merchant banker** = person who has a high position in a merchant bank **(b)** generally, a bank; **banker's bill** = order by one bank telling another bank (usually in another country) to pay money to someone; **banker's order** = order written by a customer asking a bank to make a regular payment; **he pays his subscription by banker's order**

◊ **bank giro** *noun GB* method used by clearing banks to transfer money rapidly from one account to another

◊ **bank holiday** *noun* a weekday which is a public holiday when the banks are closed; **New Year's Day is a bank holiday**

◊ **banking** *noun* the business of banks; **he is studying banking; she has gone into banking;** *US* **banking account** = account which a customer has with a bank; **a banking crisis** = crisis affecting the banks; **banking hours** = hours when a bank is open for its customers; **you cannot get money out of the bank after banking hours** NOTE: no plural

◊ **bank manager** *noun* person in charge of a branch of a bank; **he asked his bank manager for a loan**

◊ **bank note** *or* **banknote** *noun* piece of printed paper money; **he pulled out a pile of used bank notes**

◊ **bank on** *verb* to do something because you are sure something will happen; **he is banking on getting a loan from his father to set up in business; do not bank on the sale of your house**

◊ **bankroll** *verb informal* to pay for *or* to finance (a project)

◊ **bank statement** *noun* written statement from a bank showing the balance of an account

bankrupt **1** *adjective & noun* (person *or* company) which has been declared by a court not to be capable of paying its debts and whose affairs are put into the hands of a receiver; **he was adjudicated** *or* **declared bankrupt; a bankrupt property developer; he went bankrupt after two years in business; certificated bankrupt** = bankrupt who has been discharged from bankruptcy with a certificate to show he was not at fault; **discharged bankrupt** = person who has been released from being bankrupt because he has paid his debts; **undischarged bankrupt** = person who has been declared bankrupt and has not been released from that state **2** *verb* to make someone become bankrupt; **the recession bankrupted my father**

◊ **bankruptcy** *noun* state of being bankrupt; **the recession has caused thousands of bankruptcies; adjudication of bankruptcy** *or* **declaration of bankruptcy** = legal order making someone bankrupt; **discharge in bankruptcy** = being released from bankruptcy after paying debts; **to file a petition in bankruptcy** = to apply officially to be made bankrupt *or* to ask officially for someone else to be made bankrupt

bar *noun* **(a)** place where you can buy and drink alcohol; **the sales reps met in the bar of the hotel (b)** small shop; **sandwich bar** = small shop where you can buy sandwiches to take away; **snack bar** = small restaurant where you can get simple meals **(c)** thing which stops you doing something; **government legislation is a bar to foreign trade (d)** *GB* the profession of barrister; **to be called to the bar** = to become a barrister

◊ **bar chart** *noun* chart where values *or* quantities are shown as thick columns of different heights

◊ **bar code** *noun* system of lines printed on a product which when read by a computer give a reference number or price

bareboat charter *noun* system of chartering a ship where the owner provides only the ship, but not the crew, fuel or insurance

barely *adverb* almost not; **there is barely enough money left to pay the staff; she barely had time to call her lawyer**

bargain **1** *noun* **(a)** agreement on the price of something; **to make a bargain; to drive a hard bargain** = to be a difficult negotiator; **to strike a hard bargain** = to agree a deal which is favourable to you; **it is a bad bargain** = it is not worth the price **(b)** thing which is cheaper than usual; **that car is a (real) bargain at £500; bargain hunter** = person who looks for cheap deals **(c)** sale of one lot of shares on the Stock Exchange; **bargains done** = number of deals made on the Stock Exchange during a day **2** *verb* to discuss a price for something; **you will have to bargain with the dealer if you want a discount; they spent two hours bargaining about** *or* **over the price** NOTE: you bargain **with** someone **over** *or* **about** *or* **for** something

◊ **bargain basement** *noun* basement floor in a shop where goods are sold cheaply; **I'm selling this at a bargain basement price** = I'm selling this very cheaply

◊ **bargain counter** *noun* counter in a shop where goods are sold cheaply

◊ **bargain offer** *noun* sale of a particular type of goods at a cheap price; **this week's bargain offer - 30% off all carpet prices**

◊ **bargain price** *noun* cheap price; **these carpets are for sale at a bargain price**

◊ **bargain sale** *noun* sale of all goods in a store at cheap prices

◊ **bargaining** *noun* act of discussing a price, usually wage increases for workers; **(free) collective bargaining** = negotiations between employers and workers' representatives over wage increases and conditions; **bargaining power** = strength of one person or group when discussing prices *or* wage settlements; **bargaining position** = statement of position by one group during negotiations

barrel *noun* **(a)** large round container for liquids; **he bought twenty-five barrels of wine; to sell wine by the barrel (b)** amount of liquid contained in a barrel; **the price of oil has reached $30 a barrel**

> QUOTE: if signed, the deals would give effective discounts of up to $3 a barrel on Saudi oil
> *Economist*
> QUOTE: US crude oil stocks fell last week by nearly 2.6m barrels   *Financial Times*
> QUOTE: the average spot price of Nigerian light crude oil for the month of July was 27.21 dollars a barrel   *Business Times (Lagos)*

barrier *noun* thing which stops someone doing something, especially sending goods from one place to another; **customs barriers** *or* **tariff barriers** = customs duty intended to make trade more difficult; **to impose trade barriers on certain goods** = to restrict the import of certain goods by charging high duty; **the unions have asked the government to impose trade barriers on foreign cars; to lift trade barriers from imports** = to remove restrictions on imports; **the government has lifted trade barriers on foreign cars**

barrister *noun* *GB* lawyer (especially in England) who can speak *or* argue a case in one of the higher courts

barter 1 *noun* system where goods are exchanged for other goods and not sold for money; **barter agreement** *or* **barter arrangement** *or* **barter deal** = agreement to exchange goods by barter; **the company has agreed a barter deal with Bulgaria** NOTE: no plural **2** *verb* to exchange goods for other goods, but not buy them for money; **they agreed a deal to barter tractors for barrels of wine**

◊ **bartering** *noun* act of exchanging goods for other goods and not for money NOTE: no plural

> QUOTE: under the barter agreements, Nigeria will export 175,000 barrels a day of crude oil in exchange for trucks, food, planes and chemicals
> *Wall Street Journal*

base 1 *noun* **(a)** lowest or first position; **turnover increased by 200%, but starting from a low base; base year** = first year of an index, against which later years' changes are measured; **bank base rate** = basic rate of interest which a bank charges on loans to its customers; *see* DATABASE **(b)** place where a company has its main office or factory *or* place where a businessman has his office; **the company has its base in London and branches in all European countries; he has an office in Madrid which he uses as a base while he is travelling in Southern Europe 2** *verb* **(a)** to start to calculate *or* to negotiate from a position; **we based our calculations on the forecast turnover; based on** = calculating from; **based on last**

year's figures; **based on population forecasts (b)** to set up a company *or* a person in
a place; **the European manager is based in
our London office; our overseas branch is
based in the Bahamas; a London-based sales
executive**

◇ **basement** *noun* section of a shop
which is underground; **bargain basement
=** basement floor in a shop where goods
are sold cheaply; **I am selling this at a
bargain basement price**

QUOTE: the base lending rate. or prime rate. is
the rate at which banks lend to their top corporate
borrowers   *Wall Street Journal*
QUOTE: other investments include a large stake
in the Chicago-based insurance company
Lloyd's List

basic 1 *adjective* **(a)** normal; **basic pay**
or **basic salary** *or* **basic wage =** normal
salary without extra payments; **basic
discount =** normal discount without extra
percentages; **our basic discount is 20%,
but we offer 5% extra for rapid settlement
(b)** most important; **basic commodities =**
ordinary farm produce, produced in large
quantities (such as corn, rice, sugar, etc.)
(c) simple *or* from which everything starts;
**he has a basic knowledge of the market; to
work at the cash desk, you need a basic
qualification in maths**

◇ **basics** *plural noun* simple and important facts; **he has studied the basics of
foreign exchange dealing; to get back to
basics =** to consider the basic facts again

◇ **basically** *adverb* seen from the point
from which everything starts

◇ **BASIC** *noun* = BEGINNER'S ALL-
PURPOSE SYMBOLIC INSTRUCTION
CODE simple language for computer
programming

basis *noun* **(a)** point *or* number from
which calculations are made; **we forecast
the turnover on the basis of a 6% price
increase (b)** general terms of agreement;
on a short-term *or* **long-term basis =** for a
short *or* long period; **he has been appointed
on a short-term basis; we have three people
working on a freelance basis**
NOTE: the plural is **bases**

basket *noun* **(a)** container made of thin
pieces of wood *or* metal *or* plastic; **a basket
of apples; filing basket =** container kept

on a desk for documents which have to be
filed; **shopping basket =** basket used for
carrying shopping; **waste paper basket =**
container into which paper or pieces of
rubbish can be thrown **(b)** group of prices
or currencies taken as a standard; **the
pound has fallen against a basket of
European currencies; the price of the
average shopping basket** *or* *US* **the market
basket has risen by 6%**

QUOTE: as a basket of European currencies. the
ecu is protected from exchange-rate swings
Economist

batch 1 *noun* **(a)** group of items which
are made at one time; **this batch of shoes
has the serial number 25-02 (b)** group of
documents which are processed at the
same time; **a batch of invoices; today's
batch of orders; the accountant signed a
batch of cheques; we deal with the orders in
batches of fifty; batch processing =** system
of data processing where information is
collected into batches before being loaded
into the computer **2** *verb* to put items
together in groups; **to batch invoices** *or*
cheques

◇ **batch number** *noun* number attached to a batch; **when making a complaint always quote the batch number on the
packet**

battery *noun* small object for storing
electric power; **the calculator needs a new
battery; a battery-powered calculator**

battle *noun* fight; **boardroom battles =**
arguments between directors; **circulation
battle =** fight between two newspapers to
sell more copies in the same section of the
market

bay *noun* **loading bay =** section of road in
a warehouse, where lorries can drive in to
load or unload

b/d = BARRELS PER DAY

bear 1 *noun* **(a)** large wild animal
covered in fur; **their advertising symbol is
a bear (b)** (*Stock Exchange*) dealer who
sells shares because he thinks the price will
fall and he will be able to buy them again
more cheaply later; **bear market =** period
when Stock Exchange prices fall because

shareholders are selling; *see* BULL **2** *verb*
(a) to give interest; **government bonds
which bear 5% interest (b)** to have (a
name) *or* to have something written on it;
**the cheque bears the signature of the
company secretary; envelope which bears a
London postmark; a letter bearing
yesterday's date; the share certificate bears
his name (c)** to pay costs; **the costs of the
exhibition will be borne by the company; the
company bore the legal costs of both parties**
NOTE: **bearing - bore - has borne**
◊ **bearer** *noun* person who holds a
cheque *or* certificate; **the cheque is payable
to bearer** = is paid to the person who holds
it, not to any particular name written on it
◊ **bearer bond** *noun* bond which is
payable to the bearer and does not have a
name written on it
◊ **bearing** *adjective* which bears *or*
which produces; **certificate bearing interest at 5%; interest-bearing deposits**

beat *verb* **(a)** to win in a fight against
someone; **they have beaten their rivals into
second place in the computer market (b)** to
beat a ban = to do something which is
forbidden by doing it rapidly before the
ban is enforced
NOTE: **beating - beat - has beaten**

become *verb* to change into something
different; **the export market has become
very difficult since the rise in the dollar; the
company became very profitable in a short
time**
NOTE: **becoming - became - has become**

bed-and-breakfast deal *noun*
arrangement where shares are sold one day
and bought back the following day, in
order to establish a profit or loss for tax
declaration

begin *verb* to start; **the company began to
lose its market share; he began the report
which the shareholders had asked for; the
auditors' report began with a description of
the general principles adopted**
NOTE: you begin something *or* begin **to do**
something *or* begin **with** something. Note also:
beginning - began - has begun
◊ **beginning** *noun* first part; **the beginning of the report is a list of the directors and
their shareholdings**

behalf *noun* **on behalf of** = acting for
(someone *or* a company); **I am writing on
behalf of the minority shareholders; she is
acting on my behalf; solicitors acting on
behalf of the American company**

behind **1** *preposition* at the back *or* after;
**the company is No. 2 in the market, about
£4m behind their rivals 2** *adverb* after; **we
have fallen behind our rivals** = we have
fewer sales *or* make less profit than our
rivals; **the company has fallen behind with
its deliveries** = it is late with its deliveries

believe *verb* to think that something is
true; **we believe he has offered to buy 25%
of the shares; the chairman is believed to be
in South America on business**

belong *verb* **(a) to belong to** = to be the
property of; **the company belongs to an old
American banking family; the patent
belongs to the inventor's son (b) to belong
with** = to be in the correct place with;
**those documents belong with the sales
reports**

below *preposition* lower down than *or* less
than; **we sold the property at below the
market price; you can get a ticket for New
York at below £150 from a bucket shop**
◊ **below-the-line** *adjective* **below-the-
line expenditure** = exceptional payments
which are separated from a company's
normal accounts

benchmark *noun* point in an index
which is important, and can be used to
compare with other figures

QUOTE: the US bank announced a cut in its prime,
the benchmark corporate lending rate, from 10+% to
10%   *Financial Times*
QUOTE: the dollar dropped below three German
marks - a benchmark with more psychological than
economic significance - for the first time since
October   *Fortune*

beneficial *adjective* **beneficial occupier**
= person who occupies a property but
does not own it fully; **beneficial interest** =
interest which allows someone to occupy
or receive rent from a property, but not to
own it

◇ **beneficiary** *noun* person who gains money from something; **the beneficiaries of a will**

QUOTE: the pound sterling was the main beneficiary of the dollar's weakness
Business Times (Lagos)

benefit 1 *noun* **(a)** payments which are made to someone under a national or private insurance scheme; **she receives £20 a week as unemployment benefit; the sickness benefit is paid monthly; the insurance office sends out benefit cheques each week; death benefit** = money paid to the family of someone who dies in an accident at work **(b) fringe benefits** = extra items given by a company to workers in addition to their salaries (such as company cars, private health insurance) **2** *verb* **(a)** to make better *or* to improve; **a fall in inflation benefits the exchange rate (b) to benefit from** *or* **by something** = to be improved by something *or* to gain more money because of something; **exports have benefited from the fall in the exchange rate; the employees have benefited from the profit-sharing scheme**

QUOTE: the retail sector will also benefit from the expected influx of tourists
Australian Financial Review
QUOTE: what benefits does the executive derive from his directorship? Compensation has increased sharply in recent years and fringe benefits for directors have proliferated *Duns Business Month*
QUOTE: salary is negotiable to £30,000, plus car and a benefits package appropriate to this senior post *Financial Times*
QUOTE: California is the latest state to enact a program forcing welfare recipients to work for their benefits *Fortune*

bequest *noun* property, money, etc., given to someone in a will; **he made several bequests to his staff**

berth 1 *noun* place in a harbour where a ship can tie up **2** *verb* to tie up at a berth; **the ship will berth at Rotterdam on Wednesday**

BES = BUSINESS EXPANSION SCHEME

best 1 *adjective* very good *or* better than all others; **his best price is still higher than all the other suppliers; 1985 was the** company's best year ever **2** *noun* very good effort; **the salesmen are doing their best, but the stock simply will not sell at that price**

◇ **best-seller** *noun* item (especially a book) which sells very well

◇ **best-selling** *adjective* which sells very well; **these computer disks are our best-selling line**

bet 1 *noun* amount deposited when you risk money on the result of a race *or* of a game **2** *verb* to risk money on the result of something; **he bet £100 on the result of the election; I bet you £25 the dollar will rise against the pound; betting tax** = tax levied on betting on horses *or* dogs, etc.
NOTE: **betting - bet - has bet**

better *adjective* very good compared with something else; **this year's results are better than last year's; we will shop around to see if we can get a better price**

beware *verb* to be careful; **beware of imitations** = be careful not to buy cheap low-quality items which are made to look like more expensive items

bi- *prefix* twice; **bi-monthly** = twice a month; **bi-annually** = twice a year

bid 1 *noun* **(a)** offer to buy something at a certain price; **to make a bid for something** = to offer to buy something; **he made a bid for the house; the company made a bid for its rival; to make a cash bid** = to offer to pay cash for something; **to put in a bid for something** *or* **to enter a bid for something** = to offer (usually in writing) to buy something; (*at an auction*) **opening bid** = first bid; **closing bid** = last bid at an auction *or* the bid which is successful **(b)** offer to do some work at a certain price; **he made the lowest bid for the job;** *US* offer to sell something at a certain price; **they asked for bids for the supply of spare parts (c) takeover bid** = offer to buy all or a majority of shares in a company so as to control it; **to make a takeover bid for a company; to withdraw a takeover bid; the company rejected the takeover bid** = the directors recommended that the shareholders should not accept it **2** *verb* (*at an auction*) **to bid for something** = to offer to buy something; **he bid £1,000 for the jewels** = he offered to pay £1,000 for the jewels
NOTE: **bidding - bid - has bid**

◇ **bidder** *noun* person who makes a bid (usually at an auction); **several bidders made offers for the house; the property was sold to the highest bidder** = to the person who had made the highest bid *or* who offered the most money; **the tender will go to the lowest bidder** = to the person who offers the best terms *or* the lowest price for services

◇ **bidding** *noun* action of making offers to buy (usually at an auction); **the bidding started at £1,000** = the first and lowest bid was £1,000; **the bidding stopped at £250,000** = the last bid (and the successful bid) was for £250,000; **the auctioneer started the bidding at £100** = he suggested that the first bid should be £100
NOTE: no plural

Big Board *noun* *US* *informal* = NEW YORK STOCK EXCHANGE

bilateral *adjective* between two parties *or* countries; **the minister signed a bilateral trade agreement**

bill 1 *noun* **(a)** written list of charges to be paid; **the salesman wrote out the bill; does the bill include VAT? the bill is made out to Smith Ltd; the builder sent in his bill; he left the country without paying his bills; to foot the bill** = to pay the costs **(b)** list of charges in a restaurant; **can I have the bill please? the bill comes to £20 including service; does the bill include service? the waiter has added 10% to the bill for service (c)** written paper promising to pay money; **bill of exchange** = document which tells a bank to pay a person (usually used in payments in foreign currency); **accommodation bill** = bill of exchange where the person signing is helping someone else to raise a loan; **bank bill** = bill of exchange endorsed by a bank; **demand bill** = bill of exchange which must be paid when payment is asked for; **to accept a bill** = to sign a bill of exchange to show that you promise to pay it; **to discount a bill** = to buy a bill of exchange at a lower price than that written on it in order to cash it later; **bills payable** = bills which a debtor will have to pay; **bills receivable** = bills which a creditor will receive in the end **(d) bill of lading** = list of goods being shipped, which the transporter gives to the person sending the goods to show that the goods have been

loaded **(e)** *US* piece of paper money; **a $5 bill (f) bill of sale** = document which the seller gives to the buyer to show that the sale has taken place **(g)** draft of a new law which will be discussed in Parliament 2 *verb* to present a bill to someone so that it can be paid; **the builders billed him for the repairs to his neighbour's house**

◇ **billing** *noun* *US* writing of invoices or bills
NOTE: no plural

billion number one thousand million *or* one million million
NOTE: in the US it means 1,000 million, but in GB it usually means one million million. With figures it is usually written **bn: $5bn** say 'five billion dollars'

QUOTE: gross wool receipts for the selling season to end June 30 appear likely to top $2 billion   *Australian Financial Review*
QUOTE: at its last traded price the bank was capitalized at around $1.05 billion
South China Morning Post

bin *noun* large container; separate section of shelves in a warehouse; **dump bin** = display container like a large round box, filled with goods for sale

bind *verb* to tie *or* to attach; **the company is bound by its articles of association; he does not consider himself bound by the agreement which was signed by his predecessor**
NOTE: binding - bound

◇ **binder** *noun* **(a)** stiff cardboard cover for papers; **ring binder** = cover with rings in it which fit into special holes made in sheets of paper **(b)** *US* temporary agreement for insurance sent before the insurance policy is issued
NOTE: the GB English for this is **cover note**

◇ **binding** *adjective* which legally forces someone to do something; **a binding contract; this document is not legally binding; the agreement is binding on all parties** = all parties signing it must do what is agreed

black 1 *adjective* **(a) black market** = buying and selling goods in a way which is not allowed by law (as in a time of rationing); **there is a flourishing black market in spare parts for cars; you can buy gold coins on the black market; to pay**

black market prices = to pay high prices to get items which are not easily available **(b) black economy** = work which is paid for in cash, and therefore not declared for tax **(c) in the black** = in credit; **the company has moved into the black; my bank account is still in the black 2** *verb* to forbid trading in certain goods or with certain suppliers; **three firms were blacked by the government; the union has blacked a trucking firm**

◇ **blackleg** *noun* worker who goes on working when there is a strike

◇ **black list** *noun* list of goods or people or companies which have been blacked

◇ **blacklist** *verb* to put goods or people or a company on a black list; **his firm was blacklisted by the government**

blame 1 *noun* saying that someone has done something wrong or that someone is responsible; **the sales staff got the blame for the poor sales figures 2** *verb* to say that someone has done something wrong or is responsible for a mistake; **the managing director blamed the chief accountant for not warning him of the loss; the union is blaming the management for poor industrial relations**

blank 1 *adjective* with nothing written; **a blank cheque** = a cheque with no amount of money or name written on it, but signed by the drawer **2** *noun* space on a form which has to be completed; **fill in the blanks and return the form to your local office**

blanket *noun* thick woollen cover for a bed; **blanket agreement** = agreement which covers many items; **blanket insurance** = insurance which covers various items (such as a house and its contents); **blanket refusal** = refusal to accept many different items

blister pack *noun* type of packing where the item for sale is covered with a stiff plastic sheet sealed to a card backing

block 1 *noun* **(a)** series of items grouped together; **he bought a block of 6,000 shares; block booking** = booking of several seats or rooms at the same time; **the company has a block booking for twenty seats on the plane** or **for ten rooms at the**

hotel; **block vote** = voting of a large number of votes at the same time (such as those of a trade union delegation) **(b)** series of buildings forming a square with streets on all sides; **they want to redevelop a block in the centre of the town; a block of offices** or **an office block** = a large building which only contains offices **(c) block capitals** or **block letters** = capital letters (as A,B,C); **write your name and address in block letters 2** *verb* to stop something taking place; **he used his casting vote to block the motion; the planning committee blocked the redevelopment plan; blocked currency** = currency which cannot be taken out of a country because of exchange controls; **the company has a large account in blocked roubles**

blue *adjective* **blue-chip investments** or **blue-chip shares** or **blue chips** = risk-free shares in good companies; **blue-collar worker** = manual worker in a factory; **blue-collar union** = trade union formed mainly of blue-collar workers

blurb *noun* piece of advertising, especially an advertisement written by a publisher for a book

bn = BILLION

board 1 *noun* **(a)** *GB* **board of directors** = group of directors elected by the shareholders to run a company; **the bank has two representatives on the board; he sits on the board as a representative of the bank; two directors were removed from the board at the AGM; she was asked to join the board** = she was asked to become a director; **board meeting** = meeting of the directors of a company **(b)** *US* **board of directors** = group of people elected by the shareholders to draw up company policy and to appoint the president and other executive officers who are responsible for managing the company

NOTE: the board of an American company may be made up of a large number of non-executive directors and only one or two executive officers; a British board has more executive directors

(c) group of people who run a trust or a society; **advisory board** = group of advisors; **editorial board** = group of editors **(d) on board** = on a ship or plane or train; **free on board (f.o.b.)** = price includes all the seller's costs until the goods are on the ship for transportation **2** *verb* to go on to a ship *or* plane *or* train; **customs officials boarded the ship in the harbour**

◇ **boarding card** *or* **boarding pass** *noun* card given to passengers who have checked in for a flight to allow them to board the plane

◇ **boardroom** *noun* room where the directors of a company meet; **boardroom battles** = arguments between directors

QUOTE: a proxy is the written authorization an investor sends to a stockholder meeting conveying his vote on a corporate resolution or the election of a company's board of directors *Barrons*
QUOTE: CEOs, with their wealth of practical experience, are in great demand and can pick and choose the boards they want to serve on *Duns Business Month*

boat *noun* ship; **cargo boat; passenger boat; we took the night boat to Belgium; boats for Greece leave every morning**

bona fide *adjective* trustworthy *or* which can be trusted; **a bona fide offer** = an offer which is made honestly

bonanza *noun* great wealth; very profitable business; **the oil well was a bonanza for the company; 1984 was a bonanza year for the computer industry**

bond *noun* **(a)** contract document promising to repay money borrowed by a company *or* by the government; **government bonds** *or* **treasury bonds; municipal bond** *or* **local authority bond** = bond issued by a town or district **(b)** contract document promising to repay money borrowed by a person; **bearer bond** = bond which is payable to the bearer and does not have a name written on it; **debenture bond** = certificate showing that a debenture has been issued; **mortgage bond** = certificate showing that a mortgage exists and that property is security for it; *GB* **premium bond** = government bond, part of the National Savings scheme, which pays no interest, but gives the owner the chance to win a weekly or monthly prize **(c) goods (held) in bond** = goods held by the customs until duty has been paid; **entry of goods under bond** = bringing goods into a country in bond; **to take goods out of bond** = to pay duty on goods so that they can be released by the customs

◇ **bonded** *adjective* held in bond; **bonded warehouse** = warehouse where goods are stored in bond until duty is paid

◇ **bondholder** *noun* person who holds government bonds

◇ **bond-washing** *noun* selling American Treasury bonds with the interest coupon, and buying them back ex coupon, so as to reduce tax

bonus *noun* extra payment; **capital bonus** = extra payment by an insurance company which is produced by capital gain; **cost-of-living bonus** = money paid to meet the increase in the cost of living; **Christmas bonus** = extra payment made to staff at Christmas; **incentive bonus** = extra pay offered to a worker to encourage him to work harder; **productivity bonus** = extra payment made because of increased productivity; **bonus share** = extra share given to an existing shareholder; **no-claims bonus** = reduction of premiums on an insurance because no claims have been made
NOTE: plural is **bonuses**

book 1 *noun* **(a)** set of sheets of paper attached together; **a company's books** = the financial records of a company; **account book** = book which records sales and purchases; **cash book** = record of cash; **order book** = record of orders; **the company has a full order book** = it has sufficient orders to keep the workforce occupied; **purchase book** = records of purchases; **sales book** = records of sales; **book sales** = sales as recorded in the sales book; **book value** = value as recorded in the company's books **(b) bank book** = book which shows money which you have deposited or withdrawn from a bank account; **cheque book** = book of new cheques; **phone book** *or* **telephone book** = book which lists names of people or companies with their addresses and telephone numbers **2** *verb* to order *or* to reserve something; **to book a room in a hotel** *or* **a table at a restaurant** *or* **a ticket on a plane; I booked a table for 7.45; he booked a ticket through to Cairo; to book someone into a hotel** *or* **onto a flight** = to order a room *or* a plane ticket for someone; **he was booked on the 09.00 flight to Zurich; the hotel** *or* **the flight is fully booked** *or* **is booked**

up = all the rooms *or* seats are reserved; **the restaurant is booked up over the Christmas period**

◊ **booking** *noun* act of ordering a room *or* a seat; **hotel bookings have fallen since the end of the tourist season; booking clerk** = person who sells tickets in a booking office; **booking office** = office where you can book seats at a theatre *or* tickets for the railway; **block booking** = booking of several seats *or* rooms at the same time; **to confirm a booking** = to say that a booking is certain; **double booking** = booking by mistake of two people into the same hotel room *or* the same seat on a plane

◊ **bookkeeper** *noun* person who keeps the financial records of a company

◊ **bookkeeping** *noun* keeping of the financial records of a company *or* an organization; **single-entry bookkeeping** = noting a deal with only one entry; **double-entry bookkeeping** = noting of both credit and debit sides of an account
NOTE: no plural

◊ **booklet** *noun* small book with a paper cover

◊ **bookseller** *noun* person who sells books

◊ **bookshop** *noun* shop which sells books

◊ **bookstall** *noun* small open bookshop (as in a railway station)

◊ **bookstore** *noun* *US* bookshop

◊ **bookwork** *noun* keeping of financial records
NOTE: no plural

boom 1 *noun* time when sales *or* production *or* business activity are increasing; **a period of economic boom; the boom of the 1970s; boom industry** = industry which is expanding rapidly; **a boom share** = share in a company which is expanding; **the boom years** = years when there is an economic boom 2 *verb* to expand *or* to become prosperous; **business is booming; sales are booming**

◊ **booming** *adjective* which is expanding *or* becoming prosperous; **a booming industry** *or* **company; technology is a booming sector of the economy**

boost 1 *noun* help to increase; **this publicity will give sales a boost; the**

government hopes to give a boost to industrial development 2 *verb* to make something increase; **we expect our publicity campaign to boost sales by 25%; the company hopes to boost its market share; incentive schemes are boosting production**

QUOTE: the company expects to boost turnover this year to FFr 16bn from FFr 13.6bn in 1984
Financial Times

booth *noun* **(a)** small place for one person to stand or sit; **telephone booth** = public box with a telephone; **ticket booth** = place outdoors where a person sells tickets **(b)** *US* section of a commercial fair where a company exhibits its products or services
NOTE: the GB English for this is **stand**

borrow *verb* to take money from someone for a time, possibly paying interest for it, and repaying it at the end of the period; **he borrowed £1,000 from the bank; the company had to borrow heavily to repay its debts; they borrowed £25,000 against the security of the factory; to borrow short** *or* **long** = to borrow for a short *or* long period

◊ **borrower** *noun* person who borrows; **borrowers from the bank pay 12% interest**

◊ **borrowing** *noun* **(a)** action of borrowing money; **the new factory was financed by bank borrowing; borrowing power** = amount of money which a company can borrow **(b)** **borrowings** = money borrowed; **the company's borrowings have doubled; bank borrowings** = loans made by banks

boss *noun informal* employer *or* person in charge of a company *or* an office; **if you want a pay rise, go and talk to your boss; he became a director when he married the boss's daughter**

bottleneck *noun* position when business activity is slowed down because one section of the operation cannot cope with the amount of work; **a bottleneck in the supply system; there are serious bottlenecks in the production line**

bottom 1 *noun* lowest part *or* point; **sales have reached rock bottom** = the very lowest point of all; **the bottom has fallen out of the market** = sales have fallen below what previously seemed to be the lowest point; **bottom price** = lowest price; **rock-bottom price** = lowest price of all; **bottom line** = last line on a balance sheet indicating profit or loss; **the boss is interested only in the bottom line** = he is only interested in the final profit **2** *verb* **to bottom (out)** = to reach the lowest point; **the market has bottomed out** = has reached the lowest point and does not seem likely to fall further

bottomry *noun* mortgage of a ship to pay for repairs

bought *see* BUY **bought ledger** = book in which expenditure is noted; **bought ledger clerk** = office worker who deals with the bought ledger

bounce *verb* (*of a cheque*) to be returned to the person who has tried to cash it, because there is not enough money in the payer's account to pay it; **he paid for the car with a cheque that bounced**

bounty *noun* government subsidy made to help an industry

boutique *noun* small specialized shop, especially for up-to-date clothes; section of a department store selling up-to-date clothes; **a jeans boutique; a ski boutique**

box *noun* (**a**) cardboard *or* wood *or* plastic container; **the goods were sent in thin cardboard boxes; the watches are prepacked in plastic display boxes; paperclips come in boxes of two hundred** = packed two hundred to a box; **box file** = file (for papers) made like a box (**b**) **box number** = reference number used in a post office or an advertisement to avoid giving an address; **please reply to Box No. 209; our address is: P.O. Box 74209, Edinburgh** (**c**) **cash box** = metal box for keeping cash; **letter box** *or* **mail box** = place where incoming mail is put; **call box** = outdoor telephone kiosk
◊ **boxed** *adjective* put in a box *or* sold in a box; **boxed set** = set of items sold together in a box

boycott **1** *noun* refusal to buy *or* to deal in certain products; **the union organized a boycott against** *or* **of imported cars 2** *verb* to

refuse to buy *or* to deal in a certain product; **we are boycotting all imports from that country; the management has boycotted the meeting** = has refused to attend the meeting

bracket **1** *noun* group of items *or* people taken together; **people in the middle-income bracket** = people with average incomes, not high or low; **he is in the top tax bracket** = he pays the highest level of tax **2** *verb* **to bracket together** = to treat several items together in the same way; **in the sales reports, all the European countries are bracketed together**

branch **1** *noun* local office of a bank or large business; local shop of a large chain of shops; **the bank** *or* **the store has branches in most towns in the south of the country; the insurance company has closed its branches in South America; he is the manager of our local branch of Lloyds bank; we have decided to open a branch office in Chicago; the manager of our branch in Lagos** *or* **of our Lagos branch; branch manager** = manager of a branch **2** *verb* **to branch out** = to start a new (but usually related) type of business; **from car retailing, the company branched out into car leasing**

QUOTE: a leading manufacturer of business. industrial and commercial products requires a branch manager to head up its mid-western Canada operations based in Winnipeg
Globe and Mail (Toronto)

brand *noun* make of product, which can be recognized by a name *or* by a design; **the top-selling brands of toothpaste; the company is launching a new brand of soap; brand name** = name of a brand; **brand image** = idea of a product which is associated with the brand name; **brand loyalty** = loyalty by the customer who always buys the same brand; **own brand** = name of a store which is used on products which are specially packed for that store
◊ **branded** *adjective* **branded goods** = goods sold under brand names
◊ **brand new** *adjective* quite new *or* very new

breach *noun* failure to carry out the terms of an agreement; **breach of contract** = failing to do something which is in a contract; **the company is in breach of contract** = it has failed to carry out the duties of the contract; **breach of warranty** = supplying goods which do not meet the standards of the warranty applied to them

break 1 *noun* short space of time, when you can rest; **she typed for two hours without a break; coffee break** *or* **tea break** = rest time during work when the workers can drink coffee or tea 2 *verb* **(a)** to fail to carry out the duties of a contract; **the company has broken the contract** *or* **the agreement; to break an engagement to do something** = not to do what has been agreed **(b)** to cancel (a contract); **the company is hoping to be able to break the contract**
NOTE: **breaking - broke - has broken**

◇ **breakages** *plural noun* breaking of items; **customers are expected to pay for breakages**

◇ **break down** *verb* **(a)** to stop working because of mechanical failure; **the telex machine has broken down; what do you do when your photocopier breaks down? (b)** to stop; **negotiations broke down after six hours (c)** to show all the items in a total list of costs *or* expenditure; **we broke the expenditure down into fixed and variable costs; can you break down this invoice into spare parts and labour?**

◇ **breakdown** *noun* **(a)** stopping work because of mechanical failure; **we cannot communicate with our Nigerian office because of the breakdown of the telex lines (b)** stopping talking; **a breakdown in wage negotiations (c)** showing details item by item; **give me a breakdown of investment costs**

◇ **break even** *verb* to balance costs and receipts, but not make a profit; **last year the company only just broke even; we broke even in our first two months of trading**

◇ **breakeven point** *noun* point at which sales cover costs, but do not show a profit

◇ **break off** *verb* to stop; **we broke off the discussion at midnight; management broke off negotiations with the union**

◇ **break up** *verb* **(a)** to split something large into small sections; **the company was broken up and separate divisions sold off (b)** to come to an end; **the meeting broke up at 12.30**

bribe 1 *noun* money given to someone in authority to get him to help; **the minister was dismissed for taking bribes** 2 *verb* to pay someone money to get him to do something for you; **we had to bribe the minister's secretary before she would let us see her boss**

bridging loan *noun* short-term loan to help someone buy a new house when he has not yet sold his old one

brief *verb* to explain to someone in detail; **the salesmen were briefed on the new product; the managing director briefed the board on the progress of the negotiations**

◇ **briefcase** *noun* case with a handle for carrying papers and documents; **he put all the files into his briefcase**

◇ **briefing** *noun* telling someone details; **all salesmen have to attend a sales briefing on the new product**

bring *verb* to come to a place with someone or something; **he brought his documents with him; the finance director brought his secretary to take notes of the meeting; to bring a lawsuit against someone** = to tell someone to appear in court to settle an argument
NOTE: **bringing - brought**

◇ **bring down** *verb* **(a)** to reduce; **petrol companies have brought down the price of oil (b)** to add a figure to an account at the end of a period to balance expenditure and income; **balance brought down: £365.15**

◇ **bring forward** *verb* **(a)** to make earlier; **to bring forward the date of repayment; the date of the next meeting has been brought forward to March (b)** to take a balance brought down as the starting point for the next period in a balance sheet; **balance brought forward: £365.15**

◇ **bring in** *verb* to earn (an interest); **the shares bring in a small amount**

◇ **bring out** *verb* to produce something new; **they are bringing out a new model of the car for the Motor Show**

◇ **bring up** *verb* to refer to something for the first time; **the chairman brought up the question of redundancy payments**

brisk *adjective* selling actively; **sales are brisk; the market in oil shares is particularly brisk; a brisk market in oil shares**

broadside *noun*   *US* publicity leaflet

brochure *noun* publicity booklet; **we sent off for a brochure about holidays in Greece** *or* **about postal services**

broke *adjective*   *informal* having no money; **the company is broke; he cannot pay for the new car because he is broke; to go broke** = to become bankrupt; **the company went broke last month**

broker *noun* **(a)** dealer; **foreign exchange broker** = person who buys and sells foreign currency on behalf of other people; **insurance broker** = person who sells insurance to clients; **ship broker** = person who sells shipping *or* transport of goods to clients **(b) (stock)broker** = person who buys or sells shares for clients
◇ **brokerage** *or* **broker's commission** *noun* payment to a broker for a deal carried out
◇ **broking** *noun* dealing in stocks and shares

bubble pack *noun* = BLISTER PACK

buck 1 *noun US informal* dollar **2** *verb* **to buck the trend** = to go against the trend

bucket shop *noun* *informal* travel agent selling airline tickets at a discount

budget 1 *noun* **(a)** plan of expected spending and income (usually for one year); **to draw up a budget; we have agreed the budgets for next year; advertising budget** = money planned for spending on advertising; **cash budget** = plan of cash income and expenditure; **overhead budget** = plan of probable overhead costs; **publicity budget** = money allowed for expected expenditure on publicity; **sales budget** = plan of probable sales **(b) the Budget** = the annual plan of taxes and government spending proposed by a finance minister; **the minister put forward a budget aimed at boosting the economy; to balance the budget** = to plan income and expenditure so that they balance; **the president is planning for a balanced budget (c)** (*in a bank*) **budget account** = bank account where you plan income and expenditure to allow for periods when

expenditure is high, by paying a set amount each month **(d)** (*in shops*) cheap; **budget department** = cheaper department; **budget prices** = low prices **2** *verb* to plan probable income and expenditure; **we are budgeting for £10,000 of sales next year**
◇ **budgetary** *adjective* referring to a budget; **budgetary policy** = policy of planning income and expenditure; **budgetary control** = keeping check on spending; **budgetary requirements** = spending or income required to meet the budget forecasts
◇ **budgeting** *noun* preparing of budgets to help plan expenditure and income
NOTE: no plural

build *verb* to make by putting pieces together; **to build a sales structure; to build on past experience** = to use experience as a base on which to act in the future
NOTE: **building - built**
◇ **building** *noun* house *or* factory *or* office block, etc.; **they have redeveloped the site of the old office building; the Shell Building** = the office block where the head office of Shell is
◇ **building and loan association** *noun*   *US* = SAVINGS AND LOAN ASSOCIATION
◇ **building society** *noun*   *GB* financial institution which accepts and pays interest on deposits and lends money to people who are buying property; **he put his savings into a building society** *or* **into a building society account; I have an account with the Halifax Building Society; I saw the building society manager to ask for a mortgage**
◇ **build into** *verb* to add something to something being set up; **you must build all the forecasts into the budget; we have built 10% for contingencies into our cost forecast** = we have added 10% to our basic forecast to allow for items which may appear suddenly

◇ **build up** *verb* **(a)** to create something by adding pieces together; **he bought several shoe shops and gradually built up a chain (b)** to expand something gradually; **to build up a profitable business; to build up a team of salesmen**

◇ **buildup** *noun* gradual increase; **a buildup in sales** *or* **a sales buildup; there will be a big publicity buildup before the launch of the new model**

◇ **built-in** *adjective* forming part of the system *or* of a machine; **the micro has a built-in clock; the accounting system has a series of built-in checks**

bulk *noun* large quantity of goods; **in bulk** = in large quantities; **to buy rice in bulk; bulk buying** *or* **bulk purchase** = buying large quantities of goods at a lower price; **bulk carrier** = ship which carries large quantities of loose goods (such as coal); **bulk shipments** = shipments of large quantities of goods
NOTE: no plural

◇ **bulky** *adjective* large and awkward; **the Post Office does not accept bulky packages**

bull *noun* *Stock Exchange* dealer who believes the market will rise, and therefore buys shares to sell at a higher price later; **bull market** = period when share prices rise because people are optimistic and buy shares; *see* BEAR

> QUOTE: lower interest rates are always a bull factor for the stock market *Financial Times*

bullion *noun* gold or silver bars; **gold bullion; the price of bullion is fixed daily; to fix the bullion price for silver**
NOTE: no plural

bumper *noun* very large crop; **a bumper crop of corn; 1984 was a bumper year for computer sales** = 1984 was an excellent year for sales

bumping *noun* *US* situation where a senior employee takes the place of a junior (in a restaurant *or* in a job)

bureau *noun* office which specializes; **computer bureau** = office which offers to do work on its computers for companies which do not own their own computers;

employment bureau = office which finds jobs for people; **information bureau** = office which gives information; **trade bureau** = office which specializes in commercial enquiries; **visitors' bureau** = office which deals with visitors' questions; **word-processing bureau** = office which specializes in word-processing; **we farm out the office typing to a local bureau**
NOTE: the plural is **bureaux**

◇ **bureau de change** *noun* office where you can change foreign currency

burn *verb* to destroy by fire; **the chief accountant burnt the documents before the police arrived**
NOTE: **burning - burnt**

◇ **burn down** *verb* to destroy completely in a fire; **the warehouse burnt down and all the stock was destroyed; the company records were all lost when the offices were burnt down**

bus *noun* motor vehicle for carrying passengers; **he goes to work by bus; she took the bus to go to her office; bus company** = company which runs the buses in a town

bushel *noun* measure of dry goods, such as corn (= 56 pounds)

business *noun* **(a)** work in buying or selling; **business is expanding; business is slow; he does a thriving business in repairing cars; what's your line of business?; business call** = visit to talk to someone on business; **business centre** = part of a town where the main banks, shops and offices are located; **business class** = type of airline travel which is less expensive than first class and more comfortable than tourist class; **business college** *or* **business school** = place where commercial studies are taught; **business correspondent** = journalist who writes articles on business news for newspapers; **business efficiency exhibition** = exhibition which shows products (computers, word-processors) which help a business to be efficient; **business letter** = letter about commercial matters; **business lunch** = lunch to discuss business matters; **business trip** = trip to discuss business matters with clients; **to be in business** = to be in a commercial firm; **to go into business** = to start a commercial firm; **he went into business as a car dealer; to go out**

of business = to stop trading; **the firm went out of business during the recession; on business** = on commercial work; **he had to go abroad on business; the chairman is in Holland on business (b)** commercial company; **he owns a small car repair business; she runs a business from her home; he set up in business as an insurance broker; business address** = details of number, street and town where a company is located; **business card** = card showing a businessman's name and the name and address of the company he works for; **business correspondence** = letters concerned with a business; **business equipment** = machines used in an office; **business expansion scheme** = system in Britain where money invested for some years in a new company is free from tax; **business expenses** = money spent on running a business, not on stock or assets; **business hours** = time (usually 9 a.m. to 5 p.m.) when a business is open; **big business** = very large commercial firms **(c)** affairs discussed; **the main business of the meeting was finished by 3 p.m.; any other business** = item at the end of an agenda, where any matter can be raised
NOTE: no plural for meanings (a) and (c); (b) has the plural **businesses**

◇ **business agent** *noun* *US* chief local official of a trade union

◇ **businessman** *or* **businesswoman** *noun* man *or* woman engaged in business; **she's a good businesswoman** = she is good at commercial deals; **a small businessman** = man who owns a small business

bust *adjective* *informal* **to go bust** = to become bankrupt

busy *adjective* occupied in doing something/in working; **he is busy preparing the annual accounts; the manager is busy at the moment, but he will be free in about fifteen minutes; the busiest time of year for stores is the week before Christmas; summer is the busy season for hotels; the line is busy** = the telephone line is being used

buy **1** *verb* to get something by paying money; **he bought 10,000 shares; the company has been bought by its leading supplier; to buy wholesale and sell retail; to buy for cash; to buy forward** = to buy foreign currency before you need it, in order to be sure of the exchange rate
NOTE: **buying - bought**
2 *noun* **good buy** *or* **bad buy** = thing bought which is *or* is not worth the money paid for it; **that watch was a good buy; this car was a bad buy**

◇ **buy back** *verb* to buy something which you have sold; **he sold the shop last year and is now trying to buy it back**

◇ **buyer** *noun* **(a)** person who buys; **there were no buyers** = no one wanted to buy; **a buyers' market** = market where products are sold cheaply because there are few buyers; **impulse buyer** = person who buys something when he sees it, not because he was planning to buy it **(b)** person who buys a certain type of goods wholesale, which are then stocked by a large store; **head buyer** = most important buyer in a store; **she is the shoe buyer for a London department store**

◇ **buy in** *verb* (*of a seller at an auction*) to buy the thing which you are trying to sell because no one will pay the price you want

◇ **buying** *noun* getting something for money; **bulk buying** = getting large quantities of goods at low prices; **forward buying** *or* **buying forward** = buying shares *or* commodities *or* currency for delivery at a later date; **impulse buying** = buying items which you have just seen, not because you had planned to buy them; **panic buying** = rush to buy something at any price because stocks may run out; **buying department** = department in a company which buys raw materials or goods for use in the company; **buying power** = ability to buy; **the buying power of the pound has fallen over the last years**
NOTE: no plural

◇ **buyout** *noun* **management buyout** = takeover of a company by a group of employees (usually managers and directors); **leveraged buyout** = buying all the shares in a company by borrowing money against the security of the shares to be bought

QUOTE: we also invest in companies whose growth and profitability could be improved by a management buyout   *Times*
QUOTE: in a normal leveraged buyout, the acquirer raises money by borrowing against the assets or cash flow of the target company   *Fortune*

by-product *noun* product made as a result of manufacturing a main product; **soap is a useful by-product of oil**

byte *noun* storage unit in a computer, equal to one character

Cc

cabinet *noun* piece of furniture for storing records or display; **last year's correspondence is in the bottom drawer of the filing cabinet; display cabinet =** piece of furniture with a glass top or glass doors for showing goods for sale

cable 1 *noun* telegram *or* message sent by telegraph; **he sent a cable to his office asking for more money; cable address =** specially short address for sending cables 2 *verb* to send a message *or* money by telegraph; **he cabled his office to ask them to send more money; the office cabled him £1,000 to cover his expenses**
◇ **cablegram** *noun* telegram *or* message sent by telegraph

calculate *verb* (a) to find the answer to a problem using numbers; **the bank clerk calculated the rate of exchange for the dollar** (b) to estimate; **I calculate that we have six months' stock left**
◇ **calculating machine** *noun* machine which calculates
◇ **calculation** *noun* answer to a problem in mathematics; **rough calculation =** approximate answer; **I made some rough calculations on the back of an envelope; according to my calculations, we have six months' stock left; we are £20,000 out in our calculations =** we have £20,000 too much or too little
◇ **calculator** *noun* electronic machine which works out the answers to problems in mathematics; **my pocket calculator needs a new battery; he worked out the discount on his calculator**

calendar *noun* book *or* set of sheets of paper showing the days and months in a year, often attached to pictures; **for the New Year the garage sent me a calendar with photographs of old cars; calendar month =** a whole month as on a calendar, from the 1st to the 30th or 31st; **calendar year =** year from the 1st January to 31st December

call 1 *noun* (a) conversation on the telephone; **local call =** call to a number on the same exchange; **trunk call** *or* **long-distance call =** call to a number in a different zone *or* area; **overseas call** *or* **international call =** call to another country; **person-to-person call =** call where you ask the operator to connect you with a named person; **transferred charge call** *or* *US* **collect call =** call where the person receiving the call agrees to pay for it; **to make a call =** to dial and speak to someone on the telephone; **to take a call =** to answer the telephone; **to log calls =** to note all details of telephone calls made (b) demand for repayment of a loan by a lender; **money at call** *or* **money on call** *or* **call money =** money loaned for which repayment can be demanded without notice (c) *Stock Exchange* demand to pay for new shares; **call option =** option to buy shares at a certain price (d) visit; **the salesmen make six calls a day; business call =** visit to talk to someone on business; **cold call =** sales visit where the salesman has no appointment and the client is not an established customer; **call rate =** number of calls (per day or per week) made by a salesman 2 *verb* (a) to telephone to someone; **I'll call you at your office tomorrow** (b) to call on someone = to visit; **our salesmen call on their best accounts twice a month** (c) to ask someone to do something; **the union called a strike =** the union told its members to go on strike
◇ **callable bond** *noun* bond which must be repaid at notice
◇ **call-back pay** *noun* pay given to a worker who has been called back to work after his normal working hours
◇ **call box** *noun* outdoor telephone kiosk
◇ **called up capital** *noun* share capital in a company which has been paid for
◇ **caller** *noun* (a) person who telephones (b) person who visits
◇ **call in** *verb* (a) to visit; **the sales representative called in twice last week** (b) to telephone to make contact; **we ask the**

reps to call in every Friday to report the weeks' sales **(c)** to ask for a debt to be paid
◇ **call off** *verb* to ask for something not to take place; **the union has called off the strike; the deal was called off at the last moment**
◇ **call up** *verb* to ask for share capital to be paid

calm *adjective* quiet *or* not excited; **the markets were calmer after the government statement on the exchange rate**

campaign *noun* planned method of working; **sales campaign** = planned work to achieve higher sales; **publicity campaign** *or* **advertising campaign** = planned period when publicity takes place; **they are working on a campaign to launch a new brand of soap**

cancel *verb* **(a)** to stop something which has been agreed *or* planned; **to cancel an appointment** *or* **a meeting; to cancel a contract; the government has cancelled the order for a fleet of buses (b)** to cancel a cheque = to stop payment of a cheque which you have signed
NOTE: GB English: **cancelling - cancelled** but US English: **canceling - canceled**
◇ **cancellation** *noun* stopping something which has been agreed *or* planned; **cancellation of an appointment; cancellation of an agreement; cancellation clause** = clause in a contract which states the terms on which the contract may be cancelled
◇ **cancel out** *verb* to balance and so make invalid *or* even; **the two clauses cancel each other out; costs have cancelled out the sales revenue**

candidate *noun* person who applies for a job; **there are six candidates for the post of assistant manager**

canvass *verb* to visit people to ask them to buy goods *or* to vote *or* to say what they think; **he's canvassing for customers for his hairdresser's shop; we have canvassed the staff about raising the prices in the staff restaurant**
◇ **canvasser** *noun* person who canvasses

◇ **canvassing** *noun* action of asking people to buy *or* to vote *or* to say what they think; **canvassing techniques; door-to-door canvassing**
NOTE: no plural

CAP = COMMON AGRICULTURAL POLICY

capable *adjective* **(a) capable of** = able *or* clever enough to do something; **she is capable of very fast typing speeds; the sales force must be capable of selling all the stock in the warehouse (b)** efficient; **she is a very capable departmental manager**
NOTE: you are capable **of** something or **of doing** something

capacity *noun* **(a)** amount which can be produced *or* amount of work which can be done; **industrial** *or* **manufacturing** *or* **production capacity; to work at full capacity** = to do as much work as possible; **to use up spare** *or* **excess capacity** = to make use of time *or* space which is not fully used **(b)** amount of space; **storage capacity** = space available for storage; **warehouse capacity** = space available in a warehouse **(c)** ability; **he has a particular capacity for business; earning capacity** = amount of money someone is able to earn **(d) in a capacity** = acting as; **in his capacity as chairman; speaking in an official capacity** = speaking officially
NOTE: no plural for (a), (b) and (c)

QUOTE: analysts are increasingly convinced that the industry simply has too much capacity
Fortune

capita *see* PER CAPITA

capital *noun* **(a)** money, property and assets used in a business; **company with £10,000 capital** *or* **with a capital of £10,000; authorized capital** = maximum capital which is permitted by a company's articles of association; **capital account** = account of dealings (money invested in the company, or taken out of the company) by the owners of a company; **capital assets** = property *or* machines, etc. which a company owns and uses; **capital bonus** = bonus payment by an insurance company which is produced by capital gain; **capital equipment** = equipment which a factory or office uses to work; **capital expenditure** *or* **investment** *or* **outlay** = money spent on fixed assets (property, machines, furniture); **capital gains** = money made by selling a fixed asset *or* by selling shares; **capital gains tax** = tax paid on capital gains; **capital goods** = goods used to manufacture other goods (i.e. machinery); **capital levy** = tax on the value of a person's property and possessions; **capital loss** = loss made by selling assets; **capital reserves** = part of share capital which can be used only when a company is wound up; **capital structure of a company** = way in which a company's capital is set up; **capital transfer tax** = tax on gifts or bequests of money or property; **circulating capital** = capital required in the form of raw materials, finished products and work in progress for a company to carry on its business; **equity capital** = amount of a company's capital which is owned by the shareholders; **fixed capital** = capital in the form of buildings and machinery; **issued capital** = amount of capital issued as shares to the shareholders; **paid-up capital** = amount of money paid for the issued capital shares; **risk capital** *or* **venture capital** = capital for investment which may easily be lost in risky projects; **share capital** = value of the assets of a company held as shares, less its debts; **working capital** = capital in cash and stocks needed for a company to be able to work **(b)** money for investment; **movements of capital** = changes of investments from one country to another; **flight of capital** = rapid movement of capital out of one country because of lack of confidence in that country's economic future; **capital market** = places where companies can look for investment capital **(c) capital letters** *or* **block capitals** = letters written as A, B, C, D, etc., and not a, b, c, d; **write your name in block capitals at the top of the form**

NOTE: no plural for (a) and (b)

◇ **capitalism** *noun* economic system where each person has the right to invest money, to work in business, to buy and sell, with no restriction from the state

◇ **capitalist** **1** *noun* person who invests money in a business **2** *adjective* working according to the principles of capitalism; **a capitalist economy; the capitalist system; the capitalist countries** *or* **world**

◇ **capitalize** *verb* to invest money in a working company; **company capitalized at £10,000** = company with a working capital of £10,000

◇ **capitalize on** *verb* to make a profit from; **to capitalize on one's market position**

◇ **capitalization** *noun* **market capitalization** = value of a company calculated by multiplying the price of its shares on the stock exchange by the number of shares issued; **company with a £1m capitalization; capitalization of reserves** = issuing free bonus shares to shareholders

QUOTE: to prevent capital from crossing the Atlantic in search of high US interest rates and exchange-rate capital gains *Duns Business Month*
QUOTE: Canadians' principal residences have always been exempt from capital gains tax
Toronto Star
QUOTE: issued and fully paid capital is $100 million, comprising 2340 shares of $100 each and 997,660 ordinary shares of $100 each
Hongkong Standard
QUOTE: at its last traded price the bank was capitalized at around $1.05 billion with 60 per cent in the hands of the family
South China Morning Post

captive market *noun* market where one supplier has a monopoly and the buyer has no choice over the product which he must purchase

capture *verb* to take *or* to get control of something; **to capture 10% of the market** = to sell hard, and so take a 10% market share; **to capture 20% of a company's shares** = to buy shares in a company rapidly and so own 20% of it

car *noun* small motor vehicle for carrying people; **company car** = car owned by a company and lent to a member of staff to use as if it were his own

◇ **car-hire** *noun* business of lending cars to people for money; **he runs a car-hire business**

carat *noun* **(a)** measure of the quality of gold (pure gold being 24 carat); **a 22-carat gold ring (b)** measure of the weight of precious stones; **a 5-carat diamond**
NOTE: no plural

carbon *noun* **(a)** carbon paper; **you forgot to put a carbon in the typewriter (b)** carbon copy; **make a top copy and two carbons**

◇ **carbon copy** *noun* copy made with carbon paper; **give me the original, and file the carbon copy**

◇ **carbonless** *adjective* which makes a copy without using carbon paper; **our reps use carbonless order pads**

◇ **carbon paper** *noun* sheet of paper with a black material on one side, used in a typewriter to make a copy; **you put the carbon paper in the wrong way round**

card *noun* **(a)** stiff paper; **we have printed the instructions on thick white card** NOTE: no plural **(b)** small piece of stiff paper or plastic; **business card** = card showing a businessman's name and the address of the company he works for; **cash card** = plastic card used to obtain money from a cash dispenser; **charge card** = plastic card which allows you to buy goods and pay for them later; **cheque (guarantee) card** = plastic card from a bank which guarantees payment of a cheque; **credit card** = plastic card which allows you to borrow money or to buy goods without paying for them immediately; **filing card** = card with information written on it, used to classify information in correct order; **index card** = card used to make a card index; **punched card** = card with holes punched in it which a computer can read **(c)** postcard; **reply paid card** = card to be sent back to the sender with a reply on it, the sender having already paid the postage **(d) to get one's cards** = to be dismissed

◇ **cardboard** *noun* thick stiff brown paper; **cardboard box** = box made of cardboard
NOTE: no plural

◇ **card index** *noun* series of cards with information written on them, kept in special order so that the information can be found easily; **card-index file** = information kept on filing cards

◇ **card-index** *verb* to put information onto a card index

◇ **card-indexing** *noun* putting information onto a card index; **no one can understand her card-indexing system**

care of *phrase* (*in an address*) words to show that the person lives at the address, but only as a visitor; **Herr Schmidt, care of Mr W. Brown**

career *noun* job which you are trained for, and which you expect to do all your life; **he made his career in electronics; career woman** *or* **girl** = woman who is working in business and does not plan to stop working to look after the house or children

cargo *noun* load of goods which are sent in a ship *or* plane, etc.; **the ship was taking on cargo** = was being loaded with goods; **to load cargo** = to put cargo on a ship; **air cargo** = goods sent by air; **cargo ship** *or* **cargo plane** = ship *or* plane which carries only cargo and not passengers
NOTE: plural is **cargoes**

carnet *noun* international document which allows dutiable goods to cross several European countries by road without paying duty until the goods reach their final destination

carriage *noun* transporting goods from one place to another; cost of transport of goods; **to pay for carriage; to allow 10% for carriage; carriage is 15% of the total cost; carriage free** = deal where the customer does not pay for the shipping; **carriage paid** = deal where the seller has paid for the shipping; **carriage forward** = deal where the customer will pay for the shipping when the goods arrive
NOTE: no plural

carrier *noun* **(a)** company which transports goods; **we only use reputable carriers; air carrier** = company which sends cargo *or* passengers by air **(b)** vehicle *or* ship which transports goods; **bulk carrier** = ship which carries large quantities of loose goods (such as corn)

carry *verb* **(a)** to take from one place to another; **to carry goods; a tanker carrying oil from the Gulf; the train was carrying a consignment of cars for export (b)** to vote to approve; **the motion was carried** = the motion was accepted after a vote **(c)** to produce; **the bonds carry interest at 10% (d)** to keep in stock; **to carry a line of goods; we do not carry pens**

◇ **carry forward** *verb* to take a balance brought down as the starting point for the next period or page; **balance carried forward** = amount entered in an account at the end of a period to balance the income and expenditure which is then taken forward to start the next period

◇ **carrying** *noun* transporting from one place to another; **carrying charges; carrying cost**
NOTE: no plural

◇ **carry on** *verb* to continue *or* to go on doing something; **the staff carried on working in spite of the fire; to carry on a business** = to be active in running a business

◇ **carry over** *verb* **(a) to carry over a balance** = to take a balance from the end of one page or period to the beginning of the next **(b) to carry over stock** = to hold stock from the end of one stocktaking period to the beginning of the next

cartage *noun* carrying goods by road
NOTE: no plural

cartel *noun* group of companies which try to fix the price *or* to regulate the supply of a product because they can then profit from this situation

carter *noun* person who transports goods by road

carton *noun* **(a)** thick cardboard; **a folder made of carton (b)** box made of cardboard; **a carton of cigarettes**
NOTE: no plural for (a)

case 1 *noun* **(a)** suitcase *or* box with a handle for carrying clothes and personal belongings when travelling; **the customs made him open his case; she had a small case which she carried onto the plane (b)** cardboard or wooden box for packing and carrying goods; **six cases of wine** = six boxes, each containing twelve bottles; **a packing case** = large wooden box for carrying items which can be easily broken **(c) display case** = table or counter with a glass top, used for displaying items for sale **(d) court case** = legal action or trial; **the case is being heard next week** = the case is coming to court 2 *verb* to pack in a case

cash 1 *noun* **(a)** money in coins or notes; **cash in hand** = money and notes in the till, kept to pay small debts; **hard cash =** money in notes and coins, as opposed to cheques or credit cards; **petty cash** = small amounts of money; **ready cash** = money which is immediately available for payment; **cash account** = account which records the money which is received and spent; **cash advance =** loan in cash against a future payment; **cash balance** = balance in cash, as opposed to amounts owed; **cash book** = book in which cash transactions are entered; **cash box** = metal box for keeping cash; **cash budget =** plan of cash income and expenditure; **cash card** = card used to obtain money from a cash dispenser; **cash desk** = place in a store where you pay for the goods bought; **cash dispenser** = machine which gives out money when a special card is inserted and instructions given; **cash float** = cash put into the cash box at the beginning of the day or week to allow business to start; **cash offer** = offer to pay in cash; **cash payment** = payment in cash; **cash purchases** = purchases made in cash; **cash register** *or* **cash till** = machine which shows and adds the prices of items bought, with a drawer for keeping the cash received; **cash reserves** = a company's reserves in cash, deposits or bills, kept in case of urgent need **(b)** using money in coins or notes; **to pay cash down** = to pay in cash immediately; **cash price** *or* **cash terms** = lower price *or* terms which apply if the customer pays cash; **settlement in cash** *or* **cash settlement** = paying a bill in cash; **cash sale** *or* **cash transaction** = transaction paid for in cash; **terms: cash with order** = terms of sale showing the payment has to be made in cash when the order is placed; **cash on delivery** = payment in cash when goods are delivered; **cash discount** *or* **discount for cash** = discount given for payment in cash
NOTE: no plural
2 *verb* **to cash a cheque** = to exchange a cheque for cash

◇ **cashable** *adjective* which can be cashed; **a crossed cheque is not cashable at any bank**

◇ **cash and carry** *noun* large store, selling goods at low prices, where the customer pays cash and has to take the goods away himself; **cash and carry warehouse**

◇ **cash flow** *noun* cash which comes into a company from sales less the money which goes out in purchases or overhead expenditure; **cash flow forecast** = forecast of when cash will be received or paid out; **cash flow statement** = report which shows cash sales and purchases; **net cash flow** = difference between the money coming in and the money going out; **negative cash flow** = situation where more money is going out of a company than is coming in; **positive cash flow** = situation where more money is coming into a company than is going out; **the company is suffering from cash flow problems** = cash income is not coming in fast enough to pay the expenditure going out

◇ **cashier** *noun* person who takes money from customers in a shop; person who deals with customers' money in a bank

◇ **cash in** *verb* to sell (shares) for cash

◇ **cash in on** *verb* to profit from; **the company is cashing in on the interest in computer games**

◇ **cash up** *verb* to add up the cash in a shop at the end of the day

cassette *noun* small plastic box with a magnetic tape on which words or information can be recorded; **copy the information from the computer onto a cassette**

casting vote *noun* vote used by the chairman in the case where the votes for and against a proposal are equal; **the chairman has the casting vote; he used his casting vote to block the motion**

casual *adjective* not permanent *or* not regular; **casual labour** = workers who are hired for a short period; **casual work** = work where the workers are hired for a short period; **casual labourer** *or* **casual worker** = worker who can be hired for a short period

catalogue *or* US **catalog** **1** *noun* list of items for sale, usually with prices; **an office equipment catalogue; they sent us a catalogue of their new range of desks; mail order catalogue** = catalogue from which a customer orders items to be sent by mail; **catalogue price** = price as marked in a catalogue **2** *verb* to put an item into a catalogue

category *noun* type *or* sort of item; **we deal only in the most expensive categories of watches**

cater for *verb* to deal with *or* to provide for; **the store caters mainly for overseas customers**

◇ **caterer** *noun* person who supplies food and drink, especially for parties

◇ **catering** *noun* **(a)** supply of food and drink for a party, etc.; **the catering trade** = food trade, especially supplying food ready to eat NOTE: no plural **(b) catering for** = which provides for; **store catering for overseas visitors**

cause **1** *noun* thing which makes something happen; **what was the cause of the bank's collapse? the police tried to find the cause of the fire** **2** *verb* to make something happen; **the recession caused hundreds of bankruptcies**

caveat *noun* warning; **to enter a caveat** = to warn legally that you have an interest in a case, and that no steps can be taken without your permission

◇ **caveat emptor** = LET THE BUYER BEWARE phrase meaning that the buyer is himself responsible for checking that what he buys is in good order

cc = COPIES
NOTE: **cc** is put on a letter to show who has received a copy of it

ceiling *noun* **(a)** top part which covers a room; **ceiling light** = electric light attached to the ceiling **(b)** highest point; **output has reached a ceiling; to fix a ceiling to a budget; ceiling price** *or* **price ceiling** = highest price that can be reached

cent **(a)** *noun* small coin, one hundredth of a dollar; **the stores are only a 25-cent bus ride away; they sell oranges at 99 cents each** NOTE: **cent** is usually written c in prices: 25c, but not when a dollar price is mentioned: $1.25 **(b)** *see* PER CENT

centimetre *noun* measurement of length (one hundredth of a metre); **the paper is fifteen centimetres wide** NOTE: **centimetre** is usually written cm after figures: 260cm

central *adjective* organized by one main point; **central bank** = main government-controlled bank in a country, which controls the financial affairs of the country by fixing main interest rates, issuing currency and controlling the foreign exchange rate; **central office** = main office which controls all smaller offices; **central purchasing** = purchasing organized by a central office for all branches of a company

◊ **centralization** *noun* organization of everything from a central point
NOTE: no plural

◊ **centralize** *verb* to organize from a central point; **all purchasing has been centralized in our main office; the group benefits from a highly centralized organizational structure**

> QUOTE: the official use of the ecu remains limited, since most interventions by central banks on the market are conducted in dollars
> *Economist*
> QUOTE: central bankers in Europe and Japan are reassessing their intervention policy
> *Duns Business Month*

centre *or* US **center** *noun* **(a) business centre** = part of a town where the main banks, shops and offices are **(b)** important town; **industrial centre; manufacturing centre; the centre for the shoe industry (c)** *GB* **job centre** = government office which lists jobs which are vacant; **shopping centre** = group of shops linked together with car parks and restaurants **(d)** group of items in an account; **cost centre** = person or group whose costs can be itemized; **profit centre** = person or department which is considered separately for the purposes of calculating a profit

CEO *US* = CHIEF EXECUTIVE OFFICER

certain *adjective* **(a)** sure; **the chairman is certain we will pass last year's total sales (b) a certain** = one particular; **a certain number** *or* **a certain quantity** = some

certificate *noun* official document which shows that something is true; **clearance certificate** = document showing that goods have been passed by customs; **savings certificate** = document showing you have invested money in a government

savings scheme; **share certificate** = document proving that you own shares; **certificate of airworthiness** = document to show that an aircraft is safe to fly; **certificate of approval** = document showing that an item has been officially approved; **certificate of deposit** = document from a bank showing that money has been deposited; **certificate of origin** = document showing where goods were made; **certificate of registration** = document showing that an item has been registered

◊ **certificated** *adjective* **certificated bankrupt** = bankrupt who has been discharged from bankruptcy with a certificate to show that he was not at fault

certify *verb* to make an official declaration in writing; **I certify that this is a true copy; the document is certified as a true copy; certified accountant** = accountant who has passed the professional examinations and is a member of the Association of Certified Accountants; **certified cheque** *or* US **certified check** = cheque which a bank says is good and will be paid out of money put aside from the bank account

cession *noun* giving up property to someone (especially a creditor)

chain *noun* series of stores belonging to the same company; **a chain of hotels** *or* **a hotel chain; the chairman of a large do-it-yourself chain; he runs a chain of shoe shops; she bought several shoe shops and gradually built up a chain**

◊ **chain store** *noun* one store in a chain

> QUOTE: the giant US group is better known for its chain of cinemas and hotels rather than its involvement in shipping
> *Lloyd's List*

chair **1** *noun* position of the chairman, presiding over a meeting; **to be in the chair; she was voted into the chair; Mr Jones took the chair** = Mr Jones presided over the meeting; **to address the chair** = in a meeting, to speak to the chairman and not to the rest of the people at the meeting; **please address your remarks to the chair 2** *verb* to preside over a meeting; **the meeting was chaired by Mrs Smith**

◊ **chairman** *noun* **(a)** person who is in charge of a meeting; **Mr Howard was**

chairman *or* **acted as chairman; Mr Chairman** *or* **Madam Chairman** = way of speaking to the chairman **(b)** person who presides over the board meetings of a company; **the chairman of the board** *or* **the company chairman; the chairman's report** = annual report from the chairman of a company to the shareholders

◊ **chairmanship** *noun* being a chairman; **the committee met under the chairmanship of Mr Jones**

◊ **chairperson** *noun* person who is in charge of a meeting

◊ **chairwoman** *noun* woman who is in charge of a meeting

NOTE: the plurals are **chairmen, chairpersons, chairwomen.** Note also that in a US company the president is less important than the chairman of the board

QUOTE: the corporation's entrepreneurial chairman seeks a dedicated but part-time president. The new president will work a three-day week *Globe and Mail (Toronto)*

Chamber of Commerce *noun* group of local businessmen who meet to discuss problems which they have in common and to promote commerce in their town

chambers *plural noun* office of a judge; **the judge heard the case in chambers** = in his private office, and not in court

chance *noun* **(a)** being possible; **the company has a good chance of winning the contract; his promotion chances are small (b)** opportunity to do something; **she is waiting for a chance to see the managing director; he had his chance of promotion when the finance director's assistant resigned**

NOTE: you have a chance **of doing** something or **to do** something

Chancellor of the Exchequer *noun GB* chief finance minister in the government

chandler *noun* person who deals in goods, especially supplies to ships; **ship chandler**

◊ **chandlery** *noun* chandler's shop

change 1 *noun* **(a)** money in coins or small notes; **small change** = coins; **to give someone change for £10** = to give someone

coins or notes in exchange for a ten pound note; **change machine** = machine which gives small change for a larger coin **(b)** money given back by the seller, when the buyer can pay only with a larger note *or* coin than the amount asked; **he gave me the wrong change; you paid the £5.75 bill with a £10 note, so you should have £4.25 change; keep the change** = keep it as a tip (said to waiters, etc.) 2 *verb* **(a) to change a £10 note** = to give change in smaller notes or coins for a £10 note **(b)** to give one type of currency for another; **to change £1,000 into dollars; we want to change some traveller's cheques (c) to change hands** = to be sold to a new owner; **the shop changed hands for £100,000**

◊ **changer** *noun* person who changes money

channel *noun* way in which information or goods are passed from one place to another; **to go through the official channels** = to deal with government officials (especially when making a request); **to open up new channels of communication** = to find new ways of communicating with someone; **distribution channels** *or* **channels of distribution** = ways of sending goods from the manufacturer for sale by retailers

charge 1 *noun* **(a)** money which must be paid *or* price of a service; **to make no charge for delivery; to make a small charge for rental; there is no charge for service** *or* **no charge is made for service; admission charge** *or* **entry charge** = price to be paid before going into an exhibition, etc.; **bank charges** = charges made by a bank for carrying out work for a customer; **handling charge** = money to be paid for packing *or* invoicing *or* dealing with goods which are being shipped; **inclusive charge** = charge which includes all items; **interest charges** = money paid as interest on a loan; **scale of charges** = list showing various prices; **service charge** = charge added to a bill in a restaurant to pay for service; **a 10% service charge is added; does the bill include a service charge?; charge account** = arrangement which a customer has with a store to buy goods and to pay for them at a later date, usually when the invoice is sent at the end of the month; **charges forward** = charges which will be paid by the customer; **a token charge is made for heating** = a small charge

chart 46 **cheap**

is made which does not cover the real costs at all; **free of charge** = free *or* with no payment to be made **(b)** debit on an account; **it appears as a charge on the accounts (c)** being formally accused in a court; **he appeared in court on a charge of embezzling** *or* **on an embezzlement charge 2** *verb* **(a)** to ask someone to pay for services later; **to charge the packing to the customer** *or* **to charge the customer with the packing** = the customer has to pay for packing **(b)** to ask for money to be paid; **to charge £5 for delivery; how much does he charge?; he charges £6 an hour** = he asks to be paid £6 for an hour's work **(c)** (*in a court*) to accuse someone formally of having committed a crime; **he was charged with embezzling his clients' money**

◊ **chargeable** *adjective* which can be charged; **repairs chargeable to the occupier; sums chargeable to the reserve** = sums which can be debited to a company's reserves

◊ **chargee** *noun* person who has the right to force a debtor to pay

◊ **chargehand** *noun* chief of a group of workers under a foreman

QUOTE: traveller's cheques cost 1% of their face value - some banks charge more for small amounts
Sunday Times

chart *noun* diagram showing information as a series of lines *or* blocks, etc.; **bar chart** = diagram where quantities and values are shown as thick columns of different heights *or* lengths; **flow chart** = diagram showing the arrangement of various work processes in a series; **organization chart** = diagram showing how a company *or* an office is organized; **pie chart** = diagram where information is shown as a circle cut up into sections of different sizes; **sales chart** = diagram showing how sales vary from month to month

charter 1 *noun* **(a) bank charter** = official government document allowing the establishment of a bank **(b)** hiring transport for a special purpose; **charter flight** = flight in an aircraft which has been hired for that purpose; **charter plane** = plane which has been chartered; **boat on charter to Mr Smith** = boat which Mr Smith has hired for a voyage **2** *verb* to hire for a special purpose; **to charter a plane** *or* **a boat** *or* **a bus**

◊ **chartered** *adjective* **(a) chartered accountant** = accountant who has passed the professional examinations and is a member of the Institute of Chartered Accountants **(b)** (company) which has been set up by charter, and not registered as a company; **a chartered bank (c) chartered ship** *or* **bus** *or* **plane** = ship *or* bus *or* plane which has been hired for a special purpose

◊ **charterer** *noun* person who hires a ship, etc., for a special purpose

◊ **chartering** *noun* act of hiring for a special purpose

chartist *noun* person who studies stock market trends and forecasts future rises or falls

chase *verb* **(a)** to run after someone *or* something to try to catch them **(b)** to try to speed up work by asking how it is progressing; **we are trying to chase up the accounts department for the cheque; we will chase your order with the production department**

◊ **chaser** *noun* **(a) progress chaser** = person whose job is to check that work is being carried out on schedule *or* that orders are fulfilled on time **(b)** letter to remind someone of something (especially to remind a customer that an invoice has not been paid)

chattels *plural noun* goods *or* moveable property

cheap *adjective & adverb* not costing a lot of money *or* not expensive; **cheap labour** = workforce which does not earn much money; **we have opened a factory in the Far East because of the cheap labour** *or* **because labour is cheap; cheap money** = money which can be borrowed at low interest; **cheap rate** = rate which is not expensive; **cheap rate phone calls; to buy something cheap** = at a low price; **he bought two companies cheap and sold them again at a profit; they work out cheaper by the box** = these items are cheaper per unit if you buy a box of them

◊ **cheaply** *adverb* without paying much money; **the salesman was living cheaply at home and claiming a high hotel bill on his expenses**

◇ **cheapness** noun being cheap; **the cheapness of the pound means that many more tourists will come to London**
NOTE: no plural

cheat verb to trick someone so that he loses money; **he cheated the Income Tax out of thousands of pounds; she was accused of cheating clients who came to ask her for advice**

check 1 noun (a) sudden stop; **to put a check on imports** = to stop some imports (b) **check sample** = sample to be used to see if a consignment is acceptable (c) investigation or examination; **the auditors carried out checks on the petty cash book; a routine check of the fire equipment; baggage check** = examination of passengers' baggage to see if it contains bombs (d) US (in restaurant) bill (e) US = CHEQUE (f) US mark on paper to show that something is correct; **make a check in the box marked "R"** 2 verb (a) to stop or to delay; **to check the entry of contraband into the country** (b) to examine or to investigate; **to check that an invoice is correct; to check and sign for goods; he checked the computer printout against the invoices** = he examined the printout and the invoices to see if the figures were the same (c) US to mark with a sign to show that something is correct; **check the box marked "R"**
◇ **check in** verb (a) (at a hotel) to arrive at a hotel and sign for a room; **he checked in at 12.15** (b) (at an airport) to give in your ticket to show you are ready to take the flight (c) **to check baggage in** = to pass your baggage to the airline to put it on the plane for you
◇ **check-in** noun place where passengers give in their tickets for a flight; **the check-in is on the first floor; check-in counter** = counter where passengers check in; **check-in time** = time at which passengers should check in
◇ **checking** noun (a) examination or investigation; **the inspectors found some defects during their checking of the building** (b) US **checking account** = bank account on which you can write cheques
NOTE: no plural
◇ **checkoff** noun US system where union dues are automatically deducted by the employer from a worker's paycheck

◇ **check out** verb (at a hotel) to leave and pay for a room; **we will check out before breakfast**
◇ **checkout** noun (a) (in a supermarket) place where you pay for the goods you have bought (b) (in a hotel) **checkout time is 12.00** = time by which you have to leave your room
◇ **checkroom** noun US place where you leave your coat or luggage, etc.

cheque noun note to a bank asking them to pay money from your account to the account of the person whose name is written on the note; **a cheque for £10** or a **£10 cheque; cheque account** = bank account which allows the customer to write cheques; **cheque to bearer** = cheque with no name written on it, so that the person who holds it can cash it; **crossed cheque** = cheque with two lines across it showing that it can only be deposited at a bank and not exchanged for cash; **open** or **uncrossed cheque** = cheque which can be cashed anywhere; **blank cheque** = cheque with the amount of money and the payee left blank, but signed by the drawer; **pay cheque** or **salary cheque** = monthly cheque by which an employee is paid; **traveller's cheques** = cheques taken by a traveller, which can be cashed in a foreign country; **dud cheque** or **bouncing cheque** or **cheque which bounces** or US **rubber check** = cheque which cannot be cashed because the person writing it has not enough money in the account to pay it (b) **to cash a cheque** = to exchange a cheque for cash; **to endorse a cheque** = to sign a cheque on the back to show that you accept it; **to make out a cheque to someone** = to write someone's name on a cheque; **who shall I make the cheque out to?; to pay by cheque** = to pay by writing a cheque, and not using cash or a credit card; **to pay a cheque into your account** = to deposit a cheque; **the bank referred the cheque to drawer** = returned the cheque to the person who wrote it because there was not enough money in the account to pay it; **to sign a cheque** = to sign on the front of a cheque to show that you authorize the bank to pay the money from your account; **to stop a cheque** = to ask a bank not to pay a cheque which you have written
◇ **cheque book** noun booklet with new cheques

◇ **cheque guarantee card** *noun* plastic card from a bank which guarantees payment of a cheque up to a certain amount, even if there is no money in the account

chief *adjective* most important; **he is the chief accountant of an industrial group; chief executive** *or* *US* **chief executive officer** = executive in charge of a company

chip *noun* **(a) a computer chip** = a small piece of silicon able to store data, used in computers **(b) blue chip** = very safe investment *or* risk-free share in a good company

chit *noun* bill (for food or drink in a club)

choice **1** *noun* **(a)** thing which is chosen; **you must give the customer time to make his choice (b)** range of items to choose from; **we have only a limited choice of suppliers; the shop carries a good choice of paper** = the shop carries many types of paper to choose from **2** *adjective* specially selected (food); **choice meat; choice wines; choice foodstuffs**

choose *verb* to decide to do a particular thing *or* to buy a particular item (as opposed to something else); **there were several good candidates to choose from; they chose the only woman applicant as sales director; you must give the customers plenty of time to choose**
NOTE: **choosing - chose - chosen**

chronic *adjective* permanently bad; **the company has chronic cash flow problems; we have a chronic shortage of skilled staff; chronic unemployment** = being unemployed for more than six months

chronological order *noun* arrangement of records (files, invoices, etc.) in order of their dates

c.i.f. = COST, INSURANCE AND FREIGHT

circular **1** *adjective* sent to many people; **circular letter of credit** = letter of credit sent to all branches of the bank which issues it **2** *noun* leaflet *or* letter sent to many people; **they sent out a circular offering a 10% discount**

◇ **circularize** *verb* to send a circular to; **the committee has agreed to circularize the members; they circularized all their customers with a new list of prices**

◇ **circulate** *verb* **(a)** (*of money*) **to circulate freely** = to move about without restriction by the government **(b)** to send *or* to give out without restrictions; **to circulate money** = to issue money *or* to make money available to the public and industry **(c)** to send information to; **they circulated a new list of prices to all their customers**

◇ **circulating** *adjective* which is moving about freely; **circulating capital** = capital required in cash, raw materials, finished products and work in progress for a company to carry on its business

◇ **circulation** *noun* **(a)** movement; **the company is trying to improve the circulation of information between departments; circulation of capital** = movement of capital from one investment to another **(b) to put money into circulation** = to issue new notes to business and the public; **the amount of money in circulation increased more than was expected (c)** (*of newspapers*) number of copies sold; **the audited circulation of a newspaper; the new editor hopes to improve the circulation; a circulation battle** = competition between two papers to try to sell more copies in the same market
NOTE: no plural for (a) and (b)

QUOTE: the level of currency in circulation increased to N4.9 billion in the month of August
Business Times (Lagos)

city *noun* **(a)** large town; **the largest cities in Europe are linked by hourly flights; capital city** = main town in a country, where the government is located; **inter-city** = between cities; **inter-city train services are often quicker than going by air (b) the City** = old centre of London, where banks and large companies have their main offices; the British financial centre; **he works in the City** *or* **he is in the City; City desk** = section of a newspaper office which deals with business news; **City editor** = business *or* finance editor of a British paper; **they say in the City that the company has been sold** = the business world is saying that the company has been sold

civil *adjective* referring to ordinary people; **civil action** = court case brought by a person *or* a company against someone who has done them wrong; **civil law** = laws relating to people's rights and agreements between individuals

◇ **civil service** *noun* organization and personnel which administer a country; **you have to pass an examination to get a job in the civil service** *or* **to get a civil service job**

◇ **civil servant** *noun* person who works in the civil service

claim 1 *noun* **(a)** asking for money; **wage claim** = asking for an increase in wages; **the union put in a 6% wage claim** = the union asked for a 6% increase in wages for its members **(b) legal claim** = statement that you think you own something legally; **he has no legal claim to the property (c) insurance claim** = asking an insurance company to pay for damages *or* for loss; **claims department** = department of an insurance company which deals with claims; **claim form** = form to be filled in when making an insurance claim; **claims manager** = manager of a claims department; **no claims bonus** = lower premium paid because no claims have been made against the insurance policy; **to put in a claim** = to ask the insurance company officially to pay damages; **to put in a claim for repairs to the car; she put in a claim for £250,000 damages against the driver of the other car; to settle a claim** = to agree to pay what is asked for; **the insurance company refused to settle his claim for storm damage (d) small claims court** = court which deals with claims for small amounts of money **2** *verb* **(a)** to ask for money; **he claimed £100,000 damages against the cleaning firm; she claimed for repairs to the car against her insurance (b)** to say that something is your property; **he is claiming possession of the house; no one claimed the umbrella found in my office (c)** to state that something is a fact; **he claims he never received the goods; she claims that the shares are her property**

◇ **claimant** *noun* person who claims; **rightful claimant** = person who has a legal claim to something

◇ **claim back** *verb* to ask for money to be paid back

◇ **claimer** *noun* = CLAIMANT

◇ **claiming** *noun* act of making a claim

class *noun* category *or* group into which things are classified according to quality or price; **first-class** = top quality *or* most expensive; **he is a first-class accountant; economy class** *or* **tourist class** = lower quality *or* less expensive way of travelling; **I travel economy class because it is cheaper; tourist class travel is less comfortable than first class; he always travels first class because tourist class is too uncomfortable;** *GB* **first-class mail** = more expensive mail service, designed to be faster; **a first-class letter should get to Scotland in a day; second-class mail** = less expensive, slower mail service; **the letter took three days to arrive because he sent it second class**

classify *verb* to put into classes *or* categories; **classified advertisements** = advertisements listed in a newspaper under special headings (such as "property for sale" or "jobs wanted"); **classified directory** = book which lists businesses grouped under various headings (such as computer shops *or* newsagents)

◇ **classification** *noun* way of putting into classes; **job classification** = describing jobs listed in various groups

clause *noun* section of a contract; **there are ten clauses in the contract; according to clause six, payments will not be due until next year; exclusion clause** = clause in an insurance policy *or* warranty which says which items are not covered by the policy; **penalty clause** = clause which lists the penalties which will happen if the contract is not fulfilled; **termination clause** = clause which explains how and when a contract can be terminated

claw back *verb* to take back money which has been allocated; **income tax claws back 25% of pensions paid out by the government; of the £1m allocated to the project, the government clawed back £100,000 in taxes**

◇ **clawback** *noun* money taken back

clear 1 *adjective* **(a)** easily understood; **he made it clear that he wanted the manager to resign; you will have to make it clear to the staff that productivity is falling (b) clear profit** = profit after all expenses have been paid; **we made $6,000 clear profit on**

the sale **(c)** free *or* total period of time; **three clear days** = three whole working days; **allow three clear days for the cheque to be paid into the bank 2** *verb* **(a)** to sell cheaply in order to get rid of stock; **"demonstration models to clear" (b) to clear goods through the customs** = to have all documentation passed by the customs so that goods can leave the country **(c) to clear 10%** *or* **$5,000 on the deal** = to make 10% *or* $5,000 clear profit; **we cleared only our expenses** = the sales revenue only paid for the costs and expenses without making any profit **(d) to clear a cheque** = to pass a cheque through the banking system, so that the money is transferred from the payer's account to another; **the cheque took ten days to clear** *or* **the bank took ten days to clear the cheque**

◊ **clearance** *noun* **(a) customs clearance** = passing goods through the customs so that they can enter or leave the country; **to effect customs clearance** = to clear goods through the customs; **clearance certificate** = certificate showing that goods have been passed by the customs **(b) clearance sale** = sale of items at low prices to get rid of stock **(c) clearance of a cheque** = passing of a cheque through the banking system, transferring money from one account to another; **you should allow six days for cheque clearance**

◊ **clearing** *noun* **(a) clearing of goods through the customs** = passing of goods through the customs **(b) clearing of a debt** = paying all of a debt **(c) clearing bank** = bank which clears cheques, one of the major British High Street banks; **clearing house** = central office where clearing banks exchange cheques

◊ **clear off** *verb* **to clear off a debt** = to pay all of a debt

clerical *adjective* (work) done in an office *or* done by a clerk; **clerical error** = mistake made in an office; **clerical staff** = staff of an office; **clerical work** = paperwork done in an office; **clerical worker** = person who works in an office

clerk 1 *noun* **(a)** person who works in an office; **articled clerk** = clerk who is bound by a contract to work in a lawyer's office for some years to learn the trade; **chief clerk** *or* **head clerk** = most important clerk; **filing clerk** = clerk who files documents; **invoice clerk** = clerk who

deals with invoices; **shipping clerk** = clerk who deals with shipping documents **(b) bank clerk** = person who works in a bank; **booking clerk** = person who works in a booking office; *US* **sales clerk** = person who sells in a store **2** *verb US* to work as a clerk

◊ **clerkess** *noun* (*in Scotland*) woman clerk

clever *adjective* intelligent *or* able to learn quickly; **he is very clever at spotting a bargain; clever investors have made a lot of money on the share deal**

client *noun* person with whom business is done *or* person who pays for a service

◊ **clientele** *noun* all the clients of a business; all the customers of a shop
NOTE: no plural

climb *verb* to go up; **the company has climbed to No. 1 position in the market; profits climbed rapidly as the new management cut costs**

clinch *verb* to settle (a business deal) *or* to come to an agreement; **he offered an extra 5% to clinch the deal; they need approval from the board before they can clinch the deal**

clipping service *noun* service of cutting out references to a client in newspapers or magazines and sending them to him

clock *noun* machine which shows the time; **the office clock is fast; the micro has a built-in clock; digital clock** = clock which shows the time using numbers (as 12:05)

◊ **clock card** *noun* special card which a worker puts into the time clock when clocking on or off

◊ **clock in** *or* **clock on** *verb* (*of worker*) to record the time of arriving for work by putting a card into a special timing machine

◊ **clock out** *or* **clock off** *verb* (*of worker*) to record the time of leaving work by putting a card into a special timing machine

◊ **clocking in** *or* **clocking on** *noun* arriving for work and recording the time on a time-card

◇ **clocking out** *or* **clocking off** *noun* leaving work and recording the time on a time-card

close 1 *noun* end; **at the close of the day's trading the shares had fallen 20%**
NOTE: no plural
2 *adjective* **close to** = very near *or* almost; **the company was close to bankruptcy; we are close to meeting our sales targets 3** *verb* to end **(a)** to stop doing business for the day; **the office closes at 5.30; we close early on Saturdays (b) to close the accounts** = to come to the end of an accounting period and make up the profit and loss account **(c) to close an account** = (i) to stop supplying a customer on credit; (ii) to take all the money out of a bank account and stop the account; **he closed his building society account** = he took all the money out and stopped using the account **(d) the shares closed at $15** = at the end of the day's trading the price of the shares was $15

◇ **close company** *or* US **close(d) corporation** *noun* privately owned company where the public may own a small number of shares

◇ **closed** *adjective* **(a)** shut *or* not open *or* not doing business; **the office is closed on Mondays; all the banks are closed on the National Day (b)** restricted; **closed shop** = system where a company agrees to employ only union members in certain jobs; **a closed shop agreement; the union is asking the management to agree to a closed shop; closed market** = market where a supplier deals only with one agent *or* distributor and does not supply any others direct; **they signed a closed market agreement with an Egyptian company**

◇ **close down** *verb* to shut a shop *or* factory for a long period or for ever; **the company is closing down its London office; the strike closed down the railway system**

◇ **closing 1** *adjective* **(a)** final *or* coming at the end; **closing bid** = last bid at an auction *or* the bid which is successful; **closing date** = last date; **the closing date for tenders to be received is May 1st; closing price** = price of a share at the end of a day's trading **(b)** at the end of an accounting period; **closing balance; closing stock 2** *noun* **(a)** shutting of a shop *or* being shut; **Sunday closing** = not opening a shop on Sundays; **closing time** = time when a shop or office stops work;

early closing day = weekday (usually Wednesday or Thursday) when many shops close in the afternoon **(b) closing of an account** = act of stopping supply to a customer on credit
NOTE: no plural

◇ **closing down** *noun* **closing-down sale** = sale of goods when a shop is closing for ever

◇ **closing out** *noun* US selling goods cheaply to try to get rid of them

◇ **closure** *noun* act of closing

QUOTE: Toronto stocks closed at an all-time high, posting their fifth straight day of advances in heavy trading   *Financial Times*
QUOTE: the best thing would be to have a few more plants close down and bring supply more in line with current demand   *Fortune*

club *noun* group of people who have the same interest; place where these people meet; **if you want the managing director, you can phone him at his club; he has applied to join the sports club; club membership** = all the members of a club; **club subscription** = money paid to belong to a club; **staff club** = club for the staff of a company, which organizes staff parties, sports and meetings

cm = CENTIMETRE

c/o = CARE OF

Co. = COMPANY **J. Smith & Co. Ltd**

co- *prefix* working *or* acting together
◇ **co-creditor** *noun* person who is a creditor of the same company as you are
◇ **co-director** *noun* person who is a director of the same company as you
◇ **co-insurance** *noun* insurance policy where the risk is shared among several insurers

COD *or* **c.o.d.** = CASH ON DELIVERY

code *noun* **(a)** system of signs *or* numbers *or* letters which mean something; **area code** = numbers which indicate an area for telephoning; **what is the code for Edinburgh?; bar code** = system of lines printed on a product which can be read by a computer to give a reference number or price; **international dialling code =** numbers used for dialling to another country; **machine-readable codes =** sets of signs or letters (such as bar codes *or* post codes) which can be read by computers; **post code** *or* *US* **zip code =** letters and numbers used to indicate a town or street in an address on an envelope; **stock code =** numbers and letters which refer to an item of stock **(b)** set of rules; **code of practice =** rules drawn up by an association which the members must follow when doing business

◇ **coding** *noun* act of putting a code on something; **the coding of invoices**

coin *noun* piece of metal money; **he gave me two 10-franc coins in my change; I need some 10p coins for the telephone**

◇ **coinage** *noun* system of metal money used in a country
NOTE: no plural

cold *adjective* **(a)** not hot; **the machines work badly in cold weather; the office was so cold that the staff started complaining; the coffee machine also sells cold drinks (b)** without being prepared; **cold call =** sales call where the salesman has no appointment and the client is not an established customer; **cold start =** starting a new business *or* opening a new shop where there was none before

collaborate *verb* to work together; **to collaborate with a French firm on a building project; they collaborated on the new aircraft**
NOTE: you collaborate **with** someone **on** something

◇ **collaboration** *noun* working together; **their collaboration on the project was very profitable**
NOTE: no plural

collapse 1 *noun* **(a)** sudden fall in price; **the collapse of the market in silver; the collapse of the dollar on the foreign exchange markets (b)** sudden failure of a company; **investors lost thousands of pounds in the collapse of the company 2** *verb* **(a)** to fall suddenly; **the market collapsed; the yen collapsed on the foreign exchange markets (b)** to fail suddenly; **the company collapsed with £25,000 in debts**

collar *noun* part of a coat *or* shirt which goes round the neck; **blue-collar worker =** manual worker in a factory; **white-collar worker =** office worker; **he has a white-collar job =** he works in an office

collateral *adjective & noun* (security) used to provide a guarantee for a loan

QUOTE: examiners have come to inspect the collateral that thrifts may use in borrowing from the Fed   *Wall Street Journal*

collect 1 *verb* **(a)** to make someone pay money which is owed; **to collect a debt =** to go and make someone pay a debt **(b)** to take things away from a place; **we have to collect the stock from the warehouse; can you collect my letters from the typing pool?; letters are collected twice a day =** the post office workers take them from the letter box to the post office for dispatch **2** *adverb & adjective* *US* (phone call) where the person receiving the call agrees to pay for it; **to make a collect call; he called his office collect**

◇ **collecting agency** *noun* agency which collects money owed to other companies for a commission

◇ **collection** *noun* **(a)** getting money together *or* making someone pay money which is owed; **tax collection** *or* **collection of tax; debt collection =** collecting money which is owed; **debt collection agency =** company which collects debts for other companies for a commission; **bills for collection =** bills where payment is due **(b)** fetching of goods; **the stock is in the warehouse awaiting collection; collection charges** *or* **collection rates =** charge for collecting something; **to hand something in for collection =** to leave something for someone to come and collect **(c) collections =** money which has been collected **(d)** taking of letter from a letter box or mail room to the post office for dispatch; **there are six collections a day from the letter box**

◇ **collective** *adjective* working together; **free collective bargaining =** negotiations about wage increases and working conditions between management and trade unions; **collective farm =** state-owned farm which is run by the workers; **collective ownership =** ownership of a business by the workers who work in it;

they signed a collective wage agreement = an agreement was signed between management and the trade union about wages

◊ **collector** *noun* person who makes people pay money which is owed; **collector of taxes** *or* **tax collector; debt collector**

college *noun* place where people can study after they have left full-time school; **business college** *or* **commercial college** = college which teaches general business methods; **secretarial college** = college which teaches shorthand, typing and word-processing

column *noun* (a) series of numbers, one under the other; **to add up a column of figures; put the total at the bottom of the column; credit column** = right-hand side in accounts showing money received; **debit column** = left-hand side in accounts showing money paid or owed (b) section of printed words in a newspaper *or* magazine; **column-centimetre** = space in centimetres in a newspaper column, used for calculating charges for advertising

combine 1 *noun* large financial or commercial group; **a German industrial combine** 2 *verb* to join together; **the workforce and management combined to fight the takeover bid**

◊ **combination** *noun* (a) several things which are joined together; **a combination of cash flow problems and difficult trading conditions caused the company's collapse** (b) series of numbers which open a special lock; **I have forgotten the combination of the lock on my briefcase; the office safe has a combination lock**

comfort *noun* **letter of comfort** *or* **comfort letter** = letter supporting someone who is trying to get a loan

commerce *noun* business *or* buying and selling of goods and services; **Chamber of Commerce** = group of local businessmen who meet to discuss problems which they have in common and to promote business in their town

◊ **commercial** 1 *adjective* (a) referring to business; **commercial aircraft** = aircraft used to carry cargo *or* passengers for payment; **commercial artist** = artist

who designs advertisements *or* posters, etc. for payment; **commercial attaché** = diplomat who represents and tries to promote his country's business interests; **commercial college** = college which teaches business studies; **commercial course** = course where business skills are studied; **he took a commercial course by correspondence; commercial directory** = book which lists all the businesses and business people in a town; **commercial district** = part of a town where offices and shops are; **commercial law** = laws regarding business; **commercial load** = amount of goods *or* number of passengers which a bus *or* train *or* plane has to carry to make a profit; **commercial port** = port which has only goods traffic; **commercial traveller** = salesman who travels round an area visiting customers on behalf of his company; **commercial vehicle** = van *or* truck, etc. used for business purposes; **sample only - of no commercial value** = not worth anything if sold (b) profitable; **not a commercial proposition** = not likely to make a profit 2 *noun* advertisement on television

◊ **commercialization** *noun* making something into a business proposition; **the commercialization of museums** NOTE: no plural

◊ **commercialize** *verb* to make something into a business; **the holiday town has become so commercialized that it is unpleasant**

◊ **commercially** *adverb* in a business way; **not commercially viable** = not likely to make a profit

commission *noun* (a) money paid to a salesman *or* an agent, usually a percentage of the sales made; **she gets 10% commission on everything she sells; he charges 10% commission** = he asks for 10% of sales as his payment; **commission agent** = agent who is paid a percentage of sales; **commission rep** = representative who is not paid a salary, but receives a commission on sales; **commission sale** *or* **sale on commission** = sale where the salesman is paid a commission (b) group of people officially appointed to examine some problem; **the government has appointed a commission of inquiry to look into the problems of small exporters; he is the chairman of the government commission on export subsidies**

commit *verb* to carry out (a crime)
NOTE: **committing - committed**

committee *noun* official group of people who organize or plan for a larger group; **to be a member of a committee** *or* **to sit on a committee; he was elected to the committee of the staff club; the new plans have to be approved by the committee members; to chair a committee** = to be the chairman of a committee; **he is the chairman of the planning committee; she is the secretary of the finance committee; management committee** = committee which manages a club *or* a pension fund, etc.

commodity *noun* thing sold in very large quantities, especially raw materials and food such as metals or corn; **primary** *or* **basic commodities** = farm produce grown in large quantities, such as corn, rice, cotton; **staple commodity** = basic food or raw material which is most important in a country's economy; **commodity market** *or* **commodity exchange** = place where people buy and sell commodities; **commodity futures** = trading in commodities for delivery at a later date; **silver rose 5% on the commodity futures market yesterday; commodity trader** = person whose business is buying and selling commodities

common *adjective* **(a)** which happens very often; **putting the carbon paper in the wrong way round is a common mistake; being caught by the customs is very common these days (b)** belonging to several different people or to everyone; **common carrier** = firm which carries goods or passengers, and which anyone can use; **common ownership** = ownership of a company *or* a property by a group of people; **common pricing** = illegal fixing of prices by several businesses so that they all charge the same price; *US* **common stock** = ordinary shares in a company, giving shareholders a right to vote at meetings and to receive dividends; (*in the EEC*) **Common Agricultural Policy** = agreement between members of the EEC to protect farmers by paying subsidies to fix prices of farm produce
◊ **Common Market** *noun* **the European Common Market** = the European Economic Community *or* organization which links several European countries for the purposes of trade; **the Common Market finance ministers** = the finance ministers of all the Common Market countries meeting as a group

communicate *verb* to pass information to someone; **he finds it impossible to communicate with his staff; communicating with head office has been quicker since we installed the telex**
◊ **communication** *noun* **(a)** passing of information; **communication with the head office has been made easier by the telex; to enter into communication with someone** = to start discussing something with someone, usually in writing; **we have entered into communication with the relevant government department (b)** official message; **we have had a communication from the local tax inspector (c) communications** = being able to contact people *or* to pass messages; **after the flood all communications with the outside world were broken**

community *noun* **(a)** group of people living or working in the same place; **the local business community** = the business people living and working in the area **(b) the European Economic Community** = the Common Market; **the Community ministers** = the ministers of member states of the Common Market

commute *verb* **(a)** to travel to work from home each day; **he commutes from the country to his office in the centre of town (b)** to change a right into cash; **he decided to commute part of his pension rights into a lump sum payment**
◊ **commuter** *noun* person who commutes to work; **he lives in the commuter belt** = area of country where the commuters live round a town; **commuter train** = train which commuters take in the morning and evening

company *noun* business *or* group of people organized to buy, sell or provide a service **(a) to put a company into liquidation** = to close a company by selling its assets for cash; **to set up a company** = to start a company legally; **associate company** = company which is partly owned by another company; **family company** = company where most of the shares are owned by members of a family; **holding company** = company which exists only to own shares in subsidiary companies; **joint-stock company** = company whose shares are held by many people; **limited (liability) company** = company where a shareholder is responsible for repaying the company's debts only to the face value of the shares he owns; **listed company** = company whose shares can be bought or sold on the Stock Exchange; **parent company** = company which owns more than half of another company's shares; **private (limited) company** = company with a small number of shareholders, whose shares are not traded on the Stock Exchange; **public limited company (plc)** = company whose shares can be bought on the Stock Exchange; **subsidiary company** = company which is owned by a parent company **(b) finance company** = company which provides money for hire-purchase; **insurance company** = company whose business is insurance; **shipping company** = company whose business is in transporting goods; **a tractor** or **aircraft** or **chocolate company** = company which makes tractors or aircraft or chocolate **(c) company car** = car which belongs to a company and is lent to an employee to use personally; **company doctor** = (i) doctor who works for a company and looks after sick workers; (ii) specialist businessman who rescues companies which are in difficulties; **company director** = person appointed by the shareholders to help run a company; **company law** = laws which refer to the way companies may work; **company secretary** = person responsible for the company's legal and financial affairs; *GB* the **Companies Act** = Act of Parliament which states the legal limits within which companies may do their business

compare *verb* to look at several things to see how they differ; **the finance director compared the figures for the first and second quarters**

◇ **compare with** *verb* to put two things together to see how they differ; **how do the sales this year compare with last year's? compared with 1982, last year was a boom year**

◇ **comparable** *adjective* which can be compared; **the two sets of figures are not comparable; which is the nearest company**

comparable to this one in size? = which company is of a similar size and can be compared with this one?

◇ **comparability** *noun* being able to be compared; **pay comparability** = similar pay system in two different companies NOTE: no plural

◇ **comparison** *noun* way of comparing; **sales are down in comparison with last year; there is no comparison between overseas and home sales** = overseas and home sales are so different they cannot be compared

compensate *verb* to pay for damage done; **to compensate a manager for loss of commission**
NOTE: you compensate someone **for** something

◇ **compensation** *noun* **(a) compensation for damage** = payment for damage done; **compensation for loss of office** = payment to a director who is asked to leave a company before his contract ends; **compensation for loss of earnings** = payment to someone who has stopped earning money or who is not able to earn money **(b)** *US* salary; **compensation package** = salary, pension and other benefits offered with a job

> QUOTE: it was rumoured that the government was prepared to compensate small depositors
> *South China Morning Post*
> QUOTE: golden parachutes are liberal compensation packages given to executives leaving a company
> *Publishers Weekly*

compete *verb* to compete with someone or with a company = to try to do better than another person or another company; **we have to compete with cheap imports from the Far East; they were competing unsuccessfully with local companies on their home territory; the two companies are competing for a market share** or **for a contract** = each company is trying to win a larger part of the market or to win the contract

◇ **competing** *adjective* which competes; **competing firms** = firms which compete with each other; **competing products** = products from different companies which have the same use and are sold in the same markets at similar prices

◇ **competition** *noun* **(a)** trying to do better than another supplier; **free competition** = being free to compete without

government interference; **keen competition** = strong competition; **we are facing keen competition from European manufacturers (b) the competition** = companies which are trying to compete with your product; **we have lowered our prices to beat the competition; the competition have brought out a new range of products**
NOTE: singular, but can take a plural verb

◇ **competitive** *adjective* which competes fairly; **competitive price** = low price aimed to compete with a rival product; **competitive pricing** = putting low prices on goods so as to compete with other products; **competitive products** = products made to compete with existing products

◇ **competitively** *adverb* **competitively priced** = sold at a low price which competes with the price of similar products from other companies

◇ **competitiveness** *noun* being competitive
NOTE: no plural

◇ **competitor** *noun* person *or* company which competes; **two German firms are our main competitors**

QUOTE: profit margins in the industries most exposed to foreign competition are worse than usual *Sunday Times*
QUOTE: competition is steadily increasing and could affect profit margins as the company tries to retain its market share *Citizen (Ottawa)*
QUOTE: the company blamed fiercely competitive market conditions in Europe for a £14m operating loss last year *Financial Times*
QUOTE: farmers are increasingly worried by the growing lack of competitiveness for their products on world markets
Australian Financial Review
QUOTE: sterling labour costs continue to rise between 3% and 5% a year faster than in most of our competitor countries *Sunday Times*

competence *or* **competency** *noun* **the case falls within the competence of the court** = the court is legally able to deal with the case

◇ **competent** *adjective* **(a)** able to do something *or* efficient; **she is a competent secretary** *or* **a competent manager (b) the court is not competent to deal with this case** = the court is not legally able to deal with the case

complain *verb* to say that something is no good *or* does not work properly; **the office is so cold the staff have started complaining;**

she complained about the service; they are complaining that our prices are too high; if you want to complain, write to the manager

◇ **complaint** *noun* statement that you feel something is wrong; **when making a complaint, always quote the reference number; she sent her letter of complaint to the managing director; to make** *or* **lodge a complaint against someone** = to write and send an official complaint to someone's superior; **complaints department** = department which deals with complaints from customers; **complaints procedure** = agreed way for workers to make complaints to the management about working conditions

complete 1 *adjective* whole *or* with nothing missing; **the order is complete and ready for sending; the order should be delivered only if it is complete 2** *verb* to finish; **the factory completed the order in two weeks; how long will it take you to complete the job?**

◇ **completely** *adverb* all *or* totally; **the cargo was completely ruined by water; the warehouse was completely destroyed by fire**

◇ **completion** *noun* act of finishing something; **completion date** = date when something will be finished; **completion of a contract** = signing of a contract for the sale of a property when the buyer pays and the seller passes ownership to the buyer

complex 1 *noun* series of large buildings; **a large industrial complex**
NOTE: plural is **complexes**
2 *adjective* with many different parts; **a complex system of import controls; the specifications for the machine are very complex**

◇ **complimentary** *adjective* **complimentary ticket** = free ticket, given as a present

◇ **compliments slip** *noun* piece of paper with the name of the company printed on it, sent with documents *or* gifts, etc. instead of a letter

comply *verb* **to comply with a court order** = to obey an order given by a court

◇ **compliance** *noun* agreement to do what is ordered
NOTE: no plural

component *noun* piece of machinery *or* section which will be put into a final product; **the assembly line stopped because supply of a component was delayed; components factory** = factory which makes parts which are used in other factories to make finished products

composition *noun* agreement between a debtor and creditors to settle a debt by repaying only part of it

compound 1 *adjective* **compound interest** = interest which is added to the capital and then earns interest itself 2 *verb* to agree with creditors to settle a debt by paying part of what is owed

comprehensive *adjective* which includes everything; **comprehensive insurance** = insurance policy which covers you against all risks which are likely to happen

compromise 1 *noun* agreement between two sides, where each side gives way a little; **management offered £5 an hour, the union asked for £9, and a compromise of £7.50 was reached** 2 *verb* to reach an agreement by giving way a little; **he asked £15 for it, I offered £7 and we compromised on £10**

comptometer *noun* machine which counts automatically

comptroller *noun* financial controller

compulsory *adjective* which is forced *or* ordered; **compulsory liquidation** = liquidation which is ordered by a court

compute *verb* to calculate *or* to do calculations
◊ **computable** *adjective* which can be calculated
◊ **computation** *noun* calculation
◊ **computational** *adjective* **computational error** = mistake made in calculating
◊ **computer** *noun* electronic machine which calculates *or* stores information and processes it automatically; **computer bureau** = office which offers to do work on its computers for companies which do not have their own computers; **computer department** = department in a company

which manages the company's computers; **computer error** = mistake made by a computer; **computer file** = section of information on a computer (such as the payroll, list of addresses, customer accounts); **computer language** = system of signs, letters and words used to instruct a computer; **computer listing** = printout of a list of items taken from data stored in a computer; **computer manager** = person in charge of a computer department; **computer program** = instructions to a computer, telling it to do a particular piece of work; **computer programmer** = person who writes computer programs; **computer services** = work using a computer, done by a computer bureau; **computer time** = time when a computer is being used (paid for at an hourly rate); **running all those sales reports costs a lot in computer time; business computer** = powerful small computer which is programmed for special business uses; **personal computer** *or* **home computer** = small computer which can be used in the home
◊ **computerize** *verb* to change from a manual system to one using computers; **our stock control has been completely computerized**
◊ **computerized** *adjective* worked by computers; **a computerized invoicing system**
◊ **computer-readable** *adjective* which can be read and understood by a computer; **computer-readable codes**
◊ **computing** *noun* referring to computers; **computing speed** = speed at which a computer calculates

con 1 *noun* *informal* trick done to try to get money from someone; **trying to get us to pay him for ten hours' overtime was just a con** 2 *verb* *informal* to trick someone to try to get money; **they conned the bank into lending them £25,000 with no security; he conned the finance company out of £100,000**
NOTE: **con - conning - conned**

concealment *noun* hiding for criminal purposes; **concealment of assets** = hiding assets so that creditors do not know they exist

concern 1 *noun* **(a)** business *or* company; **his business is a going concern** = the company is working (and making a profit); **sold as a going concern** = sold as an actively trading company **(b)** being worried about a problem; **the management showed no concern at all for the workers' safety 2** *verb* to deal with *or* to be connected with; **the sales staff are not concerned with the cleaning of the store; he filled in a questionnaire concerning computer utilization**

concession *noun* **(a)** right to use someone else's property for business purposes; **mining concession** = right to dig a mine on a piece of land **(b)** right to be the only seller of a product in a place; **she runs a jewellery concession in a department store (c)** allowance; **tax concession** = allowing less tax to be paid
◊ **concessionnaire** *noun* person who has the right to be the only seller of a product in a place
◊ **concessionary** *adjective* **concessionary fare** = reduced fare for certain types of passenger (such as employees of the transport company)

conciliation *noun* bringing together the parties in a dispute so that the dispute can be settled

conclude *verb* **(a)** to complete successfully; **to conclude an agreement with someone (b)** to believe from evidence; **the police concluded that the thief had got into the building through the main entrance**

condition *noun* **(a)** term of a contract *or* duties which have to be carried out as part of a contract *or* something which has to be agreed before a contract becomes valid; **conditions of employment** *or* **conditions of service** = terms of a contract of employment; **conditions of sale** = agreed ways in which a sale takes place (such as discounts *or* credit terms); **on condition that** = provided that; **they were granted the lease on condition that they paid the legal costs (b)** general state; **the union has complained of the bad working conditions in the factory; item sold in good condition; what was the condition of the car when it was sold? adverse trading conditions**
◊ **conditional** *adjective* provided that certain things take place; **to give a conditional acceptance** = to accept, provided that certain things happen *or* certain

terms apply; **the offer is conditional on the board's acceptance** = provided the board accepts; **he made a conditional offer** = he offered to buy, provided that certain terms applied

condominium *noun* US system of ownership, where a person owns an apartment in a building, together with a share of the land, stairs, roof, etc.

conduct *verb* to carry on; **to conduct negotiations; the chairman conducted the negotiations very efficiently**

conference *noun* **(a)** meeting of people to discuss problems; **to be in conference** = to be in a meeting; **conference phone** = telephone so arranged that several people can speak into it from around a table; **conference room** = room where small meetings can take place; **press conference** = meeting where newspaper and TV reporters are invited to hear news of a new product *or* a takeover bid, etc.; **sales conference** = meeting of sales managers, representatives, publicity staff, etc., to discuss future sales plans **(b)** meeting of an association *or* a society *or* a union; **the annual conference of the Electricians' Union; the conference of the Booksellers' Association; the conference agenda** *or* **the agenda of the conference was drawn up by the secretary; Trades Union Conference (TUC)** = association of British trade unions

confidence *noun* **(a)** feeling sure *or* being certain; **the sales teams do not have much confidence in their manager; the board has total confidence in the managing director (b) in confidence** = in secret; **I will show you the report in confidence**
◊ **confidence trick** *noun* business deal where someone gains another person's confidence and then tricks him
◊ **confidence trickster** *noun* person who carries out a confidence trick on someone
◊ **confident** *adjective* certain *or* sure; **I am confident the turnover will increase rapidly; are you confident the sales team is capable of handling this product?**
◊ **confidential** *adjective* secret *or* not to be told or shown to other people; **he sent a confidential report to the chairman; please mark the letter "Private and Confidential"**

◇ **confidentiality** *noun* being secret; **he broke the confidentiality of the discussions** = he told someone about the secret discussions

confirm *verb* to say that something is certain; **to confirm a hotel reservation** *or* **a ticket** *or* **an agreement** *or* **a booking; to confirm someone in a job** = to say that someone is now permanently in the job
◇ **confirmation** *noun* **(a)** being certain; **confirmation of a booking** = checking that a booking is certain **(b)** document which confirms something; **he received confirmation from the bank that the deeds had been deposited**

conflict *noun* **conflict of interest** = situation where a person may profit personally from decisions which he takes in his official capacity

confuse *verb* to make it difficult for someone to understand something *or* to make something difficult; **the chairman was confused by all the journalists' questions; to introduce the problem of VAT will only confuse the issue**

conglomerate *noun* group of subsidiary companies linked together and forming a group making very different types of products

congratulate *verb* to give someone your good wishes for having done something well; **the sales director congratulated the salesmen on doubling sales; I want to congratulate you on your promotion**
◇ **congratulations** *plural noun* good wishes; **the staff sent him their congratulations on his promotion**

conman *noun* *informal* = CONFIDENCE TRICKSTER
NOTE: plural is **conmen**

connect *verb* **(a)** to link *or* to join; **the company is connected to the government because the chairman's father is a minister (b)** the flight from New York connects with a flight to Athens** = the plane from New York arrives in time for passengers to catch the plane to Athens

◇ **connecting flight** *noun* plane which a passenger will be on time to catch and which will take him to his final destination; **check at the helicopter desk for connecting flights to the city centre**
◇ **connection** *noun* **(a)** link *or* something which joins; **is there a connection between his argument with the director and his sudden move to become warehouse manager?; in connection with** = referring to; **I want to speak to the managing director in connection with the sales forecasts (b) connections** = people you know *or* customers *or* contacts; **he has useful connections in industry**

conservative *adjective* careful *or* not overestimating; **a conservative estimate of sales; his forecast of expenditure is very conservative; at a conservative estimate** = calculation which probably underestimates the final figure; **their turnover has risen by at least 20% in the last year, and that is probably a conservative estimate**
◇ **conservatively** *adverb* not overestimating; **the total sales are conservatively estimated at £2.3m**

consider *verb* to think seriously about something; **to consider the terms of a contract** = to examine and discuss if the terms are acceptable
◇ **consideration** *noun* **(a)** serious thought; **we are giving consideration to moving the head office to Scotland (b)** something valuable exchanged as part of a contract; **for a small consideration** = for a small fee *or* payment
NOTE: no plural for (a)

considerable *adjective* quite large; **we sell considerable quantities of our products to Africa; they lost a considerable amount of money on the commodity market**
◇ **considerably** *adverb* quite a lot; **sales are considerably higher than they were last year**

consign *verb* **to consign goods to someone** = to send goods to someone for him to use or to sell for you
◇ **consignation** *noun* act of consigning
◇ **consignee** *noun* person who receives goods from someone for his own use or to sell for the sender

◇ **consignment** *noun* **(a)** sending of goods to someone who will sell them for you; **consignment note** = note saying that goods have been sent; **goods on consignment** = goods kept for another company to be sold on their behalf for a commission **(b)** group of goods sent for sale; **a consignment of goods has arrived; we are expecting a consignment of cars from Japan**

◇ **consignor** *noun* person who consigns goods to someone

consist of *verb* to be formed of; **the trade mission consists of the sales directors of ten major companies; the package tour consists of air travel, six nights in a luxury hotel, all meals and visits to places of interest**

consolidate *verb* **(a)** to put the accounts of several subsidiary companies into the accounts of the main group **(b)** to group goods together for shipping

◇ **consolidation** *noun* grouping together of goods for shipping

◇ **consolidated** *adjective* **(a)** consolidated accounts = accounts of subsidiary companies grouped together into the accounts of the parent company **(b)** consolidated shipment = goods from different companies grouped together into a single shipment

consols *plural noun* *GB* government bonds which pay an interest but do not have a maturity date

consortium *noun* group of companies which work together; **a consortium of Canadian companies** *or* **a Canadian consortium; a consortium of French and British companies is planning to construct the new aircraft**

constitution *noun* written rules *or* regulations of a society *or* association *or* club *or* state; **under the society's constitution, the chairman is elected for a two-year period; payments to officers of the association are not allowed by the constitution**

◇ **constitutional** *adjective* according to a constitution; **the reelection of the chairman is not constitutional**

construct *verb* to build; **the company has tendered for the contract to construct the new airport**

◇ **construction** *noun* building; **construction company** = company which specializes in building; **under construction** = being built; **the airport is under construction**

◇ **constructive** *adjective* which helps in the making of something; **she made some constructive suggestions for improving management-worker relations; we had a constructive proposal from a distribution company in Italy; constructive dismissal** = situation when a worker leaves his job voluntarily but because of pressure from the management

◇ **constructor** *noun* person *or* company which constructs

consult *verb* to ask an expert for advice; **he consulted his accountant about his tax**

◇ **consultancy** *noun* act of giving specialist advice; **a consultancy firm; he offers a consultancy service**

◇ **consultant** *noun* specialist who gives advice; **engineering consultant; management consultant; tax consultant**

◇ **consulting** *adjective* person who gives specialist advice; **consulting engineer**

consumable *adjective* **consumable goods** = goods which are bought by members of the public and not by companies

◇ **consumables** *plural noun* = CONSUMABLE GOODS

◇ **consumer** *noun* person *or* company which buys and uses goods and services; **gas consumers are protesting at the increase in prices; the factory is a heavy consumer of water; consumer council** = group representing the interests of consumers; **consumer credit** = credit given by shops, banks and other financial institutions to consumers so that they can buy goods; **consumer durables** = items such as washing machines *or* refrigerators *or* cookers which are bought and used by the public; **consumer goods** = goods bought by consumers *or* by members of the public; **consumer panel** = group of consumers who report on products they have used so that the manufacturers can improve them or use what the panel says about them in advertising; *US* **consumer price index** = index showing how prices of consumer goods have risen over a period of time, used as a way of measuring inflation and the cost of living; **consumer protection** = protecting consumers against unfair *or* illegal traders; **consumer research** = research into why consumers buy goods and what goods they really want to buy; **consumer resistance** = lack of interest by consumers in buying a product; **the latest price increases have produced considerable consumer resistance; consumer society** = type of society where consumers are encouraged to buy goods; **consumer spending** = spending by consumers

QUOTE: analysis of the consumer price index for the first half of 1985 shows that the rate of inflation went down by about 12.9 per cent
Business Times (Lagos)

consumption *noun* buying or using goods or services; **a car with low petrol consumption; the factory has a heavy consumption of coal; home consumption** *or* **domestic consumption** = use of something in the home
NOTE: no plural

contact 1 *noun* **(a)** person you know *or* person you can ask for help or advice; **he has many contacts in the city; who is your contact in the ministry? (b)** act of getting in touch with someone; **I have lost contact with them** = I do not communicate with them any longer; **he put me in contact with a good lawyer** = he told me how to get in touch with a good lawyer
NOTE: no plural for (b)
2 *verb* to get in touch with someone *or* to communicate with someone; **he tried to contact his office by phone; can you contact the managing director at his club?**

contain *verb* to hold something inside; **each crate contains two computers and their peripherals; a barrel contains 250 litres; we have lost a file containing important documents**
◇ **container** *noun* **(a)** box *or* bottle *or* can, etc. which can hold goods; **the gas is shipped in strong metal containers; the container burst during shipping (b)** very large metal case of a standard size for loading and transporting goods on trucks,

trains and ships; **container ship; container berth; container port; container terminal; to ship goods in containers; a container-load of spare parts** = a shipment of spare parts sent in a container
◇ **containerization** *noun* putting into containers; shipping in containers
◇ **containerize** *verb* to put goods into containers; to ship goods in containers

contango *noun* payment of interest by a stockbroker for carrying payment for shares from one account day to the next; **contango day** = day when the rate of contango payments is fixed

content *noun* the ideas inside a letter, etc.; **the content of the letter** = the real meaning of the letter
◇ **contents** *plural noun* things contained *or* what is inside something; **the contents of the bottle poured out onto the floor; the customs officials inspected the contents of the crate; the contents of the letter** = the words written in the letter

contested takeover *noun* takeover where the board of the company do not recommend it to the shareholders and try to fight it

contingency *noun* possible state of emergency when decisions will have to be taken quickly; **contingency fund** *or* **contingency reserve** = money set aside in case it is needed urgently; **contingency plans** = plans which will be put into action if something happens which no one expects; **to add on 10% to provide for contingencies** = to provide for further expenditure which may be incurred; **we have built 10% for contingencies into our cost forecast**
◇ **contingent** *adjective* **(a) contingent expenses** = expenses which will be incurred only if something happens **(b) contingent policy** = policy which pays out only if something happens (as if the person named in the policy dies before the person due to benefit)

continue *verb* to go on doing something *or* to do something which you were doing earlier; **the chairman continued speaking in spite of the noise from the shareholders; the meeting started at 10 a.m. and continued until six p.m.; negotiations will continue next Monday**

◇ **continual** *adjective* which happens again and again; **production was slow because of continual breakdowns**

◇ **continually** *adverb* again and again; **the photocopier is continually breaking down**

◇ **continuation** *noun* act of continuing

◇ **continuous** *adjective* with no end *or* with no breaks; **continuous production line; continuous feed** = device which feeds continuous stationery into a printer; **continuous stationery** = paper made as one long sheet, used in the computer printers

contra 1 *noun* **contra account** = account which offsets another account; **contra entry** = entry made in the opposite side of an account to make an earlier entry worthless (i.e. a debit against a credit); **per contra** *or* **as per contra** = words showing that a contra entry has been made **2** *verb* **to contra an entry** = to enter a similar amount in the opposite side of an account

contraband *noun* **contraband (goods)** = goods brought into a country illegally, without paying customs duty

contract 1 *noun* **(a)** legal agreement between two parties; **to draw up a contract; to draft a contract; to sign a contract; the contract is binding on both parties** = both parties signing the contract must do what is agreed; **under contract** = bound by the terms of a contract; **the firm is under contract to deliver the goods by November; to void a contract** = to make a contract invalid; **contract of employment** = contract between management and employee showing all conditions of work; **service contract** = contract between a company and a director showing all conditions of work; **exchange of contracts** = point in the sale of a property when the buyer and seller both sign the contract of sale which then becomes binding **(b)** **contract law** *or* **law of contract** = laws relating to agreements; **by private contract** = by private legal agreement; **contract note** = note showing that shares have been bought or sold but not yet paid for **(c)** agreement for supply of a service or goods; **contract for the supply of spare parts; to enter into a contract to supply spare parts;** to sign a contract for £10,000 worth of spare parts; **to put work out to contract** = to decide that work should be done by another company on a contract, rather than employing members of staff to do it; **to award a contract to a company** *or* **to place a contract with a company** = to decide that a company shall have the contract to do work for you; **to tender for a contract** = to put forward an estimate of cost for work under contract; **conditions of contract** *or* **contract conditions; breach of contract** = breaking the terms of a contract; **the company is in breach of contract** = the company has failed to do what was agreed in the contract; **contract work** = work done according to a written agreement **2** *verb* to agree to do some work by contract; **to contract to supply spare parts** *or* **to contract for the supply of spare parts; the supply of spare parts was contracted out to Smith Ltd** = Smith Ltd was given the contract for supplying spare parts; **to contract out of an agreement** = to withdraw from an agreement with written permission of the other party

◇ **contracting** *adjective* **contracting party** = person or company which signs a contract

◇ **contractor** *noun* person or company which does work according to a written agreement; **haulage contractor** = company which transports goods by contract; **government contractor** = company which supplies the government with goods by contract

◇ **contractual** *adjective* according to a contract; **contractual liability** = legal responsibility for something as stated in a contract; **to fulfill your contractual obligations** = to do what you have agreed to do in a contract; **he is under no contractual obligation to buy** = he has signed no agreement to buy

◇ **contractually** *adverb* according to a contract; **the company is contractually bound to pay his expenses**

contrary *noun* opposite; **failing instructions to the contrary** = unless different instructions are given; **on the contrary** = quite the opposite; **the chairman was not annoyed with his assistant - on the contrary, he promoted him**

contribute *verb* to give money *or* to add to money; **to contribute 10% of the profits; he contributed to the pension fund for 10 years**

◇ **contribution** *noun* money paid to add to a sum; **contribution of capital** = money paid to a company as additional capital; **employer's contribution** = money paid by an employer towards a worker's pension; **National Insurance contributions** = money paid each month by a worker and the company to the National Insurance; **pension contributions** = money paid by a company or worker into a pension fund

◇ **contributor** *noun* **contributor of capital** = person who contributes capital

◇ **contributory** *adjective* (a) **contributory pension plan** *or* **scheme** = pension plan where the employee has to contribute a percentage of salary (b) which helps to cause; **falling exchange rates have been a contributory factor in** *or* **to the company's loss of profits**

con trick *noun informal* = CONFIDENCE TRICK

control 1 *noun* (a) power *or* being able to direct something; **the company is under the control of three shareholders; the family lost control of its business; to gain control of a business** = to buy more than 50% of the shares so that you can direct the business; **to lose control of a business** = to find that you have less than 50% of the shares in a company, and so are not longer able to direct it (b) restricting *or* checking something *or* making sure that something is kept in check; **under control** = kept in check; **expenses are kept under tight control; the company is trying to bring its overheads back under control; out of control** = not kept in check; **costs have got out of control; budgetary control** = keeping check on spending; **credit control** = checking that customers pay on time and do not exceed their credit limits; **quality control** = making sure that the quality of a product is good; **stock control** = making sure that movements of stock are noted (c) **exchange controls** = government restrictions on changing the local currency into foreign currency; **the government has imposed exchange controls; they say the government is going to lift exchange controls; price controls** = legal

measures to prevent prices rising too fast (d) **control group** = small group which is used to check a sample group; **control systems** = systems used to check that a computer system is working correctly 2 *verb* (a) **to control a business** = to direct a business; **the business is controlled by a company based in Luxembourg; the company is controlled by the majority shareholder** (b) to make sure that something is kept in check *or* is not allowed to develop; **the government is fighting to control inflation** *or* **to control the rise in the cost of living** NOTE: **controlling - controlled**

◇ **controlled** *adjective* ruled *or* kept in check; **government-controlled** = ruled by a government; **controlled economy** = economy where the most business activity is directed by orders from the government

◇ **controller** *noun* (a) person who controls (especially the finances of a company); **stock controller** = person who notes movements of stock (b) *US* chief accountant in a company

◇ **controlling** *adjective* **to have a controlling interest in a company** = to own more than 50% of the shares so that you can direct how the company is run

convene *verb* to ask people to come together; **to convene a meeting of shareholders**

convenience *noun* **at your earliest convenience** = as soon as you find it possible; **convenience foods** = food which is prepared by the shop before it is sold, so that it needs only heating to be made ready to eat; **ship sailing under a flag of convenience** = flying the flag of a country which may have no ships of its own but allows ships of other countries to be registered in its ports

◇ **convenient** *adjective* suitable *or* handy; **a bank draft is a convenient way of sending money abroad; is 9.30 a convenient time for the meeting?**

convenor *noun* trade unionist who organizes union meetings

conversion *noun* change (a) **conversion of funds** = using money which does not belong to you for a purpose for which it is not supposed to be used (b) **conversion price** *or* **conversion rate** = rate at which a currency is changed into a foreign currency; price at which preference shares are converted into ordinary shares

◇ **convert** *verb* to change money of one country for money of another; **we converted our pounds into Swiss francs; to convert funds to one's own use** = to use someone else's money for yourself

◇ **convertibility** *noun* ability to exchange one currency for another easily

◇ **convertible** *adjective* **convertible currency** = currency which can be exchanged for another easily; **convertible loan stock** = stock which can be exchanged for shares at a later date

conveyance *noun* legal document which transfers a property from the seller to the buyer

◇ **conveyancer** *noun* person who draws up a conveyance

◇ **conveyancing** *noun* legally transferring a property from a seller to a buyer; **do-it-yourself conveyancing** = drawing up a legal conveyance without the help of a lawyer

cooling off *noun* **cooling off period** = during an industrial dispute, a period when negotiations have to be carried on and no action can be taken by either side; period when a person is allowed to think about something which he has agreed to buy on hire-purchase and possibly change his mind

co-op *noun* = CO-OPERATIVE 2

◇ **co-operate** *verb* to work together; **the governments are co-operating in the fight against piracy; the two firms have co-operated on the computer project**

◇ **co-operation** *noun* working together; **the project was completed ahead of schedule with the co-operation of the workforce**

◇ **co-operative 1** *adjective* willing to work together; **the workforce has not been co-operative over the management's productivity plan; co-operative society** = society where the customers and workers are partners and share the profits **2** *noun* business run by a group of workers who are the owners and who share the profits; **agricultural co-operative; to set up a workers' co-operative**

co-opt *verb* **to co-opt someone onto a committee** = to ask someone to join a committee without being elected

co-owner *noun* person who owns something with another person; **the two sisters are co-owners of the property**

◇ **co-ownership** *noun* arrangement where partners *or* workers have shares in a company

copartner *noun* person who is a partner in a business with another person

◇ **copartnership** *noun* arrangement where partners *or* workers have shares in the company

cope *verb* to manage to do something; **the new assistant manager coped very well when the manager was on holiday; the warehouse is trying to cope with the backlog of orders**

copier *noun* = COPYING MACHINE, PHOTOCOPIER

coproperty *noun* ownership of property by two or more people together

◇ **coproprietor** *noun* person who owns a property with another person or several other people

copy 1 *noun* **(a)** document which is made to look the same as another; **carbon copy** = copy made with carbon paper; **certified copy** = document which is certified as being the same as another; **file copy** = copy of a document which is filed in an office for reference **(b)** document; **fair copy** *or* **final copy** = document which is written or typed with no changes or mistakes; **hard copy** = printout of a text which is on a computer *or* printed copy of something which is on microfilm; **rough copy** = draft of a document which, it is expected, will have changes made to it; **top copy** = first or top sheet of a document which is typed with carbon copies **(c)** **publicity copy** = text of a proposed advertisement before it is printed; **she writes copy for a travel firm; knocking copy** = advertising material which criticizes competing products **(d)** a book *or* a newspaper; **have you kept yesterday's copy of the "Times"? I read it in the office**

copy of "Fortune"; where is my copy of the telephone directory?
NOTE: no plural for (c)
2 *verb* to make a second document which is like the first; **he copied the company report at night and took it home**
◊ **copier** *or* **copying machine** *noun* machine which makes copies of documents
◊ **copyright 1** *noun* legal right (lasting for fifty years after the death of a writer) which a writer has to publish his own work and not to have it copied; **copyright act** = Act of Parliament making copyright legal, and controlling the copying of copyright material; **copyright law** = laws concerning copyright; **work which is out of copyright** = work by a writer who has been dead for fifty years; **work still in copyright** = work by a living writer, or by a writer who has not been dead for fifty years; **infringement of copyright** *or* **copyright infringement** = act of illegally copying a work which is in copyright; **copyright notice** = note in a book showing who owns the copyright and the date of ownership
NOTE: no plural
2 *verb* to confirm the copyright of a written work by inserting a copyright notice and publishing the work **3** *adjective* covered by the laws of copyright; **it is illegal to photocopy a copyright work**
◊ **copyrighted** *adjective* in copyright

copy typing *noun* typing documents from handwritten originals, not from dictation
◊ **copy typist** *noun* person who types documents from handwritten originals, not from dictation

copywriter *noun* person who writes advertisements

corner 1 *noun* **(a)** place where two streets *or* two walls join; **the Post Office is on the corner of the High Street and London Road; corner shop** = small general store in a town on a street corner **(b)** place where two sides join; **the box has to have specially strong corners; the corner of the crate was damaged (c)** situation where one person or a group controls the supply of a certain commodity **2** *verb* **to corner the market** = to own most or all of the supply

of a certain commodity and so control the price; **the syndicate tried to corner the market in silver**

corp *US* = CORPORATION

corporate *adjective* referring to a whole company; **corporate image** = idea which a company would like the public to have of it; **corporate plan** = plan for the future work of a whole company; **corporate planning** = planning the future work of a whole company; **corporate profits** = profits of a corporation
◊ **corporation** *noun* **(a)** large company; **finance corporation** = company which provides money for hire purchase; **corporation tax** = tax on profits made by companies **(b)** *US* company which is incorporated in the United States; **corporation income tax** = tax on profits made by incorporated companies

QUOTE: the prime rate is the rate at which banks lend to their top corporate borrowers
Wall Street Journal
QUOTE: corporate profits for the first quarter showed a 4 per cent drop from last year
Financial Times
QUOTE: if corporate forecasts are met, sales will exceed $50 million in 1985 *Citizen (Ottawa)*

correct 1 *adjective* accurate *or* right; **the published accounts do not give a correct picture of the company's financial position 2** *verb* to remove mistakes from something; **the accounts department have corrected the invoice; you will have to correct all these typing errors before you send the letter**
◊ **correction** *noun* making something correct; change which makes something correct; **he made some corrections to the text of the speech**

correspond *verb* **(a)** to correspond with someone = to write letters to someone **(b)** to correspond with something = to fit *or* to match something
◊ **correspondence** *noun* letters which are exchanged; **business correspondence** = letters concerned with a business; **to be in correspondence with someone** = to write letters to someone and receive letters

back; **correspondence clerk** = clerk whose responsibility it is to answer correspondence
NOTE: no plural

◇ **correspondent** *noun* **(a)** person who writes letters **(b)** journalist who writes articles for a newspaper on specialist subjects; **a financial correspondent; the "Times" business correspondent; he is the Paris correspondent of the "Telegraph"**

cost 1 *noun* **(a)** amount of money which has to be paid for something; **what is the cost of a first class ticket to New York? computer costs are falling each year; we cannot afford the cost of two telephones; to cover costs** = to produce enough money in sales to pay for the costs of production; **the sales revenue barely covers the costs of advertising** *or* **the manufacturing costs; to sell at cost** = to sell at a price which is the same as the cost of manufacture or the wholesale cost; **fixed costs** = business costs which do not rise with the quantity of the product made; **labour costs** = cost of hourly-paid workers employed to make a product; **manufacturing costs** *or* **production costs** = costs of making a product; **operating costs** *or* **running costs** = cost of the day-to-day organization of a company; **variable costs** = production costs which increase with the quantity of the product made (such as wages, raw materials); **cost accountant** = accountant who gives managers information about their business costs; **cost accounting** = specially prepared accounts of manufacturing and sales costs; **cost analysis** = calculating in advance what a new product will cost; **cost centre** = group *or* machine whose costs can be itemized and to which fixed costs can be allocated; **cost, insurance and freight** = estimate of a price, which includes the cost of the goods, the insurance and the transport charges; **cost price** = selling price which is the same as the price which the seller paid for the item (i.e. either the manufacturing cost or the wholesale price); **cost of sales** = all the costs of a product sold, including manufacturing costs and the staff costs of the production department **(b) costs** = expenses involved in a court case; **to pay costs** = to pay the expenses of a court case; **the judge awarded costs to the defendant; costs of the case will be borne by the**

prosecution 2 *verb* **(a)** to have a price; **how much does the machine cost? this cloth costs £10 a metre (b) to cost a product** = to calculate how much money will be needed to make a product, and so work out its selling price

◇ **cost-benefit** *noun* **cost-benefit analysis** = examining the ratio between costs and benefits, especially in comparing different production processes

◇ **cost-cutting** *noun* reducing costs; **we have taken out the telex as a cost-cutting exercise**

◇ **cost-effective** *adjective* which gives value, especially when compared with something else; **we find advertising in the Sunday newspapers very cost-effective**

◇ **cost-effectiveness** *noun* being cost-effective; **can we calculate the cost-effectiveness of air freight against shipping by sea?**

◇ **costing** *noun* calculation of the manufacturing costs, and so the selling price of a product; **the costings give us a retail price of $2.95; we cannot do the costing until we have details of all the production expenditure**

◇ **costly** *adjective* expensive *or* costing a lot of money

◇ **cost of living** *noun* money which has to be paid for food, heating, rent etc.; **to allow for the cost of living in the salaries; cost-of-living allowance** = addition to normal salary to cover increases in the cost of living; **cost-of-living bonus** = extra money paid to meet the increase in the cost of living; **cost-of-living increase** = increase in salary to allow it to keep up with the increased cost of living; **cost-of-living index** = way of measuring the cost of living which is shown as a percentage increase on the figure for the previous year

◇ **cost plus** *noun* system of charging, where the buyer pays the costs plus a percentage commission to the seller; **we are charging for the work on a cost plus basis**

◇ **cost-push inflation** *noun* inflation caused by increased wage demands which lead to higher prices and in turn lead to further wage demands

council *noun* official group chosen to run something *or* to advise on a problem; **consumer council** = group representing the interests of consumers; **town council =** representatives elected to run a town

counsel *noun* lawyer acting for one of the parties in a legal action; **defence counsel; prosecution counsel;** *GB* **Queen's Counsel =** senior lawyer
NOTE: no plural

count *verb* **(a)** to add figures together to make a total; **he counted up the sales for the six months to December (b)** to include; **did you count my trip to New York as part of my sales expenses?**
◊ **counting house** *noun* department dealing with cash
◊ **count on** *verb* to expect something to happen; **they are counting on getting a good response from the TV advertising; do not count on a bank loan to start your business**

counter *noun* long flat surface in a shop for displaying and selling goods; **over the counter =** legally; **goods sold over the counter =** retail sales of goods in shops; **some drugs are sold over the counter, but others need to be recommended by a doctor; over-the-counter sales =** legal selling of shares which are not listed in the official Stock Exchange list; **under the counter =** illegally; **under-the-counter sales =** black market sales; **bargain counter =** counter where things are sold cheaply; **check-in counter =** place where plane passengers have to check in; **ticket counter =** place where tickets are sold; **trade counter =** shop in a factory *or* warehouse where goods are sold to retailers; **glove counter =** section of a shop where gloves are sold; **counter staff =** sales staff who serve behind counters

counter- *prefix* against
◊ **counterbid** *noun* higher bid in reply to a previous bid; **when I bid £20 he put in a counterbid of £25**
◊ **counter-claim 1** *noun* claim for damages made in reply to a previous claim; **Jones claimed £25,000 in damages against Smith, and Smith entered a counter-claim of £50,000 for loss of office 2** *verb* to put in a counter-claim; **Jones claimed £25,000 in damages and Smith counter-claimed £50,000 for loss of office**

◊ **counterfeit 1** *adjective* false *or* imitation (money) **2** *verb* to make imitation money
◊ **counterfoil** *noun* slip of paper kept after writing a cheque *or* an invoice *or* a receipt, as a record of the deal which has taken place
◊ **countermand** *verb* **to countermand an order =** to say that an order must not be carried out
◊ **counter-offer** *noun* higher offer made in reply to another offer; **Smith Ltd made an offer of £1m for the property, and Blacks replied with a counter-offer of £1.4m**
◊ **counterpart** *noun* person who has a similar job in another company; **John is my counterpart in Smith's =** he has the same post as I have here
◊ **countersign** *verb* to sign a document which has already been signed by someone else; **all cheques have to be countersigned by the finance director; the sales director countersigns all my orders**

country *noun* **(a)** land which is separate and governs itself; **the contract covers distribution in the countries of the Common Market; some African countries export oil; the Organization of Petroleum Exporting Countries; the managing director is out of the country =** he is on a business trip abroad **(b)** land which is not near a town; **distribution is difficult in country areas; his territory is mainly the country, but he is based in the town**

couple *noun* two things or people taken together; **we only have enough stock for a couple of weeks; a couple of the directors were ill, so the board meeting was cancelled; the negotiations lasted a couple of hours =** the negotiations went on for about two hours

coupon *noun* **(a)** piece of paper used in place of money; **gift coupon =** coupon from a store which is given as a gift and which must be exchanged in that store **(b)** piece of paper which replaces an order form; **coupon ad =** advertisement with a form attached, which is to be cut out and returned to the advertiser with your name and address if you want further information about the product advertised; **reply coupon =** form attached to a coupon ad, which must be filled in and returned to the advertiser **(c) interest coupon** = slip of paper attached to a government bond certificate which can be cashed to provide the annual interest; **cum coupon** = with a coupon attached; **ex coupon** = without the interest coupons

courier *noun* **(a)** motorcyclist who takes messages from one place another in a town **(b)** person who goes with a party of tourists to guide them on a package tour

course *noun* **(a) in the course of** = during *or* while something is happening; **in the course of the discussion, the managing director explained the company's expansion plans; sales have risen sharply in the course of the last few months (b)** series of lessons; **she has finished her secretarial course; the company has paid for her to attend a course for trainee sales managers (c) of course** = naturally; **of course the company is interested in profits; are you willing to go on a sales trip to Australia? - of course!**

court *noun* place where a judge listens to a case and decides legally which of the parties in the argument is right; **court case** = legal action *or* trial; **to take someone to court** = to tell someone to appear in court to settle an argument; **a settlement was reached out of court** *or* **the two parties reached an out-of-court settlement** = the dispute was settled between the two parties privately without continuing the court case

covenant 1 *noun* legal contract; **deed of covenant** = official signed agreement to pay someone a sum of money each year 2 *verb* to agree to pay a sum of money each year by contract; **to covenant to pay £10 per annum**

cover 1 *noun* **(a)** thing put over a machine, etc. to keep it clean; **put the cover over your micro when you leave the office; always keep a cover over the typewriter (b) insurance cover** = protection guaranteed by an insurance policy; **do you have cover against theft?; to operate without adequate cover** = without being protected by insurance; **to ask for additional cover** = to ask the insurance company to increase the amount

for which you are insured; **full cover** = insurance against all risks; **cover note** = letter from an insurance company giving details of an insurance policy and confirming that the policy exists NOTE: the US English for this is **binder** **(c)** security to guarantee a loan; **do you have sufficient cover for this loan? (d)** (*in restaurant*) **cover charge** = charge in addition to the charge for food **(e) dividend cover** = ratio of profits to dividend **(f) to send something under separate cover** = in a separate envelope; **to send a magazine under plain cover** = in an ordinary envelope with no company name printed on it 2 *verb* **(a)** to put something over a machine, etc. to keep it clean; **don't forget to cover your micro before you go home (b) to cover a risk** = to be protected by insurance against a risk; **to be fully covered** = to have insurance against all risks; **the insurance covers fire, theft and loss of work (c)** to have enough money to pay; to ask for security against a loan which you are making; **the damage was covered by the insurance** = the insurance company paid for the damage; **to cover a position** = to have enough money to be able to pay for a forward purchase **(d)** to earn enough money to pay for costs, expenses etc.; **we do not make enough sales to cover the expense of running the shop; breakeven point is reached when sales cover all costs; the dividend is covered four times** = profits are four times the dividend paid out

◇ **coverage** *noun* **(a) press coverage** *or* **media coverage** = reports about something in the newspapers *or* on TV, etc.; **the company had good media coverage for the launch of its new model (b)** *US* protection guaranteed by insurance; **do you have coverage against fire damage?** NOTE: no plural

◇ **covering letter** *or* **covering note** *noun* letter or note sent with documents to say why you are sending them

QUOTE: three export credit agencies have agreed to provide cover for large projects in Nigeria *Business Times (Lagos)*

crane *noun* machine for lifting heavy objects; **the container slipped as the crane was lifting it onto the ship; they had to hire a crane to get the machine into the factory**

crash 1 *noun* **(a)** accident to a car *or* plane *or* train; **the car was damaged in the crash; the plane crash killed all the passengers** *or* **all the passengers were killed in the plane crash (b)** financial collapse; **financial crash; he lost all his money in the crash of 1929** 2 *verb* **(a)** to hit something and be damaged; **the plane crashed into the mountain; the lorry crashed into the post office (b)** to collapse financially; **the company crashed with debts of over £1 million**

crate 1 *noun* large wooden box; **a crate of oranges** 2 *verb* to put goods into crates

create *verb* to make something new; **by acquiring small unprofitable companies he soon created a large manufacturing group; the government scheme aims at creating new jobs for young people**
◊ **creation** *noun* making; **job creation scheme** = government-backed scheme to make work for the unemployed

> QUOTE: he insisted that the tax advantages he directed towards small businesses will help create jobs and reduce the unemployment rate
> *Toronto Star*

credere *see* DEL CREDERE

credit 1 *noun* **(a)** time given to a customer before he has to pay; **to give someone six months' credit; to sell on good credit terms; extended credit** = credit on very long repayment terms; **interest-free credit** = arrangement to borrow money without paying interest on the loan; **long credit** = terms allowing the borrower a long time to pay; **open credit** = bank credit given to good customers without security; **short credit** = terms allowing the customer only a short time to pay; **credit account** = account which a customer has with a shop which allows him to buy goods and pay for them later; **to open a credit account; credit agency** *or* *US* **credit bureau** = company which reports on the creditworthiness of customers to show whether they should be allowed credit; **credit bank** = bank which lends money; **credit control** = check that customers pay on time and do not owe more than their credit limit; **credit facilities** = arrangement with a bank or supplier to have credit

so as to buy goods; **credit freeze** *or* **credit squeeze** = period when lending by banks is restricted by the government; **letter of credit** = letter from a bank, allowing someone credit and promising to repay at a later date; **irrevocable letter of credit** = letter of credit which cannot be cancelled; **credit limit** = fixed amount which is the most a customer can owe on credit; **he has exceeded his credit limit** = he has borrowed more money than he is allowed; **to open a line of credit** *or* **a credit line** = to make credit available to someone; **credit rating** = amount which a credit agency feels a customer should be allowed to borrow; **on credit** = without paying immediately; **to live on credit; we buy everything on sixty days credit; the company exists on credit from its suppliers** NOTE: no plural **(b)** money received by a person *or* company and recorded in the accounts; **to enter £100 to someone's credit; to pay in £100 to the credit of Mr Smith; debit and credit** = money which a company owes and which it receives; **credit balance** = balance in an account showing that more money has been received than is owed by the company; **the account has a credit balance of £1,000; credit column** = right-hand column in accounts showing money received; **credit entry** = entry on the credit side of an account; **credit note** = note showing that money is owed to a customer; **the company sent the wrong order and so had to issue a credit note; credit side** = right-hand side of accounts showing money received; **account in credit** = account where the credits are higher than the debits; **bank credit** = loans or overdrafts from a bank to a customer; **tax credits** = part of a dividend on which the company has already paid tax, so that the shareholder is not taxed on it 2 *verb* to put money into someone's account; to note money received in an account; **to credit an account with £100** *or* **to credit £100 to an account**
◊ **credit card** *noun* plastic card which allows you to borrow money and to buy goods without paying for them immediately
◊ **creditor** *noun* person who is owed money; **creditors' meeting** = meeting of all persons to whom a bankrupt company owes money, to decide how to obtain the money owed

◇ **credit union** *noun US* group of people who pay regular subscriptions which are used to help members of the group who are ill or in financial difficulties

◇ **credit-worthy** *adjective* able to buy goods on credit

◇ **creditworthiness** *noun* ability of a customer to pay for goods bought on credit

crew *noun* group of people who work on a plane *or* ship, etc.; **the ship carries a crew of 250**

crime *noun* act which is against the law; **crimes in supermarkets have risen by 25%**

◇ **criminal** *adjective* illegal; **misappropriation of funds is a criminal act; criminal action** = court case brought by the state against someone who is charged with a crime

crisis *noun* serious economic situation where decisions have to be taken rapidly; **international crisis; banking crisis; financial crisis; to take crisis measures** = to take severe measures rapidly to stop a crisis developing
NOTE: plural is **crises**

criticize *verb* to say that something *or* someone is wrong *or* is working badly, etc.; **the MD criticized the sales manager for not improving the volume of sales; the design of the new catalogue has been criticized**

cross *verb* **(a)** to go across; **Concorde only takes three hours to cross the Atlantic; to get to the bank, you turn left and cross the street at the post office (b)** to **cross a cheque** = to write two lines across a cheque to show that it has to be paid into a bank; **crossed cheque** = cheque which has to be paid into a bank

◇ **cross holding** *noun* situation where two companies hold shares in each other

◇ **cross off** *verb* to remove something from a list; **he crossed my name off his list; you can cross him off our mailing list**

◇ **cross out** *verb* to put a line through something which has been written; **she crossed out £250 and put in £500**

◇ **cross rate** *noun* exchange rate between two currencies expressed in a third currency

crude (oil) *noun* raw petroleum, taken from the ground; **the price for Arabian crude has slipped**
NOTE: no plural

cubic *adjective* measured in volume by multiplying length, depth and width; **the crate holds six cubic metres; cubic measure** = volume measured in cubic feet or metres
NOTE: cubic is written in figures as ^{3}: **6m^3** = six cubic metres; **10ft^3** = ten cubic feet

cum *preposition* with; **cum dividend** = price of a share including the next dividend still to be paid; **cum coupon** = with a coupon attached

cumulative *adjective* which is added automatically each year; **cumulative interest** = interest which is added to the capital each year; **cumulative preference share** *or US* **cumulative preferred stock** = preference share which will have the dividend paid at a later date even if the company is not able to pay a dividend in the current year

currency *noun* money in coins and notes which is used in a particular country; **convertible currency** = currency which can easily be exchanged for another; **foreign currency** = currency of another country; **foreign currency account** = bank account in the currency of another country (e.g. a dollar account); **foreign currency reserves** = a country's reserves in currencies of other countries; **hard currency** = currency of a country which has a strong economy and which can be changed into other currencies easily; **to pay for imports in hard currency; to sell raw materials to earn hard currency; legal currency** = money which is legally used in a country; **soft currency** = currency of a country with a weak economy, which is cheap to buy and difficult to exchange for other currencies; **currency backing** = gold *or* securities which maintain the international strength

of a currency; **currency note** = bank note
NOTE: currency has no plural when it refers to
the money of one country: **he was arrested
trying to take currency out of the country**

QUOTE: the strong dollar's inflationary impact
on European economies, as national governments
struggle to support their sinking currencies and
push up interest rates   *Duns Business Month*
QUOTE: today's wide daily variations in
exchange rates show the instability of a system
based on a single currency, namely the dollar
                                            Economist
QUOTE: the level of currency in circulation
increased to N4.9 billion in the month of August
                              Business Times (Lagos)

current *adjective* referring to the present
time; **current account** = account in an
bank from which the customer can withdraw money when he wants; **to pay money
into a current account; current assets** =
assets used by a company in its ordinary
work (such as materials, finished products,
cash); **current cost accounting** = method
of accounting which notes the cost of
replacing assets at current prices, rather
than valuing assets at their original cost;
current liabilities = debts which a
company has to pay within the next
accounting period; **current price** =
today's price; **current rate of exchange** =
today's rate of exchange; **current yield** =
dividend calculated as a percentage of the
price paid per share
◊ **currently** *adverb* at the present time;
**we are currently negotiating with the bank
for a loan**

QUOTE: crude oil output plunged during the past
month and is likely to remain at its current level
for the near future   *Wall Street Journal*
QUOTE: customers' current deposit and current
accounts also rose to $655.31 million at the end of
December   *Hongkong Standard*

curriculum vitae *noun* summary of a
person's life story showing details of
education and work experience;
**candidates should send a letter of applica-
tion with a curriculum vitae to the personnel
officer**
NOTE: the plural is **curriculums** or **curricula
vitae.** Note also that the US English is **résumé**

curve *noun* line which bends round; **the
graph shows an upward curve; sales curve**
= graph showing how sales increase or
decrease

cushion *noun* (a) soft bag for sitting on;
**she put a cushion on her chair as it was too
hard** (b) money which allows you to make
a loss; **we have sums on deposit which are a
useful cushion when cash flow is tight**

custom *noun* (a) use of a shop by regular
shoppers; **to lose someone's custom** = to
do something which makes a regular
customer go to another shop; **custom-built**
or **custom-made** = made specially for one
customer; **he drives a custom-built Rolls
Royce** NOTE: no plural (b) **the customs of the
trade** = general way of working in a trade
◊ **customer** *noun* person *or* company
which buys goods; **the shop was full of
customers; can you serve this customer first
please? he is a regular customer of ours;
customer appeal** = what attracts customers to a product; **customer service
department** = department which deals
with customers and their complaints and
orders
◊ **customize** *verb* to change something
to fit the special needs of a customer; **we
used customized computer terminals**
◊ **customs** *plural noun* the government
department which organizes the collection
of taxes on imports; office of this
department at a port *or* airport; **to go
through the customs** = to pass through the
area of a port or airport where customs
officials examine goods; **to take something through the customs** = to carry
something illegal through the customs area
without declaring it; **he was stopped by the
customs; her car was searched by the
customs; customs barrier** = customs duty
intended to prevent imports; **customs
broker** = person *or* company which takes
goods through the customs for a shipping
company; **customs clearance** = document
given by customs to a shipper to show that
customs duty has been paid and the goods
can be shipped; **to wait for customs
clearance; customs declaration** = statement showing goods being imported on
which duty will have to be paid; **to fill in a
customs (declaration) form; customs duty**
= tax paid on goods brought into or taken
out of a country; **the crates had to go
through a customs examination** = the
crates had to be examined by customs
officials; **customs formalities** = declaration of goods by the shipper and examination of them by the customs; **customs**

officers *or* **customs officials** = people working for the customs; **customs tariff** = list of duties to be paid on imported goods; **customs union** = agreement between several countries that goods can travel between them, without paying duty, while goods from other countries have to pay special duties

cut 1 *noun* **(a)** sudden lowering of a price *or* salary *or* numbers of jobs; **price cuts** *or* **cuts in prices; salary cuts** *or* **cuts in salaries; job cuts** = reductions in the number of jobs; **he took a cut in salary** = he accepted a lower salary **(b)** share in a payment; **he introduces new customers and gets a cut of the salesman's commission 2** *verb* **(a)** to lower suddenly; **we are cutting prices on all our models; to cut (back) production** = to reduce the quantity of products made; **the company has cut back its sales force; we have taken out the telex in order to try to cut costs (b)** to stop *or* to reduce the number of something; **to cut jobs** = to reduce the number of jobs by making people redundant; **he cut his losses** = he stopped doing something which was creating a loss
NOTE: **cutting - cut - has cut**

◇ **cutback** *noun* reduction; **cutbacks in government spending**

◇ **cut down (on)** *verb* to reduce suddenly the amount of something used; **the government is cutting down on welfare expenditure; the office is trying to cut down on electricity consumption; we have installed a word-processor to cut down on paperwork**

◇ **cut in** *verb informal* **to cut someone in on a deal** = to give someone a share in the profits of a deal

◇ **cut-price** *adjective* sold at a cheaper price than usual; **cut-price goods; cut-price petrol; cut-price store** = store selling cut-price goods

◇ **cut-throat** *adjective* **cut-throat competition** = sharp competition by cutting prices and offering high discounts

◇ **cutting** *noun* **(a) cost cutting** = reducing costs; **we have made three secretaries redundant as part of our cost-cutting programme; price cutting** = sudden lowering of prices; **price-cutting war** = competition between companies to get a larger market share by cutting prices
NOTE: no plural **(b) press cutting agency** = company which cuts out references to a client from newspapers and magazines

and sends them on to him; **press cuttings** = references to a client cut out of newspapers or magazines; **we have a file of press cuttings on our rivals' products**

QUOTE: state-owned banks cut their prime rates a percentage point to 11% *Wall Street Journal*
QUOTE: the US bank announced a cut in its prime from 10+ per cent to 10 per cent *Financial Times*
QUOTE: Opec has on average cut production by one third since 1979 *Economist*

cwt = HUNDREDWEIGHT

CV *noun* = CURRICULUM VITAE **please apply in writing, enclosing a current CV**

cycle *noun* period of time when something leaves its original position and then returns to it; **economic cycle** *or* **trade cycle** *or* **business cycle** = period during which trade expands, then slows down and then expands again

◇ **cyclical** *adjective* which happens in cycles; **cyclical factors** = way in which a trade cycle affects businesses

Dd

daily *adjective* done every day; **daily consumption** = amount used each day; **daily production of cars** = number of cars produced each day; **daily sales returns** = reports of sales made each day; **a daily newspaper** *or* **a daily** = newspaper which is produced every day

damage 1 *noun* **(a)** harm done to things; **fire damage** = damage caused by a fire; **storm damage** = damage caused by a storm; **to suffer damage** = to be harmed; **we are trying to assess the damage which the shipment suffered in transit; to cause damage** = to harm something; **the fire caused damage estimated at £100,000; damage survey** = survey of damage done
NOTE: no plural **(b) damages** = money claimed as compensation for harm done; **to claim £1000 in damages; to be liable for damages; to pay £25,000 in damages; to bring an action for damages against**

someone = to take someone to court and claim damages **2** *verb* to harm; **the storm damaged the cargo; stock which has been damaged by water**

◇ **damaged** *adjective* which has suffered damage *or* which has been harmed; **goods damaged in transit; fire-damaged goods** = goods harmed in a fire

damp down *verb* to reduce; **to damp down demand for domestic consumption of oil**

danger *noun* possibility of being harmed or killed; **there is danger to the workforce in the old machinery; there is no danger of the sales force leaving** = it is not likely that the sales force will leave; **in danger of** = which may easily happen; **the company is in danger of being taken over; she is in danger of being made redundant**

◇ **danger money** *noun* extra money paid to workers in dangerous jobs; **the workforce has stopped work and asked for danger money**

◇ **dangerous** *adjective* which can be harmful; **dangerous job** = job where the workers may be killed or hurt

data *noun* information (letters or figures) available on computer; **data acquisition** = getting information; **data bank** *or* **bank of data** = store of information in a computer; **data processing** = selecting and examining data in a computer to produce special information
NOTE: **data** is usually singular: **the data is easily available**

◇ **database** *noun* store of information in a large computer; **we can extract the lists of potential customers from our database**

date 1 *noun* **(a)** number of day, month and year; **I have received your letter of yesterday's date; date stamp** = rubber stamp for marking the date on letters received; **date of receipt** = date when something is received **(b) up to date** = current *or* recent *or* modern; **an up-to-date computer system; to bring something up to date** = to add the latest information to something; **to keep something up to date** = to keep adding information to something so that it is always up to date; **we spend a lot of time keeping our mailing list up to date (c) to date** = up to now;

interest to date = interest up to the present time **(d) out of date** = old-fashioned; **their computer system is years out of date; they are still using out-of-date machinery (e) maturity date** = date when a government stock will mature; **date of bill** = date when a bill will mature **2** *verb* to put a date on a document; **the cheque was dated March 24th; you forgot to date the cheque; to date a cheque forward** = to put a later date than the present one on a cheque

◇ **dated** *adjective* with a date written on it; **thank you for your letter dated June 15th; long-dated bill** = bill which is payable more than three months from now; **short-dated bill** = bill which is payable within a few days

day *noun* **(a)** period of 24 hours; **there are thirty days in June; the first day of the month is a public holiday; settlement day** = day when accounts have to be settled; **three clear days** = three whole working days; **to give ten clear days' notice; allow four clear days for the cheque to be paid into the bank (b)** period of work from morning to night; **she took two days off** = she did not come to work for two days; **he works three days on, two days off** = he works for three days, then has two days' holiday; **to work an eight-hour day** = to spend eight hours at work each day; **day shift** = shift which works during the daylight hours such as from 8 a.m. to 5.30 p.m.; **there are 150 men on the day shift; he works the day shift; day release** = arrangement where a company allows a worker to go to college to study for one or two days each week; **the junior sales manager is attending a day release course**

◇ **daybook** *noun* book with an account of sales and purchases made each day

◇ **day-to-day** *adjective* ordinary *or* which goes on all the time; **he organizes the day-to-day running of the company; sales only just cover the day-to-day expenses**

◇ **day worker** *noun* person who works the day shift

DCF = DISCOUNTED CASH FLOW

dead *adjective* **(a)** not alive; **six people were dead as a result of the accident; the founders of the company are all dead (b)** not working; **dead account** = account which is no longer used; **the line went dead** = the telephone line suddenly stopped working; **dead loss** = total loss; **the car was written off as a dead loss**; **dead money** = money which is not invested to make a profit; **dead season** = time of year when there are few tourists about

◊ **deadline** *noun* date by which something has to be done; **to meet a deadline** = to finish something in time; **we've missed our October 1st deadline**

◊ **deadlock** **1** *noun* point where two sides in a dispute cannot agree; **the negotiations have reached a deadlock; to break a deadlock** = to find a way to start discussions again **2** *verb* to be unable to agree to continue discussing; **talks have been deadlocked for ten days** = after ten days the talks have not produced any agreement

◊ **deadweight** *noun* heavy goods like coal, iron or sand; **deadweight cargo** = heavy cargo which is charged by weight, not by volume; **deadweight capacity** *or* **deadweight tonnage** = largest amount of cargo which a ship can carry safely

deal **1** *noun* **(a)** business agreement *or* affair *or* contract; **to arrange a deal** *or* **to set up a deal** *or* **to do a deal; to sign a deal; the sales director set up a deal with a Russian bank; the deal will be signed tomorrow; they did a deal with an American airline; to call off a deal** = to stop an agreement; **when the chairman heard about the deal he called it off; cash deal** = sale done for cash; **package deal** = agreement where several different items are agreed at the same time; **they agreed a package deal, which involves the construction of the factory, training of staff and purchase of the product (b) a great deal** *or* **a good deal of something** = a large quantity of something; **he has made a good deal of money on the stock market; the company lost a great deal of time asking for expert advice 2** *verb* **(a) to deal with** = to organize; **leave it to the filing clerk - he'll deal with it; to deal with an order** = to supply an order **(b)** to trade *or* to buy and sell; **to deal with someone** = to do business with someone; **to deal in leather** *or* **to deal in options** = to buy and sell leather *or* options; **he deals on the Stock Exchange** = his work involves buying and selling shares on the Stock Exchange for clients

◊ **dealer** *noun* person who buys and sells; **dealer in tobacco** *or* **tobacco dealer; foreign exchange dealer** = person who buys and sells foreign currencies; **retail dealer** = person who sells to the general public; **wholesale dealer** = person who sells in bulk to retailers

◊ **dealing** *noun* **(a)** buying and selling on the Stock Exchange; **fair dealing** = legal trade *or* legal buying and selling of shares; **foreign exchange dealing** = buying and selling foreign currencies; **forward dealings** = buying or selling commodities forward; **insider dealing** = illegal buying or selling of shares by staff of a company who have secret information about the company's plans; **option dealing** = buying and selling share options **(b)** buying and selling goods; **to have dealings with someone** = to do business with someone

dear *adjective* **(a)** expensive *or* costing a lot of money; **property is very dear in this area; dear money** = money which has to be borrowed at a high interest rate **(b)** way of starting a letter; **Dear Sir** *or* **Dear Madam** = addressing a man or woman whom you do not know, or addressing a company; **Dear Sirs** = addressing a firm; **Dear Mr Smith** *or* **Dear Mrs Smith** *or* **Dear Miss Smith** = addressing a man or woman whom you know; **Dear James** *or* **Dear Julia** = addressing a friend *or* a person you do business with

death *noun* act of dying; **death benefit** = insurance benefit paid to the family of someone who dies in an accident at work; **death in service** = insurance benefit or pension paid when someone dies while employed by a company; *US* **death duty** *or* **death tax** = tax paid on the property left by a dead person

debenture *noun* agreement to repay a debt with fixed interest using the company's assets as security; **the bank holds a debenture on the company; mortgage debenture** = debenture where the lender can be repaid by selling the company's property; **debenture issue** *or* **issue of debentures** = borrowing money against the security of the company's assets; **debenture bond** = certificate showing that a debenture has been issued; **debenture capital** *or* **debenture stock** = capital borrowed by a company, using its fixed assets as security; **debenture holder** = person who holds a debenture for money lent; **debenture register** or **register of debentures** = list of debenture holders of a company

debit 1 *noun* money which a company owes; **debits and credits** = money which a company owes and money it receives; **debit balance** = balance in an account, showing that the company owes more money than it has received; **debit column** = left-hand column in accounts showing the money paid or owed to others; **debit entry** = entry on the debit side of an account; **debit side** = left-hand side of an account showing the money paid or owed to others; **debit note** = note showing that a customer owes money; **we undercharged Mr Smith and had to send him a debit note for the extra amount; direct debit** = system where a customer allows a company to charge costs to his bank account automatically and where the amount charged can be increased or decreased with the agreement of the customer; **I pay my electricity bill by direct debit 2** *verb* **to debit an account** = to charge an account with a cost; **his account was debited with the sum of £25**
◊ **debitable** *adjective* which can be debited

debt *noun* (a) money owed for goods or services; **the company stopped trading with debts of over £1 million; to be in debt** = to owe money; **he is in debt to the tune of £250** = he owes £250; **to get into debt** = to start to borrow more money than you can pay back; **the company is out of debt** = the company does not owe money any more; **to pay back a debt** = to pay all the money owed; **to pay off a debt** = to finish paying money owed; **to service a debt** = to pay interest on a debt; **the company is having problems in servicing its debts; bad debt** = money owed which will never be paid back; **the company has written off £30,000 in bad debts; secured debts** or **unsecured debts** = debts which are guaranteed or not guaranteed by assets; **debt collection** = collecting money which is owed; **debt collection agency** = company which collects debts for a commission; **debt collector** = person who collects debts; **debts due** = money owed which is due for repayment (b) **funded debt** = part of the British

National Debt which pays interest, but where there is no date for repayment of the principal; **the National Debt** = money borrowed by a government
◊ **debtor** *noun* person who owes money; **debtor side** = debit side of an account; **debtor nation** = country whose foreign debts are larger than money owed to it by other countries

deceit or **deception** *noun* making a wrong statement to someone in order to trick him into paying money; **he obtained £10,000 by deception**

decentralize *verb* to organize from various points, away from the centre; **the group has a policy of decentralized purchasing where each division is responsible for its own purchasing**
◊ **decentralization** *noun* organization from various points, away from the centre; **the decentralization of the buying departments**

decide *verb* to make up your mind to do something; **to decide on a course of action; to decide to appoint a new managing director**
◊ **deciding** *adjective* **deciding factor** = most important factor which influences a decision

decile *noun* one of a series of nine figures below which one tenth or several tenths of the total fall

decimal *noun* **decimal system** = system based on the number 10; **correct to three places of decimals** = correct to three figures after the decimal point (e.g. 3.485); **decimal point** = dot which indicates the division between the whole unit and its smaller parts (such as 4.75)
◊ **decimalization** *noun* changing to a decimal system
◊ **decimalize** *verb* to change to a decimal system

decision *noun* making up one's mind to do something; **to come to a decision** or **to**

reach a decision; decision making = act of coming to a decision; **the decision-making processes** = ways in which decisions are reached; **decision maker** = person who has to decide

deck *noun* flat floor in a ship; **deck cargo** = cargo carried on the open top deck of a ship; **deck hand** = ordinary sailor on a cargo ship

declaration *noun* official statement; **declaration of bankruptcy** = official statement that someone is bankrupt; **declaration of income** = statement declaring income to the tax office; **customs declaration** = statement declaring goods brought into a country on which customs duty should be paid; **VAT declaration** = statement declaring VAT income to the VAT office
◊ **declare** *verb* to make an official statement *or* to announce to the public; **to declare someone bankrupt; to declare a dividend of 10%; to declare goods to the customs** = to state that you are importing goods which are liable to duty; **the customs officials asked him if he had anything to declare; to declare an interest** = to state in public that you own shares in a company being investigated *or* that you areare related to someone who can benefit from your contacts, etc.
◊ **declared** *adjective* which has been made public or officially stated; **declared value** = value of goods entered on a customs declaration

decline 1 *noun* gradual fall; **the decline in the value of the franc; a decline in buying power; the last year has seen a decline in real wages** 2 *verb* to fall slowly; **shares declined in a weak market; imports have declined over the last year; the economy declined during the last government**

> QUOTE: in 1984 the profits again declined to L185bn from the 1983 figure of L229.7bn
> *Financial Times*
> QUOTE: Saudi oil production has declined by three quarters to around 2.5m barrels a day
> *Economist*
> QUOTE: this gives an average monthly decline of 2.15 per cent during the period
> *Business Times (Lagos)*

decontrol *verb* to stop controls; **to decontrol the price of petrol** = to stop controlling the price of petrol so that it can be reached freely by the market; **to decontrol wages** = to allow wage increases to be given freely
NOTE: **decontrolling - decontrolled**

decrease 1 *noun* fall *or* reduction; **decrease in price; decrease in value; decrease in imports; exports have registered a decrease; sales show a 10% decrease on last year** 2 *verb* to fall *or* to become less; **imports are decreasing; the value of the pound has decreased by 5%**

deduct *verb* to remove money from a total; **to deduct £3 from the price; to deduct a sum for expenses; after deducting costs the gross margin is only 23%; expenses are still to be deducted; tax deducted at source** = tax which is removed from a salary, interest payment *or* dividend payment on shares before the money is paid
◊ **deductible** *adjective* which can be deducted; **tax-deductible** = which can be deducted from an income before tax is paid; **these expenses are not tax-deductible** = tax has to be paid on these expenses
◊ **deduction** *noun* removing of money from a total *or* money removed from a total; **net salary is salary after deduction of tax and social security; deductions from salary** *or* **salary deductions** *or* **deductions at source** = money which a company removes from salaries to give to the government as tax, national insurance contributions, etc.; **tax deductions** = (i) money removed from a salary to pay tax; (ii) *US* business expenses which can be claimed against tax

deed *noun* legal document *or* written agreement; **deed of assignment** = document which legally transfers a property from a debtor to a creditor; **deed of covenant** = signed legal agreement to pay someone a sum of money every year; **deed of partnership** = agreement which sets up a partnership; **deed of transfer** = document which transfers the ownership of shares; **title deeds** = document showing who owns a property; **we have deposited the deeds of the house in the bank**

defalcation *noun* illegal use of money by someone who is not the owner but who has been trusted to look after it

default 1 *noun* failure to carry out the terms of a contract, especially failure to pay back a debt; **in default of payment** = with no payment made; **the company is in default** = the company has failed to carry out the terms of the contract; **by default** = because no one else will act; **he was elected by default** = he was elected because all the other candidates withdrew
NOTE: no plural
2 *verb* to fail to carry out the terms of a contract, especially to fail to pay back a debt; **to default on payments** = not to make payments which are due under the terms of a contract
◊ **defaulter** *noun* person who defaults

defeat 1 *noun* loss of a vote; **the chairman offered to resign after the defeat of the proposal at the AGM** 2 *verb* to beat someone *or* something in a vote; **the proposal was defeated by 10 votes to 23; he was heavily defeated in the ballot for union president**

defect *noun* something which is wrong *or* which stops a machine from working properly; **a computer defect** *or* **a defect in the computer**
◊ **defective** *adjective* (a) faulty *or* not working properly; **the machine broke down because of a defective cooling system** (b) not legally valid; **his title to the property is defective**

defence *or* *US* **defense** *noun* (a) protecting someone *or* something against attack; **the merchant bank is organizing the company's defence against the takeover bid** (b) fighting a lawsuit on behalf of a defendant; **defence counsel** = lawyer who represents the defendant in a lawsuit
◊ **defend** *verb* to fight to protect someone *or* something which is being attacked; **the company is defending itself against the takeover bid; he hired the best lawyers to defend him against the tax authorities; to defend a lawsuit** = to appear in court to state your case when accused of something

◊ **defendant** *noun* person who is sued *or* who is accused of doing something to harm someone

defer *verb* to put back to a later date *or* to postpone; **to defer payment; the decision has been deferred until the next meeting**
NOTE: deferring - deferred
◊ **deferment** *noun* postponement *or* putting back to a later date; **deferment of payment; deferment of a decision**
◊ **deferred** *adjective* put back to a later date; **deferred creditor** = person who is owed money by a bankrupt but who is paid only after all other creditors; **deferred payment** = payment for goods by instalments over a long period; **deferred stock** = shares which receive a dividend after all other dividends have been paid

deficiency *noun* lack; money lacking; **there is a £10 deficiency in the petty cash; to make up a deficiency** = to put money into an account to balance it

deficit *noun* amount by which spending is higher than income; **the accounts show a deficit** = the accounts show a loss; **to make good a deficit** = to put money into an account to balance it; **balance of payments deficit** *or* **trade deficit** = situation when a country imports more than it exports; **deficit financing** = planning by a government to borrow money to cover the shortfall between tax income and expenditure

deflate *verb* to **deflate the economy** = to reduce activity in the economy by cutting the supply of money
◊ **deflation** *noun* reduction in economic activity
◊ **deflationary** *adjective* which can cause deflation; **the government has introduced some deflationary measures in the budget**

> QUOTE: the strong dollar's deflationary impact on European economies as national governments push up interest rates *Duns Business Month*

defray *verb* to provide money to pay (costs); **the company agreed to defray the costs of the exhibition**

degearing *noun* reduction in gearing *or* reducing a company's loan capital in relation to the value of its ordinary shares NOTE: no plural

delay 1 *noun* time when someone *or* something is later than planned; **there was a delay of thirty minutes before the AGM started** *or* **the AGM started after a thirty minute delay; we are sorry for the delay in supplying your order** *or* **in replying to your letter** 2 *verb* to be late; to make someone late; **he was delayed because his taxi had an accident; the company has delayed payment of all invoices**

del credere *noun* **del credere agent** = agent who receives a high commission because he guarantees payment by customers

delegate 1 *noun* person who represents others at a meeting; **the management refused to meet the trade union delegates** 2 *verb* to pass authority or responsibility to someone else; **to delegate authority; he cannot delegate** = he wants to control everything himself and refuses to give up any of his responsibilities to his subordinates
◇ **delegation** *noun* **(a)** group of delegates; **a Chinese trade delegation; the management met a union delegation (b)** act of passing authority or responsibility to someone else

delete *verb* to cut out words in a document; **they want to delete all references to credit terms from the contract; the lawyers have deleted clause two**

deliver *verb* to transport goods to a customer; **goods delivered free** *or* **free delivered goods** = goods transported to the customer's address at a price which includes transport costs; **goods delivered on board** = goods transported free to the ship *or* plane but not to the customer's warehouse; **delivered price** = price which includes packing and transport
◇ **delivery** *noun* **(a) delivery of goods** = transport of goods to a customer's address; **parcels awaiting delivery; free delivery** *or* **delivery free; delivery date; delivery within 28 days; allow 28 days for delivery; delivery is not allowed for** *or* **is not included; delivery note** = list of goods being delivered, given

to the customer with the goods; **delivery order** = instructions given by the customer to the person holding his goods, to tell him to deliver them; **the store has a delivery service to all parts of the town** = the store will deliver goods to all parts of the town; **delivery time** = number of days before something will be delivered; **delivery van** = goods van for delivering goods to retail customers; **express delivery** = very fast delivery; **recorded delivery** = mail service where the letters are signed for by the person receiving them; **we sent the documents (by) recorded delivery; cash on delivery** = payment in cash when the goods are delivered; **to take delivery of goods** = to accept goods when they are delivered; **we took delivery of the stock into our warehouse on the 25th (b)** goods being delivered; **we take in three deliveries a day; there were four items missing in the last delivery (c)** transfer of a bill of exchange

demand 1 *noun* **(a)** asking for payment; **payable on demand** = which must be paid when payment is asked for; **demand bill** = bill of exchange which must be paid when payment is asked for; *US* **demand deposit** = money in a bank account which can be taken out when you want it by writing a cheque; **final demand** = last reminder from a supplier, after which he will sue for payment **(b)** need for goods at a certain price; **there was an active demand for oil shares on the stock market; to meet a demand** *or* **to fill a demand** = to supply what is needed; **the factory had to increase production to meet the extra demand; the factory had to cut production when demand slackened; the office cleaning company cannot keep up with the demand for its services; there is not much demand for this item** = not many people want to buy it; **this book is in great demand** *or* **there is a great demand for this book** = many people want to buy it; **effective demand** = actual demand for a product which can be paid for; **demand price** = price at which a certain quantity of goods will be bought; **supply and demand** = amount of a product which is available and the amount which is wanted by customers; **law of supply and demand** = general rule that the amount of a product which is available is related to the needs of potential customers 2 *verb* to ask for something and expect to get it; **she demanded a refund; the suppliers are demanding immediate payment of their outstanding invoices**

◊ **demand-led inflation** *noun* inflation caused by rising demand which cannot be met

---

QUOTE: spot prices are now relatively stable in the run-up to the winter's peak demand *Economist*
QUOTE: the demand for the company's products remained strong throughout the first six months of the year with production and sales showing significant increases *Business Times (Lagos)*
QUOTE: growth in demand is still coming from the private rather than the public sector
Lloyd's List

---

demarcation dispute *noun* argument between different trade unions over who shall do different parts of a job; **production of the new car was held up by demarcation disputes**

demise *noun* **(a)** death; **on his demise the estate passed to his daughter**
NOTE: no plural **(b)** granting of a property on a lease

demonetize *verb* to stop a coin or note being used as money
◊ **demonetization** *noun* stopping a coin or note being used as money

demonstrate *verb* to show how something works; **he was demonstrating a new tractor when he was killed; the managers saw the new stock control system being demonstrated**
◊ **demonstration** *noun* showing how something works; **we went to a demonstration of new telex equipment; demonstration model** = piece of equipment used in demonstrations and later sold off cheaply
◊ **demonstrator** *noun* person who demonstrates pieces of equipment

demote *verb* to give someone a less important job; **he was demoted from manager to salesman; she lost a lot of salary when she was demoted**
◊ **demotion** *noun* giving someone a less important job; **he was very angry at his demotion**

demurrage *noun* money paid to a customer when a shipment is delayed at a port *or* by the customs

denationalize *verb* to put a nationalized industry back into private ownership; **the government has plans to denationalize the steel industry**
◊ **denationalization** *noun* act of denationalizing; **the denationalization of the aircraft industry**

denomination *noun* unit of money (on a coin, banknote or stamp); **coins of all denominations; small denomination notes**

depart *verb* **(a)** to leave; **the plane departs from Paris at 11.15 (b) to depart from normal practice** = to act in a different way from the normal practice
◊ **department** *noun* **(a)** specialized section of a large company; **complaints department; design department; dispatch department; export department; legal department; accounts department** = section which deals with money paid or received; **new issues department** = section of a bank which deals with issues of new shares; **personnel department** = section of a company dealing with the staff; **head of department** *or* **department head** *or* **department manager** = person in charge of a department **(b)** section of a large store selling one type of product; **you will find beds in the furniture department; budget department** = department in a large store which sells cheaper goods **(c)** section of the British government containing several ministries; **the Department of Trade and Industry; the Department of Education and Science**
◊ **department store** *noun* large store with sections for different types of goods
◊ **departmental** *adjective* referring to a department; **departmental manager** = manager of a department

departure *noun* **(a)** going away; **the plane's departure was delayed by two hours; departures** = part of an airport terminal which deals with passengers who are leaving; **departure lounge** = room in an airport where passengers wait to get on their planes **(b)** new venture *or* a new type of business; **selling records will be a departure for the local bookshop**

depend *verb* **(a) to depend on** = to need someone *or* something to exist; **the company depends on efficient service from its suppliers; we depend on government grants to pay the salary bill (b)** to happen because of something; **the success of the launch will depend on the publicity; depending on** = varying because of something; **depending on the advertising budget, the new product will be launched on radio or on TV**

deposit **1** *noun* **(a)** money placed in a bank for safe keeping or to earn interest; **certificate of deposit** = certificate from a bank to show that money has been deposited; **bank deposits** = all the money placed in banks; **bank deposits are at an all-time high; fixed deposit** = deposit which pays a fixed interest over a fixed period; **deposit account** = bank account which pays interest but on which notice has to be given to withdraw money; **deposit at 7 days' notice** = money deposited which you can withdraw by giving seven days' notice; **deposit slip** = piece of paper stamped by the cashier to prove that you have paid money into your account **(b) safe deposit** = bank safe where you can leave jewellery or documents; **safe deposit box** = small box which you can rent, in which you can keep jewellery or documents in a bank's safe **(c)** money given in advance so that the thing which you want to buy will not be sold to someone else; **to pay a deposit on a watch; to leave £10 as deposit** **2** *verb* **(a)** to put documents somewhere for safe keeping; **to deposit shares with a bank; we have deposited the deeds of the house with the bank; he deposited his will with his solicitor (b)** to put money into a bank account; **to deposit £100 in a current account**

◇ **depositary** *noun* *US* person *or* company with whom money or documents can be deposited

◇ **depositor** *noun* person who deposits money in a bank

◇ **depository** *noun* **(a) furniture depository** = warehouse where you can store household furniture **(b)** person or company with whom money or documents can be deposited

depot *noun* central warehouse for goods; centre for transport; **bus depot; freight depot; goods depot; oil storage depot**

depreciate *verb* **(a)** to reduce the value of assets in accounts; **we depreciate our company cars over three years (b)** to lose value; **share which has depreciated by 10% over the year; the pound has depreciated by 5% against the dollar**

◇ **depreciation** *noun* **(a)** reduction in value of an asset; **depreciation rate** = rate at which an asset is depreciated each year in the accounts; **accelerated depreciation** = system of depreciation which reduces the value of assets at a high rate in the early years to encourage companies, as a result of tax advantages, to invest in new equipment; **annual depreciation** = reduction in the book value of an asset at a certain rate per year; **straight line depreciation** = depreciation calculated by dividing the cost of an asset by the number of years it is likely to be used NOTE: no plural **(b)** loss of value; **a share which has shown a depreciation of 10% over the year; the depreciation of the pound against the dollar**

> QUOTE: this involved reinvesting funds on items which could be depreciated against income for three years *Australian Financial Review*
> QUOTE: buildings are depreciated at two per cent per annum on the estimated cost of construction *Hongkong Standard*

depress *verb* to reduce; **reducing the money supply has the effect of depressing demand for consumer goods**

◇ **depressed** *adjective* **depressed area** = part of a country suffering from depression; **depressed market** = market where there are more goods than customers

◇ **depression** *noun* period of economic crisis with high unemployment and loss of trade; **an economic depression; the Great Depression** = the world economic crisis of 1929-1933

dept = DEPARTMENT

deputy *noun* person who takes the place of another; **to act as deputy for someone** *or* **to act as someone's deputy; deputy chairman; deputy manager; deputy managing director**

◇ **deputize** *verb* **to deputize for someone** = to take the place of someone who is absent; **he deputized for the chairman who had a cold**

deregulation *noun* *US* reducing government control over an industry; **the deregulation of the airlines**

describe *verb* to say what someone *or* something is like; **the leaflet describes the services the company can offer; the managing director described the company's difficulties with cash flow**
◇ **description** *noun* words which show what something is like; **false description of contents** = wrongly stating the contents of a packet to trick customers into buying it; **job description** = official document from the management which says what a job involves; **trade description** = description of a product to attract customers

design 1 *noun* planning *or* drawing of a product before it is built or manufactured; **industrial design** = design of products made by machines (such as cars and refrigerators); **product design** = design of consumer products; **design department** = department in a large company which designs the company's products or its advertising; **design studio** = independent firm which specializes in creating designs 2 *verb* to plan *or* to draw something before it is built or manufactured; **he designed a new car factory; she designs garden furniture**
◇ **designer** *noun* person who designs; **she is the designer of the new computer**

designate *adjective* person who has been appointed to a job but who has not yet started work; **the chairman designate**
NOTE: always follows a noun

desk *noun* (a) writing table in an office, usually with drawers for stationery; **desk diary; desk drawer; desk light; a three-drawer desk** = desk with three drawers; **desk pad** = pad of paper kept on a desk for writing notes (b) **cash desk** *or* **pay desk** = place in a store where you pay for goods bought; **please pay at the desk** (c) section of a newspaper; **the city desk** = the department which deals with business news

despatch = DISPATCH

destination *noun* place to which something is sent *or* to which something is going; **the ship will take ten weeks to reach** its destination; **final destination** *or* **ultimate destination** = place reached at the end of a journey after stopping at several place en route

detail 1 *noun* small part of a description; **the catalogue gives all the details of our product range; we are worried by some of the details in the contract; in detail** = giving many particulars; **the catalogue lists all the products in detail** 2 *verb* to list in detail; **the catalogue details the payment arrangements for overseas buyers; the terms of the licence are detailed in the contract**
◇ **detailed** *adjective* in detail; **detailed account** = account which lists every item

determine *verb* to fix *or* to arrange *or* to decide; **to determine prices** *or* **quantities; conditions still to be determined**

Deutschmark *noun* unit of money used in Germany
NOTE: also called a **mark;** when used with a figure, usually written **DM** before the figure: **DM250** (say "two hundred and fifty Deutschmarks")

devalue *verb* to reduce the value of a currency against other currencies; **the pound has been devalued by 7%; the government has devalued the pound by 7%**
◇ **devaluation** *noun* reduction in value of a currency against other currencies; **the devaluation of the franc**

develop *verb* (a) to plan and produce; **to develop a new product** (b) to plan and build an area; **to develop an industrial estate**
◇ **developer** *noun* **a property developer** = person who plans and builds a group of new houses *or* new factories
◇ **developing country** *or* **developing nation** *noun* country which is not fully industrialized
◇ **development** *noun* (a) planning the production of a new product; **research and development** (b) **industrial development** = planning and building of new industries in special areas; **development area** *or* **development zone** = area which has been given special help from a government to encourage businesses and factories to be set up there

device *noun* small useful machine; **he invented a device for screwing tops on bottles**

diagram *noun* drawing which shows something as a plan or a map; **diagram showing sales locations; he drew a diagram to show how the decision-making processes work; the paper gives a diagram of the company's organizational structure; flow diagram** = diagram showing the arrangement of work processes in a series
◇ **diagrammatic** *adjective* **in diagrammatic form** = in the form of a diagram; **the chart showed the sales pattern in diagrammatic form**
◇ **diagrammatically** *adverb* using a diagram; **the chart shows the sales pattern diagrammatically**

dial *verb* to call a telephone number on a telephone; **to dial a number; to dial the operator; to dial direct** = to contact a phone number without asking the operator to do it for you; **you can dial New York direct from London**
NOTE: GB English is **dialling - dialled**, but US spelling is **dialing - dialed**
◇ **dialling** *noun* act of calling a telephone number; **dialling code** = special series of numbers which you use to make a call to another town or country; **dialling tone** = noise made by a telephone to show that it is ready for you to dial a number; **international direct dialling** = calling telephone numbers in other countries direct
NOTE: no plural

diary *noun* book in which you can write notes or appointments for each day of the week; **desk diary**

Dictaphone *noun* trademark for a brand of dictating machine

dictate *verb* to say something to someone who then writes down your words; **to dictate a letter to a secretary; he was dictating orders into his pocket dictating machine; dictating machine** = machine which records what someone dictates, which a secretary can play back and type out the text

◇ **dictation** *noun* act of dictating; **to take dictation** = to write down what someone is saying; **the secretary was taking dictation from the managing director; dictation speed** = number of words per minute which a secretary can write down in shorthand

differ *verb* not to be the same as something else; **the two products differ considerably - one has an electric motor, the other runs on oil**
◇ **difference** *noun* way in which two things are not the same; **what is the difference between these two products?** differences in price *or* price differences
◇ **different** *adjective* not the same; **our product range is quite different in design from that of our rivals; we offer ten models each in six different colours**
◇ **differential 1** *adjective* which shows a difference; **differential tariffs** = different tariffs for different classes of goods **2** *noun* **price differential** = difference in price between products in a range; **wage differentials** = differences in salary between workers in similar types of jobs; **to erode wage differentials** = to reduce differences in salary gradually

difficult *adjective* not easy; **the company found it difficult to sell into the European market; the market for secondhand computers is very difficult at present**
◇ **difficulty** *noun* problem *or* thing which is not easy; **they had a lot of difficulty selling into the European market; we have had some difficulties with the customs over the export of computers**

digit *noun* single number; **a seven-digit phone number**
◇ **digital** *adjective* **digital clock** = clock which shows the time as a series of figures (such as 12:05:23); **digital computer** = computer which calculates on the basis of numbers

dilution *noun* **dilution of equity** *or* **of shareholding** = situation where the ordinary share capital of a company has been increased but without an increase in the assets, so that each share is worth less than before
NOTE: no plural

dime *noun US informal* ten cent coin

diminish *verb* to become smaller; **our share of the market has diminished over the last few years; law of diminishing returns** = general rule that as more factors of production (land, labour and capital) are added to the existing factors, so the amount they produce is proportionately smaller

dip 1 *noun* sudden small fall; **last year saw a dip in the company's performance 2** *verb* to fall in price; **shares dipped sharply in yesterday's trading**
NOTE: **dipping - dipped**

diplomat *or* **diplomatist** *noun* person (such as an ambassador) who is the official representative of his country in another country
◊ **diplomatic** *adjective* referring to diplomats; **diplomatic immunity** = being outside the control of the laws of the country you are living in because of being a diplomat; **he claimed diplomatic immunity to avoid being arrested; to grant someone diplomatic status** = to give someone the rights of a diplomat

direct 1 *verb* to manage *or* to organize; **he directs our South-East Asian operations; she was directing the development unit until last year 2** *adjective* straight *or* with no interference; **direct action** = strike *or* go-slow, etc.; **direct cost** = production cost of a product; **direct debit** = system where a customer allows a company to charge costs to his bank account automatically and where the amount charged can be increased or decreased with the agreement of the customer; **I pay my electricity bill by direct debit; direct mail** = selling a product by sending publicity material to possible buyers through the post; **these calculators are only sold by direct mail; the company runs a successful direct-mail operation; direct-mail advertising** = advertising by sending leaflets to people through the post; **direct selling** = selling a product direct to the customer without going through a shop; **direct taxation** = tax, such as income tax, which is paid direct to the government; **the government raises**

more money by direct taxation than by indirect **3** *adverb* straight *or* with no third party involved; **we pay income tax direct to the government; to dial direct** = to contact a phone number yourself without asking the operator to do it for you; **you can dial New York direct from London if you want**
◊ **direction** *noun* **(a)** organizing *or* managing; **he took over the direction of a multinational group (b) directions for use** = instructions showing how to use something
NOTE: no plural for (a)
◊ **directly** *adverb* **(a)** immediately; **he left for the airport directly after receiving the telephone message (b)** straight *or* with no third party involved; **we deal directly with the manufacturer, without using a wholesaler**
◊ **director** *noun* **(a)** person appointed by the shareholders to help run a company; **managing director** = director who is in charge of the whole company; **chairman and managing director** = managing director who is also chairman of the board of directors; **board of directors** = all the directors of a company; **directors' report** = annual report from the board of directors to the shareholders; **associate director** = director who attends board meetings but has not been elected by the shareholders; **executive director** = director who actually works full-time in the company; **non-executive director** = director who attends board meetings only to give advice; **outside director** = director who is not employed by the company **(b)** person who is in charge of a project, an official institute, etc.; **the director of the government research institute; she was appointed director of the organization**
◊ **directorate** *noun* group of directors
◊ **directorship** *noun* post of director; **he was offered a directorship with Smith Ltd**

directory *noun* list of people *or* businesses with information about their addresses and telephone numbers; **classified directory** = list of businesses grouped under various headings, such as computer shops *or* newsagents; **commercial directory** *or* **trade directory** = book which lists all the businesses and business people in a town; **street directory** = list of people living in a street; map of a town which lists all the streets in alphabetical order in an index; **telephone directory** = book which lists all people and businesses in alphabetical order with their phone numbers; **to look up a number in the telephone directory; his number is in the London directory**

disallow *verb* not to accept a claim for insurance; **he claimed £2,000 for fire damage, but the claim was disallowed**

disaster *noun* **(a)** very bad accident; **ten people died in the air disaster (b)** financial collapse; **the company is heading for disaster** *or* **is on a disaster course** = the company is going to collapse; **the advertising campaign was a disaster** = the advertising campaign was very bad *or* did not have the required effect **(c)** accident in nature; **a storm disaster on the south coast; flood disaster damage**
◇ **disastrous** *adjective* very bad; **the company suffered a disastrous drop in sales**

disburse *verb* to pay money
◇ **disbursement** *noun* payment of money

discharge 1 *noun* **(a) discharge in bankruptcy** = being released from bankruptcy after paying one's debts **(b)** payment of debt; **in full discharge of a debt** = paying a debt completely; **final discharge** = final payment of what is left of a debt **(c) in discharge of his duties as director** = carrying out his duties as director 2 *verb* **(a) to discharge a bankrupt** = to release someone from bankruptcy because he has paid his debts **(b) to discharge a debt** *or* **to discharge one's liabilities** = to pay a debt *or* one's liabilities in full **(c)** to dismiss *or* to sack; **to discharge an employee**

disciplinary *adjective* **disciplinary procedure** = way of warning a worker officially that he is breaking rules *or* that he is working badly

disclaimer *noun* legal refusal to accept responsibility

disclose *verb* to tell details; **the bank has no right to disclose details of my account to the tax office**
◇ **disclosure** *noun* act of telling details; **the disclosure of the takeover bid raised the price of the shares**

discontinue *verb* to stop stocking *or* selling *or* making (a product); **these carpets are a discontinued line**

discount 1 *noun* **(a)** percentage by which a full price is reduced to a buyer by the seller; **to give a discount on bulk purchases; to sell goods at a discount** *or* at a **discount price** = to sell goods below the normal price; **basic discount** = normal discount without extra percentages; **we give 25% as a basic discount, but can add 5% for cash payment; quantity discount** = discount given to people who buy large quantities; **10% discount for quantity purchases** = you pay 10% less if you buy a large quantity; **10% discount for cash** *or* **10% cash discount** = you pay 10% less if you pay in cash; **trade discount** = discount given to a customer in the same trade **(b) discount house** = (i) financial company which specializes in discounting bills; (ii) shop which specializes in selling cheap goods bought at a high discount; **discount rate** = percentage taken when a bank buys bills; **discount store** = shop which specializes in cheap goods bought at a high discount **(c) shares which stand at a discount** = shares which are lower in price than their face value 2 *verb* to reduce prices to increase sales; **to discount bills of exchange** = to buy bills of exchange for less than the value written on them in order to cash them later; **shares are discounting a rise in the dollar** = shares have risen in advance of a rise in the dollar price; **discounted cash flow** = calculating the forecast return on capital investment in current terms, with reductions for current interest rates; **discounted value** = difference between the face value of a share and its lower market price

◇ **discountable** *adjective* which can be discounted; **these bills are not discountable**

◇ **discounter** *noun* person *or* company which discounts bills or sells goods at a discount

> QUOTE: pressure on the Federal Reserve Board to ease monetary policy and possibly cut its discount rate mounted yesterday *Financial Times*
> QUOTE: banks refrained from quoting forward US/Hongkong dollar exchange rates as premiums of 100 points replaced the previous day's discounts of up to 50 points *South China Morning Post*
> QUOTE: a 100,000 square-foot warehouse generates ten times the volume of a discount retailer; it can turn its inventory over 18 times a year, more than triple a big discounter's turnover *Duns Business Month*

discover *verb* to find something new; **we discovered that our agent was selling our rival's products at the same price as ours; the auditors discovered some errors in the accounts**

discrepancy *noun* situation where totals do not add up correctly in accounts; **there is a discrepancy in the accounts** = there is an error; **statistical discrepancy** = amount by which sets of figures differ

discretion *noun* being able to decide correctly what should be done; **I leave it to your discretion** = I leave it for you to decide what to do; **at the discretion of someone** = if someone decides; **membership is at the discretion of the committee**
NOTE: no plural

◇ **discretionary** *adjective* which can be done if someone wants; **the minister's discretionary powers** = powers which the minister could use if he thought he should do so

discrimination *noun* treating people in different ways because of class, religion, race, language, colour or sex; **sexual discrimination** *or* **sex discrimination** *or* **discrimination on grounds of sex** = treating men and women in different ways
NOTE: no plural

discuss *verb* to talk about a problem; **they spent two hours discussing the details of the contract; the committee discussed the question of import duties on cars; the board**

will discuss wage rises at its next meeting; we discussed delivery schedules with our suppliers

◇ **discussion** *noun* talking about a problem; **after ten minutes' discussion the board agreed the salary increases; we spent the whole day in discussions with our suppliers**

disenfranchise *verb* to take away someone's right to vote; **the company has tried to disenfranchise the ordinary shareholders**

dishonour *verb* **to dishonour a bill** = not to pay a bill; **dishonoured cheque** = cheque which the bank will not pay because there is not enough money in the account to pay it

disinflation *noun* reducing inflation in the economy by increasing tax, reducing the level of money supply, etc.

disinvest *verb* to reduce investment by not replacing capital assets when they wear out

◇ **disinvestment** *noun* reduction in capital assets by not replacing them when they wear out
NOTE: no plural

disk *noun* round flat object, used to store information in computers; **floppy disk** = small disk for storing information through a computer; **hard disk** = solid disk which will store a large amount of computer information in a sealed case; **disk drive** = part of a computer which makes a disk spin round in order to read it or store information on it

◇ **diskette** *noun* very small floppy disk

dismiss *verb* **to dismiss an employee** = to remove an employee from a job; **he was dismissed for being late**

◇ **dismissal** *noun* removal of an employee from a job; **constructive dismissal** = situation where an employee leaves his job voluntarily, but because of pressure from the management; **unfair dismissal** = removing someone from a job for reasons which are not fair; **wrongful dismissal** = removing someone from a job for reasons which are wrong; **dismissal procedures** =

correct way of dismissing someone according to the contract of employment

dispatch 1 *noun* **(a)** sending of goods to a customer; **the strike held up dispatch for several weeks; dispatch department =** department which deals with the packing and sending of goods to customers; **dispatch note =** note saying that goods have been sent; **dispatch rider =** motorcyclist who delivers messages or parcels in a town **(b)** goods which have been sent; **the weekly dispatch went off yesterday** 2 *verb* to send goods to customers
◇ **dispatcher** *noun* person who sends goods to customers

dispenser *noun* machine which automatically provides something (an object *or* a drink *or* some food), often when money is put in; **automatic dispenser; towel dispenser; cash dispenser =** machine which gives out money when a special card is inserted and instructions given

display 1 *noun* showing of goods for sale; **the shop has several car models on display; an attractive display of kitchen equipment; display advertisement =** advertisement which is well designed to attract attention; **display cabinet** *or* **display case =** piece of furniture with a glass top or glass doors for showing goods for sale; **display material =** posters, photographs, etc., to be used to attract attention to goods which are for sale; **display pack** *or* **display box =** special box for showing goods for sale; **the watches are prepacked in plastic display boxes; display stand** *or* **display unit =** special stand for showing goods for sale; **visual display unit** *or* **visual display terminal =** screen attached to a computer which shows the information stored in the computer 2 *verb* to show; **the company was displaying three new car models at the show**

dispose *verb* **to dispose of =** to get rid of *or* to sell cheaply; **to dispose of excess stock; to dispose of one's business**
◇ **disposable** *adjective* **(a)** which can be used and then thrown away; **disposable cups (b) disposable personal income =** income left after tax and national insurance have been deducted

◇ **disposal** *noun* sale; **disposal of securities** *or* **of property; lease** *or* **business for disposal =** lease *or* business for sale

dispute *noun* **industrial disputes** *or* **labour disputes =** arguments between management and workers; **to adjudicate** *or* **to mediate in a dispute =** to try to settle a dispute between other parties

dissolve *verb* to bring to an end; **to dissolve a partnership** *or* **a company**
◇ **dissolution** *noun* ending (of a partnership)

distress merchandise *noun* US goods sold cheaply to pay a company's debts

distribute *verb* **(a)** to share out dividends; **profits were distributed among the shareholders (b)** to send out goods from a manufacturer's warehouse to retail shops; **Smith Ltd distributes for several smaller companies**
◇ **distribution** *noun* **(a)** act of sending goods from the manufacturer to the wholesaler and then to retailers; **distribution costs; distribution manager; channels of distribution** *or* **distribution channels =** ways of sending goods from the manufacturer to the retailer; **distribution network =** series of points *or* small warehouses from which goods are sent all over a country **(b) distribution slip =** paper attached to a document *or* a magazine showing all the people in an office who should read it
NOTE: no plural
◇ **distributor** *noun* company which sells goods for another company which makes them; **sole distributor =** retailer who is the only one in an area who is allowed by the manufacturer to sell a certain product; **a network of distributors =** a series of distributors spread all over a country
◇ **distributorship** *noun* position of being a distributor for a company

district *noun* section of a country *or* of a town; **district manager; the commercial district** *or* **the business district =** part of a town where offices and shops are located

diversification *noun* adding another quite different type of business to a firm's existing trade; **product diversification** or **diversification into new products** = adding new types of products to the range already made

◇ **diversify** verb **(a)** to add new types of business to existing ones; **to diversify into new products (b)** to invest in different types of shares or savings so as to spread the risk of loss

divest verb **to divest oneself of something** = to get rid of something; **the company had divested itself of its US interests**

divide verb to cut into separate sections; **the country is divided in six representative's areas; the two companies agreed to divide the market between them**

dividend noun percentage of profits paid to shareholders; **to raise** or **to increase the dividend** = to pay out a higher dividend than in the previous year; **to maintain the dividend** = to keep the same dividend as in the previous year; **to pass the dividend** = to pay no dividend; **final dividend** = dividend paid at the end of a year; **interim dividend** = dividend paid at the end of a half-year; **dividend cover** = the ratio of profits to dividend; **the dividend is covered four times** = the profits are four times the dividend; **dividend warrant** = cheque which makes payment of a dividend; **dividend yield** = dividend expressed as a percentage of the price of a share; **cum dividend** = share sold with the dividend still to be paid; **ex dividend** = share sold after the dividend has been paid; **the shares are quoted ex dividend** = the share price does not include the right to the dividend

division noun **(a)** main section of a large company; **marketing division; production division; retail division; the paints division of ICI; the hotel division of THF; he is in charge of one of the major divisions of the company (b)** company which is part of a large group; **Smith's is now a division of the Brown group of companies**

◇ **divisional** adjective referring to a division; **a divisional director; the divisional headquarters**

DIY = DO-IT-YOURSELF

DM or **D-mark** = DEUTSCHMARK, MARK

dock 1 noun harbour or place where ships can load or unload; **loading dock; a dock worker; the dock manager; the docks** = part of a town where the harbour is; **dock dues** = money paid by a ship going into or out of a dock, used to keep the dock in good repair **2** verb **(a)** to go into dock; **the ship docked at 17.00 (b)** to remove money from someone's wages; **we will have to dock his pay if he is late for work again; he had £20 docked from his pay for being late**

◇ **docker** noun person who works in a dock

◇ **dockyard** noun place where ships are built

docket noun list of contents of a package which is being sent

doctor noun specialist who examines people when they are sick to see how they can be made well; **the staff are all sent to see the company doctor once a year; doctor's certificate** = document written by a doctor to say that a worker is ill and cannot work; **he has been off sick for ten days and still has not sent in a doctor's certificate; company doctor** = (i) doctor who works for a company and looks after sick workers; (ii) specialist businessman who rescues businesses which are in difficulties

document noun paper with writing on it; **legal document**

◇ **documentary** adjective in the form of documents; **documentary evidence; documentary proof**

◇ **documentation** noun all documents referring to something; **please send me the complete documentation concerning the sale** NOTE: no plural

dogsbody noun informal person who does all types of work in an office for very low wages

do-it-yourself adjective done by an ordinary person, not by a skilled worker; **do-it-yourself conveyancing** = drawing up a legal conveyance by the person selling a property, without the help of a lawyer; **do-it-yourself magazine** = magazine with articles on work which the average person can do to repair or paint his house

dole *noun* money given by the government to unemployed people; **he is receiving dole payments** *or* **he is on the dole** = he is receiving unemployment benefits; **dole queues** = lines of people waiting to collect the dole

dollar *noun* **(a)** money used in the USA and other countries; **the US dollar rose 2%; fifty Canadian dollars; it costs six Australian dollars; five dollar bill** = banknote for five dollars **(b)** the currency used in the USA; **dollar area** = area of the world where the dollar is the main trading currency; **dollar balances** = a country's trade balances expressed in US dollars; **dollar crisis** = fall in the exchange rate for the US dollar; **dollar gap** *or* **dollar shortage** = situation where the supply of dollars is not enough to satisfy the demand for them from overseas buyers; **dollar stocks** = shares in US companies
NOTE: usually written $ before a figure: **$250.** The currencies used in different countries can be shown by the initial letter of the country: **C$** (Canadian dollar) **A$** (Australian dollar), etc.

domestic *adjective* referring to the home market *or* the market of the country where the business is situated; **domestic sales; domestic turnover; domestic consumption** = consumption on the home market; **domestic consumption of oil has fallen sharply; domestic market** = market in the country where a company is based; **they produce goods for the domestic market; domestic production** = production of goods for domestic consumption

domicile **1** *noun* place where someone lives *or* where a company's office is registered **2** *verb* **he is domiciled in Denmark** = he lives in Denmark officially; **bills domiciled in France** = bills of exchange which have to be paid in France

door *noun* piece of wood *or* metal, etc. which closes the entrance to a building *or* room; **the finance director knocked on the chairman's door and walked in; the sales** manager's name is on his door; **the store opened its doors on June 1st** = the store started in business on June 1st

◇ **door-to-door** *adjective* going from one house to the next, asking the occupiers to buy something or to vote for someone; **door-to-door canvassing; door-to-door salesman; door-to-door selling**

dot *noun* small round spot; **the order form should be cut off along the line shown by the row of dots**
◇ **dot-matrix printer** *noun* printer which makes letters by printing many small dots
◇ **dotted line** *noun* line made of a series of dots; **please sign on the dotted line; do not write anything below the dotted line**

double **1** *adjective* **(a)** twice as large *or* two times the size; **their turnover is double ours; to be on double time** = to earn twice the usual wages for working on Sundays or other holidays; **double-entry bookkeeping** = system of bookkeeping where both credit and debit sides of an account are noted; **double taxation** = taxing the same income twice; **double taxation agreement** = agreement between two countries that a person living in one country shall not be taxed in both countries on the income earned in the other country **(b)** **in double figures** = with two figures *or* 10 to 99; **inflation is in double figures; we have had double-figure inflation for some years** **2** *verb* to become twice as big; to make something twice as big; **we have doubled our profits this year** *or* **our profits have doubled this year; the company's borrowings have doubled**
◇ **double-book** *verb* to let the same hotel room *or* plane seat, etc., to more than one person at a time; **we had to change our flight as we were double-booked**
◇ **double-booking** *noun* letting by a travel agent of the same hotel room *or* the same plane seat to more than one person at a time

Dow Jones Average *noun* index of share prices on the New York Stock Exchange, based on a group of major companies; **the Dow Jones Average rose ten points; general optimism showed in the rise on the Dow Jones Average**

down 1 *adverb & preposition* in a lower position *or* to a lower position; **the inflation rate is gradually coming down; shares are slightly down on the day; the price of petrol has gone down; to pay money down =** to make a deposit; **he paid £50 down and the rest in monthly instalments** 2 *verb* **to down tools =** to stop working

◊ **downgrade** *verb* to reduce the importance of someone *or* of a job; **his job was downgraded in the company reorganization**

◊ **down market** *adverb & adjective* cheaper *or* appealing to a less wealthy section of the population; **the company has adopted a down-market image; the company has decided to go down market =** the company has decided to make products which appeal to a wider section of the public

◊ **down payment** *noun* part of a total payment made in advance; **he made a down payment of $100**

◊ **downside** *noun* **downside factor =** possibility of making a loss (in an investment); **the sales force have been asked to give downside forecasts =** they have been asked for pessimistic forecasts

◊ **down time** *noun* time when a machine is not working because it is broken *or* being mended, etc.; time when a worker cannot work because machines have broken down, because components are not available, etc.

◊ **downtown** *noun & adverb* in the central business district of a town; **his office is in downtown New York; a downtown store; they established a business downtown**

◊ **downturn** *noun* movement towards lower prices *or* sales *or* profits; **a downturn in the market price; the last quarter saw a downturn in the economy**

◊ **downward** *adjective* towards a lower position

◊ **downwards** *adverb* towards a lower position; **the company's profits have moved downwards over the last few years**

dozen *noun* twelve; **to sell in sets of one dozen; cheaper by the dozen =** the product is cheaper if you buy twelve at a time

draft 1 *noun* (a) order for money to be paid by a bank; **banker's draft; to make a**

draft on a bank = to ask a bank to pay money for you; **sight draft =** bill of exchange which is payable when it is presented (b) first rough plan *or* document which has not been finished; **draft of a contract** *or* **draft contract; he drew up the draft agreement on the back of an envelope; the first draft of the contract was corrected by the managing director; the finance department has passed the final draft of the accounts; rough draft =** plan of a document which may have changes made to it before it is complete 2 *verb* to make a first rough plan of a document; **to draft a letter; to draft a contract; the contract is still being drafted** *or* **is still in the drafting stage**

◊ **drafter** *noun* person who makes a draft; **the drafter of the agreement**

◊ **drafting** *noun* act of preparing the draft of a document; **the drafting of the contract took six weeks**

drain 1 *noun* (a) pipe for taking dirty water from a house (b) gradual loss of money flowing away; **the costs of the London office are a continual drain on our resources** 2 *verb* to remove something gradually; **the expansion plan has drained all our profits; the company's capital resources have drained away**

draw *verb* (a) to take money away; **to draw money out of an account; to draw a salary =** to have a salary paid by the company; **the chairman does not draw a salary** (b) to write a cheque; **he paid the invoice with a cheque drawn on an Egyptian bank**
NOTE: **drawing - drew - has drawn**

◊ **drawback** *noun* (a) thing which is not convenient *or* likely to cause problems; **one of the main drawbacks of the scheme is that it will take six years to complete** (b) paying back customs duty when imported goods are then re-exported

◊ **drawee** *noun* person *or* bank asked to make a payment by a drawer

◊ **drawer** *noun* person who writes a cheque *or* a bill asking a drawee to pay money to a payee; **the bank returned the cheque to drawer =** the bank would not pay the cheque because the person who wrote it did not have enough money in the account to pay it

◇ **drawing** *noun* **drawing account =** current account *or* account from which the customer may take money when he wants

◇ **draw up** *verb* to write a legal document; **to draw up a contract** *or* **an agreement; to draw up a company's articles of association**

drift *verb* to move slowly; **shares drifted lower in a dull market; strikers are drifting back to work**

drive 1 *noun* **(a)** energy *or* energetic way of working; **economy drive =** vigorous effort to save money or materials; **sales drive =** vigorous effort to increase sales; **he has a lot of drive =** he is very energetic in business **(b)** part of a machine which makes other parts work; **disk drive =** part of a computer which makes the disk spin round in order to store information on it 2 *verb* **(a)** to make a car *or* lorry, etc. go in a certain direction; **he was driving to work when he heard the news on the car radio; she drives a company car (b)** he drives a hard **bargain =** he is a difficult negotiator
NOTE: **driving - drove - has driven**

drop 1 *noun* **(a)** fall; **drop in sales; sales show a drop of 10%; a drop in prices (b) drop shipment =** delivery of a large order from the manufacturer direct to a customer's shop or warehouse without going through an agent or wholesaler **2** *verb* to fall; **sales have dropped by 10%** *or* **have dropped 10%; the pound dropped three points against the dollar**
NOTE: **dropping - dropped**

◇ **drop ship** *verb* to deliver a large order direct to a customer

QUOTE: while unemployment dropped by 1.6 per cent in the rural areas. it rose by 1.9 per cent in urban areas during the period under review
Business Times (Lagos)
QUOTE: corporate profits for the first quarter showed a 4 per cent drop from last year's final three months *Financial Times*
QUOTE: since last summer American interest rates have dropped by between three and four percentage points *Sunday Times*

drug *noun* medicine; **a drug on the market =** product which is difficult to sell because it has already been sold in large quantities and the market is satisfied

dry *adjective* not wet; **dry goods =** cloth, clothes and household goods; **dry measure =** way of calculating loose dry produce (such as corn)

duck *see* LAME DUCK

dud *adjective & noun informal* false *or* not good (coin or banknote); **the £50 note was a dud; dud cheque =** cheque which the bank refuses to pay because the person writing it has not enough money in his account to pay it

due *adjective* **(a)** owed; **sum due from a debtor; bond due for repayment; to fall due** *or* **to become due =** to be ready for payment; **bill due on May 1st =** bill which has to be paid on May 1st; **balance due to us =** amount owed to us which should be paid **(b)** expected to arrive; **the plane is due to arrive at 10.30** *or* **is due at 10.30 (c) in due form =** written in the correct legal form; **receipt in due form; contract drawn up in due form; after due consideration of the problem =** after thinking seriously about the problem **(d)** caused by; **supplies have been delayed due to a strike at the manufacturers; the company pays the wages of staff who are absent due to illness**

◇ **dues** *plural noun* **(a) dock dues** *or* **port dues** *or* **harbour dues =** payment which a ship makes to the harbour authorities for the right to use the harbour **(b)** orders taken but not supplied until new stock arrives

QUOTE: many expect the US economic indicators for April. due out this Thursday. to show faster economic growth *Australian Financial Review*

dull *adjective* not exciting *or* not full of life; **dull market =** market where little business is done

◇ **dullness** *noun* being dull; **the dullness of the market**

duly *adverb* **(a)** properly; **duly authorized representative (b)** as was expected; **we duly received his letter of 21st October**

dummy *noun* imitation product to test the reaction of potential customers to its design; **dummy pack =** empty pack for display

dump *verb* **to dump goods on a market** = to get rid of large quantities of excess goods cheaply in an overseas market

◇ **dump bin** *noun* display container like a large box which is filled with goods for sale

◇ **dumping** *noun* act of getting rid of excess goods cheaply in an overseas market; **the government has passed anti-dumping legislation; dumping of goods on the European market; panic dumping of sterling** = rush to sell sterling at any price because of possible devaluation

NOTE: no plural

> QUOTE: a serious threat lies in the 400,000 tonnes of subsidized beef in EEC cold stores. If dumped, this meat will have disastrous effects in Pacific Basin markets
> *Australian Financial Review*

duplicate 1 *noun* copy; **he sent me the duplicate of the contract; duplicate receipt** *or* **duplicate of a receipt** = copy of a receipt; **in duplicate** = with a copy; **receipt in duplicate** = two copies of a receipt; **to print an invoice in duplicate** 2 *verb* **(a)** (*of a bookkeeping entry*) **to duplicate with another** = to repeat another entry *or* to be the same as another entry **(b) to duplicate a letter** = to make a copy of a letter

◇ **duplicating** *noun* copying; **duplicating machine** = machine which makes copies of documents; **duplicating paper** = special paper to be used in a duplicating machine

◇ **duplication** *noun* copying of documents; **duplication of work** = work which is done twice without being necessary

◇ **duplicator** *noun* machine which makes copies of documents

durable 1 *adjective* **durable goods** = goods which will be used for a long time (such as washing machines or refrigerators); **durable effects** = effects which will be felt for a long time; **the strike will have durable effects on the economy** 2 *noun* **consumer durables** = goods bought by the public which will be used for a long time (such as washing machines or refrigerators)

Dutch *adjective* **Dutch auction** = auction where the auctioneer offers an item for sale at a high price and then gradually reduces the price until someone makes a bid; **to go Dutch** = to share the bill in a restaurant

dutiable *adjective* **dutiable goods** *or* **dutiable items** = goods on which a customs duty has to be paid

◇ **duty** *noun* tax which has to be paid; **to take the duty off alcohol; to put a duty on cigarettes; ad valorem duty** = duty calculated on the sales value of the goods; **customs duty** *or* **import duty** = tax on goods imported into a country; **excise duty** = tax on goods (such as alcohol and petrol) which are produced in the country; **goods which are liable to duty** = goods on which customs or excise tax has to be paid; **duty-paid goods** = goods where the duty has been paid; **stamp duty** = tax on legal documents (such as the conveyance of a property to a new owner); **estate duty** *or* *US* **death duty** = tax paid on the property left by a dead person

◇ **duty-free** *adjective & adverb* sold with no duty to be paid; **he bought a duty-free watch at the airport** *or* **he bought the watch duty-free; duty-free shop** = shop at an airport *or* on a ship where goods can be bought without paying duty

> QUOTE: Canadian and European negotiators agreed to a deal under which Canada could lower its import duties on $150 million worth of European goods *Globe and Mail (Toronto)*
> QUOTE: the Department of Customs and Excise collected a total of N79m under the new advance duty payment scheme *Business Times (Lagos)*

Ee

e. & o.e. = ERRORS AND OMISSIONS EXCEPTED

eager *adjective* wanting to do something; **the management is eager to get into the Far Eastern markets; our salesmen are eager to see the new product range**

early *adjective & adverb* **(a)** before the usual time; **the mail left early; early closing day** = weekday when most shops in a town close in the afternoon; **at your earliest convenience =** as soon as possible; **at an early date =** very soon **(b)** at the beginning of a period of time; **he took an early flight to Paris; we hope for an early resumption of negotiations =** we hope negotiations will start again soon

earmark *verb* to reserve for a special purpose; **to earmark funds for a project; the grant is earmarked for computer systems development**

earn *verb* **(a)** to be paid money for working; **to earn £50 a week; our agent in Paris certainly does not earn his commission;** *GB* **wife's earned income allowance =** tax allowance to be set against money earned by the wife of the taxpayer **(b)** to produce interest *or* dividends; **what level of dividend do these shares earn? account which earns interest at 10%**

◇ **earning** *noun* **earning capacity** *or* **earning power =** amount of money someone should be able to earn; **he is such a fine dress designer that his earning power is very large; earning potential =** amount of money a person should be able to earn; amount of dividend a share should produce

◇ **earnings** *plural noun* **(a)** salary *or* wages, profits and dividends *or* interest received; **compensation for loss of earnings =** payment to someone who has stopped earning money *or* who is not able to earn money; **invisible earnings =** foreign currency earned by a country in providing services (such as banking, tourism), not in selling goods **(b)** money which is earned in interest *or* dividend; **earnings per share** *or* **earnings yield =** money earned in dividends per share, shown as a percentage of the market price of one share; **gross earnings =** earnings before tax and other deductions; **price/earnings ratio (P/E ratio) =** ratio between the market price of a share and the current dividend it produces; **these shares sell at a P/E ratio of 7; retained earnings =** profits which are not paid out to shareholders as dividend

QUOTE: if corporate forecasts are met, sales will exceed \$50 million in 1985 and net earnings could exceed \$7 million *Citizen (Ottawa)*
QUOTE: the US now accounts for more than half of our world-wide sales. It has made a huge contribution to our earnings turnaround
Duns Business Month
QUOTE: last fiscal year the chain reported a 116% jump in earnings, to \$6.4 million or \$1:10 a share *Barrons*

earnest *noun* money paid as a down payment

ease *verb* to fall a little; **the share index eased slightly today**

easement *noun* right which someone has to use land belonging to someone else (such as for a path to a garage)

easy *adjective* **(a)** not difficult; **easy terms =** terms which are not difficult to accept *or* price which is easy to pay; **the shop is let on very easy terms; the loan is repayable in easy payments =** with very small sums paid back regularly; **easy money =** (i) money which can be earned with no difficulty; (ii) money available on easy repayment terms; **easy money policy =** government policy of expanding the economy by making money more easily available **(b) easy market =** market where few people are buying, so prices are low; **the Stock Exchange was easy yesterday; share prices are easier =** prices have fallen slightly

◇ **easily** *adverb* **(a)** without any difficulty; **we passed through the customs easily (b)** much *or* a lot (compared to something else); **he is easily our best salesman; the firm is easily the biggest in the market**

EC = EUROPEAN COMMUNITY
NOTE: **EC** is often used in the USA, while **EEC** is more common in GB English

ECGD = EXPORT CREDIT GUARANTEE DEPARTMENT

echelon *noun* group of people of a certain grade in an organization; **the upper echelons of industry**

econometrics *plural noun* study of the statistics of economics, using computers
NOTE: takes a singular verb

economic *adjective* **(a)** which provides enough money; **the flat is let at an economic rent; it is hardly economic for the company to run its own warehouse (b)** referring to the financial state of a country; **economic planner; economic planning; the government's economic policy; the economic situation; the country's economic system; economic trends; economic crisis** *or* **economic depression** = state where a country is in financial collapse; **the government has introduced import controls to solve the current economic crisis; economic cycle** = period during which trade expands, then slows down, then expands again; **economic development** = expansion of the commercial and financial situation; **the economic development of the region has totally changed since oil was discovered there; economic growth** = increase in the national income; **the country enjoyed a period of economic growth in the 1960s; economic indicators** = statistics which show how the economy is going to perform in the short or long term; **economic sanctions** = restrictions on trade with a country in order to make its government change policy; **the western nations imposed economic sanctions on the country; the European Economic Community** = the Common Market

◊ **economical** *adjective* which saves money or materials *or* which is cheap; **economical car** = car which does not use much petrol; **economical use of resources** = using resources as carefully as possible

◊ **economics** *plural noun* **(a)** study of production, distribution, selling and use of goods and services **(b)** study of financial structures to show how a product or service is costed and what returns it produces; **the economics of town planning; I do not understand the economics of the coal industry**
NOTE: takes a singular verb

◊ **economist** *noun* person who specializes in the study of economics; **agricultural economist**

◊ **economize** *verb* to economize on **petrol** = to save petrol

◊ **economy** *noun* **(a)** being careful not to waste money or materials; **an economy measure** = an action to save money or materials; **to introduce economies** *or* **economy measures into the system** = to start using methods to save money or materials; **economies of scale** = making a

product more profitable by manufacturing it in larger quantities; **economy car** = car which does not use much petrol; **economy class** = cheapest class on a plane; **to travel economy class; economy drive** = campaign to save money or materials; **economy size** = large size *or* large packet which is a bargain **(b)** financial state of a country *or* way in which a country makes and uses its money; **the country's economy is in ruins; black economy** = work which is paid for in cash or goods, but not declared to the tax authorities; **capitalist economy** = system where each person has the right to invest money, to work in business, to buy and sell with no restrictions from the state; **controlled economy** = system where business activity is controlled by orders from the government; **free market economy** = system where the government does not interfere in business activity in any way; **mixed economy** = system which contains both nationalized industries and private enterprise; **planned economy** = system where the government plans all business activity

QUOTE: each of the major issues on the agenda at this week's meeting is important to the government's success in overall economic management *Australian Financial Review*
QUOTE: believers in free-market economics often find it hard to sort out their views on the issue *Economist*
QUOTE: the European economies are being held back by rigid labor markets and wage structures, huge expenditures on social welfare programs and restrictions on the free movement of goods within the Common Market *Duns Business Month*

ecu *or* **ECU** *noun* = EUROPEAN CURRENCY UNIT

QUOTE: the official use of the ecu remains limited. Since its creation in 1981 the ecu has grown popular because of its stability *Economist*

edge **1** *noun* **(a)** side of a flat thing; **he sat on the edge of the managing director's desk; the printer has printed the figures right to the edge of the printout (b)** advantage; **having a local office gives us a competitive edge over Smith Ltd; to have the edge on a rival company** = to be slightly more profitable *or* to have slightly larger share of the market than a rival **2** *verb* to move a little; **prices on the stock market edged upwards today; sales figures edged downwards in January**

editor *noun* person in charge of a newspaper or a section of a newspaper; **the editor of the "Times"; the City editor =** business *or* finance editor of a British newspaper

◇ **editorial** **1** *adjective* referring to an editor; **editorial board =** group of editors (on a newspaper, etc.) **2** *noun* main article in a newspaper, written by the editor

EDP = ELECTRONIC DATA PROCESSING

EEC = EUROPEAN ECONOMIC COMMUNITY **EEC ministers met today in Brussels; the USA is increasing its trade with the EEC**

effect **1** *noun* **(a)** result; **the effect of the pay increase was to raise productivity levels; terms of a contract which take effect** *or* **come into effect from January 1st =** terms which start to operate on January 1st; **prices are increased 10% with effect from January 1st** = new prices will apply from January 1st; **to remain in effect** = to continue to be applied **(b)** meaning; **clause to the effect that** = clause which means that; **we have made provision to this effect** = we have put into the contract terms which will make this work **(c) personal effects** = personal belongings **2** *verb* to carry out; **to effect a payment** = to make a payment; **to effect customs clearance** = to clear something through customs; **to effect a settlement between two parties** = to bring two parties together and make them agree to a settlement

◇ **effective** *adjective* **(a) effective demand** = actual demand for a product which can be paid for; **effective yield** = actual yield shown as a percentage **(b) effective date** = date on which a rule *or* a contract starts to be applied; **clause effective as from January 1st** = clause which starts to be applied on January 1st **(c)** which works *or* which produces results; **advertising in the Sunday papers is the most effective way of selling;** *see* COST-EFFECTIVE

◇ **effectiveness** *noun* working *or* producing results; **I doubt the effectiveness of television advertising;** *see* COST-EFFECTIVENESS

◇ **effectual** *adjective* which produces a correct result

efficiency *noun* ability to work well *or* to produce the right result or the right work quickly; **with a high degree of efficiency; a business efficiency exhibition; an efficiency expert**

NOTE: no plural

◇ **efficient** *adjective* able to work well *or* to produce the right result quickly; the **efficient working of a system; he needs an efficient secretary to look after him; efficient machine**

◇ **efficiently** *adverb* in an efficient way; **she organized the sales conference very efficiently**

QUOTE: increased control means improved efficiency in purchasing. shipping. sales and delivery   *Duns Business Month*

efflux *noun* flowing out; **efflux of capital to North America**

effort *noun* using the mind or body to do something; **the salesmen made great efforts to increase sales; thanks to the efforts of the finance department, overheads have been reduced; if we make one more effort, we should clear the backlog of orders**

e.g. for example *or* such as; **the contract is valid in some countries (e.g. France and Belgium) but not in others**

EGM = EXTRAORDINARY GENERAL MEETING

elastic *adjective* which can expand or contract easily because of small changes in price

◇ **elasticity** *noun* ability to change easily; **elasticity of supply and demand** = changes in supply and demand of an item depending on its market price

NOTE: no plural

elect *verb* to choose someone by a vote; **to elect the officers of an association; she was elected president**

◇ **-elect** *suffix* person who has been elected but has not yet started the term of office; **she is the president-elect**

NOTE: the plural is **presidents-elect**

◇ **election** *noun* act of electing; **the election of officers of an association; the election of directors by the shareholders; general election** = choosing of representatives by all the voters in a country

electricity *noun* current used to make light *or* heat *or* power; **the electricity was cut off this morning, so the computers could not work; our electricity bill has increased considerably this quarter; electricity costs are an important factor in our overheads**
◇ **electric** *adjective* worked by electricity; **an electric typewriter**
◇ **electrical** *adjective* referring to electricity; **the engineers are trying to repair an electrical fault**

electronic *adjective* **electronic data processing** = selecting and examining data stored in a computer to produce information; **electronic engineer** = engineer who specializes in electronic machines; **electronic mail** = system of sending messages from one computer terminal to another, via telephone lines; **electronic point of sale** = system where sales are automatically charged to the customer's credit card, and stock is controlled by the shop's computer
◇ **electronics** *plural noun* applying the scientific study of electrons to produce manufactured products, such as computers, calculators or telephones; **the electronics industry; an electronics specialist** *or* **expert; electronics engineer**
NOTE: takes a singular verb

element *noun* basic part; **the elements of a settlement**

elevator *noun* *US* lift; **take the elevator to the 26th floor**

eligible *adjective* person who can be chosen; **she is eligible for re-election**
◇ **eligibility** *noun* being eligible; **the chairman questioned her eligibility to stand for re-election**

eliminate *verb* to remove; **to eliminate defects in the system; using a computer should eliminate all possibility of error**

embargo **1** *noun* government order which stops a type of trade; **to lay** *or* **put an embargo on trade with a country** = to say that trade with a country must not take place; **the government has put an embargo on the export of computer equipment; to lift an embargo** = to allow trade to start again; **the government has lifted the embargo on the export of computers; to be under an embargo** = to be forbidden

NOTE: plural is **embargoes**
2 *verb* to stop trade *or* not to allow trade; **the government has embargoed trade with the Eastern countries**

QUOTE: the Commerce Department is planning to loosen export controls for products that have been embargoed but are readily available elsewhere in the West *Duns Business Month*

embark *verb* **(a)** to go on a ship; **the passengers embarked at Southampton (b) to embark on** = to start; **the company has embarked on an expansion programme**
◇ **embarkation** *noun* going on to a ship or plane; **port of embarkation** = port at which you get on to a ship; **embarkation card** = card given to passengers getting on to a plane or ship

embezzle *verb* to use money which is not yours, or which you are looking after for someone; **he was sent to prison for six months for embezzling his clients' money**
◇ **embezzlement** *noun* act of embezzling; **he was sent to prison for six months for embezzlement**
◇ **embezzler** *noun* person who embezzles

emergency *noun* dangerous situation where decisions have to be taken quickly; **the government declared a state of emergency** = the government decided that the situation was so dangerous that the police or army had to run the country; **to take emergency measures** = to take action rapidly to stop a crisis developing; **the company had to take emergency measures to stop losing money; emergency reserves** = ready cash held in case it is needed suddenly

emoluments *plural noun* pay, salary or fees, or the earnings of directors who are not employees

employ *verb* to give someone regular paid work; **to employ twenty staff** = to have twenty people working for you; **to employ twenty new staff** = to give work to twenty new people
◇ **employed** **1** *adjective* **(a)** in regular paid work; **he is not gainfully employed** = he has no regular paid work; **self-employed** = working for yourself; **he worked**

in a bank for ten years but now is self-employed **(b)** (money) used profitably; **return against capital employed 2** *plural noun* people who are working; **the employers and the employed; the self-employed =** people who work for themselves

◇ **employee** *noun* worker *or* person employed by a company; **employees of the firm are eligible to join a profit-sharing scheme; relations between management and employees have improved; the company has decided to take on new employees**

◇ **employer** *noun* person *or* company which has regular workers and pays them; **employers' organization *or* association =** group of employers with similar interests; **employer's contribution =** money paid by an employer towards a worker's pension

◇ **employment** *noun* regular paid work; **full employment =** situation where everyone in a country who can work has a job; **full-time employment =** work for all of a working day; **to be in full-time employment; part-time employment =** work for part of a working day; **temporary employment =** work which does not last for more than a few months; **to be without employment =** to have no work; **to find someone alternative employment =** to find another job for someone; **conditions of employment =** terms of a contract where someone is employed; **contract of employment *or* employment contract =** contract between management and an employee showing all the conditions of work; **security of employment =** feeling by a worker that he has the right to keep his job until he retires; **employment office *or* bureau *or* agency =** office which finds jobs for people
NOTE: no plural

QUOTE: 70 per cent of Australia's labour force was employed in service activity
Australian Financial Review
QUOTE: the blue-collar unions are the people who stand to lose most in terms of employment growth
Sydney Morning Herald
QUOTE: companies introducing robotics think it important to involve individual employees in planning their introduction
Economist

emporium *noun* large shop
NOTE: plural is **emporia**

empower *verb* to give someone the power to do something; **she was empowered by the company to sign the contract**

emptor *see* CAVEAT

empty 1 *adjective* with nothing inside; **the envelope is empty; you can take that filing cabinet back to the storeroom as it is empty; start the computer file with an empty workspace 2** *verb* to take the contents out of something; **she emptied the filing cabinet and put the files in boxes; he emptied the petty cash box into his briefcase**

◇ **empties** *plural noun* empty bottles *or* cases; **returned empties =** empty bottles which are taken back to a shop to get back a deposit paid on them

EMS = EUROPEAN MONETARY SYSTEM

encash *verb* to cash a cheque *or* to exchange a cheque for cash

◇ **encashable** *adjective* which can be cashed

◇ **encashment** *noun* act of exchanging for cash

enc *or* **encl** = ENCLOSURE; note put on a letter to show that a document is enclosed with it

enclose *verb* to put something inside an envelope with a letter; **to enclose an invoice with a letter; I am enclosing a copy of the contract; letter enclosing a cheque; please find the cheque enclosed herewith**

◇ **enclosure** *noun* document enclosed with a letter; **letter with enclosures**

encourage *verb* **(a)** to make it easier for something to happen; **the general rise in wages encourages consumer spending; leaving your credit cards on your desk encourages people to steal *or* encourages stealing; the company is trying to encourage sales by giving large discounts (b)** to help someone to do something by giving advice; **he encouraged me to apply for the job**

◇ **encouragement** *noun* giving advice to someone to help him to succeed; **the designers produced a very marketable product, thanks to the encouragement of the sales director**

end 1 *noun* final point *or* last part; **at the end of the contract period; at the end of six months =** after six months have passed;

account end = the end of an accounting period; **month end** = the end of the month, when accounts have to be drawn up; **end product** = manufactured product, made at the end of a production process; **after six months' trial production, the end product is still not acceptable; end user =** person who actually uses a product; **the company is creating a computer with the end user in mind; in the end** = at last *or* after a lot of problems; **in the end the company had to pull out of the US market; in the end they signed the contract at the airport; in the end the company had to call in the police; on end** = for a long time *or* with no breaks; **the discussions continued for hours on end; the workforce worked at top speed for weeks on end to finish the order on time; to come to an end** = to finish; **our distribution agreement comes to an end next month 2** *verb* to finish; **the distribution agreement ends in July; the chairman ended the discussion by getting up and walking out of the meeting**

◇ **end in** *verb* to have as a result; **the AGM ended in the shareholders fighting on the floor**

◇ **end up** *verb* to finish; **we ended up with a bill for £10,000**

endorse *verb* **to endorse a bill** *or* **a cheque** = to sign a bill *or* a cheque on the back to show that you accept it

◇ **endorsee** *noun* person whose name is written on a bill *or* a cheque as having the right to cash it

◇ **endorsement** *noun* **(a)** act of endorsing; signature on a document which endorses it **(b)** note on an insurance policy which adds conditions to the policy

◇ **endorser** *noun* person who endorses a bill which is then paid to him

endowment *noun* giving money to provide a regular income; **endowment insurance** *or* **endowment policy** = insurance policy where a sum of money is paid to the insured person on a certain date, or to his heirs if he dies earlier; **endowment mortgage** = mortgage backed by an endowment policy

energy *noun* **(a)** force *or* strength; **he has not the energy to be a good salesman; they wasted their energies on trying to sell cars in the German market (b)** power from elec-

tricity *or* petrol, etc.; **we try to save energy by switching off the lights when the rooms are empty; if you reduce the room temperature to eighteen degrees, you will save energy**
NOTE: no plural for (b)

◇ **energetic** *adjective* with a lot of energy; **the salesmen have made energetic attempts to sell the product**

◇ **energy-saving** *adjective* which saves energy; **the company is introducing energy-saving measures**

enforce *verb* to make sure something is done *or* is obeyed; **to enforce the terms of a contract**

◇ **enforcement** *noun* making sure that something is obeyed; **enforcement of the terms of a contract**
NOTE: no plural

engage *verb* **(a) to engage someone to do something** = to make someone do something legally; **the contract engages us to a minimum annual purchase (b)** to employ; **we have engaged the best commercial lawyer to represent us; the company has engaged twenty new salesmen (c) to be engaged in** = to be busy with; **he is engaged in work on computers; the company is engaged in trade with Africa**

◇ **engaged** *adjective* busy (telephone); **you cannot speak to the manager - his line is engaged; engaged tone** = sound made by a telephone when the line dialled is busy; **I tried to phone the complaints department but got only the engaged tone**

◇ **engagement** *noun* **(a)** agreement to do something; **to break an engagement to do something** = not to do what you have legally agreed; **the company broke their engagement not to sell our rivals' products (b) engagements** = arrangements to meet people; **I have no engagements for the rest of the day; she noted the appointment in her engagements diary**

engine *noun* machine which drives something; **a car with a small engine is more economic than one with a large one; the lift engine has broken down again - we shall just have to walk up to the 4th floor**

◇ **engineer** *noun* person who looks after technical equipment; **civil engineer** = person who specializes in the construction of roads, bridges, railways, etc.;

consulting engineer = engineer who gives specialist advice; **product engineer** = engineer in charge of the equipment for making a product; **project engineer** = engineer in charge of a project; **programming engineer** = engineer in charge of programming a computer system

◇ **engineering** *noun* science of technical equipment; **civil engineering** = construction of roads, bridges, railways, etc.; **the engineering department** = section of a company dealing with equipment; **an engineering consultant** = an engineer who gives specialist advice
NOTE: no plural

enquire = INQUIRE
◇ **enquiry** = INQUIRY

en route *adverb* on the way; **the tanker sank when she was en route to the Gulf**

entail 1 *noun* legal condition which passes ownership of a property only to certain persons 2 *verb* to involve; **itemizing the sales figures will entail about ten days' work**

enter *verb* (a) to go in; **they all stood up when the chairman entered the room; the company has spent millions trying to enter the do-it-yourself market** (b) to write; **to enter a name on a list; the clerk entered the interest in my bank book; to enter up an item in a ledger; to enter a bid for something** = to offer (usually in writing) to buy something; **to enter a caveat** = to warn legally that you have an interest in a case, and that no steps can be taken without your permission (c) **to enter into** = to begin; **to enter into relations with someone; to enter into negotiations with a foreign government; to enter into a partnership with a legal friend; to enter into an agreement** *or* **a contract**
◇ **entering** *noun* act of writing items in a record
NOTE: no plural

enterprise *noun* (a) system of carrying on a business; **free enterprise** = system of business free from government interference; **private enterprise** = businesses which are owned privately, not nationalized; **the project is completely funded by private enterprise** (b) business; **a small-scale enterprise** = a small business; **a state**

enterprise = a state-controlled company; **bosses of state enterprises are appointed by the government**
NOTE: no plural for (a)

entertain *verb* (a) to offer meals *or* hotel accommodation *or* theatre tickets, etc. to (business) visitors (b) to be ready to consider (a proposal); **the management will not entertain any suggestions from the union representatives**
◇ **entertainment** *noun* offering meals, etc. to business visitors; **entertainment allowance** = money which a manager is allowed by his company to spend on meals with visitors; **entertainment expenses** = money spent on giving meals to business visitors

entitle *verb* to give the right to something; **he is entitled to a discount** = he has the right to be given a discount
◇ **entitlement** *noun* right; **holiday entitlement** = number of days' paid holiday which a worker has the right to take; **she has not used up all her holiday entitlement; pension entitlement** = amount of pension which someone has the right to receive when he retires

entrance *noun* way in *or* going in; **the taxi will drop you at the main entrance; deliveries should be made to the London Road entrance; entrance (charge)** = money which you have to pay to go in; **entrance is £1.50 for adults and £1 for children**

entrepot *noun* **entrepot port** = town with a large international commercial port dealing in re-exports

entrepreneur *noun* person who directs a company and takes commercial risks
◇ **entrepreneurial** *adjective* taking commercial risks; **an entrepreneurial decision**

entrust *verb* **to entrust someone with something** *or* **to entrust something to someone** = to give someone the responsibility for looking after something; **he was entrusted with the keys to the office safe**

entry *noun* (a) written information put in an accounts ledger; **credit entry** *or* **debit entry** = entry on the credit *or* debit side of an account; **single-entry bookkeeping =** noting a deal with only one entry; **double-entry bookkeeping =** noting of both debit and credit sides of an account; **to make an entry in a ledger =** to write in details of a deal; **contra entry =** entry made in the opposite side of an account to make an earlier entry worthless (such as a debit entry against a credit); **to contra an entry =** to enter a similar amount on the opposite side of the account **(b)** act of going in; place where you can go in; **to pass a customs entry point; entry of goods under bond; entry charge =** money which you have to pay before you go in; **entry visa =** visa allowing someone to go into a country; **multiple entry visa =** entry visa which allows someone to enter a country as often as he likes

envelope *noun* flat paper cover for sending letters; **airmail envelope =** very light envelope for airmail letters; **aperture envelope =** envelope with a hole in it so that the address on the letter inside can be seen; **window envelope =** envelope with a hole covered with film so that the address on the letter inside can be seen; **sealed** *or* **unsealed envelope =** envelope where the flap has been stuck down to close it *or* envelope where the flap has been pushed into the back of the envelope; **to send the information in a sealed envelope; a stamped addressed envelope =** an envelope with your own address written on it and a stamp stuck on it to pay for return postage; **please send a stamped addressed envelope for further details and our latest catalogue**

EPOS = ELECTRONIC POINT OF SALE

equal 1 *adjective* exactly the same; **male and female workers have equal pay; equal opportunities programme =** programme to avoid discrimination in employment NOTE: the US equivalent is **affirmative action 2** *verb* to be the same as; **production this month has equalled our best month ever** NOTE: **equalling - equalled** but US **equaling - equaled**
◊ **equalize** *verb* to make equal; **to equalize dividends**
◊ **equalization** *noun*
◊ **equally** *adverb* in the same way; **costs will be shared equally between the two parties; they were both equally responsible for the disastrous launch**

equip *verb* to provide with machinery; **to equip a factory with new machinery; the office is fully equipped with word-processors**
◊ **equipment** *noun* machinery and furniture required to make a factory or office work; **office equipment** *or* **business equipment; office equipment supplier; office equipment catalogue; capital equipment =** equipment which a factory *or* office uses to work; **heavy equipment =** large machines, such as for making cars or for printing NOTE: no plural

equity *noun* **(a)** right to receive dividends as part of the profit of a company in which you own shares **(b) shareholders' equity** *or* **equity capital =** amount of a company's capital which is owned by shareholders
◊ **equities** *plural noun* ordinary shares

equivalence *noun* being equivalent
◊ **equivalent** *adjective* **to be equivalent to =** to have the same value as *or* to be the same as; **the total dividend paid is equivalent to one quarter of the pretax profits**

ergonomics *plural noun* study of people at work and their working conditions NOTE: takes a singular verb
◊ **ergonomist** *noun* scientist who studies people at work and tries to improve their working conditions

erode *verb* to wear away gradually; **to erode wage differentials =** to reduce gradually differences in salary between different grades

error *noun* mistake; **he made an error in calculating the total; the secretary must have made a typing error; clerical error =** mistake made in an office; **computer error =** mistake made by a computer; **margin of error =** number of mistakes which are accepted in a document *or* in a calculation; **errors and omissions excepted =** words written on an invoice to show that the company has no responsibility for mistakes in the invoice; **error rate** = number of mistakes per thousand entries *or* per page; **in error** *or* **by error** = by mistake; **the letter was sent to the London office in error**

escalate *verb* to increase steadily
◊ **escalation** *noun* **escalation of prices** = steady increase in prices; **escalation clause** = ESCALATOR CLAUSE
◊ **escalator clause** *noun* clause in a contract allowing for regular price increases because of increased costs

escape *noun* getting away from a difficult situation; **escape clause** = clause in a contract which allows one of the parties to avoid carrying out the terms of the contract under certain conditions

escrow *noun* **in escrow** = held in safe keeping by a third party; **document held in escrow** = document given to a third party to keep and to pass on to someone when money has been paid; *US* **escrow account** = account where money is held in escrow until a contract is signed *or* until goods are delivered, etc.
NOTE: no plural

espionage *noun* **industrial espionage** = trying to find out the secrets of a competitor's work or products, usually by illegal means
NOTE: no plural

essential *adjective* very important; **it is essential that an agreement be reached before the end of the month; the factory is lacking essential spare parts**
◊ **essentials** *plural noun* goods *or* products which are very important

establish *verb* to set up *or* to make *or* to open; **the company has established a branch in Australia; the business was established in Scotland in 1823; it is a young company - it has been established for only four years; to establish oneself in business** = to become successful in a new business
◊ **establishment** *noun* **(a)** commercial business; **he runs an important printing establishment (b) establishment charges** = cost of people and property in a company's

accounts **(c)** number of people working in a company; **to be on the establishment** = to be a full-time employee; **office with an establishment of fifteen** = office with a budgeted staff of fifteen

estate *noun* **(a) real estate** = property (land or buildings); **estate agency** = office which arranges for the sale of property; **estate agent** = person in charge of an estate agency **(b) industrial estate** *or* **trading estate** = area of land near a town specially for factories and warehouses **(c)** property left by a dead person; **estate duty** = tax on property left by a dead person

estimate 1 *noun* **(a)** calculation of probable cost *or* size *or* time of something; **rough estimate** = very approximate calculation; **at a conservative estimate** = calculation which probably underestimates the final figure; **their turnover has risen by at least 20% in the last year, and that is a conservative estimate; these figures are only an estimate** = these are not the final accurate figures; **can you give me an estimate of how much time was spent on the job? (b)** calculation of how much something is likely to cost in the future, given to a client so as to get him to make an order; **estimate of costs** *or* **of expenditure; before we can give the grant we must have an estimate of the total costs involved; to ask a builder for an estimate for building the warehouse; to put in an estimate** = to give someone a written calculation of the probable costs of carrying out a job; **three firms put in estimates for the job 2** *verb* **(a)** to calculate the probable cost *or* size *or* time of something; **to estimate that it will cost £1m** *or* **to estimate costs at £1m; we estimate current sales at only 60% of last year (b) to estimate for a job** = to state in writing the future costs of carrying out a piece of work so that a client can make an order; **three firms estimated for the fitting of the offices**
◊ **estimated** *adjective* calculated approximately; **estimated sales; estimated figure**
◊ **estimation** *noun* approximate calculation
◊ **estimator** *noun* person whose job is to calculate estimates for carrying out work

etc. and so on; **the import duty is to be paid on luxury items including cars, watches, etc.**

Euro- *prefix* referring to Europe or the European Community

◇ **Eurobond** *noun* bond issued by an international corporation or government outside its country of origin and sold to Europeans who pay in Eurodollars; **the Eurobond market**

◇ **Eurocheque** *noun* British cheque which can be cashed in a European bank

◇ **Eurocurrency** *noun* European currencies used for trade within Europe but outside their countries of origin; **a Eurocurrency loan; the Eurocurrency market**

◇ **Eurodollar** *noun* US dollar in a European bank, used for trade within Europe; **a Eurodollar loan; the Eurodollar market**

◇ **Euromarket** *noun* the European Economic Community seen as a potential market for sales

◇ **Europe** *noun* group of countries to the West of Asia and the North of Africa; **most of the countries of Western Europe are members of the Common Market; Canadian exports to Europe have risen by 25%**

◇ **European** *adjective* referring to Europe; **the European Economic Community = the Common Market; the European Monetary System =** system of controlled exchange rates between some member countries of the Common Market

evade *verb* to try to avoid something; **to evade tax =** to try illegally to avoid paying tax

evaluate *verb* to calculate a value; **to evaluate costs**

◇ **evaluation** *noun* calculation of value; **job evaluation =** examining different jobs within a company to see what skills and qualifications are needed to carry them out

evasion *noun* avoiding; **tax evasion =** illegally trying not to pay tax

evidence *noun* written or spoken report at a trial; **documentary evidence =** evidence in the form of documents; **the secretary gave evidence for** *or* **against her former employer =** the secretary was a witness, and her report suggested that her former employer was not guilty *or* guilty
NOTE: no plural

ex- *preposition* **(a)** out of *or* from; **price ex warehouse =** price for a product which is to be collected from the manufacturer's or agent's warehouse and so does not include delivery; **price ex works** *or* **ex factory =** price not including transport from the maker's factory **(b) ex coupon =** bond without the interest coupon; **share quoted ex dividend =** share price not including the right to receive the next dividend; **the shares went ex dividend yesterday (c)** formerly; **Mr Smith, the ex-chairman of the company (d) ex-directory =** telephone number which is not printed in the telephone book; **he has an ex-directory number**

exact *adjective* very correct; **the exact time is 10.27; the salesgirl asked me if I had the exact sum, since the shop had no change**

◇ **exactly** *adverb* very correctly; **the total cost was exactly £6,500**

examine *verb* to look at someone *or* something very carefully to see if it can be accepted; **the customs officials asked to examine the inside of the car; the police are examining the papers from the managing director's safe**

◇ **examination** *noun* **(a)** looking at something very carefully to see if it is acceptable; **customs examination =** looking at goods *or* baggage by customs officials **(b)** test to see if someone has passed a course; **he passed his accountancy examinations; she came first in the final examination for the course; he failed his proficiency examination and so had to leave his job**

example *noun* something chosen to show; **the motor show has many examples of energy-saving cars on display; for example =** to show one thing out of many; **the government wants to encourage exports, and, for example, it gives free credit to exporters**

exceed *verb* to be more than; **discount not exceeding 15%; last year costs exceeded 20% of income for the first time; he has exceeded his credit limit =** he has borrowed more money than he is allowed

excellent *adjective* very good; **the quality of the firm's products is excellent, but its sales force is not large enough**

except *preposition & conjunction* not including; **VAT is levied on all goods and services except books, newspapers and children's clothes; sales are rising in all markets except the Far East**
◇ **excepted** *adverb* not including; **errors and omissions excepted** = note on an invoice to show that the company has no responsibility for mistakes in the invoice
◇ **exceptional** *adjective* not usual *or* different; **exceptional items** = items in a balance sheet which do not appear there each year

excess *noun* amount which is more than what is allowed; **an excess of expenditure over revenue; excess baggage** = extra payment at an airport for taking baggage which is heavier than the normal passenger's allowance; **excess capacity** = spare capacity which is not being used; **excess fare** = extra fare to be paid (such as for travelling first class with a second class ticket); **in excess of** = above *or* more than; **quantities in excess of twenty-five kilos; excess profits** = profit which is more than what is thought to be normal; **excess profits tax** = tax on excess profits
◇ **excessive** *adjective* too large; **excessive costs**

QUOTE: most airlines give business class the same baggage allowance as first class, which can save large sums in excess baggage
Business Traveller
QUOTE: control of materials provides manufacturers with an opportunity to reduce the amount of money tied up in excess materials
Duns Business Month

exchange 1 *noun* (a) giving of one thing for another; **part exchange** = giving an old product as part of the payment for a new one; **to take a car in part exchange; exchange of contracts** = point in the sale of property when the buyer and the seller both sign the contract of sale which then becomes binding (b) **foreign exchange** = (i) exchanging the money of one country for that of another; (ii) money of another country; **the company has more than £1m in foreign exchange; foreign exchange broker** = person who buys and sells foreign currency on behalf of other people; **foreign exchange market** = dealings in foreign currencies; **he trades on the foreign exchange market; foreign exchange**

markets were very active after the dollar devalued; **rate of exchange** *or* **exchange rate** = price at which one currency is exchanged for another; **the current rate of exchange is 10.95 francs to the pound; exchange control** = control by a government of the way in which its currency may be exchanged for foreign currencies; **the government had to impose exchange controls to stop the rush to buy dollars; exchange dealer** = person who buys and sells foreign currency; **exchange dealings** = buying and selling foreign currency; *GB* **Exchange Equalization Account** = account with the Bank of England used by the government when buying or selling foreign currency to influence the sterling exchange rate; **exchange premium** = extra cost above the normal rate for buying a foreign currency (c) **bill of exchange** = document which tells a bank to pay a person (usually used in foreign currency payments) (d) **Stock Exchange** = place where stocks and shares are bought and sold; **the company's shares are traded on the New York Stock Exchange; he works on the Stock Exchange; commodity exchange** = place where commodities are bought and sold
NOTE: no plural for (b)
2 *verb* (a) to exchange one article for **another** = to give one thing in place of something else; **he exchanged his motorcycle for a car; if the trousers are too small you can take them back and exchange them for a larger pair; goods can be exchanged only on production of the sales slip** (b) **to exchange contracts** = to sign a contract when buying a property (done by both buyer and seller at the same time) (c) to change money of one country for money of another; **to exchange francs for pounds**
◇ **exchangeable** *adjective* which can be exchanged
◇ **exchanger** *noun* person who buys and sells foreign currency

QUOTE: under the barter agreements, Nigeria will export crude oil in exchange for trucks, food, planes and chemicals *Wall Street Journal*
QUOTE: can free trade be reconciled with a strong dollar resulting from floating exchange rates *Duns Business Month*
QUOTE: a draft report on changes in the international monetary system casts doubt on any return to fixed exchange-rate parities
Wall Street Journal

Exchequer *noun GB* the Exchequer = government department dealing with public revenue; **the Chancellor of the Exchequer** = the chief British finance minister

excise 1 *noun* **(a)** excise duty = tax on certain goods produced in a country (such as alcohol); **to pay excise duty on wine (b) Customs and Excise** *or* **Excise Department** = government department which deals with taxes on imports and on products such as alcohol produced in the country; **Excise officer 2** *verb* to cut out; **please excise all references to the strike in the minutes**
◊ **exciseman** *noun* person who works in the Excise Department

exclude *verb* to keep out *or* not to include; **the interest charges have been excluded from the document; damage by fire is excluded from the policy**
◊ **excluding** *preposition* not including; **all salesmen, excluding those living in London, can claim expenses for attending the sales conference**
◊ **exclusion** *noun* act of not including; **exclusion clause** = clause in an insurance policy *or* warranty which says which items are not covered
◊ **exclusive** *adjective* **(a) exclusive agreement** = agreement where a person is made sole agent for a product in a market; **exclusive right to market a product** = right to be the only person to market the product **(b) exclusive of** = not including; **all payments are exclusive of tax; the invoice is exclusive of VAT**
◊ **exclusivity** *noun* exclusive right to market a product

excuse 1 *noun* reason for doing something wrong; **his excuse for not coming to the meeting was that he had been told about it only the day before; the managing director refused to accept the sales manager's excuses for the poor sales** = he refused to believe that there was a good reason for the poor sales **2** *verb* to forgive a small mistake; **she can be excused for not knowing the French for "photocopier"**

execute *verb* to carry out (an order)
◊ **execution** *noun* carrying out of an order; **stay of execution** = temporary stopping of a legal order; **the court granted the company a two-week stay of execution** NOTE: no plural
◊ **executive** 1 *adjective* which puts decisions into action; **executive committee** = committee which runs a society *or* a club; **executive director** = director who actually works full-time in the company; **executive powers** = right to put decisions into actions; **he was made managing director with full executive powers over the European operation 2** *noun* person in a business who takes decisions *or* manager *or* director; **sales executive; senior** *or* **junior executive; account executive** = employee who is the link between his company and certain customers; **chief executive** = executive director in charge of a company

executor *noun* person who sees that the terms of a will are carried out; **he was named executor of his brother's will**

exempt 1 *adjective* not covered by a law; not forced to obey a law; **exempt from tax** *or* **tax-exempt** = not required to pay tax; **as a non-profit-making organization we are exempt from tax 2** *verb* to free something from having tax paid on it or from having to pay tax; **non-profit-making organizations are exempted from tax; food is exempted from sales tax; the government exempted trusts from tax**
◊ **exemption** *noun* act of exempting something from a contract *or* from a tax; **exemption from tax** *or* **tax exemption** = being free from having to pay tax; **as a non-profit-making organization you can claim tax exemption**

exercise 1 *noun* use of something; **exercise of an option** = using an option *or* putting an option into action **2** *verb* to use; **to exercise an option** = to put an option into action; **he exercised his option to acquire sole marketing rights for the product; the chairwoman exercised her veto to block the motion**

ex gratia *adjective* **an ex gratia payment** = payment made as a gift, with no other obligations

exhibit 1 *noun* **(a)** thing which is shown; **the buyers admired the exhibits on our stand (b)** single section of an exhibition; **the British Trade Exhibit at the International Computer Fair 2** *verb* to exhibit at the

Motor Show = to display new models of cars

◇ **exhibition** *noun* showing goods so that buyers can look at them and decide what to buy; **the government has sponsored an exhibition of good design; we have a stand at the Ideal Home Exhibition; the agricultural exhibition grounds; exhibition room** *or* **hall** = place where goods are shown so that buyers can look at them and decide what to buy; **exhibition stand** = separate section of an exhibition where a company exhibits its products or services

◇ **exhibitor** *noun* person *or* company which shows products at an exhibition

exist *verb* to be; **I do not believe the document exists - I think it has been burnt**

exit *noun* way out of a building; **the customers all rushed towards the exits; fire exit** = door which leads to a way out of a building if there is a fire

ex officio *adjective & adverb* because of an office held; **the treasurer is ex officio a member** *or* **an ex officio member of the finance committee**

expand *verb* to increase *or* to get bigger *or* to make something bigger; **an expanding economy; the company is expanding fast; we have had to expand our sales force**

◇ **expansion** *noun* increase in size; **the expansion of the domestic market; the company had difficulty in financing its current expansion programme;** *GB* **business expansion scheme** = system where money invested in a new company for some years is free from tax

expect *verb* to hope that something is going to happen; **we are expecting him to arrive at 10.45; they are expecting a cheque from their agent next week; the house was sold for more than the expected price**

◇ **expectancy** *noun* **life expectancy** = number of years a person is likely to live

expenditure *noun* amounts of money spent; **below-the-line expenditure** = exceptional payments which are separated from a company's normal accounts; **capital expenditure** = money spent on fixed assets (such as property or machinery); **the company's current expenditure programme** = the company's spending according to the current plan; **heavy expenditure on equipment** = spending large sums of money on equipment
NOTE: no plural

◇ **expense** *noun* **(a)** money spent; **it is not worth the expense; the expense is too much for my bank balance; at great expense** = having spent a lot of money; **he furnished the office regardless of expense** = without thinking how much it cost
NOTE: no plural **(b) expense account** = money which a businessman is allowed by his company to spend on travelling and entertaining clients in connection with his business; **I'll put this lunch on my expense account; expense account lunches form a large part of our current expenditure**

◇ **expenses** *plural noun* money paid for doing something; **the salary offered is £10,000 plus expenses; all expenses paid** = with all costs paid by the company; **the company sent him to San Francisco all expenses paid; to cut down on expenses** = to try to reduce spending; **allowable expenses** = business expenses which are allowed against tax; **business expenses** = money spent on running a business, not on stock or assets; **entertainment expenses** = money spent on giving meals to business visitors; **fixed expenses** = money which is spent regularly (such as rent, electricity, telephone); **incidental expenses** = small amounts of money spent at various times, in addition to larger amounts; **legal expenses** = money spent on fees paid to lawyers; **overhead expenses** *or* **general expenses** *or* **running expenses** = money spent on the day-to-day cost of a business; **travelling expenses** = money spent on travelling and hotels for business purposes

◇ **expensive** *adjective* which costs a lot of money; **first-class air travel is becoming more and more expensive**

experience 1 *noun* having lived through various situations and therefore knowing how to make decisions; **he is a man of considerable experience; she has a lot of experience of dealing with German companies; he gained most of his experience in the Far East; some experience is required for this job** 2 *verb* to live through a situation; **the company experienced a period of falling sales**
◇ **experienced** *adjective* person who has lived through many situations and has learnt from them; **he is the most experienced negotiator I know; we have appointed a very experienced woman as sales director**

expert *noun* person who knows a lot about something; **an expert in the field of electronics** *or* **an electronics expert; the company asked a financial expert for advice** *or* **asked for expert financial advice; expert's report** = report written by an expert
◇ **expertise** *noun* specialist knowledge; **we hired Mr Smith because of his financial expertise** *or* **because of his expertise in the African market**
NOTE: no plural

expiration *noun* coming to an end; **expiration of an insurance policy; to repay before the expiration of the stated period; on expiration of the lease** = when the lease comes to an end
NOTE: no plural
◇ **expire** *verb* to come to an end; **the lease expires in 1987; his passport has expired** = his passport is no longer valid
◇ **expiry** *noun* coming to an end; **expiry of an insurance policy; expiry date** = date when something will end

explain *verb* to give reasons for something; **he explained to the customs officials that the two computers were presents from friends; can you explain why the sales in the first quarter are so high? the sales director tried to explain the sudden drop in unit sales**
◇ **explanation** *noun* reason for something; **the VAT inspector asked for an explanation of the invoices; at the AGM, the chairman gave an explanation for the high level of interest payments**

exploit *verb* to use something to make a profit; **the company is exploiting its contacts in the Ministry of Trade; we hope to exploit the oil resources in the China Sea**

explore *verb* to examine carefully; **we are exploring the possibility of opening an office in London**

export 1 *noun* **(a) exports** = goods sent to a foreign country to be sold; **exports to Africa have increased by 25% (b)** action of sending goods to a foreign country to be sold; **the export trade** *or* **the export market; export department** = section of a company which deals in sales to foreign countries; **export duty** = tax paid on goods sent out of a country for sale; **export house** = company which specializes in the export of goods made by other manufacturers; **export licence** = government permit allowing something to be exported; **the government has refused an export licence for computer parts; export manager** = person in charge of an export department in a company; **Export Credit Guarantee Department** = British government department which insures exports sold on credit
NOTE: usually used in the plural, but the singular form is used before a noun
2 *verb* to send goods to foreign countries for sale; **50% of our production is exported; the company imports raw materials and exports the finished products**
◇ **exportation** *noun* act of sending goods to foreign countries for sale
NOTE: no plural
◇ **exporter** *noun* person *or* company *or* country which sells goods in foreign countries; **a major furniture exporter; Canada is an important exporter of oil** *or* **an important oil exporter**
◇ **exporting** *adjective* which exports; **oil exporting countries** = countries which produce oil and sell it to other countries

exposition *noun US* = EXHIBITION

exposure *noun* amount of risk which a lender runs; **he is trying to cover his exposure in the property market**
NOTE: no plural

express 1 *adjective* **(a)** rapid *or* very fast; **express letter; express delivery (b)** clearly shown in words; **the contract has an express condition forbidding sale in**

Africa 2 *verb* **(a)** to put into words or diagrams; **this chart shows home sales expressed as a percentage of total turnover (b)** to send very fast; **we expressed the order to the customer's warehouse**

◇ **expressly** *adverb* clearly in words; **the contract expressly forbids sales to the United States**

ext = EXTENSION

extend *verb* **(a)** to make available *or* to give; **to extend credit to a customer (b)** to make longer; **to extend a contract for two years**

◇ **extended credit** *noun* credit allowing the borrower a very long time to pay; **we sell to Australia on extended credit**

◇ **extension** *noun* **(a)** allowing longer time; **to get an extension of credit =** to get more time to pay back; **extension of a contract =** continuing the contract for a further period **(b)** (*in an office*) individual telephone linked to the main switchboard; **can you get me extension 21? extension 21 is engaged; the sales manager is on extension 53**

◇ **extensive** *adjective* very large *or* covering a wide area; **an extensive network of sales outlets**

QUOTE: the White House refusal to ask for an extension of the auto import quotas
Duns Business Month

external *adjective* **(a)** outside a country; **external account =** account in a British bank of someone who is living in another country; **external trade =** trade with foreign countries **(b)** outside a company; **external audit =** audit carried out by an independent auditor

extra 1 *adjective* which is added *or* which is more than usual; **there is no extra charge for heating; to charge 10% extra for postage; he had £25 extra pay for working on Sunday; service is extra** 2 *plural noun* **extras =** items which are not included in a price; **packing and postage are extras**

extract *noun* printed document which is part of a larger document; **he sent me an extract of the accounts**

extraordinary *adjective* different from normal; **Extraordinary General Meeting =** special meeting of shareholders *or* members of a club, etc., to discuss an important matter which cannot wait until the next AGM; **to call an Extraordinary General Meeting; extraordinary items =** items in accounts which do not appear each year; **the auditors noted several extraordinary items in the accounts**

extremely *adverb* very much; **it is extremely difficult to break into the US market; their management team is extremely efficient**

Ff

face value *noun* value written on a coin *or* banknote *or* share

QUOTE: travellers cheques cost 1% of their face value - some banks charge more for small amounts
Sunday Times

facility *noun* **(a)** being able to do something easily; **we offer facilities for payment (b)** total amount of credit which a lender will allow a borrower; **credit facilities =** arrangement with a bank *or* supplier to have credit so as to buy goods; **overdraft facility =** arrangement with a bank to have an overdraft **(c) facilities =** equipment *or* buildings which make it easy to do something; **storage facilities; harbour facilities; transport facilities; there are no facilities for passengers; there are no facilities for unloading *or* there are no unloading facilities (d)** *US* single large building; **we have opened our new warehouse facility**

facsimile *noun* **facsimile copy =** exact copy of a document

fact *noun* something which is true and real; **the chairman asked to see all the facts on the income tax claim; the sales director can give you the facts and figures about the**

African operation; **the fact of the matter is = what is true is that; the fact of the matter is that the product does not fit the market; in fact =** really; **the chairman blamed the finance director for the loss when in fact he was responsible for it himself**

◇ **fact-finding** *adjective* looking for information; **a fact-finding mission =** visit, usually by a group of people, to search for information about a problem; **the minister went on a fact-finding tour of the region**

factor 1 *noun* **(a)** thing which is important *or* which influences; **the drop in sales is an important factor in the company's lower profits; cost factor =** problem of cost; **cyclical factors =** way in which a trade cycle affects businesses; **deciding factor =** most important factor which influences a decision; **load factor =** number of seats in a bus *or* plane *or* train which are occupied by passengers who have paid the full fare; **factors of production =** things needed to produce a product (land, labour and capital) **(b) by a factor of ten =** ten times **(c)** person or company which is responsible for collecting debts for companies, by buying debts at a discount on their face value 2 *verb* to buy debts from a company at a discount

◇ **factoring** *noun* business of buying debts at a discount; **factoring charges =** cost of selling debts to a factor for a commission

factory *noun* building where products are manufactured; **car factory; shoe factory; factory hand** *or* **factory worker =** person who works in a factory; **factory inspector** *or* **inspector of factories =** government official who inspects factories to see if they are well run; **the factory inspectorate =** all factory inspectors; **factory price** *or* **price ex factory =** price not including transport from the maker's factory; **factory unit =** single building on an industrial estate

fail *verb* **(a)** not to do something which you were trying to do; **the company failed to notify the tax office of its change of address; the prototype failed its first test (b)** to be unsuccessful commercially; **the company failed =** the company went bankrupt; **he lost all his money when the bank failed**

◇ **failing** 1 *noun* weakness; **the chairman has one failing - he goes to sleep at board meetings 2** *preposition* if something does not happen; **failing instructions to the contrary =** unless someone gives opposite instructions; **failing prompt payment =** if the payment is not made on time; **failing that =** if that does not work; **try the company secretary, and failing that the chairman**

◇ **failure** *noun* **(a)** breaking down *or* stopping; **the failure of the negotiations (b) failure to pay a bill =** not having paid the bill **(c) commercial failure =** financial collapse *or* bankruptcy; **he lost all his money in the bank failure**

fair 1 *noun* **trade fair =** large exhibition and meeting for advertising and selling a certain type of product; **to organize** *or* **to run a trade fair; the fair is open from 9 a.m. to 5 p.m.; the computer fair runs from April 1st to 6th; there are two trade fairs running in London at the same time - the carpet manufacturers' and the computer dealers' 2** *adjective* **(a)** honest *or* correct; **fair deal =** arrangement where both parties are treated equally; **the workers feel they did not get a fair deal from the management; fair dealing =** legal buying and selling of shares; **fair price =** good price for both buyer and seller; **fair trade =** (i) international business system where countries agree not to charge import duties on certain items imported from their trading partners; (ii) *US* = RESALE PRICE MAINTENANCE; **fair trading** *or* **fair dealing =** way of doing business which is reasonable and does not harm the consumer; *GB* **Office of Fair Trading =** government department which protects consumers against unfair *or* illegal business; **fair wear and tear =** acceptable damage caused by normal use; **the insurance policy covers most damage, but not fair wear and tear to the machine (b) fair copy =** document which is written or typed with no changes or mistakes

◇ **fairly** *adverb* quite; **the company is fairly close to financial collapse; she is a fairly fast keyboarder**

faith *noun* **to have faith in something** *or* **someone =** to believe that something *or* a person is good or will work well; **the salesmen have great faith in the product; the sales teams do not have much faith in their**

manager; the board has faith in the managing director's judgement; **to buy something in good faith** = to buy something thinking that is of good quality or that it has not been stolen or that it is not an imitation
NOTE: no plural

◇ **faithfully** adverb **yours faithfully** = used as an ending to a formal business letter not addressed to a named person
NOTE: not used in US English

fake 1 noun imitation or copy made for criminal purposes; **the shipment came with fake documentation** 2 verb to make an imitation for criminal purposes; **faked documents; he faked the results of the test**

fall 1 noun sudden drop or suddenly becoming smaller or loss of value; **a fall in the exchange rate; fall in the price of gold; a fall on the Stock Exchange; profits showed a 10% fall** 2 verb **(a)** to drop suddenly to a lower price; **shares fell on the market today; gold shares fell 10%** or **fell 45 cents on the Stock Exchange; the price of gold fell for the second day running; the pound fell against other European currencies (b)** to happen or to take place; **the public holiday falls on a Tuesday; payments which fall due** = payments which are now due to be made
NOTE: **falling - fell - has fallen**

◇ **fall away** verb to become less; **hotel bookings have fallen away since the tourist season ended**

◇ **fall back** verb to become lower or cheaper after rising in price; **shares fell back in light trading**

◇ **fall back on** verb to have to use money kept for emergencies; **to fall back on cash reserves**

◇ **fall behind** verb to be late in doing something; **he fell behind with his mortgage repayments**

◇ **falling** adjective which is growing smaller or dropping in price; **a falling market** = market where prices are coming down; **the falling pound** = the pound which is losing its value against other currencies

◇ **fall off** verb to become lower or cheaper or less; **sales have fallen off since the tourist season ended**

◇ **fall out** verb **the bottom has fallen out of the market** = sales have fallen below what previously seemed to be their lowest point

◇ **fall through** verb not to happen or not to take place; **the plan fell through at the last moment**

false adjective not true or not correct; **to make a false entry in the balance sheet; false pretences** = doing or saying something to cheat someone; **he was sent to prison for obtaining money by false pretences; false weight** = weight on shop scales which is wrong and so cheats customers

◇ **falsify** verb to change something to make it wrong; **to falsify the accounts**

◇ **falsification** noun action of making false entries in accounts

famous adjective very well known; **the company owns a famous department store in the centre of London**

fancy adjective **(a) fancy goods** = small attractive items **(b) fancy prices** = high prices; **I don't want to pay the fancy prices they ask in London shops**

fare noun price to be paid for a ticket to travel; **train fares have gone up by 5%; the government is asking the airlines to keep air fares down; concessionary fare** = reduced fare for certain types of passenger (such as employees of the transport company); **full fare** = ticket for a journey by an adult paying the full price; **half fare** = half-price ticket for a child; **single fare** or US **one-way fare** = fare for a journey from one place to another; **return fare** or US **round-trip fare** = fare for a journey from one place to another and back again

farm 1 noun property in the country where crops are grown or where animals are raised for sale; **collective farm** = state-owned farm which is run by the workers; **fish farm** = place where fish are grown for food; **mixed farm** = farm which has both

animals and crops **2** *verb* to own a farm; **he farms 150 acres**
◇ **farming** *noun* job of working on a farm *or* of raising animals for sale *or* of growing crops for food; **chicken farming; fish farming; mixed farming**
◇ **farm out** *verb* to farm out work = to hand over work for another person *or* company to do it for you; **she farms out the office typing to various local bureaux**

fast *adjective & adverb* quick *or* quickly; **the train is the fastest way of getting to our supplier's factory; home computers sell fast in the pre-Christmas period**
◇ **fast-moving** *or* **fast-selling** *adjective* **fast-selling items** = items which sell fast; **dictionaries are not fast-moving stock**

fault *noun* **(a)** being to blame for something which is wrong; **it is the stock controller's fault if the warehouse runs out of stock; the chairman said the lower sales figures were the fault of a badly motivated sales force (b)** wrong working; **the technicians are trying to correct a programming fault; we think there is a basic fault in the product design**
◇ **faulty** *adjective* which does not work properly; **faulty equipment; they installed faulty computer programs**

favour *or* *US* **favor 1** *noun* **(a)** as a **favour** = to help *or* to be kind to someone; **he asked the secretary for a loan as a favour (b) in favour of** = in agreement with *or* feeling that something is right; **six members of the board are in favour of the proposal, and three are against it 2** *verb* to agree that something is right *or* to vote for something; **the board members all favour Smith Ltd as partners in the project**
◇ **favourable** *adjective* which gives an advantage; **favourable balance of trade** = situation where a country's exports are more than the imports; **on favourable terms** = on specially good terms; **the shop is let on very favourable terms**
◇ **favourite** *adjective* which is liked best; **this brand of chocolate is a favourite with the children's market**

fax *or* **FAX** *noun & verb informal* = FACSIMILE COPY; **we will send a fax of the design plan; I've faxed the documents to our New York office**

feasibility *noun* ability to be done; **to report on the feasibility of a project; feasibility report** = report saying if something can be done; **to carry out a feasibility study on a project** = to carry out an examination of costs and profits to see if the project should be started
NOTE: no plural

federal *adjective* referring to a system of government where a group of states are linked together in a federation; especially the central government of the United States; **most federal offices are in Washington**
◇ **the Fed** *noun US informal* = FEDERAL RESERVE BOARD
◇ **Federal Reserve Bank** *noun US* one of the twelve central banks in the USA which are owned by the state and directed by the Federal Reserve Board
◇ **Federal Reserve Board** *noun US* government organization which runs the central banks in the USA
◇ **federation** *noun* group of societies *or* companies *or* organizations which have a central organization which represents them and looks after their common interests; **federation of trades unions; employers' federation**

fee *noun* **(a)** money paid for work carried out by a professional person (such as an accountant *or* a doctor *or* a lawyer); **we charge a small fee for our services; director's fees; consultant's fee (b)** money paid for something; **entrance fee *or* admission fee; registration fee**

feed 1 *noun* device which puts paper into a printer *or* into a photocopier; **the paper feed has jammed; continuous feed** = device which feeds in continuous computer stationery into a printer; **sheet feed** = device which puts in one sheet at a time into a printer **2** *verb* to put information into a computer

NOTE: **feeding - fed**

◊ **feedback** *noun* information, especially about people's reactions; **have you any feedback from the sales force about the customers' reaction to the new model?**

NOTE: no plural

feint *noun* very light lines on writing paper

ferry *noun* boat which takes passengers or goods across water; **we are going to take the night ferry to Belgium; car ferry** = ferry which carries cars; **passenger ferry** = ferry which only carries passengers

fetch *verb* **(a)** to go to bring something; **we have to fetch the goods from the docks; it is cheaper to buy at a cash and carry warehouse, provided you have a car to fetch the goods yourself (b)** to be sold for a certain price; **to fetch a high price; it will not fetch more than £200; these computers fetch very high prices on the black market**

few *adjective & noun* **(a)** not many; **we sold so few of this item that we have discontinued the line; few of the staff stay with us more than six months (b) a few** = some; **a few of our salesmen drive Rolls-Royces; we get only a few orders in the period from Christmas to the New Year**

fiat *noun* **fiat money** = coins or notes which are not worth much as paper or metal, but are said by the government to have a value

fictitious *adjective* false *or* which do not exist; **fictitious assets** = assets which do not really exist, but are entered as assets to balance the accounts

fiddle 1 *noun informal* cheating; **it's all a fiddle; he's on the fiddle** = he is trying to cheat **2** *verb informal* to cheat; **he tried to fiddle his tax returns; the salesman was caught fiddling his expense account**

fide *see* BONA FIDE

fiduciary *adjective & noun* (person) acting as trustee for someone else

field *noun* **(a)** piece of ground on a farm; **the cows are in the field (b) in the field** = outside the office *or* among the customers; **we have sixteen reps in the field; first in the field** = first company to bring out a product *or* to start a service; **Smith Ltd has a great advantage in being first in the field with a reliable electric car; field sales manager** = manager in charge of a group of salesmen; **field work** = examination of the situation among possible customers; **he had to do a lot of field work to find the right market for the product**

FIFO = FIRST IN FIRST OUT

fifty-fifty *adjective & adverb* half; **to go fifty-fifty** = to share the costs equally; **he has a fifty-fifty chance of making a profit** = he has an equal chance of making a profit or a loss

figure *noun* **(a)** number *or* cost written in numbers; **the figure in the accounts for heating is very high; he put a very low figure on the value of the lease** = he calculated the value of the lease as very low **(b) figures** = written numbers; **sales figures** = total sales; **to work out the figures** = to calculate; **his income runs into five figures** *or* **he has a five-figure income** = his income is more than £10,000; **in round figures** = not totally accurate, but correct to the nearest 10 or 100; **they have a workforce of 2,500 in round figures (c) figures** = results for a company; **the figures for last year** *or* **last year's figures**

file 1 *noun* **(a)** cardboard holder for documents, which can fit in the drawer of a filing cabinet; **put these letters in the customer file; look in the file marked "Scottish sales"; box file** = cardboard box for holding documents **(b)** documents kept for reference; **to place something on file** = to keep a record of something; **to keep someone's name on file** = to keep someone's name on a list for reference; **file copy** = copy of a document which is kept for reference in an office; **card-index file** = information kept on filing cards **(c)** section of data on a computer (such as payroll, address list, customer accounts); **how can we protect our computer files? 2** *verb* **(a) to file documents** = to put documents in order so that they can be found easily; **the correspondence is filed**

under "complaints" **(b)** to make an official request; **to file a petition in bankruptcy** = to ask officially to be made bankrupt *or* to ask officially for someone else to be made bankrupt **(c)** to register something officially; **to file an application for a patent; to file a return to the tax office**
◊ **filing** *noun* documents which have to be put in order; **there is a lot of filing to do at the end of the week; the manager looked through the week's filing to see what letters had been sent; filing basket** *or* **filing tray** = container kept on a desk for documents which have to be filed; **filing cabinet** = metal box with several drawers for keeping files; **filing card** = card with information written on it, used to classify information into the correct order; **filing clerk** = clerk who files documents; **filing system** = way of putting documents in order for reference
NOTE: no plural

fill 1 *verb* **(a)** to make something full; **we have filled our order book with orders for Africa; the production department has filled the warehouse with unsellable products (b)** to fill a gap = to provide a product *or* service which is needed, but which no one has provided before; **the new range of small cars fills a gap in the market (c) to fill a post** *or* **a vacancy** = to find someone to do a job; **your application arrived too late - the post has already been filled**
◊ **filler** *noun* something which fills a space; **stocking filler** = small item which can be used to put into a Christmas stocking; *see* SHELF FILLER
◊ **fill in** *verb* to write in the blank spaces in a form; **fill in your name and address in block capitals**
◊ **filling station** *noun* place where you can buy petrol; **he stopped at the filling station to get some petrol before going on to the motorway**
◊ **fill out** *verb* to write the required information in the blank spaces in a form; **to get customs clearance you must fill out three forms**
◊ **fill up** *verb* **(a)** to make something completely full; **he filled up the car with petrol; my appointments book is completely filled up (b)** to finish writing on a form; **he filled up the form and sent it to the bank**

final *adjective* last *or* coming at the end of a period; **to pay the final instalment; to**

make the final payment; **to put the final details on a document; final date for payment** = last date by which payment should be made; **final demand** = last reminder from a supplier, after which he will sue for payment; **final discharge** = last payment of what is left of a debt; **final dividend** = dividend paid at the end of the year; **final product** = manufactured product, made at the end of a production process
◊ **finalize** *verb* to agree final details; **we hope to finalize the agreement tomorrow; after six weeks of negotiations the loan was finalized yesterday**
◊ **finally** *adverb* in the end; **the contract was finally signed yesterday; after weeks of trials the company finally accepted the computer system**

finance 1 *noun* **(a)** money used by a company, provided by the shareholders or by loans; **where will they get the necessary finance for the project?; finance company** *or* **finance corporation** *or* **finance house** = company which provides money for hire-purchase; **finance market** = place where large sums of money can be lent or borrowed; **high finance** = lending, investing and borrowing of very large sums of money, organized by financiers **(b)** money (of a club, local authority, etc.); **she is the secretary of the local authority finance committee (c) finances** = money *or* cash which is available; **the bad state of the company's finances** 2 *verb* to provide money to pay for something; **to finance an operation**
◊ **Finance Act** *noun GB* annual act of parliament which gives the government the power to obtain money from taxes as proposed in the Budget
◊ **financial** *adjective* concerning money; **financial adviser** = person *or* company which gives advice on financial matters for a fee; **financial assistance** = help in the form of money; **financial correspondent** = journalist who writes articles on money matters for a newspaper; **financial position** = state of a company's bank balance (assets and debts); **he must think of his financial position; financial resources** = money which is available for investment; **a company with strong financial resources; financial risk** = possibility of losing money; **there is no financial risk in selling**

to East European countries on credit;
financial statement = document which
shows the financial situation of a
company; **the accounts department has
prepared a financial statement for the
shareholders; Financial Times (Ordinary)
index** = index published by the "Financial
Times", giving share prices on the London
Stock Exchange based on a group of major
companies; **financial year** = the twelve
months' period for a firm's accounts

◇ **financially** *adverb* regarding money;
company which is financially sound =
company which is profitable and has
strong assets

◇ **financier** *noun* person who lends large
amounts of money to companies

◇ **financing** *noun* providing money; **the
financing of the project was done by two
international banks; deficit financing** =
planning by a government to borrow
money to cover the shortfall between
expenditure and income from taxation

find *verb* **(a)** to get something which was
not there before; **to find backing for a
project (b)** to make a legal decision in
court; **the tribunal found that both parties
were at fault; the judge found for the
defendant** = the judge decided that the
defendant was right
NOTE: finding - found

◇ **findings** *plural noun* **the findings of a
commission of enquiry** = the recommenda-
tions of the commission

◇ **find time** *verb* to make enough time to
do something; **we must find time to visit
the new staff sports club; the chairman never
finds enough time to play golf**

fine 1 *noun* money paid because of
something wrong which has been done;
**he was asked to pay a $25,000 fine; we had
to pay a $10 parking fine 2** *verb* to punish
someone by making him pay money; **to
fine someone £2,500 for obtaining money by
false pretences 3** *adverb* very thin *or* very
small; **we are cutting our margins very fine**
= we are reducing our margins to the
smallest possible

finish 1 *noun* **(a)** final appearance; **the
product has an attractive finish (b)** end of a
day's trading on the Stock Exchange; **oil
shares rallied at the finish 2** *verb* **(a)** to do
something *or* to make something

completely; **the order was finished in time;
she finished the test before all the other
candidates (b)** to come to an end; **the
contract is due to finish next month**

◇ **finished** *adjective* **finished goods** =
manufactured goods which are ready to be
sold

fink *noun US informal* worker hired to
replace a striking worker

fire 1 *noun* thing which burns; **the
shipment was damaged in the fire on board
the cargo boat; half the stock was destroyed
in the warehouse fire; to catch fire** = to
start to burn; **the papers in the waste paper
basket caught fire; fire damage** = damage
caused by fire; **he claimed £250 for fire
damage; fire-damaged goods** = goods
which have been damaged in a fire; **fire
door** = special door to prevent fire going
from one part of a building to another;
fire escape = door *or* stairs which allow
staff to get out of a building which is on
fire; **fire hazard** *or* **fire risk** = situation *or*
goods which could start a fire; **that
warehouse full of paper is a fire hazard; fire
insurance** = insurance against damage by
fire **2** *verb* **to fire someone** = to dismiss
someone from a job; **the new managing
director fired half the sales force; to hire
and fire** = to employ new staff and dismiss
existing staff very frequently

◇ **fireproof** *adjective* which cannot be
damaged by fire; **we packed the papers in a
fireproof safe; it is impossible to make the
office completely fireproof**

firm 1 *noun* business *or* partnership; **he is
a partner in a law firm; a manufacturing
firm; an important publishing firm
2** *adjective* **(a)** which cannot be changed;
**to make a firm offer for something; to place
a firm offer for two aircraft; they are
quoting a firm price of £1.22 per unit (b)**
not dropping in price, and possibly going
to rise; **sterling was firmer on the foreign
exchange markets; shares remained firm
3** *verb* to remain at a price and seem likely
to go up; **the shares firmed at £1.50**

◇ **firmness** *noun* being steady at a price
or being likely to rise; **the firmness of the
pound**

◇ **firm up** *verb* to finalize *or* to agree final
details; **we expect to firm up the deal at the
next trade fair**

first *noun* person *or* thing which is there at the beginning *or* earlier than others; **our company was one of the first to sell into the European market; first quarter** = three months' period from January to the end of March; **first half** *or* **first half-year** = six months' period from January to the end of June; **first in first out** = (i) redundancy policy, where the people who have been working longest are the first to be made redundant; (ii) accounting policy where stock is valued at the price of the oldest purchases

◊ **first-class** *adjective & noun* **(a)** top quality *or* most expensive; **he is a first-class accountant (b)** most expensive and comfortable type of travel *or* type of hotel; **to travel first-class; first-class travel provides the best service; a first-class ticket; to stay in first-class hotels; first-class mail** = *GB* most expensive mail service, designed to be faster; *US* mail service for letters and postcards; **a first-class letter should get to Scotland in a day**

◊ **first-line** *adjective* **first-line management** = the managers who have immediate contact with the workers

fiscal *adjective* referring to tax *or* to government revenues; **the government's fiscal policies; fiscal measures** = tax changes made by a government to improve the working of the economy; **fiscal year** = twelve-month period on which taxes are calculated (in the UK, April 6th to April 5th)

fit *verb* to be the right size for something; **the paper doesn't fit the typewriter**
NOTE: **fitting - fitted**

◊ **fit in** *verb* to make something go into a space; **will the computer fit into that little room? the chairman tries to fit in a game of golf every afternoon; my appointments diary is full, but I shall try to fit you in tomorrow afternoon**

◊ **fit out** *verb* to provide equipment *or* furniture for a business; **they fitted out the factory with computers; the shop was fitted out at a cost of £10,000; fitting out of a shop** = putting shelves *or* counters in for a new shop

◊ **fittings** *plural noun* items in a property which are sold with it but are not permanently fixed (such as carpets or shelves); **fixtures and fittings** = objects in a property which are sold with the property, both those which cannot be removed and those which can

fix *verb* **(a)** to arrange *or* to agree; **to fix a budget; to fix a meeting for 3 p.m.; the date has still to be fixed; the price of gold was fixed at $300; the mortgage rate has been fixed at 11% (b)** to mend; **the technicians are coming to fix the telephone switchboard; can you fix the photocopier?**

◊ **fixed** *adjective* permanent *or* which cannot be removed; **fixed assets** = property *or* machinery which a company owns and uses; **fixed capital** = capital in the form of buildings and machinery; **fixed costs** = costs paid to produce a product which do not increase with the amount of product made (such as rent); **fixed deposit** = deposit which pays a stated interest over a set period; **fixed expenses** = money which is spent regularly (such as rent, electricity, telephone); **fixed income** = income which does not change (as from an annuity); **fixed-interest investments** = investments producing an interest which does not change; **fixed-price agreement** = agreement where a company provides a service *or* a product at a price which stays the same for the whole period of the agreement; **fixed scale of charges** = rate of charging which cannot be altered

◊ **fixer** *noun informal* person who has a reputation for arranging business deals (often illegally)

◊ **fixing** *noun* **(a)** arranging; **fixing of charges; fixing of a mortgage rate (b)** price **fixing** = illegal agreement between companies to charge the same price for competing products **(c) the London gold fixing** = system where the world price for gold is set each day in London
NOTE: no plural

◇ **fixtures** *plural noun* items in a property which are permanently attached to it (such as sinks and lavatories); **fixtures and fittings** = objects in a property which are sold with the property, both those which cannot be removed and those which can

◇ **fix up with** *verb* to arrange; **my secretary fixed me up with a car at the airport; can you fix me up with a room for tomorrow night?**

flag 1 *noun* (a) piece of cloth with a design on it which shows which country it belongs to; **a ship flying a British flag; ship sailing under a flag of convenience =** ship flying the flag of a country which may have no ships of its own, but allows ships of other countries to be registered in its ports (b) mark which is attached to information in a computer so that the information can be found easily 2 *verb* to insert marks on information in a computer so that the information can be found easily
NOTE: **flagging - flagged**

flat 1 *adjective* (a) falling because of low demand; **the market was flat today** (b) fixed *or* not changing; **flat rate =** charge which always stays the same; **we pay a flat rate for electricity each quarter; he is paid a flat rate of £2 per thousand** 2 *noun* set of rooms for one family in a building with other sets of similar rooms; **he has a flat in the centre of town; she is buying a flat close to her office; company flat =** flat owned by a company and used by members of staff from time to time
NOTE: US English is **apartment**

◇ **flat out** *adverb* working hard *or* at full speed; **the factory worked flat out to complete the order on time**

flea market *noun* market, usually in the open air, for selling cheap secondhand goods

fleet *noun* group of cars belonging to a company and used by its staff; **a company's fleet of representatives' cars; a fleet car =** car which is one of a fleet of cars; **fleet discount =** specially cheap price for purchase or rental of a company's cars; **fleet rental =** renting all a company's cars at a special price

flexible *adjective* which can be altered *or* changed; **flexible budget; flexible prices;**

flexible pricing policy; flexible working hours = system where workers can start or stop work at different hours of the morning or evening provided that they work a certain number of hours per day or week; **we work flexible hours**

◇ **flexibility** *noun* being easily changed; **there is no flexibility in the company's pricing policy**
NOTE: no plural

◇ **flexitime** *noun* system where workers can start or stop work at different hours of the morning or evening, provided that they work a certain number of hours per day or week; **we work flexitime; the company introduced flexitime working two years ago**
NOTE: no plural

flier *or* **flyer** *noun* (a) **high flier =** (i) person who is very successful *or* who is likely to rise to a very important position; (ii) share whose market price is rising rapidly (b) small advertising leaflet designed to encourage customers to ask for more information about the product for sale

flight *noun* (a) journey by an aircraft, leaving at a regular time; **flight AC 267 is leaving from Gate 46; he missed his flight; I always take the afternoon flight to Rome; if you hurry you will catch the six o'clock flight to Paris** (b) rapid movement of money out of a country because of a lack of confidence in the country's economic future; **the flight of capital from Europe into the USA; the flight from the franc into the dollar** (c) series of steps; **top-flight =** in the most important position *or* very efficient; **top-flight managers can earn very high salaries**

flip chart *noun* way of showing information to a group of people by writing on large sheets of paper which can then be turned over to show the next sheet

float 1 *noun* (a) cash taken from a central supply and used for running expenses; **the sales reps have a float of £100 each; cash float =** cash put into the cash box at the beginning of the day to allow business to start; **we start the day with a £20 float in the cash desk** (b) starting a new company by selling shares in it on the Stock Exchange; **the float of the new company was a complete failure** 2 *verb* (a) to float a company = to start a new company by selling shares in it on the Stock Exchange; **to float a loan** = to raise a loan on the financial market by asking banks and companies to subscribe to it **(b)** to let a currency find its own exchange rate on the international markets and not be fixed; **the government has let sterling float; the government has decided to float the pound**

◇ **floating** 1 *noun* **(a) floating of a company** = starting a new company by selling shares in it on the Stock Exchange **(b) the floating of the pound** = letting the pound find its own exchange rate on the international market
NOTE: no plural
2 *adjective* which is not fixed; **floating exchange rates; the floating pound**

> QUOTE: in a world of floating exchange rates the dollar is strong because of capital inflows rather than weak because of the nation's trade deficit *Duns Business Month*

flood 1 *noun* large quantity; **we received a flood of orders; floods of tourists filled the hotels** 2 *verb* to fill with a large quantity of something; **the market was flooded with cheap imitations; the sales department is flooded with orders** *or* **with complaints**

floor *noun* **(a)** part of the room which you walk on; **floor space** = area of floor in an office *or* warehouse; **we have 3,500 square metres of floor space to let; the factory floor** = main works of a factory; **on the shop floor** = in the works *or* in the factory *or* among the ordinary workers; **the feeling on the shop floor is that the manager does not know his job (b)** all rooms on one level in a building; **the shoe department is on the first floor; her office is on the 26th floor;** *US* **floor manager** = person in charge of the sales staff in a department store
NOTE: the numbering of floors is different in GB and the USA. The floor at street level is the **ground floor** in GB, but the **first floor** in the USA. Each floor in the USA is one number higher than the same floor in GB.
◇ **floorwalker** *noun* employee of a department store who advises the customers, and supervises the shop assistants in a department

flop 1 *noun* failure *or* not being a success; **the new model was a flop** 2 *verb* to fail *or* not

to be a success; **the flotation of the new company flopped badly**
NOTE: flopping - flopped
◇ **floppy** 1 *adjective* **floppy disk** = small disk for storing information in a computer 2 *noun* small disk for storing computer information; **the data is on 5 inch floppies**

flotation *noun* **the flotation of a new company** = starting a new company by selling shares in it

flotsam *noun* **flotsam and jetsam** = rubbish floating in the water after a ship has been wrecked and rubbish washed on to the land
NOTE: no plural

flourish *verb* to be prosperous *or* to do well in business; **the company is flourishing; trade with Nigeria flourished**
◇ **flourishing** *adjective* profitable; **flourishing trade** = trade which is expanding profitably; **he runs a flourishing shoe business**

flow 1 *noun* **(a)** movement; **the flow of capital into a country; the flow of investments into Japan (b) cash flow** = cash which comes into a company from sales and goes out in purchases or overhead expenditure; **discounted cash flow** = calculation of forecast sales of a product in current terms with reductions for current interest rates; **the company is suffering from cash flow problems** = cash income is not coming in fast enough to pay for the expenditure going out **(c) flow chart** *or* **flow diagram** = chart which shows the arrangement of work processes in a series 2 *verb* to move smoothly; **production is now flowing normally after the strike**

fluctuate *verb* to move up and down; **prices fluctuate between £1.10 and £1.25; the pound fluctuated all day on the foreign exchange markets**
◇ **fluctuating** *adjective* moving up and down; **fluctuating dollar prices**
◇ **fluctuation** *noun* up and down movement; **the fluctuations of the franc; the fluctuations of the exchange rate**

fly *verb* to move through the air in an aircraft; **the chairman is flying to Germany on business; the overseas sales manager flies**

about 100,000 miles a year visiting the agents

◊ **fly-by-night** *adjective* company which is not reliable *or* which might disappear to avoid paying debts; **I want a reputable builder, not one of these fly-by-night outfits**

FOB *or* **f.o.b.** = FREE ON BOARD

fold *verb* (a) to bend a flat thing, so that part of it is on top of the rest; **she folded the letter so that the address was clearly visible** (b) *informal* **to fold (up)** = to stop trading; **the business folded up last December; the company folded with debts of over £1m**

◊ **-fold** *suffix* times; **four-fold** = four times

> QUOTE: the company's sales have nearly tripled and its profits have risen seven-fold since 1982
> *Barrons*

◊ **folder** *noun* cardboard envelope for carrying papers; **put all the documents in a folder for the chairman**

folio 1 *noun* page with a number, especially two facing pages in an account book which have the same number 2 *verb* to put a number on a page

follow *verb* to come behind *or* to come afterwards; **the samples will follow by surface mail; we will pay £10,000 down, with the balance to follow in six months' time**

◊ **follow up** *verb* to examine something further; **I'll follow up your idea of putting our address list on to the computer; to follow up an initiative** = to take action once someone else has decided to do something

◊ **follow-up letter** *noun* letter sent to someone who has not acted on the instructions in a previous letter, or to discuss in more detail points which were raised earlier

food *noun* things which are eaten; **he is very fond of Indian food; the food in the staff restaurant is excellent**

◊ **foodstuffs** *plural noun* **essential foodstuffs** = very important food, such as bread or rice

foolscap *noun* large size of writing paper; **the letter was on six sheets of foolscap; a foolscap envelope** = large envelope which takes foolscap paper
NOTE: no plural

foot 1 *noun* (a) part of the body at the end of the leg; **on foot** = walking; **the reps make most of their central London calls on foot; the rush hour traffic is so bad that it is quicker to go to the office on foot** (b) bottom part; **he signed his name at the foot of the invoice** (c) measurement of length (= 30cm); **the table is six feet long; my office is ten feet by twelve**
NOTE: the plural is **feet** for (a) and (c); there is no plural for (b). In measurements, **foot** is usually written **ft** or **'** after figures: **10ft; 10'**
2 *verb* (a) **to foot the bill** = to pay the bill; **the director footed the bill for the department's Christmas party** (b) *US* **to foot up an account** = to add up a column of numbers

forbid *verb* to tell someone not to do something *or* to say that something must not be done; **the contract forbids resale of the goods to the USA; the staff are forbidden to use the front entrance**
NOTE: forbidding - forbade - forbidden

force 1 *noun* (a) strength; **to be in force** = to be operating *or* working; **the rules have been in force since 1946; to come into force** = to start to operate *or* work; **the new regulations will come into force on January 1st** (b) group of people; **labour force** *or* **workforce** = all the workers in a company *or* in an area; **the management has made an increased offer to the labour force; we are opening a new factory in the Far East because of the cheap local labour force; sales force** = group of salesmen (c) **force majeure** = something which happens which is out of the control of the parties who have signed a contract (such as strike, war, storm)
NOTE: no plural for (a) and (c)
2 *verb* to make someone do something; **competition has forced the company to lower its prices**

◊ **forced** *adjective* **forced sale** = sale which takes place because a court orders it *or* because it is the only way to avoid a financial crisis

◊ **force down** *verb* to make something become lower; **to force prices down** = to make prices come down; **competition has forced prices down**

◇ **force up** *verb* to make something become higher; **to force prices up** = to make prices go up; **the war forced up the price of oil**

forecast 1 *noun* description *or* calculation of what will probably happen in the future; **the chairman did not believe the sales director's forecast of higher turnover; we based our calculations on the forecast turnover; cash flow forecast** = forecast of when cash will be received or paid out; **population forecast** = calculation of how many people will be living in a country *or* in a town at some point in the future; **sales forecast** = calculation of future sales 2 *verb* to calculate *or* to say what will probably happen in the future; **he is forecasting sales of £2m; economists have forecast a fall in the exchange rate**
NOTE: **forecasting - forecast**
◇ **forecasting** *noun* calculating what will probably happen in the future; **manpower forecasting** = calculating how many workers will be needed in the future, and how many will actually be available
NOTE: no plural

foreclose *verb* to sell a property because the owner cannot repay money which he has borrowed (using the property as security); **to foreclose on a mortgaged property**
◇ **foreclosure** *noun* act of foreclosing

foreign *adjective* not belonging to one's own country; **foreign cars have flooded our market; we are increasing our trade with foreign countries; foreign currency** = money of another country; **foreign goods** = goods manufactured in other countries; **foreign investments** = money invested in other countries; **foreign money order** = money order in a foreign currency which is payable to someone living in a foreign country; **foreign trade** = trade with other countries
◇ **foreign exchange** *noun* **(a)** exchanging the money of one country for that of another; **foreign exchange broker** *or* **dealer** = person who deals on the foreign exchange market; **foreign exchange dealing** = buying and selling foreign currencies; **the foreign exchange markets** = market where people buy and sell foreign currencies; **foreign exchange reserves** = foreign money held by a

government to support its own currency and pay its debts; **foreign exchange transfer** = sending of money from one country to another
◇ **foreigner** *noun* person from another country

> QUOTE: the dollar recovered a little lost ground on the foreign exchanges yesterday
> *Financial Times*
> QUOTE: a sharp setback in foreign trade accounted for most of the winter slowdown *Fortune*
> QUOTE: the treasury says it needs the cash to rebuild its foreign reserves which have fallen from $19 billion when the government took office to $7 billion in August *Economist*

foreman *or* **forewoman** *noun* skilled worker in charge of several other workers
NOTE: plural is **foremen** *or* **forewomen**

forex *or* **Forex** = FOREIGN EXCHANGE

> QUOTE: the amount of reserves sold by the authorities were not sufficient to move the $200 billion Forex market permanently
> *Duns Business Month*

forfeit 1 *noun* taking something away as a punishment; **forfeit clause** = clause in a contract which says that goods *or* deposit will be taken away if the contract is not obeyed; **the goods were declared forfeit** = the court said that the goods had to be taken away from their owner 2 *verb* to have something taken away as a punishment; **to forfeit a patent** = to lose a patent because payments have not been made; **to forfeit a deposit** = to lose a deposit which was left for an item because you have decided not to buy that item
◇ **forfeiture** *noun* act of forfeiting a property
NOTE: no plural

forge *verb* to copy money or a signature illegally *or* to make a document which looks like a real one; **he tried to enter the country with forged documents**
◇ **forgery** *noun* **(a)** making an illegal copy; **he was sent to prison for forgery**
NOTE: no plural **(b)** illegal copy; **the signature was proved to be a forgery**

forget *verb* not to remember; **she forgot to put a stamp on the envelope; don't forget we're having lunch together tomorrow**
NOTE: **forgetting - forgot - forgotten**

fork-lift truck *noun* type of small tractor with two metal arms in front, used for lifting and moving pallets

form 1 *noun* **(a) form of words** = words correctly laid out for a legal document; **receipt in due form** = correctly written receipt **(b)** official printed paper with blank spaces which have to be filled in with information; **you have to fill in form A20; customs declaration form; a pad of order forms; application form** = form which has to be filled in to apply for something; **claim form** = form which has to be filled in when making an insurance claim **2** *verb* to start *or* to organize; **the brothers have formed a new company**

◊ **formation** *or* **forming** *noun* act of organizing; **the formation of a new company**
NOTE: no plural

forma *see* PRO FORMA

formal *adjective* clearly and legally written; **to make a formal application; to send a formal order**

◊ **formality** *noun* something which has to be done to obey the law; **customs formalities** = declaration of goods by the shipper and examination of them by the customs

◊ **formally** *adverb* in a formal way; **we have formally applied for planning permission for the new shopping precinct**

former *adjective* before *or* at an earlier time; **the former chairman has taken a job with the rival company**

◊ **formerly** *adverb* at an earlier time; **he is currently managing director of Smith Ltd, but formerly he worked for Jones**

fortnight *noun* two weeks; **I saw him a fortnight ago; we will be on holiday during the last fortnight of July**

fortune *noun* large amount of money; **he made a fortune from investing in oil shares; she left her fortune to her three children**

forward 1 *adjective* in advance *or* to be paid at a later date; **forward buying** *or* **buying forward** = buying shares *or* currency *or* commodities at today's price for delivery at a later date; **forward contract** = agreement to buy foreign currency *or* shares *or* commodities at a later date at a certain price; **forward market** = market for purchasing foreign currency *or* oil *or* commodities for delivery at a later date; **forward (exchange) rate** = rate for purchase of foreign currency at a fixed price for delivery at a later date; **what are the forward rates for the pound?; forward sales** = sales for delivery at a later date **2** *adverb* **(a) to date a cheque forward** = to put a later date than the present one on a cheque; **carriage forward** *or* **freight forward** = deal where the customer pays for transporting the goods; **charges forward** = charges which will be paid by the customer **(b) to buy forward** = to buy foreign currency before you need it, in order to be certain of the exchange rate; **to sell forward** = to sell foreign currency for delivery at a later date **(c) balance brought forward** *or* **carried forward** = balance which is entered in an account at the end of a period and is then taken to be the starting point of the next period **3** *verb* **to forward something to someone** = to send something to someone; **to forward a consignment to Nigeria; please forward** *or* **to be forwarded** = words written on an envelope, asking the person receiving it to send it on to the person whose name is written on it

◊ **(freight) forwarder** *noun* person *or* company which arranges shipping and customs documents for several shipments from different companies, putting them together to form one large shipment

◊ **forwarding** *noun* **(a)** arranging shipping and customs documents; **air forwarding** = arranging for goods to be shipped by air; **forwarding agent** = FORWARDER **forwarding instructions** *or* **instructions for forwarding** = instructions showing how the goods are to be shipped and delivered **(b) forwarding address** = address to which a person's mail can be sent on
NOTE: no plural

foul *adjective* **foul bill of lading** = bill of lading which says that the goods were in bad condition when received by the shipper

founder *noun* person who starts a company; **founder's shares** = special shares issued to the person who starts a company

fourth *adjective* coming after third; **fourth quarter** = period of three months from October to the end of the year

Fr = FRANC

fraction *noun* very small amount; **only a fraction of the new share issue was subscribed**
◇ **fractional** *adjective* very small; **fractional certificate** = certificate for part of a share

fragile *adjective* which can be easily broken; **there is an extra premium for insuring fragile goods in shipment**

franc *noun* money used in France, Belgium, Switzerland and many other countries; **French francs** *or* **Belgian francs** *or* **Swiss francs; it costs twenty-five Swiss francs; franc account** = bank account in francs
NOTE: in English usually written **Fr** before the figure: **Fr2,500** (say: "two thousand, five hundred francs"). Currencies of different countries can be shown by the initial letters of the countries: **FFr** (French francs); **SwFr** (Swiss francs); **BFr** (Belgian francs)

franchise 1 *noun* licence to trade using a brand name and paying a royalty for it; **he has bought a printing franchise** *or* **a hot dog franchise** 2 *verb* to sell licences for people to trade using a brand name and paying a royalty; **his sandwich bar was so successful that he decided to franchise it**
◇ **franchisee** *noun* person who runs a franchise
◇ **franchiser** *noun* person who licenses a franchise
◇ **franchising** *noun* act of selling a licence to trade as a franchise; **he runs his sandwich chain as a franchising operation**
NOTE: no plural
◇ **franchisor** *noun* = FRANCHISER

franco *adverb* free

frank *verb* to stamp the date and postage on a letter; **franking machine** = machine which marks the date and postage on letters so that the sender does not need to use stamps

fraud *noun* making money by making people believe something which is not true; **he got possession of the property by fraud; he was accused of frauds relating to foreign currency; to obtain money by fraud** = to obtain money by saying or doing something to cheat someone; **fraud squad** = special police department which investigates frauds
◇ **fraudulent** *adjective* not honest *or* aiming to cheat people; **a fraudulent transaction**
◇ **fraudulently** *adverb* not honestly; **goods imported fraudulently**

free 1 *adjective & adverb* **(a)** not costing any money; **to be given a free ticket to the exhibition; the price includes free delivery; goods are delivered free; catalogue sent free on request; carriage free** = the customer does not pay for the shipping; **free gift** = present given by a shop to a customer who buys a certain amount of goods; **there is a free gift worth £25 to any customer buying a washing machine; free sample** = sample given free to advertise a product; **free trial** = testing of a machine with no payment involved; **to send a piece of equipment for two weeks' free trial; free of charge** = with no payment to be made; **free on board** = (i) price including all the seller's costs until the goods are on the ship for transportation; (ii) *US* price includes all the seller's costs until the goods are delivered to a certain place; **free on rail** = price including all the seller's costs until the goods are delivered to the railway for shipment **(b)** with no restrictions; **free collective bargaining** = negotiations over wage increases and working conditions between the management and the trade unions; **free competition** = being free to compete without government interference; **free currency** = currency which is allowed by the government to be bought and sold without restriction; **free enterprise** = system of business with no interference from the government; **free market economy** = system where the government does not interfere in business activity in any way; **free port** *or* **free trade zone** = port *or* area where there are no customs duties; **free of tax** *or* **tax-free** = with no tax having to be paid; **he was given a tax-free sum of £25,000 when he was made redundant; interest free of tax** *or* **tax-free interest; interest-free credit** *or* **loan** =

credit _or_ loan where no interest is paid by the borrower; **free of duty** _or_ **duty-free** = with no duty to be paid; **to import wine free of duty** _or_ **duty-free**; **free trade** = system where goods can go from one country to another without any restrictions; **the government adopted a free trade policy**; **free trade area** = group of countries practising free trade; **free trader** = person who is in favour of free trade **(c)** not busy _or_ not occupied; **are there any free tables in the restaurant? I shall be free in a few minutes; the chairman always keeps Friday afternoon free for a game of bridge** **2** _verb_ to make something available _or_ easy; **the government's decision has freed millions of pounds for investment**

QUOTE: American business as a whole is increasingly free from heavy dependence on manufacturing   _Sunday Times_
QUOTE: can free trade be reconciled with a strong dollar resulting from floating exchange rates?   _Duns Business Month_
QUOTE: free traders hold that the strong dollar is the primary cause of the nation's trade problems   _Duns Business Month_

◇ **freehold** _noun_ **freehold property** = property which the owner holds for ever and on which no rent is paid

◇ **freeholder** _noun_ person who owns a freehold property

◇ **freelance** **1** _adjective & noun_ independent worker who works for several different companies but is not employed by any of them; **we have about twenty freelances working for us** _or_ **about twenty people working for us on a freelance basis; she is a freelance journalist 2** _adverb_ selling one's work to various firms, but not being employed by any of them; **he works freelance as a designer 3** _verb_ **(a)** to do work for several firms but not be employed by any of them; **she freelances for the local newspapers (b)** to send work out to be done by a freelancer; **we freelance work out to several specialists**

◇ **freelancer** _noun_ freelance worker

◇ **freely** _adverb_ with no restrictions; **money should circulate freely within the Common Market**

◇ **freephone** _noun_ _GB_ system where one can telephone to reply to an advertisement _or_ to place an order _or_ to ask for information and the seller pays for the call

◇ **freepost** _noun_ _GB_ system where one can write to an advertiser _or_ to place an order _or_ to ask for information to be sent, and the seller pays the postage

freeze **1** _noun_ **credit freeze** = period when lending by banks is restricted by the government; **wages and prices freeze** _or_ a **freeze on wages and prices** = period when wages and prices are not allowed to be increased **2** _verb_ to keep money _or_ costs, etc., at their present level and not allow them to rise; **we have frozen expenditure at last year's level; to freeze wages and prices; to freeze credits; to freeze company dividends**
NOTE: **freezing - froze - has frozen**
◇ **freeze out** _verb_ **to freeze out competition** = to trade successfully and cheaply and so prevent competitors from operating

freight **1** _noun_ **(a)** cost of transporting goods by air, sea or land; **at an auction, the buyer pays the freight; freight charges** _or_ **freight rates** = money charged for transporting goods; **freight charges have gone up sharply this year; freight costs** = money paid to transport goods; **freight forward** = deal where the customer pays for transporting the goods **(b) air freight** = shipping of goods in an aircraft; **to send a shipment by air freight; air freight charges** _or_ **rates** = money charged for sending goods by air **(c)** goods which are transported; **to take on freight** = to load goods onto a ship, train or truck; _US_ **freight car** = railway wagon for carrying goods; **freight depot** = central point where goods are collected before being shipped; **freight elevator** = strong lift for carrying goods; **freight plane** = aircraft which carries goods, not passengers; **freight train** = train used for carrying goods **2** _verb_ **to freight goods** = to send goods; **we freight goods to all parts of the USA**

◇ **freightage** _noun_ cost of transporting goods

◇ **freighter** _noun_ **(a)** aircraft or ship which carries goods **(b)** person _or_ company which organizes the transport of goods

◇ **freightliner** _noun_ train which carries goods in containers; **the shipment has to be delivered to the freightliner depot**

frequent *adjective* which comes *or* goes *or* takes place often; **there is a frequent ferry service to France; we send frequent telexes to New York; how frequent are the planes to Birmingham?**
◊ **frequently** *adverb* often; **the photocopier is frequently out of use; we telex our New York office very frequently - at least four times a day**

friendly society *noun* group of people who pay regular subscriptions which are used to help members of the group when they are ill or in financial difficulties

fringe benefits *plural noun* extra items given by a company to workers in addition to a salary (such as company cars, private health insurance)

front *noun* **(a)** part of something which faces away from the back; **the front of the office building is on the High Street; the front page of the company report has a photograph of the managing director; our ad appeared on the front page of the newspaper (b) in front of** = before *or* on the front side of something; **they put up a "for sale" sign in front of the factory; the chairman's name is in front of all the others on the staff list (c)** business or person used to hide an illegal trade; **his restaurant is a front for a drugs organization (d) money up front** = payment in advance; **they are asking for £10,000 up front before they will consider the deal; he had to put money up front before he could clinch the deal**
◊ **front-line** *adjective* **front-line management** = managers who have immediate contact with the workers
◊ **front man** *noun* person who seems honest but is hiding an illegal trade

frozen *adjective* not allowed to be changed or used; **frozen account** = bank account where the money cannot be changed or used because of a court order; **frozen assets** = a company's assets which by law cannot be sold because someone has a claim against them; **frozen credits** = credit in an account which cannot be moved; **his assets have been frozen by the court** = the court does not allow him to sell his assets; *see also* FREEZE

ft = FOOT

fuel **1** *noun* material (like oil, coal, gas) used to give power; **the annual fuel bill for the plant has doubled over the last years; he has bought a car with low fuel consumption 2** *verb* to add to; **market worries were fuelled by news of an increase in electricity charges; the rise in the share price was fuelled by rumours of a takeover bid**

fulfil *or* *US* **fulfill** *verb* to complete something in a satisfactory way; **the clause regarding payments has not been fulfilled; to fulfil an order** = to supply the items which have been ordered; **we are so understaffed that we cannot fulfil any more orders before Christmas**
◊ **fulfilment** *noun* carrying something out in a satisfactory way; **order fulfilment** = supplying items which have been ordered

full *adjective* **(a)** with as much inside it as possible; **the train was full of commuters; is the container full yet? we sent a lorry full of spare parts to our warehouse; when the disk is full, don't forget to make a backup copy (b)** complete *or* including everything; **we are working at full capacity** = we are doing as much work as possible; **full costs** = all the costs of manufacturing a product, including both fixed and variable costs; **full cover** = insurance cover against all risks; **in full discharge of a debt** = paying a debt completely; **full employment** = situation where all the people who can work have jobs; **full fare** = ticket for a journey by an adult at full price; **full price** = price with no discount; **he bought a full-price ticket (c) in full** = completely; **give your full name and address** *or* **your name and address in full; he accepted all our conditions in full; full refund** *or* **refund paid in full; he got a full refund when he complained about the service; full payment** *or* **payment in full** = paying all money owed
◊ **full-scale** *adjective* complete *or* very thorough; **the MD ordered a full-scale review of credit terms**
◊ **full-time** *adjective & adverb* working all the normal working time (i.e. about eight hours a day, five days a week); **she is in full-time work** *or* **she works full-time** *or* **she is in full-time employment; he is one of our full-time staff**
◊ **full-timer** *noun* person who works full-time

◇ **fully** *adverb* completely; **fully-paid shares** = shares where the full face value has been paid; **fully paid-up capital** = all money paid for the issued capital shares

QUOTE: a tax-free lump sum can be taken partly in lieu of a full pension *Investors Chronicle*
QUOTE: issued and fully paid capital is $100 million *Hongkong Standard*
QUOTE: the administration launched a full-scale investigation into maintenance procedures *Fortune*

function 1 *noun* duty *or* job; **management function** *or* **function of management** = the duties of being a manager **2** *verb* to work; **the advertising campaign is functioning smoothly; the new management structure does not seem to be functioning very well**

fund 1 *noun* money set aside for a special purpose; **contingency fund** = money set aside in case it is needed urgently; **pension fund** = money which provides pensions for retired members of staff; **the International Monetary Fund** = (part of the United Nations) a type of bank which helps member states in financial difficulties, gives financial advice to members and encourages world trade **2** *plural noun* **(a)** money which is available for spending; **the company has no funds to pay for the research programme; the company called for extra funds** = the company asked for more money; **to run out of funds** = to come to end of the money available; **public funds** = government money available for expenditure; **the cost was paid for out of public funds; conversion of funds** = using money which does not belong to you for a purpose for which it is not supposed to be used; **to convert funds to another purpose** = to use money for a wrong purpose; **to convert funds to one's own use** = to use someone else's money for yourself **(b)** *GB* **the Funds** = government stocks and securities **3** *verb* to provide money for a purpose; **to fund a company** = to provide money for a company to operate; **the company does not have enough resources to fund its expansion programme**

◇ **funded** *adjective* backed by long-term loans; **long-term funded capital;** *GB* **funded debt** = part of the National Debt which pays interest, but where there is no date for repayment of the principal

◇ **funding** *noun* **(a)** providing money for spending; **the bank is providing the funding for the new product launch (b)** changing a short-term debt into a long-term loan; **the capital expenditure programme requires long-term funding**
NOTE: no plural

QUOTE: the S&L funded all borrowers' development costs, including accrued interest *Barrons*
QUOTE: small innovative companies have been hampered for lack of funds *Sunday Times*
QUOTE: the company was set up with funds totalling NorKr 145m *Lloyd's List*

furnish *verb* **(a)** to supply *or* to provide **(b)** to put furniture into an office *or* room; **he furnished his office with secondhand chairs and desks; the company spent £10,000 on furnishing the chairman's office; furnished accommodation** = flat *or* house, etc. which is let with furniture in it

furniture *noun* chairs, tables, beds, etc.; **office furniture** = chairs, desks, filing cabinets used in an office; **he deals in secondhand office furniture; an office furniture store; furniture depository** = warehouse where you can store the furniture from a house

further 1 *adjective* **(a)** at a larger distance away; **the office is further down the High Street; the flight from Paris terminates in New York - for further destinations you must change to internal flights (b)** additional *or* extra; **further orders will be dealt with by our London office; nothing can be done while we are awaiting further instructions; to ask for further details** *or* **particulars; he had borrowed £100,000 and then tried to borrow a further £25,000; the company is asking for further credit; he asked for a further six weeks to pay (c) further to** = referring to something in addition; **further to our letter of the 21st** = in addition to what we said in our letter; **further to your letter of the 21st** = here is information which you asked for in your letter; **further to our telephone conversation** = here is some information which we discussed **2** *verb* to help *or* to promote; **he was accused of using his membership of the council to further his own interests**

future **1** *adjective* referring to time to come *or* to something which has not yet happened; **future delivery** = delivery at a later date **2** *noun* time which has not yet happened; **try to be more careful in future; in future all reports must be sent to Australia by air**

◇ **futures** *plural noun* trading in shares or commodities for delivery at a later date; **gold rose 5% on the commodity futures market yesterday**

Gg

g = GRAM

gain **1** *noun* **(a)** increase *or* becoming larger; **gain in experience** = getting more experience; **gain in profitability** = becoming more profitable **(b)** increase in profit *or* price *or* value; **oil shares showed gains on the Stock Exchange; property shares put on gains of 10%-15%; capital gains** = money made by selling a fixed asset; **capital gains tax** = tax paid on capital gains; **short-term gains** = increase in price made over a short period **2** *verb* **(a)** to get *or* to obtain; **he gained some useful experience working in a bank; to gain control of a business** = to buy more than 50% of the shares so that you can direct the business **(b)** to rise in value; **the dollar gained six points on the foreign exchange markets**

◇ **gainful** *adjective* **gainful employment** = employment which pays money

◇ **gainfully** *adverb* **gainfully employed** = working and earning money

gallon *noun* measure of liquids (= 4.5 litres); **the car does twenty-five miles per gallon** *or* **the car does twenty-five miles to the gallon** = the car uses one gallon of petrol in travelling twenty-five miles
NOTE: usually written **gal** after figures: **25gal**

galloping inflation *noun* very rapid inflation which is almost impossible to reduce

gap *noun* empty space; **gap in the market** = opportunity to make a product which is needed but which no one has sold before; **to look for** *or* **to find a gap in the market; this computer has filled a real gap in the market; dollar gap** = situation where the supply of dollars is not enough to satisfy the demand for them from overseas buyers; **trade gap** = difference in value between a country's imports and exports

> QUOTE: these savings are still not great enough to overcome the price gap between American products and those of other nations
> *Duns Business Month*

gate *noun* **(a)** door leading into a field **(b)** door leading to an aircraft at an airport; **flight AZ270 is now boarding at Gate 23** **(c)** number of people attending a sports match; **there was a gate of 50,000 at the football final**

gather *verb* **(a)** to collect together *or* to put together; **he gathered his papers together before the meeting started; she has been gathering information on import controls from various sources** **(b)** to understand *or* to find out; **I gather he has left the office; did you gather who will be at the meeting?**

GATT = GENERAL AGREEMENT ON TARIFFS AND TRADE

gazump *verb* **he was gazumped** = his agreement to buy the house was cancelled because someone offered more money

◇ **gazumping** *noun* offering more money for a house than another buyer has done, so as to be sure of buying it

GDP = GROSS DOMESTIC PRODUCT

gear *verb* **(a)** to link to *or* to connect with; **bank interest rates are geared to American interest rates; salary geared to the cost of living** = salary which rises as the cost of living increases **(b) a company which is highly geared** *or* **a highly-geared company** = company which has a high proportion of its funds from fixed-interest borrowings

◇ **gear up** *verb* to get ready; **to gear up for a sales drive** = to make all the plans and get ready for a sales drive; **the company is gearing itself up for expansion into the African market**

◇ **gearing** *noun* **(a)** ratio between a company's capital borrowed at fixed interest and the value of its ordinary shares **(b)** borrowing money at fixed interest which is then used to produce more money than the interest paid
NOTE: no plural

general *adjective* **(a)** ordinary *or* not special; **general expenses** = all kinds of minor expenses *or* money spent on the day-to-day costs of running a business; **general manager** = manager in charge of the administration of a company; **general office** = main administrative office of a company **(b)** dealing with everything *or* with everybody; **general audit** = examining all the books and accounts of a company; **general average** = sharing of the cost of lost goods between all parties to an insurance; **general election** = election of a government by all the voters in a country; **general meeting** = meeting of all the shareholders of a company; **general strike** = strike of all the workers in a country; **Annual General Meeting** = meeting of all the shareholders, when the company's financial situation is discussed with the directors; **Extraordinary General Meeting** = special meeting of shareholders to discuss an important matter **(c) the General Agreement on Tariffs and Trade** = international organization which aims to try to reduce restrictions in trade between countries **(d) general trading** = dealing in all types of goods; **general store** = small country shop which sells a large range of goods

◇ **generally** *adverb* normally *or* usually; the office is generally closed between Christmas and the New Year; we generally give a 25% discount for bulk purchases

generous *adjective* (person) who is glad to give money; the staff contributed a generous sum for the retirement present for the manager

gentleman *noun* **(a)** "gentlemen" = way of starting to talk to a group of men; "good morning, gentlemen; if everyone is here, the meeting can start"; "well, gentlemen, we have all read the report from our Australian office"; "ladies and gentlemen" = way of starting to talk to a group of women and men **(b)** man; **gentleman's agreement** *or* *US* **gentlemen's agreement** = verbal agreement between two parties who respect each other; they have a gentleman's agreement not to trade in each other's area

genuine *adjective* true *or* real; this old table is genuine; a genuine leather purse; **the genuine article** = real article, not an imitation; **genuine purchaser** = someone who is really interested in buying

◇ **genuineness** *noun* being real *or* not being an imitation

get *verb* **(a)** to receive; we got a letter from the solicitor this morning; when do you expect to get more stock? he gets £250 a week for doing nothing; she got £5,000 for her car **(b)** to arrive at a place; the shipment got to Canada six weeks late; she finally got to the office at 10.30
NOTE: **getting - got - has got** *or* *US* **gotten**

◇ **get across** *verb* to make someone understand something; the manager tried to get across to the workforce why some people were being made redundant

◇ **get along** *verb* to manage; we are getting along quite well with only half the staff

◇ **get back** *verb* to receive something which you had before; I got my money back after I had complained to the manager; he got his initial investment back in two months

◇ **get on** *verb* **(a)** to work *or* to manage; how is the new secretary getting on? **(b)** to succeed; my son is getting on well - he has just been promoted

◇ **get on with** *verb* **(a)** to be friendly *or* to work well with someone; she does not get on with her new boss **(b)** to go on doing work; the staff got on with the work and finished the order on time

◇ **get out** *verb* **(a)** to produce something (on time); the accounts department got out the draft accounts in time for the meeting **(b)** to sell an investment; he didn't like the annual report, so he got out before the company collapsed

◇ **get out of** *verb* to stop trading in (a product *or* an area); the company is getting out of computers; we got out of the South American market

◇ **get round** *verb* to avoid; we tried to get round the embargo by shipping from Canada

◇ **get through** *verb* (a) to speak to someone on the phone; **I tried to get through to the complaints department** (b) to be successful; **he got through his exams, so he is now a qualified engineer** (c) to try to make someone understand; **I could not get through to her that I had to be at the airport by 2.15**

gift *noun* thing given to someone; **gift coupon** *or* **gift token** *or* **gift voucher** = card, bought in a store, which is given as a present and which must be exchanged in that store for goods; **we gave her a gift token for her birthday; gift shop** = shop selling small items which are given as presents; **gift inter vivos** = present given to another living person; **free gift** = present given by a shop to a customer who buys a certain amount of goods

◇ **gift-wrap** *verb* to wrap a present in attractive paper; **do you want this book gift-wrapped?**

◇ **gift-wrapping** *noun* (a) service in a store for wrapping presents for customers (b) attractive paper for wrapping presents

gilts *plural noun* *GB* government securities

◇ **gilt-edged** *adjective* investment which is very safe; **gilt-edged stock** *or* **securities** = government securities

gimmick *noun* clever idea *or* trick; **a publicity gimmick; the PR men thought up this new advertising gimmick**

giro *noun* **the giro system** = banking system in which money can be transferred from one account to another without writing a cheque; *GB* **National Giro** = banking system, run by the Post Office, which allows account holders to move money from one account to another free of cost; **a giro cheque; giro account; giro account number; she put £25 into her giro account; to pay by bank giro transfer**

◇ **Girobank** *noun* bank in a giro system; **a National Girobank account**

give *verb* (a) to pass something to someone as a present; **the office gave him a clock when he retired** (b) to pass something to someone; **she gave the documents to the accountant; can you give me some information about the new computer system? do not**

give any details to the police (c) to organize; **the company gave a party on a boat to publicize its new discount system** NOTE: **giving - gave - has given**

◇ **give away** *verb* to give something as a free present; **we are giving away a pocket calculator with each £10 of purchases**

◇ **giveaway** 1 *adjective* **to sell at giveaway prices** = to sell at very cheap prices 2 *noun* thing which is given as a free gift when another item is bought

glue 1 *noun* material which sticks items together; **she put some glue on the back of the poster to fix it to the wall; the glue on the envelope does not stick very well** 2 *verb* to stick things together with glue; **he glued the label to the box**

glut 1 *noun* **a glut of produce** = too much produce, which is then difficult to sell; **a coffee glut** *or* **a glut of coffee; glut of money** = situation where there is too much money available to borrowers 2 *verb* to fill the market with something which is then difficult to sell; **the market is glutted with cheap cameras** NOTE: **glutting - glutted**

gm = GRAM

gnome *noun* *informal* **the gnomes of Zurich** = important Swiss international bankers

GNP = GROSS NATIONAL PRODUCT

go *verb* (a) to move from one place to another; **the cheque went to your bank yesterday; the plane goes to Frankfurt, then to Rome; he is going to our Lagos office** (b) to be placed; **the date goes at the top of the letter** NOTE: **going - went - has gone**

◇ **go-ahead** 1 *noun* **to give something the go-ahead** = to approve something *or* to say that something can be done; **his project got a government go-ahead; the board refused to give the go-ahead to the expansion plan** 2 *adjective* energetic *or* keen to do well; **he is a very go-ahead type; she works for a go-ahead clothing company**

◇ **go back on** *verb* not to do what has been promised; **two months later they went back on the agreement**

◇ **going** *adjective* **(a)** active *or* busy; **to sell a business as a going concern** = to sell a business as an actively trading company; **it is a going concern** = the company is working (and making a profit) **(b) the going price** = the usual *or* current price *or* the price which is being charged now; **what is the going price for secondhand 1975 Volkswagens?**; **the going rate** = the usual *or* current rate of payment; **we pay the going rate for typists; the going rate for offices is £10 per square metre**

◇ **going to** *verb* **to be going to do something** = to be just about to start doing something; **the firm is going to open an office in New York next year; when are you going to answer my letter?**

◇ **go into** *verb* **(a) to go into business** = to start in business; **he went into business as a car dealer; she went into business in partnership with her son (b)** to examine carefully; **the bank wants to go into the details of the inter-company loans**

◇ **go on** *verb* **(a)** to continue; **the staff went on working in spite of the fire; the chairman went on speaking for two hours (b)** to work with; **the figures for 1982 are all he has to go on; we have to go on the assumption that sales will not double next year**
NOTE: you go on **doing** something

◇ **go out** *verb* **to go out of business** = to stop trading; **the firm went out of business last week**

goal *noun* aim *or* something which you try to do; **our goal is to break even within twelve months; the company achieved all its goals**

godown *noun* warehouse (in the Far East)

gofer *noun* *US* person who does all types of work in an office for low wages

gold *noun* **(a)** very valuable yellow metal; **to buy gold; to deal in gold; gold coins; gold bullion** = bars of gold **(b) the country's gold reserves** = the country's store of gold kept to pay international debts; **the gold standard** = linking of the value of a currency to the value of a quantity of gold; **the pound came off the gold standard** = the pound stopped being linked to the value of gold **(c) gold point** = amount by which a currency which is linked to gold can vary in price **(d) gold shares** *or* **golds** = shares in gold mines
NOTE: no plural, except for (d)

◇ **golden handshake** *or* *US* **golden parachute** *noun* large, usually tax-free, sum of money given to a director who retires from a company before the end of his service contract; **when the company was taken over, the sales director received a golden handshake of £25,000**

◇ **goldmine** *noun* mine which produces gold; **that shop is a little goldmine** = that shop is a very profitable business

good *adjective* **(a)** not bad; **a good buy** = excellent item which has been bought cheaply; **to buy something in good faith** = to buy something thinking it is of good quality *or* that it has not been stolen *or* that it is not an imitation **(b) a good deal of** = a large quantity of; **we wasted a good deal of time discussing the arrangements for the AGM; the company had to pay a good deal for the building site; a good many** = very many; **a good many staff members have joined the union**

◇ **goods** *plural noun* **(a) goods and chattels** = moveable personal possessions **(b)** items which can be moved and are for sale; **goods in bond** = imported goods held by the customs until duty is paid; **capital goods** = machinery, buildings and raw materials which are used to make other goods; **consumer goods** *or* **consumable goods** = goods bought by the general public and not by businesses; **dry goods** = cloth and clothes; **finished goods** = manufactured goods which are ready to be sold; **household goods** = items which are used in the home; **luxury goods** = expensive items which are not basic necessities; **manufactured goods** = items which are made by machine **(c) goods depot** = central warehouse where goods can be stored until they are moved; **goods train** = train for carrying freight

◇ **goodwill** *noun* good reputation of a business; **he paid £10,000 for the goodwill of the shop and £4,000 for the stock**
NOTE: no plural

QUOTE: profit margins in the industries most exposed to foreign competition - machinery, transportation equipment and electrical goods
Sunday Times

QUOTE: the minister wants people buying goods ranging from washing machines to houses to demand facts on energy costs
Times

go-slow *noun* slowing down of production by workers as a protest against the management; **a series of go-slows reduced production**

govern *verb* to rule a country; **the country is governed by a group of military leaders**
◊ **government** *noun* (a) organization which administers a country; **central government** = main organization dealing with the affairs of the whole country; **local government** = organizations dealing with the affairs of a small area of the country; **provincial government** *or* **state government** = organization dealing with the affairs of a province *or* of a state (b) coming from the government *or* referring to the government; **government employees; local government staff; government intervention** *or* **intervention by the government; a government ban on the import of arms; a government investigation into organized crime; government officials prevented him leaving the country; government policy is outlined in the booklet; government regulations state that import duty has to be paid on luxury items; he invested all his savings in government securities; government support** = financial help given by the government; **the computer industry relies on government support; government annuity** = money paid each year by the government; **government contractor** = company which supplies goods or services to the government on contract
◊ **governmental** *adjective* referring to a government
◊ **government-backed** *adjective* backed by the government
◊ **government-controlled** *adjective* under the direct control of the government; **advertisements cannot be placed in the government-controlled newspapers**
◊ **government-regulated** *adjective* regulated by the government
◊ **government-sponsored** *adjective* encouraged by the government and backed by government money; **he is working in a government-sponsored scheme to help small businesses**

grace *noun* favour shown by granting a delay; **to give a creditor a period of grace** *or* **two weeks' grace**
NOTE: no plural

grade 1 *noun* level *or* rank; **top grade of civil servant; to reach the top grade in the civil service; high-grade** = of very good quality; **high-grade petrol; a high-grade trade delegation** = a delegation made up of important people; **low-grade** = not very important *or* not of very good quality; **a low-grade official from the Ministry of Commerce; the car runs well on low-grade petrol; top-grade** = most important *or* of the best quality; **top-grade petrol** 2 *verb* (a) to sort something into different levels of quality; **to grade coal** (b) to make something rise in steps according to quantity; **graded advertising rates** = rates which become cheaper as you take more advertising space; **graded tax** = tax which rises according to income (c) **graded hotel** = good quality hotel

gradual *adjective* slow *or* step by step; **1984 saw a gradual return to profits; his CV describes his gradual rise to the position of company chairman**
◊ **gradually** *adverb* slowly *or* step by step; **the company has gradually become more profitable; she gradually learnt the details of the import-export business**

graduate *noun* person who has a degree from a university or polytechnic; **graduate entry** = entry of graduates into employment with a company; **the graduate entry into the civil service; graduate training scheme** = training scheme for graduates; **graduate trainee** = person in a graduate training scheme
◊ **graduated** *adjective* rising in steps according to quantity; **graduated income tax; graduated pension scheme** = pension scheme which is calculated on the salary of each person in the scheme; **graduated taxation** = tax system where the percentage of tax paid rises as the income rises

gram *or* **gramme** *noun* measure of weight (one thousandth of a kilo)
NOTE: usually written **g** or **gm** with figures: **25g**

grand 1 *adjective* important; **grand plan** = major plan; **he explained his grand plan**

for redeveloping the factory site; **grand total** = final total made by adding several subtotals **2** *noun informal* one thousand pounds *or* dollars; **they offered him fifty grand for the information**
NOTE: no plural

grant 1 *noun* money given by the government to help pay for something; **the laboratory has a government grant to cover the cost of the development programme; the government has allocated grants towards the costs of the scheme; grant-aided scheme** = scheme which is funded by a government grant **2** *verb* to agree to give someone something; **to grant someone a loan** *or* **a subsidy; the local authority granted the company an interest-free loan to start up the new factory**

QUOTE: the budget grants a tax exemption for $500,000 in capital gains   *Toronto Star*

graph *noun* diagram which shows statistics as a drawing; **to set out the results in a graph; to draw a graph showing the rising profitability; the sales graph shows a steady rise; graph paper** = special paper with many little squares, used for drawing graphs

gratia *see* EX GRATIA

gratis *adverb* free *or* not costing anything; **we got into the exhibition gratis**

gratuity *noun* money given to someone who has helped you; **the staff are instructed not to accept gratuities**

great *adjective* large; **a great deal of** = very much; **he made a great deal of money on the Stock Exchange; there is a great deal of work to be done before the company can be made really profitable**

greenback *noun US informal* dollar bill
◇ **green card** *noun* **(a)** special British insurance certificate to prove that a car is insured for travel abroad **(b)** work permit for a person going to live in the USA
◇ **greenmail** *noun* making a profit by buying a large number of shares in a company, threatening to take the company over, and then selling the shares back to the company at a higher price

NOTE: no plural

QUOTE: proposes that there should be a limit on greenmail, permitting payment of a 20% premium on a maximum of 8% of the stock   *Duns Business Month*

◇ **Green Paper** *noun* report from the British government on proposals for a new law to be discussed in Parliament
◇ **green pound** *noun* value of the British pound as used in calculating agricultural prices and subsidies in the EEC

grid *noun* system of numbered squares; **grid structure** = structure based on a grid

grievance *noun* complaint made by a trade union or a worker to the management; **grievance procedure** = way of presenting complaints from a trade union to the management

gross 1 *noun* twelve dozen (144); **he ordered four gross of pens**
NOTE: no plural
2 *adjective* **(a)** total *or* with no deductions; **gross earnings** = total earnings before tax and other deductions; **gross income** *or* **gross salary** = salary before tax is deducted; **gross margin** = percentage difference between sales income and the cost of sales; **gross profit** = profit calculated as sales income less the cost of sales; **gross receipts** = total amount of money received before expenses are deducted; **gross yield** = profit from investments before the deduction of tax **(b)** **gross domestic product** = annual value of goods sold and services paid for inside a country; **gross national product** = annual value of goods and services in a country including income from other countries **(c)** **gross tonnage** = total amount of space in a ship; **gross weight** = weight of both the container and its contents **3** *adverb* with no deductions; **his salary is paid gross 4** *verb* to make a gross profit; **the group grossed £25m in 1985**

QUOTE: news that gross national product increased only 1.3% in the first quarter of the year sent the dollar down on foreign exchange markets   *Fortune*
QUOTE: gross wool receipts for the selling season to end June appear likely to top $2 billion   *Australian Financial Review*

ground *noun* (**a**) soil *or* earth; **the factory was burnt to the ground** = the factory was completely destroyed in a fire; **ground hostess** = woman who looks after passengers at the airport before they board the plane; **ground landlord** = person *or* company which owns the freehold of a property which is then leased and subleased; **ground lease** = first lease on a freehold building; **ground rent** = rent paid by a lessee to the ground landlord (**b**) **grounds** = basic reasons; **does he have good grounds for complaint? there are no grounds on which we can be sued; what are the grounds for the demand for a pay rise?**

◇ **ground floor** *noun* floor (in a shop *or* office) which is level with the ground; **the men's department is on the ground floor; he has a ground-floor office**

NOTE: in the USA this is the **first floor**

group 1 *noun* (**a**) several things or people together; **a group of the staff has sent a memo to the chairman complaining about noise in the office** (**b**) several companies linked together in the same organization; **the group chairman** *or* **the chairman of the group; group turnover** *or* **turnover for the group; the BPCC Group; group results** = results of a group of companies taken together 2 *verb* **to group together** = to put several items together; **sales from six different agencies are grouped together under the heading "European sales"**

grow *verb* to become larger; **the company has grown from a small repair shop to a multinational electronics business; turnover is growing at a rate of 15% per annum; the computer industry grew fast in the 1980s**

NOTE: **growing - grew - has grown**

◇ **growth** *noun* increase in size; **the company is aiming for growth** = is aiming to expand rapidly; **economic growth** = rate at which a country's national income grows; **a growth area** *or* **a growth market** = an area where sales are increasing rapidly; **a growth industry** = industry which is expanding rapidly; **growth rate** = speed at which something grows; **growth share** *or* **growth stock** = share which people think is likely to rise in value

NOTE: no plural

QUOTE: a general price freeze succeeded in slowing the growth in consumer prices
Financial Times
QUOTE: the thrift had grown from $4.7 million in assets in 1980 to $1.5 billion *Barrons*
QUOTE: growth in demand is still coming from the private rather than the public sector
Lloyd's List
QUOTE: population growth in the south-west is again reflected by the level of rental values
Lloyd's List

guarantee 1 *noun* (**a**) legal document which promises that a machine will work properly *or* that an item is of good quality; **certificate of guarantee** *or* **guarantee certificate; the guarantee lasts for two years; it is sold with a twelve-month guarantee; the car is still under guarantee** = is still covered by the maker's guarantee (**b**) promise that someone will pay another person's debts; **to go guarantee for someone** = to act as security for someone's debts (**c**) thing given as a security; **to leave share certificates as a guarantee** 2 *verb* to give a promise that something will happen; **to guarantee a debt** = to promise that you will pay a debt made by someone else; **to guarantee an associate company** = to promise that an associate company will pay its debts; **to guarantee a bill of exchange** = to promise that the bill will be paid; **the product is guaranteed for twelve months** = the manufacturer says that the product will work well for twelve months, and will mend it free of charge if it breaks down; **guaranteed wage** = wage which a company promises will not fall below a certain figure

◇ **guarantor** *noun* person who promises to pay someone's debts; **he stood guarantor for his brother**

guess 1 *noun* calculation made without any real information; **the forecast of sales is only a guess; he made a guess at the pretax profits** = he tried to calculate roughly what the pretax profits would be; **it is anyone's guess** = no one really knows what is the right answer 2 *verb* **to guess (at) something** = to try to calculate something without any information; **they could only guess at the total loss; the sales director tried to guess the turnover of the Far East division**

◇ **guesstimate** *noun* *informal* rough calculation

guideline *noun* unofficial suggestion from the government as to how something should be done; **the government has issued guidelines on increases in incomes and prices; the increase in retail price breaks** *or* **goes against the government guidelines**

guild *noun* association of merchants *or* of shopkeepers; **trade guild; the guild of master bakers**

guillotine *noun* machine for cutting paper

guilty *adjective* (person) who has done something wrong; **he was found guilty of libel; the company was guilty of not reporting the sales to the auditors**

gum *noun* glue; **he stuck the label to the box with gum**
◇ **gummed** *adjective* with glue on it; **gummed label** = label with dry glue on it, which has to be made wet to make it stick

Hh

ha = HECTARE

haggle *verb* to discuss prices and terms and try to reduce them; **to haggle about** *or* **over the details of a contract; after two days' haggling the contract was signed**

half **1** *noun* one of two parts into which something is divided; **the first half of the agreement is acceptable; the first half** *or* **the second half of the year** = the periods from January 1st to June 30th *or* from June 30th to December 31st; **we share the profits half and half** = we share the profits equally
NOTE: plural is **halves**
2 *adjective* divided into two parts; **half a per cent** *or* **a half per cent** = 0.5%; **his commission on the deal is twelve and a half per cent** = 12.5%; **half a dozen** *or* **a half-dozen** = six; **to sell goods off at half price** = at 50% of the price for which they were

sold before; **a half-price sale** = sale of all goods at half the price
◇ **half-dollar** *noun* *US* fifty cents
◇ **half-year** *noun* six months of an accounting period; **first half-year** *or* **second half-year** = first six months *or* second six months of a company's accounting year; **to announce the results for the half-year to June 30th** *or* **the first half-year's results** = results for the period January 1st to June 30th; **we look forward to improvements in the second half-year**
◇ **half-yearly** **1** *adjective* happening every six months *or* referring to a period of six months; **half-yearly accounts; half-yearly payment; half-yearly statement; a half-yearly meeting 2** *adverb* every six months; **we pay the account half-yearly**

QUOTE: economists believe the economy is picking up this quarter and will do better in the second half of the year *Sunday Times*

hallmark 1 *noun* mark put on gold or silver items to show that the metal is of the correct quality **2** *verb* to put a hallmark on a piece of gold or silver; **a hallmarked spoon**

hammer 1 *noun* **auctioneer's hammer** = wooden hammer used by an auctioneer to hit his desk, showing that an item has been sold; **to go under the hammer** = to be sold by auction; **all the stock went under the hammer** = all the stock was sold by auction **2** *verb* to hit hard; **to hammer the competition** = to attack and defeat the competition; **to hammer prices** = to reduce prices sharply
◇ **hammered** *adjective* (*on the Stock Exchange*) **he was hammered** = he was removed from the Stock Exchange because he could not pay his debts
◇ **hammering** *noun* **(a)** beating; **the company took a hammering in Europe** = the company had large losses in Europe *or* lost parts of its European markets; **we gave them a hammering** = we beat them commercially **(b)** (*on the Stock Exchange*) removal of a member because he cannot pay his debts
◇ **hammer out** *verb* **to hammer out an agreement** = to agree something after long and difficult negotiations; **the contract was finally hammered out**

hand *noun* **(a)** part of the body at the end of each arm; **to shake hands** = to hold someone's hand when meeting to show you are pleased to meet him or to show that an agreement has been reached; **the two negotiating teams shook hands and sat down at the conference table; to shake hands on a deal** = to shake hands to show that a deal has been agreed **(b) by hand** = using the hands, not a machine; **these shoes are made by hand; to send a letter by hand** = to ask someone to carry and deliver a letter personally, not sending it through the post **(c) in hand** = kept in reserve; **balance in hand** *or* **cash in hand** = cash held to pay small debts and running costs; **we have £10,000 in hand; work in hand** = work which is in progress but not finished **(d) goods left on hand** = unsold goods left with the retailer or manufacturer; **they were left with half the stock on their hands (e) to hand** = here *or* present; **I have the invoice to hand** = I have the invoice in front of me **(f) show of hands** = vote where people show how they vote by raising their hands; **the motion was carried on a show of hands (g) to change hands** = to be sold to a new owner; **the shop changed hands for £100,000 (h) note of hand** = document where someone promises to pay money at a stated time without conditions; **in witness whereof, I set my hand** = I sign as a witness **(i)** worker; **to take on ten more hands; deck hand** = ordinary sailor on a ship; **factory hand** = worker in a factory

◇ **handbill** *noun* sheet of printed paper handed out to members of the public as an advertisement

◇ **handbook** *noun* book which gives instructions on how something is to be used; **the handbook does not say how you open the photocopier; look in the handbook to see if it tells you how to clean the typewriter; service handbook** = book which shows how to service a machine

◇ **hand in** *verb* to deliver (a letter) by hand; **he handed in his notice** *or* **he handed in his resignation** = he resigned

◇ **hand luggage** *noun* small cases which passengers can carry themselves (and so can take with them into a plane)

◇ **handmade** *adjective* made by hand, not by machine; **he writes all his letters on handmade paper**

◇ **hand-operated** *adjective* worked by

hand, not automatically; **a hand-operated machine**

◇ **handout** *noun* **(a) publicity handout** = information sheet which is given to members of the public **(b)** free gift; **the company exists on handouts from the government**

◇ **hand over** *verb* to pass something to someone; **she handed over the documents to the lawyer; he handed over to his deputy** = he passed his responsibilities to his deputy

◇ **handover** *noun* passing of responsibilities to someone else; **the handover from the old chairman to the new went very smoothly; when the ownership of a company changes, the handover period is always difficult**

◇ **handshake** *noun* **golden handshake** = large, usually tax-free, sum of money given to a director who retires from a company before the end of his service contract; **the retiring director received a golden handshake of £25,000**

◇ **handwriting** *noun* writing done by hand; **send a letter of application in your own handwriting** = written by you with a pen, and not typed
NOTE: no plural

◇ **handwritten** *adjective* written by hand, not typed; **it is more professional to send in a typed rather than a handwritten letter of application**

handle *verb* **(a)** to deal with something *or* to organize something; **the accounts department handles all the cash; we can handle orders for up to 15,000 units; they handle all our overseas orders (b)** to sell *or* to trade in (a sort of product); **we do not handle foreign cars; they will not handle goods produced by other firms**

◇ **handling** *noun* moving something by hand *or* dealing with something; **handling charges** = money to be paid for packing and invoicing *or* for dealing with something in general *or* for moving goods from one place to another; **the bank adds on 5% handling charge for changing travellers' cheques; materials handling** = moving materials from one part of a factory to another in an efficient way

handy *adjective* useful *or* convenient; **they are sold in handy-sized packs; this small case is handy for use when travelling**

hang *verb* to attach something to a hook, nail, etc.; **hang your coat on the hook behind the door; he hung his umbrella over the back of his chair**
NOTE: **hanging - hung**
◇ **hang on** *verb* to wait (while phoning); **if you hang on a moment, the chairman will be off the other line soon**
◇ **hang up** *verb* to stop a telephone conversation by putting the telephone back on its hook; **when I asked him about the invoice, he hung up**

happen *verb* to take place by chance; **the contract happened to arrive when the managing director was away on holiday; he happened to be in the shop when the customer placed the order; what has happened to** = what went wrong with *or* what is the matter with *or* where is; **what has happened to that order for Japan?**

happy *adjective* very pleased; **we will be happy to supply you at 25% discount; the MD was not at all happy when the sales figures came in**

harbour *noun* port *or* place where ships come to load or unload; **harbour dues** = payment which a ship makes to the harbour authorities for the right to use the harbour; **harbour installations** *or* **harbour facilities** = buildings *or* equipment in a harbour

hard 1 *adjective* **(a)** strong *or* not weak; **to take a hard line in trade union negotiations** = to refuse to accept any proposal from the other side **(b)** difficult; **these typewriters are hard to sell; it is hard to get good people to work on low salaries (c)** solid; **hard cash** = money in notes and coins which is ready at hand; **he paid out £100 in hard cash for the chair; hard copy** = printout of a text which is on a computer *or* printed copy of a document which is on microfilm; **he made the presentation with diagrams and ten pages of hard copy; hard disk** = computer disk which has a sealed case and can store large quantities of information **(d) hard bargain** = bargain with difficult terms; **to drive a hard bargain** = to be a difficult negotiator;

to strike a hard bargain = to agree a deal where the terms are favourable to you; **after weeks of hard bargaining** = after weeks of difficult discussions **(e) hard currency** = currency of a country which has a strong economy and which can be changed into other currencies easily; **exports which can earn hard currency for the Soviet Union; these goods must be paid for in hard currency; a hard currency deal** 2 *adverb* with a lot of effort; **the sales team sold the new product range hard into the supermarkets; if all the workforce works hard, the order should be completed on time**
◇ **harden** *verb* prices are hardening = are settling at a higher price
◇ **hardening** *noun* **a hardening of prices** = becoming settled at a higher level
◇ **hardness** *noun* **hardness of the market** = being strong *or* not being likely to fall
◇ **hard sell** *noun* **to give a product the hard sell** = to make great efforts to persuade people to buy it; **he tried to give me the hard sell** = he put a lot of effort into trying to make me buy
◇ **hard selling** *noun* act of selling by using great efforts; **a lot of hard selling went into that deal**
◇ **hardware** *noun* **(a)** computer hardware = machines used in data processing, including the computers and printers, but not the programs; **hardware maintenance contract (b)** military hardware = guns *or* rockets *or* tanks, etc. **(c)** solid goods for use in the house (such as frying pans or hammers); **a hardware shop**
NOTE: no plural

QUOTE: hard disks help computers function more speedily and allow them to store more information
Australian Financial Review
QUOTE: few of the paper millionaires sold out and transformed themselves into hard cash millionaires
Investors Chronicle

harm 1 *noun* damage done; **the recession has done a lot of harm to export sales**
NOTE: no plural
2 *verb* to damage; **the bad publicity has harmed the company's reputation**

hatchet man *noun* recently appointed manager, whose job is to make staff redundant and reduce expenditure

haul *noun* distance travelled with a load of cargo; **it is a long haul from Birmingham to Athens; short-haul flight** = flight over a short distance (up to 1000 km); **long-haul flight** = long-distance flight, especially between continents

◇ **haulage** *noun* **(a) road haulage** = moving of goods by road; **road haulage depot** = centre for goods which are being moved by road, and the lorries which carry them; **haulage contractor** = company which arranges for goods to be moved by road or rail under contract; **haulage costs** *or* **haulage rates** = cost *or* rates of transporting goods by road; **haulage firm** *or* **company** = company which transports goods by road **(b)** cost of transporting goods by road; **haulage is increasing by 5% per annum**
NOTE: no plural

◇ **haulier** *noun* **road haulier** = company which transports goods by road

haven *noun* safe place; **tax haven** = country where taxes are low which encourages companies to set up their main offices there

hawk *verb* to sell goods from door to door or in the street; **to hawk something round** = to take a product *or* an idea *or* a project to various companies to see if one will accept it; **he hawked his idea for a plastic car body round all the major car constructors**

◇ **hawker** *noun* person who sells goods from door to door or in the street

hazard *noun* **fire hazard** = situation *or* goods which could start a fire; **that warehouse full of wood and paper is a fire hazard**

head **1** *noun* **(a)** most important person; **head of department** *or* **department head** = person in charge of a department **(b)** most important *or* main; **head clerk; head porter; head salesman; head waiter; head buyer** = most important buyer in a department store; **head office** = main office, where the board of directors works and meets **(c)** top part *or* first part; **write the name of the company at the head of the list (d)** person; **representatives cost on average £25,000 per head per annum (e) heads of agreement** = draft agreement with not all the details complete **2** *verb* **(a)** to be the manager *or* to be the most important person; **to head a department; he is heading a buying mission to China (b)** to be first; **the two largest oil companies head the list of stock market results**

◇ **headed** *adjective* **headed paper** = notepaper with the name of the company and its address printed on it

◇ **head for** *verb* to go towards; **the company is heading for disaster** = the company is going to collapse

◇ **headhunt** *verb* to look for managers and offer them jobs in other companies; **he was headhunted** = he was approached by a headhunter and offered a new job

◇ **headhunter** *noun* person *or* company which looks for top managers and offers them jobs in other companies

◇ **heading** *noun* **(a)** words at the top of a piece of text; **items are listed under several headings; look at the figure under the heading "Costs 85-86" (b)** letter heading *or* heading on notepaper = name and address of a company printed at the top of a piece of notepaper

◇ **headlease** *noun* lease from a freehold owner to a lessee

◇ **headquarters** *plural noun* main office, where the board of directors meets and works; **the company's headquarters are in New York; divisional headquarters** = main office of a division of a company; **to reduce headquarters staff** = to have fewer people working in the main office

◇ **head up** *verb* to be in charge of; **he has been appointed to head up our European organization**

QUOTE: reporting to the deputy managing director, the successful candidate will be responsible for heading up a team which provides a full personnel service *Times*

health *noun* **(a)** being fit and well, not ill; *GB* **Health and Safety at Work Act** = Act of Parliament which rules how the health of workers should be protected by the companies they work for; **health insurance** = insurance which pays the cost of treatment for illness, especially when travelling abroad; **a private health scheme** = insurance which will pay for the cost of treatment in a private hospital, not a state one **(b) to give a company a clean bill of health** = to report that a company is trading profitably
NOTE: no plural

◇ **healthy** *adjective* **a healthy balance sheet** = balance sheet which shows a good profit; **the company made some very healthy profits** *or* **a very healthy profit** = made a large profit

hear *verb* **(a)** to sense a sound with the ears; **you can hear the printer in the next office; the traffic makes so much noise that I cannot hear my phone ringing (b)** to have a letter *or* a phone call from someone; **we have not heard from them for some time; we hope to hear from the lawyers within a few days**
NOTE: **hearing - heard**

heavy *adjective* **(a)** large *or* in large quantities; **a programme of heavy investment overseas; he had heavy losses on the Stock Exchange; the company is a heavy user of steel** *or* **a heavy consumer of electricity; the government imposed a heavy tax on luxury goods; heavy costs** *or* **heavy expenditure** = spending large sums of money **(b)** which weighs a lot; **the Post Office refused to handle the package because it was too heavy; heavy industry** = industry which makes large products (such as steel bars, ships or railway lines); **heavy machinery** = large machines
◇ **heavily** *adverb* **he is heavily in debt** = he has many debts; **they are heavily into property** = they have large investments in property; **the company has had to borrow heavily to repay its debts** = the company has had to borrow large sums of money

QUOTE: the steel company had spent heavily on new equipment *Fortune*
QUOTE: heavy selling sent many blue chips tumbling in Tokyo yesterday *Financial Times*

hectare *noun* measurement of area of land (= 2.47 acres)
NOTE: usually written **ha** after figures: **16ha**

hectic *adjective* wild *or* very active; **a hectic day on the Stock Exchange; after last week's hectic trading, this week has been very calm**

hedge **1** *noun* protection; **a hedge against inflation** = investment which should increase in value more than the increase in the rate of inflation; **he bought gold as a hedge against exchange losses 2** *verb* **to hedge one's bets** = to make investments in several areas so as to be protected against loss in one of them; **to**

hedge against inflation = to buy investments which will rise in value faster than the increase in the rate of inflation
◇ **hedging** *noun* buying investments at a fixed price for delivery later, so as to protect oneself against possible loss

QUOTE: during the 1970s commercial property was regarded by investors as an alternative to equities, with many of the same inflation-hedge qualities *Investors Chronicle*

height *noun* **(a)** measurement of how tall *or* high something is; **what is the height of the desk from the floor? he measured the height of the room from floor to ceiling (b)** highest point; **it is difficult to find hotel rooms at the height of the tourist season**
NOTE: no plural

heir *noun* person who will receive property when someone dies; **his heirs split the estate between them**

helicopter *noun* aircraft with a large propeller on top which allows it to lift straight off the ground; **he took the helicopter from the airport to the centre of town; it is only a short helicopter flight from the centre of town to the factory site**

help 1 *noun* thing which makes it easy to do something; **she finds the word-processor a great help in writing letters; the company was set up with financial help from the government; her assistant is not much help in the office - he cannot type or drive**
NOTE: no plural
2 *verb* to make it easy for something to be done; **he helped the salesman carry his case of samples; the computers helps in the rapid processing of orders** *or* **helps us to process orders rapidly; the government helps exporting companies with easy credit**
NOTE: you help someone *or* something **to do** something

hereafter *adverb* from this time on
◇ **hereby** *adverb* in this way *or* by this letter; **we hereby revoke the agreement of January 1st 1982**
◇ **herewith** *adverb* together with this letter; **please find the cheque enclosed herewith**

hereditament *noun* property, including land and buildings

hesitate *verb* not to be sure what to do next; **the company is hesitating about starting up a new computer factory; she hesitated for some time before accepting the job**

hidden *adjective* which cannot be seen; **hidden asset** = asset which is valued much less in the company's accounts than its true market value; **hidden reserves** = illegal reserves which are not declared in the company's balance sheet; **hidden defect in the program** = defect which was not noticed when the program was tested

high 1 *adjective* **(a)** tall; **the shelves are 30 cm high; the door is not high enough to let us get the machines into the building; they are planning a 30-storey high office block (b)** large *or* not low; **high overhead costs increase the unit price; high prices put customers off; they are budgeting for a high level of expenditure; investments which bring in a high rate of return; high interest rates are killing small businesses; high finance** = lending, investing and borrowing of very large sums of money organized by financiers; **high flier** = person who is very successful *or* who is likely to get a very important job; share whose market price is rising rapidly; **high sales** = large amount of revenue produced by sales; **high taxation** = taxation which imposes large taxes on incomes *or* profits; **highest tax bracket** = the group which pays the most tax; **high volume (of sales)** = large number of items sold **(c) highest bidder** = person who offers the most money at an auction; **the property was sold to the highest bidder; a decision taken at the highest level** = decision taken by the most important person or group **2** *adverb* **prices are running high** = prices are above their usual level **3** *noun* point where prices *or* sales are very large; **share prices have dropped by 10% since the high of January 2nd; the highs and lows on the Stock Exchange; sales volume has reached an all-time high** = has reached the highest point it has ever been at

◊ **high-grade** *adjective* of very good quality; **high-grade petrol; a high-grade trade delegation** = a delegation made up of very important people

◊ **high-income** *adjective* which gives a large income; **high-income shares; a high-income portfolio**

◊ **high-level** *adjective* **(a)** very important; **a high-level meeting** *or* **delegation** = meeting *or* delegation of the most important people (such as ministers, managing directors); **a high-level decision** = decision taken by the most important person or group **(b) high-level computer language** = programming language which uses normal words and figures

◊ **highly** *adverb* very; **highly-geared company** = company which has a high proportion of its funds from fixed-interest borrowings; **highly-paid** = earning a large salary; **highly-placed** = occupying an important post; **the delegation met a highly-placed official in the Trade Ministry; highly-priced** = with a large price; **she is highly thought of by the managing director** = the managing director thinks she is very competent

◊ **high pressure** *noun* strong force by other people to do something; **working under high pressure** = working with a manager telling you what to do and to do it quickly *or* with customers asking for supplies urgently; **high-pressure salesman** = salesman who forces the customer to buy something he does not really need; **high-pressure sales techniques** *or* **high-pressure selling** = forcing a customer to buy something he does not really want

◊ **high-quality** *adjective* of very good quality; **high-quality goods; high-quality steel**

◊ **High Street** *noun* main shopping street in a British town; **the High Street shops; a High Street bookshop; the High Street banks** = main British banks which accept deposits from individual customers

QUOTE: American interest rates remain exceptionally high in relation to likely inflation rates *Sunday Times*

QUOTE: faster economic growth would tend to push US interest rates, and therefore the dollar, higher *Australian Financial Review*

QUOTE: in a leveraged buyout the acquirer raises money by selling high-yielding debentures to private investors *Fortune*

hike 1 *noun* *US* increase; **pay hike** = increase in salary **2** *verb* *US* to increase; **the union hiked its demand to $3 an hour**

hire 1 *noun* **(a)** paying money to rent a car *or* boat *or* piece of equipment for a time; **car hire; truck hire; car hire firm** *or* **equipment hire firm** = company which owns cars *or* equipment and lends them to customers for a payment; **hire car** = car which has been rented; **he was driving a hire car when the accident happened (b) "for hire"** = sign on a taxi showing it is empty **(c)** *US* **for hire contract** = freelance contract; **to work for hire** = to work freelance **2** *verb* **(a) to hire staff** = to engage new staff to work for you; **to hire and fire** = to employ new staff and dismiss existing staff frequently; **we have hired the best lawyers to represent us; they hired a small company to paint the offices (b) to hire a car** *or* **a crane** = to pay money to use a car *or* a crane for a time; **he hired a truck to move his furniture (c) to hire out cars** *or* **equipment** = to lend cars *or* equipment to customers who pay for their use

◊ **hired** *adjective* **a hired car** = car which has been rented

◊ **hire purchase** *noun* system of buying something by paying a sum regularly each month; **to buy a refrigerator on hire purchase; to sign a hire-purchase agreement** = to sign a contract to pay for something by instalments; **hire-purchase company** = company which provides money for hire purchase

◊ **hiring** *noun* employing; **hiring of new personnel has been stopped**

historic *or* **historical** *adjective* which goes back over a period of time; **historic(al) cost** = actual cost of something which was made some time ago; **historical figures** = figures which were current in the past

QUOTE: the Federal Reserve Board has eased interest rates in the past year, but they are still at historically high levels *Sunday Times*

hit *verb* **(a)** to knock against something; **he hit his head against the table; we have hit our export targets** = we have reached our targets **(b)** to hurt *or* to damage; **the company was badly hit by the falling exchange rate; our sales of summer clothes have been hit by the bad weather; the new legislation has hit the small companies hardest**
NOTE: **hitting - hit**

hive off *verb* to split off part of a large company to form a smaller subsidiary; **the new managing director hived off the retail sections of the company**

hoard *verb* to buy and store food in case of need *or* to keep cash instead of investing it

◊ **hoarder** *noun* person who buys and stores food in case of need

◊ **hoarding** *noun* **(a) hoarding of supplies** = buying large quantities of money *or* food to keep in case of need **(b) advertisement hoarding** = large board for posters
NOTE: no plural for (a)

QUOTE: as a result of hoarding, rice has become scarce with prices shooting up *Business Times (Lagos)*

hold *verb* **(a)** to own *or* to keep; **he holds 10% of the company's shares; you should hold these shares - they look likely to rise** = you should keep these shares and not sell them **(b)** to contain; **the carton holds twenty packets; each box holds 250 sheets of paper; a bag can hold twenty kilos of sugar (c)** to make something happen; **to hold a meeting** *or* **a discussion; the computer show will be held in London next month; board meetings are held in the boardroom; the AGM will be held on March 24th; the receiver will hold an auction of the company's assets; the accountants held a review of the company's accounting practices (d)** (*on telephone*) **hold the line please** = please wait; **the chairman is on the other line - will you hold?**
NOTE: **holding - held**

◊ **hold back** *verb* to wait *or* not to go forward; **investors are holding back until after the Budget** = investors are waiting until they hear the details of the Budget before they decide whether to buy or sell; **he held back from signing the lease until he had checked the details** = he delayed signing the lease until he had checked the details; **payment will be held back until the contract has been signed** = payment will not be made until the contract has been signed

◊ **hold down** *verb* **(a)** to keep at a low level; **we are cutting margins to hold our prices down (b) to hold down a job** = to manage to do a difficult job

◊ **holder** *noun* **(a)** person who owns *or* keeps something; **holders of government bonds** *or* **bondholders; holder of stock** *or* **of shares in a company; holder of an insurance policy** *or* **policy holder; credit card holder** = person who has a credit card; **debenture holder** = person who holds a debenture for money lent **(b)** thing which keeps something *or* which protects something; **card holder** *or* **message holder** = frame which protects a card *or* a message; **credit card holder** = plastic wallet for keeping credit cards

◊ **holding** *noun* **(a)** group of shares owned; **he has sold all his holdings in the Far East; the company has holdings in German manufacturing companies (b) cross holdings** = situation where two companies own shares in each other in order to stop each from being taken over; **the two companies have protected themselves from takeover by a system of cross holdings**

◊ **holding company** *noun* company which exists only to own shares in subsidiary companies

◊ **hold on** *verb* to wait *or* not to change; **the company's shareholders should hold on and wait for a better offer** = they should keep their shares and not sell them

◊ **hold out for** *verb* to wait and ask for; **you should hold out for a 10% pay rise** = do not agree to a pay rise of less than 10%

◊ **hold over** *verb* to postpone *or* to put back to a later date; **discussion of item 4 was held over until the next meeting**

◊ **hold to** *verb* not to allow something to change; **we will try to hold him to the contract** = we will try to stop him going against the contract; **the government hopes to hold wage increases to 5%** = the government hopes that wage increases will not be more than 5%

◊ **hold up** *verb* **(a)** to stay at a high level; **share prices have held up well; sales held up during the tourist season (b)** to delay; **the shipment has been held up at the customs; payment will be held up until the contract has been signed; the strike will hold up dispatch for some weeks**

◊ **hold-up** *noun* delay; **the strike caused hold-ups in the dispatch of goods**

QUOTE: real wages have been held down; they have risen at an annual rate of only 1% in the last two years
Sunday Times
QUOTE: as of last night, the bank's shareholders no longer hold any rights to the bank's shares
South China Morning Post

holiday *noun* **(a) bank holiday** = weekday which is a public holiday when the banks are closed; **New Year's Day is a bank holiday; public holiday** = day when all workers rest and enjoy themselves instead of working; **statutory holiday** = holiday which is fixed by law; **the office is closed for the Christmas holiday (b)** period when a worker does not work, but rests, goes away and enjoys himself; **to take a holiday** *or* **to go on holiday; when is the manager taking his holidays? my secretary is off on holiday tomorrow; he is away on holiday for two weeks; the job carries five weeks' holiday** = one of the conditions of the job is that you have five weeks' holiday; **the summer holidays** = holidays taken by the workers in the summer when the weather is good and children are not at school; **holiday entitlement** = number of days' paid holiday which a worker has the right to take; **holiday pay** = salary which is still paid during the holiday **(c) tax holiday** = period when a new business is exempted from paying tax

home *noun* **(a)** place where a person lives; **please send the letter to my home address, not my office (b) home country** = country where a company is based; **home sales** *or* **sales in the home market** = sales in the country where a company is based; **home-produced products** = products manufactured in the country where the company is based **(c)** house; **new home sales** = sales of new houses; **home loan** = loan by a bank *or* a building society to a person buying a house

◊ **homegrown** *adjective* which has been developed in a local area *or* in a country where the company is based; **a home-grown computer industry; India's home-grown car industry**

◊ **homemade** *adjective* made in a home; **homemade jam**

◊ **homeowner** *noun* person who owns a private house; **homeowner's insurance policy** = insurance policy covering a house and its contents and the personal liablility of the people living in it

◊ **homeward** *adjective* going towards the home country; **homeward freight; homeward journey**

◊ **homewards** *adverb* towards the home country; **cargo homewards**

hon = HONORARY **hon sec** = honorary secretary

honest *adjective* respected *or* saying what is right; **to play the honest broker** = to act for the parties in a negotiation to try to make them agree to a solution

◊ **honestly** *adverb* saying what is right *or* not cheating

honorarium *noun* money paid to a professional person, such as an accountant *or* a lawyer, when he does not ask for a fee NOTE: plural is **honoraria**

◊ **honorary** *adjective* person who is not paid a salary; **honorary secretary; honorary president; honorary member** = member who does not have to pay a subscription

honour *verb* to pay something because it is owed and is correct; **to honour a bill; to honour a signature** = to pay something because the signature is correct

hope *verb* to expect *or* to want something to happen; **we hope to be able to dispatch the order next week; he is hoping to break into the US market; they had hoped the TV commercials would help sales**

horizontal *adjective* flat *or* going from side to side, not up and down; **horizontal integration** = joining similar companies *or* taking over a company in the same line of business; **horizontal communication** = communication between workers at the same level

horse trading *noun* hard bargaining which ends with someone giving something in return for a concession from the other side

hostess *noun* woman who looks after passengers *or* clients; **air hostess** = woman who looks after passengers in a plane; **ground hostess** = woman who looks after passengers before they get into the plane

hot *adjective* **(a)** very warm; **the staff complain that the office is too hot in the summer and too cold in the winter; the drinks machines sells coffee, tea and hot soup; switch off the machine if it gets too hot (b)** not safe *or* very bad; **to make things hot for someone** = to make it difficult for someone to work *or* to trade; **customs officials are making things hot for the drug** smugglers; **hot money** = money which is moved from country to country to get the best interest rates; **he is in the hot seat** = his job involves making many difficult decisions

hotel *noun* building where you can rent a room for a night, or eat in a restaurant; **hotel bill; hotel expenses; hotel manager; hotel staff; hotel accommodation** = rooms available in hotels; **all hotel accommodation has been booked up for the exhibition; hotel chain** *or* **chain of hotels** = group of hotels owned by the same company; **the hotel trade** = business of running hotels

◊ **hotelier** *noun* person who owns *or* manages a hotel

hour *noun* **(a)** period of time lasting sixty minutes; **to work a thirty-five hour week** = to work seven hours a day each weekday; **we work an eight-hour day** = we work for eight hours a day, e.g. from 8.30 to 5.30 with one hour for lunch **(b)** sixty minutes of work; **he earns £4 an hour; we pay £6 an hour; to pay by the hour** = to pay people a fixed amount of money for each hour worked **(c) banking hours** = time when a bank is open for its customers; **you cannot get money out of a bank outside banking hours; office hours** = time when an office is open; **do not telephone during office hours; outside hours** *or* **out of hours** = when the office is not open; **he worked on the accounts out of hours; the shares rose in after-hours trading** = in trading after the Stock Exchange had closed

◊ **hourly** *adverb* per hour; **hourly-paid workers** = workers paid at a fixed rate for each hour worked; **hourly rate** = amount of money paid for an hour worked

house *noun* **(a)** building in which someone lives; **house property** = private houses, not shops, offices or factories; **house agent** = estate agent who deals in buying or selling houses **(b)** company; **a French business house; the largest London finance house; he works for a broking house** *or* **a publishing house; clearing house** = central office where clearing banks exchange cheques; **discount house** = financial company which specializes in discounting bills; **export house** = company which specializes in the export of goods manufactured by other companies; **house**

journal or **house magazine** or US **house organ** = magazine produced for the workers or shareholders in a company to give them news about the company; **house telephone** = internal telephone for calling from one office to another **(c) the House** = the London Stock Exchange

◇ **household** noun people living in a house; **household expenses** = money spent on running a private house; **household goods** = goods which are used in a house

◇ **householder** noun person who owns a private house

◇ **house starts** or US **housing starts** plural noun number of new private houses or flats of which the construction has begun during a year

◇ **house-to-house** adjective going from one house to the next, asking people to buy something or to vote for someone; **house-to-house canvassing; house-to-house salesman; house-to-house selling**

HP = HIRE PURCHASE

hundredweight noun weight of 112 pounds (about fifty kilos)
NOTE: usually written **cwt** after figures: **20cwt**

hurry 1 noun doing things fast; **there is no hurry for the figures, we do not need them until next week; in a hurry** = very fast; **the sales manager wants the report in a hurry 2** verb to do something or to make something or to go very fast; **the production team tried to hurry the order through the factory; the chairman does not want to be hurried into making a decision; the directors hurried into the meeting**

◇ **hurry up** verb to make something go faster; **can you hurry up that order - the customer wants it immediately?**

hurt verb to harm or to damage; **the bad publicity did not hurt our sales; sales of summer clothes were hurt by the bad weather; the company has not been hurt by the recession**
NOTE: **hurting - hurt**

hype 1 noun excessive claims made in advertising; **all the hype surrounding the launch of the new soap 2** verb to make excessive claims in advertising

hyper- prefix meaning very large

◇ **hyperinflation** noun inflation which is so rapid that it is almost impossible to reduce
NOTE: no plural

◇ **hypermarket** noun very large supermarket, usually on the outside of a large town

Ii

idea noun thing which you think of; **one of the salesman had the idea of changing the product colour; the chairman thinks it would be a good idea to ask all directors to itemize their expenses**

ideal adjective perfect or very good for something; **this is the ideal site for a new hypermarket**

◇ **Ideal Home Exhibition** noun annual exhibition in London showing new houses, new kitchens, etc.

idle adjective **(a)** not working; **2,000 employees were made idle by the recession (b) idle machinery** or **machines lying idle** = machinery not being used **(c) idle capital** = capital not being used productively; **money lying idle** or **idle money** = money which is not being used to produce interest or which is not invested in business

i.e. that is; **the largest companies, i.e. Smith's and Brown's, had a very good first quarter; the import restrictions apply to expensive items, i.e. items costing more than $2,500**

illegal adjective not legal or against the law

◇ **illegality** noun being illegal

◇ **illegally** adverb against the law; **he was accused of illegally importing arms into the country**

illicit adjective not legal or not permitted; **illicit sale of alcohol; trade in illicit alcohol**

ILO = INTERNATIONAL LABOUR ORGANIZATION

image *noun* general idea which the public has of a product *or* a company; **they are spending a lot of advertising money to improve the company's image; the company has adopted a down-market image; brand image** = picture which people have in their minds of a product associated with the brand name; **corporate image** = idea which a company would like the public to have of it; **to promote a corporate image** = to publicize a company so that its reputation is improved

IMF = INTERNATIONAL MONETARY FUND

imitate *verb* to do what someone else does; **they imitate all our sales gimmicks**
◇ **imitation** *noun* thing which copies another; **beware of imitations** = be careful not to buy low quality goods which are made to look like other more expensive items

immediate *adjective* happening at once; **he wrote an immediate letter of complaint; your order will receive immediate attention**
◇ **immediately** *adverb* at once; **he immediately placed an order for 2,000 boxes; as soon as he heard the news he immediately telexed his office; can you phone immediately you get the information?**

immovable *adjective* which cannot be moved; **immovable property** = houses and other buildings on land

immunity *noun* protection against arrest; **diplomatic immunity** = being outside a country's laws because of being a diplomat; **he was granted immunity from prosecution** = he was told he would not be prosecuted
NOTE: no plural

impact *noun* shock *or* strong effect; **the impact of new technology on the cotton trade; the new design has made little impact on the buying public**
NOTE: no plural

QUOTE: the strong dollar's deflationary impact on European economies as governments push up interest rates to support their sinking currencies *Duns Business Month*

imperfect *adjective* not perfect; **sale of imperfect items; to check a batch for imperfect products**
◇ **imperfection** *noun* part of an item which is not perfect; **to check a batch for imperfections**

impersonal *adjective* without any personal touch *or* as if done by machines; **an impersonal style of management**

implement 1 *noun* tool *or* instrument used to do some work **2** *verb* to put into action; **to implement an agreement**
◇ **implementation** *noun* putting into action; **the implementation of new rules**
NOTE: no plural

import 1 *noun* **(a) imports** = goods brought into a country from abroad for sale; **imports from Poland have risen to $1m a year; invisible imports** = services (such as banking, tourism) which are paid for in foreign currency; **visible imports** = real goods which are imported **(b) import ban** = forbidding imports; **the government has imposed an import ban on arms; import duty** = tax on goods imported into a country; **import levy** = tax on imports, especially in the EEC a tax on imports of farm produce from outside the EEC; **import licence** *or* **import permit** = government licence *or* permit which allows goods to be imported; **import quota** = fixed quantity of a particular type of goods which the government allows to be imported; **the government has imposed an import quota on cars; import surcharge** = extra duty charged on imported goods, to try to prevent them from being imported and to encourage local manufacture
NOTE: usually used in the plural, but the singular form is used before a noun
2 *verb* to bring goods from abroad into a country for sale; **the company imports television sets from Japan; this car was imported from France; the union organized a boycott of imported cars**

QUOTE: European manufacturers rely heavily on imported raw materials which are mostly priced in dollars *Duns Business Month*

◇ **importation** *noun* act of importing; **the importation of arms is forbidden**
NOTE: no plural

◇ **importer** *noun* person *or* company which imports goods; **a cigar importer; the company is a big importer of foreign cars**
◇ **import-export** *adjective* dealing with both bringing foreign goods into a country and sending locally made goods abroad; **import-export trade; he is in import-export**
◇ **importing** 1 *adjective* which imports; **oil-importing countries; an importing company** 2 *noun* act of bringing foreign goods into a country for sale; **the importing of arms into the country is illegal**
NOTE: no plural

importance *noun* having a value *or* mattering a lot; **the bank attaches great importance to the deal**
NOTE: no plural
◇ **important** *adjective* which matters a lot; **he left a pile of important papers in the taxi; she has an important meeting at 10.30; he was promoted to a more important job**

QUOTE: each of the major issues on the agenda at this week's meeting is important to the government's success in overall economic management *Australian Financial Review*

impose *verb* to put a tax *or* a duty on goods; **to impose a tax on bicycles; they tried to impose a ban on smoking; the government imposed a special duty on oil; the customs have imposed a 10% tax increase on luxury items; the unions have asked the government to impose trade barriers on foreign cars**
◇ **imposition** *noun* putting a tax on goods or services
NOTE: no plural

impossible *adjective* which cannot be done; **getting skilled staff is becoming impossible; government regulations make it impossible for us to export**

impound *verb* to take something away and keep it until a tax is paid; **the customs impounded the whole cargo**
◇ **impounding** *noun* act of taking something and keeping it until a tax is paid
NOTE: no plural

imprest *noun* **the imprest system =** system of controlling petty cash, where cash is paid out against a written receipt and the receipt is used to get more cash to bring the float to the original level

improve *verb* to make something better *or* to become better; **we are trying to improve our image with a series of TV commercials; they hope to improve the company's cash flow position; we hope the cash flow position will improve or we will have difficulty in paying our bills; export trade has improved sharply during the first quarter =** export trade has increased
◇ **improved** *adjective* better; **the union rejected the management's improved offer**
◇ **improvement** *noun* **(a)** getting better; **there is no improvement in the cash flow situation; sales are showing a sharp improvement over last year (b)** thing which is better; **improvement on an offer =** making a better offer
◇ **improve on** *verb* to do better than; **he refused to improve on his previous offer =** he refused to make a better offer

QUOTE: the management says the rate of loss-making has come down and it expects further improvement in the next few years *Financial Times*
QUOTE: we also invest in companies whose growth and profitability could be improved by a management buyout *Times*

impulse *noun* sudden decision; **impulse buying =** buying things which you have just seen, not because you had planned to buy them; **the store puts racks of chocolates by the checkout to attract the impulse buyer; impulse purchase =** thing bought as soon as it is seen; **to do something on impulse =** to do something because you have just thought of it, not because it was planned

in = INCH

inactive *adjective* not active *or* not busy; **inactive market =** stock market with few buyers or sellers

Inc *US* = INCORPORATED

incentive *noun* thing which encourages staff to work better; **staff incentives =** pay and better conditions offered to workers to make them work better; **incentive bonus** *or* **incentive payment =** extra pay offered to a worker to make him work better; **incentive scheme =** plan to encourage better work by paying higher commission or bonuses; **incentive schemes are boosting production**

> QUOTE: some further profit-taking was seen yesterday as investors continued to lack fresh incentives to renew buying activity
> *Financial Times*

inch *noun* measurement of length (= 2.54cm)
NOTE: usually written **in** or " after figures: **2 in** or **2"**

incidental 1 *adjective* which is not important, but connected with something else; **incidental expenses** = small amounts of money spent at various times in addition to larger amounts 2 *noun* **incidentals** = incidental expenses

include *verb* to count something along with other things; **the charge includes VAT; the total comes to £1,000 including freight; the total is £140 not including insurance and freight; the account covers services up to and including the month of June**
◇ **inclusive** *adjective* which counts something in with other things; **inclusive of tax; not inclusive of VAT; inclusive sum** *or* **inclusive charge** = charge which includes all costs; **the conference runs from the 12th to the 16th inclusive** = it starts on the morning of the 12th and ends on the evening of the 16th

income *noun* (a) money which a person receives as salary or dividends; **annual income** = money received during a calendar year; **disposable income** = income left after tax and national insurance have been deducted; **earned income** = money received as a salary or wages; **earned income allowance** = tax allowance to be set against money earned by the wife or children of the main taxpayer; **fixed income** = income which does not change from year to year; **gross income** = income before tax has been deducted; **net income** = income left after tax has been deducted; **private income** = income from dividends *or* interest *or* rent which is not part of a salary; **personal income** = income received by an individual person; **retained income** = profits which are not paid out to shareholders as dividends; **unearned income** = money received from interest or dividends; **lower** *or* **upper income bracket** = groups of people who earn low or high

salaries considered for tax purposes; **he comes into the higher income bracket** = he is in a group of people earning high incomes and therefore paying more tax **(b) the government's incomes policy** = the government's ideas on how incomes should be controlled **(c) income tax** = tax on a person's income; **income tax form** = form to be completed which declares all income to the tax office; **declaration of income** *or* **income tax return** = statement declaring income to the tax office **(d)** money which an organization receives as gifts or from investments; **the hospital has a large income from gifts (e)** *US* **income statement** = accounts for a company which show expenditure and sales balanced to give a final profit or loss

> QUOTE: there is no risk-free way of taking regular income from your money much higher than the rate of inflation   *Guardian*
> QUOTE: the company will be paying income tax at the higher rate in 1985   *Citizen (Ottawa)*

incoming *adjective* (a) **incoming call** = phone call coming into the office from someone outside; **incoming mail** = mail which comes into an office (b) which have recently been elected *or* appointed; **the incoming board of directors** = the new board which is about to start working; **the incoming chairman** *or* **president**

incompetent *adjective* who cannot work well; **the sales manager is quite incompetent; the company has an incompetent sales director**

inconvertible *adjective* (currency) which cannot be easily converted into other currencies

incorporate *verb* (a) to bring something in to form part of a main group; **income from the 1984 acquisition is incorporated into the accounts (b)** to form a registered company; **a company incorporated in the USA; an incorporated company; J. Doe Incorporated**
◇ **incorporation** *noun* act of incorporating a company

incorrect *adjective* wrong *or* not correct; **the minutes of the meeting were incorrect and had to be changed**

◇ **incorrectly** *adverb* wrongly *or* not correctly; **the package was incorrectly addressed**

increase 1 *noun* **(a)** growth *or* becoming larger; **increase in tax** *or* **tax increase; increase in price** *or* **price increase; profits showed a 10% increase** *or* **an increase of 10% on last year; increase in the cost of living** = rise in the annual cost of living **(b)** higher salary; **increase in pay** *or* **pay increase; increase in salary** *or* **salary increase; the government hopes to hold salary increases to 3%; he had two increases last year** = his salary went up twice; **cost-of-living increase** = increase in salary to allow it to keep up with higher cost of living; **merit increase** = increase in pay given to a worker whose work is good **(c) on the increase** = growing larger *or* becoming more frequent; **stealing in shops is on the increase** 2 *verb* **(a)** to grow bigger *or* higher; **profits have increased faster than the increase in the rate of inflation; exports to Africa have increased by more than 25%; the price of oil has increased twice in the past week; to increase in price** = to cost more; **to increase in size** *or* **in value** = to become larger *or* more valuable **(b) the company increased his salary to £20,000** = the company gave him a rise in salary to £20,000
◇ **increasing** *adjective* which is growing bigger; **increasing profits; the company has an increasing share of the market**
◇ **increasingly** *adverb* more and more; **the company has to depend increasingly on the export market**

QUOTE: competition is steadily increasing and could affect profit margins as the company tries to retain its market share *Citizen (Ottawa)*
QUOTE: turnover has potential to be increased to over 1 million dollars with energetic management and very little capital *Australian Financial Review*

increment *noun* regular automatic increase in salary; **annual increment; salary which rises in annual increments of £500** = each year the salary is increased by £500
◇ **incremental** *adjective* which rises automatically in stages; **incremental cost** = cost of making a single extra unit above the number already planned; **incremental increase** = increase in salary according to an agreed annual increment; **incremental**

scale = salary scale with regular annual salary increases

incur *verb* to make yourself liable to; **to incur the risk of a penalty** = to make it possible that you risk paying a penalty; **to incur debts** *or* **costs** = to do something which means that you owe money *or* that you will have to pay costs; **the company has incurred heavy costs to implement the expansion programme** = the company has had to pay large sums of money
NOTE: **incurring - incurred**

QUOTE: the company blames fiercely competitive market conditions in Europe for a £14m operating loss last year, incurred despite a record turnover *Financial Times*

indebted *adjective* owing money to someone; **to be indebted to a property company**
◇ **indebtedness** *noun* state of indebtedness = being in debt *or* owing money

indemnification *noun* payment for damage
◇ **indemnify** *verb* to pay for damage; **to indemnify someone for a loss**
◇ **indemnity** *noun* guarantee of payment after a loss; **he had to pay an indemnity of £100; letter of indemnity** = letter promising payment as compensation for a loss

indent 1 *noun* **(a)** order placed by an importer for goods from overseas; **he put in an indent for a new stock of soap (b)** line of typing which starts several spaces from the left-hand margin 2 *verb* **(a) to indent for something** = to put in an order for something; **the department has indented for a new computer (b)** to start a line of typing several spaces from the left-hand margin; **indent the first line three spaces**

indenture 1 *noun* **indentures** *or* **articles of indenture** = contract by which an apprentice works for a master for some years to learn a trade 2 *verb* to contract with an apprentice who will work for some years to learn a trade; **he was indentured to a builder**

independent *adjective* free *or* not controlled by anyone; **independent company** = company which is not controlled by another company; **independent trader** *or* **independent shop** = shop which is owned by an individual proprietor, not by a chain; **the independents** = shops or companies which are owned by private individuals

index *noun* (a) list of items classified into groups or put in alphabetical order; **index card** = small card used for filing; **card index** = series of cards with information written on them, kept in a special order so that the information can be found easily; **index letter** *or* **number** = letter or number of an item in an index (b) regular statistical report which shows rises and falls in prices, etc.; **growth index** = index showing how something has grown; **cost-of-living index** = way of measuring the cost of living, shown as a percentage increase on the figure for the previous year; **retail price index** *or* *US* **consumer price index** = index showing how prices of consumer goods have risen over a period of time, used as a way of measuring inflation and the cost of living; **wholesale price index** = index showing rises and falls of prices of manufactured goods as they leave the factory; **the Financial Times Index** = index which shows percentage rises or falls in shares prices on the London Stock Exchange based on a small group of major companies; **index number** = number which shows the percentage rise of something over a period of time
NOTE: plural is **indexes** or **indices**
◇ **indexation** *noun* linking of something to an index; **indexation of wage increases** = linking of wage increases to the percentage rise in the cost of living
NOTE: no plural
◇ **index-linked** *adjective* which rises automatically by the percentage increase in the cost of living; **index-linked pensions; his pension is index-linked; index-linked government bonds**

QUOTE: the index of industrial production sank 0.2 per cent for the latest month after rising 0.3 per cent in March *Financial Times*
QUOTE: an analysis of the consumer price index for the first half of 1985 shows that the rate of inflation went down by 12.9 per cent
Business Times (Lagos)

indicate *verb* to show; **the latest figures indicate a fall in the inflation rate; our sales for 1985 indicate a move from the home market to exports**
◇ **indicator** *noun* thing which indicates; **government economic indicators** = statistics which show how the country's economy is going to perform in the short or long term

QUOTE: it reduces this month's growth in the key M3 indicator from about 19% to 12%
Sunday Times
QUOTE: we may expect the US leading economic indicators for April to show faster economic growth *Australian Financial Review*
QUOTE: other indicators, such as high real interest rates, suggest that monetary conditions are extremely tight *Economist*

indirect *adjective* not direct; **indirect expenses** *or* **costs** = costs which are not directly attached to the making of a product (such as cleaning, rent, administration); **indirect labour costs** = costs of paying workers who are not directly involved in making a product (such as secretaries, cleaners); **indirect taxation** = taxes (such as sales tax) which are not paid direct to the government; **the government raises more money by indirect taxation than by direct**

individual 1 *noun* one single person; **savings plan made to suit the requirements of the private individual** 2 *adjective* single *or* belonging to one person; **a pension plan designed to meet each person's individual requirements; we sell individual portions of ice cream;** *US* **Individual Retirement Account** = private pension plan, where persons can make contributions separate from a company pension plan

inducement *noun* thing which helps to persuade someone to do something; **they offered him a company car as an inducement to stay**

induction *noun* starting a new person in a new job; **induction courses** *or* **induction training** = courses to train people starting new jobs
NOTE: no plural

industry *noun* (a) all factories *or* companies *or* processes involved in the manufacturing of products; **all sectors of industry have shown rises in output; basic industry** = most important industry of a country (such as coal, steel, agriculture); **a boom industry** or **a growth industry** = industry which is expanding rapidly; **heavy industry** = industry which deals in heavy raw materials (such as coal) or makes large products (such as ships or engines); **light industry** = industry making small products (such as clothes, books, calculators); **primary industry** = industry dealing with basic raw materials (such as coal, wood, farm produce); **secondary industry** = industry which uses basic raw materials to produce manufactured goods; **service industry** or **tertiary industry** = industry which does not produce raw materials or manufacture products but offers a service (such as banking, retailing, accountancy) **(b)** group of companies making the same type of product; **the aircraft industry; the building industry; the car industry; the food processing industry; the mining industry; the petroleum industry**

◊ **industrial** 1 adjective referring to manufacturing work; **industrial accident** = accident which takes place at work; **to take industrial action** = to go on strike or go-slow; **industrial capacity** = amount of work which can be done in a factory or several factories; **industrial centre** = large town with many industries; GB **industrial court** or **industrial tribunal** = court which can decide in industrial disputes if both parties agree to ask it to judge between them; **industrial design** = design of products made by machines (such as cars, refrigerators); **industrial disputes** = arguments between management and workers; **industrial espionage** = trying to find out the secrets of a competitor's work or products, usually by illegal means; **industrial estate** or **industrial park** = area of land near a town specially for factories and warehouses; **industrial expansion** = growth of industries in a country or a region; **industrial injuries** = injuries which happen to workers at work; **industrial processes** = processes involved in manufacturing products in factories; **industrial relations** = relations between management and workers; **good industrial relations** = situation where management and workers understand each others' problems and work together for the good of the company; **industrial training** = training of new workers to work in an industry; **land zoned for light industrial use** = land where planning permission has been given

to build small factories for light industry **2** noun **industrials** = shares in manufacturing companies

◊ **industrialist** noun owner or director of a factory

◊ **industrialization** noun changing of an economy from being based on agriculture to industry
NOTE: no plural

◊ **industrialize** verb to set up industries in a country which had none before; **industrialized societies** = countries which have many industries

QUOTE: indications of renewed weakness in the US economy were contained in figures on industrial production for April   *Financial Times*
QUOTE: central bank and finance ministry officials of the industrialized countries will continue work on the report *Wall Street Journal*
QUOTE: with the present overcapacity in the airline industry, discounting of tickets is widespread   *Business Traveller*

inefficiency noun lack of efficiency; **the report criticized the inefficiency of the sales staff**

◊ **inefficient** adjective not efficient or not doing a job well; **an inefficient sales director**

inertia noun being lazy; **inertia selling** = method of selling items by sending them when they have not been ordered and assuming that if the items are not returned, the person who has received them is willing to buy them
NOTE: no plural

inexpensive adjective cheap or not expensive
◊ **inexpensively** adverb without spending much money

inferior adjective not as good as others; **inferior products** or **products of inferior quality**

inflate verb **(a)** **to inflate prices** = to increase prices without any reason; **tourists don't want to pay inflated London prices (b)** **to inflate the economy** = to make the economy more active by increasing the money supply
◊ **inflated** adjective **(a)** **inflated prices** = prices which are increased without any reason **(b)** **inflated currency** = currency

which is too high in relation to other currencies

◇ **inflation** *noun* situation where prices rise to keep up with increased production costs; **we have 15% inflation** *or* **inflation is running at 15%** = prices are 15% higher than at the same time last year; **to take measures to reduce inflation; high interest rates tend to increase inflation; rate of inflation** *or* **inflation rate** = percentage increase in prices over a twelve-month period; **galloping inflation** *or* **runaway inflation** = very rapid inflation which it is almost impossible to reduce; **spiralling inflation** = inflation where price rises make workers ask for higher wages which then increase prices again
NOTE: no plural

◇ **inflationary** *adjective* which tends to increase inflation; **inflationary trends in the economy; the economy is in an inflationary spiral** = in a situation where price rises encourage higher wage demands which in turn make prices rise; **anti-inflationary measures** = measures to reduce inflation

QUOTE: the decision by the government to tighten monetary policy will push the annual inflation rate above the year's previous high
Financial Times
QUOTE: when you invest to get a return, you want a ''real'' return - above the inflation rate
Investors Chronicle

inflow *noun* flowing in; **inflow of capital into the country** = capital which is coming into a country in order to be invested

QUOTE: the dollar is strong because of capital inflows rather than weak because of the trade deficit
Duns Business Month

influence **1** *noun* effect which is had on someone *or* something; **the price of oil has a marked influence on the price of manufactured goods; we are suffering from the influence of a high exchange rate** **2** *verb* to have an effect on someone *or* something; **the board was influenced in its decision by the memo from the managers; the price of oil has influenced the price of manufactured goods; high inflation is influencing our profitability**
NOTE: you influence someone **to do** something

influx *noun* rushing in; **an influx of foreign currency into the country; an influx of cheap labour into the cities**
NOTE: plural is **influxes**

QUOTE: the retail sector will also benefit from the expected influx of tourists
Australian Financial Review

inform *verb* to tell someone officially; **I regret to inform you that your tender was not acceptable; we are pleased to inform you that your offer has been accepted; we have been informed by the Department of Trade that new tariffs are coming into force**

◇ **information** *noun* **(a)** details which explain something; **please send me information on** *or* **about holidays in the USA; have you any information on** *or* **about deposit accounts? I enclose this leaflet for your information; to disclose a piece of information; to answer a request for information; for further information, please write to Department 27; disclosure of confidential information** = telling someone information which should be secret; **flight information** = information about flight times; **tourist information** = information for tourists **(b) information technology** = working with computer data; **information retrieval** = storing and then finding data in a computer **(c) information bureau** *or* **information office** = office which gives information to tourists *or* visitors; **information officer** = person whose job is to give information about a company *or* an organization *or* a government department to the public; person whose job is to give information to other departments in the same organization
NOTE: no plural; for one item say **a piece of information**

infrastructure *noun* **(a)** basic structure; **the company's infrastructure** = how the company is organized **(b)** basic services; **a country's infrastructure** = the road and rail systems, education and legal systems, etc.

infringe *verb* to break a law *or* a right; **to infringe a copyright** = to copy a copyright text illegally; **to infringe a patent** = to make a product which works in the same way as a patented product and not pay a royalty to the patent holder

◇ **infringement** *noun* breaking a law *or* a right; **infringement of copyright** *or* **copyright infringement** = act of illegally copying a work which is in copyright; **infringement of patent** *or* **patent infringement**

ingot *noun* bar of gold or silver

inherit *verb* to get something from a person who has died; **when her father died she inherited the shop; he inherited £10,000 from his grandfather**
◇ **inheritance** *noun* property which is received from a dead person
NOTE: no plural

in-house *adverb & adjective* working inside a company's building; **the in-house staff; we do all our data processing in-house; in-house training** = training given to staff at their place of work

initial **1** *adjective* first *or* starting; **initial capital** = capital which is used to start a business; **he started the business with an initial expenditure** *or* **initial investment of £500; initial sales** = first sales of a new product; **the initial response to the TV advertising has been very good** **2** *noun* **initials** = first letters of the words in a name; **what do the initials IMF stand for? the chairman wrote his initials by each alteration in the contract he was signing 3** *verb* to write your initials on a document to show you have read it and approved; **to initial an amendment to a contract; please initial the agreement at the place marked with an X**

> QUOTE: the founding group has subscribed NKr 14.5m of the initial NKr 30m share capital
> *Financial Times*
> QUOTE: career prospects are excellent for someone with potential, and initial salary is negotiable around $45,000 per annum
> *Australian Financial Review*

initiate *verb* to start; **to initiate discussions**
◇ **initiative** *noun* decision to start something; **to take the initiative** = to decide to do something; **to follow up an initiative** = to take action once someone else has decided to do something

inject *verb* **to inject capital into a business** = to put money into a business
◇ **injection** *noun* **a capital injection of £100,000** *or* **an injection of £100,000 capital** = putting £100,000 into an existing business

injunction *noun* court order telling someone not to do something; **he got an injunction preventing the company from selling his car; the company applied for an injunction to stop their rival from marketing a similar product**

injure *verb* to hurt (someone); **two workers were injured in the fire**
◇ **injured party** *noun* party in a court case which has been harmed by another party
◇ **injury** *noun* hurt caused to a person; **injury benefit** = money paid to a worker who has been hurt at work; **industrial injuries** = injuries caused to workers at work

inking pad *noun* small pad with ink on it, used for putting ink on a rubber stamp

inland *adjective* **(a)** inside a country; **inland postage** = postage for a letter to another part of the country; **inland freight charges** = charges for carrying goods from one part of the country to another **(b)** *GB* **the Inland Revenue** = government department dealing with tax; **he received a letter from the Inland Revenue**

innovate *verb* to bring in new ideas *or* new methods
◇ **innovation** *noun* new idea *or* new method *or* new product
◇ **innovative** *adjective* (person or thing) which is new and makes changes
◇ **innovator** *noun* person who brings in new ideas and methods

> QUOTE: small innovative companies in IT have been hampered for lack of funds *Sunday Times*

input **1** *noun* **input of information** *or* **computer input** = data fed into a computer; **input lead** = lead for connecting the electric current to the machine; **input tax** = VAT paid on goods or services which a company buys **2** *verb* **to input**

information = to put data into a computer
NOTE: **inputting - inputted**

inquire *verb* to ask questions about something; **he inquired if anything was wrong; she inquired about the mortgage rate; "inquire within"** = ask for more details inside the office *or* shop

◇ **inquire into** *verb* to investigate *or* to try to find out about something; **we are inquiring into the background of the new supplier**

◇ **inquiry** *noun* official question; **I refer to your inquiry of May 25th; all inquiries should be addressed to this department**

insert 1 *noun* thing which is put inside something; **an insert in a magazine mailing** *or* **a magazine insert** = advertising sheet put into a magazine when it is mailed **2** *verb* to put something in; **to insert a clause into a contract; to insert a publicity piece into a magazine mailing**

inside 1 *adjective & adverb* in, especially in a company's office or building; **we do all our design work inside; inside worker** = worker who works in the office or factory (not in the open air, not a salesman) **2** *preposition* in; **there was nothing inside the container; we have a contact inside our rival's production department who gives us very useful information**

◇ **insider** *noun* person who works in an organization and therefore knows its secrets; **insider dealings** *or* **insider trading** = illegal buying or selling of shares by staff of a company who have secret information about the company's plans

insolvent *adjective* not able to pay debts; **he was declared insolvent** = he was officially stated to be insolvent

◇ **insolvency** *noun* not being able to pay debts; **he was in a state of insolvency** = he could not pay his debts
NOTE: no plural

inspect *verb* to examine in detail; **to inspect a machine** *or* **an installation; to inspect the accounts; to inspect products for defects** = to look at products in detail to see if they have any defects

◇ **inspection** *noun* close examination of something; **to make an inspection** *or* **to carry out an inspection of a machine** *or* **an installation; inspection of a product for** defects; **to carry out a tour of inspection** = to visit various places *or* offices *or* factories to inspect them; **to issue an inspection order** = to order an official inspection; **inspection stamp** = stamp placed on something to show it has been inspected

◇ **inspector** *noun* official who inspects; **inspector of factories** *or* **factory inspector** = government official who inspects factories to see if they are safely run; **inspector of taxes** *or* **tax inspector** = official of the Inland Revenue who examines tax returns and decides how much tax people should pay; **inspector of weights and measures** = government official who inspects weighing machines and goods sold in shops to see if the quantities and weights are correct

◇ **inspectorate** *noun* all inspectors; **the factory inspectorate** = all inspectors of factories

inst = INSTANT **your letter of the 6th inst** = your letter of the 6th of this month

instability *noun* being unstable *or* moving up and down; **period of instability in the money markets** = period when currencies fluctuate rapidly
NOTE: no plural

install *verb* to put (a machine) into an office *or* into a factory; **to install new machinery; to install a new data processing system**

◇ **installation** *noun* **(a)** machines, equipment and buildings; **harbour installations; the fire seriously damaged the oil installations (b)** putting new machines into an office *or* a factory; **to supervise the installation of new equipment**

◇ **instalment** *or* US **installment** *noun* part of a payment which is paid regularly until the total amount is paid; **the first instalment is payable on signature of the agreement; the final instalment is now due** = the last of a series of payments should be paid now; **to pay £25 down and monthly instalments of £20** = to pay a first payment of £25 and the rest in payments of £20 each month; **to miss an instalment** = not to pay an instalment at the right time

◇ **installment plan** *noun* US system of buying something by paying a sum regularly each month; **to buy a car on the installment plan**
NOTE: GB English is **hire purchase**

instance *noun* particular example *or* case; **in this instance we will overlook the delay**

instant *adjective* **(a)** this month; **our letter of the 6th instant** = our letter of the 6th of this current month **(b)** immediately available; **instant credit**

institute 1 *noun* official organization; **research institute** = organization set up to do research 2 *verb* to start; **to institute proceedings against someone**
◇ **institution** *noun* organization *or* society set up for a particular purpose; **financial institution** = bank *or* investment trust *or* insurance company whose work involves lending or investing large sums of money
◇ **institutional** *adjective* referring to a financial institution; **institutional buying** *or* **selling** = buying or selling shares by financial institutions; **institutional investors** = financial institutions who invest money in securities

> QUOTE: during the 1970s commercial property was regarded by big institutional investors as an alternative to equities   *Investors Chronicle*

instruct *verb* **(a)** to give an order to someone; **to instruct someone to do something** = to tell someone officially to do something; **he instructed the credit controller to take action (b)** to instruct a **solicitor** = to give orders to a solicitor to start legal proceedings on your behalf
◇ **instruction** *noun* order which tells what should be done *or* how something is to be used; **he gave instructions to his stockbroker to sell the shares immediately; to await instructions** = to wait for someone to tell you what to do; **to issue instructions** = to tell everyone what to do; **in accordance with** *or* **according to instructions** = as the instructions show; **failing instructions to the contrary** = unless someone tells you to do the opposite; **forwarding instructions** *or* **shipping instructions** = details of how goods are to be shipped and delivered
◇ **instructor** *noun* person who shows how something is to be done

instrument *noun* **(a)** tool *or* piece of equipment; **the technician brought instruments to measure the output of elec-** tricity **(b)** legal document; **negotiable instrument** = document (such as a bill of exchange *or* a cheque) which can be exchanged for cash

insure *verb* to have a contract with a company where, if regular small payments are made, the company will pay compensation for loss, damage, injury or death; **to insure a house against fire; to insure someone's life; he was insured for £100,000; to insure baggage against loss; to insure against bad weather; to insure against loss of earnings; the life insured** = the person whose life is covered by a life assurance; **the sum insured** = the largest amount of money that an insurer will pay under an insurance
◇ **insurable** *adjective* which can be insured
◇ **insurance** *noun* **(a)** agreement that in return for regular small payments, a company will pay compensation for loss, damage, injury or death; **to take out an insurance against fire** = to pay a premium, so that if a fire happens, compensation will be paid; **to take out an insurance on the house** = to pay a premium, so that if the house is damaged compensation will be paid; **the damage is covered by the insurance** = the insurance company will pay for the damage; **repairs will be paid for by the insurance; to pay the insurance on a car** = to pay premiums to insure a car **(b) accident insurance** = insurance which will pay if an accident takes place; **car insurance** *or* **motor insurance** = insuring a car, the driver and passengers in case of accident; **comprehensive insurance** = insurance which covers against all risks which are likely to happen; **endowment insurance** = situation where a sum of money is paid to the insured person on a certain date or to his heir if he dies before that date; **fire insurance** = insurance against damage by fire; **house insurance** = insuring a house and its contents against damage; **life insurance** = situation which pays a sum of money when someone dies; **medical insurance** = insurance which pays the cost of medical treatment, especially when travelling abroad; **term insurance** = life insurance which covers a person's life for a fixed period of time; **third-party insurance** = insurance which pays compensation if someone who is not the insured person

incurs loss or injury; **whole-life insurance** = insurance where the insured person pays premiums for all his life and the insurance company pays a sum when he dies **(c) insurance agent** or **insurance broker** = person who arranges insurance for clients; **insurance claim** = asking an insurance company to pay for damage; **insurance company** = company whose business is to receive payments and pay compensation for loss or damage; **insurance contract** = agreement by an insurance company to insure; **insurance cover** = protection guaranteed by an insurance policy; **insurance policy** = document which shows the conditions of an insurance; **insurance premium** = payment made by the insured person to the insurer **(d)** *GB* **National Insurance** = state insurance, organized by the government, which pays for medical care, hospitals, unemployment benefits, etc.; **National Insurance contributions** = money paid by a worker and the company each month to the National Insurance

◊ **insurer** *noun* company which insures
NOTE: no plural for (b), (c) and (d). Note also that for life insurance, GB English prefers to use **assurance, assure, assurer**

intangible *adjective* which cannot be touched; **intangible assets** = assets which have a value, but which cannot be seen (such as goodwill, patent or a trademark)

integrate *verb* to link things together to form one whole group

◊ **integration** *noun* bringing several businesses together under a central control; **horizontal integration** = joining similar companies or taking over a company in the same line of business as yourself; **vertical integration** = joining business together which deal with different stages in the production or sale of a product

intend *verb* to plan or to expect to do something; **the company intends to open an office in New York next year; we intend to offer jobs to 250 unemployed young people**

intensive *adjective* **intensive farming** = farming small areas of expensive land, using machines and fertilizers to obtain high crops; **capital-intensive industry** = industry which needs a large amount of capital investment in plant to make it

work; **labour-intensive industry** = industry which needs large numbers of workers or where labour costs are high in relation to turnover

intent *noun* what is planned; **letter of intent** = letter which states what a company intends to do if something happens

inter- *prefix* between; **inter-bank loan** = loan from one bank to another; **the inter-city rail services are good** = train services between cities are good; **inter-company dealings** = dealings between two companies in the same group; **inter-company comparisons** = comparing the results of one company with those of another in the same product area

interest 1 *noun* **(a)** special attention; **the MD takes no interest in the staff club; the buyers showed a lot of interest in our new product range (b)** payment made by a borrower for the use of money, calculated as a percentage of the capital borrowed; **simple interest** = interest calculated on the capital only, and not added to it; **compound interest** = interest which is added to the capital and then earns interest itself; **accrual of interest** = automatic addition of interest to capital; **accrued interest** = interest which is accumulating and is due for payment at a later date; **back interest** = interest which has not yet been paid; **fixed interest** = interest which is paid at a set rate; **high** or **low interest** = interest at a high or low percentage; **interest charges** = cost of paying interest; **interest rate** or **rate of interest** = percentage charge for borrowing money; **interest-free credit** or **loan** = credit or loan where no interest is paid by the borrower; **the company gives its staff interest-free loans (c)** money paid as income on investments or loans; **the bank pays 10% interest on deposits; to receive interest at 5%; the loan pays 5% interest; deposit which yields** or **gives** or **produces** or **bears 5% interest; account which earns interest at 10%** or **which earns 10% interest; interest-bearing deposits** = deposits which produce interest **(d)** money invested in a company or financial share in a company; **beneficial interest** = situation where someone is allowed to occupy or receive rent from a house without owning it; **he has a controlling interest in the company** = he owns more than 50% of the shares and so can direct how the company is run; **life interest =** situation where someone benefits from a property as long as he is alive; **majority interest** or **minority interest =** situation where someone owns a majority or a minority of shares in a company; **he has a majority interest in a supermarket chain; to acquire a substantial interest in the company =** to buy a large number of shares in a company; **to declare an interest =** to state in public that you own shares in a company NOTE: no plural for (a), (b) and (c) **2** verb to attract someone's attention; **he tried to interest several companies in his new invention; interested in =** paying attention to; **the managing director is interested only in increasing profitability; interested party =** person or company with a financial interest in a company

◇ **interesting** adjective which attracts attention; **they made us a very interesting offer for the factory**

QUOTE: since last summer American interest rates have dropped by between three and four percentage points *Sunday Times*
QUOTE: a lot of money is said to be tied up in sterling because of the interest-rate differential between US and British rates
Australian Financial Review

interface 1 noun link between two different computer systems or pieces of hardware **2** verb to meet and act with; **the office micros interface with the mainframe computer at head office**

interfere verb to get involved or to try to change something which is not your concern

◇ **interference** noun the act of interfering; **the sales department complained of continual interference from the accounts department**

interim noun **interim dividend =** dividend paid at the end of a half-year; **interim payment =** payment of part of a dividend; **interim report =** report given at the end of a half-year; **in the interim =** meanwhile or for the time being

QUOTE: the company plans to keep its annual dividend unchanged at Y7.5 per share. which includes a Y3.75 interim payout *Financial Times*

intermediary noun person who is the link between parties who do not agree or who are negotiating; **he refused to act as an intermediary between the two directors**

internal adjective **(a)** inside a company; **we decided to make an internal appointment =** we decided to appoint an existing member of staff to the post, and not bring someone in from outside the company; **internal audit =** audit carried out by a department within the company; **internal audit department** or **internal auditor =** department or member of staff who audits the accounts of the company he works for; **internal telephone =** telephone which is linked to other phones in an office **(b)** inside a country; **an internal flight =** flight to a town inside the same country; *US* **Internal Revenue Service =** government department which deals with tax; **internal trade =** trade between various parts of a country

◇ **internally** adverb inside a company; **the job was advertised internally**

international adjective working between countries; **international call =** telephone call to another country; **international dialling code =** number used to make a telephone call to another country; **International Labour Organization =** section of the United Nations, an organization which tries to improve working conditions and workers' pay in member countries; **international law =** laws governing relations between countries; **the International Monetary Fund =** (part of the United Nations) a type of bank which helps member states in financial difficulties, gives financial advice to members and encourages world trade; **international trade =** trade between different countries

interpret verb to translate what someone has said into another language; **my assistant knows Greek, so he will interpret for us**

◇ **interpreter** noun person who translates what someone has said into another language; **my secretary will act as interpreter**

intervene verb to try to make a change in a system; **to intervene in a dispute =** to try to settle a dispute

◊ **intervention** *noun* acting to make a change in a system; **the government's intervention in the foreign exchange markets; the central bank's intervention in the banking crisis; the government's intervention in the labour dispute; intervention price** = price at which the EEC will buy farm produce which farmers cannot sell, in order to store it

interview 1 *noun* **(a)** talking to a person who is applying for a job; **we called six people for interview; I have an interview next week** *or* **I am going for an interview next week (b)** asking a person questions as part of an opinion poll **2** *verb* to talk to a person applying for a job to see if he is suitable; **we interviewed ten candidates, but did not find anyone suitable**
◊ **interviewee** *noun* person who is being interviewed
◊ **interviewer** *noun* person who is conducting the interview

inter vivos *phrase* **gift inter vivos** = gift given to another living person

intestate *adjective* **to die intestate** = to die without having made a will

in transit *adverb* **goods in transit** = goods being transported

in tray *noun* basket on a desk for letters *or* memos which have been received and are waiting to be dealt with

introduce *verb* to make someone get to know a new person or thing; **to introduce a client** = to bring in a new client and make him known to someone; **to introduce a new product on the market** = to produce a new product and launch it on the market
◊ **introduction** *noun* **(a)** letter making someone get to know another person; **I'll give you an introduction to the MD - he is an old friend of mine (b)** bringing into use; **the introduction of new technology** = putting new machines (usually computers) into a business or industry
◊ **introductory** *adjective* **introductory offer** = special price offered on a new product to attract customers

invalid *adjective* not valid *or* not legal; **permit that is invalid; claim which has been declared invalid**
◊ **invalidate** *verb* to make something invalid; **because the company has been taken over, the contract has been invalidated**
◊ **invalidation** *noun* making invalid
◊ **invalidity** *noun* being invalid; **the invalidity of the contract**

invent *verb* to make something which has never been made before; **she invented a new type of computer terminal; who invented shorthand? the chief accountant has invented a new system of customer filing**
◊ **invention** *noun* thing which has been invented; **he tried to sell his latest invention to a US car manufacturer**
◊ **inventor** *noun* person who invents something; **he is the inventor of the all-plastic car**

inventory 1 *noun* **(a)** stock *or* goods in a warehouse or shop; **to carry a high inventory; to aim to reduce inventory; inventory control** = system of checking that there is not too much stock in a warehouse, but just enough to meet requirements **(b)** list of the contents of a house for sale, of an office for rent, etc.; **to draw up an inventory of fixtures; to agree the inventory** = to agree that the inventory is correct **2** *verb* to make a list of stock or contents

QUOTE: a warehouse needs to tie up less capital in inventory and with its huge volume spreads out costs over bigger sales   *Duns Business Month*

invest *verb* **(a)** to put money into shares, bonds, a building society, hoping that it will produce interest and increase in value; **he invested all his money in an engineering business; she was advised to invest in real estate** *or* **in government bonds; to invest abroad** = to put money into shares *or* bonds in overseas countries **(b)** to spend money on something which you believe will be useful; **to invest money in new machinery; to invest capital in a new factory**
◊ **investment** *noun* **(a)** placing of money so that it will increase in value and produce interest; **they called for more government investment in new industries; investment in real estate; to make investments in oil companies; return on**

investment = interest or dividends shown as a percentage of the money invested **(b)** shares, bonds, deposits bought with invested money; **long-term investment** or **short-term investment** = shares, etc., which are likely to increase in value over a long or short period; **safe investment** = shares, etc. which are not likely to fall in value; **blue-chip investments** = risk-free shares of good companies; **he is trying to protect his investments** = he is trying to make sure that the money he has invested is not lost **(c) investment adviser** = person who advises people on what investments to make; **investment company** or **investment trust** = company whose shares can be bought on the Stock Exchange, and whose business is to make money by buying and selling stocks and shares; **investment grant** = government grant to a company to help it to invest in new machinery; **investment income** = income (such as interest and dividends) from investments

◇ **investor** *noun* person who invests money; **the small investor** or **the private investor** = person with a small sum of money to invest; **the institutional investor** = organization (like a pension fund or insurance company) with large sums of money to invest

QUOTE: we have substantial venture capital to invest in good projects   *Times*
QUOTE: investment trusts, like unit trusts, consist of portfolios of shares and therefore provide a spread of investments
                    Investors Chronicle
QUOTE: investment companies took the view that prices had reached rock bottom and could only go up   *Lloyd's List*

investigate *verb* to examine something which may be wrong
◇ **investigation** *noun* examination to find out what is wrong; **to conduct an investigation into irregularities in share dealings**
◇ **investigator** *noun* person who investigates; **government investigator**

invisible 1 *adjective* **invisible assets** = assets which have a value but which cannot be seen (such as goodwill or patents); **invisible earnings** = foreign currency earned by a country by providing services, not selling goods; **invisible imports** or **exports** = services which are

paid for in foreign currency or earn foreign currency without actually selling a product (such as banking or tourism) **2** *plural noun* **invisibles** = invisible imports and exports

invite *verb* to ask someone to do something or to ask for something; **to invite someone to an interview; to invite someone to join the board; to invite shareholders to subscribe a new issue; to invite tenders for a contract**
◇ **invitation** *noun* asking someone to do something; **to issue an invitation to someone to join the board; invitation to tender for a contract; invitation to subscribe a new issue**

invoice 1 *noun* **(a)** note asking for payment for goods or services supplied; **your invoice dated November 10th; they sent in their invoice six weeks late; to make out an invoice for £250; to settle** or **to pay an invoice; the total is payable within thirty days of invoice** = the total sum has to be paid within thirty days of the date on the invoice; **VAT invoice** = invoice which includes VAT **(b) invoice clerk** = office worker who deals with invoices; **invoice price** = price as given on an invoice (including discount and VAT); **total invoice value** = total amount on an invoice, including transport, VAT, etc. **2** *verb* to send an invoice to someone; **to invoice a customer; we invoiced you on November 10th** = we sent you the invoice on November 10th
◇ **invoicing** *noun* sending of an invoice; **our invoicing is done by the computer; invoicing department** = department in a company which deals with preparing and sending invoices; **invoicing in triplicate** = preparing three copies of invoices; **VAT invoicing** = sending of an invoice including VAT
NOTE: no plural

inward *adjective* towards the home country; **inward bill** = bill of lading for goods arriving in a country; **inward mission** = visit to your home country by a group of foreign businessmen

IOU *noun* = I OWE YOU signed document promising that you will pay back money borrowed; **to pay a pile of IOUs**

IRA *US* = INDIVIDUAL RETIREMENT ACCOUNT

irrecoverable *adjective* which cannot be recovered; **irrecoverable debt** = debt which will never be paid

irredeemable *adjective* which cannot be redeemed; **irredeemable bond** = bond which has no date of maturity and which therefore provides interest but can never be redeemed at full value

irregular *adjective* not correct *or* not done in the correct way; **irregular documentation; this procedure is highly irregular**
◊ **irregularity** *noun* **(a)** not being regular *or* not being on time; **the irregularity of the postal deliveries (b) irregularities** = things which are not done in the correct way and which are possibly illegal; **to investigate irregularities in the share dealings**

irrevocable *adjective* which cannot be changed; **irrevocable acceptance** = acceptance which cannot be withdrawn; **irrevocable letter of credit** = letter of credit which cannot be cancelled or changed

IRS *US* = INTERNAL REVENUE SERVICE

issue **1** *noun* giving out new shares; **bonus issue** *or* **scrip issue** = new shares given free to shareholders; **issue of debentures** *or* **debenture issue** = borrowing money by giving lenders debentures; **issue of new shares** *or* **share issue** = selling new shares in a company to the public; **rights issue** = giving shareholders the right to buy more shares at a lower price; **new issues department** = section of a bank which deals with issues of new shares in companies; **issue price** = price of shares when they are offered for sale for the first time **2** *verb* to put out *or* to give out; **to issue a letter of credit; to issue shares in a new company; to issue a writ against someone; the government issued a report on London's traffic**
◊ **issued** *adjective* **issued capital** = amount of capital which is given out as shares to shareholders; **issued price** =

price of shares in a new company when they are offered for sale for the first time
◊ **issuing** *noun* which organizes an issue of shares; **issuing bank** *or* **issuing house** = bank which organizes the selling of shares in a new company

---

QUOTE: the rights issue should overcome the cash flow problems *Investors Chronicle*
QUOTE: the company said that its recent issue of 10.5 per cent convertible preference shares at A$8.50 a share has been oversubscribed
Financial Times
QUOTE: issued and fully paid capital is $100 million *Hongkong Standard*

IT = INFORMATION TECHNOLOGY

item *noun* **(a)** thing for sale; **cash items** = goods sold for cash; **we are holding orders for out of stock items** = for goods which are not in stock; **please find enclosed an order for the following items from your catalogue (b)** piece of information; **items on a balance sheet; extraordinary items** = items in accounts which do not appear each year and need to be noted; **item of expenditure** = goods or services which have been paid for and appear in the accounts **(c)** point on a list; **we will now take item four on the agenda** = we will now discuss the fourth point on the agenda
◊ **itemize** *verb* to make a detailed list of things; **itemizing the sales figures will take about two days; itemized account** = detailed record of money paid or owed; **itemized invoice** = invoice which lists each item separately

itinerary *noun* list of places to be visited on one journey; **a salesman's itinerary**

Jj

jam **1** *noun* **(a)** sweet food made with fruit and sugar **(b)** blocking; **traffic jam** = situation where there is so much traffic on the road that it moves only very slowly **2** *verb* to stop working *or* to be blocked; **the paper feed has jammed; the switchboard was jammed with calls**
NOTE: **jamming - jammed**

jetsam *noun* **flotsam and jetsam** = rubbish floating in the water after a ship has been wrecked and rubbish washed on to the land
NOTE: no plural

jettison *verb* to throw cargo from a ship into the sea to make the ship lighter

jingle *noun* **advertising jingle** *or* **publicity jingle** = short and easily remembered tune to advertise a product on television, etc.

job *noun* **(a)** piece of work; **to do a job of work** = to be given a job of work to do; **to do odd jobs** = to do various pieces of work; **he does odd jobs for us around the house**; **odd-job-man** = person who does various pieces of work; **to be paid by the job** = to be paid for each piece of work done **(b)** order being worked on; **we are working on six jobs at the moment; the shipyard has a big job starting in August (c)** regular paid work; **he is looking for a job in the computer industry; he lost his job when the factory closed; she got a job in a factory; to apply for a job in an office; office job** *or* **white-collar job** = job in an office; **to give up one's job** = to resign from one's work; **to look for a job** = to try to find work; **to retire from one's job** = to leave work and take a pension; **to be out of a job** = to have no work **(d) job analysis** = detailed examination and report on the duties of a job; **job application** *or* **application for a job** = asking for a job in writing; **you have to fill in a job application form; job centre** = government office which lists jobs which are vacant; **job classification** = describing jobs listed under various classes; **job creation scheme** = government-backed plan to make work for the unemployed; **job description** = official document from the management which says what a job involves; **job evaluation** = examining different jobs within an organization to see what skills and qualifications are needed to carry them out; **job satisfaction** = a worker's feeling that he is happy in his place of work and pleased with the work he does; **job security** = feeling which a worker has that he has a right to keep his job, or that his job will never end; **job specification** = very detailed description of what is involved in a job; **job title** = name given to a person in a certain job; **her job title is "Chief Buyer"; on-the-job training** = training given to workers at

their place of work; **off-the-job training** = training given to workers away from their place of work (i.e. at a college) **(e) job lot** = group of miscellaneous items sold together; **he sold the household furniture as a job lot (f)** difficulty; **they will have a job to borrow the money they need for the expansion programme; we had a job to find a qualified secretary**

◊ **jobber** *noun* **(a) (stock) jobber** = person who buys and sells shares from other traders on the Stock Exchange **(b)** *US* wholesaler

◊ **jobbing** *noun* **(a) (stock) jobbing** = buying and selling shares from other traders on the Stock Exchange **(b)** doing small pieces of work; **jobbing gardener** *or* **jobbing printer** = person who does odd jobs in the garden *or* who does small printing jobs

◊ **jobless** *noun* **the jobless** = people with no jobs *or* the unemployed
NOTE: takes a plural verb

QUOTE: he insisted that the tax advantages he directed toward small businesses will help create jobs
Toronto Star
QUOTE: the contradiction between the jobless figures and latest economic review *Sunday Times*
QUOTE: warehouse clubs buy directly from manufacturers, eliminating jobbers and wholesale middlemen
Duns Business Month

join *verb* **(a)** to put things together; **the offices were joined together by making a door in the wall; if the paper is too short to take all the accounts, you can join an extra piece on the bottom (b) to join a firm** = to start work with a company; **he joined on January 1st** = he started work on the January 1st **(c) to join an association** *or* **a group** = to become a member of an association *or* a group; **all the staff have joined the company pension plan; he was asked to join the board; Smith Ltd has applied to join the trade association**

joint *adjective* **(a)** combined *or* with two or more organizations linked together; **joint commission of inquiry** *or* **joint committee** = commission *or* committee with representatives of various organizations on it; **joint discussions** = discussions between management and workers before something is done; **joint management** = management done by two or more people; **joint venture** = very large business project where two or more companies join together **(b) joint account** = bank account for two people; **joint-stock bank** = bank which is a public company quoted on the Stock Exchange; **joint-stock company** = public company whose shares are owned by very many people **(c)** one of two or more people who work together *or* who are linked; **joint beneficiary; joint managing director; joint owner; joint signatory; joint ownership** = owning of a property by several owners

◊ **jointly** *adverb* together with one or more other people; **to own a property jointly; to manage a company jointly; they are jointly liable for damages**

journal *noun* **(a)** book with the account of sales and purchases made each day **(b)** magazine; **house journal** = magazine produced for the workers in a company to give them news about the company; **trade journal** = magazine produced for people or companies in a certain trade

◊ **journalist** *noun* person who writes for a newspaper

journey *noun* long trip, especially a trip done by a salesman; **he planned his journey to visit all his accounts in two days; journey order** = order given by the shopkeeper to a salesman when he calls

judge **1** *noun* person who decides in a legal case; **the judge sent him to prison for embezzlement 2** *verb* to decide; **he judged it was time to call an end to the discussions**

◊ **judgement** *or* **judgment** *noun* legal decision *or* official decision; **to pronounce judgement** *or* **to give one's judgement on something** = to give an official or legal decision about something; **judgment debtor** = debtor who has been ordered by a court to pay a debt
NOTE: the spelling **judgment** is used by lawyers

judicial *adjective* referring to the law; **judicial processes** = the ways in which the law works

jumble sale *noun* sale of odd secondhand items organized by a club or organization to raise money

jump **1** *noun* sudden rise; **jump in prices; jump in unemployment figures 2** *verb* **(a)** to

go up suddenly; **oil prices have jumped since the war started; share values jumped on the Stock Exchange (b)** to go away suddenly; **to jump bail** = not to appear in court after having been released on bail; **to jump the gun** = to start to do something too early *or* before you should; **to jump the queue** = to go in front of someone who has been waiting longer; **they jumped the queue and got their export licence before we did; to jump ship** = to leave a ship where you work as a sailor and not to go back

◊ **jumpy** *adjective* nervous *or* excited; **the market is jumpy** = the stock market is nervous and share prices are likely to fluctuate

junior **1** *adjective* younger *or* lower in rank; **junior clerk** = clerk, usually young, who has lower status than a senior clerk; **junior executive** *or* **junior manager** = young manager in a company; **junior partner** = person who has been made a partner more recently than others; **John Smith, Junior** = the younger John Smith (i.e. the son of John Smith, Senior) **2** *noun* **(a)** barrister who is not a Queen's counsel **(b) office junior** = young man or woman who does all types of work in an office

junk *noun* rubbish *or* useless items; **you should throw away all that junk; junk bonds** = bonds raised as debentures on the security of a company which is the subject of a takeover bid; **junk mail** = advertising material sent through the post
NOTE: no plural

jurisdiction *noun* **within the jurisdiction of the court** = in the legal power of a court

Kk

K *abbreviation* one thousand; **"salary: £15K + "** = salary more than £15,000 per annum

keen *adjective* **(a)** eager *or* active; **keen competition** = strong competition; **we are facing some keen competition from European manufacturers; keen demand** = wide demand; **there is a keen demand for home**

computers **(b) keen prices** = prices which are kept low so as to be competitive; **our prices are the keenest on the market**

keep *verb* **(a)** to go on doing something; **they kept working, even when the boss told them to stop; the other secretaries complain that she keeps singing when she is typing (b)** to do what is necessary; **to keep an appointment** = to be there when you said you would be; **to keep the books of a company** *or* **to keep a company's books** = to note the accounts of a company accurately **(c)** to hold items for sale *or* for information; **we always keep this item in stock** = we always have this item in our warehouse *or* shop; **to keep someone's name on file** = to have someone's name on a list for reference **(d)** to hold things at a certain level; **we must keep our mailing list up to date; to keep spending to a minimum; the price of oil has kept the pound at a high level; the government is encouraging firms to keep prices low; lack of demand for typewriters has kept prices down**
NOTE: keeping - kept
◇ **keep back** *verb* to hold on to something which you could give to someone; **to keep back information** *or* **to keep something back from someone; to keep £10 back from someone's salary**
◇ **keeping** *noun* **safe keeping** = being looked after carefully; **we put the documents into the bank for safe keeping**
NOTE: no plural
◇ **keep on** *verb* to continue to do something; **the factory kept on working in spite of the fire; we keep on receiving orders for this item although it was discontinued two years ago**
◇ **keep up** *verb* to hold at a certain high level; **we must keep up the turnover in spite of the recession; she kept up a rate of sixty words per minute for several hours**

key *noun* **(a)** piece of metal used to open a lock; **we have lost the keys to the computer room; key money** = premium paid when taking over the keys of a flat or office which you are renting **(b)** part of a computer *or* typewriter which you press with your fingers; **there are sixty-four keys on the keyboard; control key** = key on a computer which works part of a program; **shift key** = key which makes a typewriter *or* computer move to capital letters **(c)** important; **key factor; key**

industry; **key personnel; key post; key staff**
◇ **keyboard** 1 *noun* part of a typewriter or computer with keys which are pressed to make a letter or figure; **qwerty keyboard** = English language keyboard, where the first letters are Q-W-E-R-T-Y; **the computer has a normal qwerty keyboard** 2 *verb* to press the keys on a keyboard to type something; **he is keyboarding our address list**
◇ **keyboarder** *noun* person who types information into a computer
◇ **keyboarding** *noun* act of typing on a keyboard; **keyboarding costs have risen sharply**
NOTE: no plural
◇ **keypad** *noun* small keyboard; **numeric keypad** = part of a computer keyboard which is a programmable set of numbered keys

kg = KILOGRAM

kickback *noun* illegal commission paid to someone (especially a government official) who helps in a business deal

killing *noun* *informal* huge profit; **he made a killing on the stock market**

kilo *or* **kilogram** *noun* measure of weight (= one thousand grams)
◇ **kilobyte** *noun* unit of storage in a computer (= 1,024 bytes)
◇ **kilometre** *or* *US* **kilometer** *noun* measure of length (= one thousand metres); **the car does fifteen kilometres to the litre** = the car uses a litre of petrol to travel fifteen kilometres

kind *noun* sort *or* type; **the printer produces two kinds of printout; our drinks machine has three kinds of soups; payment in kind** = payment made by giving goods or food, but not money

kiosk *noun* small wooden shelter, for selling goods out of doors; **a newspaper kiosk; telephone kiosk** = shelter with a public telephone in it

kite *noun* **(a) to fly a kite** = to put forward an proposal to try to interest people; **kite flier** = person who tries to impress by putting forward a proposal;

kite-flying = trying to impress by putting forward grand plans **(b)** *GB* **kite mark** = mark on goods to show they meet official standards

kitty *noun* money which has been collected by a group of people to be used later (such as for an office party)

km = KILOMETRE

knock *verb* **(a)** to hit something; **he knocked on the door and went in; she knocked her head on the filing cabinet (b) to knock the competition** = to hit competing firms hard by vigorous selling; **knocking copy** = advertising material which criticizes competing products
◇ **knock down** *verb* **to knock something down to a bidder** = to sell something at an auction; **the stock was knocked down to him for £10,000**
◇ **knockdown** *noun* **knockdown prices** = very low prices; **he sold me the car at a knockdown price**
◇ **knock off** *verb* **(a)** to stop work **(b)** to reduce a price by an amount; **he knocked £10 off the price for cash**
◇ **knock-on effect** *noun* effect which an action will have on other situations; **the strike by customs officers has had a knock-on effect on car production by slowing down exports of cars**

know *verb* **(a)** to learn *or* to have information about something; **I do not know how a computer works; does he know how long it takes to get to the airport? the managing director's secretary does not know where he is (b)** to have met someone; **do you know Mr Jones, our new sales director? he knows the African market very well**
NOTE: **knowing - known**
◇ **know-how** *noun* knowledge about how something works *or* how something is made; **electronic know-how; to acquire computer know-how**
NOTE: no plural
◇ **knowledge** *noun* what is known; **he had no knowledge of the contract** = he did not know that the contract existed
NOTE: no plural

LI

l = LITRE

label 1 *noun* **(a)** piece of paper *or* card attached to something to show its price *or* an address *or* instructions for use; **gummed label** = label which you wet to make it stick on the item; **self-sticking label** = sticky label, ready to stick on an item; **tie-on label** = label with a piece of string attached so that it can be tied on to an item **(b) address label** = label with an address on it; **price label** = label showing a price; **quality label** = label which states the quality of something **(c) own label goods** = goods specially produced for a store with the store's name on them **2** *verb* to attach a label to something; **incorrectly labelled parcel** = parcel with the wrong information on the label
NOTE: **labelling - labelled** but US **labeling - labeled**
◇ **labelling** *noun* putting a label on something; **labelling department** = section of a factory where labels are attached to the product
NOTE: no plural

laboratory *noun* place where scientific research is carried out; **the product was developed in the company's laboratories; all products are tested in our own laboratories**

labour *or* US **labor** *noun* **(a)** heavy work; **manual labour** = work done by hand; **to charge for materials and labour** = to charge for both the materials used in a job and also the hours of work involved; **labour costs** *or* **labour charges** = cost of the workers employed to make a product (not including materials or overheads); **indirect labour costs** = cost of wages of workers who are not directly involved in making the product (such as secretaries, cleaners); **labour is charged at £5 an hour** = each hour of work costs £5 **(b)** workers *or* the workforce; **casual labour** = workers who are hired for a short period; **cheap labour** = workers who do not earn much money; **local labour** = workers recruited near a factory, not brought in from somewhere else; **organized labour** = workers who are members of trade unions; **skilled labour** = workers who have special knowledge or qualifications; **labour force** = all workers; **the management has made**

an increased offer to the labour force; **we are setting up a factory in the Far East because of the cheap labour force available; labour market** = number of workers who are available for work; **25,000 young people have left school and have come on to the labour market** = 25,000 people have left school and become available for work; **labour shortage** or **shortage of labour** = situation where there are not enough workers to fill jobs; **labour-intensive industry** = industry which needs large numbers of workers or where labour costs are high in relation to turnover **(c) labour disputes** = arguments between management and workers; **labour laws** or **labour legislation** = laws relating to the employment of workers; **labour relations** = relations between management and workers; *US* **labor union** = organization which represents workers who are its members in discussions about wages and conditions of work with management **(d) International Labour Organization** = section of the United Nations which tries to improve working conditions and workers' pay in member countries
NOTE: no plural

◇ **labourer** *noun* person who does heavy work; **agricultural labourer** = person who does heavy work on a farm; **casual labourer** = worker who can be hired for a short period; **manual labourer** = person who does heavy work with his hands

◇ **labour-saving** *adjective* which saves you doing hard work; **a labour-saving device**

QUOTE: the possibility that British goods will price themselves back into world markets is doubtful as long as sterling labour costs continue to rise faster than in competitor countries
Sunday Times

QUOTE: 70 per cent of Australia's labour force is employed in service activity
Australian Financial Review

QUOTE: European economies are being held back by rigid labor markets and wage structures
Duns Business Month

---

lack **1** *noun* not having enough; **lack of data** or **lack of information** = not having enough information; **the decision has been put back for lack of up-to-date information; lack of funds** = not enough money; **the project was cancelled because of lack of funds**
NOTE: no plural
2 *verb* not to have enough of something;

the company lacks capital; the sales staff lack motivation = the sales staff are not motivated enough

ladder *noun* series of steps made of wood or metal which can be moved about, and which you can climb; **you will need a ladder to look into the machine; promotion ladder** = series of steps by which people can be promoted; **by being appointed sales manager, he moved several steps up the promotion ladder**

laden *adjective* loaded; **fully-laden ship** = ship with a full cargo; **ship laden in bulk** = ship which has a loose cargo (such as corn) which is not packed in containers

lading *noun* loading or putting goods on a ship; **bill of lading** = list of goods being shipped, which the transporter gives to the person sending the goods to show that they have been loaded
NOTE: no plural

laissez-faire economy *noun* economy where the government does not interfere because it believes it is right to let the economy run itself

lame *adjective* walking badly because of a bad leg
◇ **lame duck** *noun* company which is in financial difficulties; **the government has refused to help lame duck companies**

land **1** *noun* area of earth; **land agent** = person who runs a farm or a large area of land for someone; *GB* **land register** = register of land, showing who owns it and what buildings are on it; **land registration** = system of registering land and its owners; **land registry** = government office where land is registered; **land taxes** = taxes on the amount of land someone owns **2** *verb* **(a)** to put goods or passengers on to land after a voyage by sea or by air; **to land goods at a port; to land passengers at an airport; landed costs** = costs of goods which have been delivered to a port, unloaded and passed through customs **(b)** to come down to earth after a flight; **the plane landed ten minutes late**
◇ **landing** *noun* **landing card** = card given to passengers who have passed customs and can land from a ship or an aircraft; **landing charges** = payment for

putting goods on land and the customs duties; **landing order** = permit which allows goods to be unloaded into a bonded warehouse without paying customs duty

◇ **landlady** *noun* woman who owns a property which she lets

◇ **landlord** *noun* person *or* company which owns a property which is let; **ground landlord** = person *or* company which owns the freehold of a property which is then let and sublet; **our ground landlord is an insurance company**

◇ **landowner** *noun* person who owns large areas of land

language *noun* words spoken or written by people in a certain country; **the managing director conducted the negotiations in three languages; programming language** = system of signs, letters and words used to instruct a computer; **what language does the program run on?**

lapse 1 *noun* **a lapse of time** = a period of time which has passed 2 *verb* to stop being valid *or* to stop being active; **the guarantee has lapsed; to let an offer lapse** = to allow time to pass so that an offer is no longer valid

large *adjective* very big *or* important; **our company is one of the largest suppliers of computers to the government; he is our largest customer; why has she got an office which is larger than mine?**

◇ **largely** *adverb* mainly *or* mostly; **our sales are largely in the home market; they have largely pulled out of the American market**

◇ **large-scale** *adjective* working in a large way, with large numbers of people *or* large amounts of money involved; **large-scale investment in new technology; large-scale redundancies in the construction industry**

last 1 *adjective & adverb* **(a)** coming at the end of a series; **out of a queue of twenty people, I was served last; this is our last board meeting before we move to our new offices; we finished the last items in the order just two days before the promised delivery date; last quarter** = period of three months to the end of the financial year **(b)** most recent *or* most recently; **where is the last batch of orders? the last ten**

orders were only for small quantities; **last week** *or* **last month** *or* **last year** = the week *or* month *or* year before this one; **last week's sales were the best we have ever had; the sales managers have been asked to report on last month's drop in unit sales; last year's accounts have to be ready by the AGM (c) the week** *or* **month** *or* **year before last** = the week *or* month *or* year before the one before this; **last year's figures were bad, but they were an improvement on those of the year before last** 2 *verb* to go on *or* to continue; **the boom started in the 1970s and lasted until the early 1980s; the discussions over redundancies lasted all day**

◇ **last in first out** *noun* **(a)** redundancy policy, where the people who have been most recently appointed are the first to be made redundant **(b)** accounting method where stock is valued at the price of the latest purchases

late 1 *adjective* **(a)** after the time stated or agreed; **we apologize for the late arrival of the plane from Amsterdam; there is a penalty for late delivery** = if delivery is later than the agreed date, the supplier has to pay a fine **(b)** at the end of a period of time; **latest date for signature of the contract** = the last acceptable date for signing the contract **(c) latest** = most recent; **he always drives the latest model of car; here are the latest sales figures** 2 *adverb* after the time stated or agreed; **the shipment was landed late; the plane was two hours late**

◇ **late-night** *adjective* happening late at night; **he had a late-night meeting at the airport; their late-night negotiations ended in an agreement which was signed at 3 a.m.**

launch 1 *verb* to put a new product on the market (usually spending money on advertising it); **they launched their new car model at the motor show; the company is spending thousands of pounds to launch a new brand of soap** 2 *noun* act of putting a new product on the market; **the launch of the new model has been put back three months; the company is geared up for the launch of the new brand of soap; the management has decided on a September launch date**

◇ **launching** *noun* act of putting a new product on the market; **launching costs** = costs of publicity for a new product; **launching date** = date when a new product

is officially shown to the public for the first time; **launching party** = party held to advertise the launching of a new product
NOTE: no plural

launder *verb* to pass illegal profits *or* money which has not been taxed, etc. into the normal banking system; **to launder money through an offshore bank**

law *noun* **(a) laws** = rules by which a country is governed and the activities of people and organizations controlled; **labour laws** = laws concerning the employment of workers **(b) law** = all the laws of a country taken together; **civil law** = laws relating to arguments between individuals and the rights of individuals; **commercial law** = laws regarding business; **company law** = laws which refer to the way companies work; **contract law** *or* **the law of contract** = laws relating to private agreements; **copyright law** = laws concerning the protection of copyright; **criminal law** = laws relating to crime; **international law** = laws referring to the way countries deal with each other; **maritime law** *or* **the law of the sea** = laws referring to ships, ports, etc.; **law courts** = place where a judge listens to cases and decides who is right legally; **to take someone to law** = to tell someone to appear in court to settle an argument; **inside the law** *or* **within the law** = obeying the laws of a country; **against** *or* **outside the law** = not according to the laws of a country; **the company is operating outside the law; to break the law** = to do something which is not allowed by law; **he is breaking the law by selling goods on Sunday; you will be breaking the law if you try to take that computer out of the country without an export licence (c)** general rule; **law of supply and demand** = general rule that the amount of a product which is available is related to the needs of the possible customers; **law of diminishing returns** = general rule that as more factors of production (land, labour and capital) are added to the existing factors, so the amount they produce is proportionately smaller
NOTE: no plural for (b)

◇ **lawful** *adjective* acting within the law; **lawful practice** = action which is permitted by the law; **lawful trade** = trade which is allowed by law

◇ **lawfully** *adverb* acting within the law

◇ **lawsuit** *noun* case brought to a court; **to bring a lawsuit against someone** = to tell someone to appear in court to settle an argument; **to defend a lawsuit** = to appear in court to state your case

◇ **lawyer** *noun* person who has studied law and can act for people on legal business; **commercial lawyer** *or* **company lawyer** = person who specializes in company law *or* who advises companies on legal problems; **international lawyer** = person who specializes in international law; **maritime lawyer** = person who specializes in laws concerning ships

lay *verb* to put; **to lay an embargo on trade with a country** = to forbid trade with a country
NOTE: **laying - laid**

◇ **lay off** *verb* **(a) to lay off workers** = to dismiss workers for a time (until more work is available); **the factory laid off half its workers because of lack of orders (b) to lay off risks** = to protect oneself against risk in one investment by making other investments

◇ **lay-off** *noun* action of dismissing a worker for a time; **the recession has caused hundreds of lay-offs in the car industry**

◇ **lay out** *verb* to spend money; **we had to lay out half our cash budget on equipping the new factory**

◇ **layout** *noun* arrangement of the inside of a building; **they have altered the layout of the offices**

◇ **lay up** *verb* to stop using a ship because there is no work; **half the shipping fleet is laid up by the recession**

QUOTE: the company lost $52 million last year, and has laid off close to 2,000 employees
Toronto Star
QUOTE: while trading conditions for the tanker are being considered, it is possible that the ship could be laid up
Lloyd's List

---

lazy *adjective* (person) who does not want to work; **she is too lazy to do any overtime; he is so lazy he does not even send in his expense claims on time**

lb = pound

L/C = LETTER OF CREDIT

lead *verb* **(a)** to be the first *or* to be in front; **the company leads the market in cheap computers (b)** to be the main person in a group; **she will lead the trade mission to Nigeria; the tour of American factories will be led by the minister**
NOTE: **leading - led**

◇ **leader** *noun* **(a)** person who manages *or* directs others; **the leader of the construction workers' union** *or* **the construction workers' leader; she is the leader of the trade mission to Nigeria; the minister was the leader of the party of industrialists on a tour of American factories (b)** product which sells best; **a market leader =** product which sells most in a market *or* company which has the largest share of a market; **loss-leader =** article which is sold very cheaply to attract customers **(c)** important share *or* share which is often bought or sold on the Stock Exchange

◇ **leading** *adjective* most important; **leading industrialists feel the end of the recession is near; leading shares rose on the Stock Exchange; leading shareholders in the company forced a change in management policy; they are the leading company in the field**

◇ **lead time** *noun* time between deciding to place an order and receiving the product; **the lead time on this item is more than six weeks**

◇ **lead (up) to** *verb* to be the cause of; **the discussions led to a big argument between the management and the union; we received a series of approaches leading up to the takeover bid**

leaflet *noun* sheet of paper giving information, used to advertise something; **to mail leaflets** *or* **to hand out leaflets describing services; they made a leaflet mailing to 20,000 addresses**

leak *verb* to pass on a secret; **information on the contract was leaked to the press; they discovered the managing director was leaking information to a rival company**

◇ **leakage** *noun* amount of goods lost in storage (by going bad *or* by being stolen *or* by escaping from the container)

leap-frogging *adjective* **leap-frogging pay demands =** pay demands where each section of workers asks for higher pay to do better than another section, which then asks for further increases in turn

lease 1 *noun* **(a)** written contract for letting or renting of a building *or* a piece of land *or* a piece of equipment for a period against payment of a fee; **long lease** *or* **short lease =** lease which runs for fifty years or more *or* for up to two or three years; **to take an office building on a long lease; we have a short lease on our current premises; to rent office space on a twenty-year lease; full repairing lease =** lease where the tenant has to pay for all repairs to the property; **headlease =** lease from the freeholder to a tenant; **sublease** *or* **underlease =** lease from a tenant to another tenant; **the lease expires** *or* **runs out in 1989 =** the lease comes to an end in 1989; **on expiration of the lease =** when the lease comes to an end **(b) to hold an oil lease in the North Sea =** to have a lease on a section of the North Sea to explore for oil **2** *verb* **(a)** to let or rent offices *or* land *or* machinery for a period; **to lease offices to small firms; to lease equipment (b)** to use an office *or* land *or* machinery for a time and pay a fee; **to lease an office from an insurance company; all our company cars are leased**

◇ **lease back** *verb* to sell a property *or* machinery to a company and then take it back on a lease; **they sold the office building to raise cash, and then leased it back for twenty-five years**

◇ **lease-back** *noun* arrangement where property is sold and then taken back on a lease; **they sold the office building and then took it back under a lease-back arrangement**

◇ **leasehold** *noun* & *adjective* holding property on a lease; **leasehold property; the company has some valuable leaseholds; to buy a property leasehold**

◇ **leaseholder** *noun* person who holds a property on a lease

◇ **leasing** *noun* which leases *or* working under a lease; **the company has branched out into car leasing; an equipment-leasing company; to run a copier under a leasing arrangement**
NOTE: no plural. See also LESSEE

leave 1 *noun* permission to be away from work; **six weeks' annual leave =** six weeks' holiday each year; **leave of absence =** being allowed to be away from work; **maternity leave =** permission given to woman to be away from work to have a

baby; **sick leave** = period when a worker is away from work because of illness; **to go on leave** or **to be on leave** = to be away from work; **she is away on sick leave** or **on maternity leave**
NOTE: no plural
2 verb **(a)** to go away from; **he left his office early to go to the meeting; the next plane leaves at 10.20 (b)** to resign; **he left his job and bought a farm**
NOTE: **leaving - left**
◊ **leave out** verb not to include; **she left out the date on the letter; the contract leaves out all details of marketing arrangements**

ledger noun book in which accounts are written; **bought ledger** or **purchase ledger** = book in which expenditure is noted; **bought ledger clerk** or **sales ledger clerk** = office worker who deals with the bought ledger or the sales ledger; **nominal ledger** = book which records a company's income and expenditure in general; **payroll ledger** = list of staff and their salaries; **sales ledger** = book in which sales are noted

left adjective on the side of the body which usually has the weaker hand or not right; **the numbers run down the left side of the page; put the debits in the left column;** see also LEAVE
◊ **left-hand** adjective belonging to the left side; **the debits are in the left-hand column in the accounts; he keeps the personnel files in the left-hand drawer of his desk**
◊ **left luggage office** noun room where suitcases can be left while passengers are waiting for a plane or train

legacy noun property given by someone to someone else at his death

legal adjective **(a)** according to the law or allowed by the law; **the company's action was completely legal (b)** referring to the law; **to take legal action** = to sue someone or to take someone to court; **to take legal advice** = to ask a lawyer to advise about a legal problem; **legal adviser** = person who advises clients about the law; GB **legal aid** = government scheme where someone who has little money can have his legal expenses paid for him; **legal claim** = statement that someone owns something legally; **he has no legal claim to the property; legal costs** or **legal charges** or

legal expenses = money spent on fees to lawyers; **legal currency** = money which is legally used in a country; **legal department** or **legal section** = section of a company dealing with legal matters; **legal expert** = person who knows a lot about the law; **legal holiday** = day when banks and other businesses are closed; **legal tender** = coins or notes which can be legally used to pay a debt (small denominations cannot be used to pay large debts)
◊ **legality** noun being allowed by law; **there is doubt about the legality of the company's action in dismissing him**
◊ **legalize** verb to make something legal
◊ **legalization** noun making something legal
◊ **legally** adverb according to the law; **the contract is legally binding** = according to the law, the contract has to be obeyed; **the directors are legally responsible** = the law says that the directors are responsible

legatee noun person who receives property from someone who has died

legislation noun laws; **labour legislation** = laws concerning the employment of workers
NOTE: no plural

lend verb to allow someone to use something for a period; **to lend something to someone** or **to lend someone something; he lent the company money** or **he lent money to the company; to lend money against security; the bank lent him £50,000 to start his business**
NOTE: **lending - lent**
◊ **lender** noun person who lends money; **lender of the last resort** = central bank which lends money to commercial banks
◊ **lending** noun act of letting someone use money for a time; **lending limit** = limit on the amount of money a bank can lend
NOTE: no plural

length noun **(a)** measurement of how long something is; **the boardroom table is twelve feet in length; inches and centimetres are measurements of length (b)** to go to **great lengths to get something** = to do anything (even commit a crime) to get something; **they went to considerable lengths to keep the turnover secret**

less 1 *adjective* smaller than *or* of a smaller size *or* of a smaller value; **we do not grant credit for sums of less than £100; he sold it for less than he had paid for it** 2 *preposition* minus *or* with a sum removed; **purchase price less 15% discount; interest less service charges**

lessee *noun* person who has a lease *or* who pays money for a property he leases ◊ **lessor** *noun* person who grants a lease on a property

let 1 *verb* to lend a house *or* an office *or* a farm to someone for a payment; **to let an office** = to allow someone to use an office for a time in return for payment of rent; **offices to let** = offices which are available to be leased by companies
NOTE: **letting - let**
2 *noun* period of the lease of a property; **they took the office on a short let**
◊ **let-out clause** *noun* clause which allows someone to avoid doing something in a contract; **he added a let-out clause to the effect that the payments would be revised if the exchange rate fell by more than 5%**

letter *noun* **(a)** piece of writing sent from one person *or* company to another to give information; **business letter** = letter which deals with business matters; **circular letter** = letter sent to many people; **covering letter** = letter sent with documents to say why they are being sent; **follow-up letter** = letter sent to someone after a previous letter *or* after a visit; **private letter** = letter which deals with personal matters; **standard letter** = letter which is sent without change to various correspondents **(b) letter of acknowledgement** = letter which says that something has been received; **letters of administration** = letter given by a court to allow someone to deal with the estate of someone who has died; **letter of allotment** *or* **allotment letter** = letter which tells someone how many shares in a new company he has been allotted; **letter of application** = letter in which someone applies for a job; **letter of appointment** = letter in which someone is appointed to a job; **letter of comfort** = letter supporting

someone who is trying to get a loan; **letter of complaint** = letter in which someone complains; **letter of credit** = letter from a bank allowing someone credit and promising to repay at a later date; **letter of indemnity** = letter promising payment of compensation for a loss; **letter of intent** = letter which states what a company intends to do if something happens; **letters patent** = official document which gives someone the exclusive right to make and sell something which he has invented; **letter of reference** = letter in which an employer recommends someone for a new job **(c) air letter** = special thin blue paper which when folded can be sent by air without an envelope; **airmail letter** = letter sent by air; **express letter** = letter sent very fast; **registered letter** = letter which is noted by the post office before it is sent, so that compensation can be claimed if it is lost **(d) to acknowledge receipt by letter** = to write a letter to say that something has been received **(e)** written or printed sign (such as A, B, C, etc.); **write your name and address in block letters** *or* **in capital letters**
◊ **letterhead** *noun* name and address of a company printed at the top of a piece of notepaper

letting *noun* **letting agency** = agency which deals in property to let; **furnished lettings** = furnished property to let

level 1 *noun* position where high is large and low is small; **low level of productivity** *or* **low productivity levels; to raise the level of employee benefits; to lower the level of borrowings; high level of investment** = large amount of money invested; **a decision taken at the highest level** = decision taken by the most important person or group; **low-level** = not very important; **a low-level delegation; high-level** = very important; **a high-level meeting** *or* **decision; decisions taken at managerial level** = decisions taken by managers; **manning levels** *or* **staffing levels** = number of people required in each department of a company to do the work efficiently 2 *verb* **to level off** *or* **to level out** = to stop rising or falling; **profits have levelled off over the last few years; prices are levelling out**
NOTE: **levelling - levelled** but US **leveling - leveled**

QUOTE: figures from the Fed on industrial production for April show a decline to levels last seen in June 1984   *Sunday Times*
QUOTE: applications for mortgages are running at a high level   *Times*
QUOTE: employers having got their staff back up to a reasonable level are waiting until the scope for overtime working is exhausted before hiring   *Sydney Morning Herald*

leverage *noun* **(a)** influence which you can use to achieve an aim; **he has no leverage over the chairman (b)** relation between a company's capital borrowed at a fixed interest and the value of its ordinary shares **(c)** borrowing money at fixed interest which is then used to produce more money than the interest paid
NOTE: no plural
◇ **leveraged buyout** *noun* buying all the shares in a company by borrowing money against the security of the shares to be bought

QUOTE: the offer came after management had offered to take the company private through a leveraged buyout for $825 million   *Fortune*

levy **1** *noun* money which is demanded and collected by the government; **capital levy** = tax on the value of a person's property and possessions; **import levy** = tax on imports, especially in the EEC a tax on imports of farm produce from outside the EEC; **levies on luxury items** = taxes on luxury items; **training levy** = tax to be paid by companies to fund the government's training schemes **2** *verb* to demand payment of a tax or an extra payment and to collect it; **the government has decided to levy a tax on imported cars; to levy a duty on the import of luxury items; to levy members for a new club house** = to ask members of the club to pay for the new building

QUOTE: royalties have been levied at a rate of 12.5% of full production   *Lloyd's List*

liability *noun* **(a)** being legally responsible for damage or loss, etc.; **to accept liability for something** = to agree that you are responsible for something; **to refuse liability for something** = to refuse to agree that you are responsible for something; **contractual liability** = legal responsibility for something as stated in a contract;

employers' liability insurance = insurance to cover accidents which may happen at work, and for which the company may be responsible; **limited liability** = situation where someone's liability for debt is limited by law; **limited liability company** = company where a shareholder is responsible for repaying the company's debts only to the face value of the shares he owns **(b) liabilities** = debts of a business; **the balance sheet shows the company's assets and liabilities; current liabilities** = debts which a company should pay within the next accounting period; **long-term liabilities** = debts which are not due to be paid for some time; **he was not able to meet his liabilities** = he could not pay his debts; **to discharge one's liabilities in full** = to pay everything which you owe
NOTE: no plural for (a)
◇ **liable** *adjective* **(a) liable for** = legally responsible for; **the customer is liable for breakages; the chairman was personally liable for the company's debts (b) liable to** = which is officially due to be paid; **goods which are liable to stamp duty**

libel **1** *noun* untrue written statement which damages someone's character; **action for libel** or **libel action** = case in a law court where someone says that another person has written a libel **2** *verb* **to libel someone** = to damage someone's character in writing
NOTE: **libelling - libelled** but US **libeling - libeled**. Compare **SLANDER**

licence or US **license** *noun* **(a)** official document which allows someone to do something; **driving licence** = document which allows someone to drive a car or a truck, etc.; **applicants should hold a valid driving licence; import licence** or **export licence** = documents which allow goods to be exported or imported; **liquor licence** = government document allowing someone to sell alcohol; **off licence** = licence to sell alcohol to be drunk away from the place where it is bought; shop which sells alcohol for drinking at home **(b) goods manufactured under licence** = goods made with the permission of the owner of the copyright or patent
◇ **license** **1** *noun* US = LICENCE **2** *verb* to give someone official permission to do something; **licensed to sell beers, wines and spirits; to license a company to manu-**

facture spare parts; she is licensed to run an employment agency

◇ **licensee** *noun* person who has a licence, especially a licence to sell alcohol *or* to manufacture something

◇ **licensing** *noun* which refers to licences; **a licensing agreement; licensing laws;** *GB* **licensing hours** = hours of the day when alcohol can be sold

lien *noun* legal right to hold someone's goods and keep them until a debt has been paid

lieu *noun* **in lieu of** = instead of; **she was given two months' salary in lieu of notice** = she was given the salary and asked to leave immediately

life *noun* **(a)** time when a person is alive; **for life** = for as long as someone is alive; **his pension gives him a comfortable income for life; life annuity** *or* **annuity for life** = annual payments made to someone as long as he is alive; **life assurance** *or* **life insurance** = insurance which pays a sum of money when someone dies, or at a certain date if he is still alive; **the life assured** *or* **the life insured** = the person whose life has been covered by the life assurance; **life expectancy** = number of years a person is likely to live; **life interest** = interest in a property which stops when a person dies **(b)** period of time something exists; **the life of a loan; during the life of the agreement; shelf life of a product** = length of time during which a product can stay in the shop and still be good to use

◇ **lifeboat** *noun* boat used to rescue passengers from sinking ships; **lifeboat operation** = rescue of a company (especially of a bank) which is in difficulties

LIFO = LAST IN FIRST OUT

lift 1 *noun* machine which takes people or goods from one floor to another in a building; **he took the lift to the 27th floor; the staff could not get into their office when the lift broke down 2** *verb* to take away *or* to remove; **the government has lifted the ban on imports from Japan; to lift trade**

barriers; **the minister has lifted the embargo on the export of computers to East European countries**

light *adjective* not heavy; **shares fell back in light trading** = shares lost value on a day when there was little business done on the Stock Exchange; **light industry** = industry which makes small products (such as clothes, books, calculators)

limit 1 *noun* point at which something ends *or* point where you can go no further; **to set limits to imports** *or* **to impose import limits** = to allow only a certain amount of imports; **age limit** = top age at which you are allowed to do a job; **there is an age limit of thirty-five on the post of buyer; credit limit** = largest amount of money which a customer can borrow; **he has exceeded his credit limit** = he has borrowed more money than he is allowed; **lending limit** = restriction on the amount of money a bank can lend; **time limit** = to set a time limit for acceptance of the offer maximum time which can be taken to do something; **weight limit** = maximum weight **2** *verb* to stop something from going beyond a certain point; **the banks have limited their credit** = the banks have allowed their customers only a certain amount of credit; **each agent is limited to twenty-five units** = each agent is allowed only twenty-five units to sell

◇ **limitation** *noun* **(a)** act of allowing only a certain quantity of something; **limitation of liability** = making someone liable for only a part of the damage or loss; **time limitation** = amount of time available; **the contract imposes limitations on the number of cars which can be imported (b) statute of limitations** = law which allows only a certain amount of time (a few years) for someone to claim damages or property

◇ **limited** *adjective* restricted *or* not open; **limited market** = market which can take only a certain quantity of goods; **limited liability company** = company where a shareholder is responsible for the company's debts only to the face value of his shares; **private limited company** = company with a small number of shareholders, whose shares are not traded on the Stock Exchange; **Smith and Sons, Ltd; Public Limited Company** = company whose shares can be bought on the Stock Exchange; **Smith and Sons, plc** ◇ **limiting** *adjective* which limits; **a limiting clause in a contract; the short holiday season is a limiting factor on the hotel trade**

line *noun* **(a)** long mark; **paper with thin blue lines; I prefer notepaper without any lines; he drew a thick line across the bottom of the column to show which figure was the total (b) shipping line** *or* **airline** = large shipping or aircraft company which carries passengers or cargo; **profits of major airlines have been affected by the rise in fuel prices (c) line of business** *or* **line of work** = type of business or work; **what is his line?; line of product** *or* **product line** = series of different products which form a group, all made by the same company; **we do not stock that line; computers are not one of our best-selling lines; they produce an interesting line in garden tools (d)** row of letters *or* figures on a page; **bottom line** = last line in accounts, showing the net profit; **the boss is interested only in the bottom line; to open a line of credit** *or* **a credit line** = to make credit available to someone **(e) assembly line** *or* **production line** = production system where the product (such as a car) moves slowly through a factory with new sections added to it as it goes along; **he works on the production line** *or* **he is a production line worker in the car factory (f) line chart** *or* **line graph** = chart or graph using lines to indicate values; **line printer** = machine which prints information from a computer one line at a time **(g) line of command** *or* **line management** *or* **line organization** = organization of a business where each manager is responsible for doing what his superior tells him to do **(h) telephone line** = wire along which telephone messages travel; **the line is bad** = it is difficult to hear clearly what someone is saying; **a crossed line** = when two telephone conversations get mixed; **the line is engaged** = the person is already speaking on the phone; **the chairman is on the other line** = the chairman is speaking on his second telephone; **outside line** = line from an internal office telephone system to the main telephone exchange ◇ **lined** *adjective* with lines; **he prefers lined paper for writing notes** ◇ **liner** *noun* large passenger ship

QUOTE: the best thing would be to have a few more plants close down and bring supply more in line with current demand *Fortune*
QUOTE: cash paid for overstocked lines, factory seconds, slow sellers, etc.
Australian Financial Review

link *verb* to join *or* to attach to something else; **to link pensions to inflation; his salary is linked to the cost of living; to link bonus payments to productivity**

liquid *adjective* **liquid assets** = cash, or bills which can easily be changed into cash; **to go liquid** = to convert as many assets as possible into cash ◇ **liquidate** *verb* **to liquidate a company** = to close a company and sell its assets; **to liquidate a debt** = to pay a debt in full; **to liquidate stock** = to sell stock to raise cash ◇ **liquidation** *noun* **(a) liquidation of a debt** = payment of a debt **(b)** closing of a company and selling of its assets; **the company went into liquidation** = the company was closed and its assets sold; **compulsory liquidation** = liquidation which is ordered by a court; **voluntary liquidation** = situation where a company itself decides it must close ◇ **liquidator** *noun* person named to supervise the closing of a company which is in liquidation ◇ **liquidity** *noun* having cash or assets which can be changed into cash; **liquidity crisis** = not having enough liquid assets

lira *noun* money used in Italy; **the book cost 2,700 lira** *or* **L2,700**
NOTE: **lira** is usually written **L** before figures: **L2,700**

list 1 *noun* **(a)** several items written one after the other; **list of products** *or* **product list; stock list; to add an item to a list; to cross an item off a list; address list** *or* **mailing list** = list of names and addresses of people and companies; **black list** = list of goods *or* companies *or* countries which are banned for trade; **picking list** = list of items in an order, but listed according to where they can be found in the warehouse **(b)** catalogue; **list price** = price as given in a catalogue; **price list** = sheet giving prices of goods for sale **2** *verb* **(a)** to write a series of items one after the other; **to list products by category; to list representatives**

by area; **to list products in a catalogue; the catalogue lists twenty-three models of washing machines (b) listed company =** company whose shares can be bought or sold on the Stock Exchange; **listed securities =** shares which can be bought or sold on the Stock Exchange *or* shares which appear on the official Stock Exchange list

◊ **listing** *noun* **(a)** Stock Exchange **listing =** being on the official list of shares which can be bought or sold on the Stock Exchange; **the company is planning to obtain a Stock Exchange listing (b)** computer **listing =** printout of a list of items taken from the data stored in a computer; **listing paper =** paper made as a long sheet, used in computer printers

literature *noun* written information about something; **please send me literature about your new product range**
NOTE: no plural

litigation *noun* the bringing of a lawsuit against someone
NOTE: no plural

litre *or* *US* **liter** *noun* measure of liquids; **the car does fifteen kilometres to the litre** *or* **fifteen kilometres per litre =** the car uses one litre of petrol to travel fifteen kilometres
NOTE: usually written l after figures: **25l**

lively *adjective* **lively market =** active stock market, with many shares being bought or sold

living *noun* **cost of living =** money which a person has to pay for rent, food, heating, etc.; **cost-of-living index =** way of measuring the cost of living which is shown as a percentage increase on the figure for the previous year; **he does not earn a living wage =** he does not earn enough to pay for essentials (food, heat, rent); **standard of living** *or* **living standards =** quality of personal home life (amount of food, clothes bought, size of the family car, etc.); **living standards fell as unemployment rose**
NOTE: no plural

Lloyd's *noun* central London insurance market; **Lloyd's Register =** classified list showing details of all the ships in the world; **ship which is A1 at Lloyd's =** ship in very good condition

load 1 *noun* **(a)** goods which are transported; **load of a lorry** *or* **of a container =** goods carried by a lorry or container; **lorry-load** *or* **container-load =** amount of goods carried on a lorry or container; **a container-load of spare parts is missing; they delivered six lorry-loads of coal; commercial load =** amount of goods *or* number of passengers which a bus *or* train *or* plane has to carry to make a profit; **maximum load =** largest weight of goods which a lorry *or* plane can carry; **load-carrying capacity =** amount of goods which a lorry is capable of carrying; **load factor =** number of seats in a bus *or* train *or* plane which are occupied by passengers who have paid the full fare **(b) workload =** amount of work which a person has to do; **he has difficulty in coping with his heavy workload 2** *verb* **(a) to load a lorry** *or* **a ship =** to put goods into a lorry *or* a ship for transporting; **to load cargo onto a ship; a truck loaded with boxes; a ship loaded with iron; fully loaded ship =** ship which is full of cargo **(b)** (*of ship*) to take on cargo; **the ship is loading a cargo of wood (c)** to put a program into a computer; **load the word-processing program before you start keyboarding**

◊ **loading** *noun* **loading bay =** section of road in a warehouse where lorries can drive in to be loaded; **loading dock =** part of a harbour where ships can load or unload; **loading ramp =** raised platform which makes it easier to load goods onto a lorry
NOTE: no plural

◊ **load line** *noun* line painted on the side of a ship to show where the water should reach for maximum safety if the ship is fully loaded

loan 1 *noun* money which has been lent; **loan capital =** part of a company's capital which is a loan to be repaid at a later date; **loan stock =** money lent to a company at a fixed rate of interest; **convertible loan stock =** money which can be exchanged for shares at a later date; **bank loan =** money lent by a bank; **bridging loan =** short-term loan to help someone buy a new house when he has not yet sold his old one; **government loan =** money lent by the government; **home loan =** loan by a bank or building society to help someone buy a house; **short-term loan** *or* **long-term loan =** loans which have to be repaid within a few weeks or some years; **soft loan** = loan (from a company to an employee *or* from one government to another) with no interest payable; **unsecured loan** = loan made with no security **2** *verb* to lend

lobby 1 *noun* group of people who try to influence members of parliament, members of town councils, etc.; **the energy-saving lobby** = people who try to persuade members of parliament to pass laws to save energy **2** *verb* to try to influence members of parliament, members of town councils, etc.; **the group lobbied the chairmen of all the committees**

local 1 *adjective* referring to a particular area, especially one near where a factory *or* an office is based; **local authority** = elected section of government which runs a small area of the country; **local call** = telephone call to a number in the same area as the person making the call; **local government** = elected administrative bodies which run areas of the country; **local labour** = workers who are recruited near a factory, and are not brought there from a distance **2** *noun* *US* branch of a trade union
◇ **locally** *adverb* in the area near where an office or factory is based; **we recruit all our staff locally**

> QUOTE: each cheque can be made out for the local equivalent of £100 rounded up to a convenient figure *Sunday Times*
> QUOTE: the business agent for Local 414 of the Store Union said his committee will recommend that the membership ratify the agreement *Toronto Star*
> QUOTE: EEC regulations insist that customers can buy cars anywhere in the EEC at the local pre-tax price *Financial Times*

locate *verb* **to be located** = to be in a certain place; **the warehouse is located near to the motorway**
◇ **location** *noun* place where something is; **the company has moved to a new location** = the company has moved to a new office or a different town

lock 1 *noun* device for closing a door *or* box so that it can be opened only with a key; **the lock is broken on the petty cash box; I have forgotten the combination of the lock on my briefcase 2** *verb* to close a door with a key, so that it cannot be opened; **the manager forgot to lock the door of the**

computer room; **the petty cash box was not locked**
◇ **lock out** *verb* **to lock out workers** = to shut the factory door so that workers cannot get in and so force them not to work until the conditions imposed by the management are met
◇ **lockout** *noun* industrial dispute where the management will not let the workers into the factory until they have agreed to the management's conditions
◇ **lock up** *verb* **to lock up a shop** *or* **an office** = to close and lock the door at the end of the day's work; **to lock up capital** = to have capital invested in such a way that it cannot be used for other investments
◇ **locking up** *noun* **the locking up of money in stock** = investing money in stock so that it cannot be used for other, possibly more profitable, investments
◇ **lock-up** *adjective* **lock-up shop** = shop which has no living accommodation and which the proprietor locks at night when it is closed

lodge *verb* **to lodge a complaint against someone** = to make an official complaint about someone; **to lodge money with someone** = to deposit money with someone; **to lodge securities as collateral** = to put securities into a bank to be used as collateral for a loan

log *verb* to write down all that happens; **to log phone calls** = to note all details of phone calls made
NOTE: **logging - logged**

logo *noun* symbol *or* design *or* group of letters used by a company as a mark on its products and in advertising

long 1 *adjective* for a large period of time; **long credit** = credit terms which allow the borrower a long time to pay; **in the long term** = over a long period of time; **to take the long view** = to plan for a long period before current investment becomes profitable **2** *noun* **longs** = government stocks which mature in over fifteen years' time
◇ **long-dated** *adjective* **long-dated bills** = bills which are payable in more than three months' time
◇ **long-distance** *adjective* **a long-distance call** = telephone call to a number

which is not near; **long-distance flight** = flight to a destination which is a long way away

◊ **longhand** *noun* handwriting where the words are written out in full and not typed or in shorthand; **applications should be written in longhand and sent to the personnel officer**

◊ **long-haul** *adjective* over a long distance; **long-haul flight** = long-distance flight especially between continents

◊ **long-range** *adjective* for a long period of time in the future; **long-range economic forecast** = forecast which covers a period of several years

◊ **long-standing** *adjective* which has been arranged for a long time; **long-standing agreement; long-standing customer** *or* **customer of long standing** = person who has been a customer for many years

◊ **long-term** *adjective* **on a long-term basis** = for a long period of time; **long-term debts** = debts which will be repaid many years later; **long-term forecast** = forecast for a period of over three years; **long-term loan** = loan to be repaid many years later; **long-term objectives** = aims which will take years to achieve

QUOTE: land held under long-term leases is not amortized   *Hongkong Standard*
QUOTE: the company began to experience a demand for longer-term mortgages when the flow of money used to finance these loans diminished
Globe and Mail (Toronto)

loophole *noun* **to find a loophole in the law** = to find a means of legally avoiding the law; **to find a tax loophole** = to find a means of legally not paying tax

QUOTE: because capital gains are not taxed but money taken out in profits is taxed, owners of businesses will be using accountants and tax experts to find loopholes in the law *Toronto Star*

loose *adjective* not packed together; **loose change** = money in coins; **to sell loose sugar** *or* **to sell sugar loose** = to sell sugar in separately weighed quantities, not in packets

◊ **loose-leaf book** *noun* book with loose pages which can be taken out and fixed back in again on rings

lorry *noun* large motor vehicle for carrying goods; **he drives a five-ton lorry; heavy lorry** = very large lorry which carries heavy loads; **lorry driver** = person who drives a lorry
NOTE: US English is **truck**

lose *verb* **(a)** not to have something any more; **to lose an order** = not to get an order which you were hoping to get; **during the strike, the company lost six orders to American competitors; to lose control of a company** = to find that you have less than 50% of the shares and so are no longer able to direct the company; **to lose customers** = to have fewer customers; **their service is so slow that they have been losing customers; she lost her job when the factory closed** = she was made redundant **(b)** to have less money; **he lost £25,000 in his father's computer company; the pound has lost value** = the pound is worth less **(c)** to drop to a lower price; **the dollar lost two cents against the yen; gold shares lost 5% on the market yesterday**
NOTE: **losing - lost**

◊ **lose out** *verb* to suffer as a result of something; **the company has lost out in the rush to make cheap computers**

loss *noun* **(a) loss of customers** = not keeping customers because of bad service *or* high prices, etc.; **loss of an order** = not getting an order which was expected; **the company suffered a loss of market penetration** = the company found it had a smaller share of the market; **compensation for loss of earnings** = payment to someone who has stopped earning money *or* who is not able to earn money; **compensation for loss of office** = payment to a director who is asked to leave a company before his contract ends **(b)** having less money than before *or* not making a profit; **the company suffered a loss** = the company did not make a profit; **to report a loss** = not to show a profit in the accounts at the end of the year; **the company reported a loss of £1m on the first year's trading; capital loss** = loss made by selling assets; **the car was written off as a dead loss** *or* **a total loss** = the car was so badly damaged that the insurers said it had no value; **paper loss** = loss made when an asset has fallen in value but has not been sold; **trading loss** = situation where the company's receipts are less than its expenditure; **at a loss** = making a loss *or* not making any profit;

the company is trading at a loss; he sold the shop at a loss; **to cut one's losses** = to stop doing something which was losing money **(c)** being worth less *or* having a lower value; **shares showed losses of up to 5% on the Stock Exchange (d) loss in weight** = goods which weigh less than when they were packed; **loss in transport** = amount of weight which is lost while goods are being transported

◊ **loss-leader** *noun* article which is sold at a loss to attract customers; **we use these cheap films as a loss-leader**

QUOTE: against losses of FFr 7.7m in 1983, the company made a net profit of FFr 300,000 last year
Financial Times

lot *noun* **(a)** large quantity; **a lot of people** *or* **lots of people are out of work (b)** group of items sold together at an auction; **to bid for lot 23; at the end of the auction half the lots were unsold (c)** group of shares which are sold; **to sell a lot of shares; to sell shares in small lots (d)** *US* piece of land, especially one to be used for redevelopment

lottery *noun* game where numbered tickets are sold and prizes given for some of the numbers

lounge *noun* comfortable room; **departure lounge** = room in an airport where passengers wait to board their planes; **transit lounge** = room in an airport where passengers wait for connecting flights

low 1 *adjective* small *or* not high; **low overhead costs keep the unit cost low; we try to keep our wages bill low; the company offered him a mortgage at a low rate of interest; the pound is at a very low rate of exchange against the dollar; our aim is to buy at the lowest price possible; shares are at their lowest for two years; low sales** = small amount of money produced by sales; **low volume of sales** = small number of items sold; **the tender will go to the lowest bidder** = the contract will be awarded to the person who offers the best terms **2** *noun* point where prices *or* sales are very small; **sales have reached a new low; the highs and lows on the stock market; shares have hit an all-time low** = shares have reached their lowest price ever

◊ **lower 1** *adjective* smaller *or* less high; **a lower rate of interest; sales were lower in**

December than in November **2** *verb* to make smaller *or* less expensive; **to lower prices to secure a larger market share; to lower the interest rate**

◊ **lowering** *noun* making smaller *or* less expensive; **lowering of prices; we hope to achieve low prices with no lowering of quality**
NOTE: no plural

◊ **low-grade** *adjective* not very important *or* not of very good quality; **a low-grade official from the Ministry of Commerce; the car runs best on low-grade petrol**

◊ **low-level** *adjective* **(a)** not very important; **a low-level delegation visited the ministry; a low-level meeting decided to put off making a decision (b)** low-level **computer language** = programming language similar to machine code

◊ **low-pressure** *adjective* **low-pressure sales** = sales where the salesman does not force someone to buy, but only encourages him to do so

◊ **low-quality** *adjective* not of good quality; **they tried to sell us some low-quality steel**

QUOTE: after opening at 79.1 the index touched a peak of 79.2 and then drifted to a low of 78.8
Financial Times
QUOTE: the pound which had been as low as $1.02 earlier this year, rose to $1.30 *Fortune*
QUOTE: Canadian and European negotiators agreed to a deal under which Canada could keep its quotas but lower its import duties
Globe and Mail (Toronto)

loyalty *noun* **brand loyalty** = feeling of a customer who always buys the same brand of product; **customer loyalty** = feeling of customers who always shop at the same shop

Ltd = LIMITED

luggage *noun* suitcases *or* bags for carrying clothes when travelling; **hand luggage** *or* **cabin luggage** = small cases which passengers can take with them into the cabin of a plane *or* ship; **free luggage allowance** = amount of luggage which a passenger can take with him free of charge
NOTE: no plural; to show one suitcase, etc., say **a piece of luggage**

lull *noun* quiet period; **after last week's hectic trading this week's lull was welcome**

lump *noun* **lump sum** = money paid in one single amount, not in several small sums; **when he retired he was given a lump-sum bonus; she sold her house and invested the money as a lump sum**

lunch *noun* meal eaten in the middle of the day; **the hours of work are from 9.30 to 5.30 with an hour off for lunch; the chairman is out at lunch; business lunch** = meeting between businessmen where they have lunch together to discuss business deals
◊ **lunch hour** *or* **lunchtime** *noun* time when people have lunch; **the office is closed during the lunch hour** *or* **at lunchtimes**
◊ **luncheon voucher** *noun* ticket given by an employer to a worker in addition to his wages, which can be exchanged for food in a restaurant

luxury *noun* expensive thing which is not necessary but which is good to have; **luxury items** *or* **luxury goods; a black market in luxury articles**

Mm

m = METRE, MILE, MILLION

M1 British measure of money supply, including all coins and notes plus personal money in current accounts
◊ **M2** British measure of money supply, including coins and notes and personal money in current and deposit accounts
◊ **M3** British measure of money supply, including coins and notes, personal money in current and deposit accounts, government deposits and deposits in currencies other than sterling; **£M3** = British measure of sterling money supply, including coins and notes, personal money in current and deposit accounts and government deposits
NOTE: say "sterling M3"

machine *noun* (a) device which works with power from a motor; **adding machine** = machine which adds numbers; **copying machine** *or* **duplicating machine** = machine

which makes copies of documents; **dictating machine** = machine which records what someone dictates, which a typist can then play back and type out; **automatic vending machine** = machine which provides food or drink when money is put in it; **machine shop** = place where working machines are placed; **machine tools** = tools worked by motors, used to work on wood or metal (b) **machine-made** *or* **machine-produced** = manufactured by a machine, not by people (c) **machine code** *or* **machine language** = instructions and information shown as a series of figures (0 and 1) which can be read by a computer; **machine-readable codes** = sets of signs or letters (such as bar codes, post codes) which a computer can read
◊ **machinery** *noun* (a) machines; **idle machinery** *or* **machinery lying idle** = machines not being used; **machinery guards** = pieces of metal to prevent workers from getting hurt by the moving parts of a machine (b) organization *or* system; **the government machinery; the machinery of local government; administrative machinery; the machinery for awarding government contracts**
NOTE: no plural
◊ **machinist** *noun* person who works a machine

macro- *prefix* very large, covering a wide area; **macro-economics** = study of the economics of a whole area *or* whole industry *or* whole group of the population *or* whole country, in order to help in economic planning

Madam *noun* formal way of addressing a woman, especially one whom you do not know; **Dear Madam** = beginning of a letter to a woman whom you do not know; **Madam Chairman** = way of addressing a woman who is in the chair at the meeting

made *adjective* produced *or* manufactured; **made in Japan** *or* **Japanese made;** *see also* MAKE

magazine *noun* paper, usually with pictures, which comes out regularly, every month or every week; **computer magazine** = magazine with articles on computers and programs; **do-it-yourself magazine** = magazine with articles on work which the average person can do to repair or paint the house; **house magazine** = magazine produced for the workers in a company to give them news of the company's affairs; **trade magazine** = magazine produced for people or companies in certain trades; **travel magazine** = magazine with articles on holidays and travel; **women's magazine** = magazine aimed at the women's market; **magazine insert** = advertising sheet put into a magazine when it is mailed or sold; **to insert a leaflet in a specialist magazine** = to put an advertising leaflet into a magazine before it is mailed or sold; **magazine mailing** = sending of copies of a magazine by post to subscribers

magnate *noun* important businessman; **a shipping magnate**

magnetic tape *or informal* **mag tape** *noun* plastic tape for recording information on a large computer

mail 1 *noun* **(a)** system of sending letters and parcels from one place to another; **to put a letter in the mail; the cheque was lost in the mail; the invoice was put in the mail yesterday; mail to some of the islands in the Pacific can take six weeks; by mail** = using the postal services, not sending something by hand or by messenger; **to send a package by surface mail** = to send a package by land or sea, not by air; **by sea mail** = sent by post abroad, using a ship; **to receive a sample by air mail** = by post using a plane; **we sent the order by first-class mail** = by the most expensive mail service, designed to be faster; **electronic mail** = system of sending messages from one computer to another, using the telephone lines **(b)** letters sent or received; **has the mail arrived yet? to open the mail; your cheque arrived in yesterday's mail; my secretary opens my mail as soon as it arrives; the receipt was in this morning's mail; incoming mail** = mail which arrives; **outgoing mail** = mail which is sent out; **mail room** = room in an office where incoming letters are sorted and sent to each department, and where outgoing mail is collected for sending **(c) direct mail** = selling a product by sending publicity material to possible buyers through the post; **the company runs a successful direct-mail operation; these calculators are sold only by direct mail; direct-mail advertising** = advertising by sending leaflets to people

by post; **mail shot** = leaflets sent by mail to possible customers
NOTE: no plural
2 *verb* to send something by post; **to mail a letter; we mailed our order last Wednesday**

◊ **mail box** *noun* one of several boxes where incoming mail is put in a large building; box for putting letters, etc. which you want to post

◊ **mailing** *noun* sending something in the post; **the mailing of publicity material; direct mailing** = sending of publicity material by post to possible buyers; **mailing list** = list of names and addresses of people who might be interested in a product *or* list of names and addresses of members of a society; **his name is on our mailing list; to build up a mailing list; to buy a mailing list** = to pay a society, etc. money to buy the list of members so that you can use it to mail publicity material; **mailing piece** = leaflet suitable for sending by direct mail; **mailing shot** = leaflets sent by mail to possible customers

◊ **mail-order** *noun* system of buying and selling from a catalogue, placing orders and sending goods by mail; **mail-order business** *or* **mail-order firm** *or* **mail-order house** = company which sells a product by mail; **mail-order catalogue** = catalogue from which a customer can order items to be sent by mail

main *adjective* most important; **main office; main building; one of our main customers;** *US* **Main Street** = most important street in a town, where the shops and banks are

◊ **mainframe** *noun* large computer; **the office micro interfaces with the mainframe in the head office**

◊ **mainly** *adverb* mostly *or* usually; **their sales are mainly in the home market; we are interested mainly in buying children's gift items**

maintain *verb* **(a)** to keep something going *or* working; **to maintain good relations with one's customers; to maintain contact with an overseas market (b)** to keep something working at the same level; **the company has maintained the same volume of business in spite of the recession; to maintain an interest rate at 5%; to maintain a dividend** = to pay the same dividend as the previous year

◇ **maintenance** *noun* **(a)** keeping things going *or* working; **maintenance of contacts; maintenance of supplies (b)** keeping a machine in good working order; **maintenance contract** = contract by which a company keeps a piece of equipment in good working order; **we offer a full maintenance service**

QUOTE: responsibilities include the maintenance of large computerized databases *Times*
QUOTE: the federal administration launched a full-scale investigation into the airline's maintenance procedures *Fortune*

majeure *see* FORCE MAJEURE

major *adjective* important; **major shareholder** = shareholder with a large number of shares

◇ **majority** *noun* larger group than all others; **majority of the shareholders** = more than 50% of the shareholders; **the board accepted the proposal by a majority of three to two** = three members of the board voted to accept and two voted against; **majority vote** *or* **majority decision** = decision made after a vote according to the wishes of the largest group; **majority shareholding** *or* **majority interest** = group of more than half the shares in a company; **a majority shareholder** = person who owns more than half the shares

QUOTE: if the share price sinks much further the company is going to look tempting to any major takeover merchant *Australian Financial Review*
QUOTE: monetary officials have reasoned that coordinated greenback sales would be able to drive the dollar down against other major currencies *Duns Business Month*
QUOTE: a client base which includes many major commercial organizations and nationalized industries *Times*

make 1 *noun* type of product manufactured; **Japanese makes of cars; a standard make of equipment; what make is the new computer system** *or* **what is the make of the new computer system? 2** *verb* **(a)** to produce *or* to manufacture; **to make a car** *or* **to make a computer; the workmen spent ten weeks making the table; the factory makes three hundred cars a day (b)** to sign *or* to agree; **to make a deal** *or* **to make an agreement; to make a bid for something** = to offer to buy something; **to make a payment** = to pay; **to make a deposit** = to

pay money as a deposit **(c)** to earn *or* to increase in value; **he makes £50,000 a year** *or* **£25 an hour; the shares made $2.92 in today's trading (d)** to make a profit *or* to **make a loss** = to have more money *or* less money after a deal; **to make a killing** = to make a very large profit
NOTE: **making - made**

◇ **make good** *verb* **(a)** to repair *or* to compensate; **the company will make good the damage; to make good a loss (b)** to be a success; **a local boy made good** = local person who becomes successful

◇ **make out** *verb* to write; **to make out an invoice; the bill is made out to Smith & Co.; to make out a cheque to someone** = to write someone's name on a cheque

◇ **make over** *verb* to transfer property legally; **to make over the house to one's children**

◇ **make up** *verb* **(a)** to compensate for something; **to make up a loss** *or* **to make up the difference** = to pay extra so that the loss or difference is covered **(b)** to **make up accounts** = to complete the accounts

◇ **make up for** *verb* to compensate for something; **to make up for a short payment** *or* **to make up for a late payment**

◇ **maker** *noun* person who makes something; **a major car maker; a furniture maker; decision maker** = person who decides *or* who takes decisions

◇ **making** *noun* production of an item; **ten tons of concrete were used in the making of the wall; decision making** = act of coming to a decision

maladministration *noun* incompetent administration

mall *noun US* **shopping mall** = enclosed covered area for shopping, with shops, restaurants, banks and other facilities

man 1 *noun* person *or* ordinary worker; **all the men went back to work yesterday 2** *verb* to provide the workforce for something; **to man a shift; to man an exhibition; the exhibition stand was manned by three salesgirls;** *see also* MANNED, MANNING

manage *verb* **(a)** to direct *or* to be in charge of; **to manage a department; to manage a branch office (b) to manage property** = to look after rented property for the owner **(c) to manage to** = to be able to do something; **did you manage to see the head buyer? she managed to write six orders and take three phone calls all in two minutes**

◇ **manageable** *adjective* which can be dealt with easily; **difficulties which are still manageable; the problems are too large to be manageable**

◇ **management** *noun* **(a)** directing *or* running a business; **to study management; good management** *or* **efficient management; bad management** *or* **inefficient management; a management graduate** *or* **a graduate in management; line management** = organization of a business where each manager is responsible for doing what his superior tells him to do; **portfolio management** = buying and selling shares by a person or by a specialist on behalf of a client; **product management** = directing the making and selling of a product as an independent item; **management accountant** = accountant who prepares specialized information for managers so that they can make decisions; **management accounts** = financial information (on sales, costs, credit, profitability) prepared for a manager; **management committee** = committee which manages a club, a pension fund, etc.; **management consultant** = person who gives advice on how to manage a business; **management course** = training course for managers; **management by objectives** = way of managing a business by planning work for the managers and testing to see if it is completed correctly and on time; **management team** = a group of managers working together; **management techniques** = ways of managing a business; **management training** = training managers by making them study problems and work out ways of solving them; **management trainee** = young person being trained to be a manager **(b)** group of managers or directors; **the management has decided to give an overall pay increase; top management** = the main directors of a company; **middle management** = the department managers of a company who carry out the policy set by the directors and organize the work of a group of workers NOTE: no plural for (a)

◇ **manager** *noun* **(a)** head of a department in a company; **a department manager; personnel manager; production manager; sales manager; accounts**

manager = head of the accounts department; **area manager** = manager who is responsible for the company's work (usually sales) in an area; **general manager** = manager in charge of the administration in a large company **(b)** person in charge of a branch or shop; **Mr Smith is the manager of our local Lloyds Bank; the manager of our Lagos branch is in London for a series of meetings; bank manager** = person in charge of a branch of a bank; **branch manager** = person in charge of a branch of a company

◇ **manageress** *noun* woman who runs a shop, or a department

◇ **managerial** *adjective* referring to managers; **managerial staff; to be appointed to a managerial position** = to be appointed a manager; **decisions taken at managerial level** = decisions taken by managers

◇ **managership** *noun* job of being a manager; **after six years, he was offered the managership of a branch in Scotland**

◇ **managing** *adjective* **managing director** = director who is in charge of a whole company; **chairman and managing director** = managing director who is also chairman of the board of directors

QUOTE: the management says that the rate of loss-making has come down and it expects further improvement in the next few years
Financial Times
QUOTE: the research director will manage and direct a team of graduate business analysts reporting on consumer behaviour throughout the UK *Times*
QUOTE: the No. 1 managerial productivity problem in America is managers who are out of touch with their people and out of touch with their customers *Fortune*

mandate *noun* **bank mandate** = written order allowing someone to sign cheques on behalf of a company

mandatory *adjective* **mandatory meeting** = meeting which all members have to attend

man-hour *noun* work done by one man in one hour; **one million man-hours were lost through industrial action**

manifest *noun* list of goods in a shipment; **passenger manifest** = list of passengers on a ship or plane

manilla *noun* thick brown paper; **a manilla envelope**
NOTE: no plural

manipulate *verb* **to manipulate the accounts** = to make false accounts so that the company seems profitable; **to manipulate the market** = to work to influence share prices in your favour
◊ **manipulation** *noun* **stock market manipulation** = trying to influence the price of shares
◊ **manipulator** *noun* **stock market manipulator** = person who tries to influence the price of shares in his own favour

manned *adjective* with someone working on it; **the switchboard is manned twenty-four hours a day; the stand was manned by our sales staff**
◊ **manning** *noun* people who are needed to do a work process; **manning levels** = number of people required in each department of a company to do the work efficiently; **manning agreement** *or* **agreement on manning** = agreement between the company and the workers about how many workers are needed for a certain job
NOTE: no plural

manpower *noun* number of workers; **manpower forecasting** = forecasting how many workers will be needed, and how many will be available; **manpower planning** = planning to obtain the right number of workers in each job; **manpower requirements** = number of workers needed; **manpower shortage** *or* **shortage of manpower** = lack of workers
NOTE: no plural

manual 1 *adjective* done by hand *or* done using the hands; **manual labour** *or* **manual work** = heavy work done by hand; **manual labourer** = person who does heavy work with his hands; **manual worker** = person who works with his hands 2 *noun* book of instructions; **operating manual** = book showing how to operate a machine; **service manual** = book showing how to service a machine
◊ **manually** *adverb* done by hand, not by a machine; **invoices have had to be made manually because the computer has broken down**

manufacture 1 *verb* to make a product for sale, using machines; **manufactured goods; the company manufactures spare parts for cars** 2 *noun* making a product for sale, using machines; **products of foreign manufacture** = products made in foreign countries
NOTE: no plural
◊ **manufacturer** *noun* person *or* company which produces machine-made products; **foreign manufacturers; cotton manufacturer; sports car manufacturer; manufacturer's recommended price** = price at which the manufacturer suggests the product should be sold on the retail market, though often reduced by the retailer; **all typewriters - 20% off the manufacturer's recommended price**
◊ **manufacturing** *noun* producing machine-made products for sale; **manufacturing overheads; manufacturing processes; manufacturing capacity** = amount of a product which a factory is capable of making; **manufacturing costs** = costs of making a product; **manufacturing industries** = industries which take raw materials and make them into finished products
NOTE: no plural

margin *noun* (a) difference between the money received when selling a product and the money paid for it; **gross margin** = percentage difference between the unit manufacturing cost and the received price; **net margin** = percentage difference between received price and all costs, including overheads; **we are cutting our margins very fine** = we are reducing our margins to the smallest possible to be competitive; **our margins have been squeezed** = profits have been reduced because our margins have to be smaller to stay competitive (b) extra space *or* time allowed; **margin of error** = number of mistakes which are accepted in a document *or* in a calculation; **safety margin** = time *or* space allowed for something to be safe; **margin of safety** = sales which are above the breakeven point
◊ **marginal** *adjective* (a) **marginal cost** = cost of making a single extra unit above the number already planned; **marginal pricing** = making the selling price the same as the marginal cost; **marginal rate of tax** = percentage of tax which a taxpayer pays at the top rate; **marginal**

revenue = income from selling a single extra unit above the number already sold **(b)** not very profitable *or* hardly worth the money paid; **marginal return on investment; marginal land** = land which is almost not worth farming; **marginal purchase** = thing which a buyer feels is only just worth buying

QUOTE: profit margins in the industries most exposed to foreign competition - machinery, transportation equipment and electrical goods - are significantly worse than usual
QUOTE: pensioner groups claim that pensioners have the highest marginal rates of tax. Income earned by pensioners above $30 a week is taxed at 62.5 per cent. more than the highest marginal rate   *Australian Financial Review*

marine 1 *adjective* referring to the sea; **marine insurance** = insurance of ships and their cargoes; **marine underwriter** = person who insures ships and their cargoes **2** *noun* **the merchant marine** = all the commercial ships of a country
◊ **maritime** *adjective* referring to the sea; **maritime law** = laws referring to ships, ports, etc.; **maritime lawyer** = lawyer who specializes in legal matters concerning ships and cargoes; **maritime trade** = transporting commercial goods by sea

mark 1 *noun* **(a)** sign put on an item to show something; **assay mark** = hallmark *or* mark put on gold or silver items to show that the metal is of the correct quality; *GB* **kite mark** = mark on goods to show that they meet official standards **(b)** money used in Germany; **the price is twenty-five marks; the mark rose against the dollar**
NOTE: usually written **DM** after a figure: **25DM**. Also called **Deutschmark, D-Mark**
2 *verb* to put a sign on something; **to mark a product "for export only"; article marked at £1.50; to mark the price on something**
◊ **mark down** *verb* to make lower; **to mark down a price** = to lower the price of something; **this range has been marked down to $24.99; we have marked all prices down by 30% for the sale**
◊ **mark-down** *noun* **(a)** reduction of the price of something to less than its usual price **(b)** percentage amount by which a price has been lowered; **we have used a 30% mark-down to fix the sale price**

◊ **marker pen** *noun* felt pen which makes a wide coloured mark
◊ **mark up** *verb* to increase; **to mark prices up** = to increase prices; **these prices have been marked up by 10%**
◊ **mark-up** *noun* **(a)** increase in price; **we put into effect a 10% mark-up of all prices in June (b)** amount added to the cost price to give the selling price; **we work to a 3.5 times mark-up** *or* **to a 350% mark-up** = we take the unit cost and multiply by 3.5 to give the selling price

market 1 *noun* **(a)** place (often in the open air) where farm produce is sold; **fish market; flower market; open-air market; here are this week's market prices for sheep; flea market** = market for secondhand goods; **market day** = day when a market is regularly held; **Tuesday is market day, so the streets are closed to traffic; market dues** = rent for a stall in a market **(b) the Common Market** = the European Economic Community; **the Common Market agricultural policy** *or* **the Common Market ministers (c)** place where a product might be sold *or* group of people who might buy a product; **home** *or* **domestic market** = market in the country where the selling company is based; **sales in the home market rose by 22% (d)** possible sales of a certain type of product *or* demand for a certain type of product; **the market for home computers has fallen sharply; we have 20% of the British car market; there is no market for electric typewriters; a growth market** = market where sales are likely to rise rapidly; **the labour market** = number of workers available for work; **25,000 graduates have come on to the labour market** = they have become available for work because they have left college; **the property market** = sales of houses **(e) the black market** = buying and selling goods in a way which is not allowed by law; **there is a flourishing black market in spare parts for cars; to pay black market prices** = to pay high prices to get items which are not easily available **(f) a buyer's market** = market where goods are sold cheaply because there is little demand; **a seller's market** = market where the seller can ask high prices because there is a large demand for the product **(g) closed market** = market where a supplier deals with only one agent or distributor and does not supply any others direct; **free market**

economy = system where the government does not interfere in business activity in any way; **open market** = market where anyone can buy and sell **(h) capital market** = place where companies can look for investment capital; **the foreign exchange markets** = places where currencies are bought or sold; **forward markets** = places where foreign currency or commodities can be bought or sold for delivery at a later date; **money market** or **finance market** = place where large sums of money are lent or borrowed **(i) commodity market** = place where commodities are bought or sold; **stock market** = place where shares are bought and sold; **the market in oil shares was very active** or **there was a brisk market in oil shares; to buy shares in the open market** = to buy shares on the Stock Exchange, not privately; **over-the-counter market** = secondary market in shares which are not listed on the main Stock Exchange **(j) market analysis** = detailed examination and report on a market; **market capitalization** = value of a company calculated by multiplying the price of its shares on the Stock Exchange by the number of shares issued; **market economist** = person who specializes in the study of financial structures and the return on investments in the stock market; **market forces** = influences on the sales of a product; **market forecast** = forecast of prices on the stock market; **market leader** = company with the largest market share; **we are the market leader in home computers; market opportunities** = possibility of finding new sales in a market; **market penetration** or **market share** = percentage of a total market which the sales of a company cover; **we hope our new product range will increase our market share; market price** = price at which a product can be sold; **market rate** = normal price in the market; **we pay the market rate for secretaries** or **we pay secretaries the market rate; market research** = examining the possible sales of a product before it is put on the market; **market trends** = gradual changes taking place in a market; **market value** = value of a product or of a company if sold today **(k) up market** or **down market** = more expensive or less expensive; **to go up market** or **to go down market** = to make products which appeal to a wealthy section of the market or to a wider, less wealthy, section of the market **(l) to be in the market for secondhand cars** = to look for

secondhand cars to buy; **to come on to the market** = to start to be sold; **this soap has just come on to the market; to put something on the market** = to start to offer something for sale; **they put their house on the market; I hear the company has been put on the market; the company has priced itself out of the market** = the company has raised its prices so high that its products do not sell **2** verb to sell (products); **this product is being marketed in all European countries**

◇ **marketable** adjective which can be sold easily

◇ **marketing** noun techniques used in selling a product (such as packaging, advertising, etc.); **marketing agreement** = contract by which one company will market another company's products; **marketing department** = department in a company which specializes in using marketing techniques to sell a product; **marketing manager** = person in charge of a marketing department; **marketing policy** or **marketing plans** = ideas of how the company's products are going to be marketed; **to plan the marketing of a new product**
NOTE: no plural

◇ **marketplace** noun **(a)** open space in the middle of a town where a market is held **(b)** place where goods are sold; **our salesmen find life difficult in the marketplace; what is the reaction to the new car in the marketplace?** or **what is the marketplace reaction to the new car?**

mart noun market or place where things are sold; **car mart; auction mart** = auction rooms

mass noun **(a)** large group of people; **mass marketing** = marketing which aims at reaching large numbers of people; **mass media** = means of communication which reach large numbers of people (such as radio, television, newspapers); **mass unemployment** = unemployment of large numbers of workers **(b)** large number; **we have a mass of letters** or **masses of letters to write; they received a mass of orders** or **masses of orders after the TV commercials**

◊ **mass-produce** *verb* to manufacture in large quantities; **to mass-produce cars**

◊ **mass production** *noun* manufacturing large quantities of products

master *noun* main or original; **master copy of a file** = main copy of a computer file, kept for security purposes

material *noun* **(a)** substance which can be used to make a finished product; **building materials** = bricks, cement, etc., used in building; **raw materials** = substances which have not been manufactured (such as wool, wood, sand); **synthetic materials** = substances made as products of a chemical process; **materials control** = system to check that a company has enough materials in stock to do its work; **materials handling** = moving materials from one part of a factory to another in an efficient way **(b) display material** = posters, photographs, etc., which can be used to attract attention to goods which are for sale

maternity *noun* becoming a mother; **maternity benefit** = money paid by the National Insurance to a mother when she has her child; **maternity leave** = permission for a woman to be away from work to have a baby

matter 1 *noun* **(a)** problem; **it is a matter of concern to the members of the committee** = the members of the committee are worried about it **(b) printed matter** = printed books, newspapers, publicity sheets, etc.; **publicity matter** = sheets or posters or leaflets used for publicity **(c)** question or problem to be discussed; **the most important matter on the agenda; we shall consider first the matter of last month's fall in prices**
NOTE: no plural for (b)
2 *verb* to be important; **does it matter if one month's sales are down?**

mature 1 *adjective* **mature economy** = fully developed economy 2 *verb* **bills which mature in three weeks' time** = bills which will be due for payment in three weeks

◊ **maturity** *noun* **date of maturity** or **maturity date** = date when a government stock or an assurance policy or a debenture will become due for payment; **amount payable on maturity** = amount received by the insured person when the policy becomes mature

maximization *noun* making as large as possible; **profit maximization** or **maximization of profit**

◊ **maximize** *verb* to make as large as possible; **to maximize profits**

maximum 1 *noun* largest possible number or price or quantity; **up to a maximum of £10** = no more than £10; **to increase exports to the maximum** = as much as possible; **it is the maximum the insurance company will pay**
NOTE: plural is **maxima**
2 *adjective* largest possible; **maximum income tax rate** or **maximum rate of tax; maximum load; maximum production levels; maximum price; to increase production to the maximum level** = as much as possible

MD = MANAGING DIRECTOR **the MD is in his office; she was appointed MD of a property company**

mean 1 *adjective* average; **mean annual increase; mean price** = average price of a share in a day's trading 2 *noun* average or number calculated by adding several figures together and dividing by the number of figures added; **unit sales are over the mean for the first quarter** or **above the mean for the first quarter**

◊ **means** *plural noun* **(a)** way of doing something; **air freight is the fastest means of getting stock to South America; do we have any means of copying all these documents quickly? (b)** money or resources; **the company has the means to launch the new product; such a level of investment is beyond the means of a small private company; means test** = inquiry into how much money someone earns to see if he is eligible for state benefits; **he has private means** = he has income from dividends or interest or rent which is not part of his salary

measure 1 noun **(a)** way of calculating size or quantity; **cubic measure** = volume in cubic feet or metres, calculated by multiplying height, width and length; **dry measure** = way of calculating the quantity of loose dry goods (such as corn); **square measure** = area in square feet or metres, calculated by multiplying width and length; **inspector of weights and measures** = government inspector who inspects weighing machines and goods sold in shops to see if the quantities and weights are correct; **as a measure of the company's performance** = as a way of judging if the company's results are good or bad **(b) made to measure** = made specially to fit; **he has his clothes made to measure (c) tape measure** = long tape with centimetres or inches marked on it, used to measure how long something is **(d)** type of action; **to take measures to prevent something happening** = to act to stop something happening; **to take crisis** or **emergency measures** = to act rapidly to stop a crisis developing; **an economy measure** = an action to save money; **fiscal measures** = tax changes made by the government to improve the working of the economy; **as a precautionary measure** = to prevent something taking place; **safety measures** = actions to make sure that something is safe **2** verb **(a)** to find out the size or quantity of something; to be of a certain size or quantity; **to measure the size of a package; a package which measures 10cm by 25cm** or **a package measuring 10cm by 25cm (b)** to measure the government's performance = to judge how well the government is doing
◊ **measurement** noun **(a)** measurements = size (in inches, centimetres, etc.); **to write down the measurements of a package (b)** way of judging something; **performance measurement** or **measurement of performance; measurement of profitability** = way of calculating how profitable something is
◊ **measuring tape** noun long tape with centimetres or inches marked on it, used to measure how long something is

mechanic noun person who works with engines or machines; **car mechanic**
◊ **mechanical** adjective worked by a machine; **a mechanical pump**

◊ **mechanism** noun way in which something works; **a mechanism to slow down inflation; the company's discount mechanism**
◊ **mechanize** verb to use machines in place of workers; **the country is aiming to mechanize its farming industry**
◊ **mechanization** noun using machines in place of workers; **farm mechanization** or **the mechanization of farms**

media noun **the media** or **the mass media** = means of communicating information to the public (such as television, radio, newspapers); **the product attracted a lot of interest in the media** or **a lot of media interest; media analysis** or **media research** = examining different types of media (such as the readers of newspapers, television viewers) to see which is best for promoting a certain type of product; **media coverage** = reports about something in the media; **we got good media coverage for the launch of the new model**
NOTE: **media** is followed by a singular or plural verb

median noun point in the middle of a list of numbers

mediate verb to try to make the two sides in an argument come to to an agreement; **to mediate between the manager and his staff; the government offered to mediate in the dispute**
◊ **mediation** noun attempt by a third party to make the two sides in an argument agree; **the employers refused an offer of government mediation; the dispute was ended through the mediation of union officials**
◊ **mediator** noun official mediator = government official who tries to make the two sides in an industrial dispute agree

medical noun referring to the study or treatment of illness; **medical certificate** = certificate from a doctor to show that a worker has been ill; **medical inspection** = examining a place of work to see if the conditions will not make the workers ill; **medical insurance** = insurance which pays the cost of medical treatment especially when travelling abroad; **medical officer of health** = person responsible for the health services in a town; **he resigned for medical reasons** = he resigned because he was too ill to work

medium 1 *adjective* middle *or* average; **the company is of medium size** 2 *noun* **(a)** way of doing something *or* means of doing something; **advertising medium** = type of advertisement (such as a TV commercial); **the product was advertised through the medium of the trade press** NOTE: plural is **media (b) mediums** = government stocks which mature in five to fifteen years' time

◇ **medium-sized** *adjective* **a medium-sized engineering company** = company which is neither very large nor very small

◇ **medium-term** *adjective* referring to a point between short term and long terms; **medium-term forecast** = forecast for two or three years

meet *verb* **(a)** to come together with someone; **to meet a negotiating committee; to meet an agent at his hotel; the two sides met in the lawyer's office (b)** to be satisfactory for; **to meet a customer's requirements; to meet the demand for a new product** = to fill the demand for a product; **we will try to meet your price** = we will try to offer a price which is acceptable to you; **they failed to meet the deadline** = they were not able to complete in time **(c)** to pay for; **to meet someone's expenses; the company will meet your expenses; he was unable to meet his mortgage repayments** NOTE: **meeting - met**

◇ **meet with** *verb* **(a)** *US* to come together with someone; **I hope to meet with him in New York** = I hope to meet him in New York **(b) his request met with a refusal** = his request was refused

◇ **meeting** *noun* **(a)** coming together of a group of people; **management meeting; staff meeting; board meeting** = meeting of the directors of a company; **general meeting** *or* **meeting of shareholders** *or* **shareholders' meeting** = meeting of all the shareholders of a company *or* meeting of all the members of a society; **Annual General Meeting** = meeting of all the shareholders when a company's financial situation is discussed with the directors; **Extraordinary General Meeting** = special meeting of shareholders to discuss an important matter **(b) to hold a meeting** = to organize a meeting of a group of people; **the meeting will be held in the committee room; to open a meeting** = to start a meeting; **to conduct a meeting** = to be in the chair for a meeting; **to close a meeting**

= to end a meeting; **to address a meeting** = to speak to a meeting; **to put a resolution to a meeting** = to ask a meeting to vote on a proposal

QUOTE: if corporate forecasts are met, sales will exceed $50 million in 1985 *Citizen (Ottawa)*
QUOTE: in proportion to your holding you have a stake in every aspect of the company, including a vote in the general meetings *Investors Chronicle*

megabyte *noun* storage unit in computers, equal to 1,048,576 bytes

member *noun* **(a)** person who belongs to a group *or* a society; **members of a committee** *or* **committee members; they were elected members of the board; ordinary member** = person who pays a subscription to belong to a group; **honorary member** = special person who does not have to pay a subscription **(b)** organization which belongs to a society; **the member countries of the EEC; the members of the United Nations; the member companies of a trade association**

◇ **membership** *noun* **(a)** belonging to a group; **membership qualifications; conditions of membership; membership card; to pay your membership** *or* **your membership fees; is Austria going to apply for membership of the Common Market? (b)** all the members of a group; **the membership was asked to vote for the new president; the club's membership secretary** = committee member who deals with the ordinary members of a society; **the club has a membership of five hundred** = the club has five hundred members

QUOTE: it will be the first opportunity for party members and trade union members to express their views on the tax package
Australian Financial Review
QUOTE: the bargaining committee will recommend that its membership ratify the agreement at a meeting called for June *Toronto Star*
QUOTE: in 1984 exports to Canada from the member-states of the European Community jumped 38 per cent *Globe and Mail (Toronto)*
QUOTE: for EMS members, which means all EEC countries except Britain, the ecu has performed well *Economist*

memo *noun* short message sent from one person to another in the same organization; **to write a memo to the finance**

director; **to send a memo to all the sales representatives; according to your memo about debtors; I sent the managing director a memo about your complaint**

◇ **memo pad** *noun* pad of paper for writing short notes

◇ **memorandum** *noun* short message; **memorandum (and articles) of association** = legal document setting up a limited company and giving details of its aims, directors, and registered office

memory *noun* facility for storing of data in a computer

mention *verb* to talk about something for a short time; **the chairman mentioned the work of the retiring managing director; can you mention to the secretary that the date of the next meeting has been changed?**

mercantile *adjective* commercial; **mercantile country** = country which earns income from trade; **mercantile law** = laws relating to business; **mercantile marine** = all the commercial ships of a country

merchandise 1 *noun* goods which are for sale *or* which have been sold; **the merchandise is shipped through two ports** NOTE: no plural
2 *verb* to sell goods by a wide variety of means, including display, advertising, sending samples, etc.; **to merchandise a product**

◇ **merchandiser** *noun* person *or* company which organizes the display and promotion of goods

◇ **merchandising** *noun* organizing the display and promotion of goods for sale; **merchandising of a product; merchandising department**

QUOTE: fill huge warehouses with large quantities but limited assortments of top-brand, first-quality merchandise and sell the goods at rock-bottom prices *Duns Business Month*

merchant *noun* **(a)** businessman who buys and sells goods (especially imported goods) in bulk for retail sale; **coal merchant; tobacco merchant; wine merchant (b) merchant bank** = bank which lends money to companies and deals in international finance; **merchant banker** = person who has a high position in a

merchant bank; **merchant navy** *or* **merchant marine** = all the commercial ships of a country; **merchant ship** *or* **merchant vessel** = commercial ship *or* ship which carries a cargo

◇ **merchantman** *noun* commercial ship

merge *verb* to join together; **the two companies have merged; the firm merged with its main competitor**

◇ **merger** *noun* joining together of two or more companies; **as a result of the merger, the company is the largest in the field**

merit *noun* being good or efficient; **merit award** *or* **merit bonus** = extra money given to a worker because he has worked well; **merit increase** = increase in pay given to someone because his work is good; **merit rating** = judging how well a worker does his work, so that he can be paid according to merit

message *noun* piece of news which is sent to someone; **to send a message; I will leave a message with his secretary; can you give the director a message from his wife? he says he never received the message**

messenger *noun* person who brings a message; **he sent the package by special messenger** *or* **by motorcycle messenger; office messenger** = person who carries messages from one person to another in a large office; **messenger boy** = young man who carries messages

Messrs *noun* plural form of Mr, used only in names of firms; **Messrs White and Smith**

method *noun* way of doing something; **a new method of making something** *or* **of doing something; what is the best method of payment? his organizing methods are out of date; their manufacturing methods** *or* **production methods are among the most modern in the country; time and method study** = examining the way in which something is done to see if a cheaper or quicker way can be found

metre *or* *US* **meter** *noun* measure of length (= 3.4 feet) NOTE: usually written **m** after figures: **the case is 2m wide by 3m long**

◊ **metric** *adjective* using the metre as a basic measurement; **metric ton** *or* **metric tonne** = 1000 kilograms; **the metric system** = system of measuring, using metres, litres and grams

mg = MILLIGRAM

mi = MILE

micro *noun* microcomputer; **we put the sales statistics on to the office micro; our office micro interfaces with the mainframe computer in London**
◊ **micro-** *prefix* very small; **micro-economics** = study of the economics of persons or single companies
◊ **microcomputer** *noun* small computer for general use in the home or office
◊ **microfiche** *noun* index sheet, made of several microfilm photographs; **we hold our records on microfiche**
◊ **microfilm** 1 *noun* roll of film on which a document is photographed in very small scale; **we hold our records on microfilm** 2 *verb* to make a very small scale photograph; **send the 1980 correspondence to be microfilmed** *or* **for microfilming**
◊ **microprocessor** *noun* small computer processing unit

mid- *prefix* middle; **from mid-1982** = from the middle of 1982; **the factory is closed until mid-July**
◊ **mid-month** *adjective* taking place in the middle of the month; **mid-month accounts**
◊ **mid-week** *adjective* which happens in the middle of a week; **the mid-week lull in sales**

middle *adjective* in the centre *or* between two points; **middle management** = department managers in a company, who carry out the policy set by the directors and organize the work of a group of workers
◊ **middle-income** *adjective* **people in the middle-income bracket** = people with average incomes, not very high or very low
◊ **middleman** *noun* businessman who buys from the manufacturer and sells to the public; **we sell direct from the factory to the customer and cut out the middleman**
NOTE: plural is **middlemen**

◊ **middle-sized** *adjective* neither small nor large; **a middle-sized company**

mile *noun* measure of length (= 1.625 kilometres); **the car does twenty-five miles to the gallon** *or* **twenty-five miles per gallon** = the car uses one gallon of petrol to travel twenty-five miles
NOTE: miles per gallon is usually written **mpg** after figures: **the car does 25mpg**
◊ **mileage** *noun* distance travelled in miles; **mileage allowance** = money allowed as expenses to someone who uses his own car for business travel; **the salesman's average annual mileage** = the number of miles which a salesman drives in a year
NOTE: no plural

mill *noun* building where a certain type of material is processed or made; **after lunch the visitors were shown round the mill; cotton mill** = factory where raw cotton is processed; **paper mill** = factory where wood is made into paper

milligram *noun* one thousandth of a gram
NOTE: usually written **mg** after figures
◊ **millilitre** *noun* one thousandth of a litre
NOTE: usually written **ml** after figures
◊ **millimetre** *noun* one thousandth of a metre
NOTE: usually written **mm** after figures

million number 1,000,000; **the company lost £10 million in the African market; our turnover has risen to $13.4 million**
NOTE: can be written **m** after figures: **$5m** (say "five million dollars")
◊ **millionaire** *noun* person who has more than one million pounds; **dollar millionaire** = person who has more than one million dollars; **paper millionaire** = person who owns shares which, if sold, would be worth one million pounds or dollars

min = MINUTE, MINIMUM

mine 1 *noun* hole in the ground for digging out coal, gold, iron etc.; **the mines have been closed by a strike** 2 *verb* to dig and bring out coal, gold, etc.; **the company is mining coal in the south of the country; mining concession** = right to use a piece of land for mining

mini- *prefix* very small

◇ **minibudget** *noun* interim statement about financial plans from a finance minister

◇ **minicomputer** *noun* computer which is larger than a micro but smaller than a mainframe

◇ **minicontainer** *noun* small container

◇ **minimarket** *noun* very small self-service store

minimal *adjective* the smallest possible; **there was a minimal quantity of imperfections in the batch; the head office exercises minimal control over the branch offices**

◇ **minimize** *verb* to make something seem to be very small and not very important; **do not minimize the risks involved; he tends to minimize the difficulty of the project**

◇ **minimum** 1 *noun* smallest possible quantity *or* price *or* number; **to keep expenses to a minimum; to reduce the risk of a loss to a minimum**
NOTE: plural is **minima** or **minimums**
2 *adjective* smallest possible; **minimum dividend** = smallest dividend which is legal and accepted by the shareholders; **minimum payment** = smallest payment necessary; **minimum quantity** = smallest quantity which is acceptable; **minimum wage** = lowest hourly wage which a company can legally pay its workers

minister *noun* member of a government who is in charge of a ministry; **a government minister; the Minister of Trade** *or* **the Trade Minister; the Minister of Foreign Affairs** *or* **the Foreign Minister**
NOTE: in the USA, they are called **secretary: the Secretary for Commerce**

◇ **ministry** *noun* department in the government; **he works in the Ministry of Finance** *or* **the Finance Ministry; he is in charge of the Ministry of Information** *or* **of the Information Ministry; a ministry official** *or* **an official from the ministry**
NOTE: in GB and the USA, important ministries are called **departments: the Department of Trade and Industry; the Commerce Department**

minor *adjective* less important; **minor expenditure; minor shareholders; a loss of minor importance** = not a very serious loss

◇ **minority** *noun* number *or* quantity which is less than half of the total; **a minority of board members opposed the chairman; minority shareholding** *or* **minority interest** = group of shares which are less than one half of the shares in a company; **minority shareholder** = person who owns a group of shares but less than half of the shares in a company; **in the minority** = being fewer than half; **good salesmen are in the minority in our sales team**

mint 1 *noun* factory where coins are made 2 *verb* to make coins

minus 1 *adverb* less *or* without; **net salary is gross salary minus tax and National Insurance deductions; gross profit is sales minus production costs** 2 *adjective* **the accounts show a minus figure** = show that more has been spent than has been received; **minus factor** = unfavourable factor; **to have lost sales in the best quarter of the year is a minus factor for the sales team**

minute 1 *noun* (a) one sixtieth part of an hour; **I can see you for ten minutes only; if you do not mind waiting, Mr Smith will be free in about twenty minutes'** time (b) **the minutes of the meeting** = notes of what happened at a meeting, written by the secretary; **to take the minutes** = to write notes of what happened at a meeting; **the chairman signed the minutes of the last meeting** = he signed them to show that they are a correct record of what was said and what decisions were taken; **this will not appear in the minutes of the meeting** = this is unofficial and will not be noted as having been said 2 *verb* to put something into the minutes of a meeting; **the chairman's remarks about the auditors were minuted; I do not want that to be minuted** *or* **I want that not to be minuted** = do not put that remark into the minutes of the meeting

◇ **minutebook** *noun* book in which the minutes of a meeting are kept

misappropriate *verb* to use illegally money which is not yours, but with which you have been trusted

◇ **misappropriation** *noun* illegal use of money by someone who is not the owner but who has been trusted to look after it

misc = MISCELLANEOUS

miscalculate *verb* to calculate wrongly; **the salesman miscalculated the discount, so we hardly broke even on the deal**
◊ **miscalculation** *noun* mistake in calculating

miscellaneous *adjective* various *or* mixed *or* not all of the same sort; **miscellaneous items; a box of miscellaneous pieces of equipment; miscellaneous expenditure**

miscount **1** *noun* mistake in counting **2** *verb* to count wrongly; **the shopkeeper miscounted, so we got twenty-five bars of chocolate instead of two dozen**

misdirect *verb* to give wrong directions

mismanage *verb* to manage badly
◊ **mismanagement** *noun* bad management; **the company failed because of the chairman's mismanagement**
NOTE: no plural

misrepresent *verb* to report facts wrongly
◊ **misrepresentation** *noun* wrongly reporting facts; **fraudulent misrepresentation** = giving someone wrong information in order to cheat him

Miss *noun* title given to a woman who is not married; **Miss Smith is our sales manager**

miss *verb* **(a)** not to hit; **the company has missed its profit forecast again; the sales team has missed its sales targets (b)** not to meet; **I arrived late, so missed most of the discussion; he missed the chairman by ten minutes** = he left ten minutes before the chairman arrived

mission *noun* group of people going on a journey for a special purpose; **trade mission** = visit by a group of businessmen to discuss trade; **he led a trade mission to China; inward mission** = visit to your home country by a group of foreign businessmen; **outward mission** = visit by a group of businessmen to a foreign country; **a fact-finding mission** = visit to an area to search for information about a problem

mistake *noun* wrong action *or* wrong decision; **to make a mistake** = to do something wrong; **the shop made a mistake and sent the wrong items; there was a mistake in the address; she made a mistake in the address; by mistake** = in error *or* wrongly; **they sent the wrong items by mistake; she put my letter into an envelope for the chairman by mistake**

misunderstanding *noun* lack of agreement *or* mistake; **there was a misunderstanding over my tickets**

misuse *noun* wrong use; **misuse of funds** *or* **of assets**

mix **1** *noun* things put together; **product mix** = range of different products which a company has for sale; **sales mix** = sales and profitability of a wide range of different products **2** *verb* to put different things together; **I like to mix business with pleasure - why don't we discuss the deal over lunch?**
◊ **mixed** *adjective* **(a)** of different sorts *or* of different types together; **mixed economy** = system which contains both nationalized industries and private enterprise; **mixed farm** = farm which has both animals and crops **(b)** neither good nor bad

QUOTE: prices closed on a mixed note after a moderately active trading session
Financial Times

ml = MILLILITRE

mm = MILLIMETRE

mobile *adjective* which can move about; **mobile shop** = van fitted out like a small shop which travels round selling groceries or vegetables; **mobile workforce** = workers who move from place to place to get work
◊ **mobility** *noun* being able to move from one place to another; **mobility of labour** = situation when workers agree to move from one place to another to get work
NOTE: no plural

◇ **mobilize** *verb* to bring together, especially to fight; **to mobilize capital** = to collect capital to support something; **to mobilize resources to defend a takeover bid** = to get the support of shareholders, etc., to stop a company being taken over

mock-up *noun* model of a new product for testing or to show to possible buyers

mode *noun* way of doing something; **mode of payment** = way in which payment is made (such as cash or cheque)

model 1 *noun* **(a)** small copy of something to show what it will look like when finished; **he showed us a model of the new office building** **(b)** style *or* type of product; **this is the latest model; the model on display is last year's; he drives a 1985 model Ford; demonstration model** = piece of equipment used in demonstrations and then sold cheaply **(c)** person whose job is to wear new clothes to show them to possible buyers **(d) economic model** = computerized plan of a country's economic system, used for forecasting economic trends **2** *adjective* which is a perfect example to be copied; **a model agreement** **3** *verb* to wear new clothes to show them to possible buyers
NOTE: **modelling - modelled** but US **modeling - modeled**

modem *noun* device which links a computer to the telephone line, allowing data to be sent from one computer to another

moderate 1 *adjective* not too large; **the trade union made a moderate claim; the government proposed a moderate increase in the tax rate** **2** *verb* to make less strong *or* less large; **the union was forced to moderate its claim**

modern *adjective* referring to the recent past or the present time; **it is a fairly modern invention - it was patented only in the 1960s**
◇ **modernize** *verb* to make modern; **he modernized the whole product range**
◇ **modernization** *noun* making modern; **the modernization of the workshop**

modest *adjective* small; **oil shares showed modest gains over the week's trading**

modify *verb* to change *or* to make something fit a different use; **the management modified its proposals; this is the new modified agreement; the car will have to be modified to pass the government tests; the refrigerator was considerably modified before it went into production**
◇ **modification** *noun* change; **to make** *or* **to carry out modifications to the plan; the new model has had several important modifications; we asked for modifications to the contract**

modular *adjective* made of various sections

momentum *noun* movement forwards; **to gain** *or* **to lose momentum** = to move faster or more slowly; **the strike is gaining momentum** = more workers are joining the strike
NOTE: no plural

monetary *adjective* referring to money or currency; **the government's monetary policy** = the government's policy relating to finance (bank interest rates, taxes, government expenditure and borrowing); **monetary standard** = fixing of a fixed exchange rate for a currency; **the international monetary system** = methods of controlling and exchanging currencies between countries; **the European Monetary System** = system of controlled exchange rates between some member countries of the Common Market; **The International Monetary Fund** = (part of the United Nations) a type of bank which helps member states in financial difficulties, gives financial advice to members and encourages world trade; **monetary unit** = standard currency in a country (the pound, the dollar, the franc, etc.)
◇ **monetarism** *noun* idea that inflation can be controlled by regulating the amount of money available in the economy
NOTE: no plural
◇ **monetarist** 1 *noun* person who believes in monetarism and acts accordingly **2** *adjective* according to monetarism; **monetarist theories**

money *noun* (a) coins and notes used for buying and selling; **to earn money** = to have a salary; **to earn good money** = to have a large salary; **to lose money** = to make a loss *or* not to make a profit; **the company has been losing money for months** = the company has been working at a loss; **to get your money back** = to earn enough to cover your original investment; **to make money** = to make a profit; **to put money into the bank** = to deposit money into a bank account; **to put money into a business** = to invest money in a business; **he put all his redundancy money into a shop; to put money down** = to pay cash, especially as a deposit; **he put £25 down and paid the rest in instalments; cheap money** = money which can be borrowed at a low rate of interest; **danger money** = extra salary paid to workers in dangerous jobs; **dear money** = money which has to be borrowed at a high rate of interest; **easy money** = money which can be earned with no difficulty; **selling insurance is easy money; hot money** = money which is moved from country to country to get the best returns; **paper money** = money in notes, not coins; **ready money** = cash *or* money which is immediately available; **money lying idle** = money not being used to produce interest; **they are worth a lot of money** = they are valuable (b) **money supply** = amount of money which exists in a country; **money markets** = markets for buying and selling short-term loans; **the international money markets are nervous; money rates** = rates of interest for borrowers or lenders (c) **money order** = document which can be bought for sending money through the post; **foreign money order** *or* **international money order** *or* **overseas money order** = money order in a foreign currency which is payable to someone living in a foreign country
NOTE: no plural for (a), (b) and (c) (d) **monies** = sums of money; **monies owing to the company; to collect monies due**

◇ **moneylender** *noun* person who lends money at interest
◇ **money-making** *adjective* which makes money; **a money-making plan**
◇ **money-spinner** *noun* item which sells very well *or* which is very profitable

monitor 1 *noun* screen (like a TV screen) on a computer 2 *verb* to check *or* to examine how something is working; **he is monitoring the progress of sales; how do you monitor the performance of the sales reps?**

monopoly *noun* situation where one person or company controls all the market in the supply of a product; **to have the monopoly of alcohol sales** *or* **to have the alcohol monopoly; to be in a monopoly situation; the company has the absolute monopoly of imports of French wine; the factory has the absolute monopoly of jobs in the town; public monopoly** *or* **state monopoly** = situation where the state is the only suppliers of a product or service (such as the Post Office, the coal industry,etc.); *GB* **the Monopolies Commission** = organization which examines takeovers and mergers to make sure that a monopoly is not being created
NOTE: **trust** is mainly used in US English
◇ **monopolize** *verb* to create a monopoly *or* to get control of all the supply of a product
◇ **monopolization** *noun* making a monopoly

month *noun* one of twelve periods which make a year; **the company pays him £100 a month; he earns £2,000 a month; bills due at the end of the current month; calendar month** = whole month as on a calendar; **paid by the month** = paid once each month; **to give a customer two months' credit** = to allow a customer to pay not immediately, but after two months
◇ **month end** *noun* the end of a calendar month, when accounts have to be drawn up; **month-end accounts**
◇ **monthly** 1 *adjective* happening every month *or* which is received every month; **monthly statement; monthly payments; he is paying for his car by monthly instalments; my monthly salary cheque is late; monthly ticket** = ticket for travel which is good for one month 2 *adverb* every month; **to pay monthly; the account is credited monthly**

moonlight *verb* *informal* to do a second job for cash (often in the evening) as well as a regular job

◇ **moonlighter** *noun* person who moonlights

◇ **moonlighting** *noun* doing a second job; **he makes thousands a year from moonlighting**

mooring *noun* place where boats can be tied up in a harbour

moratorium *noun* temporary stop to repayments of money owed; **the banks called for a moratorium on payments**
NOTE: plural is **moratoria**

mortality tables *plural noun* chart, used by insurers, which shows how long a person of a certain age can be expected to live on average

mortgage 1 *noun* agreement where someone lends money to another person so that he can buy a property, the property being the security; money lent in this way; **to take out a mortgage on the a house; to buy a house with a £20,000 mortgage; mortgage payments** = money paid each month as interest on a mortgage, plus repayment of a small part of the capital borrowed; **endowment mortgage** = mortgage backed by an endowment policy; **first mortgage** = main mortgage on a property; **second mortgage** = further mortgage on a property which is already mortgaged; **to foreclose on a mortgaged property** = to sell a property because the owner cannot repay money which he has borrowed, using the property as security; **to pay off a mortgage** = to pay back the principal and all the interest on a loan to buy a property; **mortgage bond** = certificate showing that a mortgage exists and that property is security for it; **mortgage debenture** = debenture where the lender can be repaid by selling the company's property; **mortgage famine** = situation where there is not enough money available to offer mortgages to house buyers; **mortgage queue** = list of people waiting for mortgages 2 *verb* to accept a loan with a property as security; **the house is mortgaged; he mortgaged his house to set up in business**

◇ **mortgagee** *noun* person or company which lends money for someone to buy a property

◇ **mortgager** *or* **mortgagor** *noun* person who borrows money to buy a property

QUOTE: mortgage money is becoming tighter. Applications for mortgages are running at a high level and some building societies are introducing quotas
Times
QUOTE: for the first time since mortgage rates began falling a financial institution has raised charges on homeowner loans
Globe and Mail (Toronto)

most 1 *noun* very large amount *or* quantity; **most of the staff are graduates; most of our customers live near the factory; most of the orders come in the early part of the year** 2 *adjective* very large number of; **most orders are dealt with the same day; most salesmen have had a course of on-the-job training**

◇ **most favoured nation** *noun* country which has the best trade terms; **most-favoured-nation clause** = agreement between two countries that each will offer the best possible terms in commercial contracts

◇ **mostly** *adverb* mainly *or* generally; **the staff are mostly girls of twenty to thirty years of age; he works mostly in the London office**

motion *noun* (a) moving about; **time and motion study** = study in an office *or* factory of the time taken to do certain jobs and the movements workers have to make to do them (b) proposal which will be put to a meeting to vote on; **to propose *or* to move a motion; the meeting voted on the motion; to speak against *or* for a motion; the motion was carried *or* was defeated by 220 votes to 196; to table a motion** = to put forward a proposal for discussion by putting details of it on the table at a meeting
NOTE: no plural

motivated *adjective* **highly motivated sales staff** = sales staff who are very eager to sell

◇ **motivation** *noun* encouragement *or* being eager to sell; **the sales staff lack motivation** = the sales staff are not motivated enough
NOTE: no plural

motor *noun* car; **motor insurance** = insuring a car, the driver and the passengers in case of accident

mountain *noun* pile *or* large heap; **I have mountains of typing to do; there is a mountain of invoices on the sales manager's desk; butter mountain** = large amount of unsold butter kept in storage

mounting *adjective* increasing; **he resigned in the face of mounting pressure from the shareholders; the company is faced with mounting debts**
◇ **mount up** *verb* to increase rapidly; **costs are mounting up**

move *verb* **(a)** to go from one place to another; **the company is moving from London Road to the centre of town; we have decided to move our factory to a site near the airport (b)** to be sold *or* to sell; **the stock is starting to move; the salesmen will have to work hard if they want to move all that stock by the end of the month (c)** to propose formally that a motion be accepted by a meeting; **he moved that the accounts be agreed; I move that the meeting should adjourn for ten minutes**
◇ **moveable** 1 *adjective* which can be moved; **moveable property** 2 *plural noun* **moveables** = moveable property
◇ **movement** *noun* **(a)** changing position *or* going up or down; **movements in the money markets; cyclical movements of trade; movements of capital** = changes of investments from one country to another; **stock movements** = passing of stock into *or* out of the warehouse; **all stock movements are logged by the computer (b)** group of people working towards the same aim; **the labour movement; the free trade movement**
◇ **mover** *noun* person who proposes a motion

mpg = MILES PER GALLON

Mr *noun* title given to a man; **Mr Smith is the Managing Director**

MRP = MANUFACTURER'S RECOMMENDED PRICE

Mrs *noun* title given to a married woman; **the chair was taken by Mrs Smith**

Ms *noun* title given to a woman where it is not known if she is married, or where she does not wish to indicate if she is married or not; **Ms Smith is the personnel officer**

multi- *prefix* referring to many things
◇ **multilateral** *adjective* between several parties; **a multilateral agreement; multilateral trade** = trade between several countries
◇ **multimillion** *adjective* referring to several million pounds or dollars; **they signed a multimillion pound deal**
◇ **multimillionaire** *noun* person who owns several million pounds or dollars
◇ **multinational** *noun* company which has branches *or* subsidiary companies in several countries; **the company has been bought by one of the big multinationals**

QUOTE: factory automation is a multi-billion-dollar business   *Duns Business Month*

multiple 1 *adjective* many; **multiple entry visa** = visa which allows a visitor to enter a country many times; **multiple store** = one store in a chain of stores; **multiple ownership** = situation where something is owned by several parties jointly 2 *noun* company with stores in several different towns

multiply *verb* **(a)** to calculate the sum of various numbers repeated a certain number of times; **to multiply twelve by three; square measurements are calculated by multiplying length by width (b)** to grow *or* to increase; **profits multiplied in the boom years**
◇ **multiplication** *noun* act of multiplying; **multiplication sign** = sign used to show that a number is being multiplied by another
NOTE: no plural

municipal *adjective* referring to a town; **municipal taxes; municipal offices**

Murphy's law *noun* law, based on wide experience, which says that in commercial life if something can go wrong it will go wrong

mutual *adjective* belonging to two or more people; **mutual (insurance) company**

= company which belongs to insurance policy holders; *US* **mutual funds** = organizations which take money from small investors and invest it in stocks and shares for them, the investment being in the form of shares in the fund

Nn

nail *noun* small piece of metal, used to attach things together; **to pay on the nail** = to pay promptly *or* to pay rapidly

naira *noun* money used in Nigeria
NOTE: no plural; naira is usually written **N** before figures: **N2,000** say "two thousand naira"

name *noun* word used to call a thing *or* a person; **I cannot remember the name of the managing director of Smith's Ltd; his first name is John, but I am not sure of his other names; brand name** = name of a particular make of product; **corporate name** = name of a large corporation; **under the name of** = using a particular name; **trading under the name of "Best Foods"** = using the name "Best Foods" as a commercial name, but not the name of the company
◊ **named** *adjective* **person named in the policy** = person whose name is given on an insurance policy as the person insured

nation *noun* country and the people living in it; **most favoured nation** = country which has the best trade terms; **most-favoured-nation clause** = agreement between two countries that each will give the other the best possible trade terms in commercial contracts; **the United Nations** = organization linking almost all countries in the world
◊ **national** *adjective* referring to a particular country; **national advertising** = advertising in every part of a country, not just in the capital; **we took national advertising to promote our new 24-hour delivery service; national campaign** = sales or publicity campaign in every part of a country; **the National Debt** = money borrowed by a government; *GB* **National**

Health Service = scheme for free medical and hospital service for everyone, paid for by the National Insurance; **national income** = value of income from the sales of goods and services in a country; *GB* **National Insurance** = state insurance which pays for medical care, hospitals, unemployment benefits, etc.; **National Insurance contributions** = money paid into the National Insurance scheme by the employer and the worker; **national newspapers** *or* **the national press** = newspapers which sell in all parts of a country; **gross national product** = annual value of goods and services in a country including income from other countries; *GB* **National Savings** = savings scheme for small investors run by the Post Office (including a savings bank, savings certificates and premium bonds)
◊ **nationality** *noun* **he is of British nationality** = he is a British citizen
◊ **nationalize** *verb* to put a privately-owned industry under state ownership and control; **the government are planning to nationalize the banking system**
◊ **nationalized** *adjective* **nationalized industry** = industry which was privately owned, but is now owned by the state
◊ **nationalization** *noun* taking over of private industry by the state
◊ **nationwide** *adjective* all over a country; **the union called for a nationwide strike; we offer a nationwide delivery service; the new car is being launched with a nationwide sales campaign**

nature *noun* kind *or* type; **what is the nature of the contents of the parcel? the nature of his business is not known**
◊ **natural** *adjective* **(a)** found in the earth; **natural gas; natural resources** = raw materials (such as coal, gas, iron) which are found in the earth and not made by people; **natural fibres (c)** normal; **it was natural for the shopkeeper to feel annoyed when the hypermarket was set up close to his shop; natural wastage** = losing workers because they resign or retire, not through redundancy or dismissals; **the company is hoping to avoid redundancies and reduce its staff by natural wastage**

navy *noun* **merchant navy** = all the commercial ships of a country

NB = NOTE

necessary *adjective* which has to be done *or* which is needed; **it is necessary to fill in the form correctly if you are not to have difficulty at the customs; is it really necessary for the chairman to have six personal assistants? you must have all the necessary documentation before you apply for a subsidy**

◇ **necessity** *noun* thing which is absolutely important, without which nothing can be done; **being unemployed makes it difficult to afford even the basic necessities**

negative *adjective* meaning "no"; **the answer was in the negative** = the answer was "no"; **negative cash flow** = situation where a company is spending more money than it receives

neglected *adjective* not well looked after; **neglected shares** = shares which are not bought or sold often; **bank shares have been a neglected sector of the market this week; neglected business** = company which has not been actively run by its owners and could therefore do better

negligence *noun* lack of proper care *or* not doing a duty; **criminal negligence** = not doing a duty with the result that harm is done to the interests of people
NOTE: no plural

◇ **negligible** *adjective* very small *or* not worth bothering about; **not negligible** = quite large

negotiable *adjective* **not negotiable** = which cannot be exchanged for cash; **"not negotiable"** = words written on a cheque to show that it can be paid only to a certain person; **negotiable cheque** = cheque made payable to bearer (i.e. to anyone who holds it); **negotiable instrument** = document (such as a bill of exchange, or cheque) which can be exchanged for cash

◇ **negotiate** *verb* **to negotiate with someone** = to discuss a problem formally with someone, so as to reach an agreement; **the management refused to negotiate with the union; to negotiate terms and conditions** *or* **to negotiate a contract** = to discuss and agree terms of a contract; **he negotiated a £250,000 loan with the bank** =

he came to an agreement with the bank for a loan of £250,000; **negotiating committee** = group of representatives of management or unions who negotiate a wage settlement

◇ **negotiation** *noun* discussion of terms and conditions to reach an agreement; **contract under negotiation** = contract which is being discussed; **a matter for negotiation** = something which must be discussed before a decision is reached; **to enter into negotiations** *or* **to start negotiations** = to start discussing a problem; **to resume negotiations** = to start discussing a problem again, after talks have stopped for a time; **to break off negotiations** = to refuse to go on discussing a problem; **to conduct negotiations** = to negotiate; **negotiations broke down after six hours** = discussions stopped because no agreement was possible; **pay negotiations** *or* **wage negotiations** = discussions between management and workers about pay

◇ **negotiator** *noun* **(a)** person who discusses with the aim of reaching an agreement; **an experienced union negotiator** = member of a union who has a lot of experience of discussing terms of employment with management **(b)** *GB* person who works in an estate agency

net 1 *adjective* **(a)** price *or* weight *or* pay, etc. after all deductions have been made; **net assets** *or* **net worth** = value of all the property of a company after taking away what the company owes; **net cash flow** = difference between money coming in and money going out of a firm; **net earnings** *or* **net income** = total earnings of a business after tax and other deductions; **net income** *or* **net salary** = person's income which is left after taking away tax and other deductions; **net loss** = actual loss, after deducting overheads; **net margin** = net profit shown as a percentage of sales; **net price** = price which cannot be reduced by a discount; **net profit** = result where income from sales is more than all expenditure; **net receipts** = receipts after deducting commission *or* tax *or* discounts, etc.; **net sales** = sales less damaged or returned items; **net weight** = weight of goods after deducting the weight of packaging material and container; **net yield** = profit from investments after deduction of tax **(b) terms strictly net** = payment has to be the full price, with no discount allowed

NOTE: the spelling **nett** is sometimes used on containers

2 *verb* to make a true profit; **to net a profit of £10,000**

NOTE: **netting - netted**

QUOTE: out of its earnings a company will pay a dividend. When shareholders receive this it will be net, that is it will have had tax deducted at 30 per cent   *Investors Chronicle*

network 1 *noun* system which links different points together; **a network of distributors** *or* **a distribution network** = series of points *or* warehouses from which goods are sent all over a country; **computer network** = computer system where several micros are linked so that they all draw on the same database; **television network** = system of linked television stations covering the whole country **2** *verb* to link together in a network; **to network a television programme** = to send out the same television programme through several TV stations; **networked system** = computer system where several micros are linked together so that they all draw on the same database

new *adjective* recent *or* not old; **under new management** = with a new owner; **new issue** = issues of new shares; **new issues department** = section of a bank which deals with issues of new shares; **new technology** = electronic instruments which have recently been invented

◇ **news** *noun* information about things which have happened; **business news; financial news; financial markets were shocked by the news of the devaluation; news agency** = office which distributes news to newspapers and television companies; **news release** = sheet giving information about a new event which is sent to newspapers and TV and radio stations so that they can use it; **the company sent out a news release about the new managing director**

◇ **newsagent** *noun* person who runs a shop selling newspapers and magazines

◇ **newsletter** *noun* **company newsletter** = printed sheet or small newspaper giving news about a company

niche *noun* special place in a market, occupied by one company

nickel *noun* *US* five cent coin

night *noun* period of time from evening to morning; **night safe** = safe in the outside wall of a bank where money and documents can be deposited at night using a special door; **night shift** = shift which works at night; **there are thirty men on the night shift; he works nights** *or* **he works the night shift**

nil *noun* zero *or* nothing; **to make a nil return; the advertising budget has been cut to nil**

No = NUMBER

no-claims bonus *noun* reduction of premiums on an insurance policy because no claims have been made

nominal *adjective* **(a)** very small (payment); **we make a nominal charge for our services; they are paying a nominal rent (b) nominal capital** = the total of the face value of all the shares in a company; **nominal ledger** = general accounts book showing income and expenditure; **nominal value** = face value *or* value written on a share *or* a coin *or* a banknote

nominate *verb* to suggest someone *or* to name someone for a job; **to nominate someone to a post** = to appoint someone to a post without an election; **to nominate someone as proxy** = to name someone as your proxy

◇ **nomination** *noun* act of nominating

◇ **nominee** *noun* person who is nominated, especially someone who is appointed to deal with financial matters on your behalf; **nominee account** = account held on behalf of someone

non- *prefix* not

◇ **non-acceptance** *noun* situation

where the person who is to pay a bill of exchange does not accept it

◇ **non-contributory** *adjective* **non-contributory pension scheme** = pension scheme where the employee does not make any contributions and the company pays everything; **the company pension scheme is non-contributory**

◇ **non-delivery** *noun* situation where something is not delivered

◇ **non-durables** *plural noun* goods which are used up soon after they have been bought (such as food, newspapers)

◇ **non-executive** *adjective* **non-executive director** = director who attends board meetings and gives advice, but does not work full-time for the company

◇ **non-feasance** *noun* not doing something which should be done by law

◇ **non-negotiable** *adjective* **non-negotiable instrument** = document (such as a crossed cheque) which cannot be exchanged for cash

◇ **non-payment** *noun* **non-payment of a debt** = not paying a debt due

◇ **non profit-making organization** *or* US **non-profit corporation** *noun* organization (such as a club) which is not allowed by law to make a profit; **non-profit-making organizations are exempted from tax**

◇ **non-recurring** *adjective* **non-recurring items** = special items in a set of accounts which appear only once

◇ **non-refundable** *adjective* which will not be refunded; **non-refundable deposit**

◇ **non-resident** *noun* person who is not considered a resident of a country for tax purposes; **he has a non-resident bank account**

◇ **non-returnable** *adjective* which cannot be returned; **non-returnable packing** = packing which is to be thrown away when it has been used and not returned to the sender

◇ **non-stop** *adjective & adverb* without stopping; **they worked non-stop to finish the audit on time**

◇ **non-taxable** *adjective* which is not subject to tax; **non-taxable income**

◇ **non-union** *adjective* **company using non-union labour** = company employing workers who do not belong to trade unions

◇ **non-voting** *adjective* **non-voting**

shares = shares which do not allow the shareholder to vote at meetings

norm *noun* the usual quantity *or* the usual rate; **the output from this factory is well above the norm for the industry** *or* **well above the industry norm**

◇ **normal** *adjective* usual *or* which happens regularly; **normal deliveries are made on Tuesdays and Fridays; now that the strike is over we hope to resume normal service as soon as possible; under normal conditions** = if things work in the usual way; **under normal conditions a package takes two days to get to Copenhagen**

notary public *noun* lawyer who has the authority to witness documents and spoken statements, making them official NOTE: plural is **notaries public**

note 1 *noun* **(a)** short document *or* short piece of information; **advice note** = written notice to a customer giving details of goods ordered and shipped but not yet delivered; **contract note** = note showing that shares have been bought or sold but not yet paid for; **cover note** = letter from an insurance company giving details of an insurance policy and confirming that the policy exists; **covering note** = letter sent with documents to explain why you are sending them; **credit note** = note showing that money is owed to a customer; **debit note** = note showing that a customer owes money; **we undercharged Mr Smith and had to send him a debit note for the extra amount; delivery note** = list of goods being delivered, given to the customer with the goods; **dispatch note** = note saying that goods have been sent; **note of hand** *or* **promissory note** = document stating that someone promises to pay an amount of money on a certain date **(b)** short letter *or* short piece of information; **to send someone a note; I left a note on his desk; she left a note for the managing director with his secretary (c)** bank note *or* **currency note** = piece of printed paper money; **a £5 note; he pulled out a pile of used notes 2** *verb* to write down details of something and remember them; **we note that the goods were delivered in bad condition; your order has been noted and will be dispatched as soon as we have stock; your complaint has been noted**

◇ **notebook** *noun* book for writing notes in

◇ **notepad** *noun* pad of paper for writing short notes

◇ **notepaper** *noun* good quality paper for letters

notice *noun* (a) piece of written information; **the company secretary pinned up a notice about the pension scheme; copyright notice** = note in a book showing who owns the copyright and the date of ownership (b) official warning that a contract is going to end *or* that terms are going to be changed; **until further notice** = until different instructions are given; **you must pay £200 on the 30th of each month until further notice** (c) written announcement that a worker is leaving his job on a certain date; **period of notice** = time stated in the contract of employment which the worker or company has to allow between resigning or being fired and the worker actually leaving his job; **we require three months' notice; he gave six months' notice; we gave him three months' wages in lieu of notice; she gave in** *or* **handed in her notice** = she resigned; **he is working out his notice** = he is working during the time between resigning and actually leaving the company (d) time allowed before something takes place; **at short notice** = with very little warning; **the bank manager will not see anyone at short notice; you must give seven days' notice of withdrawal** = you must ask to take money out of the account seven days before you want it (e) legal document (such as telling a tenant to leave property which he is occupying); **to give a tenant notice to quit; to serve notice on someone** = to give someone a legal notice NOTE: no plural for (b), (c), (d) and (e)

◇ **noticeboard** *noun* board fixed to a wall where notices can be put up; **did you see the new list of prices on the noticeboard?**

notify *verb* **to notify someone of something** = to tell someone something formally; **they were notified of the arrival of the shipment**

◇ **notification** *noun* informing someone

notional *adjective* probable but not known exactly *or* not quantifiable; **notional income** = invisible benefit which is not money or goods and services; **notional**

rent = sum put into accounts as rent where the company owns the building it is occupying and so does not pay an actual rent

nought number 0; **a million pounds can be written as "£1m" or as one and six noughts**
NOTE: **nought** is commoner in GB English; in US English, **zero** is more usual

null *adjective* with no meaning *or* which cannot legally be enforced; **contract was declared null and void** = the contract was said to be not valid; **to render a decision null** = to make a decision useless *or* to cancel a decision

◇ **nullification** *noun* act of making something invalid

◇ **nullify** *verb* to make something invalid *or* to cancel something

number 1 *noun* (a) quantity of things *or* people; **the number of persons on the payroll has increased over the last year; the number of days lost through strikes has fallen; the number of shares sold; a number of** = some; **a number of the staff will be retiring this year** (b) written figure; **account number; batch number; cheque number; invoice number; order number; page number; serial number; phone number** *or* **telephone number; box number** = reference number used when asking for mail to be sent to a post office or when asking for replies to an advertisement to be sent to the newspaper's offices; **please reply to Box No. 209; index number** = (i) number of something in an index; (ii) number showing the percentage rise of something over a period
NOTE: often written **No.** with figures
2 *verb* to put a figure on a document; **to number an order; I refer to your invoiced numbered 1234; numbered account** = bank account (usually in Switzerland) which is referred to only by a number, the name of the person holding it being kept secret

◇ **numeric** *or* **numerical** *adjective* referring to numbers; **in numerical order** = in the order of figures (such as 1 before 2, 33 before 34); **file these invoices in numerical order; numeric data** = data in the form of figures; **numeric keypad** = part of a computer keyboard which is a programmable set of numbered keys

Oo

O & M = ORGANIZATION AND METHODS

OAP = OLD AGE PENSIONER

oath *noun* legal promise stating that something is true; **he was under oath** = he had promised in court to say what was true

object *verb* to refuse to do something *or* to say that you do not accept something; **to object to a clause in a contract**
NOTE: you object **to** something
◇ **objection** *noun* **to raise an objection to something** = to object to something; **the union delegates raised an objection to the wording of the agreement**

objective **1** *noun* something which you try to do; **the company has achieved its objectives; we set the sales forces certain objectives; long-term objective** *or* **short-term objective** = aim which you hope to achieve within a few years or a few months; **management by objectives** = way of managing a business by planning work for the managers to do and testing if it is completed correctly and on time **2** *adjective* considered from a general point of view not from that of the person involved; **you must be objective in assessing the performance of the staff; to carry out an objective survey of the market**

obligate *verb* **to be obligated to do something** = to have a legal duty to do something
◇ **obligation** *noun* **(a)** duty to do something; **to be under an obligation to do something** = to feel it is your duty to do something; **there is no obligation to buy; to be under no obligation to do something; he is under no contractual obligation to buy** = he has signed no contract which forces him to buy; **to fulfill one's contractual obligations** = to do what is stated in a contract; **two weeks' free trial without obligation** = the customer can try the item at home for two weeks without having to buy it at the end of the test **(b)** debt; **to meet one's obligations** = to pay one's debts

◇ **obligatory** *adjective* necessary according to the law or rules; **each person has to pass an obligatory medical examination**
◇ **oblige** *verb* **to oblige someone to do something** = to make someone feel he must do something; **he felt obliged to cancel the contract**

obsolescence *noun* act of going out of date, and therefore becoming less useful and valuable; **built-in obsolescence** *or* **planned obsolescence** = situation where the manufacturer designs his products to become out of date so that the customers can be pressed to replace them with new models
NOTE: no plural
◇ **obsolescent** *adjective* becoming out of date
◇ **obsolete** *adjective* no longer used; **when the office was equipped with word-processors the typewriters became obsolete**

obtain *verb* to get; **to obtain supplies from abroad; we find these items very difficult to obtain; to obtain an injunction against a company; he obtained control by buying the founder's shareholding**
◇ **obtainable** *adjective* which can be got; **prices fall when raw materials are easily obtainable; our products are obtainable in all computer shops**

occasional *adjective* which happens from time to time

occupancy *noun* act of occupying a property (such as a house, an office, a room in a hotel); **with immediate occupancy** = empty and available to be occupied immediately; **occupancy rate** = average number of rooms occupied in a hotel over a period of time shown as a percentage of the total number of rooms; **during the winter months the occupancy rate was down to 50%**
NOTE: no plural
◇ **occupant** *noun* person or company which occupies a property
◇ **occupation** *noun* **(a) occupation of a building** = act of occupying a building **(b)** job *or* work; **what is her occupation? his main occupation is house building (c) occupations** = types of work; **people in professional occupations**

◇ **occupational** *adjective* referring to a job; **occupational accident** = accident which takes place at work; **occupational disease** = disease which affects people in certain jobs; **occupational hazards** = dangers which apply to certain jobs; **heart attacks are one of the occupational hazards of directors; occupational pension scheme** = pension scheme where the worker gets a pension from the company he has worked for

◇ **occupier** *noun* person who lives in a property; **beneficial occupier** = person who occupies a property but does not own it fully; **owner-occupier** = person who owns the property in which he lives

◇ **occupy** *verb* **(a)** to live or work in a property (such as a house, an office, a hotel room); **all the rooms in the hotel are occupied; the company occupies three floors of an office block (b) to occupy a post** = to be employed in a job

> QUOTE: while occupancy rates matched those of 1984 in July, August has been a much poorer month than it was the year before *Economist*
> QUOTE: employment in professional occupations increased by 40 per cent between 1974 and 1983, while the share of white-collar occupations in total employment rose from 44 per cent to 49 per cent *Sydney Morning Herald*

odd *adjective* **(a) odd numbers** = numbers (like 17 or 33) which cannot be divided by two; **odd-numbered buildings** *or* **buildings with odd numbers are on the south side of the street (b) a hundred odd** = approximately one hundred; **keep the odd change** = keep the small change which is left over **(c)** one of a group; **an odd shoe** = one shoe of a pair; **we have a few odd boxes left** = we have a few boxes left out of the total shipment; **odd lot** = group of miscellaneous items for sale at an auction; **to do odd jobs** = to do various pieces of work **(d) odd sizes** = strange sizes which are not usual

◇ **odd-job-man** *noun* person who does various pieces of work

◇ **oddments** *plural noun* items left over; pieces of large items sold separately

off 1 *adverb* **(a)** not working *or* not in operation; **the agreement is off; they called the strike off (b)** taken away from a price; **these carpets are sold at £25 off the marked price; we give 5% off for quick settlement** 2 *preposition* **(a)** away from a price; **to take £25 off the price; we give 10% off our normal prices (b)** away from work; **to take time off work; we give the staff four days off at Christmas; it is the secretary's day off tomorrow**

offer 1 *noun* **(a)** statement that you are willing to pay a certain amount of money to buy something; **to make an offer for a company; he made an offer of £10 a share; we made a written offer for the house; £1,000 is the best offer I can make; to accept an offer of £1,000 for the car; the house is under offer** = someone has made an offer to buy the house and the offer has been accepted provisionally; **we are open to offers** = we are ready to discuss the price which we are asking; **cash offer** = being ready to pay in cash; **or near offer** = or an offer of a price which is slightly less than the price asked; **the car is for sale at £2,000 or near offer** NOTE: often shortened to **o.n.o. (b)** statement that you are willing to sell something; **offer for sale** = situation where a company advertises new shares for sale; **offer price** = price at which new shares are put on sale **(c) he received six offers of jobs** *or* **six job offers** = six companies told him he could have a job with them **(d) bargain offer** = sale of a particular type of goods at a cheap price; **this week's bargain offer - 30% off all carpet prices; introductory offer** = special price offered on a new product to attract customers; **special offer** = goods put on sale at a specially low price; **we have a range of men's shirts on special offer** 2 *verb* **(a) to offer someone a job** = to tell someone that he can have a job in your company; **he was offered a directorship with Smith Ltd (b)** to say that you are willing to pay a certain amount of money for something; **to offer someone £100,000 for his house; he offered £10 a share (c)** to say that you are willing to sell something; **we offered the house for sale**

office *noun* **(a)** set of rooms where a company works *or* where business is done; **branch office** = less important office, usually in a different town or country from the main office; **head office** *or* **main office** = office building where the board of directors works and meets; *GB* **registered office** = office address of a company which is officially registered with the Companies' Registrar **(b) office block** or **a block of offices** = building which contains only offices; **office boy** = young man who works in an office, usually taking messages from one department to another; **office equipment** = furniture and machines needed to make an office work; **office hours** = time when an office is open; **open during normal office hours; do not telephone during office hours; the manager can be reached at home out of office hours; office junior** = young man or woman who does all types of work in an office; **office space** or **office accommodation** = space available for offices or occupied by offices; **we are looking for extra office space; office staff** = people who work in offices; **office supplies** = stationery and furniture used in an office; **an office supplies firm** = company which sells office supplies; **for office use only** = something which must only be used in an office; **office worker** = person who works in an office **(c)** room where someone works and does business; **come into my office; the manager's office is on the third floor (d) booking office** = office where you can book seats at a theatre or tickets for the railway; **box office** = office at a theatre where tickets can be bought; **employment office** = office which finds jobs for people; **general office** = main administrative office in a company; **information office** = office which gives information to tourists or visitors; **inquiry office** = office where someone can answer questions from members of the public; **ticket office** = office where tickets can be bought **(e)** *GB* government department; **the Foreign Office** = ministry dealing with foreign affairs; **the Home Office** = ministry dealing with the internal affairs of the country; **Office of Fair Trading** = government department which protects consumers against unfair or illegal business **(f)** post or position; **he holds** or **performs the office of treasurer; high office** = important position or job; **compensation for loss of office** = payment to a director who is asked to leave a company before his contract ends

officer *noun* **(a)** person who has an official position; **customs officer** = person working for the customs; **fire safety officer** = person responsible for fire safety

in a building; **information officer** = person who gives information about a company or about a government department to the public; **personnel officer** = person who deals with the staff, especially interviewing new workers; **training officer** = person who deals with the training of staff; **the company officers** or **the officers of a company** = the main executives or directors of a company **(b)** official (usually unpaid) of a club or society, etc.; **the election of officers of an association**

official 1 *adjective* **(a)** from a government department or organization; **on official business; he left official documents in his car; she received an official letter of explanation; speaking in an official capacity** = speaking officially; **to go through official channels** = to deal with officials, especially when making a request; **the official exchange rate** = exchange rate which is imposed by the government; **the official exchange rate is ten to the dollar, but you can get twice that on the black market (b)** done or approved by a director or by a person in authority; **this must be an official order - it is written on the company's notepaper; the strike was made official** = the local strike was approved by the main trade union office **(c) the official receiver** = government official who is appointed to close down a company which is in liquidation **2** *noun* person working in a government department; **airport officials inspected the shipment; government officials stopped the import licence; customs official** = person working for the customs; **high official** = important person in a government department; **minor official** = person in a low position in a government department; **some minor official tried to stop my request for building permission; top official** = very important person in a government department; **union officials** = paid organizers in a trade union

◇ **officialese** *noun* language used in government documents which can be difficult to understand

◇ **officially** *adverb* in an official way; **officially he knows nothing about the problem, but unofficially he has given us a lot of advice about it**

officio *see* EX OFFICIO

off-licence *noun GB* **(a)** licence to sell alcohol for drinking away from the place where you buy it **(b)** shop which sells alcohol for drinking at home

offload *verb* to pass something which is not wanted to someone else; **to offload excess stock** = to try to sell excess stock; **to offload costs onto a subsidiary company** = to try to get a subsidiary company to pay some charges so as to reduce tax
NOTE: you offload something **from** a thing or person **onto** another thing or person

off-peak *adjective* not during the most busy time; **during the off-peak period** = at the time when business is less busy; **off-peak tariff** *or* **rate** = lower charges used when the service is not busy

off-season **1** *adjective* off-season tariff *or* **rate** = cheap fares which are charged in a season when there is less business **2** *noun* less busy season for travel (usually during the winter); **to travel in the off-season; air fares are cheaper in the off-season**

offset *verb* to balance one thing against another so that they cancel each other out; **to offset losses against tax; foreign exchange losses more than offset profits in the domestic market**
NOTE: **offsetting - offset**

off-shore *adjective & adverb* **(a)** on an island *or* in the sea near to land; **off-shore oil field; off-shore oil platform (b)** on an island which is a tax haven; **off-shore fund** = fund which is based in the Bahamas, etc.

off-the-job *adjective* off-the-job training = training given to workers away from their place of work (such as at a college or school)

oil *noun* natural liquid found in the ground, used to burn to give power; **oil-exporting countries** = countries which produce oil and sell it to others; **oil field** = area of land or sea under which oil is found; **the North Sea oil fields; oil-importing countries** = countries which import oil; **oil-producing countries** = countries which produce oil; **oil platform** *or* **oil rig** = large construction with equipment for making holes in the ground to

find oil; **oil well** = hole in the ground from which oil is pumped

old *adjective* having existed for a long time; **the company is 125 years old next year; we have decided to get rid of our old computer system and install a new one**
◇ **old age** *noun* period when a person is old; **old age pension** = state pension given to a man who is 65 or a woman who is 60; **old age pensioner** = person who receives the old age pension
◇ **old-established** *adjective* (company *or* brand) which has been in existence for a long time
◇ **old-fashioned** *adjective* out of date *or* not modern; **he still uses an old-fashioned typewriter**

ombudsman *noun* official who investigates complaints by the public against government departments
NOTE: plural is **ombudsmen**

omit *verb* **(a)** to leave something out *or* not to put something in; **the secretary omitted the date when typing the contract (b)** not to do something; **he omitted to tell the managing director that he had lost the documents**
NOTE: **omitting - omitted**
◇ **omission** *noun* thing which has been omitted; **errors and omissions excepted** = words written on an invoice to show that the company has no responsibility for mistakes in the invoice

omnibus *noun* omnibus agreement = agreement which covers many different items

on *preposition* **(a)** being a member of a group; **to sit on a committee; she is on the boards of two companies; we have 250 people on the payroll; she is on our full-time staff (b)** in a certain way; **on a commercial basis; to buy something on approval; on the average; to buy a car on hire-purchase; to get a mortgage on easy terms (c)** at a time; **on weekdays; the shop is closed on Wednesday afternoons; on May 24th (d)** doing something; **the director is on holiday; she is in the States on business; the switchboard operator is on duty from 6 to 9**

oncosts *plural noun* fixed costs *or* money paid in producing a product which does not rise with the quantity of the product made

on line *or* **online** *adverb* linked directly to a mainframe computer; **the sales office is on line to the warehouse; we get our data on line from the stock control department**

on-the-job *adjective* **on-the-job training** = training given to workers at their place of work

one-man *adjective* **one-man business** *or* **firm** *or* **company** *or* **operation** = business run by one person alone with no staff or partners

◊ **one-off** *adjective* done or made only once; **one-off item; one-off deal**

◊ **one-sided** *adjective* which favours one side and not the other in a negotiation; **one-sided agreement**

◊ **one-way** *adjective* **one-way ticket** = ticket for a journey from one place to another; *US* **one-way fare** = fare for a journey from one place to another; **one-way trade** = situation where one country sells to another, but does not buy anything in return

◊ **one-way street** *noun* street where the traffic is allowed to go only in one direction; **the shop is in a one-way street, which makes it very difficult for parking**

onerous *adjective* heavy *or* needing a lot of effort or money; **the repayment terms are particularly onerous** = the loan is particularly difficult to pay back

o.n.o. = OR NEAR OFFER

OPEC = ORGANIZATION OF PETRO-LEUM EXPORTING COUNTRIES

open 1 *adjective* **(a)** at work *or* not closed; **the store is open on Sunday mornings; our offices are open from 9 to 6; they are open for business every day of the week (b)** ready to accept something; **the job is open to all applicants** = anyone can apply for the job; **we will keep the job open for you until you have passed your driving test** = we will not give the job to anyone else, and will wait until you have passed your test; **open to offers** = ready to accept

a reasonable offer; **the company is open to offers for the empty factory** = the company is ready to discuss an offer which is lower than the suggested price **(c) open account** = unsecured credit *or* amount owed with no security; **open cheque** = cheque which is not crossed and can be cashed anywhere; **open credit** = bank credit given to good customers without security up to a certain maximum sum; **open market** = market where anyone can buy or sell; **to buy shares on the open market** = to buy shares on the Stock Exchange, not privately; **open ticket** = ticket which can be used on any date **2** *verb* **(a)** to start a new business working; **she has opened a shop in the High Street; we have opened an office in London (b)** to start work *or* to be at work; **the office opens at 9 a.m.; we open for business on Sundays (c)** to begin; **to open negotiations** = to begin negotiating; **he opened the discussions with a description of the product; the chairman opened the meeting at 10.30 (d)** to start *or* to allow something to start; **to open a bank account; to open a line of credit; to open a loan (e) the shares opened lower** = share prices were lower at the beginning of the day's trading

◊ **open-ended** *or* *US* **open-end** *adjective* with no fixed limit *or* with some items not specified; **open-ended agreement**

◊ **opening 1** *noun* **(a)** act of starting a new business; **the opening of a new branch; the opening of a new market** *or* **of a new distribution network (b) opening hours** = hours when a shop *or* business is open **(c) job openings** = jobs which are empty and need filling; **we have openings for office staff; a market opening** = possibility of starting to do business in a new market **2** *adjective* at the beginning *or* first; **opening balance** = balance at the beginning of an accounting period; **opening bid** = first bid at an auction; **opening entry** = first entry in an account; **opening price** = price at the start of the day's trading; **opening stock** = stock at the beginning of the accounting period

◊ **open-plan** *adjective* **open-plan office** = large room divided into smaller working spaces with no fixed divisions between them

◊ **open up** *verb* **to open up new markets** = to work to start business in markets where such business has not been done before

operate *verb* **(a)** to work; **the new terms of service will operate from January 1st; the rules operate on inland postal services (b) to operate a machine** = to make a machine work; **he is learning to operate the new telephone switchboard**

◊ **operating** *noun* general running of a business *or* of a machine; **operating budget** = forecast of income and expenditure over a period of time; **operating costs** *or* **operating expenses** = costs of the day-to-day organization of a company; **operating manual** = book which shows how to work a machine; **operating profit** *or* **operating loss** = profit or loss made by a company in its usual business; **operating system** = the main program which operates a computer
NOTE: no plural

◊ **operation** *noun* **(a)** business organization and work; **the company's operations in West Africa; he heads up the operations in Northern Europe; operations review** = examining the way in which a company or department works to see how it can be made more efficient and profitable; **a franchising operation** = selling licences to trade as a franchise **(b) Stock Exchange operation** = buying or selling of shares on the Stock Exchange **(c) in operation** = working *or* being used; **the system will be in operation by June; the new system came into operation on June 1st**

◊ **operational** *adjective* **(a)** referring to how something works; **operational budget** = forecast of expenditure on running a business; **operational costs** = costs of running a business; **operational planning** = planning how a business is to be run; **operational research** = study of a company's way of working to see if it can be made more efficient and profitable **(b) the system became operational on June 1st** = the system began working on June 1st

◊ **operative 1** *adjective* **to become operative** = to start working; **the new system has been operative since June 1st 2** *noun* person who operates a machine which makes a product

◊ **operator** *noun* **(a)** person who works a machine; **a keyboard operator; a telex operator (b)** person who works a tele-phone switchboard; **switchboard operator; to call the operator** *or* **to dial the operator; to place a call through** *or* **via the operator (c)** (*on the Stock Exchange*) person who buys and sells shares hoping to make a quick profit **(d) tour operator** = person *or* company which organizes package tours

opinion *noun* **(a) public opinion** = what people think about something; **opinion poll** *or* **opinion research** = asking a sample group of people what their opinion is, so as to guess the opinion of the whole population; **opinion polls showed that the public preferred butter to margarine; before starting the new service, the company carried out nationwide opinion polls (b)** piece of expert advice; **the lawyers gave their opinion; to ask an adviser for his opinion on a case**

opportunity *noun* situation where you can do something successfully; **investment opportunities** *or* **sales opportunities** = possibilities for making investments or sales which will be profitable; **a market opportunity** = possibility of going into a market for the first time; **employment opportunities** *or* **job opportunities** = new jobs being available; **the increase in export orders has created hundreds of job opportunities**

oppose *verb* to try to stop something happening; to vote against something; **a minority of board members opposed the motion; we are all opposed to the takeover**

opposite *noun* **opposite number** = person who has a similar job in another company; **John is my opposite number in Smith's** = John has the same job in Smith's as I have here

optimal *adjective* best

◇ **optimism** *noun* being sure that everything will work out well; **he has considerable optimism about sales possibilities in the Far East; market optimism** = feeling that the stock market will rise

NOTE: no plural

◇ **optimistic** *adjective* feeling sure that everything will work out well; **he takes an optimistic view of the exchange rate** = he expects the exchange rate will go in his favour

◇ **optimum** *adjective* best; **the market offers optimum conditions for sales**

option *noun* (a) **option to purchase** *or* **to sell** = giving someone the possibility to buy or sell something within a period of time; **first option** = allowing someone to be the first to have the possibility of deciding something; **to grant someone a six-month option on a product** = to allow someone six months to decide if he wants to be the agent *or* if he wants to manufacture the product; **to take up an option** *or* **to exercise an option** = to accept the option which has been offered and to put it into action; **he exercised his option** *or* **he took up his option to acquire sole marketing rights to the product; I want to leave my options open** = I want to be able to decide what to do when the time is right; **to take the soft option** = to decide to do something which involves the least risk, effort or problems (b) (*Stock Exchange*) **call option** = option to buy shares at a certain price; **put option** = option to sell shares at a certain price; **share option** = right to buy or sell shares at a certain price at a time in the future; **stock option** = right to buy shares at a cheap price given by a company to its employees; **option contract** = right to buy or sell shares at a fixed price; **option dealing** *or* **option trading** = buying and selling share options

◇ **optional** *adjective* which can be added if the customer wants; **the insurance cover is optional; optional extras** = items (such as a radio) which can be added (to a car) if wanted

order 1 *noun* (a) arrangement of records (filing cards, invoices, etc.); **alphabetical order** = arrangement by the letters of the alphabet (A, B, C, etc.); **chronological order** = arrangement by the order of the dates; **the reports are filed in chronological order; numerical order** = arrangement by numbers; **put these invoices in numerical order** (b) working arrangement; **machine in full working order** = machine which is ready and able to work properly; **the telephone is out of order** = the telephone is not working; **is all the documentation in order?** = are all the documents valid and correct? (c) **pay to Mr Smith or order** = pay money to Mr Smith or as he orders; **pay to the order of Mr Smith** = pay money directly into Mr Smith's account (d) official request for goods to be supplied; **to give someone an order** *or* **to place an order with someone for twenty filing cabinets; to fill** *or* **to fulfil an order** = to supply items which have been ordered; **we are so understaffed we cannot fulfil any more orders before Christmas; to supply an order for twenty filing cabinets; purchase order** = official paper which places an order for something; **order fulfilment** = supplying items which have been ordered; **terms: cash with order** = the goods will be supplied only if payment in cash is made at the same time as the order is placed; **items available to order only** = items which will be manufactured only if someone orders them; **on order** = ordered but not delivered; **this item is out of stock, but is on order; unfulfilled orders** *or* **back orders** *or* **outstanding orders** = orders received in the past and not yet supplied; **order book** = record of orders; **the company has a full order book** = it has enough orders to work at full capacity; **telephone orders** = orders received over the telephone; **since we mailed the catalogue we have had a large number of telephone orders; a pad of order forms** = a pad of blank sheet for orders to be written on (e) item which has been ordered; **the order is to be delivered to our warehouse; order picking** = collecting various items in a warehouse to make up an order to be sent to a customer (f) instruction; **delivery order** = instructions given by the customer to the person holding his goods, telling him to deliver them **(g)** document which allows money to be paid to someone; **he sent us an order on the Chartered Bank; banker's order** *or* **standing order** = order written by a customer asking a bank to make a regular payment; **he pays his subscription by banker's order; money order** = document which can be bought for sending money through the post **2** *verb* **(a)** to ask for goods to be supplied; **to order twenty filing cabinets to be delivered to the warehouse; they ordered a new Rolls Royce for the managing director (b)** to put in a certain way; **the address list is ordered by country; that filing cabinet contains invoices ordered by date**

ordinary *adjective* normal *or* not special; **ordinary member** = person who pays a subscription to belong to a group; **ordinary shares** = normal shares in a company, which have no special bonuses or restrictions; **ordinary shareholder** = person who owns ordinary shares in a company

organization *noun* **(a)** way of arranging something so that it works efficiently; **the chairman handles the organization of the AGM; the organization of the group is too centralized to be efficient; the organization of the head office into departments; organization and methods** = examining how an office works, and suggesting how it can be made more efficient; **organization chart** = list of people working in various departments, showing how a company *or* office is organized; **line organization** = organization of a business where each manager is responsible for doing what his superior tells him to do **(b)** group or institution which is arranged for efficient work; **the Organization of Petroleum Exporting Countries** = group of major countries who are producers and exporters of oil; **a government organization** = official body, run by the government; **a travel organization** = body representing companies in the travel business; **an employers' organization** = group of employers with similar interests
NOTE: no plural for (a)

◇ **organize** *verb* to arrange something so that it works efficiently; **the company is organized into six profit centres; the group is organized by areas of sales; organized**

labour = workers who are members of trade unions

◇ **organizational** *adjective* referring to the way in which something is organized; **the paper gives a diagram of the company's organizational structure**

◇ **organizer** *noun* person who arranges things efficiently

◇ **organizing committee** *noun* group of people who arrange something; **he is a member of the organizing committee for the conference**

QUOTE: working with a client base which includes many major commercial organizations and nationalized industries *Times*
QUOTE: we organize a rate with importers who have large orders and guarantee them space at a fixed rate so that they can plan their costs *Lloyd's List*
QUOTE: governments are coming under increasing pressure from politicians, organized labour and business to stimulate economic growth *Duns Business Month*

oriented *or* **orientated** *adjective* working in a certain direction; **profit-oriented company** = company which does everything to make a profit; **export-oriented company** = company which produces goods mainly for export

origin *noun* where something comes from; **spare parts of European origin; certificate of origin** = document showing where goods were made; **country of origin** = country where a product is manufactured

◇ **original 1** *adjective* which was used or made first; **they sent a copy of the original invoice; he kept the original receipt for reference 2** *noun* first copy made; **send the original and file two copies**

◇ **originally** *adverb* first *or* at the beginning

ounce *noun* measure of weight (= 28 grams)
NOTE: usually written **oz** after figures

out *adverb* **(a)** on strike; **the workers have been out on strike for four weeks; as soon as the management made the offer, the staff came out; the shop stewards called the**

workforce out **(b) to be out** = to be wrong in calculating something; **the balance is £10 out; we are £20,000 out in our calculations** = we have £20,000 too much *or* too little

◇ **outbid** *verb* to offer a better price than someone else; **we offered £100,000 for the warehouse, but another company outbid us** NOTE: **outbidding - outbid**

◇ **outfit** *noun* small, sometimes badly run, company; **they called in a public relations outfit; he works for some finance outfit**

◇ **outflow** *noun* **outflow of capital from a country** = capital which is sent out of a country for investment abroad

◇ **outgoing** *adjective* **(a) outgoing mail** = mail which is being sent out **(b) the outgoing chairman** *or* **the outgoing president** = chairman *or* president who is about the retire

◇ **outgoings** *plural noun* money which is paid out

◇ **out-house** *adjective* working outside a company's buildings; **the out-house staff; we do all our data processing out-house**

◇ **outlay** *noun* money spent *or* expenditure; **capital outlay** = money spent on fixed assets (such as property, machinery, furniture); **for a modest outlay** = for a small sum

◇ **outlet** *noun* place where something can be sold; **retail outlets** = shops which sell to the general public

◇ **outline** **1** *noun* general description, without giving many details; **they drew up the outline of a plan** *or* **an outline plan; outline planning permission** = general permission to build a property on a piece of land, but not final because there are no details **2** *verb* to make a general description; **the chairman outlined the company's plans for the coming year**

◇ **outlook** *noun* view of what is going to happen in the future; **the economic outlook is not good; the stock market outlook is worrying**

◇ **out of court** *adverb* & *adjective* **a settlement was reached out of court** = a dispute was settled between two parties privately without continuing a court case; **they are hoping to reach an out-of-court settlement**

◇ **out of date** *adjective* & *adverb* old-fashioned *or* no longer modern; **their computer system is years out of date; they are still using out-of-date equipment**

◇ **out of pocket** *adjective* & *adverb* having paid out money personally; **the deal has left me out of pocket; out-of-pocket expenses** = amount of money to pay a worker back for his own money which he has spent on company business

◇ **out of stock** *adjective* & *adverb* with no stock left; **those records are temporarily out of stock; several out-of-stock items have been on order for weeks**

◇ **out of work** *adjective* & *adverb* with no job; **the recession has put millions out of work; the company was set up by three out-of-work engineers**

◇ **output 1** *noun* **(a)** amount which a company or a person or a machine produces; **output has increased by 10%; 25% of our output is exported; output per hour** = amount produced in one hour; **output bonus** = extra payment for increased production; **output tax** = VAT charged by a company on goods or services sold **(b)** information which is produced by a computer NOTE: no plural **2** *verb* to produce (by a computer); **the printer will output colour graphs; that is the information outputted from the computer** NOTE: **outputting - outputted**

◇ **outright** *adverb* & *adjective* completely; **to purchase something outright** *or* **to make an outright purchase** = to buy something completely, including all rights in it

◇ **outsell** *verb* to sell more than someone; **the company is easily outselling its competitors** NOTE: **outselling - outsold**

◇ **outside** *adjective* & *adverb* not in a company's office or building; **to send work to be done outside** = to send work to be done in other offices; **outside office hours** = when the office is not open; **outside dealer** = person who is not a member of the Stock Exchange but is allowed to trade; **outside director** = director who is not employed by the company; **outside line** = line from an internal office telephone system to the main telephone exchange; **you dial 9 to get an outside line; outside worker** =

worker who does not work in a company's offices

◇ **outsize** *noun* size which is larger than usual; **an outsize order** = a very large order

◇ **outstanding** *adjective* not yet paid or completed; **outstanding debts** = debts which are waiting to be paid; **outstanding orders** = orders received but not yet supplied; **what is the amount outstanding?** = how much money is still owed?; **matters outstanding from the previous meeting** = questions which were not settled at the previous meeting

◇ **out tray** *noun* basket on a desk for letters or memos which have been dealt with and are ready to be dispatched

◇ **outturn** *noun* amount produced by a country *or* company

◇ **outvote** *verb* to defeat in a vote; **the chairman was outvoted** = the majority voted against the chairman

◇ **outward** *adjective* going away from the home country; **the ship is outward bound; on the outward voyage the ship will call in at the West Indies; outward cargo** *or* **outward freight** = goods which are being exported; **outward mission** = visit by a group of businessmen to a foreign country

◇ **outwork** *noun* work which a company pays someone to do at home

◇ **outworker** *noun* person who works at home for a company

QUOTE: crude oil output plunged during the last month and is likely to remain near its present level for the near future   *Wall Street Journal*
QUOTE: American demand has transformed the profit outlook for many European manufacturers
Duns Business Month
QUOTE: Nigeria recorded foreign exchange outflow of N972.9 million for the month of June 1985   *Business Times (Lagos)*

over 1 *preposition* **(a)** more than; **the carpet costs over £100; packages not over 200 grams; the increase in turnover was over 25%** **(b)** compared with; **increase in output over last year; increase in debtors over the last quarter's figure** **(c)** during; **over the last half of the year profits doubled 2** *adverb* **held over to the next meeting** = postponed *or* put back to the next meeting; **to carry over a balance** = to take a balance from the end of one page or period to the beginning of the next **3** *plural noun* **overs** = extra items above the agreed total; **the**

price includes 10% overs to compensate for damage

◇ **over-** *prefix* more than; **shop which caters to the over-60s** = shop which has goods which appeal to people who are more than sixty years old

◇ **overall** *adjective* covering *or* including everything; **although some divisions traded profitably, the company reported an overall fall in profits** = the company reported a general fall in profits; **overall plan** = plan which covers everything

◇ **overbook** *verb* to book more people than there are seats or rooms available; **the hotel** *or* **the flight was overbooked**

◇ **overbooking** *noun* booking of more people than there are seats or rooms available

◇ **overbought** *adjective* having bought too much; **the market is overbought** = prices on the stock market are too high, because there have been too many buyers

◇ **overcapacity** *noun* unused capacity for producing something

◇ **overcapitalized** *adjective* with more capital in a company than it needs

◇ **overcharge 1** *noun* charge which is higher than it should be; **to pay back an overcharge 2** *verb* to ask too much money; **they overcharged us for meals; we asked for a refund because we had been overcharged**

◇ **overdraft** *noun* amount of money which a person withdraws from his account and which is more than he has in the account; **the bank has allowed me an overdraft of £5,000; overdraft facilities** = arrangement with a bank to have an overdraft; **we have exceeded our overdraft facilities** = we have taken out more than the overdraft allowed by the bank

◇ **overdraw** *verb* to take out more money from a bank account than there is in it; **your account is overdrawn** *or* **you are overdrawn** = you have paid out more money from your account than you have in it
NOTE: **overdrawing - overdrew - overdrawn**

◇ **overdue** *adjective* which has not been paid on time; **interest payments are three weeks overdue** = interest payments which should have been made three weeks ago

◇ **overestimate** *verb* to think something is larger or worse than it really is; **he overestimated the amount of time needed to fit out the factory**

◇ **overextend** *verb* **the company overextended itself** = the company borrowed more money than its assets would allow

◇ **overhead** **1** *adjective* **overhead costs** *or* **expenses** = money spent on the day-to-day cost of a business; **overhead budget** = plan of probable overhead costs **2** *noun* **overheads** *or* *US* **overhead** = costs of the day-to-day running of a business; **the sales revenue covers the manufacturing costs but not the overheads**

◇ **overlook** *verb* **(a)** to look out over; **the Managing Director's office overlooks the factory (b)** not to pay attention to; **in this instance we will overlook the delay**

◇ **overmanning** *noun* having more workers than are needed to do a company's work; **to aim to reduce overmanning**

◇ **overpaid** *adjective* paid too much; **our staff are overpaid and underworked**

◇ **overpayment** *noun* paying too much

◇ **overproduce** *verb* to produce too much

◇ **overproduction** *noun* manufacturing too much of a product

◇ **overrated** *adjective* valued more highly than it should be; **the effect of the dollar on European business cannot be overrated; their "first-class service" is very overrated**

◇ **overrider** *or* **overriding commission** *noun* special extra commission which is above all other commissions

◇ **overrun** *noun* to go beyond a limit; **the company overran the time limit set to complete the factory**
NOTE: overrunning - overran - overrun

◇ **overseas** **1** *adjective* across the sea *or* to foreign countries; **an overseas call** = phone call to another country; **the overseas division** = section of a company dealing with trade with other countries; **overseas markets** = markets in foreign countries; **overseas trade** = trade with foreign countries **2** *noun* foreign countries; **the profits from overseas are far higher than those of the home division**

◇ **overseer** *noun* person who supervises other workers

◇ **oversell** *verb* to sell more than you can produce; **he is oversold** = he has agreed to sell more product than he can produce;

the market is oversold = stock market prices are too low, because there have been too many sellers
NOTE: overselling - oversold

◇ **overspend** *verb* to spend too much; **to overspend one's budget** = to spend more money than is allowed in the budget
NOTE: overspending - overspent

◇ **overspending** *noun* spending more than is allowed; **the board decided to limit the overspending by the production departments**

◇ **overstaffed** *adjective* with more workers than are needed to do the work of the company

◇ **overstock** **1** *verb* to have more stock than is needed; **to be overstocked with spare parts** = to have too many spare parts in stock **2** *plural noun* *US* **overstocks** = more stock than is needed to supply orders; **we will have to sell off the overstocks to make room in the warehouse**

◇ **oversubscribe** *verb* **the share offer was oversubscribed six times** = people applied for six times as many new shares as were available

◇ **over-the-counter** *adjective* over-the-counter sales = legal selling of shares which are not listed in the official Stock Exchange list; **this share is available on the over-the-counter market**

◇ **overtime** **1** *noun* hours worked more than the normal working time; **to work six hours' overtime; the overtime rate is one and a half times normal pay; overtime ban** = order by a trade union which forbids overtime work by its members; **overtime pay** = pay for extra time worked
NOTE: no plural
2 *adverb* **to work overtime** = to work longer hours than in the contract of employment

◇ **overvalue** *verb* to give a higher value than is right; **these shares are overvalued at £1.25** = the shares are worth less than the £1.25 for which they are selling; **the pound is overvalued against the dollar** = the exchange rate gives too many dollars to the pound, given the strength of the two countries' economies

◇ **overweight** *adjective* **the package is sixty grams overweight** = the package weighs sixty grams too much

◇ **overworked** *adjective* having too much work to do; **our staff complain of being underpaid and overworked**

owe *verb* to have to pay money; **he owes the bank £250,000; he owes the company for the stock he purchased** = he has not paid for the stock

◇ **owing** *adjective* (a) which is owed; **money owing to the directors; how much is still owing to the company by its debtors?** (b) **owing to** = because of; **the plane was late owing to fog; I am sorry that owing to pressure of work, we cannot supply your order on time**

own *verb* to have *or* to possess; **he owns 50% of the shares; a wholly-owned subsidiary** = a subsidiary which belongs completely to the parent company; **a state-owned industry** = industry which is nationalized

◇ **own brand goods** *noun* products specially packed for a store with the store's name on them

◇ **owner** *noun* person who owns something; **sole owner** = person who owns something by himself; **owner-occupier** = person who owns and lives in a house; **goods sent at owner's risk** = situation where the owner has to insure the goods while they are being transported

◇ **ownership** *noun* act of owning something; **common** *or* **collective ownership** = situation where a business is owned by the workers who work in it; **joint ownership** = situation where two people own the same property; **public ownership** *or* **state ownership** = situation where an industry is nationalized; **private ownership** = situation where a company is owned by private shareholders; **the ownership of the company has passed to the banks** = the banks have become owners of the company
NOTE: no plural

◇ **own label goods** *noun* goods specially produced for a store with store's name on them

oz = OUNCE(S)

Pp

PA = PERSONAL ASSISTANT

p.a. = PER ANNUM

pack 1 *noun* **pack of items** = items put together in a container for selling; **pack of cigarettes; pack of biscuits; pack of envelopes; items sold in packs of 200** = sold in boxes containing 200 items; **blister pack** *or* **bubble pack** = type of packing where the item for sale is covered with a stiff plastic cover sealed to a card backing; **display pack** = specially attractive box for showing goods for sale; **dummy pack** = empty pack for display in a shop; **six-pack** = box containing six items (often bottles) **2** *verb* to put things into a container for selling *or* sending; **to pack goods into cartons; the biscuits are packed in plastic wrappers; the computer is packed in expanded polystyrene before being shipped**

◇ **package 1** *noun* (a) goods packed and wrapped for sending by mail; **the Post Office does not accept bulky packages; the goods are to be sent in airtight packages** (b) group of different items joined together in one deal; **pay package** *or* **salary package** *or* **US compensation package** = salary and other benefits offered with a job; **the job carries an attractive salary package; package deal** = agreement where several different items are agreed at the same time; **we are offering a package deal which includes the whole office computer system, staff training and hardware maintenance; package holiday** *or* **package tour** = holiday *or* tour where the hotel, travel and meals are all included in the price; **the travel company is arranging a package trip to the international computer exhibition 2** *verb* (a) **to package goods** = to wrap and pack goods in an attractive way (b) **to package holidays** = to sell a holiday package including travel hotels and food

◇ **packaging** *noun* **(a)** the action of putting things into packages **(b)** material used to protect goods which are being packed; **airtight packaging; packaging material (c)** attractive material used to wrap goods for display
NOTE: no plural

◇ **packager** *noun* person who creates a book for a publisher

◇ **packer** *noun* person who packs goods

◇ **packet** *noun* small box of goods for selling; **packet of cigarettes; packet of biscuits; packet of filing cards; item sold in packets of 20** = sold in boxes containing 20 items each; **postal packet** = small container of goods sent by post

◇ **packing** *noun* **(a)** action of putting goods into boxes and wrapping them for shipping; **what is the cost of the packing? packing is included in the price; packing case** = large wooden box for carrying easily broken items; **packing charges** = money charged for putting goods into boxes; **packing list** *or* **packing slip** = list of goods which have been packed, sent with the goods to show they have been checked **(b)** material used to protect goods; **packed in airtight packing; non-returnable packing** = packing which is to be thrown away when it has been used and not returned to the sender
NOTE: no plural

pad *noun* **(a)** pile of sheets of paper attached together on one side; **desk pad** = pad of paper kept on a desk for writing notes; **memo pad** *or* **note pad** = pad of paper for writing memos or notes; **phone pad** = pad of paper kept by a telephone for noting messages **(b)** soft material like a cushion; **the machine is protected by rubber pads; inking pad** = cushion with ink in it, used to put ink on a rubber stamp

paid *adjective* with money given **(a) paid holidays** = holidays where the worker's wages are still paid even though he is not working **(b) paid assistant** = assistant who receives a salary **(c)** which has been settled; **carriage paid; tax paid; paid bills** = bills which have been settled; **the invoice is marked "paid" (d) paid-up capital** = all money paid for the issued capital shares; **paid-up shares** = shares which have been completely paid for by the shareholder

pallet *noun* flat wooden base on which goods can be stacked for easy handling by a fork-lift truck

◇ **palletize** *verb* to put goods on pallets; **palletized cartons**

pamphlet *noun* small booklet of advertising material or of information

panel *noun* **(a)** flat surface standing upright; **display panel** = flat area for displaying goods in a shop window; **advertisement panel** = specially designed large advertising space in a newspaper **(b) panel of experts** = group of people who give advice on a problem; **consumer panel** = group of consumers who report on goods they have used so that the manufacturer can improve the goods, or use the consumers' reports in his advertising

panic *adjective* frightened; **panic buying** = rush to buy something at any price because stocks may run out or because the price may rise; **panic buying of sugar** *or* **of dollars; panic selling of sterling** = rush to sell sterling at any price because of possible devaluation

paper *noun* **(a)** thin material for writing on *or* for wrapping; **brown paper** = thick paper for wrapping parcels; **carbon paper** = sheet of paper with a black stuff on one side used in a typewriter to make a copy; **she put the carbon paper in the wrong way round; duplicating paper** = special paper to be used in a duplicating machine; **graph paper** = paper with small squares printed on it, used for drawing graphs; **headed paper** = notepaper with the name and address of the company printed on it; **lined paper** = paper with thin lines printed on it; **typing paper** = thin paper for use in a typewriter; **wrapping paper** = paper for wrapping NOTE: no plural **(b) paper bag =** bag made of paper; **paper feed =** device which puts paper into a printer or photocopier **(c) papers =** documents; **he sent me the relevant papers on the case; he has lost the customs papers; the office is asking for the VAT papers (d) on paper =** in theory; **on paper the system is ideal, but we have to see it working before we will sign the contract; paper loss =** loss made when an asset has fallen in value but has not been sold; **paper profit =** profit made when an asset has increased in value but has not been sold; **paper millionaire =** person who owns shares which, if he sold them, would make him a millionaire **(e)** documents which can represent money (bills of exchange, promissory notes, etc.); **bankable paper =** document which a bank will accept as security for a loan; **negotiable paper =** document which can be transferred from one owner to another for money **(f) paper money** or **paper currency =** banknotes **(g)** newspaper; **trade paper =** newspaper aimed at people working in a certain industry; **free paper** or **giveaway paper =** newspaper which is given away free, and which relies for its income on its advertising

◊ **paperclip** noun piece of bent wire, used to hold pieces of paper together

◊ **paperwork** noun office work, especially writing memos and filling in forms; **exporting to Russia involves a large amount of paperwork**
NOTE: no plural

> QUOTE: the profits were tax-free and the interest on the loans they incurred qualified for income tax relief; the paper gains were rarely changed into spending money *Investors Chronicle*

par adjective equal or at the same price; **par value =** face value or the value printed on a share certificate; **shares at par =** shares whose market price is the same as their face value; **shares above par** or **below par =** shares with a market price higher or lower than their par value

parachute noun US **golden parachute =** large, usually tax-free, sum of money given to an executive who retires from a company before the end of his service contract

paragraph noun group of several lines of writing which makes a separate section; **the first paragraph of your letter** or **paragraph one of your letter; please refer to the paragraph in the contract on "shipping instructions"**

parameter noun fixed limit; **the budget parameters are fixed by the finance director; spending by each department has to fall within certain parameters**

parastatal noun in Africa large state-controlled organization

parcel 1 noun **(a)** goods wrapped up in paper or plastic, etc., to be sent by post; **to do up goods into parcels; to tie up a parcel =** to fasten a parcel with string; **parcel delivery service =** private company which delivers parcels within a certain area; **parcels office =** office where parcels can be handed in for sending by mail; **parcel post =** mail service for sending parcels; **to send a box by parcel post; parcel rates =** charges for sending parcels by post **(b) parcel of shares =** group of shares (such as 50 or 100) which are sold as a group; **the shares are on offer in parcels of 50 2** verb to wrap and tie to make a parcel; **to parcel up a consignment of books**
NOTE: **parcelling - parcelled** but US **parceling - parceled**

parent noun **parents =** father and mother; **parent company =** company which owns more than 50% of the shares of another company

pari passu phrase equally; **the new shares will rank pari passu with the existing ones**

parity noun being equal; **the female staff want parity with the men =** they want to have the same rates of pay and perks as the men; **the pound fell to parity with the dollar =** the pound fell to a point where one pound equalled one dollar
NOTE: no plural

> QUOTE: the draft report on changes in the international monetary system casts doubt about any return to fixed exchange-rate parities *Wall Street Journal*

park 1 *noun* open space with grass and trees; **business park** = group of small factories or warehouses, especially near a town; **car park** = place where you can leave your car; **he left his car in the hotel car park; if the car park is full, you can park in the street for thirty minutes; industrial park** = area of land near a town specially set aside for factories and warehouses; **science park** = area near a town or university set aside for technological industries 2 *verb* to leave your car in a place while you are not using it; **the rep parked his car outside the shop; you cannot park here during the rush hour; parking is difficult in the centre of the city**

Parkinson's law *noun* law, based on wide experience, that in business as in government the amount of work increases to fill the time available for it

part *noun* (a) piece *or* section; **part of the shipment was damaged; part of the workforce is on overtime; part of the expenses will be refunded** = some of the expenses, but not all (b) **in part** = not completely; **to contribute in part to the costs** *or* **to pay the costs in part** (c) **spare part** = small piece of machinery to replace a part of a machine which is broken; **the photocopier will not work - we need to replace a part** *or* **a part needs replacing** (d) **part-owner** = person who owns something jointly with one or more other persons; **he is part-owner of the restaurant; part-ownership** = situation where two or more persons own the same property (e) **part exchange** = giving an old product as part of the payment for a new one; **they refused to take my old car as part exchange for the new one; part payment** = paying of part of a whole payment; **I gave him £250 as part payment for the car; part delivery** *or* **part order** *or* **part shipment** = delivering or shipping only some items of an order

◊ **part-time** *adjective & adverb* not working for the whole working day; **she works part-time; he is trying to find part-time work when the children are in school; a part-time worker; we are looking for part-time staff to work our computers; part-time work** *or* **part-time employment** = work for part of a working day

◊ **part-timer** *noun* person who works part-time

partial *adjective* not complete; **partial loss** = situation where only part of the insured property has been damaged or lost; **he got partial compensation for the damage to his house** = he was compensated for part of the damage

participation *noun* taking part; **worker participation** = situation where the workers take part in making management decisions
NOTE: no plural
◊ **participative** *adjective* where both sides take part; **we do not treat management-worker relations as a participative process**

particular 1 *adjective* special *or* different from others; **the photocopier only works with a particular type of paper; particular average** = situation where part of a shipment is lost or damaged and the insurance costs are borne by the owner of the lost goods and not shared among all the owners of the shipment 2 *noun* (a) **particulars** = details; **sheet which gives particulars of the items for sale; the inspector asked for particulars of the missing car; to give full particulars of something** = to list all the known details about something (b) **in particular** = specially *or* as a special point; **fragile goods, in particular glasses, need special packing**

partly *adverb* not completely; **partly-paid capital** = capital which represents partly-paid shares; **partly-paid up shares** = shares where the shareholders have not paid the full face value; **partly-secured creditors** = creditors whose debts are not fully covered by the value of the security

partner *noun* person who works in a business and has an equal share in it with other partners; **he became a partner in a firm of solicitors; active partner** *or* **working partner** = partner who works in a partnership; **junior partner** *or* **senior partner** = person who has a small or large part of the shares in a partnership; **sleeping partner** = partner who has a share in a business but does not work in it

◇ **partnership** *noun* **(a)** unregistered business where two or more people share the risks and profits equally; **to go into partnership with someone; to join with someone to form a partnership; to offer someone a partnership** *or* **to take someone into partnership with you** = to have a working business and bring someone in to share it with you; **to dissolve a partnership** = to bring a partnership to an end **(b) limited partnership** = registered business where the liability of the partners is limited to the amount of capital they have each provided to the business and where the partners may not take part in the running of the business

party *noun* **(a)** company *or* person involved in a legal dispute *or* legal agreement; **one of the parties to the suit has died; the company is not a party to the agreement (b) third party** = any third person, in addition to the two main people involved in a contract; **third party insurance** *or* **third party policy** = insurance to cover damage to any person who is not one of the people named in the insurance contract (that is, not the insured person nor the insurance company) **(c) working party** = group of experts who study a problem; **the government has set up a working party to study the problems of industrial waste; Professor Smith is the chairman of the working party on computers in society**

pass 1 *noun* permit to allow someone to go into a building; **you need a pass to enter the ministry offices; all members of staff must show a pass** 2 *verb* **(a) to pass a dividend** = to pay no dividend in a certain year **(b)** to approve; **the finance director has to pass an invoice before it is sent out; the loan has been passed by the board; to pass a resolution** = to vote to agree to a resolution; **the meeting passed a proposal that salaries should be frozen (c)** to be successful; **he passed his typing test; she has passed all her exams and now is a qualified accountant**
◇ **passbook** *noun* book given by a bank *or* building society which shows money which you deposit *or* withdraw from your savings account *or* building society account

◇ **pass off** *verb* **to pass something off as something else** = to pretend that it is another thing in order to cheat a customer; **he tried to pass off the wine as French, when in fact it came from outside the Common Market**

passage *noun* voyage by ship

passenger *noun* person who travels in a plane, bus, taxi, plane, etc., but is not the driver or member of the crew; **passenger terminal** = air terminal for people going on planes, not for cargo; **passenger train** = train which carries passengers but not freight

passport *noun* official document proving that you are a citizen of a country, which you have to show when you travel from one country to another; **we had to show our passports at the customs post; his passport is out of date; the passport officer stamped my passport**

patent 1 *noun* **(a)** official document showing that a person has the exclusive right to make and sell an invention; **to take out a patent for a new type of light bulb; to apply for a patent for a new invention; letters patent** = official term for a patent; **patent applied for** *or* **patent pending** = words on a product showing that the inventor has applied for a patent for it; **to forfeit a patent** = to lose a patent because payments have not been made; **to infringe a patent** = to make and sell a product which works in the same way as a patented product and not pay a royalty for it; **infringement of patent** *or* **patent infringement** = act of illegally making or selling a product which is patented **(b) patent agent** = person who advises on patents and applies for patents on behalf of clients; **to file a patent application** = to apply for a patent; **patent medicine** = medicine which is registered as a patent; **patent office** = government office which grants patents and supervises them; **patent rights** = rights which an inventor holds under a patent 2 *verb* **to patent an invention**

= to register an invention with the patent office to prevent other people from copying it

◊ **patented** *adjective* which is protected by a patent

paternity *noun* **paternity leave** = permission for a man to be away from work when his wife is having a baby

pattern *noun* (a) **pattern book** = book showing examples of design (b) general way in which something usually happens; **pattern of prices** *or* **price pattern; pattern of sales** *or* **sales pattern; pattern of trade** *or* **trading pattern** = general way in which trade is carried on; **the company's trading pattern shows high export sales in the first quarter and high home sales in the third quarter**

pawn 1 *noun* **to put something in pawn** = to leave a valuable object with someone in exchange for a loan which has to be repaid if you want to take back the object; **to take something out of pawn** = to repay the loan and so get back the object; **pawn ticket** = receipt given by the pawnbroker for the object left in pawn
NOTE: no plural
2 *verb* **to pawn a watch** = to leave a watch with a pawnbroker who gives a loan against it

◊ **pawnbroker** *noun* person who lends money against the security of valuable objects

◊ **pawnshop** *noun* pawnbroker's shop

pay 1 *noun* (a) salary *or* wage *or* money given to someone for regular work; **back pay** = salary which has not been paid; **basic pay** = normal salary without extra payments; **take-home pay** = pay left after tax and insurance have been deducted; **holidays with pay** = holiday which a worker can take by contract and for which he is paid; **unemployment pay** = dole *or* money given by the government to someone who is unemployed (b) **pay cheque** = monthly cheque which pays a salary to a worker; **pay day** = day on which wages are paid to workers (usually Friday for workers paid once a week, and during the last week of the month for workers who are paid once a month); **pay negotiations** *or* **pay talks** = discussions

between management and workers about pay increases; **pay packet** = envelope containing the pay slip and the cash pay; **pay rise** = increase in pay; **pay slip** = piece of paper showing the full amount of a worker's pay, and the money deducted as tax, pension and insurance contributions (c) **pay desk** = place in a store where you pay for goods bought; **pay phone** = telephone which works if you put coins into it 2 *verb* (a) to give money to buy an item or a service; **to pay £1,000 for a car; how much did you pay to have the office cleaned?; to pay in advance** = to give money before you receive the item bought *or* before the service has been completed; **we had to pay in advance to have the new telephone system installed; to pay in instalments** = to give money for an item by giving small amounts regularly; **we are paying for the computer by paying instalments of £50 a month; to pay cash** = to pay the complete sum in cash; **"pay cash"** = words written on a crossed cheque to show that it can be paid in cash if necessary; **to pay by cheque** = to pay by giving a cheque, not by using cash or credit card; **to pay by credit card** = to pay, using a credit card and not a cheque or cash (b) to give money; **to pay on demand** = to pay money when it is asked for, not after a period of credit; **please pay the sum of £10** = please give £10 in cash or by cheque; **to pay a dividend** = to give shareholders a part of the profits of a company; **these shares pay a dividend of 1.5p; to pay interest** = to give money as interest on money borrowed or invested; **building societies pay an interest of 10%; pay as you earn** *or* *US* **pay-as-you-go** = tax system, where income tax is deducted from the salary before it is paid to the worker (c) to give a worker money for work done; **the workforce has not been paid for three weeks; we pay good wages for skilled workers; how much do they pay you per hour?; to be paid by the hour** = to get money for each hour worked; **to be paid at piece-work rates** = to get money for each piece of work finished (d) to give money which is owed *or* which has to be paid; **to pay a bill; to pay an invoice; to pay duty on imports; to pay tax (e) to pay a cheque into an account** = to deposit money in the form of a cheque
NOTE: **paying - paid**

◊ **payable** *adjective* which is due to be

paid; **payable in advance** = which has to be paid before the goods are delivered; **payable on delivery** = which has to be paid when the goods are delivered; **payable on demand** = which must be paid when payment is asked for; **payable at sixty days** = which has to be paid by sixty days after the date of invoice; **cheque made payable to bearer** = cheque which will be paid to the person who has it, not to any particular name written on it; **shares payable on application** = shares which must be paid for when you apply to buy them; **accounts payable** = money owed by a company; **bills payable** = bills which a debtor will have to pay; **electricity charges are payable by the tenant** = the tenant (and not the landlord) must pay for the electricity

◇ **pay back** *verb* to give money back to someone; **to pay back a loan; I lent him £50 and he promised to pay me back in a month; he has never paid me back for the money he borrowed**

◇ **payback** *noun* paying back money which has been borrowed; **payback clause** = clause in a contract which states the terms for repaying a loan; **payback period** = period of time over which a loan is to be repaid *or* an investment is to pay for itself
NOTE: no plural

◇ **paycheck** *noun* salary cheque given to an employee

◇ **pay down** *verb* **to pay money down** = to make a deposit; **he paid £50 down and the rest in monthly instalments**

◇ **PAYE** = PAY AS YOU EARN

◇ **payee** *noun* person who receives money from someone *or* person whose name is on a cheque

◇ **payer** *noun* person who gives money to someone; **slow payer** = person *or* company which does not pay debts on time; **he is well known as a slow payer**

◇ **paying** **1** *adjective* which makes a profit; **it is a paying business; it is not a paying proposition** = it is not a business which is going to make a profit **2** *noun* giving money; **paying of a debt; paying-in book** = book of forms for paying money into a bank account *or* building society; **paying-in slip** = form which is filled in when money is being deposited in a bank account *or* building society
NOTE: no plural

◇ **payload** *noun* cargo *or* passengers carried by a ship *or* train *or* plane for which payment is made

◇ **payment** *noun* **(a)** giving money; **payment in cash** *or* **cash payment; payment by cheque; payment of interest** *or* **interest payment; payment on account** = paying part of the money owed; **full payment** *or* **payment in full** = paying all money owed; **payment on invoice** = paying money as soon as an invoice is received; **payment in kind** = paying by giving goods or food, but not money; **payment by results** = money given which increases with the amount of work done or goods produced **(b)** money paid; **back payment** = paying money which is owed; **deferred payments** = money paid later than the agreed date; **the company agreed to defer payments for three months; down payment** = part of a total payment made in advance; **repayable in easy payments** = repayable with small sums regularly; **incentive payments** = extra pay offered to a worker to make him work better; **balance of payments** = the international financial position of a country including visible and invisible trade

◇ **pay off** *verb* **(a)** to finish paying money which is owed; **to pay off a mortgage; to pay off a loan (b)** to pay all the money owed to someone and terminate his employment; **when the company was taken over the factory was closed and all the workers were paid off**

◇ **payoff** *noun* money paid to finish paying something which is owed

◇ **pay out** *verb* to give money; **the company pays out thousands of pounds in legal fees; we have paid out half our profits in dividends**

◇ **payout** *noun* money paid to help a company in difficulty *or* subsidy; **the company only exists on payouts from the government**

◇ **payroll** *noun* list of people employed and paid by a company *or* money paid by a company in salaries; **the company has 250 on the payroll; payroll ledger** = list of staff and their salaries; **payroll tax** = tax on the people employed by a company

◇ **pay up** *verb* to give money which is owed; **the company only paid up when we sent them a letter from our solicitor; he finally paid up six months late**

P/E *abbreviation* = PRICE/EARNINGS
P/E ratio = ratio between the market price of a share and the current dividend it produces; **the shares sell at a P/E ratio of 7**

peak 1 *noun* highest point; **peak period** = time of the day when most commuters are travelling *or* when most electricity is being used, etc.; **time of peak demand** = time when something is being used most; **peak output** = highest output; **peak year** = best year *or* year when the largest quantity of products was produced *or* when sales were highest; **the shares reached their peak in January; the share index has fallen 10% since the peak in January 2** *verb* to reach the highest point; **productivity peaked in January; shares have peaked and are beginning to slip back**

pecuniary *adjective* referring to money; **he gained no pecuniary advantage** = he made no profit

peddle *verb* to sell goods from door to door *or* in the street

peg *verb* to hold something at a certain point; **to peg prices** = to fix prices to stop them rising; **to peg wage increases to the cost-of-living index** = to limit increases in wages to the increases in the cost-of-living index
NOTE: **pegging - pegged**

pen *noun* thing for writing with, using ink; **felt pen** = pen with a point made of hard cloth; **light pen** = type of pen which when passed over a bar code can read it and send information back to a computer; **marker pen** = pen which makes a wide coloured mark

penalty *noun* punishment (such as a fine) which is imposed if something is not done; **penalty clause** = clause which lists the penalties which will be imposed if the contract is not obeyed; **the contract contains a penalty clause which fines the company 1% for every week the completion date is late**
◇ **penalize** *verb* to punish *or* to fine; **to penalize a supplier for late deliveries; they were penalized for bad service**

pence *see* PENNY

pending 1 *adjective* waiting; **pending tray** = basket on a desk for papers which cannot be dealt with immediately; **patent pending** = situation where an invention is put on the market before a patent is granted **2** *adverb* **pending advice from our lawyers** = while waiting for advice from our lawyers

penetrate *verb* **to penetrate a market** = to get into a market and capture a share of it
◇ **penetration** *noun* **market penetration** = percentage of a total market which the sales of a company cover
NOTE: no plural

penny *noun* **(a)** *GB* small coin, of which one hundred make a pound
NOTE: usually written **p** after a figure: **26p;** the plural is **pence**
(b) *US informal* small coin, one cent
◇ **penny share** *or US* **penny stock** *plural noun* very cheap share, costing about 10p or less than $1

pension 1 *noun* **(a)** money paid regularly to someone who no longer works; **retirement pension** *or* **old age pension** = state pension given to a man who is over 65 or and woman who is over 60; **government pension** *or* **state pension** = pension paid by the state; **occupational pension** = pension which is paid by the company by which a worker has been employed; **portable pension** = pension entitlement which can be moved from one company to another without loss (as a worker changes jobs); **pension contributions** = money paid by a company or worker into a pension fund **(b)** **pension plan** *or* **pension scheme** = plan worked out by an insurance company which arranges for a worker to pay part of his salary over many years and receive a regular payment when he retires; **company pension scheme** = pension which is organized by a company for its staff; **he decided to join the company's pension scheme; contributory pension scheme** = scheme where the worker has to pay a proportion of his salary; **graduated pension scheme** = pension scheme where the benefit is calculated as a percentage of the salary of each person in the scheme; **non-contributory pension scheme** = scheme where the employer pays in all the money on behalf of the worker; **personal pension plan** = pension plan which applies to one worker only, usually a self-employed person, not to a group; **portable pension plan** = pension plan which a worker can carry from one company to another as he changes jobs **(c) pension entitlement** = amount of pension which someone has the right to receive when he retires; **pension fund** = money which provides pensions for retired members of staff **2** *verb* **to pension someone off** = to ask someone to retire and take a pension

◇ **pensionable** *adjective* able to receive a pension; **pensionable age** = age after which someone can take a pension

◇ **pensioner** *noun* person who receives a pension; **old age pensioner** = person who receives the retirement pension

peppercorn rent *noun* very small *or* nominal rent; **to pay a peppercorn rent; to lease a property for** *or* **at a peppercorn rent**

per *preposition* **(a) as per** = according to; **as per invoice** = as stated in the invoice; **as per sample** = as shown in the sample; **as per previous order** = according to the details given in our previous order **(b)** at a rate of; **per hour** *or* **per day** *or* **per week** *or* **per year** = for each hour *or* day *or* week *or* year; **the rate is £5 per hour; he makes about £250 per month; we pay £10 per hour** = we pay £10 for each hour worked; **the car was travelling at twenty-five miles per hour** = at a speed which covered 25 miles in one hour; **the earnings per share** = dividend received by each share; **the average sales per representative** = the average sales achieved by one representative; **per head** = for each person; **allow £15 per head for expenses; representatives cost on average £25,000 per head per annum**

(c) out of; **the rate of imperfect items is about twenty-five per thousand; the birth rate has fallen to twelve per hundred**

◇ **per annum** *adverb* in a year; **what is their turnover per annum?**

◇ **per capita** *adjective & adverb* for each person; **average income per capita** *or* **per capita income** = average income of one person; **per capita expenditure** = total money spent divided by the number of people involved

◇ **per cent** *adjective & adverb* out of each hundred *or* for each hundred; **10 per cent** = ten in every hundred; **what is the increase per cent? fifty per cent of nothing is still nothing**

◇ **percentage** *noun* amount shown as part of one hundred; **percentage discount** = discount calculated at an amount per hundred; **percentage increase** = increase calculated on the basis of a rate for one hundred; **percentage point** = 1 per cent

◇ **percentile** *noun* one of a series of ninety-nine figures below which a certain percentage of the total falls

---

QUOTE: a 100,000 square-foot warehouse generates $600 in sales per square foot of space
Duns Business Month
QUOTE: this would represent an 18 per cent growth rate - a slight slackening of the 25 per cent turnover rise in the first half
Financial Times
QUOTE: buildings are depreciated at two per cent per annum on the estimated cost of construction
Hongkong Standard
QUOTE: state-owned banks cut their prime rates a percentage point to 11%
Wall Street Journal
QUOTE: a good percentage of the excess stock was taken up during the last quarter
Australian Financial Review

---

perfect 1 *adjective* completely correct *or* with no mistakes; **we check each batch to make sure it is perfect; she did a perfect typing test 2** *verb* to make something which is completely correct; **he perfected the process for making high grade steel**

◇ **perfectly** *adverb* with no mistakes *or* correctly; **she typed the letter perfectly**

perform *verb* to do well or badly; **how did the shares perform?** = did the shares go up or down?; **the company** *or* **the shares performed badly** = the company's share price fell

◇ **performance** *noun* way in which someone *or* something acts; **the poor performance of the shares on the stock market** = the fall in the share price on the stock market; **last year saw a dip in the company's performance; as a measure of the company's performance** = as a way of judging if the company's results are good or bad; **performance of personnel against objectives** = how personnel have worked, measured against the objectives set; **performance review** = yearly interview between a manager and each worker to discuss how the worker has worked during the year; **earnings performance** = way in which shares earn dividends; **job performance** = doing a job well or badly

QUOTE: inflation-adjusted GNP edged up at a 1.3% annual rate, its worst performance since the economic expansion began *Fortune*

period *noun* (a) length of time; **for a period of time** *or* **for a period of months** *or* **for a six-year period; sales over a period of three months; sales over the holiday period; to deposit money for a fixed period (b) accounting period** = period of time at the end of which the firm's accounts are made up
◇ **periodic** *or* **periodical 1** *adjective* from time to time; **a periodic review of the company's performance 2** *noun* **periodical** = magazine which comes out regularly

peripherals *plural noun* items of hardware (such as terminals, printers, monitors, etc.) which are attached to a main computer system

perishable 1 *adjective* which can go bad *or* become rotten easily; **perishable goods** *or* **items** *or* **cargo 2** *plural noun* **perishables** = goods which can go bad easily

perjury *noun* telling lies when you have made an oath to say what is true in court; **he was sent to prison for perjury; she appeared in court on a perjury charge**
◇ **perjure** *verb* **to perjure yourself** = to tell lies when you have made an oath to say what is true

perks *plural noun* extra items given by a company to workers in addition to their salaries (such as company cars, private health insurance)

permanent *adjective* which will last for a very long time *or* for ever; **he has found a permanent job; she is in permanent employment; the permanent staff and part-timers**
◇ **permanency** *noun* being permanent
NOTE: no plural
◇ **permanently** *adverb* for ever

permission *noun* being allowed to do something; **written permission** = document which allows someone to do something; **verbal permission** = telling someone that he is allowed to do something; **to give someone permission to do something** = to allow someone to do something; **he asked the manager's permission to take a day off**

permit 1 *noun* official document which allows someone to do something; **building permit** = official document which allows someone to build on a piece of land; **export permit** *or* **import permit** = official document which allows goods to be exported *or* imported; **work permit** = official document which allows someone who is not a citizen to work in a country **2** *verb* to allow someone to do something; **this document permits you to export twenty-five computer systems; the ticket permits three people to go into the exhibition**

per pro = PER PROCURANTIONEM with the authority of; **the secretary signed per pro the manager**

perquisites *plural noun* = PERKS

person *noun* (a) someone *or* man *or* woman; **insurance policy which covers a named person; the persons named in the contract** = people whose names are given in the contract; **the document should be witnessed by a third person** = someone who is not named in the document should witness it **(b) in person** = someone himself *or* herself; **this important package is to be delivered to the chairman in person** = the package has to be given to the chairman himself (and not to his secretary, assistant, etc.); **he came to see me in person** = he himself came to see me

◇ **person-to-person call** *noun* telephone call where you ask the operator to connect you with a named person

◇ **personal** *adjective* **(a)** referring to one person; **personal allowances** = part of a person's income which is not taxed; **personal assets** = moveable assets which belong to a person; **personal call** = telephone call where you ask the operator to connect you with a particular person; **personal computer** = small computer which can be used home; **personal effects** *or* **personal property** = things which belong to someone; **personal income** = income received by an individual person before tax is paid; **apart from the family shares, he has a personal shareholding in the company** = he has shares which belong to himself; **the car is for his personal use** = the car is for him to use himself **(b)** private; **I want to see the director on a personal matter; personal assistant** = secretary who also helps the boss in various ways

◇ **personalized** *adjective* with the name or initials of a person printed on it; **personalized cheques; personalized briefcase**

◇ **personally** *adverb* in person; **he personally opened the envelope; she wrote to me personally**

personnel *noun* people who work in a certain place *or* for a certain company; **the personnel of the warehouse** *or* **the warehouse personnel; the personnel department** = section of the company which deals with the staff; **personnel management** = organizing and training of staff so that they work well and profitably; **personnel manager** = head of the personnel department

persuade *verb* to talk to someone and get him to do what you want; **after ten hours of discussion, they persuaded the MD to resign; we could not persuade the French company to sign the contract**

peseta *noun* money used in Spain
NOTE: usually written **ptas** after a figure: **2,000ptas**

peso *noun* money used in Mexico and many other countries

pessimism *noun* expecting that everything will turn out badly; **market pessimism** *or* **pessimism on the market** = feeling that the stock market prices will fall; **there is considerable pessimism about job opportunities**
NOTE: no plural

◇ **pessimistic** *adjective* feeling sure that things will work out badly; **he takes a pessimistic view of the exchange rate** = he expects the exchange rate to fall

peter out *verb* to come to an end gradually

QUOTE: economists believe the economy is picking up this quarter and will do better in the second half of the year, but most expect growth to peter out in 1986 *Sunday Times*

Peter principle *noun* law, based on wide experience, that people are promoted until they occupy positions for which they are incompetent

petition **1** *noun* official request; **to file a petition in bankruptcy** = to ask officially to be made bankrupt *or* to ask officially for someone else to be made bankrupt **2** *verb* to make an official request; **he petitioned the government for a special pension**

petrodollar *noun* dollar earned by a country from exporting oil, then invested outside that country

petrol *noun* liquid, made from petroleum, used to drive a car engine; **the car is very economic on petrol; we are looking for a car with a low petrol consumption**
NOTE: no plural

◇ **petroleum** *noun* raw natural oil, found in the ground; **crude petroleum** = raw petroleum which has not been processed; **petroleum exporting countries** = countries which produce petroleum and sell it to others; **petroleum industry** = industry which uses petroleum to make other products (petrol, soap, etc.); **petroleum products** = products (such as petrol, soap, paint) which are made from crude petroleum; **petroleum revenues** = income from selling oil

petty *adjective* not important; **petty cash** = small amount of money kept in an office to pay small debts; **petty cash book** =

book in which petty cash payments are noted; **petty cash box** = locked metal box in an office where the petty cash is kept; **petty expenses** = small sums of money spent

phase *noun* period *or* part of something which takes place; **the first phase of the expansion programme**
◊ **phase in** *verb* to bring something in gradually; **the new invoicing system will be phased in over the next two months**
◊ **phase out** *verb* to remove something gradually; **Smith Ltd will be phased out as a supplier of spare parts**

> QUOTE: the budget grants a tax exemption for $500,000 in capital gains, phased in over the next six years   *Toronto Star*

phone 1 *noun* telephone *or* machine used for speaking to someone over a long distance; **we had a new phone system installed last week; house phone** *or* **internal phone** = telephone for calling from one office to another; **by phone** = using the telephone; **to place an order by phone; to be on the phone** = to be speaking to someone on the telephone; **she has been on the phone all morning; he spoke to the manager on the phone; phone book** = book which lists names of people and companies with their addresses and phone numbers; **look up his address in the phone book; phone call** = speaking to someone on the phone; **to make a phone call** = to speak to someone on the telephone; **to answer the phone** *or* **to take a phone call** = to reply to a call on the phone; **phone number** = set of figures for a particular telephone; **he keeps a list of phone numbers in a little black book; the phone number is on the company notepaper; can you give me your phone number?** 2 *verb* to phone someone = to call someone by telephone; **don't phone me, I'll phone you; his secretary phoned to say he would be late; he phoned the order through to the warehouse; to phone for something** = to make a phone call to ask for something; **he phoned for a taxi; to phone about something** = to make a phone call to speak about something; **he phoned about the January invoice**
◊ **phone back** *verb* to reply by phone; **the chairman is in a meeting, can you phone back in about half an hour? Mr Smith called while you were out and asked if you would phone him back**

photocopier *noun* machine which makes a copy of a document by photographing and printing it
◊ **photocopy** 1 *noun* copy of a document made by photographing and printing it; **make six photocopies of the contract** 2 *verb* to make a copy of a document by photographing and printing it; **she photocopied the contract**
◊ **photocopying** *noun* making photocopies; **photocopying costs are rising each year; photocopying bureau** = office which photocopies documents for companies which do not possess their own photocopiers; **there is a mass of photocopying to be done** = there are many documents waiting to be photocopied
NOTE: no plural
◊ **photostat** 1 *noun* trademark for a type of photocopy 2 *verb* to make a photostat of a document

pick 1 *noun* thing chosen; **take your pick** = choose what you want; **the pick of the group** = the best item in the group 2 *verb* to choose; **the board picked the finance director to succeed the retiring MD; the Association has picked Paris for its next meeting**
◊ **picking** *noun* **order picking** = collecting various items in a warehouse to make up an order to be sent to a customer; **picking list** = list of items in an order, listed according to where they can be found in the warehouse
◊ **pick out** *verb* to choose (something *or* someone) out of a lot; **he was picked out for promotion by the chairman**
◊ **pick up** *verb* to get better *or* to improve; **business** *or* **trade is picking up**
◊ **pickup** *noun* **pickup (truck)** = type of small van for transporting goods; **pickup and delivery service** = service which takes goods from the warehouse and delivers them to the customer

picket 1 *noun* striking worker who stands at the gate of a factory to try to persuade other workers not to go to work; **flying pickets** = pickets who travel round the country to try to stop workers going to work; **picket line** = line of pickets at the

gate of a factory; **to man a picket line** *or* **to be on the picket line; to cross a picket line** = to go into a factory to work, even though pickets are trying to prevent workers from going in **2** *verb* **to picket a factory** = to put pickets at the gate of a factory to try to prevent other workers from going to work ◊ **picketing** *noun* act of standing at the gates of a factory to prevent workers going to work; **lawful picketing** = picketing which is allowed by law; **mass picketing** = picketing by large numbers of pickets who try to frighten workers who want to work; **peaceful picketing** = picketing which does not involve fighting; **secondary picketing** = picketing of another factory, not directly connected with the strike, to prevent it supplying the striking factory *or* receiving supplies from it
NOTE: no plural

piece *noun* small part of something; **to sell something by the piece; the price is 25p the piece; mailing piece** = leaflet suitable for sending by direct mail
◊ **piece rate** *noun* rate of pay for a product produced *or* for a piece of work done and not paid for at an hourly rate; **to earn piece rates**
◊ **piecework** *noun* work for which workers are paid for the products produced *or* the piece of work done and not at an hourly rate
NOTE: no plural

pie chart *noun* diagram where information is shown as a circle cut up into sections of different sizes

pigeonhole **1** *noun* one of a series of small spaces for filing documents *or* for putting letters for delivery to separate offices **2** *verb* to file a plan or document as the best way of forgetting about it; **the whole expansion plan was pigeonholed**

pile **1** *noun* lot of things put one on top of the other; **the Managing Director's desk is covered with piles of paper; she put the letter on the pile of letters waiting to be signed 2** *verb* to put things on top of one another; **he piled the papers on his desk**
◊ **pile up** *verb* to put *or* get into a pile; **the invoices were piled up on the table; complaints are piling up about the after-sales service**

pilferage *or* **pilfering** *noun* stealing small amounts of money *or* small items from an office or shop
NOTE: no plural

pilot *noun* **(a)** person who flies a plane *or* guides a ship into port **(b)** used as a test, which if successful will then be expanded into a full operation; **the company set up a pilot project to see if the proposed manufacturing system was efficient; the pilot factory has been built to test the new production processes; he is directing a pilot scheme for training unemployed young people**

pin **1** *noun* sharp piece of metal for attaching papers together, etc.; **drawing pin** = pin with a flat head for attaching a sheet of paper to something hard; **she used drawing pins to pin the poster to the door 2** *verb* to attach with a pin; **she pinned the papers together; pin your cheque to the application form**
◊ **pin up** *verb* to attach something with pins to a wall; **they pinned the posters up at the back of the exhibition stand**

pint *noun* measure of liquids (= 0.568 of a litre)

pioneer **1** *noun* first to do a type of work; **pioneer project** *or* **pioneer development** = project or development which is new and has never been tried before **2** *verb* to be the first to do something; **the company pioneered developments in the field of electronics**

pirate **1** *noun* person who copies a patented invention or a copyright work and sells it; **a pirate copy of a book 2** *verb* to copy a copyright work; **a pirated book** *or* **a pirated design; the designs for the new dress collection were pirated in the Far East**
◊ **piracy** *noun* copying of patented inventions or copyright works
NOTE: no plural

pit *noun* coal mine

pitch *noun* **sales pitch** = talk by a salesman to persuade someone to buy

pix *plural noun* *informal* pictures (used in advertising or design)

place 1 *noun* **(a)** where something is *or* where something happens; **to take place** = to happen; **the meeting will take place in our offices**; **meeting place** = room *or* area where people can meet; **place of work** = office *or* factory, etc. where people work **(b)** position (in a competition); **three companies are fighting for first place in the home computer market** **(c)** job; **he was offered a place with an insurance company; she turned down three places before accepting the one we offered** **(d)** position in a text; **she marked her place in the text with a red pen; I have lost my place and cannot remember where I have reached in my filing** 2 *verb* **(a)** to put; **to place money in an account** = to deposit money; **to place a block of shares** = to find a buyer for a block of shares; **to place a contract** = to decide that a certain company shall have the contract to do work; **to place something on file** = to file something **(b) to place an order** = to order something; **he placed an order for 250 cartons of paper** **(c) to place staff** = to find jobs for staff; **how are you placed for work?** = have you enough work to do?

◊ **placement** *noun* finding work for someone

◊ **placing** *noun* **the placing of a line of shares** = finding a buyer for a large number of shares in a new company or a company which is going public
NOTE: no plural

plain *adjective* **(a)** easy to understand; **we made it plain to the union that 5% was the management's final offer; the manager is a very plain-spoken man** = the manager says exactly what he thinks **(b)** simple; **the design of the package is in plain blue and white squares; we want the cheaper models to have a plain design**

◊ **plain cover** *noun* **to send something under plain cover** = to send something in an ordinary envelope with no company name printed on it

plaintiff *noun* person who starts a legal action against someone

plan 1 *noun* **(a)** organized way of doing something; **contingency plan** = plan which will be put into action if something happens which no one expects to happen;

the government's economic plans = the government's proposals for running the country's economy; **a Five-Year Plan** = proposals for running a country's economy over a five-year period **(b)** way of saving or investing money; **investment plan; pensions plan; savings plan** **(c)** drawing which shows how something is arranged *or* how something will be built; **the designers showed us the first plans for the new offices; floor plan** = drawing of a floor in a building, showing where different departments are; **street plan** *or* **town plan** = map of a town showing streets and buildings 2 *verb* to organize carefully how something should be done; **to plan for an increase in bank interest charges** = to change a way of doing things because you think there will be an increase in bank interest charges; **to plan investments** = to propose how investments should be made
NOTE: **planning - planned**

◊ **planned** *adjective* **planned economy** = system where the government plans all business activity

◊ **planner** *noun* **(a)** person who plans; **the government's economic planners** = people who plan the future economy of the country for the government **(b) desk planner** *or* **wall planner** = book *or* chart which shows days *or* weeks *or* months so that the work of an office can be shown by diagrams

◊ **planning** *noun* **(a)** organizing how something should be done, especially how a company should be run to make increased profits; **long-term planning** *or* **short-term planning; economic planning** = planning the future financial state of the country for the government; **corporate planning** = planning the future financial state of a group of companies; **manpower planning** = planning to get the right number of workers in each job **(b)** *GB* **planning permission** = official document allowing a person *or* company to plan new buildings on empty land; **to be refused planning permission; we are waiting for planning permission before we can start building; the land is to be sold with planning permission; the planning department** = section of a local government office which deals with requests for planning permission
NOTE: no plural

plane *noun* aircraft *or* machine which flies in the air, carrying passengers or cargo; **I plan to take the 5 o'clock plane to New York; he could not get a seat on Tuesday's plane, so he had to wait until Wednesday; there are ten planes a day from London to Paris**

plant *noun* **(a)** machinery; **plant-hire firm** = company which lends large machines (such as cranes and tractors) to building companies **(b)** large factory; **they are planning to build a car plant near the river; to set up a new plant; they closed down six plants in the north of the country; he was appointed plant manager**
NOTE: no plural for **(a)**

platform *noun* high pavement in a station, so that passengers can get on or off trains; **the train for Birmingham leaves from Platform 12; the ticket office is on Platform 2**

PLC *or* **plc** = PUBLIC LIMITED COMPANY

plead *verb* to speak on behalf of a client in court

pledge **1** *noun* object given to a pawnbroker as security for money borrowed; **to redeem a pledge** = to pay back a loan and interest and so get back the security; **unredeemed pledge** = pledge which the borrower has not claimed back by paying back his loan **2** *verb* **to pledge share certificates** = to deposit share certificates with the lender as security for money borrowed

plenary *noun* **plenary meeting** *or* **plenary session** = meeting at a conference when all the delegates meet together

plough back *verb* to plough back profits into the company = to invest the profits in the business (and not pay them out as dividends to the shareholders) by using

them to buy new equipment *or* create new products

plug **1** *noun* **(a)** device at the end of a wire for connecting a machine to the electricity supply; **the printer is supplied with a plug (b)** to give a plug to a new **product** = to publicize a new product **2** *verb* **(a)** to plug in = to attach a machine to the electricity supply; **the computer was not plugged in (b)** to publicize *or* to advertise; **they ran six commercials plugging holidays in Spain (c)** to block *or* to stop; **the company is trying to plug the drain on cash reserves**
NOTE: **plugging - plugged**

plummet *or* **plunge** *verb* to fall sharply; **share prices plummeted *or* plunged on the news of the devaluation**

plus **1** *preposition* **(a)** added to; **his salary plus commission comes to more than £25,000; production costs plus overheads are higher than revenue (b)** more than; **houses valued at £100,000 plus** = houses valued at over £100,000 **2** *adjective* favourable *or* good and profitable; **a plus factor for the company is that the market is much larger than they had originally thought; the plus side of the account** = the credit side of the account; **on the plus side** = this is a favourable point; **on the plus side, we must take into account the new product line 3** *noun* a good *or* favourable point; **to have achieved £1m in new sales in less than six months is certainly a plus for the sales team**

p.m. *adverb* in the afternoon *or* in the evening *or* after 12 o'clock midday; **the train leaves at 6.50 p.m.; if you phone New York after 6 p.m. the calls are at a cheaper rate**

PO = POST OFFICE

pocket *noun* **pocket calculator** *or* **pocket diary** = calculator *or* diary which can be carried in the pocket; **to be £25 in pocket** = to have made a profit of £25; **to be £25**

out of pocket = to have lost £25; **out-of-pocket expenses** = amount of money to pay back a worker for his own money which he has spent on company business

point 1 *noun* **(a)** place *or* position; **point of sale** = place where a product is sold (such as a shop); **point of sale material** = display material (such as posters, dump bins) to advertise a product where it is being sold; **breakeven point** = position at which sales cover costs but do not show a profit; **customs entry point** = place at a border between two countries where goods are declared to customs; **starting point** = place where something starts **(b)** **decimal point** = dot which indicates the division between a whole unit and its smaller parts (such as 4.25); **percentage point** = 1 per cent; **half a percentage point** = 0.5 per cent; **the dollar gained two points** = the dollar increased in value against another currency by two hundredths of a cent; **the exchange fell ten points** = the stock market index fell by ten units **2** *verb* **to point out** = to show; **the report points out the mistakes made by the company over the last year; he pointed out that the results were better than in previous years**

QUOTE: sterling M3, the most closely watched measure, rose by 13% in the year to August – seven percentage points faster than the rate of inflation *Economist*
QUOTE: banks refrained from quoting forward US/Hongkong dollar exchange rates as premiums of 100 points replaced discounts of up to 50 points *South China Morning Post*

policy *noun* **(a)** decisions on the general way of doing something; **government policy on wages** *or* **government wages policy; the government's prices policy** *or* **incomes policy; the country's economic policy; a company's trading policy; the government made a policy statement** *or* **made a statement of policy** = the government declared in public what its plans were; **budgetary policy** = policy of expected income and expenditure **(b)** **company policy** = the company's agreed plan of action *or* the company's way of doing things; **what is the company policy on credit? it is against company policy to give more than thirty days' credit; our policy is to submit all contracts to the legal department (c) insurance policy** = document which shows the conditions of an insurance contract;

an accident policy = an insurance contract against accidents; **all-risks policy** = insurance policy which covers risks of any kind, with no exclusions; **a comprehensive** *or* **an all-in policy** = an insurance which covers all risks; **contingent policy** = policy which pays out only if something happens (as if the person named in the policy dies before the person due to benefit); **endowment policy** = policy where a sum of money is paid to the insured person on a certain date, or to his estate if he dies earlier; **policy holder** = person who is insured by an insurance company; **to take out a policy** = to sign the contract for an insurance and start paying the premiums; **she took out a life insurance policy** *or* **a house insurance policy; the insurance company made out a policy** *or* **drew up a policy** = the company wrote the details of the contract on the policy

polite *adjective* behaving in a pleasant way; **we stipulate that our salesgirls must be polite to customers; we had a polite letter from the MD**
◇ **politely** *adverb* in a pleasant way; **she politely answered the customers' questions**

political *adjective* referring to a certain idea of how a country should be run; **political levy** = part of the subscription of a member of a trade union which the union pays to support a political party; **political party** = group of people who believe a country should be run in a certain way

poll 1 *noun* **opinion poll** = asking a sample group of people, taken at random, what they feel about something, so as to guess the opinion of the whole population; **opinion polls showed the public preferred butter to margarine; before starting the service the company carried out a nationwide opinion poll 2** *verb* **to poll a sample of the population** = to ask a sample group of people what they feel about something; **to poll the members of the club on an issue** = to ask the members for their opinion on an issue
◇ **pollster** *noun* expert in understanding what polls mean

polystyrene *noun* **expanded polystyrene** = light solid plastic used for packing; **the computer is delivered packed in expanded**

polystyrene
NOTE: no plural

pool 1 *noun* **(a) typing pool** = group of typists, working together in a company, offering a secretarial service to several departments **(b)** unused supply; **a pool of unemployed labour** *or* **of expertise** 2 *verb* **to pool resources** = to put all resources together so as to be more powerful or profitable

poor *adjective* **(a)** without much money; **the company tries to help the poorest members of staff with soft loans; it is one of the poorest countries in the world (b)** not very good; **poor quality; poor service; poor turnround time of orders** *or* **poor order turnround time**
◇ **poorly** *adverb* badly; **the offices are poorly laid out; the plan was poorly presented; poorly-paid staff** = staff with low wages

popular *adjective* liked by many people; **this is our most popular model; the South Coast is the most popular area for holidays; popular prices** = prices which are low and therefore liked

population *noun* number of people who live in a country *or* in a town; **Paris has a population of over one million; the working population; population statistics; population trends; floating population** = people who move from place to place

port *noun* **(a)** harbour *or* place where ships come to load or unload; **the port of Rotterdam; inland port** = port on a river *or* canal; **to call at a port** = to stop at a port to load or unload cargo; **port authority** = organization which runs a port; **port of call** = port at which a ship often stops; **port charges** *or* **port dues** = payment which a ship makes to the port authority for the right to use the port; **port of embarkation** = port at which you get on a ship; **port installations** = buildings and equipment of a port; **commercial port** = port which has only goods traffic; **fishing port** = port which is used mainly by fishing boats; **free port** = port where there are no customs duties to be paid **(b)** part of a computer where a lead can be attached

portable 1 *adjective* which can be carried; **a portable computer** *or* **a portable typewriter; portable pension** = pension rights which a worker can take with him from one company to another as he changes jobs 2 *noun* **a portable** = a computer *or* typewriter which can be carried

portfolio *noun* **a portfolio of shares** = all the shares owned by someone; **portfolio management** = buying and selling shares to make profits for a person

portion *noun* small quantity, especially enough food for one person; **we serve ice cream in individual portions**

p.o.s. = POINT OF SALE

position *noun* **(a)** situation *or* state of affairs; **what is the cash position?** = what is the state of the company's current account?; **bargaining position** = statement of position by one group during negotiations; **to cover a position** = to have enough money to pay for a forward purchase **(b)** job *or* paid work in a company; **to apply for a position as manager; we have several positions vacant; all the vacant positions have been filled; she retired from her position in the accounts department; he is in a key position** = he has an important job

positive *adjective* meaning "yes"; **the board gave a positive reply; positive cash flow** = situation where more money is coming in than is being spent

possess *verb* to own; **the company possesses property in the centre of the town; he lost all he possessed in the collapse of his company**
◇ **possession** *noun* **(a)** owning something; **the documents are in his possession** = he is holding the documents; **vacant possession** = being able to occupy a property immediately after buying it because it is empty; **the property is to be sold with vacant possession (b) possessions** = property *or* things owned; **they lost all their possessions in the fire**
NOTE: no plural for **(a)**

possible *adjective* which might happen; **the 25th and 26th are possible dates for our next meeting; it is possible that production will be held up by industrial action; there are two possible candidates for the job** = two candidates are good enough to be appointed
◇ **possibility** *noun* being likely to happen; **there is a possibility that the plane will be early; there is no possibility of the chairman retiring before next Christmas**

post **1** *noun* **(a)** system of sending letters and parcels from one place to another; **to send an invoice by post; he put the letter in the post; the cheque was lost in the post; to send a reply by return of post** = to reply to a letter immediately; **letter post** *or* **parcel post** = service for sending letters or parcels; **post room** = room in an office where the post is sorted and sent to each department or collected from each department for sending **(b)** letters sent or received; **has the post arrived yet? my secretary opens the post as soon as it arrives; the receipt was in this morning's post; the letter did not arrive by first post this morning (c)** job *or* paid work in a company; **to apply for a post as cashier; we have three posts vacant; all our posts have been filled; we advertised three posts in the "Times"**
NOTE: no plural for (a) or (b)
2 *verb* **(a)** to send something by post; **to post a letter** *or* **to post a parcel (b) to post an entry** = to transfer an entry to an account; **to post up a ledger** = to keep a ledger up to date **(c) to post up a notice** = to put a notice on a wall *or* on a noticeboard **(d) to post an increase** = to let people know that an increase has taken place

> QUOTE: Toronto stocks closed at an all-time high, posting their fifth day of advances in heavy trading *Financial Times*

post- *prefix* later

postage *noun* payment for sending a letter or parcel by post; **what is the postage to Nigeria?; postage paid** = words printed on an envelope to show that the sender has paid the postage even though there is no stamp on it; **postage stamp** = small piece of paper attached to a letter or parcel to show that you have paid for it to be sent through the post
NOTE: no plural

postal *adjective* referring to the post; **postal charges** *or* **postal rates** = money to be paid for sending letters or parcels by post; **postal charges are going up by 10% in September; postal order** = document bought at a post office, as a method of paying small amounts of money by post

postcard *noun* piece of cardboard for sending a message by post (often with a picture on one side)

postcode *noun* letters and numbers used to indicate a town *or* street in an address on an envelope
NOTE: US English is **zip code**

postdate *verb* to put a later date on a document; **he sent us a postdated cheque; his cheque was postdated to June**

poster *noun* large notice *or* advertisement to be stuck up on a wall

poste restante *noun* system where letters can be addressed to someone at a post office, where they can be collected; **send any messages to "Poste Restante, Athens"**

post free *adverb* without having to pay any postage; **the game is obtainable post free from the manufacturer**

postmark **1** *noun* mark stamped by the Post Office on a letter, covering the postage stamp, to show that the Post Office has accepted it; **letter with a London postmark 2** *verb* to stamp a letter with a postmark; **the letter was postmarked New York**

post office *noun* **(a)** building where the postal services are based *or* shop where you can buy stamps, send parcels, etc.; **main post office; sub-post office** = small post office, usually part of a general store **(b) the Post Office** = national organization which deals with sending letters and parcels; **Post Office officials** *or* **officials of the Post Office; Post Office van; Post Office box number** = reference number given for delivering mail to a post office, so as not to give the actual address of the person who will receive it

postpaid *adjective* with the postage already paid; **the price is £5.95 postpaid**

postpone *verb* to arrange for something to take place later than planned; **he postponed the meeting to tomorrow; they asked if they could postpone payment until the cash situation was better**

◇ **postponement** *noun* arranging for something to take place later than planned; **I had to change my appointments because of the postponement of the board meeting**

potential 1 *adjective* possible; **potential customers** = people who could be customers; **potential market** = market which could be exploited; **the product has potential sales of 100,000 units** = the product will possibly sell 100,000 units; **he is a potential managing director** = he is the sort of man who could become managing director 2 *noun* possibility of becoming something; **share with a growth potential** *or* **with a potential for growth** = share which is likely to increase in value; **product with considerable sales potential** = product which is likely to have very large sales; **to analyze the market potential** = to examine the market to see how large it possibly is; **earning potential** = amount of money which someone should be able to earn *or* amount of dividend which a share is capable of earning

pound *noun* **(a)** measure of weight (= 0.45 kilos); **to sell oranges by the pound; a pound of oranges; oranges cost 50p a pound** NOTE: usually written **lb** after a figure: **25lb (b)** money used in the UK and many other countries; **pound sterling** = official term for the British currency; **a pound coin; a five pound note; it costs six pounds; the pound/dollar exchange rate**

NOTE: usually written **£** before a figure: **£25**

◇ **poundage** *noun* (i) rate charged per pound in weight; (ii) tax charged per pound in value
NOTE: no plural

power *noun* **(a)** strength *or* ability; **purchasing power** = quantity of goods which can be bought by a group of people *or* with a sum of money; **the purchasing power of the school market; the purchasing power of the pound has fallen over the last five years; the power of a consumer group** = ability of a group to influence the government *or* manufacturers; **bargaining power** = strength of one person *or* group when discussing prices or wages; **earning power** = amount of money someone should be able to earn; **he is such a fine designer that his earning power is very large; borrowing power** = amount of money which a company can borrow **(b)** force *or* legal right; **executive power** = right to act as director *or* to put decisions into action; **power of attorney** = legal document which gives someone the right to act on someone's behalf in legal matters; **the full power of the law** = the full force of the law when applied; **we will apply the full power of the law to get possession of our property again**

p.p. *verb* = PER PROCURANTIONEM **to p.p. a letter** = to sign a letter on behalf of someone; **the secretary p.p.'d the letter while the manager was at lunch**

PR = PUBLIC RELATIONS **a PR firm is handling all our publicity; he is working in PR; the PR people gave away 100,000 balloons**

practice *noun* **(a)** way of doing things; **his practice was to arrive at work at 7.30 and start counting the cash; business practices** *or* **industrial practices** *or* **trade practices** = ways of managing *or* working in business, industry or trade; **restrictive practices** = ways of working which make people less free (such as stopping, by trade unions, of workers from doing certain jobs *or* not allowing customers a free choice of product); **sharp practice** = way of doing business which is not honest, but is not illegal; **code of practice** = rules drawn up by an association which the members must follow when doing business **(b) in practice**

= when actually done; **the marketing plan seems very interesting, but what will it cost in practice?**

QUOTE: the EC demanded international arbitration over the pricing practices of the provincial boards   *Globe and Mail (Toronto)*

pre- *prefix* before; **a pre-stocktaking sale; there will be a pre-AGM board meeting** *or* **there will be a board meeting pre the AGM; the pre-Christmas period is always very busy**

precautionary *adjective* **as a precautionary measure** = in case something takes place
◊ **precautions** *plural noun* care taken to avoid something unpleasant; **to take precautions to prevent thefts in the office; the company did not take proper fire precautions; safety precautions** = actions to try to make sure that something is safe

precinct *noun* **(a) pedestrian precinct** *or* **shopping precinct** = part of a town which is closed to traffic so that people can walk about and shop **(b)** *US* administrative district in a town

predecessor *noun* person who had a job *or* position before someone else; **he took over from his predecessor last May; she is using the same office as her predecessor**

predict *verb* to say that something will certainly happen

QUOTE: lower interest rates are a bull factor for the stock market and analysts predict that the Dow Jones average will soon challenge the 1,300 barrier   *Financial Times*

pre-empt *verb* to get an advantage by doing something quickly before anyone else; **they staged a management buyout to pre-empt a takeover bid**
◊ **pre-emptive** *adjective* which has an advantage by acting early; **pre-emptive strike against a takeover bid** = rapid action taken to prevent a takeover bid; **a pre-emptive right** = (i) right of a government *or* of a local authority to buy a property before anyone else; (ii) *US* right of a shareholder to be first to buy a new stock issue

prefer *verb* to like something better than another thing; **we prefer the small corner shop to the large supermarket; most customers prefer to choose clothes themselves, rather than take the advice of the sales assistant**
◊ **preference** *noun* thing which is preferred; **the customers' preference for small corner shops; preference shares** = shares (often with no voting rights) which receive their dividend before all other shares and which are repaid first (at face value) if the company is liquidated; **preference shareholders** = owners of preference shares; **cumulative preference share** = preference share where the dividend will be paid at a later date even if the company cannot pay a dividend in the current year
◊ **preferential** *adjective* showing that something is preferred more than another; **preferential creditor** = creditor who must be paid first if a company is in liquidation; **preferential duty** *or* **preferential tariff** = special low rate of tax; **preferential terms** *or* **preferential treatment** = terms or way of dealing which is better than usual; **subsidiary companies get preferential treatment when it comes to subcontracting work**
◊ **preferred** *adjective* **preferred creditor** = creditor who must be paid first if a company is in liquidation; **preferred shares** *or* *US* **preferred stock** = shares which receive their dividend before all other shares, and which are repaid first (at face value) if the company is in liquidation; *US* **cumulative preferred stock** = preference share where the dividend will be paid at a later date even if the company cannot pay a dividend in the current year

pre-financing *noun* financing in advance

prejudice 1 *noun* harm done to someone; **without prejudice** = without harming any interests (words written on a letter to indicate that the writer is not legally bound to do what he offers to do in the letter); **to act to the prejudice of a claim** = to do something which may harm a claim **2** *verb* to harm; **to prejudice someone's claim**

preliminary *adjective* early *or* happening before anything else; **preliminary discussion** *or* **a preliminary meeting** =

discussion _or_ meeting which takes place before the main discussion or meeting starts

QUOTE: preliminary indications of the level of business investment and activity during the March quarter will be available this week
Australian Financial Review

premises _plural noun_ building and the land it stands on; **business premises** _or_ **commercial premises** = building used for commercial use; **office premises** _or_ **shop premises** = building which houses an office or shop; **lock-up premises** = shop which is locked up at night when the owner goes home; **licensed premises** = shop _or_ restaurant _or_ public house which is licensed to sell alcohol; **on the premises** = in the building; **there is a doctor on the premises at all times**

premium _noun_ **(a) premium offer** = free gift offered to attract more customers **(b) insurance premium** = annual payment made by the insured person _or_ a company to an insurance company; **additional premium** = payment made to cover extra items in an existing insurance; **you pay either an annual premium of £360 or twelve monthly premiums of £32 (c)** amount to be paid to a landlord or a tenant for the right to take over a lease; **flat to let with a premium of £10,000; annual rent: £8,500, premium: £25,000 (d)** extra charge; **exchange premium** = extra cost above the normal rate for buying foreign currency; **the dollar is at a premium; shares sold at a premium** = shares whose price is higher than their face value; new shares whose market price is higher than their issue price **(e)** _GB_ **premium bonds** = government bonds, part of the national savings scheme, which pay no interest, but give the owner the chance to win a weekly _or_ monthly prize **(f) premium quality** = top quality

QUOTE: greenmail. the practice of buying back stock at a premium from an acquirer who threatens a takeover _Duns Business Month_
QUOTE: responsibilities include the production of premium quality business reports
Times

prepack _or_ **prepackage** _verb_ to pack something before putting it on sale; **the**

fruit are prepacked _or_ prepackaged in plastic trays; the watches are prepacked in attractive display boxes

prepaid _adjective_ paid in advance; **carriage prepaid** = note showing that the transport costs have been paid in advance; **prepaid reply card** = stamped addressed card which is sent to someone so that he can reply without paying the postage
◊ **prepay** _verb_ to pay in advance
NOTE: prepaying - prepaid
◊ **prepayment** _noun_ payment in advance; **to ask for prepayment of a fee** = to ask for the fee to be paid before the work is done

present 1 _noun_ thing which is given; **these calculators make good presents; the office gave her a present when she got married 2** _adjective_ **(a)** happening now; **the shares are too expensive at their present price; what is the present address of the company? (b)** being there when something happens; **only six directors were present at the board meeting 3** _verb_ **(a)** to give someone something; **he was presented with a watch on completing twenty-five years' service with the company (b)** to bring _or_ send and show a document; **to present a bill for acceptance** = to send a bill for payment by the person who has accepted it; **to present a bill for payment** = to send a bill to be paid
◊ **presentation** _noun_ **(a)** showing a document; **cheque payable on presentation** = cheque which will be paid when it is presented; **free admission on presentation of the card** = you do not pay to go in if you show this card **(b)** demonstration _or_ exhibition of a proposed plan; **the manufacturer made a presentation of his new product line to possible customers; the distribution company made a presentation of the services they could offer; we have asked two PR firms to make presentations of proposed publicity campaigns**
◊ **present value** _noun_ **(a)** the value something has now; **in 1974 the pound was worth five times its present value (b)** sum of money which if invested now at a given rate of interest would produce a certain amount in the future

preside _verb_ to be chairman; **to preside over a meeting; the meeting was held in the committee room, Mr Smith presiding**

◇ **president** *noun* head of a company *or* a club; **he was elected president of the sports club; A.B.Smith has been appointed president of the company**
NOTE: in GB, president is sometimes a title given to a non-executive former chairman of a company; in the USA, the president is the main executive director of a company

press *noun* newspapers and magazines; **the local press** = newspapers which are sold in a small area of the country; **the national press** = newspapers which sell in all parts of the country; **the new car has been advertised in the national press; we plan to give the product a lot of press publicity; there was no mention of the new product in the press; press conference** = meeting where reporters from newspapers are invited to hear news of a new product *or* of a court case *or* of a takeover bid, etc.; **press coverage** = reports about something in the press; **we were very disappointed by the press coverage of the new car; press cutting** = piece cut out of a newspaper *or* magazine, which refers to an item which you find interesting; **we have kept a file of press cuttings about the new car; press release** = sheet giving news about something which is sent to newspapers and TV and radio stations so that they can use the information; **the company sent out a press release about the launch of the new car**
NOTE: no plural
◇ **pressing** *adjective* urgent; **pressing engagements** = meetings which have to be attended; **pressing bills** = bills which have to be paid

pressure *noun* something which forces you to do something; **he was under considerable financial pressure** = he was forced to act because he owed money; **to put pressure on someone to do something** = to try to force someone to do something; **the group tried to put pressure on the government to act; the banks put pressure on the company to reduce its borrowings; working under high pressure** = working with customers asking for supplies urgently *or* with a manager telling you to work faster; **high-pressure salesman** = salesman who forces a customer to buy something he does not really need; **pressure group** = group of people who try to influence the government *or* the local town council, etc.

prestige *noun* importance because of high quality *or* high value, etc.; **prestige advertising** = advertising in high quality magazines to increase a company's reputation; **prestige product** = expensive luxury product; **prestige offices** = expensive offices in a good area of the town

presume *verb* to suppose something is correct; **I presume the account has been paid; the company is presumed to be still solvent; we presume the shipment has been stolen**
◇ **presumption** *noun* thing which is assumed to be correct

pre-tax *or* **pretax** *adjective* before tax has been deducted *or* paid; **pretax profit** = profit before tax has been paid; **the dividend paid is equivalent to one quarter of the pretax profit**

QUOTE: the company's goals are a growth in sales of up to 40 per cent, a rise in pre-tax earnings of nearly 35 per cent and a rise in after-tax earnings of more than 25 per cent
Citizen (Ottawa)
QUOTE: EEC regulations which came into effect in July insist that customers can buy cars anywhere in the EEC at the local pre-tax price
Financial Times

pretences *plural noun* **false pretences** = doing or saying something to cheat someone; **he was sent to prison for obtaining money by false pretences**

pretend *verb* to act like someone else in order to trick *or* to act as if something is true when it really is not; **he got in by pretending to be a telephone engineer; the chairman pretended he knew the final profit; she pretended she had 'flu and asked to have the day off**

prevent *verb* to stop something happening; **we must try to prevent the takeover bid; the police prevented anyone from leaving the building; we have changed the locks on the doors to prevent the former MD from getting into the building**
◇ **preventive** *adjective* which tries to stop something happening; **to take preventive measures against theft** = to try to stop things from being stolen

previous *adjective* which happens earlier; **he could not accept the invitation because he had a previous engagement** = because he had earlier accepted another invitation to go somewhere

◊ **previously** *adverb* happening earlier

price **1** *noun* money which has to be paid to buy something; **agreed price** = price which has been accepted by both the buyer and seller; **all-in price** = price which covers all items in a purchase (goods, insurance, delivery, etc.); **asking price** = price which the seller is hoping to be paid for the item when it is sold; **bargain price** = very cheap price; **catalogue price** *or* **list price** = price as marked in a catalogue or list; **competitive price** = low price aimed to compete with a rival product; **cost price** = selling price which is the same as the price which the seller paid for the item (either the manufacturing price or the wholesale price); **cut price** = very cheap price; **discount price** = full price less a discount; **factory price** *or* **price ex factory** = price not including transport from the maker's factory; **fair price** = good price for both buyer and seller; **firm price** = price which will not change; **they are quoting a firm price of $1.23 a unit; going price** *or* **current price** *or* **usual price** = the price which is being charged now; **to sell goods off at half price** = to sell goods at half the price at which they were being sold before; **market price** = price at which a product can be sold; **net price** = price which cannot be reduced by a discount; **retail price** = price at which the retailer sells to the final customer; **retail price index** = index which shows how prices of consumer goods have increased or decreased over a period of time; **spot price** = price for immediate delivery of a commodity; **the spot price of oil on the commodity markets; price ceiling** = highest price which can be reached; **price control** = legal measures to stop prices rising too fast; **price cutting** = sudden lowering of prices; **price war** *or* **price-cutting war** = competition between companies to get a larger market share by cutting prices; **price differential** = difference in price between products in a range; **price fixing** = illegal agreement between companies to charge the same price for competing products; **price label** *or* **price tag** = label which shows a price;

the takeover bid put a $2m price tag on the company; price list = sheet giving prices of goods for sale; **price range** = series of prices for similar products from different suppliers; **cars in the £6-7,000 price range** = cars of different makes, selling for between £6,000 and £7,000; **price-sensitive product** = product which will not sell if the price is increased **(b) to increase in price** = to become more expensive; **petrol has increased in price** *or* **the price of petrol has increased; to increase prices** *or* **to raise prices** = to make items more expensive; **we will try to meet your price** = we will try to offer a price which is acceptable to you; **to cut prices** = to reduce prices suddenly; **to lower prices** *or* **to reduce prices** = to make items cheaper **(c)** (*on the Stock Exchange*) **asking price** = price which sellers are asking for shares; **closing price** = price at the end of a day's trading; **opening price** = price at the start of a day's trading; **price/earnings ratio** = ratio between the market price of a share and the current earnings it produces **2** *verb* to give a price to a product; **car priced at £5,000; competitively priced** = sold at a low price which competes with that of similar goods from other companies; **the company has priced itself out of the market** = the company has raised its prices so high that its products do not sell

◊ **pricing** *noun* giving a price to a product; **pricing policy** = a company's policy in giving prices to its products; **our pricing policy aims at producing a 35% gross margin; common pricing** = illegal fixing of prices by several businesses so that they all charge the same price; **competitive pricing** = putting a low price on a product so that it competes with similar products from other companies; **marginal pricing** = making the selling price the same as the cost of a single extra unit above the number already planned

NOTE: no plural

QUOTE: that British goods will price themselves back into world markets is doubtful as long as sterling labour costs continue to rise

Sunday Times

QUOTE: the average price per kilogram for this season has been 300c

Australian Financial Review

QUOTE: European manufacturers rely heavily on imported raw materials which are mostly priced in dollars

Duns Business Month

primary *adjective* basic; **primary commodities** = raw materials or food; **primary industry** = industry dealing with basic raw materials (such as coal, wood, farm produce); **primary products** = products (such as wood, milk, fish) which are basic raw materials

◇ **primarily** *adverb* mainly

QUOTE: farmers are convinced that primary industry no longer has the capacity to meet new capital taxes or charges on farm inputs
Australian Financial Review

prime *adjective* (a) most important; **prime time** = most expensive advertising time for TV commercials; **we are putting out a series of prime-time commercials** (b) basic; **prime bills** = bills of exchange which do not involve any risk; **prime cost** = cost involved in producing a product, excluding overheads; **prime rate** *or* **prime** = best rate of interest at which a bank lends to its customers

◇ **Prime Minister** *noun* head of a government; **the Australian Prime Minister** *or* **the Prime Minister of Australia**

◇ **priming** *noun* see PUMP PRIMING

QUOTE: the base lending rate, or prime rate, is the rate at which banks lend to their top corporate borrowers
Wall Street Journal

principal **1** *noun* (a) person *or* company which is represented by an agent; **the agent has come to London to see his principals** (b) money invested *or* borrowed on which interest is paid; **to repay principal and interest** **2** *adjective* most important; **the principal shareholders asked for a meeting; the country's principal products are paper and wood**

QUOTE: the company was set up with funds totalling NorKr 145m with the principal aim of making capital gains on the secondhand market
Lloyd's List

principle *noun* basic point *or* general rule; **in principle** = in agreement with a general rule; **agreement in principle** = agreement with the basic conditions of a proposal

print **1** *noun* words made (on paper) with a machine; **to read the small print** *or* **the fine print on a contract** = to read the conditions of a contract which are often printed very small so that people will not be able to read them easily **2** *verb* (a) to make letters on paper with a machine; **printed agreement; printed regulations** (b) to write in capital letters; **please print your name and address on the top of the form**

◇ **printer** *noun* machine which prints; **computer printer** *or* **line printer** = machine which prints information from a computer, printing one line at a time; **dot-matrix printer** = machine which prints by forming letter from many tiny dots

◇ **print out** *verb* to print information from a computer through a printer

◇ **printout** *noun* computer printout = printed copy of information from a computer; **the sales director asked for a printout of the agents' commissions**

prior *adjective* earlier; **prior agreement** = agreement which was reached earlier; **without prior knowledge** = without knowing before; **prior charge** = security (such as a preference share) which is repaid before other securities when a company goes into liquidation

◇ **priority** *noun* to have priority = to have the right to be first; **to have priority over** *or* **to take priority over something** = to be more important than something; **reducing overheads takes priority over increasing turnover; debenture holders have priority over ordinary shareholders; to give something top priority** = to make something the most important item

private *adjective* (a) belonging to a single person, not a company *or* the state; **letter marked "private and confidential"** = letter which must not be opened by anyone other than the person it is addressed to; **private client** *or* **private customer** = client dealt with by a salesman as a person, not as a company; **private income** = income from dividends *or* interest *or* rents which is not part of a salary; **private investor** = ordinary person with money to invest; **private property** = property which belongs to a private person, not to the public (b) **in private** = away from other people; **he asked to see the managing director in private; in public he said the company would break even soon, but in private he was less optimistic** (c) **private limited company** = company with a small number of shareholders whose shares are not traded on the Stock Exchange **(d) private enterprise =** businesses which are owned by private shareholders, not by the state; **the project is funded by private enterprise; the private sector =** all companies which are owned by private shareholders, not by the state ◊ **privately** *adverb* away from other people; **the deal was negotiated privately** ◊ **privatization** *noun* selling a nationalized industry to private owners

◊ **privatize** *verb* to sell a nationalized industry to private owners

QUOTE: in the private sector the total number of new house starts was 3 per cent higher than in the corresponding period last year, while public sector starts were 23 per cent lower
Financial Times
QUOTE: management had offered to take the company private through a leveraged buyout for $825 million   *Fortune*

pro *preposition* for; **pro tem =** for the time being *or* temporarily; **per pro =** with the authority of; **the secretary signed per pro the manager; pro forma =** invoice sent to a buyer before the goods are sent, so that payment can be made in advance *or* that business documents can be produced; **pro rata =** at a rate which varies according to the size or importance of something; **dividends are paid pro rata =** dividends are paid according to the number of shares held

probable *adjective* likely to happen; **he is trying to prevent the probable collapse of the company** ◊ **probably** *adverb* likely; **the MD is probably going to retire next year; this shop is probably the best in town for service**

probate *noun* proving legally that a document, especially a will, is valid; **the executor was granted probate =** the executor was told officially that the will was valid; **probate court =** court which examines wills to see if they are valid
NOTE: no plural
◊ **probation** *noun* period when a new worker is being tested before getting a permanent job; **he is on three months' probation; to take someone on probation**
NOTE: no plural
◊ **probationary** *adjective* while someone is being tested; **a probationary**

period of three months; after the probationary period the company decided to offer him a full-time contract

problem *noun* thing to which it is difficult to find an answer; **the company suffers from cash flow problems** *or* **staff problems; to solve a problem =** to find an answer to a problem; **problem solving is a test of a good manager; problem area =** area of a company's work which is difficult to run; **overseas sales is one of our biggest problem areas**

QUOTE: everyone blames the strong dollar for US trade problems, but they differ on what should be done   *Duns Business Month*

procedure *noun* way in which something is done; **to follow the proper procedure; this procedure is very irregular =** this is not the set way to do something; **accounting procedures =** set ways of doing the accounts of a company; **disciplinary procedure =** way of warning a worker that he is breaking the rules of a company; **complaints procedure** *or* **grievance procedure =** way of presenting complaints formally from a trade union to a management; **the trade union has followed the correct complaints procedure; dismissal procedures =** correct way to dismiss someone, following the rules in the contract of employment

proceed *verb* to go on *or* to continue; **the negotiations are proceeding slowly; to proceed against someone =** to start a legal action against someone; **to proceed with something =** to go on doing something; **shall we proceed with the committee meeting?** ◊ **proceedings** *plural noun* **(a) conference proceedings =** written report of what has taken place at a conference **(b) legal proceedings =** legal action *or* lawsuit; **to take proceedings against someone; the court proceedings were adjourned; to institute proceedings against someone =** to start a legal action against someone ◊ **proceeds** *plural noun* **the proceeds of a sale =** money received from a sale after deducting expenses; **he sold his shop and invested the proceeds in a computer repair business**

process 1 *noun* **(a) industrial processes** = processes involved in manufacturing products in factories; **decision-making processes** = ways in which decisions are reached **(b) the due processes of the law** = the formal work of a legal action 2 *verb* **(a) to process figures** = to sort out information to make it easily understood; **the sales figures are being processed by our accounts department; data is being processed by our computer (b)** to deal with something in the usual routine way; **to process an insurance claim; orders are processed in our warehouse**

◇ **processing** *noun* **(a)** sorting of information; **processing of information** *or* **of statistics; batch processing** = computer system, where information is collected into batches before being loaded into the computer; **data processing** *or* **information processing** = selecting and examining data in a computer to produce information in a special form; **word processing** *or* **text processing** = working with words, using a computer to produce, check and change texts, reports, letters, etc. **(b) the processing of a claim for insurance** = putting a claim for insurance through the usual office routine in the insurance company; **order processing** = dealing with orders
NOTE: no plural

◇ **processor** *noun* **word processor** = small computer which is used for working with words, to produce texts, reports, letters, etc.

produce 1 *noun* foodstuffs grown on the land; **home produce; agricultural produce** *or* **farm produce**
NOTE: no plural
2 *verb* **(a)** to bring out; **he produced documents to prove his claim; the negotiators produced a new set of figures; the customs officer asked him to produce the relevant documents (b)** to make *or* to manufacture; **to produce cars** *or* **engines** *or* **books; to mass produce** = to make large quantities of a product **(c)** to give an interest; **investments which produce about 10% per annum**

◇ **producer** *noun* person *or* company *or* country which manufactures; **country which is a producer of high quality watches; the company is a major car producer**

◇ **producing** *adjective* which produces;

producing capacity = capacity to produce; **oil-producing country** = country which produces oil

product *noun* **(a)** thing which is made *or* manufactured; **basic product** = main product made from a raw material; **by-product** = secondary product made as a raw material is being processed; **end product** *or* **final product** *or* **finished product** = product made at the end of a production process **(b)** manufactured item for sale; **product advertising** = advertising a particular named product, not the company which makes it; **product analysis** = examining each separate product in a company's range to see why it sells *or* who buys it, etc.; **product design** = design of consumer products; **product development** = improving an existing product line to meet the needs of the market; **product engineer** = engineer in charge of the equipment for making a product; **product line** *or* **product range** = series of different products made by the same company which form a group (such as cars in different models, pens in different colours, etc.); **product management** = directing the making and selling of a product as an independent item; **product mix** = group of quite different products made by the same company **(c) gross domestic product** = annual value of goods sold and services paid for inside a country; **gross national product** = annual value of goods and services in a country, including income from other countries

◇ **production** *noun* **(a)** showing something; **on production of** = when something is shown; **the case will be released by the customs on production of the relevant documents; goods can be exchanged only on production of the sales slip (b)** making *or* manufacturing of goods for sale; **production will probably be held up by industrial action; we are hoping to speed up production by installing new machinery; batch production** = production in batches; **domestic production** = production of goods in the home market; **mass production** = manufacturing of large quantities of goods; **mass production of cars** *or* **of calculators; rate of production** *or* **production rate** = speed at which items are made; **production cost** = cost of making a product; **production department** = section of a company which deals with the making

of the company's products; **production line** = system of making a product, where each item (such as a car) moves slowly through the factory with new sections added to it as it goes along; **he works on the production line; she is a production line worker; production manager** = person in charge of the production department; **production unit** = separate small group of workers producing a certain product
NOTE: no plural

◇ **productive** *adjective* which produces; **productive capital** = capital which is invested to give interest; **productive discussions** = useful discussions which lead to an agreement *or* decision

◇ **productively** *adverb* in a productive way

◇ **productivity** *noun* rate of output per worker *or* per machine in a factory; **bonus payments are linked to productivity; the company is aiming to increase productivity; productivity has fallen** *or* **risen since the company was taken over; productivity agreement** = agreement to pay a productivity bonus; **productivity bonus** = extra payments made to workers because of increased production; **productivity drive** = extra effort to increase productivity
NOTE: no plural

QUOTE: though there has been productivity growth, the absolute productivity gap between many British firms and their foreign rivals remains *Sunday Times*

profession *noun* (a) work which needs special skills learnt over a period of time; **the managing director is an accountant by profession** (b) group of specialized workers; **the legal profession** = all lawyers; **the medical profession** = all doctors

◇ **professional** 1 *adjective* (a) referring to one of the professions; **the accountant sent in his bill for professional services; we had to ask our lawyer for professional advice on the contract; a professional man** = man who works in one of the professions (such as a lawyer, doctor, accountant); **professional qualifications** = documents showing that someone has successfully finished a course of study which allows him to work in one of the professions (b) expert *or* skilled; **his work is very professional; they did a very**

professional job in designing the new office (c) doing work for money; **a professional tennis player; he is a professional troubleshooter** = he makes his living by helping companies to sort out their problems **2** *noun* skilled person *or* person who does skilled work for money

proficiency *noun* skill *or* being capable for doing something; **she has a certificate of proficiency in English; to get the job he had to pass a proficiency test**
NOTE: no plural

◇ **proficient** *adjective* capable of doing something well; **she is quite proficient in English**

profile *noun* brief description; **he asked for a company profile of the possible partners in the joint venture; the customer profile shows our average buyer to be male, aged 25-30, and employed in the service industries**

profit *noun* money gained from a sale which is more than the money spent; **clear profit** = profit after all expenses have been paid; **we made $6,000 clear profit on the deal; gross profit** = profit calculated as sales income less the cost of the goods sold; **net profit** = result where income from sales is larger than all expenditure; **operating profit** = result where sales from normal business activities are higher than the costs; **trading profit** = result where the company's receipts are higher than its expenditure; **profit and loss account** = accounts for a company which show expenditure and income balanced to show a final profit *or* loss; **profit margin** = percentage difference between sales income and the cost of sales; **profits tax** *or* **tax on profits** = tax to be paid on profits; **profit before tax** *or* **pretax profit** = profit before any tax has been paid; **profit after tax** = profit after tax has been paid; **to take one's profit** = to sell shares at a higher price than was paid for them, rather than to keep them as an investment; **to show a profit** = to make a profit and state it in the company accounts; **we are showing a small profit for the first quarter; to make a profit** = to have more money as a result of a deal; **to move into profit** = to start to make a profit; **the company is breaking even now, and expects to move into profit within the next two months; to sell at a**

profit = to sell at a price which gives you a profit; **excess profit** = profit which is higher than what is thought to be normal; **excess profits tax** = tax on excess profits; **healthy profit** = quite a large profit; **paper profit** = profit on an asset which has increased in price but has not been sold; **he is showing a paper profit of £25,000 on his investment**

◇ **profit centre** *noun* person *or* department which is considered separately for the purposes of calculating a profit

◇ **profit-making** *adjective* which makes a profit; **the whole project was expected to be profit-making by 1985; non profit-making** = (organization, such as a club) which is not allowed by law to make a profit; **non profit-making organizations are exempt from tax**

◇ **profit-sharing** *noun* arrangement where workers get a share of the profits of the company they work for; **the company runs a profit-sharing scheme**
NOTE: no plural

◇ **profit-taking** *noun* selling investments to realize the profit, rather than keeping them; **share prices fell under continued profit-taking**
NOTE: no plural

◇ **profitability** *noun* (a) ability to make a profit (b) amount of profit made as a percentage of costs; **measurement of profitability** = way of calculating how profitable something is
NOTE: no plural

◇ **profitable** *adjective* which makes a profit

◇ **profitably** *adverb* making a profit

◇ **profiteer** *noun* person who makes too much profit, especially when goods are rationed *or* in short supply

◇ **profiteering** *noun* making too much profit

pro forma *noun* pro forma (invoice) = invoice sent to a buyer before the goods are sent, so that payment can be made or that business documents can be produced; **they sent us a pro forma**

program 1 *noun* computer program = instructions to a computer telling it to do a particular piece of work; **to buy a word-processing program; the accounts department is running a new payroll program** 2 *verb* to write a program for a computer; **to program a computer** = to install a program in a computer; **the computer is programmed to print labels**
NOTE: programming - programmed

◇ **programme** *or* US **program** *noun* plan of things which will be done; **development programme; research programme; training programme; to draw up a programme of investment** *or* **an investment programme**

◇ **programmable** *adjective* which can be programmed

◇ **programmer** *noun* computer programmer = person who writes computer programs

◇ **programming** *noun* computer programming = writing programs for computers; **programming engineer** = engineer in charge of programming a computer system; **programming language** = system of signs, letters and words used to instruct a computer

progress 1 *noun* movement of work forward; **to report on the progress of the work** *or* **of the negotiations; to make a progress report** = to report how work is going; **in progress** = which is being done but is not finished; **negotiations in progress; work in progress; progress payments** = payments made as each stage of a contract is completed; **the fifth progress payment is due in March**
NOTE: no plural
2 *verb* to move forward *or* to go ahead; **the contract is progressing through various departments**

◇ **progress chaser** *noun* person whose job is to check that work is being carried out on schedule *or* that orders are being fulfilled on time, etc.

◇ **progressive** *adjective* which moves forward in stages; **progressive taxation**

prohibitive *adjective* with a price so high that you cannot afford to pay it; **the cost of redeveloping the product is prohibitive**

project *noun* (a) plan; **he has drawn up a project for developing new markets in Europe** (b) particular job of work which follows a plan; **we are just completing an engineering project in North Africa; the company will start work on the project next month; project analysis** = examining all costs *or* problems of a project before work on it is started; **project engineer** = engineer in charge of a project; **project manager** = manager in charge of a project
◇ **projected** *adjective* planned *or* expected; **projected sales** = forecast of sales; **projected sales in Europe next year should be over £1m**
◇ **projection** *noun* forecast of something which will happen in the future; **projection of profits for the next three years; the sales manager was asked to draw up sales projections for the next three years**

promise 1 *noun* saying that you will do something; **to keep a promise** = to do what you said you would do; **he says he will pay next week, but he never keeps his promises; to go back on a promise** = not to do what you said you would do; **the management went back on its promise to increase salaries across the board; a promise to pay** = a promissory note 2 *verb* to say that you will do something; **they promised to pay the last instalment next week; the personnel manager promised he would look into the grievances of the office staff**
◇ **promissory note** *noun* document stating that someone promises to pay an amount of money on a certain date

promote *verb* (a) to give someone a more important job; **he was promoted from salesman to sales manager** (b) to advertise; **to promote a new product** = to increase the sales of a new product by a sales campaign *or* TV commercials *or* free gifts (c) **to promote a new company** = to organize the setting up of a new company
◇ **promoter** *noun* **company promoter** = person who organizes the setting up of a new company
◇ **promotion** *noun* (a) moving up to a more important job; **promotion chances** *or*

promotion prospects; he ruined his chances of promotion when he argued with the managing director; to earn promotion = to work hard and efficiently and so be promoted (b) **promotion of a company** = setting up a new company (c) **promotion of a product** = selling a new product by publicity *or* sales campaign *or* TV commercials *or* free gifts; **promotion budget; promotion team; sales promotion; special promotion**
◇ **promotional** *adjective* used in an advertising campaign; **the admen are using balloons as promotional material; promotional budget** = forecast cost of promoting a new product

prompt *adjective* rapid *or* done immediately; **prompt service; prompt reply to a letter; prompt payment** = payment made rapidly; **prompt supplier** = supplier who delivers orders rapidly
◇ **promptly** *adverb* rapidly; **he replied to my letter very promptly**

QUOTE: they keep shipping costs low and can take advantage of quantity discounts and other allowances for prompt payment
Duns Business Month

proof *noun* thing which shows that something is true; **documentary proof** = proof in the form of a document
◇ **-proof** *suffix* which prevents something getting in or out *or* harming; **dustproof cover; inflation-proof pension; soundproof studio**

property *noun* (a) personal property = things which belong to a person; **the storm caused considerable damage to personal property; the management is not responsible for property left in the hotel rooms** (b) land and buildings; **property tax; damage to property** *or* **property damage; the commercial property market is booming; the office has been bought by a property company** = by a company which buys buildings to lease them; **property developer** = person who buys old buildings *or* empty land and builds new buildings for sale or rent; **private property** = property which belongs to a private person and not to the public (c) a building; **we have several properties for sale in the centre of the town**
NOTE: no plural for (a) or (b)

proportion *noun* part (of a total); **a proportion of the pre-tax profit is set aside for contingencies; only a small proportion of our sales comes from retail shops; in proportion to** = showing how something is related to something else; **profits went up in proportion to the fall in overhead costs; sales in Europe are small in proportion to those in the USA**
◇ **proportional** *adjective* directly related; **the increase in profit is proportional to reduction in overheads**
◇ **proportionately** *adverb* in proportion

proposal *noun* (a) suggestion *or* thing suggested; **to make a proposal** *or* **to put forward a proposal to the board; the committee turned down the proposal** = the committee refused to accept what was suggested (b) official document with details of a property *or* person to be insured which is sent to the insurance company when asking for an insurance
◇ **propose** *verb* (a) to suggest that something should be done; **to propose a motion** = to ask a meeting to vote for a motion and explain the reasons for this; **to propose someone as president** = to ask a group to vote for someone to become president (b) **to propose to** = to say that you intend to do something; **I propose to repay the loan at £20 a month**
◇ **proposer** *noun* person who proposes a motion at a meeting
◇ **proposition** *noun* commercial deal which is suggested; **it will never be a commercial proposition** = it is not likely to make a profit

proprietary *adjective* (a) product (such as a medicine) which is made and owned by a company; **proprietary drug** = drug which is made by a particular company and marketed under a brand name (b) (*in South Africa and Australia*) **proprietary company** = private limited company
◇ **proprietor** *noun* owner; **the proprietor of a hotel** *or* **a hotel proprietor**
◇ **proprietress** *noun* woman owner; **the proprietress of an advertising consultancy**

pro rata *adjective & adverb* at an amount which varies according to the rate applied; **a pro rata payment; to pay someone pro rata**

prosecute *verb* to bring (someone) to court to answer a criminal charge; **he was prosecuted for embezzlement**
◇ **prosecution** *noun* (a) act of bringing someone to court to answer a charge; **his prosecution for embezzlement** (b) people who have prosecuted someone; **the costs of the case will be borne by the prosecution; prosecution counsel** *or* **counsel for the prosecution** = lawyer acting for the prosecution
NOTE: no plural for (b)

prospect *noun* (a) **prospects** = possibilities for the future; **his job prospects are good** = he is very likely to find a job; **prospects for the market** *or* **market prospects are worse than those of last year** = sales in the market are likely to be lower than they were last year (b) possibility that something will happen; **there is no prospect of negotiations coming to an end soon** (c) person who may become a customer; **the salesmen were looking out for possible prospects**
◇ **prospective** *adjective* which may happen in the future; **a prospective buyer** = someone who may buy in the future; **there is no shortage of prospective buyers for the computer**
◇ **prospectus** *noun* (a) document which gives information to attract buyers *or* customers; **the restaurant has girls handing out prospectuses in the street** (b) document which gives information about a company whose shares are being sold to the public for the first time
NOTE: plural is **prospectuses**

prosperous *adjective* rich; **a prosperous shopkeeper; a prosperous town**
◇ **prosperity** *noun* being rich; **in times of prosperity** = when people are rich
NOTE: no plural

protect *verb* to defend something against harm; **the workers are protected from unfair dismissal by government legislation; the computer is protected by a plastic cover; the cover is supposed to protect the machine from dust; to protect an industry by imposing tariff barriers** = to stop a local industry from being hit by foreign competition by stopping foreign products from being imported

◇ **protection** *noun* thing which protects; **the legislation offers no protection to part-time workers; consumer protection** = protecting consumers against unfair *or* illegal traders
NOTE: no plural

◇ **protective** *adjective* which protects; **protective tariff** = tariff which tries to ban imports to stop them competing with local products; **protective cover** = cover which protects a machine

pro tem *adverb* temporarily *or* for a time

protest 1 *noun* **(a)** statement *or* action to show that you do not approve of something; **to make a protest against high prices; sit-down protest** = action by members of the staff who occupy their place of work and refuse to leave; **in protest at** = showing that you do not approve of something; **the staff occupied the offices in protest at the low pay offer; to do something under protest** = to do something, but say that you do not approve of it **(b)** official document which proves that a bill of exchange has not been paid **2** *verb* **(a) to protest against something** = to say that you do not approve of something; **the importers are protesting against the ban on luxury goods**
NOTE: GB English is **to protest against something**, but US English is **to protest something**
(b) to protest a bill = to draw up a document to prove that a bill of exchange has not been paid

prototype *noun* first model of a new machine before it goes into production; **prototype car** *or* **prototype plane; the company is showing the prototype of the new model at the exhibition**

provide *verb* **(a) to provide for** = to allow for something which may happen in the future; **the contract provides for an annual increase in charges; £10,000 of expenses have been provided for in the budget (b)** to put money aside in accounts to cover expenditure *or* loss in the future; **£25,000 is provided against bad debts (c) to provide someone with something** = to supply something to someone; **each rep is provided with a company car; staff uniforms are provided by the hotel**
◇ **provided that** *or* **providing** *conjunction* on condition that; **the goods will be** delivered next week provided *or* providing the drivers are not on strike

◇ **provident** *adjective* which provides benefits in case of illness *or* old age, etc.; **a provident fund; a provident society**

province *noun* **(a)** large division of a country; **the provinces of Canada (b) the provinces** = parts of any country away from the main capital town; **there are fewer retail outlets in the provinces than in the capital**
◇ **provincial** *adjective* referring to a province *or* to the provinces; **a provincial government; a provincial branch of a national bank**

provision *noun* **(a) to make provision for** = to see that something is allowed for in the future; **there is no provision for** *or* **no provision has been made for car parking in the plans for the office block** = the plans do not include space for cars to park **(b)** money put aside in accounts in case it is needed in the future; **the bank has made a £2m provision for bad debts (c)** legal condition; **we have made provision to this effect** = we have put into the contract terms which will make this work **(d) provisions** = food
◇ **provisional** *adjective* temporary *or* not final or permanent; **provisional forecast of sales; provisional budget; they telexed their provisional acceptance of the contract**
◇ **provisionally** *adverb* not finally; **the contract has been accepted provisionally**

> QUOTE: landlords can create short lets of dwellings which will be free from the normal security of tenure provisions   *Times*

proviso *noun* condition in a contract; **we are signing the contract with the proviso that the terms can be discussed again after six months**

proxy *noun* **(a)** document which gives someone the power to act on behalf of someone else; **to sign by proxy; proxy vote** = votes made by proxy; **the proxy votes were all in favour of the board's recommendation (b)** person who acts on behalf of someone else; **to act as proxy for someone**

P.S. *noun* = POST SCRIPTUM additional note at the end of a letter; **did you read the P.S. at the end of the letter?**

PSBR = PUBLIC SECTOR BORROWING REQUIREMENT

pt = PINT

ptas = PESETAS

Pty = PROPRIETARY COMPANY

public 1 *adjective* **(a)** referring to all the people in general; **public holiday** = day when all workers rest and enjoy themselves instead of working; **public image** = idea which the people have of a company *or* a person; **the minister is trying to improve his public image; public transport** = transport (such as buses, trains) which is used by any member of the public **(b)** referring to the government or the state; **public expenditure** = spending of money by the local *or* central government; **public finance** = the raising of money by governments (by taxes or borrowing) and the spending of it; **public funds** = government money available for expenditure; **public ownership** = situation where an industry is nationalized **(c) Public Limited Company** = company whose shares can be bought on the Stock Exchange; **the company is going public** = the company is going to place some of its shares for sale on the stock market so that anyone can buy them **2** *noun* **the public** *or* **the general public** = the people; **in public** = in front of everyone; **in public he said that the company would soon be in profit, but in private he was less optimistic** NOTE: no plural
◊ **public relations** *plural noun* keeping good relations between a company *or* a group and the public so that people know what the company is doing and can approve of it; **a public relations man; he works in public relations; a public relations firm handles all our publicity; a public relations exercise** = a campaign to improve public relations
◊ **public sector** *noun* nationalized industries and services; **a report on wage rises in the public sector** *or* **on public sector wage settlements; public sector borrowing requirement** = amount of money which a government has to borrow to pay for its own spending

publication *noun* **(a)** making something public; **the publication of the latest trade figures (b)** printed document which is to be sold *or* given to the public; **he asked the library for a list of government publications; the company has six business publications** = the company publishes six magazines or newspapers referring to business NOTE: no plural for (a)

publicity *noun* attracting the attention of the public to products or services by mentioning them in the media; **publicity agency** *or* **publicity bureau** = office which organizes publicity for companies who do not have publicity departments; **publicity budget** = money allowed for expenditure on publicity; **publicity campaign** = period when planned publicity takes place; **publicity copy** = text of an advertisement before it is printed; **publicity department** = section of a company which organizes the company's publicity; **publicity expenditure** = money spent on publicity; **publicity manager** = person in charge of a publicity department; **publicity matter** = sheets *or* posters *or* leaflets used for publicity NOTE: no plural
◊ **publicize** *verb* to attract people's attention to a product for sale *or* a service *or* an entertainment; **the campaign is intended to publicize the services of the tourist board; we are trying to publicize our products by advertisements on buses**

publish *verb* to have a document (such as a catalogue *or* book *or* magazine *or* newspaper) written and printed and then sell it *or* give it to the public; **the society publishes its list of members annually; the government has not published the figures on which its proposals are based; the company publishes six magazines for the business market**
◊ **publisher** *noun* person *or* company which publishes

pull off *verb informal* to succeed in negotiating a deal
◊ **pull out** *verb* to stop being part of a deal *or* agreement; **our Australian partners pulled out of the contract**

pump priming *noun* government investment in new projects which it hopes will benefit the economy

punched card *noun* card with holes in it which a computer can read and store as information

punt 1 *noun* money used in the Republic of Ireland 2 *verb* to gamble *or* to bet (on something)
◊ **punter** *noun* person who gambles *or* who hopes to make money on the Stock Exchange

purchase 1 *noun* thing which has been bought; **to make a purchase** = to buy something; **purchase book** = records of purchases; **purchase ledger** = book in which expenditure is noted; **purchase order** = official order made out by a purchasing department for goods which a company wants to buy; **we cannot supply you without a purchase order number;** **purchase price** = price paid for something; **purchase tax** = tax paid on things which are bought; **bulk purchase** *or* **quantity purchase** = buying of large quantities of goods at low prices; **cash purchase** = purchase made in cash; **hire purchase** = system of buying something by paying a sum regularly each month; **he is buying a refrigerator on hire purchase; hire purchase agreement** = contract to pay for something by instalments 2 *verb* to buy; **to purchase something for cash** = to pay cash for something
◊ **purchaser** *noun* person *or* company which purchases; **the company is looking for a purchaser** = the company is trying to find someone who will buy it; **the company has found a purchaser for its warehouse**
◊ **purchasing** *noun* buying; **purchasing department** = section of a company which deals with buying of stock, raw materials, equipment, etc.; **purchasing manager** = head of a purchasing department; **purchasing officer** = person in a company *or* organization who is responsible for buying stock, raw materials, equipment, etc.; **purchasing power** = quantity of goods which can be bought by a group of people *or* with an amount of money; **the decline in the purchasing power of the pound; central purchasing** = purchasing organized by the main office for all departments or branches
NOTE: no plural

purpose *noun* aim *or* plan; **we need the** invoice for tax purposes *or* **for the purpose of declaration to the tax authorities** = in order for it to be declared to the tax authorities

put 1 *noun* **put option** = right to sell shares at a certain price at a certain date 2 *verb* to place *or* to fix; **the accounts put the stock value at £10,000** = the accounts state that the value of the stock is £10,000; **to put a proposal to the vote** = to ask a meeting to vote for *or* against the proposal; **to put a proposal to the board** = to ask the board to consider a suggestion
NOTE: **putting - put**
◊ **put down** *verb* **(a)** to make a deposit; **to put down money on a house** **(b)** to write an item in a ledger *or* an account book; **to put down a figure for expenses**
◊ **put in** *verb* **to put an ad in a paper** = to have an ad printed in a newspaper; **to put in a bid for something** = to offer (usually in writing) to buy something; **to put in an estimate for something** = to give someone a written calculation of the probable costs of carrying out a job; **to put in a claim for damage** = to ask an insurance company to pay for damage; **the union put in a 6% wage claim** = the union asked for a 6% increase in wages
◊ **put into** *verb* to **put money into a business** = to invest money in a business
◊ **put off** *verb* to arrange for something to take place later than planned; **the meeting was put off for two weeks; he asked if we could put the visit off until tomorrow**
◊ **put on** *verb* to put an item on the agenda = to list an item for discussion at a meeting; **to put an embargo on trade** = to forbid trade; **property shares put on gains of 10%-15%** = shares in property companies increased in value by 10%-15%
◊ **put out** *verb* to send out; **to put work out to freelancers; we put all our typing out to a bureau; to put work out to contract** = to decide that work should be done by a company on a contract, rather than employ members of staff to do it
◊ **put up** *verb* **(a) who put up the money for the shop?** = who provided the investment money for the shop to start?; **to put something up for sale** = to advertise that something is for sale; **when he retired he decided to put his town flat up for sale** **(b)** to increase *or* to make higher; **the shop has put up all its prices by 5%**

Qq

quadruplicate *noun* **in quadruplicate** = with the original and three copies; **the invoices are printed in quadruplicate**
NOTE: no plural

qualification *noun* **(a)** proof that you have completed a specialized course of study; **to have the right qualifications for the job**; **professional qualifications** = documents which show that someone has successfully finished a course of study which allows him to work in one of the professions **(b)** period of qualification = time which has to pass before someone qualifies for something
◇ **qualify** *verb* **(a) to qualify for** = to be in the right position for *or* to be entitled to; **the company does not qualify for a government grant; she qualifies for unemployment pay (b) to qualify as** = to follow a specialized course and pass examinations so that you can do a certain job; **she has qualified as an accountant; he will qualify as a solicitor next year (c)** the auditors have qualified the accounts = the auditors have found something in the accounts of the company which they do not agree with, and have noted it
◇ **qualified** *adjective* **(a)** having passed special examinations in a subject; **she is a qualified accountant; we have appointed a qualified designer to supervise the new factory project; highly qualified** = with very good results in examinations; **all our staff are highly qualified; they employ twenty-six highly qualified engineers (b)** with some reservations *or* conditions; **qualified acceptance of a contract; the plan received qualified approval from the board (c) qualified accounts** = accounts which have been noted by the auditors because they contain something with which the auditors do not agree
◇ **qualifying** *adjective* **(a) qualifying period** = time which has to pass before something qualifies for a grant *or* subsidy, etc.; **there is a six-month qualifying period before you can get a grant from the local authority (b) qualifying shares** = number of shares which you need to earn to get a bonus issue *or* to be a director of the company, etc.

quality *noun* **(a)** what something is like *or* how good or bad something is; **good quality** *or* **bad quality; we sell only quality farm produce** = we sell only farm produce of the best quality; **there is a market for good quality secondhand computers; high quality** *or* **top quality** = very best quality; **the store specializes in high quality imported items (b) quality control** = checking that the quality of a product is good; **quality controller** = person who checks the quality of a product
NOTE: no plural

quango *noun* official body, set up by a government to investigate or deal with a special problem

quantify *verb* **to quantify the effect of something** = to show the effect of something in figures; **it is impossible to quantify the effect of the new legislation on our turnover**
◇ **quantifiable** *adjective* which can be quantified; **the effect of the change in the discount structure is not quantifiable**

quantity *noun* **(a)** amount *or* number of items; **a small quantity of illegal drugs; he bought a large quantity of spare parts (b)** large amount; **the company offers a discount for quantity purchase; quantity discount** = discount given to a customer who buys large quantities of goods **(c) to carry out a quantity survey** = to estimate the amount of materials and the cost of the labour required for a construction project; **quantity surveyor** = person who carries out a quantity survey

quart *noun* old measure of liquids *or* of loose goods, such as seeds (= 1.136 litres)

quarter *noun* **(a)** one of four equal parts; **a quarter of a litre** *or* **a quarter litre** = 250 millilitres; **a quarter of an hour** = 15 minutes; **three quarters** = 75%; **three**

quarters of the staff are less than thirty years old; he paid only a quarter of the list price **(b)** period of three months; **first quarter** or **second quarter** or **third quarter** or **fourth quarter** or **last quarter** = periods of three months from January to the end of March or from April to the end of June or from July to the end of September or from October to the end of the year; **the instalments are payable at the end of each quarter; the first quarter's rent is payable in advance; quarter day** = day at the end of a quarter, when rents or fees, etc. should be paid **(c)** *US informal* 25 cent coin

◊ **quarterly** *adjective & adverb* happening every three months or happening four times a year; **there is a quarterly charge for electricity; the bank sends us a quarterly statement; we agreed to pay the rent quarterly** or **on a quarterly basis**

QUOTE: corporate profits for the first quarter showed a 4 per cent drop from last year's final three months *Financial Times*
QUOTE: economists believe the economy is picking up this quarter and will do better still in the second half of the year *Sunday Times*

quartile *noun* one of three figures below which 25%, 50% or 75% of a total falls

quasi- *prefix* almost or which seems like; **a quasi-official body**

quay *noun* place in a harbour where ships tie up; **price ex quay** = price of goods after they have been unloaded, not including transport from the harbour

QC = QUEEN'S COUNSEL

query 1 *noun* question; **the chief accountant had to answer a mass of queries from the auditors 2** *verb* to ask a question about something or to suggest that something may be wrong; **the shareholders queried the payments to the chairman's son**

question 1 *noun* **(a)** words which need an answer; **the managing director refused to answer questions about redundancies; the market research team prepared a series of questions to test the public's reactions to colour and price (b)** problem; **he raised the question of moving to less expensive offices; the main question is that of cost; the board discussed the question of redundancy pay-**

ments **2** *verb* **(a)** to ask questions; **the police questioned the accounts staff for four hours; she questioned the chairman on the company's investment policy (b)** to query or to suggest that something may be wrong; **we all question how accurate the computer printout is**

◊ **questionnaire** *noun* printed list of questions, especially used in market research; **to send out a questionnaire to test the opinions of users of the system; to answer** or **to fill in a questionnaire about holidays abroad**

queue 1 *noun* **(a)** line of people waiting one behind the other; **to form a queue** or **to join a queue; queues formed at the doors of the bank when the news spread about its possible collapse; dole queue** = line of people waiting to collect their unemployment money **(b)** series of documents (such as orders, application forms) which are dealt with in order; **his order went to the end of the queue** = his order was dealt with last; **mortgage queue** = list of people waiting for mortgages **2** *verb* to form a line one after the other for something; **when food was rationed, people had to queue for bread; we queued for hours to get tickets; a list of companies queueing to be launched on the Stock Exchange**

quick *adjective* fast or not taking any time; **the company made a quick recovery; he is looking for a quick return on his investments; we are hoping for a quick sale** ◊ **quickly** *adverb* without taking much time; **the sale of the company went through quickly; the accountant quickly looked through the pile of invoices**

quiet *adjective* calm or not excited; **the market is very quiet; currency exchanges were quieter after the government's statement on exchange rates; on the quiet** = in secret; **he transferred his bank account to Switzerland on the quiet**

quit *verb* to resign or to leave (a job); **he quit after an argument with the managing director; several of the managers are quitting to set up their own company** NOTE: **quitting - quit**

quite *adverb* **(a)** more or less; **he is quite a good salesman; she can type quite fast; sales are quite satisfactory in the first**

quarter (b) very *or* completely; **he is quite capable of running the department alone; the company is quite possibly going to be sold** (c) **quite a few** *or* **quite a lot** = many; **quite a few of our sales staff are women; quite a lot of orders come in the pre-Christmas period**

quorum *noun* number of people who have to be present at a meeting to make it valid; **to have a quorum** = to have enough people present for a meeting to go ahead; **do we have a quorum?**

quota *noun* fixed amount of something which is allowed; **import quota** = fixed quantity of a particular type of goods which the government allows to be imported; **the government has imposed a quota on the importation of cars; the quota on imported cars has been lifted; quota system** = system where imports *or* supplies are regulated by fixing maximum amounts; **to arrange distribution through a quota system** = to arrange distribution by allowing each distributor only a certain number of items

QUOTE: Canada agreed to a new duty-free quota of 600,000 tonnes a year
Globe and Mail (Toronto)

quote 1 *verb* (a) to repeat words used by someone else; to repeat a reference number; **he quoted figures from the annual report; in reply please quote this number; when making a complaint please quote the batch number printed on the box; he replied, quoting the number of the account** (b) to estimate *or* to say what costs may be; **to quote a price for supplying stationery; their prices are always quoted in dollars; he quoted me a price of £1,026; can you quote for supplying 20,000 envelopes?** 2 *noun informal* estimate of how much something will cost; **to give someone a quote for supplying computers; we have asked for quotes for refitting the shop; his quote was the lowest of three; we accepted the lowest quote**
◇ **quotation** *noun* (a) estimate of how much something will cost; **they sent in their quotation for the job; to ask for quotations for refitting the shop; his quotation was much lower than all the others; we accepted the lowest quotation** (b) quotation on the Stock Exchange *or* Stock Exchange

quotation = listing of the price of a share on the Stock Exchange; **the company is going for a quotation on the Stock Exchange** = the company has applied to the Stock Exchange to have its shares listed; **we are seeking a stock market quotation**
◇ **quoted** *adjective* quoted company = company whose shares can be bought or sold on the Stock Exchange; **quoted shares** = shares which can be bought or sold on the Stock Exchange

QUOTE: a Bermudan-registered company quoted on the Luxembourg stock exchange *Lloyd's List*
QUOTE: banks operating on the foreign exchange market refrained from quoting forward US/Hongkong dollar exchange rates *South China Morning Post*

qty = QUANTITY

qwerty *or* **QWERTY** *noun* **qwerty keyboard** = English language keyboard for a typewriter or computer, where the first letters are Q-W-E-R-T-Y; **the computer has a normal qwerty keyboard**

Rr

R&D = RESEARCH AND DEVELOPMENT **the R&D department; the company spends millions on R&D**

rack *noun* (a) frame to hold items for display; **card rack; display rack; magazine rack; rack jobber** = wholesaler who sells goods by putting them on racks in retail shops (b) **rack rent** = (i) very high rent; (ii) full yearly rent of a property let on a normal lease

racket *noun* illegal deal which makes a lot of money; **he runs a cut-price ticket racket**
◇ **racketeer** *noun* person who runs a racket

raid *noun* **dawn raid** = buying large numbers of shares in a company at the beginning of a day's trading; **bear raid** = selling large numbers of shares to try to bring down prices

◇ **raider** *noun* company which buys shares in another company before making a takeover bid

rail *noun* railway *or* system of travel using trains; **six million commuters travel to work by rail each day; we ship all our goods by rail; rail travellers are complaining about rising fares; rail travel is cheaper than air travel; free on rail** = price including all the seller's costs until the goods are delivered to the railway for shipment

◇ **railhead** *noun* end of a railway line; **the goods will be sent to the railhead by lorry**

◇ **railroad** *noun* *US* system using trains to carry passengers and goods

◇ **railway** *noun* system using trains to carry passengers and goods; **a railway station; a railway line; the British railway network**

raise **1** *noun* *US* increase in salary; **he asked the boss for a raise; she is pleased - she has had her raise**
NOTE: GB English is **rise**
2 *verb* **(a)** to ask a meeting to discuss a question; **to raise a question** *or* **a point at a meeting; in answer to the questions raised by Mr Smith; the chairman tried to prevent the question of redundancies being raised (b) to raise an invoice** = to write out an invoice **(c)** to increase *or* to make higher; **the government has raised the tax levels; air fares will be raised on June 1st; the company raised its dividend by 10%; when the company raised its prices, it lost half of its share of the market (d)** to obtain (money) *or* to organize (a loan); **the company is trying to raise the capital to fund its expansion programme; the government raises more money by indirect taxation than by direct; where will he raise the money from to start up his business?**

QUOTE: the company said yesterday that its recent share issue has been oversubscribed, raising A$225.5m   *Financial Times*
QUOTE: investment trusts can raise capital, but this has to be done as a company does, by a rights issue of equity   *Investors Chronicle*

rake in *verb* to gather together; **to rake in cash** *or* **to rake it in** = to make a lot of money

◇ **rake-off** *noun* commission; **the group gets a rake-off on all the company's sales; he**

got a **£100,000 rake-off for introducing the new business**
NOTE: plural is **rake-offs**

rally **1** *noun* rise in price when the trend has been downwards; **shares staged a rally on the Stock Exchange; after a brief rally shares fell back to a new low 2** *verb* to rise in price, when the trend has been downwards; **shares rallied on the news of the latest government figures**

ramp *noun* **loading ramp** = raised platform which makes it easier to load goods onto a lorry

random *adjective* done without making any special choice; **random check** = check on items taken from a group without any special choice; **random error** = computer error which has no special reason; **random sample** = sample for testing taken without any choice; **random sampling** = choosing samples for testing without any special selection; **at random** = without special choice; **the chairman picked out two salesmen's reports at random**

range **1** *noun* **(a)** series of items from which the customer can choose; **we offer a wide range of sizes** *or* **range of styles; their range of products** *or* **product range is too narrow; we have the most modern range of models** *or* **model range on the market (b)** variation from small to large; **I am looking for something in the £2 - 3 price range; we make shoes in a wide range of prices (c)** type of variety; **this falls within the company's range of activities 2** *verb* to vary *or* to be different; **the company sells products ranging from the cheap downmarket pens to imported luxury items; the company's salary scale ranges from £5,000 for a trainee to £50,000 for the managing director; our activities range from mining in the USA to computer servicing in Scotland**

rank **1** *noun* position in a company *or* an organization; **all managers are of equal rank; in rank order** = in order according to position of importance **2** *verb* **(a)** to classify in order of importance; **candidates are ranked in order of appearance (b)** to be in a certain position; **the non-voting shares rank equally with the voting shares; all managers rank equally** = all managers have the same status in the company

◇ **rank and file** *noun* ordinary members of a trade union; **the rank and file of the trade union membership; the decision was not liked by the rank and file; rank-and-file members** = ordinary members

◇ **ranking** *adjective* in a certain position; **high-ranking official; he is the top-ranking** *or* **the senior-ranking official in the delegation** = the member of the delegation who occupies the highest official post

rapid *adjective* fast *or* quick; **we offer 5% discount for rapid settlement** = we take 5% off the price if the customer pays quickly

◇ **rapidly** *adverb* quickly *or* fast; **the company rapidly ran up debts of over £1m; the new clothes shop rapidly increased sales**

rare *adjective* not common; **experienced salesmen are rare these days; it is rare to find a small business with good cash flow**

◇ **rarely** *adverb* not often; **the company's shares are rarely sold on the Stock Exchange; the chairman is rarely in his office on Friday afternoons**

rata *see* PRO RATA

rate 1 *noun* **(a)** money charged for time worked or work completed; **all-in rate** = price which covers all items in a purchase (such as delivery, tax and insurance, as well as the goods themselves); **fixed rate** = charge which cannot be changed; **flat rate** = charge which always stays the same; **a flat-rate increase of 10%; we pay a flat rate for electricity each quarter; he is paid a flat rate of £2 per thousand; full rate** = full charge, with no reductions; **the going rate** = the usual *or* the current rate of payment; **the market rate** = normal price in the market; **we pay the going rate** *or* **the market rate for typists; the going rate for offices is £10 per square foot; reduced rate** = specially cheap charge **(b) discount rate** = percentage taken by a bank when it buys bills; **insurance rates** = amount of premium which has to be paid per £1000 of insurance; **interest rate** *or* **rate of interest** = percentage charge for borrowing money; **rate of return** = amount of interest *or* dividend which comes from an investment, shown as a percentage of the money invested **(c) bank base rates** = basic rate of interest which a bank uses to

calculate the actual rate of interest on loans to customers; **cross rate** = exchange rate between two currencies expressed in a third currency; **exchange rate** *or* **rate of exchange** = rate at which one currency is exchanged for another; **what is today's rate** *or* **the current rate for the dollar?; to calculate costs on a fixed exchange rate** = to calculate costs on an exchange rate which does not change; **forward rate** = rate for purchase of foreign currency at a fixed price for delivery at a later date; **freight rates** = charges for transporting goods; **letter rate** *or* **parcel rate** = postage (calculated by weight) for sending a letter *or* a parcel; **it is more expensive to send a packet letter rate but it will get there quicker; night rate** = cheap telephone calls at night **(d)** amount *or* number *or* speed compared with something else; **the rate of increase in redundancies; the rate of absenteeism** *or* **the absenteeism rate always increases in fine weather; birth rate** = number of children born per 1,000 of the population; **call rate** = number of calls (per day *or* per week) which a salesman makes on customers; **depreciation rate** = rate at which an asset is depreciated each year in the company accounts; **error rate** = number of mistakes per thousand entries *or* per page; **rate of sales** = speed at which units are sold **(e)** *GB* local taxes on property; **the local authority has fixed** *or* **has set the rate for next year; our rates have gone up by 25% this year** 2 *verb* **(a)** to **rate someone highly** = to value someone *or* to think someone is very good **(b) highly-rated part of London** = part of London with high local taxes

◇ **rateable** *adjective* **rateable value** = value of a property as a basis for calculating local taxes

◇ **ratepayer** *noun* **domestic ratepayer** = person who pays local taxes on a house *or* flat; **business ratepayer** = business which pays local taxes on a shop *or* factory, etc.

QUOTE: state-owned banks cut their prime rate a percentage point to 11% *Wall Street Journal*
QUOTE: the unions had argued that public sector pay rates had slipped behind rates applying in private sector employment
Australian Financial Review
QUOTE: royalties have been levied at a rate of 12.5% of full production *Lloyd's List*

ratify *verb* to approve officially; **the agreement has to be ratified by the board**

◊ **ratification** *noun* official approval; **the agreement has to go to the board for ratification**

rating *noun* **(a)** valuing of property; **rating officer** = official in a local authority who decides the rateable value of a house **(b) credit rating** = amount which a credit agency feels a customer will be able to repay; **merit rating** = judging how well a worker does his work, so that he can be paid according to merit; **performance rating** = judging how well a share *or* a company has performed **(c) ratings** = estimated number of people who watch TV programmes; **the show is high in the ratings, which means it will attract good publicity**

ratio *noun* proportion *or* quantity of something compared to something else; **the ratio of successes to failures; our product outsells theirs by a ratio of two to one; price/earnings ratio (P/E ratio)** = comparison between the market price of a share and the current dividend it produces; **the shares sell at a P/E ratio of 7**

ration *verb* to allow someone only a certain amount (of food *or* money); **to ration investment capital** *or* **to ration funds for investment; to ration mortgages** = to make only a certain amount of money available for house mortgages, and so restrict the number of mortgages which can be given; **mortgages are rationed for first-time buyers**
◊ **rationing** *noun* allowing only a certain amount of something to be sold; **there may be a period of food rationing this winter; building societies are warning of mortgage rationing**
NOTE: no plural

rationale *noun* set of reasons for doing something; **I do not understand the rationale behind the decision to sell the warehouse**

rationalization *noun* streamlining *or* making more efficient
◊ **rationalize** *verb* to streamline *or* to make more efficient; **the rail company is trying to rationalize its freight services**

rat race *noun* competition for success in business *or* in a career; **he decided to get out of the rat race and buy a small farm**
NOTE: no plural

raw *adjective* in the original state *or* not processed; **raw data** = data as it is put into a computer, without being analyzed; **raw materials** = substances which have not been manufactured (such as wool, wood, sand)

QUOTE: it makes sense for them to produce goods for sale back home in the US from plants in Britain where raw materials are relatively cheap
Duns Business Month

re *preposition* about *or* concerning *or* referring to; **re your inquiry of May 29th; re: Smith's memo of yesterday; re: the agenda for the AGM**

re- *prefix* again

reach *verb* **(a)** to arrive at a place *or* at a point; **the plane reaches Hong Kong at midday; sales reached £1m in the first four months of the year; I did not reply because your letter never reached me (b)** to come to; **to reach an agreement** = to agree; **to reach an accommodation with creditors** = to agree terms for a settlement with creditors; **to reach a decision** = to decide; **the two parties reached an agreement over the terms for the contract; the board reached a decision about closing the factory**

react *verb* **to react to** = to do *or* to say something in reply to what someone has done *or* said; **shares reacted sharply to the fall in the exchange rate; how will the chairman react when we tell him the news?**
◊ **reaction** *noun* change *or* action in reply to something said or done; **the reaction of the shares to the news of the takeover bid**

read *verb* to look at printed words and understand them; **the terms and conditions are printed in very small letters so that they are difficult to read; has the managing director read your report on sales in India?; can the computer read this information?** = can the computer take in this information and understand it or analyze it?
◊ **readable** *adjective* which can be read; **machine-readable codes** = sets of signs or letters (such as bar codes, post codes) which can be read and understood by a

computer; **the data has to be presented in computer-readable form** = in a form which a computer can read

readjust *verb* to adjust again; **to readjust prices to take account of the rise in the costs of raw materials; shares prices readjusted quickly to the news of the devaluation**
◇ **readjustment** *noun* act of readjusting; **a readjustment in pricing; after the devaluation there was a period of readjustment in the exchange rates**

readvertise *verb* to advertise again; **to readvertise a post** = to put in a second advertisement for a vacant post; **all the candidates failed the test, so we will just have to readvertise**
◇ **readvertisement** *noun* second advertisement for a vacant post

ready *adjective* **(a)** fit to be used *or* to be sold; **the order will be ready for delivery next week; the driver had to wait because the shipment was not ready; make-ready time** = time to get a machine ready to start production **(b) ready cash** = money which is immediately available for payment; **these items find a ready sale in the Middle East** = these items sell rapidly *or* easily in the Middle East
◇ **ready-made** *or* **ready-to-wear** *adjective* (clothes) which are mass-produced, not made for each customer personally; **the ready-to-wear trade has suffered from foreign competition**

real *adjective* **(a)** true *or* not an imitation; **his case is made of real leather** *or* **he has a real leather case; that car is a real bargain at £300; real income** *or* **real wages** = income which is available for spending after tax, etc. has been deducted; **in real terms** = actually *or* really; **prices have gone up by 3% but with inflation running at 5% that is a fall in real terms (b) real time** = time when a computer is working on the processing of data while the problem to which the data refers is actually taking place; **real-time system** = computer system where data is inputted directly into the computer which automatically processes it to produce information which can be used immediately **(c) real estate** = property (land or buildings); **he made his money from real estate deals in the 1970s;** *US* **real estate agent** =

person who sells property for customers
◇ **really** *adverb* in fact; **the company is really making an acceptable profit; the office building really belongs to the chairman's father; the shop is really a general store, though it does carry some books**
◇ **realtor** *noun US* estate agent *or* person who sells real estate for customers
◇ **realty** *noun* property *or* real estate

QUOTE: real wages have been held down dramatically: they have risen as an annual rate of only 1% in the last two years *Sunday Times*
QUOTE: sterling M3 rose by 13.5% in the year to August - seven percentage points faster than the rate of inflation and the biggest increase in real terms since 1972-3 *Economist*
QUOTE: on top of the cost of real estate. the investment in inventory and equipment to open a typical warehouse comes to around $5 million *Duns Business Month*

realize *verb* **(a)** to understand clearly; **he soon realized the meeting was going to vote against his proposal; the small shopkeepers realized that the hypermarket would take away some of their trade; when she went into the manager's office she did not realize she was going to be promoted (b)** to make something become real; **to realize a project** *or* **a plan** = to put a project *or* a plan into action **(c)** to sell for money; **to realize property** *or* **assets; the sale realized £100,000**
◇ **realizable** *adjective* **realizable assets** = assets which can be sold for money
◇ **realization** *noun* **(a)** gradual understanding; **the chairman's realization that he was going to be outvoted (b)** making real; **the realization of a project** = putting as project into action; **the plan moved a stage nearer realization when the contracts were signed (c) realization of assets** = selling of assets for money

reapply *verb* to apply again; **when he saw that the job had still not been filled, he reapplied for it**
◇ **reapplication** *noun* second application

reappoint *verb* to appoint someone again; **he was reappointed chairman for a further three-year period**

◇ **reappointment** *noun* being reappointed

reason *noun* thing which explains why something has happened; **the airline gave no reason for the plane's late arrival; the personnel officer asked him for the reason why he was late again; the chairman was asked for his reasons for closing the factory**
◇ **reasonable** *adjective* **(a)** sensible *or* not annoyed; **the manager of the shop was very reasonable when she tried to explain that she had left her credit cards at home; no reasonable offer refused** = we will accept any offer which is not extremely low **(b)** moderate *or* not expensive; **the restaurant offers good food at reasonable prices**

reassess *verb* to assess again
◇ **reassessment** *noun* new assessment

reassign *verb* to assign again
◇ **reassignment** *noun* new assignment

reassure *verb* **(a)** to make someone calm *or* less worried; **the markets were reassured by the government statement on import controls; the manager tried to reassure her that she would not lose her job (b)** to reinsure *or* to spread the risk of an insurance by asking another insurance company to cover part of it and receive part of the premium
◇ **reassurance** *noun* making someone calm
NOTE: no plural

rebate *noun* **(a)** reduction in the amount of money to be paid; **to offer a 10% rebate on selected goods (b)** money returned to someone because he has paid too much; **he got a tax rebate at the end of the year**

rebound *verb* to go back up again quickly; **the market rebounded on the news of the government's decision**

recd = RECEIVED

receipt 1 *noun* **(a)** paper showing that money has been paid *or* that something has been received; **customs receipt; rent receipt; receipt for items purchased; please produce your receipt if you want to exchange items; receipt book** *or* **book of receipts** = book of blank receipts to be filled in when purchases are made **(b)** act of receiving something; **to acknowledge receipt of a letter** = to write to say that you have received a letter; **we acknowledge receipt of your letter of the 15th; goods will be supplied with thirty days of receipt of order; invoices are payable within thirty days of receipt; on receipt of the notification, the company lodged an appeal (c) receipts** = money taken in sales; **to itemize receipts and expenditure; receipts are down against the same period of last year**
NOTE: no plural for (b)
2 *verb* to stamp *or* to sign a document to show that it has been received *or* to stamp an invoice to show that it has been paid

QUOTE: the public sector borrowing requirement is kept low by treating the receipts from selling public assets as a reduction in borrowing
Economist
QUOTE: gross wool receipts for the selling season to end June appear likely to top $2 billion
Australian Financial Review

receive *verb* to get something which has been delivered; **we received the payment ten days ago; the workers have not received any salary for six months; the goods were received in good condition; "received with thanks"** = words put on an invoice to show that a sum has been paid
◇ **receivable** *adjective* which can be received; **accounts receivable** = money owed to a company; **bills receivable** = bills which a creditor will receive
◇ **receivables** *plural noun* money which is owed to a company
◇ **receiver** *noun* **(a)** person who receives something; **the receiver of the shipment (b) official receiver** = government official who is appointed to run a company which is in financial difficulties, to pay off its debts as far as possible, and to close it down; **the court appointed a receiver for the company; the company is in the hands of the receiver**
◇ **receivership** *noun* **the company went into receivership** = the company was put into the hands of a receiver
◇ **receiving** *noun* **(a)** act of getting something which has been delivered; **receiving clerk** = official who works in a receiving office; **receiving department** =

section of a company which deals with incoming goods *or* payments; **receiving office** = office where goods *or* payments are received **(b) receiving order** = order from a court appointing a receiver to a company
NOTE: no plural

recent *adjective* which happened not very long ago; **the company's recent acquisition of a chain of shoe shops; his recent appointment to the board; we will mail you our most recent catalogue**
◊ **recently** *adverb* not very long ago; **the company recently started on an expansion programme; they recently decided to close the branch office in Australia**

reception *noun* place (in a hotel *or* office) where visitors register *or* say who they have come to see; **reception clerk** = person who works at the reception desk; **reception desk** = desk where customers *or* visitors check in
◊ **receptionist** *noun* person in a hotel *or* office who meets guests *or* clients, answers the phone, etc.

recession *noun* fall in trade *or* in the economy; **the recession has reduced profits in many companies; several firms have closed factories because of the recession**

recipient *noun* person who receives; **the recipient of an allowance from the company**

reciprocal *adjective* applying from one country *or* person *or* company to another and vice versa; **reciprocal agreement; reciprocal contract; reciprocal holdings** = situation where two companies own shares in each other to prevent takeover bids; **reciprocal trade** = trade between two countries
◊ **reciprocate** *verb* to do the same thing to someone as he has just done to you; **they offered us an exclusive agency for their cars and we reciprocated with an offer of the agency for our buses**

QUOTE: in 1934 Congress authorized President Roosevelt to seek lower tariffs with any country willing to reciprocate   *Duns Business Month*

reckon *verb* **(a)** to calculate; **to reckon the costs at £25,000; we reckon the loss to be**

over £1m; **they reckon the insurance costs to be too high (b) to reckon on** = to depend on *or* to expect something to happen; **they reckon on being awarded the contract; he can reckon on the support of the managing director**

recognize *verb* **(a)** to know someone *or* something because you have seen *or* heard them before; **I recognized his voice before he said who he was; do you recognize the handwriting on the letter? (b) to recognize a union** = to accept that a union can act on behalf of staff; **although all the staff had joined the union, the management refused to recognize it; recognized agent** = agent who is approved by the company for which he acts
◊ **recognition** *noun* act of recognizing; **to grant a trade union recognition** = to recognize a trade union

recommend *verb* **(a)** to suggest that something should be done; **the investment adviser recommended buying shares in aircraft companies; we do not recommend bank shares as a safe investment; manufacturer's recommended price (MRP)** *or* **recommended retail price (RRP)** = price which a manufacturer suggests the product should be sold at on the retail market, though often reduced by the retailer; **"all typewriters - 20% off MRP" (b)** to say that someone *or* something is good; **he recommended a shop in the High Street for shoes; I certainly would not recommend Miss Smith for the job; the board meeting recommended a dividend of 10p a share; can you recommend a good hotel in Amsterdam?**
◊ **recommendation** *noun* saying that someone *or* something is good; **we appointed him on the recommendation of his former employer**

reconcile *verb* to make two accounts *or* statements agree; **to reconcile one account with another; to reconcile the accounts**
◊ **reconciliation** *noun* making two accounts *or* statements agree; **reconciliation statement** = statement which explains why two accounts do not agree

reconstruction *noun* building again; **the economic reconstruction of an area after a disaster**

record 1 *noun* **(a)** report of something which has happened; **the chairman signed the minutes as a true record of the last meeting; for the record** *or* **to keep the record straight** = to note something which has been done; **for the record, I would like these sales figures to be noted in the minutes; on record** = correctly reported; **the chairman is on record as saying that profits are set to rise; off the record** = unofficially *or* in private; **he made some remarks off the record about the disastrous home sales figures (b) records** = documents which give information; **the names of customers are kept in the company's records; we find from our records that our invoice number 1234 has not been paid (c)** description of what has happened in the past; **the salesman's record of service** *or* **service record; the company's record in industrial relations; track record** = success or failure of a company *or* salesman in the past; **he has a good track record as a salesman; the company has no track record in the computer market (d)** success which is better than anything before; **record sales** *or* **record losses** *or* **record profits** = sales *or* losses *or* profits which are higher than ever before; **1985 was a record year for the company; sales for 1983 equalled the record of 1980; our top salesman has set a new record for sales per call; we broke our record for June** = we sold more than we have ever sold before in June **2** *verb* to note *or* to report; **the company has recorded another year of increased sales; your complaint has been recorded and will be investigated; recorded delivery** = mail service where the letters are signed for by the person receiving them

◇ **record-breaking** *adjective* which is better than anything which has happened before; **we are proud of our record-breaking profits in 1984**

◇ **recording** *noun* making of a note; **the recording of an order** *or* **of a complaint**

recoup *verb* **to recoup one's losses** = to get back money which you thought you had lost

recourse *noun* **to decide to have recourse to the courts** = to decide in the end to sue someone

recover *verb* **(a)** to get back something which has been lost; **he never recovered his** money; **the initial investment was never recovered; to recover damages from the driver of the car; to start a court action to recover property (b)** to get better *or* to rise; **the market has not recovered from the rise in oil prices; the stock market fell in the morning, but recovered during the afternoon**

◇ **recoverable** *adjective* which can be got back

◇ **recovery** *noun* **(a)** getting back something which has been lost; **we are aiming for the complete recovery of the money invested; to start an action for recovery of property (b)** movement upwards of shares *or* of the economy; **the economy staged a recovery; the recovery of the economy after a slump; recovery shares** = shares which are likely to go up in value because the company's performance is improving

recruit *verb* **to recruit new staff** = to get new staff to join a company; **we are recruiting staff for our new store**

◇ **recruitment** *or* **recruiting** *noun* the **recruitment of new staff** = looking for new staff to join a company

rectify *verb* to correct something *or* to make something right; **to rectify an entry**

◇ **rectification** *noun* correction

recurrent *adjective* which happens again and again; **a recurrent item of expenditure**

recycle *verb* to take waste material and process it so that it can be used again; **recycled paper** = paper made from waste paper

red *noun* **in the red** = showing a debit or loss; **my bank account is in the red; the company went into the red in 1984; the company is out of the red for the first time since 1950**
NOTE: no plural

◇ **red tape** *noun* official paperwork which takes a long time to complete; **the Australian joint venture has been held up by government red tape**
NOTE: no plural

redeem *verb* **(a)** to pay off a loan *or* a debt; **to redeem a mortgage; to redeem a debt (b) to redeem a bond** = to sell a bond for cash

◇ **redeemable** *adjective* which can be sold for cash

redemption *noun* **(a)** repayment of a loan; **redemption date** = date on which a loan, etc., is due to be repaid; **redemption before due date** = paying back a loan before the date when repayment is due; **redemption value** = value of a security when redeemed; **redemption yield** = yield on a security including interest and its redemption value **(b)** repayment of a debt; **redemption of a mortgage**
NOTE: no plural

redeploy *verb* to move workers from one place to another *or* to give workers totally different jobs to do; **we closed the design department and redeployed the workforce in the publicity and sales departments**
◇ **redeployment** *noun* moving workers from one place to another

redevelop *verb* to knock down the buildings on a site, and build new ones
◇ **redevelopment** *noun* knocking down of existing buildings to replace them with new ones; **the redevelopment plan was rejected by the planning committee**

redistribute *verb* to move items *or* work *or* money to different areas *or* people; **the government aims to redistribute wealth by taxing the rich and giving grants to the poor; the orders have been redistributed among the company's factories**
◇ **redistribution** *noun* **redistribution of wealth** = sharing wealth among the whole population

redraft *verb* to draft again; **the whole contract had to be redrafted to take in the objections from the chairman**

reduce *verb* to make smaller *or* lower; **to reduce expenditure; to reduce a price; to reduce taxes; we have made some staff redundant to reduce overmanning; prices have been reduced by 15%; carpets are reduced from £100 to £50; the company reduced output because of a fall in demand; the government's policy is to reduce inflation to 5%; to reduce staff** = to sack employees in order to have a smaller number of staff

◇ **reduced** *adjective* lower; **reduced prices have increased unit sales; prices have fallen due to a reduced demand for the goods**

reduction *noun* lowering (of prices, etc.); **price reductions; tax reductions; staff reductions; reduction of expenditure; reduction in demand; the company was forced to make job reductions**

redundancy *noun* **(a)** being no longer employed, because the job is no longer necessary; **redundancy payment** = payment made to a worker to compensate for losing his job; **voluntary redundancy** = situation where the worker asks to be made redundant, usually in return for a large payment **(b)** person who has lost a job because he is not needed any more; **the takeover caused 250 redundancies**
◇ **redundant** *adjective* **(a)** more than is needed *or* useless; **redundant capital; redundant clause in a contract; the new legislation has made clause 6 redundant (b) to make someone redundant** = to decide that a worker is not needed any more; **redundant staff** = staff who have lost their jobs because they are not needed any more

re-elect *verb* to elect again; **he was re-elected chairman**
◇ **re-election** *noun* being elected again; **she is eligible to stand for re-election** = it is possible for her to be re-elected if she wants

re-employ *verb* to employ someone again
◇ **re-employment** *noun* employing someone again

re-engage *verb* **to re-engage staff** = to employ staff again

re-entry *noun* coming back in again; **re-entry visa** *or* **permit** = visa which allows someone to leave a country and go back in again

re-examine *verb* to examine something again
◇ **re-examination** *noun* examining something which has already been examined before

re-export 1 *noun* exporting of goods which have been imported; **re-export trade; we import wool for re-export; the value of re-exports has increased** 2 *verb* to export something which has been imported

◊ **re-exportation** *noun* exporting goods which have been imported

ref = REFERENCE

refer *verb* (a) to mention *or* to deal with *or* to write about something; **we refer to your estimate of May 26th; he referred to an article which he had seen in the "Times"; referring to your letter of June 4th** (b) to pass a problem on to someone else to decide; **to refer a question to a committee; we have referred your complaint to our supplier** (c) **the bank referred the cheque to drawer** = the bank returned the cheque to person who wrote it because there was not enough money in the account to pay it; **"refer to drawer"** = words written on a cheque which a bank refuses to pay
NOTE: **referring - referred**

◊ **referee** *noun* person who can give a report on someone's character *or* ability *or* speed of work, etc.; **to give someone's name as referee; she gave the name of her boss as referee; when applying please give the names of three referees**

◊ **reference** *noun* (a) **terms of reference** = areas which a committee *or* an inspector can deal with; **under the terms of reference of the committee, it cannot investigate complaints from the public; the committee's terms of reference do not cover exports** (b) mentioning *or* dealing with; **with reference to your letter of May 25th** (c) numbers *or* letters which make it possible to find a document which has been filed; **our reference: PC/MS 1234; thank you for your letter (reference 1234); please quote this reference in all correspondence; when replying please quote reference 1234** (d) written report on someone's character *or* ability, etc.; **to write someone a reference *or* to give someone a reference; to ask applicants to supply references; to ask a company for trade references *or* for bank references** = to ask for reports from traders *or* a bank on the company's financial status and reputation; **letter of reference** = letter in which an employer *or* former employer recommends someone for a job; **he enclosed letters of reference from his two previous employers** (e) person who reports on someone's character *or* ability, etc.; **to give someone's name as reference; please use me as a reference if you wish**

refinancing *noun* **refinancing of a loan** = floating a new loan to pay back a previous loan

refit *verb* to fit out (a shop *or* factory *or* office) again
NOTE: **refitting - refitted**
◊ **refitting** *noun* fitting out (of a shop *or* factory *or* office) again

reflate *verb* **to reflate the economy** = to stimulate the economy by increasing the money supply *or* by reducing taxes, leading to increased inflation; **the government's attempts to reflate the economy were not successful**

◊ **reflation** *noun* act of stimulating the economy by increasing the money supply *or* by reducing taxes
NOTE: no plural

◊ **reflationary** *adjective* **reflationary measures** = acts which are likely to stimulate the economy

refresher course *noun* course of study to make you practise your skills again in order to improve them; **he went on a refresher course in bookkeeping**

refund 1 *noun* money paid back; **to ask for a refund; she got a refund after she had complained to the manager; full refund *or* refund in full** = refund of all the money paid; **he got a full refund when he complained about the service** 2 *verb* to pay back money; **to refund the cost of postage; all money will be refunded if the goods are not satisfactory**

◊ **refundable** *adjective* which can be paid back; **refundable deposit; the entrance fee is refundable if you purchase £5 worth of goods**

refuse *verb* to say that you will not do something *or* will not accept something; **they refused to pay; the bank refused to lend the company any more money; he asked for a rise but it was refused; the loan was refused by the bank; the customer refused the goods *or* refused to accept the goods**
NOTE: you refuse **to do something** or refuse **something**

◊ **refusal** *noun* saying no; **his request met with a refusal** = his request was refused; **to give someone first refusal of something** = to allow someone to be the first to decide if they want something or not; **blanket refusal** = refusal to accept many different items

regard *noun* **with regard to** = concerning *or* dealing with; **with regard to your request for unpaid leave**

◊ **regarding** *preposition* concerning *or* dealing with; **instructions regarding the shipment of goods to Africa**

◊ **regardless** *adjective* **regardless of** = in spite of; **the chairman furnished his office regardless of expense** = without thinking of how much it would cost

region *noun* large area of a country; **in the region of** = about *or* approximately; **he was earning a salary in the region of £25,000; the house was sold for a price in the region of £100,000**

◊ **regional** *adjective* referring to a region; **regional planning** = planning the industrial development of a region

register 1 *noun* (a) official list; **to enter something in a register; to keep a register up to date; companies' register** *or* **register of companies** = list of companies, showing their directors and registered addresses; **register of debentures** *or* **debenture register** = list of debenture holders of a company; **register of directors** = official list of the directors of a company which has to be sent to the registrar of companies; **land register** = list of pieces of land, showing who owns it and what buildings are on it; **Lloyd's register** = classified list showing details of all the ships in the world; **register of shareholders** *or* **share register** = list of shareholders in a company with their addresses (b) large book for recording details (as in a hotel, where guests sign in, or in a registry where deaths are recorded) (c) **cash register** = machine which shows and adds the prices of items bought in a shop, with a drawer for keeping the cash received 2 *verb* (a) to write something in an official list; **to register a company; to register a sale; to register a property; to register a trademark** (b) to arrive at a hotel *or* at a conference, sign your name and write your address on a

list; **they registered at the hotel under the name of Macdonald (c)** to send (a letter) by registered post; **I registered the letter, because it contained some money**

◊ **registered** *adjective* (a) which has been noted on an official list; **registered share transaction; registered trademark; the company's registered office** = the head office of the company as noted in the register of companies (b) **registered letter** *or* **registered parcel** = letter *or* parcel which is noted by the post office before it is sent, so that compensation can be claimed if it is lost; **to send documents by registered mail** *or* **registered post**

◊ **registrar** *noun* person who keeps official records; **registrar of companies** *or* **the company registrar**

◊ **registration** *noun* (a) act of having something noted on an official list; **registration of a trademark** *or* **of a share transaction; certificate of registration** *or* **registration certificate** = document showing that an item has been registered; **registration fee** = money paid to have something registered *or* money paid to attend a conference; **registration number** = official number (such as the number of a car) (b) **land registration** = system of registering land and its owners

◊ **registry** *noun* (a) place where official records are kept; *GB* **land registry** = government office where details of land are kept; **registry office** = office where records of births, marriages and deaths are kept (b) **port of registry** = port where a ship is registered

regret *verb* to be sorry; **I regret having to make so many staff redundant; we regret the delay in answering your letter; we regret to inform you of the death of the chairman** NOTE: you **regret doing something** *or* **regret to do something** *or* **regret something**. Note also: **regretting - regretted**

regular *adjective* (a) which happens *or* comes at the same time each day *or* each week *or* each month *or* each year; **his regular train is the 12.45; the regular flight to Athens leaves at 06.00; regular customer** = customer who always buys from the same shop; **regular income** = income which comes in every week or month; **she works freelance so she does not have a regular income; regular staff** = full-time staff (b) ordinary *or* standard; **the regular**

price is $1.25, but we are offering them at 99c; regular size = ordinary size (smaller than economy size, family size, etc.)

◇ **regularly** *adverb* happening often each day *or* week *or* /month *or* year; **the first train in the morning is regularly late**

◇ **regulate** *verb* **(a)** to adjust something so that it works well *or* is correct **(b)** to change *or* maintain something by law; **prices are regulated by supply and demand** = prices are increased or lowered according to supply and demand; **government-regulated price** = price which is imposed by the government

◇ **regulation** *noun* **(a)** act of making sure that something will work well; **the regulation of trading practices (b)** regulations = laws *or* rules; **the new government regulations on housing standards; fire regulations** *or* **safety regulations; regulations concerning imports and exports**
NOTE: no plural for (a)

> QUOTE: EEC regulations which came into effect in July insist that customers can buy cars anywhere in the EEC at the local pre-tax price
> *Financial Times*
> QUOTE: a unit trust is established under the regulations of the Department of Trade, with a trustee, a management company and a stock of units
> *Investors Chronicle*

reimburse *verb* to reimburse someone his expenses = to pay someone back for money which he has spent; **you will be reimbursed for your expenses** *or* **your expenses will be reimbursed**

◇ **reimbursement** *noun* paying back money; **reimbursement of expenses**

reimport **1** *noun* importing of goods which have been exported from the same country **2** *verb* to import goods which have been exported

◇ **reimportation** *noun* importing goods which have been exported

reinstate *verb* to put someone back into a job from which he was dismissed; **the union demanded that the sacked workers should be reinstated**

◇ **reinstatement** *noun* putting someone back into a job from which he was dismissed

reinsure *verb* to spread the risk of an insurance, by asking another insurance company to cover part of it and receive part of the premium

◇ **reinsurance** *noun* act of reinsuring

◇ **reinsurer** *noun* insurance company which accepts to insure part of the risk for another insurer

reinvest *verb* to invest again; **he reinvested the money in government stocks**

◇ **reinvestment** *noun* investing again in the same securities; investing a company's earnings in its own business by using them to create new products for sale

reissue **1** *noun* issue of something again **2** *verb* to issue something again; **the company reissued its catalogue with a new price list**

reject 1 *noun* thing which has been thrown out because it is not of the usual standard; **sale of rejects** *or* **of reject items; to sell off reject stock; reject shop** = shop which specializes in the sale of rejects **2** *verb* to refuse to accept *or* to say that something is not satisfactory; **the union rejected the management's proposals; the company rejected the takeover bid** = the directors recommended that the shareholders should not accept the bid

◇ **rejection** *noun* refusal to accept

related *adjective* connected *or* linked; **related items on the agenda; related company** = company which is partly owned by another company; **earnings-related pension** = pension which is linked to the size of the salary

◇ **relating to** *adverb* referring to *or* connected with; **documents relating to the agreement**

◇ **relation** *noun* **(a)** in relation to = referring to *or* connected with; **documents in relation to the agreement (b)** relations = links (with other people *or* other companies); **we try to maintain good relations with our customers; to enter into relations with a company** = to start discussing a business deal with a company; **to break off relations with someone** = to stop dealing with someone; **industrial relations** *or* **labour relations** = relations between management and workers; **the company has a history of bad labour relations (c)**

public relations (PR) = keeping good links between a company *or* a group and the public so that people know what the company is doing and approve of it; **public relations department** = section of a company which deals with relations with the public; **public relations officer** = official who deals with relations with the public

◊ **relatively** *adverb* more or less; **we have appointed a relatively new PR firm to handle our publicity**

release 1 *noun* (a) setting free; **release from a contract; release of goods from customs (b) day release** = arrangement where a company allows a worker to go to college to study for one day each week; **the junior sales manager is attending a day release course (c) press release** = sheet giving news about something which is sent to newspapers and TV and radio stations so that they can use the information in it; **the company sent out** *or* **issued a press release about the launch of the new car (d) new releases** = new records put on the market
NOTE: no plural for (a)
2 *verb* (a) to free; **to release goods from customs; the customs released the goods against payment of a fine; to release someone from a debt (b)** to make something public; **the company released information about the new mine in Australia; the government has refused to release figures for the number of unemployed women (c)** to put on the market; **to release a new record; to release dues** = to send off orders which had been piling up while a product was out of stock

QUOTE: pressure to ease monetary policy mounted yesterday with the release of a set of pessimistic economic statistics *Financial Times*
QUOTE: the national accounts for the March quarter released by the Australian Bureau of Statistics showed a real increase in GDP
Australian Financial Review

relevant *adjective* which has to do with what is being discussed; **which is the relevant government department? can you give me the relevant papers?**

reliable *adjective* which can be trusted; **reliable company; the sales manager is completely reliable; we have reliable information about our rival's sales; the**

company makes a very reliable product
◊ **reliability** *noun* being reliable; **the product has passed its reliability tests**
NOTE: no plural
◊ **rely on** *verb* to depend on *or* to trust; **the chairman relies on the finance department for information on sales; we rely on part-time staff for most of our mail-order business; do not rely on the agents for accurate market reports**

relief *noun* help; **tax relief** = allowing someone to pay less tax; **there is full tax relief on mortgage interest payments** = no tax is payable on income used to pay interest on a mortgage; **mortgage relief** = allowing someone to pay no tax on mortgage interest payments; **relief shift** = shift which comes to take the place of another shift, usually the shift between the day shift and the night shift
NOTE: no plural

remain *verb* (a) to be left; **half the stock remained unsold; we will sell off the old stock at half price and anything remaining will be thrown away (b)** to stay; **she remained behind at the office after 6.30 to finish her work**
◊ **remainder** 1 *noun* (a) things left behind; **the remainder of the stock will be sold off at half price (b) remainders** = new books sold cheaply; **remainder merchant** = book dealer who buys unsold new books from publishers at a very low price
NOTE: in (a) **remainder** is usually singular and is written with **the**
2 *verb* **to remainder books** = to sell new books off cheaply; **the shop was full of piles of remaindered books**

remember *verb* to bring back into your mind something which you have seen *or* heard *or* read before; **do you remember the name of the Managing Director of Smith Ltd? I cannot remember the make of photocopier which he said was so good; did you remember to ask the switchboard to put my calls through to the boardroom? she remembered seeing the item in a supplier's catalogue**
NOTE: you **remember doing something** which you did in the past; you **remember to do something** in the future

remind *verb* to make someone remember; **I must remind my secretary to book the**

flight for New York; he reminded the chairman that the meeting had to finish at 6.30

◇ **reminder** *noun* letter to remind a customer that he has not paid an invoice; **to send someone a reminder**

remission *noun* **remission of taxes** = refund of taxes which have been overpaid

remit *verb* to send (money); **to remit by cheque**
NOTE: **remitting - remitted**

◇ **remittance** *noun* money which is sent; **please send remittances to the treasurer; the family lives on a weekly remittance from their father in the USA**

remnant *noun* odd piece of a large item sold separately; **remnant sale** *or* **sale of remnants**

remove *verb* to take something away; **we can remove his name from the mailing list; the government has removed the ban on imports from Japan; the minister has removed the embargo on the sale of computer equipment; two directors were removed from the board at the AGM** = two directors were dismissed from the board

◇ **removal** *noun* **(a)** moving to a new house *or* office; **removal** *or* **removals company** = company which specializes in moving the contents of a house *or* an office to a new building **(b)** sacking someone (usually a director) from a job; **the removal of the managing director is going to be very difficult**

remunerate *verb* to pay someone for doing something; **to remunerate someone for their services**

◇ **remuneration** *noun* payment for services; **she has a monthly remuneration of £400**
NOTE: no plural

◇ **remunerative** *adjective* (job) which pays well; **he is in a very remunerative job**

render *verb* **to render an account** = to send in an account; **payment for account rendered; please find enclosed payment per account rendered**

renew *verb* to continue something for a further period of time; **to renew a bill of exchange** *or* **to renew a lease; to renew a**

subscription = to pay a subscription for another year; **to renew an insurance policy** = to pay the premium for another year's insurance

◇ **renewal** *noun* act of renewing; **renewal of a lease** *or* **of a subscription** *or* **of a bill; the lease is up for renewal next month; when is the renewal date of the bill?; renewal notice** = note sent by an insurance company asking the insured person to renew the insurance; **renewal premium** = premium to be paid to renew an insurance
NOTE: no plural

rent **1** *noun* money paid to use an office *or* house *or* factory for a period of time; **high rent** *or* **low rent** = expensive *or* cheap rent; **rents are high in the centre of the town; we cannot afford to pay High Street rents; to pay three months' rent in advance; back rent** = rent owed; **the flat is let at an economic rent** = at a rent which covers all costs to the landlord; **ground rent** = rent paid by the main tenant to the ground landlord; **nominal rent** = very small rent; **rent control** = government regulation of rents; **income from rents** *or* **rent income** = income from letting office *or* houses, etc. **2** *verb* **(a)** to pay money to hire an office *or* house *or* factory *or* piece of equipment for a period of time; **to rent an office** *or* **a car; he rents an office in the centre of town; they were driving a rented car when they were stopped by the police** **(b) to rent (out)** = to own a car *or* office, etc. and let it to someone for money; **we rented part of the building to an American company**

◇ **rental** *noun* money paid to use an office *or* house *or* factory *or* car *or* piece of equipment, etc., for a period of time; **the telephone rental bill comes to over £500 a quarter; rental income** *or* **income from rentals** = income from letting offices *or* houses, etc.; **car rental firm** = company which specializes in offering cars for rent; **fleet rental** = renting all a company's cars from the same company at a special price

QUOTE: top quality office furniture: short or long-term rental 50% cheaper than any other rental company *Australian Financial Review*
QUOTE: office rental growth has been faster in Britain in the first six months of 1985 than in 1984 *Lloyd's List*

renunciation *noun* act of giving up ownership of shares; **letter of renunciation**

= form sent with new shares, which allows the person who has been allotted the shares to refuse to accept them and so sell them to someone else
NOTE: no plural

reopen *verb* to open again; **the office will reopen soon after its refit**
◊ **reopening** *noun* opening again; **the reopening of the store after refitting**

reorder 1 *noun* further order for something which has been ordered before; **the product has only been on the market ten days and we are already getting reorders; reorder level** = minimum amount of stock of an item which must be reordered when stock falls to this amount 2 *verb* to place a new order for something; **we must reorder these items because stock is getting low**

reorganize *verb* to organize in a new way
◊ **reorganization** *noun* new way of organizing; **his job was downgraded in the office reorganization** *or* **in the reorganization of the office; the reorganization of a company** *or* **a company reorganization** = restructuring the finances of a company

rep 1 *noun* = REPRESENTATIVE **to hold a reps' meeting; our reps make on average six calls a day; commission rep** = representative who is not paid a salary but receives a commission on sales 2 *verb informal* = REPRESENT **he reps for two firms on commission**
NOTE: repping - repped

repack *verb* to pack again
◊ **repacking** *noun* packing again

repair 1 *noun* mending *or* making good something which was broken; **to carry out repairs to the machinery; his car is in the garage for repair** 2 *verb* to mend *or* to make good something which is broken; **the photocopier is being repaired; repairing lease** = lease where the tenant is responsible for repairs to the building which he is renting
◊ **repairer** *or* **repair man** *noun* person who carries out repairs; **the repair man has come to mend the photocopier**

repay *verb* to pay back; **to repay money owed; the company had to cut back on expenditure in order to repay its debts; he repaid me in full** = he paid me back all the money he owed me
NOTE: **repaying - repaid**
◊ **repayable** *adjective* which can be paid back; **loan which is repayable over ten years**
◊ **repayment** *noun* paying back; money which is paid back; **the loan is due for repayment next year; he fell behind with his mortgage repayments** = he was late in paying back the instalments on his mortgage

repeat *verb* **(a)** to say something again; **he repeated his address slowly so that the salesgirl could write it down; when asked what the company planned to do, the chairman repeated "Nothing" (b)** to repeat an order = to order something again
◊ **repeat order** *noun* new order for something which has been ordered before; **the product has been on the market only ten days and we are already flooded with repeat orders**

replace *verb* to put someone *or* something in the place of something else; **the cost of replacing damaged stock is very high; the photocopier needs replacing; the company will replace any defective item free of charge; we are replacing all our salaried staff with freelancers**
◊ **replacement** *noun* **(a)** replacement cost *or* **cost of replacement** = cost of an item to replace an existing asset; **replacement value** = value of something for insurance purposes if it were to be replaced; **the computer is insured at its replacement value (b)** item which replaces something; **we are out of stock and are waiting for replacements (c)** person who replaces someone; **my secretary leaves us next week, so we are advertising for a replacement**
NOTE: no plural for (a)

reply 1 *noun* answer; **there was no reply to my letter** *or* **to my phone call; I am writing in reply to your letter of the 24th; the company's reply to the takeover bid; reply coupon** = form attached to a coupon ad which has to be filled in and returned to the advertiser; **international postal reply**

coupon = coupon which can be used in another country to pay the postage of replying to a letter; **he enclosed an international reply coupon with his letter; reply paid card** *or* **letter** = card or letter to be sent back to the sender with a reply, the sender having already paid for the return postage **2** *verb* to answer; **to reply to a letter; the company has replied to the takeover bid by offering the shareholders higher dividends**

report 1 *noun* **(a)** statement describing what has happened *or* describing a state of affairs; **to draft a report; to make a report** *or* **to present a report** *or* **to send in a report; the sales manager reads all the reports from the sales team; the chairman has received a report from the insurance company; the company's annual report** *or* **the chairman's report** *or* **the directors' report** = document sent each year by the chairman of a company or the directors to the shareholders, explaining what the company has done during the year; **confidential report** = secret document which must not be shown to other people; **feasibility report** = document which says if something can be done; **financial report** = document which gives the financial position of a company *or* of a club, etc.; **progress report** = document which describes what progress has been made; **the treasurer's report** = document from the honorary treasurer of a society to explain the financial state of the society to its members **(b) a report in a newspaper** *or* **a newspaper report** = article *or* news item; **can you confirm the report that the company is planning to close the factory? (c)** official document from a government committee; **the government has issued a report on the credit problems of exporters 2** *verb* **(a)** to make a statement describing something; **the salesmen reported an increased demand for the product; he reported the damage to the insurance company; we asked the bank to report on his financial status; he reported seeing the absentee in a shop (b)** to report to **someone** = to be responsible to *or* to be under someone; **he reports direct to the managing director; the salesmen report to the sales director (c)** to go to a place *or* to attend; **to report for an interview; please report to our London office for training** NOTE: for (a), you **report something** or **report on something** or **report doing something**

repossess *verb* to take back an item which someone is buying under a hire-purchase agreement, because the purchaser cannot continue the payments

represent *verb* **(a)** to work for a company, showing goods or services to possible buyers; **he represents an American car firm in Europe; our French distributor represents several other competing firms (b)** to act for someone; **he sent his solicitor and accountant to represent him at the meeting; three managers represent the workforce in discussions with the directors**
◊ **re-present** *verb* to present something again; **he re-presented the cheque two weeks later to try to get payment from the bank**
◊ **representation** *noun* **(a)** act of selling goods for a company; **we offered them exclusive representation in Europe; they have no representation in the USA (b)** having someone to act on your behalf; **the minority shareholders want representation on the board (c)** complaint made on behalf of someone; **the managers made representations to the board on behalf of the hourly-paid members of staff**
◊ **representative 1** *adjective* which is an example of what all others are like; **we displayed a representative selection of our product range; the sample chosen was not representative of the whole batch 2** *noun* **(a) sales representative** = person who works for a company, showing goods or services for sale; **we have six representatives in Europe; they have vacancies for representatives to call on accounts in the north of the country (b)** company which works for another company, selling their goods; **we have appointed Smith & Co our exclusive representatives in Europe (c)** person who acts on someone's behalf; **he**

sent his solicitor and accountant to act as his representatives at the meeting; the board refused to meet the representatives of the workforce

repudiate *verb* to refuse to accept; **to repudiate an agreement** = to refuse to continue with an agreement
◇ **repudiation** *noun* refusal to accept

reputable *adjective* with a good reputation; **we only use reputable carriers; a reputable firm of accountants**
◇ **reputation** *noun* opinion of someone *or* something held by other people; **company with a reputation for quality; he has a reputation for being difficult to negotiate with**

request 1 *noun* asking for something; **they put in a request for a government subsidy; his request for a loan was turned down by the bank; on request** = if asked for; **we will send samples on request** *or* "samples available on request" 2 *verb* to ask for; **to request assistance from the government; I am sending a catalogue as requested**

require *verb* (a) to ask for *or* to demand something; **to require a full explanation of expenditure; the law requires you to submit all income to the tax authorities** (b) to need; **the document requires careful study; to write the program requires a computer specialist**
◇ **requirement** *noun* what is needed; **public sector borrowing requirement** = amount of money which a government has to borrow to pay for its own spending
◇ **requirements** *plural noun* things which are needed; **to meet a customer's requirements; if you will supply us with a list of your requirements, we shall see if we can meet them; the requirements of a market** *or* **market requirements** = things which are needed by the market; **budgetary requirements** = spending or income needed to meet the budget forecasts; **manpower requirements** = number of workers needed

requisition 1 *noun* official order for something; **what is the number of your latest requisition?; cheque requisition** = official note from a department to the company accounts staff asking for a

cheque to be written 2 *verb* to put in an official order for something; to ask for supplies to be sent

resale *noun* selling goods which have been bought; **to purchase something for resale; the contract forbids resale of the goods to the USA**
NOTE: no plural
◇ **resale price maintenance** *noun* system where the price for an item is fixed by the manufacturer and the retailer is not allowed to sell it for a lower price

rescind *verb* to annul *or* to cancel; **to rescind a contract** *or* **an agreement**

rescue 1 *noun* saving someone *or* something from danger; **rescue operation** = arrangement by a group of people to save a company from collapse; **the banks planned a rescue operation for the company** 2 *verb* to save someone *or* something from danger; **the company nearly collapsed, but was rescued by the banks**

research 1 *noun* trying to find out facts *or* information; **consumer research** = research into why consumers buy goods and what goods they may want to buy; **market research** = examining the possible sales of a product and the possible customers for it before it is put on the market; **research and development** = scientific investigation which leads to making new products or improving existing products; **the company spends millions on research and development; scientific research** = study to try to find out information; **he is engaged in research into the packaging of the new product line; the company is carrying out research into finding a medicine to cure colds; research department** = section of a company which does research; **a research institute** *or* **organization** = place which exists only to carry out research; **research unit** = separate small group of research workers; **research worker** = person who works in a research department 2 *verb* to study *or* to try to find out information about something; **to research the market for a product**
◇ **researcher** *noun* person who carries out research

reservation *noun* booking a seat *or* table *or* room; **I want to make a reservation on**

the train to Plymouth tomorrow evening; **room reservations** = department in a hotel which deals with bookings for rooms; **can you put me through to reservations?**

reserve 1 *noun* **(a)** money from profits not paid as dividend, but kept back by a company in case it is needed for a special purpose; **bank reserves** = cash and securities held by a bank to cover deposits; **capital reserves** = money from profits, which forms part of the capital of a company and can be used for distribution to shareholders only when a company is wound up; **capitalization of reserves** = issuing free bonus shares to shareholders; **cash reserves** = a company's reserves in cash deposits or bills kept in case of urgent need; **the company was forced to fall back on its cash reserves; to have to draw on reserves to pay the dividend; contingency reserve** *or* **emergency reserves** = money set aside in case it is needed urgently; **reserve for bad debts** = money kept by a company to cover debts which may not be paid; **hidden reserves** = illegal reserves which are not declared in the company's balance sheet; **sums chargeable to the reserve** = sums which can be debited to a company's reserves; **reserve fund** = profits in a business which have not been paid out as dividend but have been ploughed back into the business **(b) reserve currency** = strong currency held by other countries to support their own weaker currencies; **currency reserves** = foreign money held by a government to support its own currency and to pay its debts; **a country's foreign currency reserves** = a country's reserves in currencies of other countries; **the UK's gold and dollar reserves fell by $200 million during the quarter (c) in reserve** = kept to be used at a later date; **to keep something in reserve; we are keeping our new product in reserve until the launch date (d) reserves** = supplies kept in case of need; **our reserves of fuel fell during the winter; the country's reserves of gas** *or* **gas reserves are very large (e) reserve price** = lowest price which a seller will accept at an auction; **the painting was withdrawn when it did not reach its reserve 2** *verb* **to reserve a room** *or* **a table** *or* **a seat** = to book a room *or* table *or* seat *or* to ask for a room *or* table *or* seat to be kept free for you; **I want to reserve a table for four people; can your secretary reserve a seat for me on the train to Glasgow?**

residence *noun* **(a)** house *or* flat where someone lives; **he has a country residence where he spends his weekends (b)** act of living *or* operating officially in a country; **residence permit** = official document allowing a foreigner to live in a country; **he has applied for a residence permit; she was granted a residence permit for one year** NOTE: no plural for (b)

◊ **resident** *noun* person *or* company living *or* operating in a country; **the company is resident in France; non-resident** = person *or* company which is not officially resident in a country; **he has a non-resident account with a French bank; she was granted a non-resident visa**

residue *noun* money left over; **after paying various bequests the residue of his estate was split between his children**

◊ **residual** *adjective* remaining after everything else has gone

resign *verb* to give up a job; **he resigned from his post as treasurer; he has resigned with effect from July 1st; she resigned as finance director**

◊ **resignation** *noun* act of giving up a job; **he wrote his letter of resignation to the chairman; to hand in** *or* **to give in** *or* **to send in one's resignation** = to resign from a job

resist *verb* to fight against something *or* not to give in to something; **the chairman resisted all attempts to make him resign; the company is resisting the takeover bid**

◊ **resistance** *noun* showing that people are opposed to something; **there was a lot of resistance from the shareholders to the new plan; the chairman's proposal met with strong resistance from the banks; consumer resistance** = lack of interest by consumers in buying a new product; **the new product met no consumer resistance even though the price was high** NOTE: no plural

resolution *noun* decision to be reached at a meeting; **to put a resolution to a meeting** = to ask a meeting to vote on a proposal; **the meeting passed** *or* **carried** *or* **adopted a resolution to go on strike; the meeting rejected the resolution** *or* **the resolution was defeated by ten votes to twenty**

resolve *verb* to decide to do something; **the meeting resolved that a dividend should not be paid**

resources *plural noun* **(a)** source of supply of something; **natural resources** = supplies of gas, oil, coal, etc. which are available in the ground; **the country is rich in natural resources; we are looking for a site with good water resources** = a site with plenty of water available **(b) financial resources** = supply of money for something; **the costs of the London office are a drain on the company's financial resources; the company's financial resources are not strong enough to support the cost of the research programme; the cost of the new project is easily within our resources** = we have enough money to pay for the new project

respect 1 *noun* **with respect to** = concerning **2** *verb* to pay attention to; **to respect a clause in an agreement; the company has not respected the terms of the contract**
◊ **respectively** *adverb* referring to each one separately; **Mr Smith and Mr Jones are respectively MD and Sales Director of Smith Ltd**

response *noun* reply *or* reaction; **there was no response to our mailing shot; we got very little response to our complaints**

responsibility *noun* **(a)** being responsible; **there is no responsibility on the company's part for loss of customers' property; the management accepts no responsibility for loss of goods in storage (b) responsibilities** = duties; **he finds the responsibilities of being managing director too heavy**
NOTE: no plural for (a)
◊ **responsible** *adjective* **(a) responsible for** = directing *or* being in charge of; **he is responsible for all sales (b) responsible to someone** = being under someone's authority; **he is directly responsible to the managing director (c) a responsible job** = job where important decisions have to be taken *or* where the employee has many responsibilities; **he is looking for a responsible job in marketing**

rest *noun* what is left; **the chairman went home, but the rest of the directors stayed in**

the boardroom; **we sold most of the stock before Christmas and hope to clear the rest in a sale; the rest of the money is invested in gilts**
NOTE: usually singular, written with **the**

restaurant *noun* place where you can buy a meal; **he runs a French restaurant in New York**
◊ **restaurateur** *noun* person who runs a restaurant

restitution *noun* **(a)** giving back (property); **the court ordered the restitution of assets to the company (b)** compensation *or* payment for damage or loss **(c)** (*in the EEC*) **export restitution** = subsidies to European food exporters
NOTE: no plural

restock *verb* to order more stock; **to restock after the Christmas sales**
◊ **restocking** *noun* ordering more stock
NOTE: no plural

restraint *noun* control; **pay restraint** *or* **wage restraint** = keeping increases in wages under control; **restraint of trade** = (i) situation where a worker is not allowed to use his knowledge in another company if he changes jobs; (ii) attempt by companies to fix prices *or* create monopolies *or* reduce competition, which could affect free trade

restrict *verb* to limit *or* to impose controls on; **to restrict credit; we are restricted to twenty staff by the size of our offices; to restrict the flow of trade** *or* **to restrict imports; to sell into a restricted market** = to sell goods into a market where the supplier has agreed to limit sales to avoid competition
◊ **restriction** *noun* limit *or* controlling; **import restrictions** *or* **restrictions on imports; to impose restrictions on imports** *or* **on credit** = to start limiting imports *or* credit; **to lift credit restrictions** = to allow credit to be given freely
◊ **restrictive** *adjective* which limits; **restrictive trade practices** = arrangement between companies to fix prices *or* to share the market, etc.

restructure *verb* to reorganize the financial basis of a company

◇ **restructuring** *noun* **the restructuring of the company** = reorganizing the financial basis of a company
NOTE: no plural

result 1 *noun* **(a)** profit or loss account for a company at the end of a trading period; **the company's results for 1984 (b)** something which happens because of something else; **what was the result of the price investigation? the company doubled its sales force with the result that the sales rose by 26%; the expansion programme has produced results** = has produced increased sales; **payment by results** = being paid for profits *or* increased sales **2** *verb* **(a) to result in** = to produce as a result **(b) to result from** = to happen because of something; **the increase in debt resulted from the expansion programme; the doubling of the sales force resulted in increased sales; the extra orders resulted in overtime work for all the factory staff**

QUOTE: the company has received the backing of a number of oil companies who are willing to pay for the results of the survey *Lloyd's List*
QUOTE: some profit-taking was noted, but underlying sentiment remained firm in a steady stream of strong corporate results *Financial Times*

resume *verb* to start again; **the discussions resumed after a two hour break**

résumé *noun* *US* summary of a person's life story with details of education and work experience
NOTE: GB English is **curriculum vitae**

resumption *noun* starting again; **we expect an early resumption of negotiations** = we expect negotiations will start again soon
NOTE: no plural

retail 1 *noun* sale of small quantities of goods to ordinary customers; **retail dealer** = person who sells to the general public; **retail price** = full price paid by a customer in a shop; **retail price index** = index showing how prices of retail goods have risen over a period of time; **retail shop** *or* **retail outlet** = shop which sells goods to the general public; **the retail trade** = all people *or* businesses selling goods retail; **the goods in stock have a retail value of £1m** = the value of the goods if sold to the

public is £1m, before discounts etc. are taken into account **2** *adverb* **he sells retail and buys wholesale** = he buys goods in bulk at a wholesale discount and sells in small quantities to the public **3** *verb* **(a) to retail goods** = to sell goods direct to the public **(b)** to sell for a price; **these items retail at** *or* **for 25p** = the retail price of these items is 25p
◇ **retailer** *noun* person who runs a retail business, selling goods direct to the public
◇ **retailing** *noun* selling of full price goods to the public; **from car retailing the company branched out into car leasing**
NOTE: no plural

retain *verb* **(a)** to keep; **out of the profits, the company has retained £50,000 as provision against bad debts; retained income** = profit not distributed to the shareholders as dividend; **the balance sheet has £50,000 in retained income (b) to retain a lawyer to act for a company** = to agree with a lawyer that he will act for you (and pay him a fee in advance)
◇ **retainer** *noun* money paid in advance to someone so that he will work for you, and not for someone else; **we pay him a retainer of £1,000**

retire *verb* **(a)** to stop work and take a pension; **she retired with a £6,000 pension; the founder of the company retired at the age of 85; the shop is owned by a retired policeman (b)** to make a worker stop work and take a pension; **they decided to retire all staff over 50 (c)** to come to the end of an elected term of office; **the treasurer retires from the council after six years; two retiring directors offer themselves for re-election**
◇ **retiral** *noun* *US* = RETIREMENT
◇ **retirement** *noun* act of retiring from work; **to take early retirement** = to leave work before the usual age; **retirement age** = age at which people retire (in the UK usually 65 for men and 60 for women); **retirement pension** = pension which someone receives when he retires
NOTE: no plural

retrain *verb* to train someone for a new job, or to do the same job in a more modern way
◇ **retraining** *noun* act of training again; **the shop is closed for staff retraining; he had**

to attend a retraining session
NOTE: no plural

retrenchment *noun* reduction of expenditure *or* of new plans; **the company is in for a period of retrenchment**

retrieve *verb* to get back (something) which has been lost; to get back (information) which is stored in a computer; **the company is fighting to retrieve its market share; all of the information was accidentally wiped off the computer so we cannot retrieve our sales figures for the last month**

◊ **retrieval** *noun* getting back; **data retrieval** *or* **information retrieval** = getting information from the data stored in a computer; **retrieval system** = system which allows information to be retrieved
NOTE: no plural

retroactive *adjective* which takes effect from a time in the past; **retroactive pay rise; they got a pay rise retroactive to last January**

◊ **retroactively** *adverb* going back to a time in the past

return 1 *noun* **(a)** going back *or* coming back; **return journey** = journey back to where you came from; **a return ticket** *or* **a return** = a ticket for a journey to a place and back again; **I want two returns to Edinburgh; return fare** = fare for a journey from one place to another and back again **(b)** sending back; **he replied by return of post** = he replied by the next post service back; **return address** = address to send back something; **these goods are all on sale or return** = if the retailer does not sell them, he sends them back to the supplier, and pays only for the items sold **(c)** profit *or* income from money invested; **to bring in a quick return; what is the gross return on this line?; return on investment (ROI)** *or* **on capital** = profit shown as a percentage of money invested; **rate of return** = amount of interest *or* dividend produced by an investment, shown as a percentage **(d)** official **return** = official report; **to make a return to the tax office** *or* **to make an income tax return** = to send a statement of income to the tax office; **to fill in a VAT return** = to complete the form showing VAT receipts and expenditure; **nil return** = report

showing no sales *or* income *or* tax etc.; **daily** *or* **weekly** *or* **quarterly sales return** = report of sales made each day *or* week *or* quarter **2** *verb* **(a)** to send back; **to return unsold stock to the wholesaler; to return a letter to sender; returned empties** = empty bottles *or* containers which are sent back to a supplier **(b)** to make a statement; **to return income of £15,000 to the tax authorities**

◊ **returnable** *adjective* which can be returned; **these bottles are not returnable**

◊ **returns** *plural noun* **(a)** profits *or* income from investment; **the company is looking for quick returns on its investment; law of diminishing returns** = general rule that as more factors of production (land, labour and capital) are added to the existing factors, so the amount they produce is proportionately smaller **(b)** unsold goods, especially books *or* newspapers *or* magazines sent back to the supplier

revalue *verb* to value something again (at a higher value than before); **the company's properties have been revalued; the dollar has been revalued against all world currencies**

◊ **revaluation** *noun* act of revaluing; **the balance sheet takes into account the revaluation of the company's properties; the revaluation of the dollar against the franc**

revenue *noun* **(a)** money received; **revenue from advertising** *or* **advertising revenue; oil revenues have risen with the rise in the dollar; revenue accounts** = accounts of a business which record money received as sales, commission etc. **(b)** money received by a government in tax; **Inland Revenue** *or* *US* **Internal Revenue Service** = government department which deals with tax; **revenue officer** = person working in the government tax offices

reversal *noun* change from being profitable to unprofitable; **the company suffered a reversal in the Far East**

reverse 1 *adjective* opposite *or* in the opposite direction; **reverse takeover** = takeover of a large company by a small company; **reverse charge call** = telephone call where the person receiving the call agrees to pay for it **2** *verb* **(a)** to change a decision to the opposite; **the committee**

reversed its decision on import quotas (b) to reverse the charges = to make a phone call, asking the person receiving it to pay for it

QUOTE: the trade balance sank $17 billion, reversing last fall's brief improvement *Fortune*

reversion *noun* return of property to an original owner; **he has the reversion of the estate** = he will receive the estate when the present lease ends
◇ **reversionary** *adjective* (property) which passes to another owner on the death of the present one; **reversionary annuity** = annuity paid to someone on the death of another person

review 1 *noun* **(a)** general examination; **to conduct a review of distributors; financial review** = examination of an organization's finances; **wage review** *or* **salary review** = examination of salaries *or* wages in a company to see if the workers should earn more; **she had a salary review last April** = her salary was examined (and increased) in April **(b)** magazine *or* monthly or weekly journal **2** *verb* to examine something generally; **to review salaries** = to look at all salaries in a company to decide on increases; **his salary will be reviewed at the end of the year; the company has decided to review freelance payments in the light of the rising cost of living; to review discounts** = to look at discounts offered to decide whether to change them

revise *verb* to change something which has been calculated *or* planned; **sales forecasts are revised annually; the chairman is revising his speech to the AGM**

revive *verb* to make more lively; to increase (after a recession); **the government is introducing measures to revive trade; industry is reviving after the recession**
◇ **revival** *noun* **revival of trade** = increase in trade after a recession

revoke *verb* to cancel; **to revoke a clause in an agreement; the quota on luxury items has been revoked**

revolving *adjective* **revolving credit** = system where someone can borrow money at any time up to an agreed amount, and continue to borrow while still paying off the original loan

rich *adjective* **(a)** having a lot of money; **a rich stockbroker; a rich oil company (b)** having a lot of natural resources; **the country is rich in minerals; oil-rich territory**

rid *verb* **to get rid of something** = to throw something away because it is useless; **the company is trying to get rid of all its old stock; our department has been told to get rid of twenty staff**
NOTE: **getting rid - got rid**

rider *noun* additional clause; **to add a rider to a contract**

rig 1 *noun* **oil rig** = platform which holds the equipment for taking oil out of the earth **2** *verb* to arrange for a result to be changed; **they tried to rig the election of officers; to rig the market** = to make share prices go up or down so as to make a profit; **rigging of ballots** *or* **ballot-rigging** = trying to change the result of an election by altering or destroying voting papers
NOTE: **rigging - rigged**

right 1 *adjective* **(a)** good *or* correct; **the chairman was right when he said the figures did not add up; this is not the right plane for Paris (b)** not left; **the credits are on the right side of the page** **2** *noun* **(a)** legal title to something; **right of renewal of a contract; she has a right to the property; he has no right to the patent; the staff have a right to know how the company is doing; foreign rights** = legal title to sell something (especially a book) in a foreign country; **right to strike** = legal title for workers to stop working if they have a good reason for it; **right of way** = legal title to go across someone's property **(b) rights issue** = giving shareholders the right to buy more shares at a lower price
◇ **rightful** *adjective* legally correct; **rightful claimant** = person who has a legal claim to something; **rightful owner** = legal owner
◇ **right-hand** *adjective* belonging to the right side; **the credit side is the right-hand column in the accounts; he keeps the address list in the right-hand drawer of his desk; right-hand man** = main assistant

ring 1 *noun* group of people who try to fix prices so as not to compete with each other and still make a large profit **2** *verb* to call using the telephone; **he rang (up) his stockbroker**
NOTE: ringing - rang - has rung
◊ **ring back** *verb* to telephone in reply to a phone call; **the managing director rang - can you ring him back?**

rise 1 *noun* **(a)** increase *or* growing high; **rise in the price of raw materials; oil price rises brought about a recession in world trade; there is a rise in sales of 10% or sales show a rise of 10%; salaries are increasing to keep up with the rises in the cost of living; the recent rise in interest rates has made mortgages dearer (b)** increase in salary; **she asked her boss for a rise; he had a 6% rise in January**
NOTE: US English for (b) is **raise**
2 *verb* to move upwards *or* to become higher; **prices are rising faster than inflation; interest rates have risen to 15%**
NOTE: rising - rose - has risen

> QUOTE: the index of industrial production sank 0.2 per cent for the latest month after rising 0.3 per cent in March *Financial Times*
> QUOTE: the stock rose to over $20 a share, higher than the $18 bid *Fortune*
> QUOTE: customers' deposit and current accounts also rose to $655.31 million at the end of December *Hongkong Standard*

risk *noun* **(a)** possible harm *or* chance of danger; **to run a risk** = to be likely to suffer harm; **to take a risk** = to do something which may make you lose money or suffer harm; **financial risk** = possibility of losing money; **there is no financial risk in selling to East European countries on credit; he is running the risk of overspending his promotion budget; the company is taking a considerable risk in manufacturing 25m units without doing any market research (b) risk capital** = capital for investment which may easily be lost in risky projects, but which can also provide high returns **(c) at owner's risk** = situation where goods shipped *or* stored are insured by the owner, not by the transport company or the storage company; **goods left here are at owner's risk; the shipment was sent at owner's risk (d)** loss *or* damage against which you are insured; **fire risk** = situation *or* goods which could start a fire; **that warehouse full of paper is a fire risk (e)**

he is a good *or* **bad risk** = it is not likely *or* it is very likely that the insurance company will have to pay out against claims where he is concerned
◊ **risk-free** *adjective* with no risk involved; **a risk-free investment**
◊ **risky** *adjective* dangerous *or* which may cause harm; **he lost all his money is some risky ventures in South America**

> QUOTE: there is no risk-free way of taking regular income from your money higher than the rate of inflation and still preserving its value *Guardian*

rival *noun* person *or* company which competes in the same market; **a rival company; to undercut a rival; we are analyzing the rival brands on the market**

road *noun* **(a)** way used by cars *or* lorries, etc. to move from one place to another; **to send** *or* **to ship goods by road; road transport costs have risen; the main office is in London Road; use the Park Road entrance to get to the buying department (b) on the road** = travelling; **the salesmen are on the road thirty weeks a year; we have twenty salesmen on the road**

robot *noun* machine which can be programmed to work like a person; **the car is made by robots**
◊ **robotics** *noun* study of robots *or* making of robots
NOTE: takes a singular verb

rock *noun* large stone; **the company is on the rocks** = the company is in great financial difficulties
◊ **rock bottom** *noun* **rock-bottom prices** = the lowest prices possible; **sales have reached rock bottom** = sales have reached the lowest point possible

> QUOTE: investment companies took the view that secondhand prices had reached rock bottom and that levels could only go up *Lloyd's List*

rocket *verb* to rise fast; **rocketing prices; prices have rocketed**

ROI = RETURN ON INVESTMENT

roll 1 *noun* something which has been turned over and over to wrap round itself;

the desk calculator uses a roll of paper **2** *verb* to make something go forward by turning it over; **they rolled the computer into position**

◇ **roll on/roll off** *adjective* (ferry) where lorries and cars can drive straight into or off the boat

◇ **roll over** *verb* **to roll over credit** *or* **a debt** = to make credit available over a continuing period *or* to allow a debt to stand after the repayment date

◇ **rolling plan** *noun* plan which runs for a period of time and is updated regularly for the same period

◇ **rolling stock** *noun* wagons, etc., used on the railway

room *noun* **(a)** part of a building, divided off from other parts by walls; **the chairman's room is at the end of the corridor; conference room** = room where a small meeting can take place; **mail room** = section of a building where incoming letters are sorted and distributed to departments **(b)** bedroom in a hotel; **I want a room with bath for two nights; double room** = room with two beds, for two people; **room service** = arrangement in a hotel where food or drink can be served in a guest's bedroom **(c)** space; **the filing cabinets take up a lot of room; there is no more room in the computer file**
NOTE: no plural for (c)

rotation *noun* taking turns; **to fill the post of chairman by rotation** = each member of the group is chairman for a period then gives the post to another member; **two directors retire by rotation** = two directors retire because they have been directors longer than any others, but can offer themselves for re-election
NOTE: no plural

rouble *noun* money used in Russia

rough *adjective* **(a)** approximate *or* not very accurate; **rough calculation** *or* **rough estimate** = approximate answer; **I made some rough calculations on the back of an envelope (b)** not finished; **rough copy** = draft of a document which will have changes made to it before it is complete; **he made a rough draft of the new design**

◇ **roughly** *adverb* more or less; **the turnover is roughly twice last year's; the**

development cost of the project will be roughly £25,000

◇ **rough out** *verb* to make a draft *or* a general design; **the finance director roughed out a plan of investment**

round 1 *adjective* **(a) in round figures** = not totally accurate, but correct to the nearest 10 or 100 **(b) round trip** = journey from one place to another and back again; **round-trip ticket; round-trip fare**

◇ **round down** *verb* to decrease to the nearest full figure

◇ **round up** *verb* to increase to the nearest full figure; **to round up the figures to the nearest pound**

QUOTE: each cheque can be made out for the local equivalent of £100 rounded up to a convenient figure
Sunday Times

---

route *noun* **(a)** way which is regularly taken; **bus route** = normal way taken by a bus from one place to another; **companies were warned that normal shipping routes were dangerous because of the war (b) en route** = on the way; **the tanker sank when she was en route to the Gulf**

routine 1 *noun* normal *or* regular way of doing something; **he follows a daily routine - he takes the 8.15 train to London, then the bus to his office, and returns by the same route in the evening; refitting the conference room has disturbed the office routine 2** *adjective* normal *or* which happens regularly; **routine work; routine call; a routine check of the fire equipment**

royalty *noun* money paid to an inventor *or* writer *or* the owner of land for the right to use his property (usually a certain percentage of sales, or a certain amount per sale); **oil royalties; he is receiving royalties from his invention**

RPM = RESALE PRICE MAINTENANCE

RRP = RECOMMENDED RETAIL PRICE

RSVP = REPONDEZ S'IL VOUS PLAIT letters on an invitation showing the person to whom replies should be sent

rubber *noun* elastic material from the juice of a tree; *US* **rubber check** = cheque which cannot be cashed because the person writing it does not have enough money in the account to pay it

◊ **rubber stamp 1** *noun* stamp with rubber letters or figures on it to put the date *or* a note on a document; **he stamped the invoice with the rubber stamp "Paid" 2** *verb* to agree to something without discussing it; **the board simply rubber stamped the agreement**

rule 1 *noun* **(a)** general way of conduct; **as a rule** = usually; **as a rule, we do not give discounts over 20%; company rules** = general way of working in a company; **it is a company rule that smoking is not allowed in the offices (b) to work to rule** = to work strictly according to the rules agreed by the company and union, and therefore to work very slowly **2** *verb* **(a)** to give an official decision; **the commission of inquiry ruled that the company was in breach of contract; the judge ruled that the documents had to be deposited with the court (b)** to be in force *or* to be current; **prices which are ruling at the moment**

◊ **ruling 1** *adjective* in operation at the moment *or* current; **we will invoice at ruling prices 2** *noun* decision; **the inquiry gave a ruling on the case; according to the ruling of the court, the contract was illegal**

run 1 *noun* **(a)** making a machine work; **a cheque run** = series of cheques processed through a computer; **a computer run** = period of work of a computer; **test run** = trial made on a machine **(b)** rush to buy something; **the Post Office reported a run on the new stamps; a run on the bank** = rush by customers to take deposits out of a bank which they think may close down; **a run on the pound** = rush to sell pounds and buy other currencies **(c)** regular route (of a plane *or* bus) **2** *verb* **(a)** to be in force; **the lease runs for twenty years; the lease has only six months to run (b)** to amount to; **the costs ran into thousands of pounds (c)** to manage *or* to organize; **she runs a mail-order business from home; they run a staff sports club; he is running a multimillion-pound company (d)** to work on a machine; **do not run the photocopier for more than four hours at a time; the computer was running invoices all night (e)** (*of buses,*

trains etc.) to be working; **there is an evening plane running between Manchester and Paris; this train runs on weekdays**
NOTE: **running - ran - has run**

◊ **runaway** *adjective* **runaway inflation** = very rapid inflation, which is almost impossible to reduce

◊ **run down** *verb* **(a)** to reduce a quantity gradually; **to run down stocks** *or* **to let stocks run down (b)** to slow down the business activities of a company before it is going to be closed; **the company is being run down**

◊ **run into** *verb* **(a) to run into debt** = to start to have debts **(b)** to amount to; **costs have run into thousands of pounds; he has an income running into five figures** = he earns more than £10,000

◊ **running** *noun* **(a) running total** = total carried from one column of figures to the next **(b) running costs** *or* **running expenses** *or* **costs of running a business** = money spent on the day-to-day cost of keeping a business going **(c) the company has made a profit for six years running** = the company has made a profit for six years one after the other

◊ **run out of** *verb* to have nothing left *or* to use up all the stock; **we have run out of headed notepaper; the printer has run out of paper**

◊ **run up** *verb* to make debts go up quickly; **he quickly ran up a bill for £250**

rupee *noun* money used in India and some other countries

rush 1 *noun* doing something fast; **rush hour** = time when traffic is worst *or* when everyone is trying to travel to work or from work back home; **the taxi was delayed in the rush hour traffic; rush job** = job which has to be done fast; **rush order** = order which has to be supplied fast **2** *verb* to make something go fast; **to rush an order through the factory; to rush a shipment to Africa**

Ss

sack 1 *noun* **(a)** large bag made of strong cloth or plastic; **a sack of potatoes; we sell onions by the sack (b) to get the sack** = to be dismissed from a job
NOTE: no plural for (b)
2 *verb* **to sack someone** = to dismiss someone from a job; **he was sacked after being late for work**
◊ **sacking** *noun* dismissal from a job; **the union protested against the sackings**

SAE *or* **s.a.e.** = STAMPED ADDRESSED ENVELOPE

safe 1 *noun* heavy metal box which cannot be opened easily, in which valuable documents, money, etc. can be kept; **put the documents in the safe; we keep the petty cash in the safe; fire-proof safe** = safe which cannot be harmed by fire; **night safe** = safe in the outside wall of a bank, where money and documents can be deposited at night, using a special door; **wall safe** = safe installed in a wall **2** *adjective* **(a)** out of danger; **keep the documents in a safe place** = in a place where they cannot be stolen or destroyed; **safe keeping** = being looked after carefully; **we put the documents into the bank for safe keeping (b) safe investments** = shares, etc., which are not likely to fall in value
◊ **safe deposit** *noun* bank safe where you can leave jewellery or documents
◊ **safe deposit box** *noun* small box which you can rent to keep jewellery or documents in a bank's safe
◊ **safely** *adverb* without being harmed; **the cargo was unloaded safely from the sinking ship**
◊ **safeguard** *verb* to protect; **to safeguard the interests of the shareholders**
◊ **safety** *noun* **(a)** being free from danger or risk; **safety margin** = time *or* space allowed for something to be safe; **margin of safety** = sales which are above the breakeven point; **to take safety precautions** *or* **safety measures** = to act to make sure something is safe; **safety regulations** = rules to make a place of work safe for the workers **(b) fire safety** =

making a place of work safe for the workers in case of fire; **fire safety officer** = person in a company responsible for seeing that the workers are safe if a fire breaks out **(c) for safety** = to make something safe *or* to be safe; **put the documents in the cupboard for safety; to take a copy of the disk for safety**
NOTE: no plural

sail *verb* to travel on water *or* to leave harbour; **the ship sails at 12.00**
◊ **sailing** *noun* departure (of a ship); **there are no sailings to France because of the strike**

salary *noun* payment for work, made to an employee usually as a cheque at the end of each month; **she got a salary increase in June; the company froze all salaries for a six-month period; basic salary** = normal salary without extra payments; **gross salary** = salary before tax is deducted; **net salary** = salary which is left after deducting tax and national insurance contributions; **starting salary** = amount of payment for an employee when starting work; **he was appointed at a starting salary of £10,000; salary cut** = sudden reduction in salary; **salary cheque** = monthly cheque by which an employee is paid; **salary deductions** = money which a company removes from salaries to give to the government as tax, national insurance contributions, etc.; **salary review** = examination of salaries in a company to see if workers should earn more; **she had a salary review last April** *or* **her salary was reviewed last April; scale of salaries** *or* **salary scale** = list of salaries showing different levels of pay in different jobs in the same company; **the company's salary structure** = organization of salaries in a company, with different rates for different types of job
◊ **salaried** *adjective* earning a salary; **the company has 250 salaried staff**

QUOTE: the union of hotel and personal service workers has demanded a new salary structure and uniform conditions of service for workers in the hotel and catering industry
Business Times (Lagos)

sale *noun* **(a)** act of selling *or* of giving an item in exchange for money; **cash sale** = selling something for cash; **credit card sale**

= selling something for credit, using a credit card; **forced sale** = selling something because a court orders it or because it is the only thing to do to avoid a financial crisis; **sale and lease-back** = situation where a company sells a product to raise cash and then leases it back from the purchaser; **sale or return** = system where the retailer sends goods back if they are not sold, and pays the supplier only for goods sold; **we have taken 4,000 items on sale or return; bill of sale** = document which the seller gives to the buyer to show that a sale has taken place; **conditions of sale** = agreed ways in which a sale takes place (such as discounts and credit terms) **(b) for sale** = ready to be sold; **to offer something for sale** or **to put something up for sale** = to announce that something is ready to be sold; **they put the factory up for sale; his shop is for sale; these items are not for sale to the general public (c) on sale** = ready to be sold in a shop; **these items are on sale in most chemists (d) sales** = money received for selling something or number of items sold; **sales have risen over the first quarter; sales analysis** = examining the reports of sales to see why items have or have not sold well; **sales appeal** = quality which makes customers want to buy; **sales book** = record of sales; **book sales** = sales as recorded in the sales book; **sales budget** = plan of probable sales; **sales campaign** = planned work to achieve higher sales; **sales conference** or **sales meeting** = meeting of sales managers, representatives, publicity staff, etc, to discuss results and future sales plans; **cost of sales** = all the costs of a product sold, including manufacturing costs and the staff costs of the production department; **sales department** = section of a company which deals in selling the company's products or services; **domestic sales** or **home sales** = sales in the home market; **sales drive** = vigorous work to increase sales; **sales executive** = person in a company in charge of sales; **sales figures** = total sales, or sales broken down by category; **sales force** = group of salesmen; **sales forecast** = calculation of future sales; **forward sales** = sales (of shares, commodities, foreign exchange) for delivery at a later date; **sales ledger** = book in which income from sales are recorded; **sales ledger clerk** = office worker who deals with the sales ledger; **sales literature** = printed information (such as leaflets, prospectuses) which help

sales; **sales manager** = person in charge of a sales department; **monthly sales report** = report made showing the number of items or amount of money received for selling stock; **in the sales reports all the European countries are bracketed together; sales revenue** = money received from sales; **sales tax** = tax to be paid on each item sold; **sales volume** or **volume of sales** = number of units sold **(e)** selling of goods at specially low prices; **the shop is having a sale to clear old stock; the sale price is 50% of the normal price; bargain sale** = sale of all goods in a store at cheap prices; **clearance sale** = sale of items at low prices to get rid of the stock; **half-price sale** = sale of items at half the usual price; **jumble sale** = sale of old used household goods; **the sales** = period when major stores sell many items at specially low prices; **I bought this in the sales** or **at the sales** or **in the January sales**

◇ **saleability** *noun* quality of an item which makes it easy to sell
NOTE: no plural

◇ **saleable** *adjective* which can easily be sold

◇ **saleroom** *noun* room where an auction takes place

◇ **salesclerk** *noun* *US* person who sells goods to customers in a store

◇ **salesgirl** *noun* girl who sells goods to customers in a store

◇ **saleslady** *noun* woman who sells goods to customers in a store

◇ **salesman** *noun* **(a)** man who sells goods or services to members of the public; **he is the head salesman in the carpet department; a used car salesman; door-to-door salesman** = man who goes from one house to the next, asking people to buy something; **insurance salesman** = man who encourages clients to take out insurance policies **(b)** person who represents a company, selling its products or services to retail shops; **we have six salesmen calling on accounts in central London**
NOTE: plural is **salesmen**

◇ **salesmanship** *noun* art of selling or of persuading customers to buy
NOTE: no plural

◇ **saleswoman** *noun* woman in a shop who sells goods to customers
NOTE: plural is **saleswomen**

salvage 1 *noun* **(a)** saving a ship *or* a cargo from being destroyed; **salvage money** = payment made by the owner of a ship *or* a cargo to the person who has saved it; **salvage vessel** = ship which specializes in saving other ships and their cargoes **(b)** goods saved from a wrecked ship *or* from a fire, etc.; **a sale of flood salvage items**
NOTE: no plural
2 *verb* **(a)** to save goods *or* a ship from being wrecked; **we are selling off a warehouse full of salvaged goods (b)** to save something from loss; **the company is trying to salvage its reputation after the managing director was sent to prison for fraud; the receiver managed to salvage something from the collapse of the company**

sample 1 *noun* **(a)** specimen *or* a small part of an item which is used to show what the whole item is like; **a sample of the cloth** *or* **a cloth sample; check sample** = sample to be used to see if a whole consignment is acceptable; **free sample** = sample given free to advertise a product; **sample book** *or* **book of samples** = book showing samples of different types of cloth *or* paper, etc. **(b)** small group taken to show what a larger group is like; **we interviewed a sample of potential customers; a random sample** = a sample taken without any selection 2 *verb* **(a)** to test *or* to try something by taking a small amount; **to sample a product before buying it (b)** to ask a representative group of people questions to find out what the reactions of a much larger group would be; **they sampled 2,000 people at random to test the new drink**
◇ **sampling** *noun* **(a)** testing a product by taking a small amount; **sampling of Common Market produce; acceptance sampling** = testing a small sample of a batch to see if the whole batch is good enough to be accepted **(b)** testing the reactions of a small group of people to find out the reactions of a larger group of consumers; **random sampling**

sanction 1 *noun* **(a)** permission; **you will need the sanction of the local authorities** before you can knock down the office block **(b) economic sanctions** = restrictions on trade with a country in order to influence its political situation *or* in order to make its government change its policy; **to impose sanctions on a country** *or* **to lift sanctions** 2 *verb* to approve; **the board sanctioned the expenditure of £1.2m on the development project**

sandwich *noun* two pieces of bread with meat *or* cheese, etc. between them
◇ **sandwich boards** *noun* boards carried in front of and behind a person to carry advertisements
◇ **sandwich course** *noun* course of study where students spend a period of time working in a factory *or* office as part of a college course
◇ **sandwich man** *noun* man who carries sandwich boards

satisfaction *noun* feeling of being happy *or* good feeling; **customer satisfaction** = making a customer pleased with what he has bought; **job satisfaction** = a worker's feeling that he is happy in his place of work and pleased with the work he does
NOTE: no plural
◇ **satisfy** *verb* **(a) to satisfy a client** = to make a client pleased with what he has purchased; **a satisfied customer** = a customer who has got what he wanted **(b) to satisfy a demand** = to fill a demand; **we cannot produce enough to satisfy the demand for the product**

saturation *noun* filling completely; **saturation of the market** *or* **market saturation** = situation where the market has taken as much of the product as it can buy; **the market has reached saturation point** = the market is at a point where it cannot buy any more of the product
NOTE: no plural
◇ **saturate** *verb* to fill something completely; **to saturate the market; the market for home computers is saturated**

save *verb* **(a)** to keep (money) *or* not to spend (money); **he is trying to save money by walking to work; she is saving to buy a house (b)** not to waste *or* to use less; **to save time, let us continue the discussion in the taxi to the airport; the government is encouraging companies to save energy (c)**

to store data on a computer disk; **do not forget to save your files when you have finished keyboarding them**

◇ **save-as-you-earn** *noun* *GB* **save-as-you-earn scheme** = scheme where workers can save money regularly by having it deducted automatically from their wages and invested in National Savings

◇ **save on** *verb* not to waste *or* to use less; **by introducing shift work we find we can save on fuel**

◇ **saver** *noun* person who saves money

◇ **save up** *verb* to put money aside for a special purpose; **they are saving up for a holiday in the USA**

◇ **saving** **1** *noun* using less; **we are aiming for a 10% saving in fuel** **2** *suffix* which uses less; **an energy-saving** *or* **labour-saving device** = machine which saves energy *or* labour; **time-saving** = which takes less time

◇ **savings** *plural noun* money saved; **he put all his savings into a deposit account;** *GB* **National Savings** = scheme run by the Post Office, where small investors can invest in government savings certificates, premium bonds, etc.; **savings certificate** *or* *US* **savings bond** = document showing that you have invested money in a government savings scheme; **savings account** = bank account where you can put money in regularly and which pays interest, often at a higher rate than a deposit account

◇ **savings bank** *noun* bank where you can deposit money and receive interest on it

◇ **savings and loan (association)** *noun* *US* financial association which accepts and pays interest on deposits from investors and lends money to people who are buying property

SAYE = SAVE-AS-YOU-EARN

scab *noun* *informal* worker who goes on working when there is a strike

scale **1** *noun* **(a)** system which is graded into various levels; **scale of charges** *or* **scale of prices** = list showing various prices; **fixed scale of charges** = rate of charging which does not change; **scale of salaries** *or* **salary scale** = list of salaries showing different levels of pay in different jobs in

the same company; **he was appointed at the top end of the salary scale; incremental scale** = salary scale with regular annual salary increases **(b) large scale** *or* **small scale** = working with large or small amounts of investment *or* staff, etc.; **to start in business on a small scale** = to start in business with a small staff *or* few products *or* little investments; **economies of scale** = making a product more economical by manufacturing it or buying it in larger quantities **(c) scales** = machine for weighing **2** *verb* **to scale down** *or* **to scale up** = to lower *or* to increase in proportion

scam *noun* *US* *informal* case of fraud

scarce *adjective* not easily found *or* not common; **scarce raw materials; reliable trained staff are scarce**

◇ **scarceness** *or* **scarcity** *noun* lack *or* being scarce; **the scarceness of trained staff; there is a scarcity of trained staff; scarcity value** = value of something because it is rare and there is a large demand for it
NOTE: no plural

schedule **1** *noun* **(a)** timetable *or* plan of time drawn up in advance; **to be ahead of schedule** = to be early; **to be on schedule** = to be on time; **to be behind schedule** = to be late; **the project is on schedule; the building was completed ahead of schedule; I am sorry to say that we are three months behind schedule; the managing director has a busy schedule of appointments; his secretary tried to fit me into his schedule (b)** list (especially additional documents attached to a contract); **please find enclosed our schedule of charges; schedule of territories to which a contract applies; see the attached schedule** *or* **as per the attached schedule (c)** *GB* **tax schedules** = six types of income as classified for tax **2** *verb* **(a)** to list officially; **scheduled prices** *or* **scheduled charges (b)** to plan the time when something will happen; **the building is scheduled for completion in May; scheduled flight** = regular flight which is in the airline timetable; **he left for Helsinki on a scheduled flight**

◇ **scheduling** *noun* drawing up a plan *or* a timetable
NOTE: no plural

scheme 270 **season**

scheme *noun* plan *or* arrangement *or* way of working; **bonus scheme; pension scheme; profit-sharing scheme**

science *noun* study *or* knowledge based on observing and testing; **business science** *or* **management science** = the study of business *or* management techniques; **he has a master's degree in business science; science park** = area near a town or university set aside for technological industries

scope *noun* opportunity *or* possibility; **there is scope for improvement in our sales performance** = the sales performance could be improved; **there is considerable scope for expansion into the export market**

scrap 1 *noun* waste material *or* pieces of metal to be melted down to make new metal ingots; **to sell a ship for scrap; its scrap value is £2,500; scrap dealer** *or* **scrap merchant** = person who deals in scrap 2 *verb* **(a)** to give up *or* to stop working on; **to scrap plans for expansion (b)** to throw (something) away as useless; **they had to scrap 10,000 spare parts**
NOTE: **scrapping - scrapped**

screen 1 *noun* glass surface on which computer information *or* TV pictures, etc., can be shown; **a TV screen; he brought up the information on the screen** 2 *verb* to **screen candidates** = to examine candidates to see if they are completely suitable
◇ **screening** *noun* **the screening of candidates** = examining candidates to see if they are suitable

scrip *noun* **scrip issue** = new shares given free to shareholders

sea *noun* area of salt water; **to send a shipment by sea; by sea mail** = sent by post abroad, using a ship, not by air
◇ **seaport** *noun* port by the sea

seal 1 *noun* **(a) common seal** *or* **company's seal** = metal stamp for stamping documents with the name of the company to show they have been approved officially; **to attach the company's seal to a document; contract under seal** = contract which has been legally approved with the seal of the company **(b)** piece of paper *or* metal *or* wax attached to close something, so that it can be opened only if the paper *or* metal *or* wax is removed or broken; **customs seal** = seal attached by customs office to a box, to show that the contents have not passed through the customs 2 *verb* **(a)** to close something tightly; **the computer disks were sent in a sealed container; sealed envelope** = envelope where the back has been stuck down to close it; **the information was sent in a sealed envelope; sealed tenders** = tenders sent in sealed envelopes, which will all be opened at a certain time; **the company has asked for sealed bids for the warehouse (b)** to attach a seal *or* to stamp something with a seal; **the customs sealed the shipment**

search *noun* examination of records by the lawyer acting for someone who wants to buy a property, to make sure that the vendor has the right to sell it

season *noun* **(a)** one of four parts which a year is divided into (spring, summer, autumn, winter) **(b)** a period of time when something usually takes place; **low season** *or* **high season** = period when there are few travellers *or* lots of travellers; **air fares are cheaper in the low season; tourist season** *or* **holiday season** = period when there are many people on holiday; **busy season** *or* **slack season** = period when a company is busy *or* not very busy; **dead season** = time of year when there are few tourists about; **end of season sale** = selling goods cheaply when the season in which they would be used is over (such as summer clothes sold cheaply in the autumn)
◇ **seasonal** *adjective* which lasts for a season *or* which only happens during a particular season; **the demand for this item is very seasonal; seasonal variations in sales patterns; seasonal adjustments** = changes made to figures to take account of seasonal variations; **seasonal demand** = demand which exists only during the high season; **seasonal unemployment** = unemployment which rises and falls according to the season
◇ **seasonally** *adverb* **seasonally adjusted figures** = statistics which are adjusted to take account of seasonal variations
◇ **season ticket** *noun* rail *or* bus ticket which can be used for any number of

journeys over a period (normally 1, 3, 6 or 12 months)

sec = SECRETARY **hon sec** = honorary secretary

second 1 *adjective* (thing) which comes after the first; **second half-year** = six month period from July to the end of December; **second mortgage** = further mortgage on a property which is already mortgaged; **second quarter** = three month period from April to the end of June **2** *verb* **(a) to second a motion** = to be the first person to support a proposal put forward by someone else; **Mrs Smith seconded the motion** *or* **the motion was seconded by Mrs Smith (b)** to lend a member of staff to another company *or* to a government department, etc., for a fixed period of time; **he was seconded to the Department of Trade for two years**
◊ **secondary** *adjective* second in importance; **secondary banks** = companies which provide money for hire-purchase deals; **secondary industry** = industry which uses basic raw materials to make manufactured goods; **secondary picketing** = picketing of a second factory, which is not directly connected with a strike, to prevent it supplying a striking factory or receiving supplies from it
◊ **second-class** *adjective & adverb* less expensive *or* less comfortable way of travelling; **to travel second-class; the price of a second-class ticket is half that of a first class; I find second-class hotels are just as comfortable as the best ones; second-class mail** = (i) *GB* less expensive, slower, mail service; (ii) *US* mail service for sending newspapers and magazines; **a second-class letter is slower than a first-class; send it second-class if it is not urgent**
◊ **seconder** *noun* person who seconds a proposal; **there was no seconder for the motion so it was not put to the vote**
◊ **second half** *noun* period of six months from 1st July to end of December; **the figures for the second half are up on those for the first part of the year**
◊ **secondhand** *adjective & adverb* used *or* not new *or* which has been owned by someone before; **a secondhand car salesman; the secondhand computer market** *or* **the market in secondhand computers; to buy**
something secondhand; **look at the prices of secondhand cars** *or* **look at secondhand car prices; secondhand dealer** = dealer who buys and sells secondhand items
◊ **secondment** *noun* being seconded to another job for a period; **he is on three years' secondment to an Australian college**
◊ **second-rate** *adjective* not of good quality; **never buy anything second-rate**
◊ **seconds** *plural noun* items which have been turned down by the quality controller as not being top quality; **the shop has a sale of seconds**

secret *noun & adjective* (something) hidden *or* not known by many people; **the MD kept the contract secret from the rest of the board; they signed a secret deal with their main rivals; to keep a secret** = not to tell someone a secret which you know
◊ **secretary** *noun* **(a)** person who helps to organize work *or* types letters *or* files documents *or* arranges meetings, etc. for someone; **secretary and personal assistant; my secretary deals with incoming orders; his secretary phoned to say he would be late (b)** official of a company *or* society; **company secretary** = person who is responsible for a company's legal and financial affairs; **honorary secretary** = person who keeps the minutes and official documents of a committee *or* club, but is not paid a salary; **he was elected secretary of the committee** *or* **committee secretary; membership secretary** = committee member who deals with the ordinary members of a society **(c)** *GB* member of the government in charge of a department; **Education Secretary; Foreign Secretary;** *US* **Secretary of the Treasury** = senior member of the government in charge of financial affairs
◊ **Secretary of State** *noun* **(a)** *GB* member of the government in charge of a department **(b)** *US* senior member of the government in charge of foreign affairs
◊ **secretarial** *adjective* referring to the work of a secretary; **she is taking a secretarial course; he is looking for secretarial work; we need extra secretarial help to deal with the mailings; secretarial college** = college which teaches typing, shorthand and word-processing
◊ **secretariat** *noun* important office and the officials who work in it; **the United Nations secretariat**

section *noun* part of something; **legal section** = department of a company dealing with legal matters

sector *noun* part of the economy *or* the business organization of a country; **all sectors of the economy suffered from the fall in the exchange rate; technology is a booming sector of the economy; public sector** = nationalized industries and public services; **public sector borrowing requirement** = amount of money which a government has to borrow to pay for its own spending; **private sector** = all companies which are owned by private shareholders, not by the state; **the expansion is funded completely by the private sector; salaries in the private sector have increased faster than in the public**

QUOTE: government services form a large part of the tertiary or service sector
Sydney Morning Herald
QUOTE: in the dry cargo sector, a total of 956 dry cargo vessels are laid up - 3% of world dry cargo tonnage
Lloyd's List

secure **1** *adjective* safe *or* which cannot change; **secure job** = job from which you are not likely to be made redundant; **secure investment** = investment where you are not likely to lose money **2** *verb* **(a) to secure a loan** = to pledge a property as a security for a loan **(b)** to get (something) safely into your control; **to secure funds; he secured the backing of an Australian group**

◊ **secured** *adjective* **secured loan** = loan which is guaranteed by the borrower giving valuable property as security; **secured creditor** = person who is owed money by someone, and can legally claim the same amount of the borrower's property if he fails to pay back the money owed; **secured debts** = debts which are guaranteed by assets

◊ **securities** *plural noun* investments in stocks and shares; certificates to show that someone owns stock; **gilt-edged securities** *or* **government securities** = investments in British government stock; **listed securities** = shares which can be bought or sold on the Stock Exchange *or* shares which appear on the official Stock Exchange list; **the securities market** = Stock Exchange *or* place where stocks and shares can be bought or sold; **securities trader** = person whose business is buying and selling stocks and shares

◊ **security** *noun* **(a) job security** = feeling which a worker has that he has a right to keep his job *or* that his job will never end; **security of employment** = feeling by a worker that he has the right to keep his job until he retires; **security of tenure** = right to keep a job *or* rented accommodation, provided that certain conditions are met **(b)** being protected; **airport security** = actions taken to protect aircraft and passengers against attack; **security guard** = person who protects an office *or* factory against burglars; **office security** = protecting an office against theft **(c)** being secret; **security in this office is nil** = nothing can be kept secret in this office; **security printer** = printer who prints paper money, secret government documents, etc. **(d) social security** = money *or* help provided by the government to people who need it; **he lives on social security payments (e)** guarantee that someone will repay money borrowed; **to stand security for someone** = to guarantee that if the person does not repay a loan, you will repay it for him; **to give something as security for a debt; to use a house as security for a loan; the bank lent him £20,000 without security**
NOTE: no plural

see-safe *noun* agreement where a supplier will give credit for unsold goods at the end of a period; **we bought the stock see-safe**

seek *verb* to ask for; **they are seeking damages for loss of revenue; to seek an interview** = to ask if you can see someone; **she sought an interview with the minister**
NOTE: **seeking - sought**

seize *verb* to take hold of something *or* to take possession of something; **the customs seized the shipment of books; the court ordered the company's funds to be seized**

◊ **seizure** *noun* taking possession of something; **the court ordered the seizure of the shipment *or* of the company's funds**

select **1** *adjective* of top quality *or* specially chosen; **our customers are very select; a select range of merchandise 2** *verb* to choose; **selected items are reduced by 25%** = some items have been reduced by 25%

◊ **selection** *noun* choice; thing which has been chosen; **a selection of our product line; selection board** *or* **selection committee** = committee which chooses a candidate for a job; **selection procedure** = general method of choosing a candidate for a job

◊ **selective** *adjective* which chooses; **selective strikes** = strikes in certain areas *or* at certain factories, but not everywhere

self *pronoun* your own person; (*on cheques*) **"pay self"** = pay the person who has signed the cheque

◊ **self-** *prefix* referring to oneself

◊ **self-contained office** *noun* office which has all facilities inside it, and its own entrance, so that it is separate from other offices in the same building

◊ **self-employed** *adjective* working for yourself *or* not on the payroll of a company; **a self-employed engineer; he worked for a bank for ten years but now is self-employed; the self-employed** = people who work for themselves
NOTE: can be followed by a verb in the plural

◊ **self-financed** *adjective* **the project is completely self-financed** = the project pays its development costs out of its own revenue, with no subsidies

◊ **self-financing 1** *noun* the financing of development costs, purchase of capital assets etc., of a company from its own resources
NOTE: no plural
2 *adjective* **the company is completely self-financing** = the company finances its development costs *or* capital assets, etc. from its own resources

◊ **self-made man** *noun* person who is rich and successful because of his own work, not because he inherited money or position

◊ **self-regulatory** *adjective* (group) which regulates itself

◊ **self-service** *adjective* **a self-service store** = shop where customers take goods from the shelves and pay for them at the checkout; **self-service petrol station** = petrol station where the customers put the petrol in their cars themselves

◊ **self-sufficiency** *noun* being self-sufficient
NOTE: no plural

◊ **self-sufficient** *adjective* producing enough food *or* raw materials for its own needs; **the country is self-sufficient in oil**

◊ **self-supporting** *adjective* which finances itself from its own resources, with no subsidies

sell 1 *noun* act of selling; **to give a product the hard sell** = to make great efforts to persuade customers to buy it; **he tried to give me the hard sell** = he put a lot of effort into trying to persuade me to buy his product; **soft sell** = persuading people to buy, by encouraging and not forcing them to do so
NOTE: no plural
2 *verb* **(a)** to give goods in exchange for money; **to sell cars** *or* **to sell refrigerators; they have decided to sell their house; they tried to sell their house for £100,000; to sell something on credit; her house is difficult to sell; their products are easy to sell; to sell forward** = to sell foreign currency, commodities, etc., for delivery at a later date **(b)** to be bought; **these items sell well in the pre-Christmas period; those packs sell for £25 a dozen**
NOTE: **selling - sold**

◊ **sell-by date** *noun* date on a food packet which is the last date on which the food is guaranteed to be good

◊ **seller** *noun* **(a)** person who sells; **there were few sellers in the market, so prices remained high; seller's market** = market where the seller can ask high prices because there is a large demand for the product **(b)** thing which sells; **this book is a steady seller; best-seller** = item (especially a book) which sells very well

◊ **selling 1** *noun* **direct selling** = selling a product direct to the customer without going through a shop; **mail-order selling** = selling by taking orders and supplying a product by post; **selling costs** = amount of money to be paid for advertising, reps' commissions, etc., involved in selling something; **selling price** = price at which someone is willing to sell **2** *suffix* **fast-selling items** = items which sell quickly; **best-selling car** = car which sells better than other models

◊ **sell off** *verb* to sell goods quickly to get rid of them

◊ **sell out** *verb* **(a)** to sell all stock; **to sell out of a product line; we have sold out of electronic typewriters; this item has sold out (b) to sell out** = to sell one's business; **he sold out and retired to the seaside**

◇ **sellout** *noun* this item has been a sellout = all the stock of the item has been sold
◇ **sell up** *verb* to sell a business and all the stock

semi- *prefix* half
◇ **semi-finished** *adjective* **semi-finished products** = products which are partly finished
◇ **semi-skilled** *adjective* **semi-skilled workers** = workers who have had some training

send *verb* to make someone *or* something go from one place to another; **to send a letter** *or* **an order** *or* **a shipment; the company is sending him to Australia to be general manager of the Sydney office; send the letter airmail if you want it to arrive next week; the shipment was sent by rail**
NOTE: **sending - sent**
◇ **send away for** *verb* to write asking something to be sent to you; **we sent away for the new catalogue**
◇ **sender** *noun* person who sends; **"return to sender"** = words on an envelope *or* parcel to show that it is to be sent back to the person who sent it
◇ **send in** *verb* to send (a letter); **he sent in his resignation; to send in an application**
◇ **send off** *verb* to put (a letter) in the post
◇ **send off for** *verb* to write asking for something to be sent to you; **we sent off for the new catalogue**
◇ **send on** *verb* to post a letter which you have received, and address it to someone else; **he sent the letter on to his brother**

senior *adjective* older; more important; (worker) who has been employed longer than another; **senior manager** *or* **senior executive** = manager *or* director who has a higher rank than others; **senior partner** = most important partner in a firm of solicitors *or* accountants; **John Smith, Senior** = the older John Smith (i.e. the father of John Smith, Junior)
◇ **seniority** *noun* being older; being an employee of the company longer; **the managers were listed in order of seniority** = the manager who had been an employee the longest was put at the top of the list
NOTE: no plural

sensitive *adjective* able to feel something sharply; **the market is very sensitive to the result of the elections; price-sensitive product** = product which will sell less if the price is increased

separate 1 *adjective* not together; **to send something under separate cover** = to send something in a different envelope **2** *verb* to divide; **the personnel are separated into part-timers and full-time staff**
◇ **separately** *adverb* not together; **each job was invoiced separately**
◇ **separation** *noun* *US* leaving a job (resigning, retiring, or being fired or made redundant)

sequester *or* **sequestrate** *verb* to take and keep (property) because a court has ordered it
◇ **sequestration** *noun* taking and keeping of property on the order of a court
◇ **sequestrator** *noun* person who takes and keeps property on the order of a court

serial number *noun* number in a series; **this batch of shoes has the serial number 25-02**

series *noun* group of items following one after the other; **a series of successful takeovers made the company one of the largest in the trade**
NOTE: plural is **series**

serious *adjective* bad *or* important; **the storm caused serious damage; the management is making serious attempts to improve working conditions; the damage to the computer was not very serious**
◇ **seriously** *adverb* badly; **the cargo was seriously damaged by water**

servant *noun* person who is paid to work in someone's house; **civil servant** = person who works for the government

serve *verb* to deal with (a customer); **to serve a customer** = to take a customer's order and provide what he wants; **to serve in a shop** *or* **in a restaurant** = to deal with customers' orders; **to serve someone with a writ** *or* **to serve a writ on someone** = to give someone a writ officially, so that he has to obey it

service 1 *noun* **(a)** working for a company *or* in a shop, etc.; **length of service** = number of years someone has worked; **service agreement** *or* **service contract** = contract between a company and a director showing all conditions of work **(b)** the work of dealing with customers *or* payment for help for the customer; **the service in that restaurant is extremely slow; to add on 10% for service; the bill includes service** = includes a charge added for the work involved; **is the service included?; service charge** = charge added to the bill in a restaurant to pay for service *or* amount paid by tenants in a block of flats for general cleaning **(c)** keeping a machine in good working order; **the machine has been sent in for service; the routine service of equipment; service contract** = contract by which a company keeps a piece of equipment in good working order; **after-sales service** = service of a machine carried out by the seller for the buyer; **service centre** = office *or* workshop which specializes in keeping machines in good working order; **service department** = section of a company which keeps customers' machines in good working order; **service engineer** = engineer who specializes in keeping machines in good working order; **service handbook** *or* **service manual** = book which shows how to service a machine; **service station** = garage where you can buy petrol and have small repairs done to a car **(d)** business *or* office which gives help when it is needed; **answering service** = office which answers the telephone and takes messages for a company; **24-hour service** = help which is available for the whole day; **service bureau** = office which specializes in helping other offices; **service department** = department of a company which does not deal with production or sales (accounts, personnel, etc.); **service industry** = industry which does not make products, but offers a service (such as banking, insurance, transport) **(e) to put a machine into service** = to start using a machine **(f)** regular working of a public organization; **the postal service is efficient; the bus service is very irregular; we have a good train service to London; the civil service** = the administration of a country; **he has a job in the civil service; civil service pensions are index-linked** 2 *verb* **(a)** to keep a machine in good working order;

the car needs to be serviced every six months; the computer has gone back to the manufacturer for servicing **(b) to service a debt** = to pay interest on a debt; **the company is having problems in servicing its debts**

session *noun* meeting *or* period when a group of people meets; **the morning session** *or* **the afternoon session will be held in the conference room; opening session** *or* **closing session** = first part *or* last part of a conference

set 1 *noun* group of items which go together *or* which are used together *or* which are sold together; **set of tools** *or* **set of equipment; boxed set** = set of items sold together in a box 2 *adjective* fixed *or* which cannot be changed; **set price; set menu** = cheaper menu in a restaurant where there are only a few choices 3 *verb* to fix *or* to arrange; **we have to set a price for the new computer; the price of the calculator has been set low, so as to achieve maximum unit sales; the auction set a record for high prices** = the prices at the auction were the highest ever reached

NOTE: **setting - set**

◊ **set against** *verb* to balance one group of figures against another group to try to make them cancel each other out; **to set the costs against the invoice; can you set the expenses against tax?**

◊ **set aside** *verb* to decide not to apply a decision; **the arbitrator's award was set aside on appeal**

◊ **set back** *verb* to make something late; **the project was set back six weeks by bad weather**

◊ **setback** *noun* stopping progress; **the company suffered a series of setbacks in 1984; the shares had a setback on the Stock Exchange**

◊ **set out** *verb* to put clearly in writing; **to set out the details in a report**

◊ **set up** *verb* **(a)** to begin (something) *or* to organize (something) new; **to set up an inquiry** *or* **a working party; to set up a company** = to start a company legally **(b) to set up in business** = to start a new business; **he set up in business as an insurance broker; he set himself up as a freelance engineer**

◊ **setting up costs** *or* **setup costs**

plural noun costs of getting a machine *or* a factory ready to make a new product after finishing work on another one

◇ **setup** *noun* **(a)** arrangement *or* organization; **the setup in the office** = the way the office is organized **(b)** commercial firm; **he works for a PR setup**

QUOTE: the concern announced that it had acquired a third large tanker since being set up in 1983 *Lloyd's List*
QUOTE: a sharp setback in foreign trade accounted for most of the winter slowdown *Fortune*
QUOTE: for sale: top quality office furniture, which includes executive desks, filing cabinets, typewriters and complete office setup
Australian Financial Review

settle *verb* **(a) to settle an account** = to pay what is owed **(b) to settle a claim** = to agree to pay what is asked for; **the insurance company refused to settle his claim for storm damage; the two parties settled out of court** = the two parties reached an agreement privately without continuing the court case

◇ **settlement** *noun* **(a)** payment of an account; **settlement day** = day when accounts have to be settled; **our basic discount is 20% but we offer an extra 5% for rapid settlement** = we take a further 5% off the price if the customer pays quickly; **settlement in cash** *or* **cash settlement** = payment of an invoice in cash, not by cheque **(b)** agreement after an argument; **to effect a settlement between two parties** = to bring two parties together to make them agree

◇ **settle on** *verb* to leave property to someone when you die; **he settled his property on his children**

QUOTE: he emphasised that prompt settlement of all forms of industrial disputes would guarantee industrial peace in the country and ensure increased productivity *Business Times (Lagos)*

several *adjective* more than a few *or* some; **several managers are retiring this year; several of our products sell well in Japan**

◇ **severally** *adverb* separately *or* not jointly; **they are jointly and severally liable** = they are liable both as a group and as individuals

severance pay *noun* money paid as compensation to someone who is losing his job

severe *adjective* bad *or* serious; **the company suffered severe losses in the European market; the government imposed severe financial restrictions**

◇ **severely** *adverb* badly *or* in a serious way; **train services have been severely affected by snow**

shady *adjective* not honest; **shady deal**

shake *verb* **(a)** to move something quickly from side to side **(b)** to surprise *or* to shock; **the markets were shaken by the company's results**
NOTE: **shaking - shook - has shaken**

◇ **shakeout** *noun* reorganization, where some people are left, but others go; **a shakeout in the top management; only three companies were left after the shakeout in the computer market**

◇ **shakeup** *noun* total reorganization; **the managing director ordered a shakeup of the sales departments**

◇ **shaky** *adjective* not very sure *or* not very reliable; **the year got off to a shaky start**

share 1 *noun* **(a) to have a share in** = to take part in *or* to contribute to; **to have a share in management decisions; market share** *or* **share of the market** = percentage of a total market which the sales of a company cover; **the company hopes to boost its market share; their share of the market has gone up by 10% (b)** one of many parts into which a company's capital is divided; **he bought a block of shares in Marks and Spencer; shares fell on the London market; the company offered 1.8m shares on the market; "A" shares** = ordinary shares with limited voting rights; **"B" shares** = ordinary shares with special voting rights (often owned by the founder of the company and his family); **bonus share** = extra share given to an existing shareholder; **deferred shares** = shares which receive a dividend only after all other dividends have been paid; **founder's shares** = special shares issued to the person who starts a company; **ordinary shares** = normal shares in a company, which have no special benefits or restrictions; **preference shares** = shares (often with no voting rights) which receive their dividend before all other shares and are repaid first (at face value) if the company goes into liquidation; **share allocation** or **share allotment** = sharing of a small number of shares among a large number of people who have applied to buy them; **to allot shares** = to give a certain number of shares to people who have applied to buy them; **share capital** = value of the assets of a company held as shares; **share certificate** = document proving that someone owns shares; **share issue** = selling new shares in a company to the public **2** verb **(a)** to own or use something together with someone else; **to share a telephone; to share an office (b)** to divide something up among several people; **three companies share the market; to share computer time; to share the profits among the senior executives; to share information** or **to share data** = to give someone information which you have

◊ **shareholder** noun person who owns shares in a company; **to call a shareholders' meeting; shareholders' equity** = ordinary shares owned by shareholders in a company; **majority** or **minority shareholder** = person who owns more or less than half the shares in a company; **the solicitor acting on behalf of the minority shareholders**

◊ **shareholding** noun group of shares in a company owned by one person; **a majority shareholding** or **a minority shareholding** = group of shares which are more or less than half the total; **he acquired a minority shareholding in the company; she has sold all her shareholdings; dilution of shareholding** = situation where the ordinary share capital of a company has been increased, but without an increase in the assets so that each share is worth less than before

◊ **shareout** noun dividing something among many people; **a shareout of the profits**

◊ **sharing** noun dividing up; **profit sharing** = dividing profits among workers; **the company operates a profit-sharing scheme; time-sharing** = (i) owning a property in part, with the right to use it for a period each year; (ii) sharing a computer system with different users using different terminals

NOTE: no plural

shark noun **loan shark** = person who lends money at a very high interest rate

sharp adjective **(a)** sudden; **sharp rally on the stock market; sharp drop in prices (b) sharp practice** = way of doing business which is not honest, but not illegal

◊ **sharply** adverb suddenly; **shares dipped sharply in yesterday's trading**

sheet noun **(a) sheet of paper** = piece of paper; **sheet feed** = device which puts one sheet at a time into a computer printer or photocopier; **sales sheet** = paper which gives details of a product and explains why it is good; **time sheet** = paper showing when a worker starts work and when he leaves work in the evening **(b) balance sheet** = statement of the financial position of a company at the end of a financial year or at the end of a period; **the company's balance sheet for 1984; the accountants prepared a balance sheet for the first half-year**

shelf noun flat surface attached to a wall or in a cupboard on which items for sale are displayed; **the shelves in the supermarket were full of items before the Christmas rush; shelf filler** = person whose job it is to make sure that the shelves in a shop are kept full of items for sale; **shelf life of a product** = number of days or weeks when the product will stay on the shelf in the shop and still be good to use; **shelf space** = amount of space on shelves in a shop
NOTE: plural is **shelves**

shell company noun company which does not trade, but exists only as a name to be used to hold shares in other companies

shelter *noun* protected place; **tax shelter** = financial arrangement (such as a pension scheme) where investments can be made without tax

shelve *verb* to postpone *or* to put back to another date; **the project was shelved; discussion of the problem has been shelved** ◇ **shelving** *noun* **(a)** rows of shelves *or* space on shelves; **we installed metal shelving in the household goods department (b)** postponing; **the shelving of the project has resulted in six redundancies**

shift 1 *noun* **(a)** group of workers who work for a period, and then are replaced by another group; period of time worked by a group of workers; **day shift** = shift worked during the daylight hours (from early morning to late afternoon); **night shift** = shift worked during the night; **there are 150 men on the day shift; he works the day shift** *or* **night shift; we work an 8-hour shift; the management is introducing a shift system** *or* **shift working; they work double shifts** = two groups of workers are working shifts together **(b)** movement *or* change; **a shift in the company's marketing strategy; the company is taking advantage of a shift in the market towards higher priced goods 2** *verb* to move *or* to sell; **we shifted 20,000 items in one week** ◇ **shift key** *noun* key on a typewriter *or* computer which makes capital letters ◇ **shift work** *noun* system of work in a factory with shifts

shilling *noun* money used in Kenya

ship 1 *noun* large boat for carrying passengers and cargo on the sea; **cargo ship** = ship which carries cargo, not passengers; **container ship** = ship made specially to carry containers; **ship chandler** = person who supplies goods (such as food) to ships; **to jump ship** = to leave the ship on which you are working and not come back **2** *verb* to send (goods), but not always on a ship; **to ship goods to the USA; we ship all our goods by rail; the consignment of cars was shipped abroad last week; to drop ship** = to deliver a large order direct to a customer's shop or warehouse, without going through an agent
NOTE: **shipping - shipped**

ship broker *noun* person who arranges shipping *or* transport of goods for customers on behalf of ship owners ◇ **shipment** *noun* goods sent; **two shipments were lost in the fire; a shipment of computers was damaged; we make two shipments a week to France; bulk shipment** = shipments of large quantities of goods; **consolidated shipment** = goods from different companies grouped together into a single shipment; **drop shipment** = delivery of a large order from a manufacturer direct to a customer's shop or warehouse, without going through an agent ◇ **shipper** *noun* person who sends goods *or* who organizes the sending of goods for other customers ◇ **shipping** *noun* sending of goods; **shipping charges** *or* **shipping costs; shipping agent** = company which specializes in the sending of goods; **shipping clerk** = clerk who deals with shipping documents; **shipping company** *or* **shipping line** = company which owns ships; **shipping instructions** = details of how goods are to be shipped and delivered; **shipping note** = note which gives details of goods being shipped
NOTE: no plural. Note also that **shipping** does not always mean using a ship
◇ **shipyard** *noun* factory where ships are built

shoot up *verb* to go up fast; **prices have shot up during the strike**
NOTE: **shooting - shot**

shop 1 *noun* **(a)** place where goods are stored and sold; **bookshop; computer shop; electrical goods shop; he has bought a shoe shop in the centre of town; she opened a women's wear shop; all the shops in the centre of town close on Sundays; retail shop** = shop where goods are sold only to the public; **the corner shop** = small privately owned general store; **shop assistant** = person who serves customers in a shop; **shop front** = part of a shop which faces the street, including the entrance and windows; **shop window** = window in a shop where goods are displayed so that customers can see them *or* place where goods or services can be exhibited NOTE: US English usually uses **store (b)** place where goods are made *or* workshop; **machine shop** = place where working machines are kept; **repair shop** = small factory where machines are repaired; **on**

the shop floor = in the factory *or* in the works *or* among the ordinary workers; **the feeling on the shop floor is that the manager does not know his job** **(c) closed shop** = system where a company agrees to employ only union members in certain jobs; **the union is asking the management to agree to a closed shop** **2** *verb* **to shop (for)** = to look for things in shops

NOTE: **shopping** - **shopped**

◊ **shop around** *verb* to go to various shops or offices and compare prices before making a purchase *or* before placing an order; **you should shop around before getting your car serviced; he is shopping around for a new computer; it pays to shop around when you are planning to ask for a mortgage**

◊ **shopkeeper** *noun* person who owns or runs a shop

◊ **shoplifter** *noun* person who steals goods from shops

◊ **shoplifting** *noun* stealing goods from shops

NOTE: no plural

◊ **shopper** *noun* person who buys goods in a shop; **the store stays open to midnight to cater for late-night shoppers; shoppers' charter** = law which protects the rights of shoppers against shopkeepers who are not honest

◊ **shopping** *noun* **(a)** buying goods in a shop; goods bought in a shop; **to go shopping; to buy one's shopping** *or* **to do one's shopping in the local supermarket** **(b)** **shopping basket** = basket for carrying shopping; **shopping centre** = group of shops linked together with car parks and restaurants; *US* **shopping mall** = enclosed covered area for shopping, with shops, restaurants, banks and other facilities; **shopping precinct** = part of town which is closed to traffic so that people can walk about and shop; **window shopping** = looking at goods in shop windows, without buying anything; **shopping around** = looking at prices in various shops before buying what you want

NOTE: no plural

◊ **shop-soiled** *adjective* dirty because of having been on display in a shop

◊ **shop steward** *noun* elected trade union representative of workers who reports their complaints to the management

◊ **shopwalker** *noun* employee of a department store who advises the customers and supervises the shop assistants in a department

short **1** *adjective* **(a)** for a small period of time; **short credit** = terms which allow the customer only a little time to pay; **in the short term** = in the near future *or* quite soon **(b)** not as much as should be; **the shipment was three items short; when we cashed up we were £10 short** = we had £10 less than we should have had; **to give short weight** = to sell something which is lighter than it should be **(c)** **short of** = with less than needed *or* with not enough of; **we are short of staff** *or* **short of money; the company is short of new ideas** **(d)** **to sell short** = to agree to sell something (such as shares) which you do not possess, but which you think you will be able to buy for less; **short selling** *or* **selling short** = arranging to sell something in the future which you think you can buy for less than the agreed selling price; **to borrow short** = to borrow for a short period **2** *noun* **shorts** = government stocks which mature in less than five years time

◊ **shortage** *noun* lack *or* not having enough; **a chronic shortage of skilled staff; we employ part-timers to make up for staff shortages; the import controls have resulted in the shortage of spare parts; manpower shortage** *or* **shortage of manpower** = lack of workers; **there is no shortage of investment advice** = there are plenty of people who want to give advice on investments

◊ **short change** *verb* to give a customer less change than is right, hoping that he will not notice

◊ **short-dated** *adjective* **short-dated bills** = bills which are payable within a few days; **short-dated securities** = government stocks which mature in less than five years time

◊ **shorten** *verb* to make shorter; **to shorten credit terms**

◊ **shortfall** *noun* amount which is missing which would make the total expected sum; **we had to borrow money to cover the shortfall between expenditure and revenue**

◊ **shorthand** *noun* rapid way of writing using a system of signs; **shorthand secretary** = secretary who takes dictation in shorthand; **shorthand typist** = typist who can take dictation in shorthand and then type it; **to take shorthand** = to write using shorthand; **he took down the minutes in shorthand**

◇ **shorthanded** *adjective* without enough staff; **we are rather shorthanded at the moment**

◇ **short-haul** *adjective* **short-haul flight** = flight over a short distance (up to 1,000 km)

◇ **shortlist 1** *noun* list of some of the better people who have applied for a job, who can be asked to come for a test or an interview; **to draw up a shortlist; he is on the shortlist for the job 2** *verb* to make a shortlist; **four candidates have been shortlisted; shortlisted candidates will be asked for an interview**

◇ **short-range** *adjective* **short-range forecast** = forecast which covers a period of a few months

◇ **short-staffed** *adjective* with not enough staff; **we are rather short-staffed at the moment**

◇ **short-term** *adjective* for a short period; **to place money on short-term deposit; short-term contract; on a short-term basis** = for a short period; **short-term debts** = debts which have to be repaid within a few weeks; **short-term forecast** = forecast which covers a period of a few months; **short-term gains** = gains made over a short period (less than 12 months); **short-term loan** = loan which has to be repaid within a few weeks

◇ **short time** *noun* shorter working hours than usual; **to be on short time; the company has had to introduce short-time working because of lack of orders**

shot *noun* **mail shot** *or* **mailing shot** = leaflets sent by post to possible customers

show 1 *noun* **(a)** exhibition *or* display of goods or services for sale; **motor show; computer show; show house** *or* **show flat** = house *or* flat built and furnished so that possible buyers can see what similar houses could be like **(b) show of hands** = vote where people show how they vote by raising their hands; **the motion was carried on a show of hands 2** *verb* to make something be seen; **to show a gain** *or* **a fall; to show a profit** *or* **a loss**
NOTE: **showing - showed - has shown**

◇ **showcard** *noun* piece of cardboard with advertising material, put near an item for sale

◇ **showcase** *noun* cupboard with a glass front or top to display items

◇ **showroom** *noun* room where goods are displayed for sale; **car showroom**

shrink *verb* to get smaller; **the market has shrunk by 20%; the company is having difficulty selling into a shrinking market**
NOTE: **shrinking - shrank - has shrunk**

◇ **shrinkage** *noun* **(a)** amount by which something gets smaller; **to allow for shrinkage (b)** *informal* losses of stock through theft (especially by members of the staff of the shop)

◇ **shrink-wrapped** *adjective* covered in tight plastic protective cover

◇ **shrink-wrapping** *noun* act of covering (a book, fruit, record etc.) in a tight plastic cover

shut 1 *adjective* closed *or* not open; **the office is shut on Saturdays 2** *verb* to close; **to shut a shop** *or* **a warehouse**
NOTE: **shutting - shut**

◇ **shut down** *verb* **to shut down a factory** = to make a factory stop working for a time; **the offices will shut down for Christmas; six factories have shut down this month**

◇ **shutdown** *noun* shutting of a factory

◇ **shutout** *noun* locking of the door of a factory *or* office to stop the staff getting in

sick *adjective* ill *or* not well; **sick leave** = time when a worker is away from work because of illness; **sick pay** = pay paid to a worker who is sick, even if he cannot work

◇ **sickness** *noun* being ill; **sickness benefit** = payment paid by the government or private insurance to someone who is ill and cannot work; **the sickness benefit is paid monthly**

side *noun* **(a)** part of something near the edge; **credit side** = right-hand side of accounts showing money received; **debit side** = left-hand side of accounts showing money owed or paid **(b)** one of the surfaces of a flat object; **please write on one side of the paper only (c) on the side** = separate from your normal work, and hidden from your employer; **he works in an accountant's office, but he runs a construction company on the side; her salary is too small to live on, so the family lives on what she can make on the side**

◊ **sideline** *noun* business which is extra to your normal work; **he runs a profitable sideline selling postcards to tourists**

sight *noun* seeing; **bill payable at sight =** bill which must be paid when it is presented; **sight bill** *or* **sight draft =** bill of exchange which is payable at sight; **to buy something sight unseen =** to buy something without having inspected it

NOTE: no plural

sign 1 *noun* advertising board *or* notice which advertises something; **they have asked for planning permission to put up a large red shop sign; advertising signs cover most of the buildings in the centre of the town** 2 *verb* to write your name in a special way on a document to show that you have written it or approved it; **to sign a letter** *or* **a contract** *or* **a document** *or* **a cheque; the letter is signed by the managing director; the cheque is not valid if it has not been signed by the finance director; the warehouse manager signed for the goods =** the manager signed a receipt to show that the goods had been received; **he signed the goods in** *or* **he signed the goods out =** he signed the stock report to show that the goods had arrived *or* had been dispatched

◊ **signatory** *noun* person who signs a contract, etc.; **you have to get the permission of all the signatories to the agreement if you want to change the terms**

◊ **signature** *noun* name written in a special way by someone; **a pile of letters waiting for the managing director's signature; he found a pile of cheques on his desk waiting for signature; all cheques need two signatures**

◊ **sign on** *verb* to start work, by signing your name in the personnel office; **to sign on for the dole =** to register as unemployed

silent *adjective* not speaking; **silent partner =** partner who has a share of the business but does not work in it

simple interest *noun* interest calculated on the capital only, and not added to it

sincerely *adverb* **Yours sincerely** *or* *US* **Sincerely yours =** words used as an ending to a business letter addressed to a named person

sine die *phrase* **to adjourn a case sine die =** to postpone the hearing of a case without fixing a new date for it

single *adjective* one alone **(a) single fare** *or* **single ticket** *or* **a single =** fare *or* ticket for one journey from one place to another; **I want two singles to London (b) single premium policy =** insurance policy where only one premium is paid rather than regular annual premiums; **single-entry bookkeeping =** method of bookkeeping where payments or sales are noted with only one entry; **in single figures =** less than ten; **sales are down to single figures; inflation is now in single figures; single-figure inflation =** inflation rising at less than 10% per annum

sink *verb* **(a)** to go to the bottom of the water; **the ship sank in the storm and all the cargo was lost (b)** to go down suddenly; **prices sank at the news of the closure of the factory (c)** to invest money (into something); **he sank all his savings into a car-hire business**

NOTE: **sinking - sank - sunk**

◊ **sinking fund** *noun* fund built up out of amounts of money put aside regularly to meet a future need

sir *noun* **Dear Sir =** way of addressing a letter to a man whom you do not know or to a limited company; **Dear Sirs =** way of addressing a letter to a firm

sister *adjective* **sister company =** one of several companies which are part of the same group; **sister ship =** ship which is of the same design and belongs to the same company as another ship

sit-down *adjective* **sit-down protest** *or* **sit-down strike =** strike where the workers stay in their place of work and refuse to work or to leave

◊ **sit-in** *noun* strike where the workers stay in their place of work and refuse to work or leave

NOTE: plural is **sit-ins**

site 1 *noun* place where something is built; **we have chosen a site for the new factory; the supermarket is to be built on a site near the station; building site** *or* **construction site** = place where a building is being constructed; **all visitors to the site must wear safety helmets; green field site** = site for a factory which is in the country, and not surrounded by other buildings; **site engineer** = engineer in charge of a building being constructed 2 *verb* to be **sited** = to be placed; **the factory will be sited near the motorway**

situated *adjective* placed; **the factory is situated on the edge of the town; the office is situated near the railway station**
◊ **situation** *noun* **(a)** state of affairs; **financial situation of a company; the general situation of the economy (b)** job; **situations vacant** *or* **situations wanted** = list in a newspaper of vacancies for workers *or* of people wanting work **(c)** place where something is; **the factory is in a very pleasant situation by the sea**

size *noun* measurements of something *or* how big something is *or* how many there are of something; **what is the size of the container? the size of the staff has doubled in the last two years; this packet is the maximum size allowed by the post office**

skeleton *noun* **skeleton staff** = few staff left to carry on essential work while most of the workforce is away

skill *noun* ability to do something because you have been trained; **she has acquired some very useful office management skills; he will have to learn some new skills if he is going to direct the factory**
◊ **skilled** *adjective* having learnt certain skills; **skilled workers** *or* **skilled labour** = workers who have special skills *or* who have had long training

slack *adjective* not busy; **business is slack at the end of the week; January is always a slack period**
◊ **slacken off** *verb* to become less busy; **trade has slackened off**

slander 1 *noun* untrue spoken statement which damages someone's character; **action for slander** *or* **slander action** = case in a

law court where someone says that another person had slandered him 2 *verb* **to slander someone** = to damage someone's character by saying untrue things about him
NOTE: compare **LIBEL**

slash *verb* to cut *or* to reduce sharply; **to slash prices** *or* **credit terms; prices have been slashed in all departments; the bank has been forced to slash interest rates**

sleeper *noun* share which has not risen in value for some time, but which may suddenly do so in the future
◊ **sleeping** *adjective* **sleeping partner** = partner who has a share in the business but does not work in it

slide *verb* to move down steadily; **prices slid after the company reported a loss**
NOTE: **sliding - slid**
◊ **sliding** *adjective* which rises in steps; **a sliding scale of charges** = list of charges which rises gradually according to value *or* quantity *or* time, etc.

slight *adjective* not very large *or* not very important; **there was a slight improvement in the balance of trade; we saw a slight increase in sales in February**
◊ **slightly** *adverb* not very much; **sales fell slightly in the second quarter; the Swiss bank is offering slightly better terms**

slip 1 *noun* **(a)** small piece of paper; **compliments slip** = piece of paper with the name of the company printed on it, sent with documents, gifts, etc., instead of a letter; **deposit slip** = piece of paper stamped by the cashier to prove that you have paid money into your account; **distribution slip** = paper attached to a document *or* to a magazine, showing all the people in an office who should read it; **pay slip** = piece of paper showing the full amount of a worker's pay, and the money deducted as tax, pension and insurance contributions; **paying-in slip** = printed form which is filled in when money is being deposited in a bank; **sales slip** = paper showing that an article was bought at a certain shop; **goods can be exchanged only on production of a sales slip (b)** mistake; **he made a couple of slips in calculating the discount** 2 *verb* to go down and back; **profits slipped to £1.5m; shares**

slipped back at the close
NOTE: **slipping - slipped**
◇ **slip up** *verb* to make a mistake; **we slipped up badly in not signing the agreement with the Chinese company**
◇ **slip-up** *noun* mistake
NOTE: plural is **slip-ups**

slogan *noun* **publicity slogan** = group of words which can be easily remembered, and which is used in publicity for a product; **we are using the slogan "Smiths can make it" on all our publicity**

slot machine *noun* machine which provides drinks *or* cigarettes, plays music, etc., when a coin is put in it

slow 1 *adjective* not going fast; **a slow start to the day's trading; the sales got off to a slow start, but picked up later; business is always slow after Christmas; they were slow to reply *or* slow at replying to the customer's complaints; the board is slow to come to a decision; there was a slow improvement in sales in the first half of the year 2** *adverb* **to go slow** = to protest against management by working slowly
◇ **slow down** *verb* to stop rising *or* moving *or* falling; **inflation is slowing down; the fall in the exchange rate is slowing down; the management decided to slow down production**
◇ **slowdown** *noun* becoming less busy; **a slowdown in the company's expansion**
◇ **slowly** *adverb* not fast; **the company's sales slowly improved; we are slowly increasing our market share**

QUOTE: a general price freeze succeeded in slowing the growth in consumer prices
Financial Times
QUOTE: cash paid for stock: overstocked lines. factory seconds. slow sellers
Australian Financial Review
QUOTE: the fall in short-term rates suggests a slowing economy   *Financial Times*

slump 1 *noun* **(a)** rapid fall; **slump in sales; slump in profits; slump in the value of the pound; the pound's slump on the foreign exchange markets (b)** period of economic collapse with high unemployment and loss of trade; **we are experiencing slump conditions; the Slump** = the world economic crisis of 1929 - 1933 **2** *verb* to fall

fast; **profits have slumped; the pound slumped on the foreign exchange markets**

slush fund *noun* money kept to one side to give to people to persuade them to do what you want

small *adjective* not large; **small ads** = short private advertisements in a newspaper (selling small items, asking for jobs, etc.); **small businesses** = little companies with low turnover and few employees; **small businessman** = man who runs a small business; **small change** = loose coins; *GB* **small claims court** = court which deals with disputes over small amounts of money; **the small investor** = person who has a small amount of money to invest; **small shopkeepers** = owners of small shops
◇ **small-scale** *adjective* working in a small way, with few staff and not much money; **a small-scale enterprise** = a small business

smash *verb* to break (a record) *or* to do better than (a record); **to smash all production records; sales have smashed all records for the first half of the year**

smuggle *verb* to take goods into a country without declaring them to the customs; **they had to smuggle the spare parts into the country**
◇ **smuggler** *noun* person who smuggles
◇ **smuggling** *noun* taking goods illegally into a country; **he made his money in arms smuggling**
NOTE: no plural

snap *adjective* rapid *or* sudden; **the board came to a snap decision; they carried out a snap check *or* a snap inspection of the expense accounts**
◇ **snap up** *verb* to buy something quickly; **to snap up a bargain; he snapped up 15% of the company's shares**
NOTE: **snapping - snapped**

snip *noun informal* bargain; **these typewriters are a snip at £50**

soar *verb* to go up rapidly; **food prices soared during the cold weather; share prices soared on the news of the takeover bid *or* the news of the takeover bid sent share prices soaring**

social *adjective* referring to society in general; **social costs** = ways in which something will affect people; **the report examines the social costs of building the factory in the middle of the town; social security** = money from contributions paid to the National Insurance provided by the government to people who need it; **he gets weekly social security payments; the social system** = the way society is organized

◇ **society** *noun* **(a)** way in which people in a country are organized; **consumer society** = type of society where consumers are encouraged to buy goods; **the affluent society** = type of society where most people are rich **(b)** club *or* group of people with the same interests; **he has joined a computer society; building society** = financial institution which accepts and pays interest on deposits, and lends money to people who are buying property; **cooperative society** = organization where customers and workers are partners and share the profits; **friendly society** = group of people who pay regular subscriptions to a fund which is used to help members who are ill or in financial trouble

◇ **socio-economic** *adjective* referring to social and economic conditions; **the socio-economic system in capitalist countries; socio-economic groups** = groups in society divided according to income and position

soft *adjective* not hard; **soft currency** = currency of a country with a weak economy, which is cheap to buy and difficult to exchange for other currencies; **soft loan** = loan (from a company to an employee or from a government to another government) at very low or nil interest; **to take the soft option** = to decide to do something which involves least risk, effort or problems; **soft sell** = persuading people to buy by encouraging them, but not forcing them to do so

◇ **software** *noun* computer programs (as opposed to machines)
NOTE: no plural

sole *adjective* only; **sole agency** = agreement to be the only person to represent a company *or* to sell a product in a certain area; **he has the sole agency for Ford cars; sole agent** = person who has the sole agency for a product in an area; **sole distributor** = retailer who is the only one in an area who is allowed to sell a certain product; **sole owner** = person who owns a business on his own, with no partners; **sole trader** = person who runs a business by himself but has not registered it as a company

solemn *adjective* **solemn and binding agreement** = agreement which is not legally binding, but which all parties are supposed to obey

solicit *verb* **to solicit orders** = to ask for orders *or* to try to get people to order goods

◇ **solicitor** *noun* *GB* lawyer who gives advice to members of the public and acts for them legally; **to instruct a solicitor** = to give orders to a solicitor to start legal proceedings on your behalf

solus **(advertisement)** *noun* advertisement which does not appear near other advertisements for similar products

solution *noun* answer to a problem; **to look for a solution to the financial problems; the programmer came up with a solution to the systems problem; we think we have found a solution to the problem of getting skilled staff**

solve *verb* **to solve a problem** = to find an answer to a problem; **the loan will solve some of our short-term problems**

solvent *adjective* having enough money to pay debts; **when he bought the company it was barely solvent**

◇ **solvency** *noun* being able to pay all debts
NOTE: no plural

sort *verb* to put (a lot of things) in order; **she is sorting index cards into alphabetical order**

◇ **sort out** *verb* to put into order; to settle (a problem); **did you sort out the accounts problem with the auditors?**

sound *adjective* reasonable *or* which can be trusted; **the company's financial situation is very sound; he gave us some very sound advice**

◇ **soundness** *noun* being reasonable
NOTE: no plural

source *noun* place where something comes from; **source of income; you must declare income from all sources to the tax office; income which is taxed at source =** where the tax is removed before the income is paid

space *noun* empty place *or* empty area; **advertising space =** space in a newspaper set aside for advertisements; **to take advertising space in a newspaper =** to place a large advertisement in a newspaper; **floor space =** area of the floor in an office; **office space =** area available for offices or used by offices; **we are looking for extra office space for our new accounts department**

◇ **space bar** *noun* key on a typewriter *or* computer which makes a single space between letters

◇ **space out** *verb* to place things with spaces between them; **the company name is written in spaced-out letters; payments can be spaced out over a period of ten years**

spare *adjective* extra *or* not being used; **he has invested his spare capital in a computer shop; to use up spare capacity =** to make use of time or space which has not been fully used; **spare part =** small piece of machinery used to replace part of a machine which is broken; **the photocopier will not work - it needs a spare part; spare time =** time when you are not at work; **he built himself a car in his spare time**

spec *noun* **to buy something on spec =** to buy something as a speculation, without being sure of its value

◇ **specs** *plural noun* = SPECIFICATIONS

special *adjective* different *or* not normal *or* referring to one particular thing; **he offered us special terms; the car is being offered at a special price; special deposits =** large sums of money which banks have to deposit with the Bank of England

◇ **specialist** *noun* person *or* company which deals with one particular type of product or one subject; **you should go to a specialist in computers *or* to a computer specialist for advice**

◇ **speciality** *or* **specialty** *noun* particular interest *or* special type of product which a company deals in; **their speciality is computer programs;** *US* spe-

cialty store = shop selling a limited range of items of good quality

◇ **specialization** *noun* study of one particular thing *or* dealing with one particular type of product; **the company's area of specialization is accounts packages for small businesses**

◇ **specialize** *verb* to trade in one particular type of product or service; **the company specializes in electronic components; they have a specialized product line; he sells very specialized equipment for the electronics industry**

> QUOTE: the group specializes in the sale. lease and rental of new and second-user hardware
> *Financial Times*
>
> QUOTE: airlines offer special stopover rates and hotel packages to attract customers to certain routes
> *Business Traveller*

specie *plural noun* coins

specify *verb* to state clearly what is needed; **to specify full details of the goods ordered; do not include VAT on the invoice unless specified**

◇ **specification** *noun* detailed information about what is needed *or* about a product to be supplied; **to detail the specifications of a computer system; job specification =** very detailed description of what is involved in a job; **to work to standard specifications =** to work to specifications which are acceptable anywhere in the industry; **the work is not up to specification *or* does not meet our specifications =** the product is not made in the way which was detailed

specimen *noun* thing which is given as a sample; **to give specimen signatures on a bank mandate =** to write the signatures of all people who can sign cheques for an account so that the bank can recognize them

speculate *verb* to take a risk in business which you hope will bring you profits; **to speculate on the Stock Exchange =** to buy shares which you hope will rise in value

◇ **speculation** *noun* risky deal which may produce a short-term profit; **he bought the company as a speculation; she lost all her money in Stock Exchange speculations**

◇ **speculative** *adjective* **speculative builder** = builder who builds houses in the hope that someone will want to buy them; **speculative share** = share which may go up or down in value

◇ **speculator** *noun* person who buys goods *or* shares *or* foreign currency in the hope that they will rise in value; **a property speculator; a currency speculator; a speculator on the Stock Exchange** *or* **a Stock Exchange speculator**

speed *noun* rate at which something moves; **dictation speed** = number of words per minute which a secretary can write down in shorthand; **typing speed** = number of words per minute which a typist can type

◇ **speed up** *verb* to make something go faster; **we are aiming to speed up our delivery times**

spend *verb* **(a)** to pay money; **they spent all their savings on buying the shop; the company spends thousands of pounds on research (b)** to use time; **the company spends hundreds of man-hours on meetings; the chairman spent yesterday afternoon with the auditors**
NOTE: **spending - spent**

◇ **spending** *noun* paying money; **cash spending** *or* **credit card spending; consumer spending** = spending by consumers; **spending money** = money for ordinary personal expenses; **spending power** = having money to spend on goods; amount of goods which can be bought for a certain sum of money; **the spending power of the pound has fallen over the last ten years; the spending power of the student market**
NOTE: no plural

sphere *noun* area; **sphere of activity; sphere of influence**

spin off *verb* **to spin off a subsidiary company** = to take a part of a large company and make a smaller subsidiary from it
NOTE: **spinning - span - spun**

◇ **spinoff** *noun* useful product developed as a secondary product from a main item; **one of the spinoffs of the research programme has been the development of the electric car**

spiral 1 *noun* thing which twists round and round getting higher all the time; **the economy is in an inflationary spiral** *or* **wage-price spiral** = the economy is in a situation where price rises encourage higher wage demands which in turn make prices rise **2** *verb* to twist round and round, getting higher all the time; **a period of spiralling prices; spiralling inflation** = inflation where price rises make workers ask for higher wages which then increase prices again
NOTE: **spiralling - spiralled** but US English **spiraling - spiraled**

split 1 *noun* **(a)** dividing up; **share split** = dividing of shares into smaller denominations; **the company is proposing a five for one split** = the company is proposing that each existing share should be divided into five smaller shares **(b)** lack of agreement; **a split in the family shareholders 2** *verb* **(a) to split shares** = to divide shares into smaller denominations; **the shares were split five for one** = five new shares were given for each existing share held **(b) to split the difference** = to come to an agreement over a price by dividing the difference between the amount the seller is asking and amount the buyer wants to pay and agreeing on a price between the two
NOTE: **splitting - split**

spoil *verb* to ruin *or* to make something bad; **half the shipment was spoiled by water; the company's results were spoiled by a disastrous last quarter**

sponsor 1 *noun* **(a)** person who pays money to help research *or* to pay for a business venture; company which pays to help a sport, in return for advertising rights **(b)** company which advertises on TV **2** *verb* to pay money to help research *or* business development; **to sponsor an television programme; the company has sponsored the football match; government-sponsored trade exhibition**

◇ **sponsorship** *noun* act of sponsoring; **government sponsorship of overseas selling missions**

spot *noun* **(a)** buying something for immediate delivery; **spot cash** = cash paid for something bought immediately; **the spot market in oil** = the market for buying oil for immediate delivery; **spot**

price or **spot rate** = price or rate for something which is delivered immediately **(b)** place; **to be on the spot** = to be at a certain place; **we have a man on the spot to deal with any problems which happen on the building site (c)** TV **spot** = period on TV which is used for commercials; **we are running a series of TV spots over the next three weeks**

QUOTE: with most of the world's oil now traded on spot markets. Opec's official prices are much less significant than they once were *Economist*
QUOTE: the averager spot price of Nigerian light crude oil for the month of July was 27.21 dollars per barrel *Business Times (Lagos)*

spread 1 *noun* **(a)** range; **he has a wide spread of investments** or **of interests** = he has shares in many different types of companies **(b)** (*on the Stock Exchange*) difference between buying and selling prices 2 *verb* to space out over a period of time; **to spread payments over several months; to spread a risk** = to make the risk of insurance less great by asking other companies to help cover it
NOTE: spreading - spread
◇ **spreadsheet** *noun* computer print-out showing a series of columns of figures

QUOTE: dealers said markets were thin. with gaps between trades and wide spreads between bid and ask prices on the currencies *Wall Street Journal*
QUOTE: to ensure an average return you should hold a spread of different shares covering a wide cross-section of the market *Investors Chronicle*

square *noun* **(a)** shape with four equal sides and four right angles; **graph paper is drawn with a series of small squares (b)** way of measuring area, by multiplying the length by the width; **the office is ten metres by twelve - its area is one hundred and twenty square metres; square measure** = area in square feet or metres
NOTE: written with figures as ² : **10ft²** = ten square feet; **6m²** = six square metres
◇ **squared paper** *noun* graph paper or paper printed with a series of small squares

squeeze 1 *noun* government control carried out by reducing amounts available; **credit squeeze** = period when lending by the banks is restricted by the government; **profit squeeze** = control of

the amount of profits which companies can pay out as dividend 2 *verb* to crush or to press; to make smaller; **to squeeze margins** or **profits** or **credit; our margins have been squeezed by the competition** = profits have been reduced because our margins have to be smaller for us to stay competitive

stability *noun* being steady or not moving up or down; **price stability; a period of economic stability; the stability of the currency markets**
NOTE: no plural
◇ **stabilization** *noun* making stable or preventing sudden changes in prices, etc.; **stabilization of the economy** = keeping the economy stable by preventing inflation from rising, cutting high interest rates and excess money supply
◇ **stabilize** *verb* to make steady; **prices have stabilized** = prices have stopped moving up or down; **to have a stabilizing effect on the economy** = to make the economy more stable
◇ **stable** *adjective* steady or not moving up or down; **stable prices; stable exchange rate; stable currency; stable economy**

stack 1 *noun* pile or heap of things on top of each other; **there is a stack of replies to our advertisement** 2 *verb* to pile things on top of each other; **the boxes are stacked in the warehouse**

staff 1 *noun* people who work for a company or for an organization; **to be on the staff** or **a member of staff** or **a staff member** = to be employed permanently by a company; **staff agency** = agency which looks for office staff for companies; **staff appointment** = a job on the staff; **staff association** = society formed by members of staff of a company to represent them to the management and to organize entertainments; **accounts staff** = people who work in the accounts department; **clerical staff** or **office staff** = people who work in offices; **counter staff** = sales staff who work behind counters; **senior staff** or **junior staff** = older or younger members of staff; people in more important or less important positions in a company
NOTE: **staff** refers to a group of people and so is often followed by a verb in the plural
2 *verb* to employ workers; **to be staffed**

with skilled part-timers; **to have difficulty in staffing the factory**
◇ **staffer** *noun* *US* member of the permanent staff
◇ **staffing** *noun* providing workers for a company; **staffing levels** = numbers of members of staff required in a department of a company for it work efficiently; **the company's staffing policy** = the company's views on staff - how many are needed for each department *or* if they should be full-time or part-time *or* what the salaries should be, etc.
NOTE: no plural

stag **1** *noun* person who buys new issues of shares and sells them immediately to make a profit **2** *verb* **to stag an issue** = to buy a new issue of shares not as an investment, but to sell immediately at a profit
NOTE: **stagging - stagged**

stage **1** *noun* period *or* one of several points of development; **the different stages of the production process; the contract is still in the drafting stage** = the contract is still being drafted; **in stages** = in different steps; **the company has agreed to repay the loan in stages** **2** *verb* **(a)** to put on *or* to organize (a show); **the exhibition is being staged in the conference centre; to stage a recovery** = to recover; **the company has staged a strong recovery from a point of near bankruptcy** **(b) staged payments** = payments made in stages

stagflation *noun* inflation and stagnation of an economy

stagger *verb* to arrange (holidays, working hours) so that they do not all begin and end at the same time; **staggered holidays help the tourist industry; we have to stagger the lunch hour so that there is always someone on the switchboard**

stagnant *adjective* not active *or* not increasing; **turnover was stagnant for the first half of the year; a stagnant economy**
◇ **stagnate** *verb* not to increase *or* not to make progress; **the economy is stagnating; after six hours the talks were stagnating**
◇ **stagnation** *noun* not increasing *or* not making any progress; **the country entered a period of stagnation; economic**

stagnation = lack of expansion in the economy
NOTE: no plural

stake **1** *noun* money invested; **to have a stake in a business** = to have money invested in a business; **to acquire a stake in a business** = to buy shares in a business; **he acquired a 25% stake in the business** **2** *verb* **to stake money on something** = to risk money on something

QUOTE: other investments include a large stake in a Chicago-based insurance company, as well as interests in tobacco products and hotels
Lloyd's List

stamp **1** *noun* **(a)** device for making marks on documents; mark made in this way; **the invoice has the stamp "Received with thanks" on it; the customs officer looked at the stamps in his passport; date stamp** = stamp with rubber figures which can be moved, used for marking the date on documents; **rubber stamp** = stamp made of hard rubber cut to form words; **stamp pad** = soft pad of cloth with ink on which a stamp is pressed, before marking the paper **(b)** small piece of gummed paper which you buy from a post office and stick on a letter *or* parcel to pay for the postage; **a postage stamp; a £1 stamp (c) stamp duty** = tax on legal documents (such as the conveyance of a property to a new owner) **2** *verb* **(a)** to mark a document with a stamp; **to stamp an invoice "Paid"; the documents were stamped by the customs officials (b)** to put a postage stamp on (an envelope, etc.); **stamped addressed envelope** = envelope with your own address written on it and a stamp stuck on it to pay for the return postage; **send a stamped addressed envelope for further details and catalogue**

stand **1** *noun* arrangement of shelves *or* tables, etc. at an exhibition for showing a company's products; **display stand** = special stand for displaying goods for sale; **exhibition stand** = separate section of an exhibition where a company exhibits its products or services; **news stand** = small wooden shop on a pavement, for selling newspapers **2** *verb* to be *or* to stay; **to stand liable for damages** = to be liable to pay damages; **the company's balance stands at £24,000** = the balance is £24,000
NOTE: **standing - stood**

◇ **stand down** *verb* to withdraw your name from an election

◇ **stand in for** *verb* to take someone's place; **Mr Smith is standing in for the chairman, who is ill**

standard 1 *noun* normal quality *or* normal conditions which other things are judged against; **standard of living** *or* **living standards** = quality of personal home life (such as amount of food or clothes bought, size of family car, etc.); **production standards** = quality of production; **up to standard** = of acceptable quality; **this batch is not up to standard** *or* **does not meet our standards; gold standard** = linking of the value of a currency to value of a quantity of gold 2 *adjective* normal *or* usual; **a standard model car; we have a standard charge of £25 for a thirty-minute session; standard agreement** *or* **standard contract** = normal printed contract form; **standard letter** = letter which is sent without any change to various correspondents; **standard rate** = basic rate of income tax which is paid by most taxpayers

◇ **standardization** *noun* making sure that everything fits a standard *or* is produced in the same way; **standardization of design; standardization of measurements; standardization of products** = reducing a large number different products to a series which have the same measurements *or* design *or* packaging, etc. NOTE: no plural

◇ **standardize** *verb* to make sure that everything fits a standard *or* is produced in the same way

standby *noun* **(a) standby ticket** = cheap air ticket which allows the passenger to wait until the last moment to see if there is an empty seat on the plane; **standby fare** = cheap fare for a standby ticket **(b) standby arrangements** = plans for what should be done if an emergency happens, especially money held in reserve in the International Monetary Fund for use by a country in financial difficulties; **standby credit** = credit which is available if a company needs it

standing 1 *adjective* **standing order** = order written by a customer asking a bank to pay money regularly to an account; **I pay my subscription by standing order** 2 *noun* **(a) long-standing customer** *or* **customer of long standing** = person who has been a customer for many years **(b)** good reputation; **the financial standing of a company; company of good standing** = very reputable company NOTE: no plural

standstill *noun* situation where work has stopped; **production is at a standstill; the strike brought the factory to a standstill**

staple 1 *adjective* **(a) staple commodity** = basic food or raw material; **staple industry** = main industry in a country; **staple product** = main product **(b)** small piece of bent metal for attaching papers together; **he used a pair of scissors to take the staples out of the documents** 2 *verb* to **staple papers together** = to attach papers with staples; **he could not take away separate pages, because the documents were stapled together**

◇ **stapler** *noun* small device used to attach papers together with staples

start 1 *noun* beginning; **cold start** = beginning a new business *or* opening a new shop with no previous turnover to base it on; **house starts** *or* **US housing starts** = number of new private houses or flats of which construction has been started during a year 2 *verb* **to start a business from cold** = to begin a new business, with no previous turnover to base it on

◇ **starting** *noun* beginning; **starting date** = date on which something starts; **starting salary** = salary for an employee when he starts work with a company

◇ **start-up** *noun* beginning of a new company *or* new product; **start-up costs** NOTE: plural is **start-ups**

state 1 *noun* **(a)** independent country; semi-independent section of a federal country (such as the USA) **(b)** government of a country; **state enterprise** = company run by the state; **the bosses of state industries are appointed by the government; state ownership** = situation where an industry is nationalized 2 *verb* to say clearly; **the document states that all revenue has to be declared to the tax office**

◇ **state-controlled** *adjective* run by the

state; **state-controlled television**
◇ **state-of-the-art** *adjective* technically as advanced as possible
◇ **state-owned** *adjective* owned by the state or by a state

> QUOTE: the unions had argued that public sector pay rates had slipped behind rates applying in state and local government areas
> *Australian Financial Review*
> QUOTE: state-owned banks cut their prime rates a percentage point to 11% *Wall Street Journal*
> QUOTE: each year American manufacturers increase their budget for state-of-the-art computer-based hardware and software
> *Duns Business Month*

statement *noun* saying something clearly; **to make a false statement** = to give wrong details; **statement of expenses** = detailed list of money spent; **bank statement** = written document from a bank showing the balance of an account; **monthly** *or* **quarterly statement** = statement which is sent every month *or* every quarter by the bank **(b) financial statement** = document which shows the financial situation of a company; **the accounts department have prepared a financial statement for the shareholders (c) statement of account** = list of invoices and credits and debits sent by a supplier to a customer at the end of each month

station *noun* **(a)** place where trains stop for passengers; **the train leaves the Central Station at 14.15 (b) TV station** *or* **radio station** = building where TV or radio programmes are produced

stationery *noun* office supplies for writing, such as paper, carbons, pens, etc.; **stationery supplier; office stationery; continuous stationery** = paper made as a long sheet used in computer printers
NOTE: no plural

statistics *plural noun* study of facts in the form of figures; **to examine the sales statistics for the previous six months; government trade statistics show an increase in imports**
◇ **statistical** *adjective* based on figures; **statistical analysis; statistical information; statistical discrepancy** = amount by which sets of figures differ

◇ **statistician** *noun* person who analyzes statistics

status *noun* **(a)** importance *or* position in society; **the chairman's car is a status symbol** = the size of the car shows how important the company is; **loss of status** = becoming less important in a group; **status inquiry** = checking on a customer's credit rating **(b) legal status** = legal position
NOTE: no plural
◇ **status quo** *noun* state of things as they are now; **the contract does not alter the status quo**

statute *noun* law made by parliament; **statute book** = list of laws passed by parliament; **statute of limitations** = law which allows only a certain amount of time (a few years) for someone to claim damages or property
◇ **statutory** *adjective* fixed by law; **there is a statutory period of probation of thirteen weeks; statutory holiday** = holiday which is fixed by law

stay 1 *noun* **(a)** length of time spent in one place; **the tourists were in town only for a short stay; short-stay guests** = customers who spend only a few nights at a hotel **(b) stay of execution** = temporary stopping of a legal order; **the court granted the company a two-week stay of execution** 2 *verb* to stop at a place; **the chairman is staying at the Hotel London; profits have stayed below 10% for two years; inflation has stayed high in spite of the government's efforts to bring it down**

STD = SUBSCRIBER TRUNK DIALLING

steady 1 *adjective* continuing in a regular way; **steady increase in profits; the market stayed steady; there is a steady demand for computers** 2 *verb* to become firm *or* to stop fluctuating; **the markets steadied after last week's fluctuations; prices steadied on the commodity markets; the government's figures had a steadying influence on the exchange rate**
◇ **steadily** *adverb* in a regular *or* continuous way; **output increased steadily over the last two quarters; the company has steadily increased its market share**
◇ **steadiness** *noun* being firm *or* not

fluctuating; **the steadiness of the markets is due to the government's intervention** NOTE: no plural

steal *verb* to take something which does not belong to you; **the rival company stole our best clients; one of our biggest problems is stealing in the wine department** NOTE: **stealing - stole - has stolen**

steep *adjective* very sharp *or* very high (price); **a steep increase in interest charges; a steep decline in overseas sales**

stencil *noun* sheet of special paper which can be written or typed on, and used in a duplicating machine

stenographer *noun* official person who can write in shorthand

step *noun* **(a)** type of action; **the first step taken by the new MD was to analyse all the expenses; to take steps to prevent something happening** = to act to stop something happening **(b)** movement; **becoming assistant to the MD is a step up the promotion ladder; in step with** = moving at the same rate as; **the pound rose in step with the dollar; out of step with** = not moving at the same rate as; **the pound was out of step with other European currencies; wages are out of step with the cost of living** ◇ **step up** *verb* to increase; **to step up industrial action; the company has stepped up production of the latest models** NOTE: **stepping - stepped**

sterling *noun* standard currency used in the United Kingdom; **to quote prices in sterling** *or* **to quote sterling prices; pound sterling** = official term for the British currency; **sterling area** = area of the world where the pound sterling is the main trading currency; **sterling balances** = a country's trade balances expressed in pounds sterling; **sterling crisis** = fall in the exchange rate of the pound sterling NOTE: no plural

QUOTE: it is doubtful that British goods will price themselves back into world markets as long as sterling labour costs continue to rise faster than in competitor countries *Sunday Times*

stevedore *noun* person who works in a port, loading or unloading ships

steward *noun* **(a)** man who serves drinks *or* food on a ship *or* plane **(b) shop steward** = elected union representative of workers, who represents their complaints to the management ◇ **stewardess** *noun* woman who serves drinks *or* food on a ship *or* plane

stick *verb* **(a)** to attach with glue; **to stick a stamp on a letter; they stuck a poster on the door (b)** to stay still *or* not to move; **sales have stuck at £2m for the last two years** NOTE: **sticking - stuck** ◇ **sticker** **1** *noun* small piece of gummed paper or plastic to be stuck on something as an advertisement *or* to indicate a price; **airmail sticker** = blue sticker with the words "By air mail" which can be stuck on an envelope or parcel to show that it is being sent by air **2** *verb* to put a price sticker on an article for sale; **we had to sticker all the stock**

stiff *adjective* strong *or* difficult; **stiff competition; he had to take a stiff test before he qualified**

stimulate *verb* to encourage *or* to make (something) become more active; **to stimulate the economy; to stimulate trade with the Middle East** ◇ **stimulus** *noun* thing which encourages activity NOTE: plural is **stimuli**

stipulate *verb* to demand that a condition be put into a contract; **to stipulate that the contract should run for five years; to pay the stipulated charges; the company failed to pay on the date stipulated in the contract; the contract stipulates that the seller pays the buyer's legal costs** ◇ **stipulation** *noun* condition in a contract

stock **1** *noun* **(a)** quantity of raw materials; **we have large stocks of oil** *or* **coal; the country's stocks of butter** *or* **sugar (b)** quantity of goods for sale; **opening stock** = details of stock at the beginning of an accounting period; **closing stock** = details of stock at the end of an accounting period; **stock code** = number and letters which indicate an item of stock; **stock control** = making sure that enough stock is kept and that quantities and movements of stock are noted; **stock depreciation =** reduction in value of stock which is held in a warehouse for some time; **stock figures =** details of how many goods are in the warehouse *or* store etc.; **stock level =** quantity of goods kept in stock; **we try to keep stock levels low during the summer; stock turn** *or* **stock turnround** *or* **stock turnover =** total value of stock sold in a year divided by the average value of goods in stock; **stock valuation =** estimating the value of stock at the end of an accounting period; **to buy a shop with stock at valuation =** to pay for the stock the same amount as its value as estimated by the valuer; **stock in hand =** stock held in a shop *or* warehouse; **to purchase stock at valuation =** to pay for stock the price it is valued at **(c) in stock** *or* **out of stock =** available *or* not available in the warehouse *or* store; **to hold 2,000 lines in stock; the item went out of stock just before Christmas but came back into stock in the first week of January; we are out of stock of this item; to take stock =** to count the items in a warehouse **(d) stocks and shares =** shares in ordinary companies; **stock certificate =** document proving that someone owns stock in a company; **debenture stock =** capital borrowed by a company, using its fixed assets as security; **dollar stocks =** shares in American companies; **government stock =** government securities; **loan stock =** money lent to a company at a fixed rate of interest; **convertible loan stock =** money lent to a company which can be converted into shares at a later date; *US* **common stock =** ordinary shares in a company giving the shareholders the right to vote at meetings and receive a dividend **(e) the stock market =** place where shares are bought and sold; **stock market price** *or* **price on the stock market; stock market valuation =** value of shares based on the current market price **(f)** normal *or* usually kept in stock; **butter is a stock item for any good grocer; stock size =** normal size; **we only carry stock sizes of shoes 2** *verb* to hold goods for sale in a warehouse *or* store; **to stock 200 lines**

◇ **stockbroker** *noun* person who buys or sells shares for clients; **stockbroker's commission =** payment to a broker for a deal carried out on behalf of a client

◇ **stockbroking** *noun* trade of dealing in shares for clients; **a stockbroking firm** NOTE: no plural

◇ **stock controller** *noun* person who notes movements of stock

◇ **Stock Exchange** *noun* place where stocks and shares are bought and sold; **he works on the Stock Exchange; shares in the company are traded on the Stock Exchange; Stock Exchange listing =** official list of shares which can be bought or sold on the Stock Exchange

◇ **stockholder** *noun* person who holds shares in a company

◇ **stockholding** *noun* shares in a company held by someone

◇ **stock-in-trade** *noun* goods held by a business for sale NOTE: no plural

◇ **stockist** *noun* person *or* shop which stocks a certain item

◇ **stock jobber** *noun* person who buys and sells shares from other traders on the Stock Exchange

◇ **stock jobbing** *noun* buying and selling shares from other traders on the Stock Exchange NOTE: no plural

◇ **stocklist** *noun* list of items carried in stock

◇ **stockpile 1** *noun* supplies kept by a country *or* a company in case of need; **a stockpile of raw materials 2** *verb* to buy items and keep them in case of need; **to stockpile raw materials**

◇ **stockroom** *noun* room where stores are kept

◇ **stocktaking** *noun* counting of goods in stock at the end of an accounting period; **the warehouse is closed for the annual stocktaking; stocktaking sale =** sale of goods cheaply to clear a warehouse before stocktaking NOTE: no plural

◇ **stock up** *verb* to buy supplies of something which you will need in the future; **they stocked up with computer paper**

QUOTE: US crude oil stocks fell last week by nearly 2.5m barrels *Financial Times*
QUOTE: to stock rose to over $20 a share, higher than the $18 bid *Fortune*
QUOTE: the news was favourably received on the Sydney Stock Exchange, where the shares gained 40 cents to A$9.80 *Financial Times*

stop 1 *noun* **(a)** end of an action; **work came to a stop when the company could not pay the workers' wages; the new finance director put a stop to the reps' expense claims (b)** not supplying; **account on stop** = account which is not supplied because it has not paid its latest invoices; **to put an account on stop; to put a stop on a cheque** = to tell the bank not to pay a cheque which you have written **2** *verb* **(a)** to make (something) not to move any more; **the shipment was stopped by the customs; the government has stopped the import of cars (b)** not to do anything any more; **the work force stopped work when the company could not pay their wages; the office staff stop work at 5.30; we have stopped supplying Smith & Co. (c) to stop an account** = not to supply an account any more on credit because bills have not been paid; **to stop a cheque** = to ask a bank not to pay a cheque you have written; **to stop payments** = not to make any further payments **(d) to stop someone's wages** = to take money out of someone's wages; **we stopped £25 from his pay because he was late**
NOTE: **stopping - stopped**

◊ **stop over** *verb* to stay for a short time in a place on a long journey; **we stopped over in Hong Kong on the way to Australia**

◊ **stopover** *noun* staying for a short time in a place on a long journey; **the ticket allows you two stopovers between London and Tokyo**

◊ **stoppage** *noun* **(a)** act of stopping; **stoppage of deliveries; stoppage of payments; deliveries will be late because of stoppages on the production line (b)** money take from a worker's wage packet for insurance, tax, etc.

storage *noun* **(a)** keeping in store or in a warehouse; **we put our furniture into storage; storage capacity** = space available for storage; **storage company** = company which keeps items for customers; **storage facilities** = equipment and buildings suitable for storage; **storage unit** = device attached to a computer for storing information on disk or tape; **cold storage** = keeping food, etc., in a cold store to prevent it going bad; **to put a plan into cold storage** = to postpone work on a plan, usually for a very long time **(b)** cost of keeping goods in store; **storage was 10% of value, so we scrapped the stock (c)**

facility for storing data in a computer; **disk with a storage capacity of 10Mb**
NOTE: no plural

◊ **store** 1 *noun* **(a)** place where goods are kept; **cold store** = warehouse or room where food can be kept cold **(b)** quantity of items or materials kept because they will be needed; **I always keep a store of envelopes ready in my desk (c)** large shop; **a furniture store; a big clothing store; chain store** = one store in a number of stores; **department store** = large store with sections for different types of goods; **discount store** = shop which specializes in cheap goods sold at a high discount; **general stores** = small country shop which sells a wide range of products **2** *verb* **(a)** to keep in a warehouse; **to store goods for six months (b)** to keep for future use; **we store our pay records on computer**

◊ **storekeeper** *or* **storeman** *noun* person in charge of a storeroom

◊ **storeroom** *noun* room where stock can be kept or small warehouse attached to a factory

straight line *noun* **straight line depreciation** = depreciation calculated by dividing the cost of an asset by the number of years it is likely to be used

strategy *noun* plan of future action; **business strategy; company strategy; marketing strategy; financial strategy**

◊ **strategic** *adjective* based on a plan of action; **strategic planning** = planning the future work of a company

stream *noun* mass of people or traffic, all going in the same direction; **we had a stream of customers on the first day of the sale; to come on stream** = to start production

◊ **streamer** *noun* device for attaching a tape storage unit to a computer

◊ **streamline** *verb* to make (something) more efficient or more simple; **to streamline the accounting system; to streamline distribution services**

◊ **streamlined** *adjective* efficient or rapid; **streamlined production; the company introduced a streamlined system of distribution**

◊ **streamlining** *noun* making efficient
NOTE: no plural

street *noun* road in a town; **High Street** = main shopping street in a British town; **the High Street banks** = main British banks which accept deposits from individual customers; **street directory** = (i) list of people living in a street; (ii) map of a town with all the streets listed in alphabetical order in an index

strength *noun* being strong *or* at a high level; **the company took advantage of the strength of the demand for home computers; the strength of the pound increases the possibility of high interest rates**

stretch *verb* to pull out *or* make longer; **the investment programme has stretched the company's resources; he is not fully stretched** = his job does not make him work as hard as he could

strict *adjective* exact; **in strict order of seniority**
◇ **strictly** *adverb* exactly; **the company asks all staff to follow strictly the buying procedures**

strike 1 *noun* **(a)** stopping of work by the workers (because of lack of agreement with management *or* because of orders from a union); **all-out strike** = complete strike by all workers; **general strike** = strike of all the workers in a country; **official strike** = strike which has been approved by the main office of a union; **protest strike** = strike in protest at a particular grievance; **sit-down strike** = strike where workers stay in their place of work and refuse to work or leave; **sympathy strike** = strike to show that workers agree with another group of workers who are on strike; **token strike** = short strike to show that workers have a grievance; **unofficial strike** = strike by local workers, which has not been approved by the main union; **wildcat strike** = strike organized by workers without the main union office knowing about it **(b) to take strike action** = to go on strike; **strike call** = demand by a union for a strike; **no-strike agreement** *or* **no-strike clause** = (clause in an) agreement where the workers say that they will never strike; **strike fund** = money collected by a trade union from its members, used to pay strike pay; **strike pay** = wages paid to striking workers by their trade union; **strike ballot** *or* **strike**

vote = vote by workers to decide if a strike should be held **(c) to come out on strike** *or* **to go on strike** = to stop work; **the office workers are on strike for higher pay; to call the workforce out on strike** = to tell the workers to stop work; **the union called its members out on strike** 2 *verb* **(a)** to stop working because there is no agreement with management; **to strike for higher wages** *or* **for shorter working hours; to strike in protest against bad working conditions; to strike in sympathy with the postal workers** = to strike to show that you agree with the postal workers who are on strike **(b) to strike a bargain with someone** = to come to an agreement; **a deal was struck at £25 a unit** = we agreed the price of £25 a unit
NOTE: **striking - struck**
◇ **strikebound** *adjective* not able to work *or* to move because of a strike; **six ships are strikebound in the docks**
◇ **strikebreaker** *noun* worker who goes on working while everyone else is on strike
◇ **striker** *noun* worker who is on strike

stripper *noun* **asset stripper** = person who buys a company to sell its assets
◇ **stripping** *noun* **asset stripping** = buying a company in order to sell its assets

strong *adjective* with a lot of force *or* strength; **a strong demand for home computers; the company needs a strong chairman; strong pound** = pound which is high against other currencies
◇ **strongbox** *noun* safe *or* heavy metal box which cannot be opened easily, in which valuable documents, money, etc., can be kept
◇ **strongroom** *noun* special room (in a bank) where valuable documents, money, golds, etc., can be kept

QUOTE: everybody blames the strong dollar for US trade problems *Duns Business Month*
QUOTE: in a world of floating exchange rates the dollar is strong because of capital inflows rather than weak because of the nation's trade deficit *Duns Business Month*

structure 1 *noun* way in which something is organized; **the paper gives a diagram of the company's organizational structure; the price structure in the small car market; the career structure within a cor-**

poration; the company is reorganizing its discount structure; **capital structure of a company** = way in which a company's capital is set up; **the company's salary structure** = organization of salaries in a company with different rates of pay for different types of job **2** *verb* to arrange in a certain way; **to structure a meeting**

◇ **structural** *adjective* referring to a structure; **to make structural changes in a company; structural unemployment** = unemployment caused by the changing structure of an industry *or* society

stub *noun* **cheque stub** = piece of paper left in a cheque book after a cheque has been written and taken out

studio *noun* place where designers, film producers, artists, etc., work; **design studio** = independent firm which specializes in creating designs for companies

study 1 *noun* examining something carefully; **the company has asked the consultants to prepare a study of new production techniques; he has read the government study on sales opportunities; to carry out a feasibility study on a project** = to examine the costs and possible profits to see if the project should be started **2** *verb* to examine (something) carefully; **we are studying the possibility of setting up an office in New York; the government studied the committee's proposals for two months; you will need to study the market carefully before deciding on the design of the product**

stuff *verb* to put papers, etc., into envelopes; **we pay casual workers £2 an hour for stuffing envelopes** *or* **for envelope stuffing**

◇ **stuffer** *noun* *US* advertising paper to be put in an envelope for mailing

style *noun* way of doing *or* making something; **a new style of product; old-style management techniques**

sub *noun* **(a)** wages paid in advance **(b)** = SUBSCRIPTION

sub- *prefix* under *or* less important

◇ **sub-agency** *noun* small agency which is part of a large agency

◇ **sub-agent** *noun* person who is in charge of a sub-agency

◇ **subcommittee** *noun* small committee which is part of *or* set up by a main committee; **the next item on the agenda is the report of the finance subcommittee**

◇ **subcontract 1** *noun* contract between the main contractor for a whole project and another firm who will do part of the work; **they have been awarded the subcontract for all the electrical work in the new building; we will put the electrical work out to subcontract 2** *verb* to agree with a company that they will do part of the work for a project; **the electrical work has been subcontracted to Smith Ltd**

◇ **subcontractor** *noun* company which has a contract to do work for a main contractor

◇ **subdivision** *noun* *US* piece of empty land to be used for building new houses

subject to *adjective* **(a)** depending on; **the contract is subject to government approval** = the contract will be valid only if it is approved by the government; **agreement** *or* **sale subject to contract** = agreement *or* sale which is not legal until a proper contract has been signed; **offer subject to availability** = the offer is valid only if the goods are available **(b)** these **articles are subject to import tax** = import tax has to be paid on these articles

sub judice *adverb* being considered by a court (and so not to be mentioned in the media); **the papers cannot report the case because it is still sub judice**

sublease 1 *noun* lease from a tenant to another tenant **2** *verb* to lease a leased property from another tenant; **they subleased a small office in the centre of town**

◇ **sublessee** *noun* person *or* company which takes a property on a sublease

◇ **sublessor** *noun* tenant who lets a leased property to another tenant

◇ **sublet** *verb* to let a leased property to another tenant; **we have sublet part of our office to a financial consultancy**
NOTE: **subletting - sublet**

submit *verb* to put (something) forward to be examined; **to submit a proposal to the committee; he submitted a claim to the**

insurers; the reps are asked to submit their expenses claims once a month
NOTE: **submitting - submitted**

subordinate 1 *adjective* less important; **subordinate to** = governed by *or* which depends on 2 *noun* member of staff who is directed by someone; **his subordinates find him difficult to work with**

subpoena 1 *noun* order telling someone to appear in court as a witness 2 *verb* to order someone to appear in court; **the finance director was subpoenaed by the prosecution**

subscribe *verb* (a) **to subscribe to a magazine** = to pay for a series of issues of a magazine (b) **to subscribe for shares** = to apply for shares in a new company
◇ **subscriber** *noun* (a) **subscriber to a magazine** *or* **magazine subscriber** = person who has paid in advance for a series of issues of a magazine; **the extra issue is sent free to subscribers** (b) **subscriber to a share issue** = person who has applied for shares in a new company (c) **telephone subscriber** = person who has a telephone; **subscriber trunk dialling** = telephone system where you can dial international numbers direct from your own telephone without going through the operator
◇ **subscription** *noun* (a) money paid in advance for a series of issues of a magazine *or* for membership of a society; **did you remember to pay the subscription to the computer magazine? he forgot to renew his club subscription; to take out a subscription to a magazine** = to start paying for a series of issues of a magazine; **to cancel a subscription to a magazine** = to stop paying for a magazine; **subscription rates** = amount of money to be paid for a series of issues of a magazine (b) **subscription to a new share issue** = offering shares in a new company for sale; **subscription list** = list of subscribers to a new share issue; **the subscription lists close at 10.00 on September 24th** = no new applicants will be allowed to subscribe for the share issue after that date

subsidiary 1 *adjective* (thing) which is less important; **they agreed to most of the conditions in the contract but queried one or two subsidiary items; subsidiary company** = company which is owned by a parent company 2 *noun* company which is owned by a parent company; **most of the group profit was contributed by the subsidiaries in the Far East**

subsidize *verb* to help by giving money; **the government has refused to subsidize the car industry; subsidized accommodation** = cheap accommodation which is partly paid for by an employer or a local authority, etc.
◇ **subsidy** *noun* (a) money given to help something which is not profitable; **the industry exists on government subsidies; the government has increased its subsidy to the car industry** (b) money given by a government to make something cheaper; **the subsidy on butter** *or* **the butter subsidy**

subsistence *noun* minimum amount of food, money, housing, etc., which a person needs; **subsistence allowance** = money paid by a company to cover the cost of hotels, meals, etc., for a member of staff who is travelling on business; **to live at subsistence level** = to have only just enough money to live on
NOTE: no plural

substantial *adjective* large *or* important; **she was awarded substantial damages** = she received a large sum of money as damages; **to acquire a substantial interest in a company** = to buy a large number of shares in a company

substitute 1 *noun* person *or* thing which takes the place of someone *or* something else 2 *verb* to take the place of something else

subtenancy *noun* agreement to sublet a property
◇ **subtenant** *noun* person *or* company to which a property has been sublet

subtotal *noun* total of one section of a complete set of figures

subtract *verb* to take away (something) from a total; **if the profits from the Far Eastern operations are subtracted, you will see that the group has not been profitable in the European market**

subvention *noun* subsidy

succeed *verb* (a) to do well *or* to be profitable; **the company has succeeded best in the overseas markets; his business has succeeded more than he had expected** (b) to do what was planned; **she succeeded in passing her shorthand test; they succeeded in putting their rivals out of business** (c) to follow (someone); **Mr Smith was succeeded as chairman by Mr Jones**
◇ **success** *noun* (a) doing something well; **the launch of the new model was a great success; the company has had great success in the Japanese market** (b) doing what was intended; **we had no success in trying to sell the lease; he has been looking for a job for six months, but with no success**
◇ **successful** *adjective* which does well; **a successful businessman; a successful selling trip to Germany**
◇ **successfully** *adverb* done well; **he successfully negotiated a new contract with the unions; the new model was successfully launched last month**
◇ **successor** *noun* person who takes over from someone; **Mr Smith's successor as chairman will be Mr Jones**

sue *verb* to take someone to court *or* to start legal proceedings against someone to get money as compensation; **to sue someone for damages; he is suing the company for $50,000 compensation**

suffer *verb* to be in a bad situation *or* to do badly; **exports have suffered during the last six months; to suffer from something** = to do badly because of something; **the company's products suffer from bad design; the group suffers from bad management**

QUOTE: the bank suffered losses to the extent that its capital has been wiped out
South China Morning Post
QUOTE: the holding company has seen its earnings suffer from big writedowns in conjunction with its agricultural loan portfolio
Duns Business Month

sufficient *adjective* enough; **the company has sufficient funds to pay for its expansion programme**

suggest *verb* to put forward a proposal; **the chairman suggested (that) the next meeting should held in October; we suggested Mr Smith for the post of treasurer**
◇ **suggestion** *noun* proposal *or* idea which is put forward; **suggestion box** = place in a company where members of staff can put forward their ideas for making the company more efficient and profitable

suitable *adjective* convenient *or* which fits; **Wednesday is the most suitable day for board meetings; we had to readvertise the job because there were no suitable candidates**

suitcase *noun* box with a handle for carrying clothes and personal belongings when travelling; **the customs officer made him open his three suitcases**

sum *noun* (a) quantity of money; **a sum of money was stolen from the personnel office; he lost large sums on the Stock Exchange; she received the sum of £500 in compensation; the sum insured** = the largest amount which an insurer will pay under the terms of an insurance; **lump sum** = money paid in one payment, not in several small payments (b) total of a series of figures added together

summary *noun* short account of what has happened *or* of what has been written; **the chairman gave a summary of his discussions with the German trade delegation; the sales department has given a summary of sales in Europe for the first six months**

summons *noun* official order to appear in court to be tried; **he threw away the summons and went on holiday to Spain**

sundry *adjective & noun* various; **sundry items** *or* **sundries** = small items which are not listed in detail

superannuation *noun* pension paid to someone who is too old *or* ill to work any more; **superannuation plan** *or* **scheme** = pension plan *or* scheme
NOTE: no plural

superintend *verb* to be in charge of; **he superintends the company's overseas sales**
◇ **superintendent** *noun* person in charge

superior 1 *adjective* better *or* of better quality; **our product is superior to all competing products; their sales are higher because of their superior distribution service** 2 *noun* more important person; **each manager is responsible to his superior for accurate reporting of sales**

supermarket *noun* large store, usually selling food, where customers serve themselves and pay at a checkout; **sales in supermarkets** *or* **supermarket sales account for half the company's turnover**

superstore *noun* very large self-service store which sells a wide range of goods

supertanker *noun* very large oil tanker

supervise *verb* to watch work carefully to see if it is well done; **the move to the new offices was supervised by the administrative manager; she supervises six girls in the accounts department**
◇ **supervision** *noun* being supervised; **new staff work under supervision for the first three months; she is very experienced and can be left to work without any supervision; the cash was counted under the supervision of the finance manager**
NOTE: no plural
◇ **supervisor** *noun* person who supervises
◇ **supervisory** *adjective* as a supervisor; **supervisory staff; he works in a supervisory capacity**

supplement 1 *noun* thing which is added; **the company gives him a supplement to his pension** 2 *verb* to add; **we will supplement the warehouse staff with six part-timers during the Christmas rush**
◇ **supplementary** *adjective* in addition to; **supplementary benefit** = payments from the government to people with very low incomes

supply 1 *noun* **(a)** providing something which is needed; **money supply** = amount of money which exists in a country; **supply price** = price at which something is

provided; **supply and demand** = amount of a product which is available and the amount which is wanted by customers; **the law of supply and demand** = general rule that the amount of a product which is available is related to the needs of the possible customer **(b) in short supply** = not available in large enough quantities to meet the demand; **spare parts are in short supply because of the strike (c)** stock of something which is needed; **the factory is running short of coal; supplies of coal have been reduced; office supplies** = goods needed to run an office (such as paper, pens, typewriters) 2 *verb* to provide something which is needed; **to supply a factory with spare parts; the finance department supplied the committee with the figures; details of staff addresses and phone numbers can be supplied by the personnel staff**
◇ **supply side economics** *noun* economic theory, that governments should encourage producers and suppliers of goods by cutting taxes, rather than encourage demand by making more money available in the economy
◇ **supplier** *noun* person *or* company which supplies *or* sells goods or services; **office equipment supplier; they are major suppliers of spare parts to the car industry**

support 1 *noun* **(a)** giving money to help; **the government has provided support to the electronics industry; we have no financial support from the banks (b)** agreement *or* encouragement; **the chairman has the support of the committee; support price** = price (in the EEC) at which a government will buy agricultural produce to stop the price falling
NOTE: no plural
2 *verb* **(a)** to give money to help; **the government is supporting the electronics industry to the tune of $2m per annum; we hope the banks will support us during the expansion period (b)** to encourage *or* to agree with; **she hopes the other members of the committee will support her; the market will not support another price increase**

surcharge *noun* extra charge; **import surcharge** = extra duty charged on imported goods, to try to stop them from being imported and to encourage local manufacture

surety *noun* (a) person who guarantees that someone will do something; **to stand surety for someone** (b) deeds *or* share certificates, etc., deposited as security for a loan

surface *noun* top part of the earth; **to send a package by surface mail** = to send it by land or sea, but not by air; **surface transport** = transport on land or sea
NOTE: no plural

surplus *noun* extra stock *or* something which is more than is needed; **surplus government equipment; surplus butter is on sale in the shops; we are holding a sale of surplus stock; governments are trying to find ways of reducing the agricultural surpluses in the Common Market; we are trying to let surplus capacity in the warehouse; a budget surplus** = more revenue than was planned for in the budget; **these items are surplus to our requirements** = we do not need these items; **to absorb a surplus** = to take a surplus into a larger amount

surrender 1 *noun* giving up of an insurance policy before the contracted date for maturity; **surrender value** = money which an insurer will pay if an insurance policy is given up 2 *verb* **to surrender a policy** = to give up an insurance

surtax *noun* extra tax on high income

survey 1 *noun* (a) general report on a problem; **the government has published a survey of population trends; we have asked the sales department to produce a survey of competing products** (b) examining something to see if it is in good condition; **we have asked for a survey of the house before buying it; the insurance company is carrying out a survey of the damage; damage survey** = survey of damage done (c) measuring exactly; **quantity survey** = calculating the amount of materials and cost of labour needed for a construction project 2 *verb* to examine (something) to see if it is in good condition
◇ **surveyor** *noun* person who examines buildings to see if they are in good condition; **quantity surveyor** = person who calculates the amount of materials

and cost of labour needed for a construction project

suspend *verb* (a) to stop (something) for a time; **we have suspended payments while we are waiting for news from our agent; sailings have been suspended until the weather gets better; work on the construction project has been suspended; the management decided to suspend negotiations** (b) to stop (someone) working for a time; **he was suspended on full pay while the police investigations were going on**
◇ **suspension** *noun* stopping something for a time; **suspension of payments; suspension of deliveries**

swap 1 *noun* exchange of one thing for another 2 *verb* to exchange one thing for another; **he swapped his old car for a new motorcycle; they swapped jobs** = each of them took the other's job
NOTE: swapping - swapped

swatch *noun* small sample; **colour swatch** = small sample of colour which the finished product must look like

sweat *noun* drops of liquid which come through your skin when you are hot
◇ **sweated labour** *noun* (a) people who work hard for very little money; **of course the firm makes a profit - it employs sweated labour** (b) hard work which is very badly paid
◇ **sweatshop** *noun* factory using sweated labour

switch *verb* to change from one thing to another; **to switch funds from one investment to another; the job was switched from our British factory to the States**
◇ **switchboard** *noun* central point in a telephone system, where all lines meet; **switchboard operator** = person who works the central telephone system
◇ **switch over to** *verb* to change to something quite different; **we have switched over to a French supplier; the factory has switched over to gas for heating**

swop = SWAP

symbol *noun* sign *or* picture *or* object which represents something; **they use a bear as their advertising symbol**

sympathy *noun* feeling sorry because someone else has problems; **the manager had no sympathy for his secretary who complained of being overworked; sympathy strike** = strike to show that workers agree with another group of workers who are on strike; **to strike in sympathy** = to stop work to show that you agree with another group of workers who are on strike; **the postal workers went on strike and the telephone engineers came out in sympathy**

◇ **sympathetic** *adjective* showing sympathy; **sympathetic strike** = sympathy strike

syndicate 1 *noun* group of people *or* companies working together to make money; **a German finance syndicate; arbitrage syndicate** = group of people who together raise the capital to invest in arbitrage deals; **underwriting syndicate** = group of underwriters who insure a large risk **2** *verb* to produce an article, drawing, etc., which is published in several newspapers or magazines

◇ **syndicated** *adjective* published in several newspapers or magazines; **he writes a syndicated column on personal finance**

synergy *noun* producing greater effects by joining forces than by acting separately

synthetic *adjective* artificial *or* made by man; **synthetic fibres** *or* **synthetic materials** = materials made as products of a chemical process

system *noun* **(a)** arrangement *or* organization of things which work together; **our accounting system has worked well in spite of the large increase in orders; decimal system** = system of mathematics based on the number 10; **filing system** = way of putting documents in order for easy reference; **to operate a quota system** = to regulate supplies by fixing quantities which are allowed; **we arrange our distribution using a quota system - each agent is allowed only a certain number of units (b) computer system** = set of programs, commands, etc., which run a computer **(c) systems analysis** = using a computer to suggest how a company should work by analyzing the way in which it works at present; **systems analyst** = person who

specializes in systems analysis

◇ **systematic** *adjective* in order *or* using method; **he ordered a systematic report on the distribution service**

Tt

tab *noun* = TABULATOR

table 1 *noun* **(a)** piece of furniture with a flat top and legs; **typing table** = table for a typewriter **(b)** list of figures *or* facts set out in columns; **table of contents** = list of contents in a book; **actuarial tables** = lists showing how long people of certain ages are likely to live **2** *verb* to put items of information on the table before a meeting; **the report of the finance committee was tabled; to table a motion** = to put forward a proposal for discussion by putting details of it on the table at a meeting

◇ **tabular** *adjective* **in tabular form** = arranged in a table

◇ **tabulate** *verb* to set out in a table

◇ **tabulation** *noun* arrangement of figures in a table

◇ **tabulator** *noun* part of a typewriter *or* computer which sets words or figures automatically in columns

tachograph *noun* device in a lorry, which shows details of distance travelled and time of journeys

tacit *adjective* agreed but not stated; **tacit approval; tacit agreement to a proposal**

tactic *noun* way of doing things so as to be at an advantage; **his usual tactic is to buy shares in a company, then mount a takeover bid, and sell out at a profit; the directors planned their tactics before going into the meeting with the union representatives**

tag *noun* label; **price tag; name tag**

take 1 *noun* money received in a shop **2** *verb* **(a)** to receive *or* to get; **the shop takes £2,000 a week** = the shop receives £2,000 a week in cash sales; **he takes home £250 a**

week = his salary, after deductions for tax, etc., is £250 a week **(b)** to do a certain action; **to take action** = to do something; **you must take immediate action if you want to stop thefts; to take a call** = to answer the telephone; **to take the chair** = to be chairman of a meeting; **in the absence of the chairman his deputy took the chair; to take dictation** = to write down what someone is saying; **the secretary was taking dictation from the managing director; to take stock** = to count the items in a warehouse; **to take stock of a situation** = to examine the state of things before deciding what to do **(c)** to need (a time *or* a quantity); **it took the factory six weeks** *or* **the factory took six weeks to clear the backlog of orders; it will take her all morning to do my letters; it took six men and a crane to get the computer into the office**

NOTE: **taking - took - has taken**

◊ **take away** *verb* **(a)** to remove one figure from a total; **if you take away the home sales, the total turnover is down (b)** to remove; **we had to take the work away from the supplier because the quality was so bad; the police took away piles of documents from the office; sales of food to take away** = cooked food sold by a shop to be eaten at some other place

◊ **takeaway** *noun* shop which sells food to be eaten at some other place; **a takeaway meal; a Chinese takeaway**

◊ **take back** *verb* **(a)** to return with something; **when the watch went wrong, he took it back to the shop; if you do not like the colour, you can take it back to change it (b) to take back dismissed workers** = to allow former workers to join the company again

◊ **take-home pay** *noun* amount of money received in wages, after tax, etc., has been deducted

NOTE: no plural

◊ **take into** *verb* to take inside; **to take items into stock** *or* **into the warehouse**

◊ **take off** *verb* **(a)** to remove *or* to deduct; **he took £25 off the price (b)** to start to rise fast; **sales took off after the TV commercials (c) she took the day off** = she decided not to work for the day

◊ **take on** *verb* to agree to employ someone *or* to agree to do something; **she took on the job of preparing the VAT**

returns; **to take on more staff; he has taken on a lot of extra work**

◊ **take out** *verb* to remove; **to take out a patent for an invention** = to apply for and receive a patent; **to take out insurance against theft** = to pay a premium to an insurance company, so that if a theft takes place the company will pay compensation

◊ **take over** *verb* **(a)** to start to do something in place of someone else; **Miss Black took over from Mr Jones on May 1st; the new chairman takes over on July 1st; the take-over period is always difficult** = the period when one person is taking over work from another **(b) to take over a company** = to buy (a business) by offering to buy most of its shares; **the buyer takes over the company's liabilities; the company was taken over by a large multinational**

◊ **takeover** *noun* buying a business; **takeover bid** = offer to buy all or most of the shares in a company so as to control it; **to make a takeover bid for a company** = to offer to buy most of the shares in a company; **to withdraw a takeover bid** = to say that you no longer offer to buy the shares in a company; **the company rejected the takeover bid** = the directors recommended that the shareholders should not accept the offer; **the disclosure of the takeover bid raised share prices; contested takeover** = takeover where the board of the company which is being bought do not recommend it, and try to fight it

◊ **taker** *noun* buyer *or* person who wants to buy; **there were no takers for the new shares**

◊ **take up** *verb* **to take up an option** = to accept an option which has been offered and put into action; **half the rights issue was not taken up by the shareholders; take up rate** = percentage of acceptances for a rights issue

◊ **takings** *plural noun* money received in a shop *or* a business; **the week's takings were stolen from the cash desk**

QUOTE: many takeovers result in the new managers/owners rationalizing the capital of the company through better asset management

Duns Business Month

QUOTE: capital gains are not taxed, but money taken out in profits and dividends is taxed

Toronto Star

tally 1 *noun* note of things counted *or* recorded; **to keep a tally of stock move-**

ments *or* of expenses; **tally clerk** = person whose job is to note quantities of cargo; **tally sheet** = sheet on which quantities are noted **2** *verb* to agree *or* to be the same; **the invoices do not tally; the accounts department tried to make the figures tally**

tangible *adjective* **tangible assets** = assets which are solid (such as furniture, jewellery, etc.)

tanker *noun* special ship for carrying liquids (especially oil)

tap *noun* GB government stocks issued direct to the Bank of England
◇ **tap stock** *noun* issue of government securities

tape *noun* long, flat, narrow piece of plastic; **magnetic tape** = sensitive tape for recording information; **computer tape** = magnetic tape used in computers; **measuring tape** *or* **tape measure** = long tape with centimetres *or* inches marked on it for measuring how long something is

tare *noun* (allowance made for the) weight of a container and packing which is deducted from the total weight; (allowance made for the) weight of a vehicle in calculating transport costs; **to allow for tare**
NOTE: no plural

target **1** *noun* thing to aim for; **production targets** = amount of units a factory is expected to produce; **sales targets** = amount of sales a representative is expected to achieve; **target market** = market in which a company is planning to sell its goods; **to set targets** = to fix amounts *or* quantities which workers have to produce *or* reach; **to meet a target** = to produce the quantity of goods *or* sales which are expected; **to miss a target** = not to produce the amount of goods *or* sales which are expected; **they missed the target figure of £2m turnover 2** *verb* to aim to sell; **to target a market** = to plan to sell goods in a certain market

> QUOTE: in a normal leveraged buyout the acquirer raises money by borrowing against the assets of the target company *Fortune*
> QUOTE: the minister is persuading the oil, gas, electricity and coal industries to target their advertising towards energy efficiency *Times*

tariff *noun* **(a) customs tariffs** = tax to be paid for importing *or* exporting goods; **tariff barriers** = customs duty intended to make imports more difficult; **to impose tariff barriers on** *or* **to lift tariff barriers from a product; differential tariffs** = different duties for different types of goods; **General Agreement on Tariffs and Trade** = international agreement to try to reduce restrictions in trade between countries **(b)** rate of charging for electricity, hotel rooms, train tickets, etc.

task *noun* **(a)** work which has to be done; **to list task processes** = to make a list of various parts of a job which have to be done **(b) task force** = special group of workers *or* managers who are chosen to carry out a special job *or* to deal with a special problem

tax **1** *noun* **(a)** money taken by the government *or* by an official body to pay for government services; **airport tax** = tax added to the price of an air ticket to cover the cost of running an airport; **capital gains tax** = tax on capital gains; **capital transfer tax** = tax on gifts or bequests of money or property; **corporation tax** = tax on profits made by companies; **excess profits tax** = tax on profits which are higher than what is thought to be normal; **income tax** = tax on salaries and wages; **land tax** = tax on the amount of land owned; **sales tax** = tax on the price of goods sold; **turnover tax** = tax on company turnover; **value added tax** = tax on goods and services, added as a percentage to the invoiced sales price **(b) ad valorem tax** = tax calculated according to the value of the goods taxed; **back tax** = tax which is owed; **basic tax** = tax paid at the normal rate; **direct tax** = tax paid directly to the government (such as income tax); **indirect tax** = tax paid to someone who then pays it to the government (such as VAT); **to levy a tax** *or* **to impose a tax** = to make a tax payable; **the government has imposed a 15% tax on petrol; to lift a tax** = to remove a tax; **the tax on company profits has been lifted; exclusive of tax** = not including tax; **tax abatement** = reduction of tax; **tax adjustments** = changes made to tax; **tax adviser** *or* **tax consultant** = person who gives advice on tax problems; **tax allowance** *or* **allowances against tax** = part of the income which a person is allowed to earn and not pay tax on; **tax avoidance** = trying (legally) to minimize the amount of tax to be paid; **in the top tax bracket** = paying the highest level of tax; **tax code** = number given to indicate the amount of tax allowances a person has; **tax concession** = allowing less tax to be paid; **tax credit** = part of a dividend on which the company has already paid tax, so that the shareholder is not taxed on it again; **tax deductions** = (i) money removed from a salary to pay tax; (ii) *US* business expenses which can be claimed against tax; **tax deducted at source** = tax which is removed from a salary or interest before the money is paid out; **tax evasion** = trying illegally not to pay tax; **tax exemption** = (i) being free from payment of tax; (ii) *US* part of income which a person is allowed to earn and not pay tax on; **tax form** = blank form to be filled in with details of income and allowances and sent to the tax office each year; **tax haven** = country where taxes are low, encouraging companies to set up their main offices there; **tax holiday** = period when a new company pays no tax; **tax inspector** *or* **inspector of taxes** = official of the Inland Revenue who examines tax returns and decides how much tax someone should pay; **tax loophole** = legal means of not paying tax; **tax relief** = allowing someone not to pay tax on certain parts of his income; **tax return** *or* **tax declaration** = completed tax form, with details of income and allowances; **tax shelter** = financial arrangement (such as a pension scheme) where investments can be made without tax; **tax year** = twelve month period on which taxes are calculated (in the UK, 6th April to 5th April of the following year) **2** *verb* to make someone pay a tax *or* to impose a tax on something; **to tax businesses at 50%; income is taxed at 35%; luxury items are heavily taxed**

◇ **taxable** *adjective* which can be taxed; **taxable items** = items on which a tax has to be paid; **taxable income** = income on which a person has to pay tax

◇ **taxation** *noun* act of taxing; **direct taxation** = taxes (such as income tax) which are paid direct to the government; **indirect taxation** = taxes (such as sales tax) which are not paid direct to the government; **the government raises more money by indirect taxation than by direct;**

double taxation = taxing the same income twice; **double taxation agreement** = agreement between two countries that a person living in one country will not be taxed in both countries on the income earned in the other country
NOTE: no plural

◇ **tax-deductible** *adjective* which can be deducted from an income before tax is calculated; **these expenses are not tax-deductible** = tax has to be paid on these expenses

◇ **tax-exempt** *adjective* not required to pay tax; (income *or* goods) which are not subject to tax

◇ **tax-free** *adjective* on which tax does not have to be paid

◇ **taxpayer** *noun* person *or* company which has to pay tax; **basic taxpayer** *or* **taxpayer at the basic rate; corporate taxpayers**

taxi *noun* car which takes people from one place to another for money; **he took a taxi to the airport; taxi fares are very high in New York**

team *noun* group of people who work together; **management team** = group of all the managers working in the same company; **sales team** = all representatives, salesmen and sales managers working in a company

◇ **teamster** *noun US* truck driver

◇ **teamwork** *noun* being able to work together as a group
NOTE: no plural

technical *adjective* **(a)** referring to particular machine *or* process; **the document gives all the technical details on the new computer (b) technical correction** = situation where a share price *or* a currency moves up or down because it was previously too low or too high

◇ **technician** *noun* person who is specialized in industrial work; **computer technician; laboratory technician** = person who deals with practical work in a laboratory

◇ **technique** *noun* skilled way of doing a job; **the company has developed a new technique for processing steel; he has a special technique for answering complaints from customers; management techniques**

= skill in managing a business; **marketing techniques** = skill in marketing a product

◇ **technology** *noun* applying scientific knowledge to industrial processes; **information technology** = working with data stored on computers; **the introduction of new technology** = putting new electronic equipment into a business or industry

◇ **technological** *adjective* referring to technology; **the technological revolution** = changing of industry by introducing new technology

QUOTE: market analysts described the falls in the second half of last week as a technical correction

Australian Financial Review

tel = TELEPHONE

telecommunications *plural noun* systems of passing messages over long distances (by cable, radio, etc.)

telegram *noun* message sent to another country by telegraph; **to send an international telegram**

◇ **telegraph** **1** *noun* system of sending messages along wires; **to send a message by telegraph; telegraph office** = office from which telegrams can be sent **2** *verb* to send a message by telegram; **to telegraph an order**

◇ **telegraphic** *adjective* referring to a telegraph system; **telegraphic address** = short address used for sending telegrams

◇ **telemessage** *noun GB* message sent by telephone, and delivered as a card

telephone **1** *noun* machine used for speaking to someone over a long distance; **we had a new telephone system installed last week; to be on the telephone** = to be speaking to someone using the telephone; **the managing director is on the telephone to Hong Kong; she has been on the telephone all day; by telephone** = using the telephone; **to place an order by telephone; to reserve a room by telephone; house telephone** *or* **internal telephone** = telephone for calling from one room to another in an office or hotel; **telephone book** *or* **telephone directory** = book which lists all people and businesses in alphabetical order with their telephone numbers; **he looked up the number of the company in the telephone book; telephone call** = speaking to someone on the telephone; **to make a telephone call** = to speak to someone on the telephone; **to answer the telephone** *or* **to take a telephone call** = to speak in reply to a call on the telephone; **telephone exchange** = central office where the telephones of a whole district are linked; **telephone number** = set of figures for a particular telephone subscriber; **can you give me your telephone number?; telephone operator** = person who operates a telephone switchboard; **telephone orders** = orders received by telephone; **since we mailed the catalogue we have received a large number of telephone orders; telephone subscriber** = person who has a telephone; **telephone switchboard** = central point in a telephone system where all internal and external lines meet **2** *verb* **to telephone a place** *or* **a person** = to call a place *or* someone by telephone; **his secretary telephoned to say he would be late; he telephoned the order through to the warehouse** = he telephoned the warehouse to place an order; **to telephone about something** = to make a telephone call to speak about something; **he telephoned about the January invoice; to telephone for something** = to make a telephone call to ask for something; **he telephoned for a taxi**

◇ **telephonist** *noun* person who works a telephone switchboard

◇ **teleprinter** *noun* machine like a typewriter, which can send messages by telegraph and print incoming messages; **teleprinter operator**

◇ **telesales** *plural noun* sales made by telephone

◇ **teletypewriter** *noun US* = TELEPRINTER

telex **1** *noun* **(a)** system of sending messages by teleprinter; **to send information by telex; the order came by telex; telex line** = wire linking a telex machine to the telex system; **we cannot communicate with our Nigerian office because of the breakdown of the telex lines; telex operator** = person who operates a telex machine; **telex subscriber** = company which has a telex **(b) a telex** = (i) machine for sending and receiving telex messages; (ii) a message sent by telex; **he sent a telex to his head office; we received his telex this morning 2** *verb* to send a message using a teleprinter; **can you telex the Canadian office before they open? he telexed the**

details of the contract to New York

teller *noun* person who takes cash or pays cash to customers at a bank

tem *see* PRO TEM

temp 1 *noun* temporary secretary; **we have had two temps working in the office this week to clear the backlog of letters; temp agency** = office which deals with finding temporary secretaries for offices 2 *verb* to work as a temporary secretary ◇ **temping** *noun* working as a temporary secretary; **she can earn more money temping than from a full-time job** NOTE: no plural

temporary *adjective* which only lasts a short time; **he was granted a temporary export licence; to take temporary measures; he has a temporary post with a construction company; he has a temporary job as a filing clerk** *or* **he has a job as a temporary filing clerk; temporary employment** = full-time work which does not last for more than a few days or months; **temporary staff** = staff who are appointed for a short time ◇ **temporarily** *adverb* lasting only for a short time

tenancy *noun* (i) agreement by which a tenant can occupy a property; (ii) period during which a tenant has an agreement to occupy a property ◇ **tenant** *noun* person *or* company which rents a house *or* flat *or* office to live or work in; **the tenant is liable for repairs; sitting tenant** = tenant who is living in a house when the freehold or lease is sold

tend *verb* to be likely to do something; **he tends to appoint young girls to his staff** ◇ **tendency** *noun* being likely to do something; **the market showed an upward tendency; there has been a downward tendency in the market for several days; the market showed a tendency to stagnate** = the market seemed to stagnate rather than advance

tender 1 *noun* (a) offer to work for a certain price; **a successful tender** *or* **an unsuccessful tender; to put a project out to tender** *or* **to ask for** *or* **to invite tenders for a**

project = to ask contractors to give written estimates for a job; **to put in a tender** *or* **to submit a tender** = to make an estimate for a job; **to sell shares by tender** = to ask people to offer in writing a price for shares; **sealed tenders** = tenders sent in sealed envelopes which will all be opened together at a certain time **(b) legal tender** = coins or notes which can be legally used to pay a debt (small denominations cannot be used to pay large debts) 2 *verb* **(a) to tender for a contract** = to put forward an estimate of cost for work to be carried out under contract; **to tender for the construction of a hospital (b) to tender one's resignation** = to give in one's resignation ◇ **tenderer** *noun* person *or* company which tenders for work; **the company was the successful tenderer for the project** ◇ **tendering** *noun* act of putting forward an estimate of cost; **to be successful, you must follow the tendering procedure as laid out in the documents**

tentative *adjective* not certain; **they reached a tentative agreement over the proposal; we suggested Wednesday May 10th as a tentative date for the next meeting** ◇ **tentatively** *adverb* not sure; **we tentatively suggested Wednesday as the date for our next meeting**

tenure *noun* **(a)** right to hold property *or* position; **security of tenure** = right to keep a job *or* rented accommodation provided certain conditions are met **(b)** time when a position is held; **during his tenure of the office of chairman**

term *noun* **(a)** period of time when something is legally valid; **the term of a lease; the term of the loan is fifteen years; to have a loan for a term of fifteen years; during his term of office as chairman; term deposit** = money invested for a fixed period at a higher rate of interest; **term insurance** = life assurance which covers a person's life for a period of time; **he took out a ten-year term insurance; term loan** = loan for a fixed period of time; **term shares** = type of building society deposit for a fixed period of time at a higher rate of interest; **short-term** = for a period of months; **long-term** = for a long period of time; **medium-term** = for a period of one or two years **(b) terms** = conditions *or* duties which have to be carried out as part of a contract *or* arrangements which have to be agreed before a contract is valid; **he refused to agree to some of the terms of the contract; by** *or* **under the terms of the contract, the company is responsible for all damage to the property; to negotiate for better terms; terms of payment** *or* **payment terms** = conditions for paying something; **terms of sale** = conditions attached to a sale; **cash terms** = lower terms which apply if the customer pays cash; **"terms: cash with order"** = terms of sale showing that payment has to be made in cash when the order is placed; **easy terms** = terms which are not difficult to accept *or* price which is easy to pay; **the shop is let on very easy terms; to pay for something on easy terms; on favourable terms** = on especially good terms; **the shop is let on very favourable terms; trade terms** = special discount for people in the same trade **(c)** part of a legal *or* university year **(d) terms of employment** = conditions set out in a contract of employment

QUOTE: companies have been improving communications, often as part of deals to cut down demarcation and to give everybody the same terms of employment *Economist*

QUOTE: the Federal Reserve Board has eased interest rates in the past year, but they are still at historically high levels in real terms *Sunday Times*

terminal 1 *noun* **(a) computer terminal** = keyboard and screen, by which information can be put into a computer or can be called up from a database; **computer system consisting of a microprocessor and six terminals (b) air terminal** = building in a town where passengers meet to be taken by bus to an airport outside the town; **airport terminal** *or* **terminal building** = main building at an airport where passengers arrive and leave; **container terminal** = area of a harbour where container ships are loaded or unloaded; **ocean terminal** = building at a port where passengers arrive and depart 2 *adjective* at the end; **terminal bonus** = bonus received when an insurance comes to an end

terminate *verb* to end (something) *or* to bring (something) to an end; **to terminate an agreement; his employment was terminated; the offer terminates on July**

31st; the flight from Paris terminates in New York

◊ **terminable** *adjective* which can be terminated

◊ **termination** *noun* **(a)** bringing to an end; **termination clause** = clause which explains how and when a contract can be terminated **(b)** *US* leaving a job (resigning, retiring, or being fired or made redundant)

territory *noun* area visited by a salesman; **a rep's territory; his territory covers all the north of the country**

tertiary *adjective* **tertiary industry** = service industry *or* industry which does not produce or manufacture but offers a service (such as banking, retailing or accountancy); **tertiary sector** = section of the economy containing the service industries

test 1 *noun* **(a)** examination to see if something works well *or* is possible; **test certificate** = certificate to show that something has passed a test; **driving test** = examination to see if someone is able to drive a car; **feasibility test** = test to see if something is possible; **market test** = examination to see if a sample of a product will sell in a market **(b) test case** = legal action where the decision will fix a principle which other cases can follow 2 *verb* to examine something to see if it is working well; **to test a computer system; to test the market for a product** *or* **to test market a product** = to show samples of a product in a market to see if it will sell well; **we are test marketing the toothpaste in Scotland**

◊ **test-drive** *verb* **to test-drive a car** = to drive a car (before buying it) to see if it works well

◊ **testing** *noun* examining something to see if it works well; **during the testing of the system several defects were corrected**

testimonial *noun* written report about someone's character *or* ability; **to write someone a testimonial; unsolicited testimonial** = letter praising someone *or* a product, without the writer having been asked to write it

text *noun* written part of something; **he wrote notes at the side of the text of the agreement; text processing** = working with words, using a computer to produce, check and change documents, reports, letters, etc.

thank *verb* to show someone that you are grateful for what has been done; **the committee thanked the retiring chairman for his work; "Thank you for your letter of June 25th"**
◊ **thanks** *plural noun* word showing that someone is grateful; **"many thanks for your letter of June 25th"; vote of thanks** = official vote at a meeting to show that the meeting is grateful for what someone has done; **the meeting passed a vote of thanks to the organizing committee for their work in setting up the international conference**
◊ **thanks to** *adverb* because of; **the company was able to continue trading thanks to a loan from the bank; it was no thanks to the bank that we avoided making a loss** = we avoided making a loss in spite of the bank's actions

theft *noun* stealing; **we have brought in security guards to protect the store against theft; they are trying to cut their losses by theft; to take out insurance against theft**

theory *noun* statement of the general principle of how something should work; **in theory the plan should work** = the plan may work, but it has not been tried in practice

think tank *noun* group of experts who advise *or* put forward plans

third *noun* part of something which is divided into three; **to sell everything at one third off** = to sell everything at a discount of 33%; **the company has two thirds of the total market** = the company has 66% of the total market
◊ **third party** *noun* any person other than the two main parties involved in a contract; **third-party insurance** = insurance to cover damage to any person who is not one of the people named in the insurance contract; **the case is in the hands of a third party** = the case is being dealt with by someone who is not one of the main interested parties

◊ **third quarter** *noun* three months' period from July to September
◊ **Third World** *noun* countries of Africa, Asia and South America which do not have highly developed industries; **we sell tractors into the Third World** *or* **to Third World countries**

threshold *noun* limit *or* point at which something changes; **threshold agreement** = contract which says that if the cost of living goes up by more than a certain amount, pay will go up to match it; **threshold price** = in the EEC, the lowest price at which farm produce imported into the EEC can be sold; **pay threshold** = point at which pay increases because of a threshold agreement; **tax threshold** = point at which another percentage of tax is payable; **the government has raised the minimum tax threshold from £6,000 to £6,500**

thrift *noun* (a) saving money by spending carefully (b) *US* private local bank *or* savings and loan association *or* credit union, which accepts and pays interest on deposits from small investors
NOTE: no plural for (a)
◊ **thrifty** *adjective* careful not to spend too much money

QUOTE: the thrift, which had grown from $4.7 million in assets in 1980 to 1.5 billion this year, has ended in liquidation *Barrons*

thrive *verb* to grow well *or* to be profitable; **a thriving economy; thriving black market in car radios; the company is thriving in spite of the recession**

throughput *noun* amount of work done *or* of goods produced in a certain time; **we hope to increase our throughput by putting in two new machines; the invoice department has a throughput of 6,000 invoices a day**

throw out *verb* (a) to reject *or* to refuse to accept; **the proposal was thrown out by the planning committee; the board threw out the draft contract submitted by the union** (b) to get rid of (something which is not wanted); **we threw out the old telephones and installed a computerized system; the AGM threw out the old board of directors**
NOTE: **throwing - threw - has thrown**

tick 1 *noun* **(a)** *informal* credit; **all the furniture in the house is bought on tick (b)** mark on paper to show that something is correct *or* that something is approved; **put a tick in the box marked "R"**
NOTE: no plural for (a). Note also US English for (b) is **check**
2 *verb* to mark with a sign to show that something is correct; **tick the box marked "R" if you require a receipt**

◇ **ticker** *noun* *US* machine (operated by telegraph) which prints details of share prices and transactions rapidly on paper tape

ticket *noun* **(a)** piece of paper *or* card which allows you to do something; **entrance ticket** *or* **admission ticket** = ticket which allows you to go in; **theatre ticket** = ticket which allows you a seat in a theatre **(b)** piece of paper *or* card which allows you to travel; **train ticket** *or* **bus ticket** *or* **plane ticket**; **season ticket** = train *or* bus ticket which can be used for any number of journeys over a period (usually one, three, six or twelve months); **single ticket** *or* *US* **one-way ticket** = ticket for one journey from one place to another; **return ticket** *or* *US* **round-trip ticket** = ticket for a journey from one place to another and back again **(c) ticket agency** = shop which sells tickets to theatres; **ticket counter** = counter where tickets are sold **(d)** paper which shows something; **baggage ticket** = paper showing that you have a left a piece of baggage with someone; **price ticket** = piece of paper showing a price

tie *verb* to attach *or* to fasten (with string, wire, etc.); **he tied the parcel with thick string; she tied two labels on to the parcel**
NOTE: tying - tied
◇ **tie-on label** *noun* label with a piece of string attached so that it can be tied to an item

◇ **tie up** *verb* **(a)** to attach *or* to fasten tightly; **the parcel is tied up with string; the ship was tied up to the quay; he is rather tied up at the moment** = he is very busy **(b)** to invest money in one way, so that it cannot be used for other investments; **he has £100,000 tied up in long-dated gilts; the company has £250,000 tied up in stock which no one wants to buy**

◇ **tie-up** *noun* link *or* connection; **the company has a tie-up with a German distributor**
NOTE: plural is **tie-ups**

QUOTE: a lot of speculator money is said to be tied up in sterling because of the interest-rate differential between US and British rates
Australian Financial Review

tight *adjective* which is controlled *or* which does not allow any movement; **the manager has a very tight schedule today - he cannot fit in any more appointments; expenses are kept under tight control; tight money** = money which is borrowed at a high interest rate; **tight money policy** = government policy to restrict money supply

◇ **-tight** *suffix* which prevents something getting in; **the computer is packed in a watertight case; send the films in an airtight container**

◇ **tighten** *verb* to make (something) tight *or* to control (something); **the accounts department is tightening its control over departmental budgets**

◇ **tighten up on** *verb* to control (something) more; **the government is tightening up on tax evasion; we must tighten up on the reps' expenses**

QUOTE: mortgage money is becoming tighter
Times
QUOTE: the decision by the government to tighten monetary policy will push the annual inflation rate above the previous high
Financial Times

till *noun* drawer for keeping cash in a shop; **cash till** = cash register *or* machine which shows and adds prices of items bought, with a drawer for keeping the cash received; **there was not much money in the till at the end of the day**

time *noun* **(a)** period when something takes place (such as one hour, two days, fifty minutes, etc.); **computer time** = time when a computer is being used (paid for at an hourly rate); **real time** = time when a computer is working on the processing of data while the problem to which the data refers is actually taking place; **time and motion study** = study in an office *or* factory of how long it takes to do certain jobs and the movements workers have to make to do them; **time and motion expert** = person who analyzes time and motion studies and

suggests changes in the way work is done **(b)** hour of the day (such as 9.00, 12.15, ten o'clock at night, etc.); **the time of arrival** *or* **the arrival time is indicated on the screen; departure times are delayed by up to fifteen minutes because of the volume of traffic; on time** = at the right time; **the plane was on time; you will have to hurry if you want to get to the meeting on time** *or* **if you want to be on time for the meeting; opening time** *or* **closing time** = time when a shop or office starts or stops work **(c)** system of hours on the clock; **Summer Time** *or* **Daylight Saving Time** = system where clocks are set back one hour in the summer to take advantage of the longer hours of daylight; **Standard Time** = normal time as in the winter months **(d)** hours worked; **he is paid time and a half on Sundays** = he is paid the normal rate plus 50% extra when he works on Sundays; **full-time** = working for the whole normal working day; **overtime** = hours worked more than the normal working time; **part-time** = not working for a whole working day **(e)** period before something happens; **time deposit** = deposit of money for a fixed period, during which it cannot be touched; **delivery time** = number of days before something will be delivered; **lead time** = time between placing an order and receiving the goods; **time limit** = period during which something should be done; **to keep within the time limits** *or* **within the time schedule** = to complete work by the time stated
NOTE: no plural for (a), (c) and (d)

◇ **time-card** *or* *US* **time-clock card** *noun* card which is put into a timing machine when a worker clocks in *or* clocks out, and records the time when he starts and stops work

◇ **time-keeping** *noun* being on time for work; **he was warned for bad time-keeping**
NOTE: no plural

◇ **time rate** *noun* rate for work which is calculated as money per hour *or* per week, and not money for work completed

◇ **time saving 1** *adjective* which saves time; **a time-saving device 2** *noun* trying to save time; **the management is keen on time saving**

◇ **time scale** *noun* time which will be taken to complete work; **our time scale is that all work should be completed by the end of August; he is working to a strict time scale**

◇ **time share** *noun* system where several people each own part of a property (such as a holiday flat), each being able to use it for a certain period each year

◇ **time-sharing** *noun* **(a)** = TIME SHARE **(b)** sharing a computer system, with different users using different terminals
NOTE: no plural

◇ **time sheet** *noun* paper showing when a worker starts work in the morning and leaves work in the evening

◇ **timetable 1** *noun* **(a)** list showing times of arrivals *or* departures of buses *or* trains *or* planes, etc.; **according to the timetable, there should be a train to London at 10.22; the bus company has brought out its winter timetable (b)** list of appointments *or* events; **the manager has a very full timetable, so I doubt if he will be able to see you today; conference timetable** = list of speakers *or* events at a conference **2** *verb* to make a list of times

◇ **time work** *noun* work which is paid for at a rate per hour *or* per day, not per piece of work completed

◇ **timing** *noun* way in which something happens at a particular time; **the timing of the conference is very convenient, as it comes just before my annual holiday; his arrival ten minutes after the meeting finished was very bad timing**
NOTE: no plural

tip 1 *noun* **(a)** money given to someone who has helped you; **I gave the taxi driver a 10 cent tip; the staff are not allowed to accept tips (b)** advice on something to buy *or* to do which could be profitable; **a stock market tip; he gave me a tip about a share which was likely to rise because of a takeover bid; tip sheet** = newspaper which gives information about shares which should be bought or sold **2** *verb* **(a)** to give money to someone who has helped you; **he tipped the receptionist £5 (b)** to say that something is likely to happen *or* that something might be profitable; **two shares were tipped in the business section of the paper; he is tipped to become the next chairman**
NOTE: **tipping - tipped**

TIR = TRANSPORT INTERNATIONAL ROUTIER

title *noun* **(a)** right to own a property; **she has no title to the property; he has a good title to the property; title deeds** = document showing who is the owner of a property **(b)** name given to a person in a certain job; **he has the title "Chief Executive" (c)** name of a book *or* film, etc.

token *noun* **(a)** thing which acts as a sign *or* symbol; **token charge** = small charge which does not cover the real costs; **a token charge is made for heating; token payment** = small payment to show that a payment is being made; **token rent** = very low rent payment to show that a rent is being asked; **token strike** = short strike to show that workers have a grievance **(b) book token** *or* **flower token** *or* **gift token** = card bought in a store which is given as a present and which must be exchanged in that store for goods; **we gave her a gift token for her birthday**

toll *noun* payment for using a service (usually a bridge or a ferry); **we had to cross a toll bridge to get to the island; you have to pay a toll to cross the bridge**
◇ **toll call** *noun US* long-distance telephone call
◇ **toll free** *adverb US* without having to pay a charge for a long-distance telephone call; **to call someone toll free; toll free number**

tombstone *noun informal* official announcement in a newspaper showing that a loan has been subscribed

ton *noun* measure of weight; *GB* **long ton** = measure of weight (= 1016 kilos); *US* **short ton** = measure of weight (= 907 kilos); **metric ton** = 1,000 kilos
◇ **tonne** *noun* metric ton *or* 1,000 kilos
◇ **tonnage** *noun* space for cargo in a ship, measured in tons; **gross tonnage** = amount of total space in a ship; **deadweight tonnage** = largest amount of cargo which a ship can carry safely
NOTE: no plural

QUOTE: Canada agreed to the new duty-free quota of 600,000 tonnes a year
Globe and Mail (Toronto)
QUOTE: in the dry cargo sector a total of 956 cargo vessels of 11.6m tonnes are laid up - 3% of world dry cargo tonnage *Lloyd's List*

tone *noun* **dialling tone** = noise made by a telephone to show that it is ready for you to dial a number

tool *noun* instrument used for doing manual work (such as a hammer, screwdriver); **machine tools** = tools worked by motors, used to work on wood or metal
◇ **tool up** *verb* to put machinery into a factory

top 1 *adjective & noun* **(a)** upper surface *or* upper part; **do not put coffee cups on top of the computer; top copy** = first sheet of a document which is typed with several carbon copies or photocopies **(b)** highest point *or* most important place; **the company is in the top six exporters; top-flight** *or* **top-ranking** = in the most important position; **top-flight managers can earn very high salaries; he is the top-ranking official in the delegation; top-grade** = most important *or* of the best quality; **the car only runs on top-grade petrol; top management** = the main directors of a company; **to give something top priority** = to make something the most important item, so that it is done very fast; **top quality** = very best quality; **we specialize in top quality imported goods** 2 *verb* to go higher than; **sales topped £1m in the first quarter**
NOTE: **topping - topped**
◇ **top-hat pension** *noun* special extra pension for senior managers
◇ **top-selling** *adjective* which sells better than all other products; **top-selling brands of toothpaste**
◇ **top up** *verb* to fill up something which is not full; **to top up stocks before the Christmas rush**

QUOTE: gross wool receipts for the selling season appear likely to top $2 billion
Australian Financial Review
QUOTE: the base lending rate, or prime rate, is the rate at which banks lend to their top corporate borrowers *Wall Street Journal*
QUOTE: fill huge warehouses with large quantities of top-brand, first-quality merchandise, sell the goods at rock-bottom prices
Duns Business Month

tort *noun* harm done to someone *or* property which can be the basis of a lawsuit

total 1 *adjective* complete *or* with everything added together; **total amount; total assets; total cost; total expenditure; total income; total output; total revenue; the cargo was written off as a total loss** = the cargo was so badly damaged that the insurers said it had no value 2 *noun* amount which is complete *or* with everything added up; **the total of the charges comes to more than £1,000; grand total** = final total made by adding several subtotals 3 *verb* to add up to; **costs totalling more than £25,000**
NOTE: **totalling** - **totalled** but US English **totaling** - **totaled**
◇ **totally** *adverb* completely; **the factory was totally destroyed in the fire; the cargo was totally ruined by water**

tour *noun* (holiday) journey to various places, coming back in the end to the place the journey started from; **the group went on a tour of Italy; the minister went on a fact-finding tour of the region; conducted tour** = tour with a guide who shows places to the tourists; **package tour** = tour where the hotel, travel, and meals are all arranged in advance and paid for in one payment; **tour operator** = person *or* company which organizes tours; **to carry out a tour of inspection** = to visit various places *or* offices *or* factories to inspect them
◇ **tourism** *noun* business of providing travel, hotel rooms, food, entertainment, etc., for tourists
NOTE: no plural
◇ **tourist** *noun* person who goes on holiday to visit places away from his home; **tourist bureau** *or* **tourist information office** = office which gives information to tourists about the place where it is situated; **tourist class** = lower quality or less expensive way of travelling; **he always travel first class, because he says tourist class is too uncomfortable; tourist visa** = visa which allows a person to visit a country for a short time on holiday

tout 1 *noun* person who sells tickets (to games *or* shows) for more than the price printed on them 2 *verb* **to tout for custom** = to try to attract customers

track record *noun* success or failure of a company *or* salesman in the past; **he has a good track record as a secondhand car salesman; the company has no track record in the computer market**

trade 1 *noun* **(a)** business of buying and selling; **export trade** *or* **import trade** = the business of selling to other countries *or* buying from other countries; **foreign trade** *or* **overseas trade** *or* **external trade** = trade with other countries; **home trade** = trade in the country where a company is based; **trade cycle** = period during which trade expands, then slows down, then expands again; **balance of trade** *or* **trade balance** = international trading position of a country, excluding invisible trade; **the country had an adverse balance of trade for the second month running; favourable balance of trade** = situation where a country's exports are larger than its imports **(b) to do a good trade in a range of products** = to sell a large number of the range of products; **fair trade** = international business system where countries agree not to charge import duties on certain items imported from their trading partners; **free trade** = system where goods can go from one country to another without any restrictions; **free trade area** = group of countries practising free trade; **trade agreement** = international agreement between countries over general terms of trade; **trade bureau** = office which specializes in commercial enquiries; **to impose trade barriers on** = to restrict the import of certain goods by charging high duty; **trade deficit** *or* **trade gap** = difference in value between a country's high imports and low exports; **trade description** = description of a product to attract customers; GB **Trade Descriptions Act** = act which limits the way in which products can be described so as to protect customers from wrong descriptions made by manufacturers; **trade directory** = book which lists all the businesses and business people in a town; **trade mission** = visit to a country by a group of foreign businessmen to discuss trade; **to ask a company to supply trade references** = to ask a company to give names of traders who can report on the company's financial situation and reputation **(c)** people *or* companies dealing in the same type of product; **he is in the secondhand car trade; she is very well known in the clothing trade; trade association** = group which links together companies in the same trade; **trade counter** = shop in a factory *or* warehouse where goods are sold to retailers; **trade discount** *or* **trade terms** = reduction in price given to a customer in the same trade; **trade fair** = large exhibition and meeting for advertising and selling a certain type of product; **there were two trade fairs running in London at the same time; to organize** or **to run a trade fair; trade journal** or **trade magazine** or **trade paper** or **trade publication** = magazine or newspaper produced for people and companies in a certain trade; **trade press** = all magazines produced for people working in a certain trade; **trade price** = special wholesale price paid by a retailer to the manufacturer or wholesaler

NOTE: no plural for (a) or (b)

2 verb to buy and sell or to carry on a business; **to trade with another country; to trade on the Stock Exchange; the company has stopped trading; the company trades under the name "Eeziphitt"**

◇ **trade in** verb **(a)** to buy and sell certain items; **the company trades in imported goods; he trades in French wine (b)** to give in an old item as part of the payment for a new one; **the chairman traded in his old Rolls Royce for a new model**

◇ **trade-in** noun old item (such as a car or washing machine) given as part of the payment for a new one; **to give the old car as a trade-in; trade-in price** = amount allowed by the seller for an old item being traded in for a new one

◇ **trademark** or **trade name** noun particular name, design, etc., which has been registered by the manufacturer and which cannot be used by other manufacturers; **you cannot call your beds "Softn'kumfi" - it is a registered trademark**

◇ **trade-off** noun exchanging one thing for another as part of a business deal

◇ **trader** noun person who does business; **commodity trader** = person whose business is buying and selling commodities; **free trader** = person who is in favour of free trade; **sole trader** = person who runs a business, usually by himself, but has not registered it as a company

◇ **tradesman** noun shopkeeper or person who runs a shop

NOTE: plural is **tradesmen**

◇ **tradespeople** plural noun shopkeepers

◇ **trade union** or **trades union** noun organization which represents workers who are its members in discussions with employers about wages and conditions of employment; **they are members of a trades union** or **they are trade union members; he has applied for trade union membership** or **he has applied to join a trades union; Trades Union Congress** = organization linking all British trade unions

NOTE: although **Trades Union Congress** is the official name for the organization, **trade union** is commoner than **trades union** in GB English. US English is **labor union**

◇ **trade unionist** noun member of a trade union

◇ **trading** noun business of buying and selling; **trading account** = account of a company's gross profit; **trading area** = group of countries which trade with each other; **trading company** = company which specializes in buying and selling goods; **adverse trading conditions** = bad conditions for trade; **trading estate** = area of land near a town specially for factories and warehouses; **trading loss** = situation where a company's receipts are less than its expenditure; **trading partner** = company or country which trades with another; **trading profit** = situation where a company's gross receipts are more than its gross expenditure; **trading stamp** = special stamp given away by a shop, which the customer can collect and exchange later for free goods; **fair trading** = way of doing business which is reasonable and does not harm the customer; *GB* **Office of Fair Trading** = government department which protects consumers against unfair or illegal business; **insider trading** = illegal buying or selling of shares by staff of a company who have secret information about the company's plans

NOTE: no plural

QUOTE: a sharp setback in foreign trade accounted for most of the winter slowdown. The trade balance sank $17 billion *Fortune*
QUOTE: at its last traded price, the bank was capitalized around $1.05 billion
South China Morning Post
QUOTE: with most of the world's oil now traded on spot markets. Opec's official prices are much less significant than they once were *Economist*

traffic noun **(a)** movement of cars or lorries or trains or planes; movement of people or goods in vehicles; **there is an increase in commuter traffic** or **goods traffic on the motorway; passenger traffic on the commuter lines has decreased during the summer; air traffic controller** = person

who controls the landing and taking off of planes at an airport **(b)** illegal trade; **drugs traffic** or **traffic in drugs**
NOTE: no plural

train 1 *noun* set of coaches *or* wagons pulled by an engine along railway lines; **a passenger train** *or* **a goods train; to take the 09.30 train to London; he caught his train** *or* **he missed his train; to ship goods by train; freight train** *or* **goods train** = train used for carrying goods **2** *verb* to teach (someone) to do something; to learn how to do something; **he trained as an accountant; the company has appointed a trained lawyer as its managing director**
◇ **trainee** *noun* person who is learning how to do something; **we employ a trainee accountant to help in the office at peak periods; graduate trainees come to work in the laboratory when they have finished their courses at university; management trainee** = young member of staff being trained to be a manager
◇ **traineeship** *noun* post of trainee
◇ **training** *noun* being taught how to do something; **there is a ten-week training period for new staff; the shop is closed for staff training; industrial training** = training of new workers to work in an industry; **management training** = training staff to be managers, by making them study problems and work out solutions to them; **on-the-job training** = training given to workers at their place of work; **off-the-job training** = training given to workers away from their place of work (such as at a college or school); **training levy** = tax to be paid by companies to fund the government's training schemes; **training officer** = person who deals with the training of staff; **training unit** = special group of teachers who organize training for companies
NOTE: no plural

transact *verb* **to transact business** = to carry out a piece of business
◇ **transaction** *noun* **business transaction** = piece of business or buying or selling; **cash transaction** = transaction paid for in cash; **a transaction on the Stock Exchange** = purchase *or* sale of shares on the Stock Exchange; **the paper publishes a daily list of Stock Exchange transactions; exchange transaction** = purchase *or* sale of foreign currency; **fraudulent transaction** =

transaction which aims to cheat someone

transfer 1 *noun* moving someone *or* something to a new place; **he applied for a transfer to our branch in Scotland; transfer of property** *or* **transfer of shares** = moving the ownership of property *or* shares from one person to another; **airmail transfer** = sending money from one bank to another by airmail; **bank transfer** = moving money from a bank account to an account in another country; **credit transfer** *or* **transfer of funds** = moving money from one account to another; **stock transfer form** = form to be signed by the person transferring shares **2** *verb* **(a)** to move someone *or* something to a new place; **the accountant was transferred to our Scottish branch; he transferred his shares to a family trust; she transferred her money to a deposit account; transferred charge call** = phone call where the person receiving the call agrees to pay for it **(b)** to change from one type of travel to another; **when you get to London airport, you have to transfer onto an internal flight**
NOTE: transferring - transferred
◇ **transferable** *adjective* which can be passed to someone else; **the season ticket is not transferable** = the ticket cannot be given or lent to someone else to use

tranship *verb* to move cargo from one ship to another
NOTE: transhipping - transhipped

transit *noun* **(a)** movement of passengers *or* goods on the way to a destination; **to pay compensation for damage suffered in transit** *or* **for loss in transit; some of the goods were damaged in transit; goods in transit** = goods being transported from warehouse to customer **(b) transit lounge** = room in an airport where passengers wait for connecting flights; **transit visa** *or* **transit permit** = document which allows someone to spend a short time in one country while travelling to another country
NOTE: no plural

translate *verb* to put something which is said *or* written in one language into another language; **he asked his secretary to translate the letter from the German agent; we have had the contract translated from French into Japanese**

◊ **translation** *noun* something which has been translated; **she passed the translation of the letter to the accounts department; translation bureau** = office which translates documents for companies

◊ **translator** *noun* person who translates

transmission *noun* sending; **transmission of a message**

◊ **transmit** *verb* to send (a message)

NOTE: **transmitting - transmitted**

transport 1 *noun* moving of goods or people; **air transport** *or* **transport by air; rail transport** *or* **transport by rail; road transport** *or* **transport by road; passenger transport** *or* **the transport of passengers; the passenger transport services of British Rail; what means of transport will you use to get to the factory?; the visitors will be using public transport** *or* **private transport** = the visitors will be coming by bus *or* train, etc., or in their own cars; **public transport system** = system of trains, buses, etc., used by the general public

NOTE: no plural

2 *verb* to move goods *or* people from one place to another in a vehicle; **the company transports millions of tons of goods by rail each year; the visitors will be transported to the factory by air** *or* **by helicopter** *or* **by taxi**

◊ **transportable** *adjective* which can be moved

◊ **transportation** *noun* **(a)** moving goods *or* people from one place to another **(b)** vehicles used to move goods *or* people from from place to another; **the company will provide transportation to the airport; ground transportation** = buses, taxis, etc., available to take passengers from an airport to the town

NOTE: no plural

◊ **transporter** *noun* company which transports goods

◊ **Transport International Routier** *noun* system with international documents which allows dutiable goods to cross several European countries by road without paying duty until they reach their final destination

travel 1 *noun* moving of people from one place to another *or* from one country to another; **business travel is a very important part of our overhead expenditure; travel agent** = person in charge of a travel agency; **travel agency** = office which arranges travel for customers; **travel allowance** = money which an employee is allowed to spend on travelling; **travel magazine** = magazine with articles on holidays and travel; **the travel trade** = all businesses which organize travel for people

NOTE: no plural

2 *verb* **(a)** to move from one place to another *or* from one country to another; **he travels to the States on business twice a year; in her new job, she has to travel abroad at least ten times a year (b)** to go from one place to another, showing a company's goods to buyers and taking orders from them; **he travels in the north of the country for an insurance company**

NOTE: **travelling - travelled** but US **traveling - traveled**

◊ **traveller** *or* US **traveler** *noun* **(a)** person who travels; **business traveller** = person who is travelling on business; **traveller's cheques** *or* US **traveler's checks** = cheques taken by a traveller which can be cashed in a foreign country **(b) commercial traveller** = salesman who travel round an area visiting customers on behalf of his company

◊ **travelling** *noun* **travelling expenses** = money spent on travelling and hotels for business purposes

tray *noun* **filing tray** = container kept on a desk for documents which have to be filed; **in tray** = basket on a desk for letters *or* memos which have been received and are waiting to be dealt with; **out tray** = basket on a desk for letters *or* memos which have been dealt with and are ready to be sent out; **pending tray** = basket on a desk for papers which cannot be dealt with immediately

treasurer *noun* **(a)** person who looks after the money *or* finances of a club or society, etc.; **honorary treasurer** = treasurer who does not receive any fee **(b)** US main financial officer of a company

◊ **treasury** *noun* **the Treasury** = government department which deals with the country's finance; **treasury bill** = bill of exchange which does not give any interest and is sold by the government at a discount; **treasury bonds** = bonds issued by the Treasury of the USA

treaty *noun* (a) agreement between countries; **commercial treaty** (b) agreement between individual persons; **to sell a house by private treaty** = to sell a home to another person not by auction

treble *verb* to increase three times; **the company's borrowings have trebled**

trend *noun* general way things are going; **there is a trend away from old-established food stores; a downward trend in investment; we notice a general trend to sell to the student market; the report points to inflationary trends in the economy; an upward trend in sales; economic trends** = way in which a country's economy is moving; **market trends** = gradual changes taking place in a market

QUOTE: the quality of building design and ease of accessibility will become increasingly important, adding to the trend towards out-of-town office development *Lloyd's List*

trial *noun* (a) court case to judge a person accused of a crime; **he is on trial** *or* **is standing trial for embezzlement** (b) test to see if something is good; **on trial** = being tested; **the product is on trial in our laboratories; trial period** = time when a customer can test a product before buying it; **trial sample** = small piece of a product used for testing; **free trial** = testing of a machine *or* product with no payment involved (c) **trial balance** = draft adding of debits and credits to see if they balance

tribunal *noun* official court which examines special problems and makes judgements; **adjudication tribunal** = group which adjudicates in industrial disputes; **industrial tribunal** = court which can decide in disputes about employment; **rent tribunal** = court which can decide if a rent is too high or low

trick *noun* clever act to make someone believe something which is not true; **confidence trick** = business where someone gains another person's confidence and then tricks him
◇ **trickster** *noun* **confidence trickster** = person who carries out a confidence trick on someone

trip *noun* journey; **business trip** = journey to discuss business matters with people who live a long way away or overseas

triple 1 *verb* to multiply three times; **the company's debts tripled in twelve months; the acquisition of the chain of stores has tripled the group's turnover** 2 *adjective* three times as much; **the cost of airfreighting the goods is triple their manufacturing cost**

triplicate *noun* **in triplicate** = with an original and two copies; **to print an invoice in triplicate; invoicing in triplicate** = preparing three copies of invoices

trouble *noun* problem *or* difficult situation; **we are having some computer trouble** *or* **some trouble with the computer; there was some trouble in the warehouse after the manager was fired**
◇ **troubleshooter** *noun* person whose job is to solve problems in a company

trough *noun* low point in the economic cycle

truck *noun* (a) large motor vehicle for carrying goods; **fork-lift truck** = type of small tractor with two metal arms in front, used for lifting and moving pallets (b) open railway wagon for carrying goods
◇ **trucker** *noun* person who drives a truck
◇ **trucking** *noun* carrying goods in trucks; **trucking firm**
NOTE: no plural

true *adjective* correct *or* accurate; **true copy** = exact copy; **I certify that this is a true copy; certified as a true copy**

truly *adverb* **Yours truly** *or* *US* **Truly yours** = ending to a formal business letter where you do not know the person you are writing to

trunk call *noun* telephone call to a number which is in a different area

trust 1 *noun* (a) being confident that something is correct, will work, etc.; **we took his statement on trust** = we accepted his statement without examining it to see if it was correct (b) passing goods *or* money *or* secrets to someone who will look after them well; **he left his property in trust for his grandchildren; he was guilty of a breach of trust** = he did not act correctly *or* honestly when people expected him to; **he has a position of trust** = his job shows that people believe he will act correctly and honestly **(c)** management of money *or* property for someone; **they set up a family trust for their grandchildren;** *US* **trust company** = organization which supervises the financial affairs of private trusts, executes wills, and acts as a bank to a limited number of customers; **trust deed** = document which sets out the details of a private trust; **trust fund** = assets (money, securities, property) held in trust for someone; **investment trust** = company whose shares can be bought on the Stock Exchange and whose business is to make money by buying and selling stocks and shares; **unit trust** = organization which takes money from investors and invests it in stocks and shares for them under a trust deed **(d)** *US* small group of companies which control the supply of a product NOTE: no plural for (a) and (b) **2** *verb* **to trust someone with something** = to give something to someone to look after; **can he be trusted with all that cash?**

◇ **trustbusting** *noun US* breaking up monopolies to encourage competition

◇ **trustee** *noun* person who has charge of money in trust *or* person who is responsible for a family trust; **the trustees of the pension fund; Trustee Savings Bank** = bank which takes savings from small savers, and is guaranteed by the government

◇ **trustworthy** *adjective* (person) who can be trusted; **our cashiers are completely trustworthy**

TUC – TRADES UNION CONGRESS

tune *noun* piece of music; **the bank is backing him to the tune of £10,000** = the bank is helping him with a loan of £10,000

turn 1 *noun* **(a)** movement in a circle *or* change of direction **(b)** profit *or* commission; **jobber's turn** = profit made by a stock jobber **(c) stock turn** = total value of stocks sold in a year divided by the average value of goods in stock; **the company has a stock turn of 6.7 2** *verb* to change direction *or* to go round in a circle

◇ **turn down** *verb* to refuse; **the board turned down their takeover bid; the bank turned down their request for a loan; the application for a licence was turned down**

◇ **turnkey** *noun* **turnkey operation** = deal where a company takes all responsibility for constructing, fitting and staffing a building (such as a school *or* hospital *or* factory) so that it is completely ready for the purchaser to take over

◇ **turn out** *verb* to produce; **the factory turns out fifty units per day**

◇ **turn over** *verb* to have a certain amount of sales; **we turn over £2,000 a week**

◇ **turnover** *noun* **(a)** *GB* amount of sales; **the company's turnover has increased by 235%; we based our calculations on the forecast turnover; stock turnover** = total value of stock sold in a year divided by the average value of goods held in stock **(b)** changes in staff, when some leave and others join; **staff turnover** *or* **turnover of staff (c)** *US* number of times something is used *or* sold in a period (usually one year), expressed as a percentage of a total

◇ **turn round** *verb* to make (a company) change from making a loss to become profitable; **he turned the company round in less than a year** = he made the company profitable in less than a year

◇ **turnround** *noun* **(a)** value of goods sold during a year divided by the average value of goods held in stock **(b)** action of emptying a ship, plane, etc., and getting it ready for another commercial journey **(c)** making a company profitable again

---

QUOTE: a 100,000 square foot warehouse can turn its inventory over 18 times a year, more than triple a discounter's turnover

Duns Business Month

QUOTE: he is turning over his CEO title to one of his teammates, but will remain chairman for a year *Duns Business Month*

QUOTE: the US now accounts for more than half our world-wide sales; it has made a huge contribution to our earnings turnround

Duns Business Month

---

two-part *noun* paper (for computers *or* typewriters) with a top sheet for the original and a second sheet for a copy; **two-part invoices; two-part stationery**

tycoon *noun* important businessman

type *verb* to write with a typewriter; **he can type quite fast; all his reports are typed on his portable typewriter**

◇ **typewriter** *noun* machine which prints letters *or* figures on a piece of paper when a key is pressed; **portable typewriter; electronic typewriter**

◇ **typewritten** *adjective* written on a typewriter; **he sent in a typewritten job application**

◇ **typing** *noun* writing letters with a typewriter; **typing error** = mistake made when using a typewriter; **the secretary must have made a typing error; typing pool** = group of typists, working together in a company, offering a secretarial service to several departments; **copy typing** = typing documents from handwritten originals, not from dictation
NOTE: no plural

◇ **typist** *noun* person whose job is to write letters using a typewriter; **copy typist** = person who types documents from handwritten originals not from dictation; **shorthand typist** = typist who takes dictation in shorthand and then types it

Uu

ultimate *adjective* last *or* final; **ultimate consumer** = the person who actually uses the product

◇ **ultimately** *adverb* in the end; **ultimately, the management had to agree to the demands of the union**

◇ **ultimatum** *noun* statement to a someone that unless he does something within a period of time, action will be taken against him; **the union officials argued among themselves over the best way to deal with the ultimatum form the management**
NOTE: plural is **ultimatums** or **ultimata**

umbrella *noun* **umbrella organization** = large organization which includes several smaller ones

UN = THE UNITED NATIONS

unable *adjective* not able; **the chairman was unable to come to the meeting**

unacceptable *adjective* which cannot be accepted; **the terms of the contract are quite unacceptable**

unaccounted for *adjective* lost, without any explanation; **several thousand units are unaccounted for in the stocktaking**

unanimous *adjective* where everyone votes in the same way; **there was a unanimous vote against the proposal; they reached unanimous agreement**

◇ **unanimously** *adverb* with everyone agreeing; **the proposals were adopted unanimously**

unaudited *adjective* which has not been audited; **unaudited accounts**

unauthorized *adjective* not permitted; **unauthorized access to the company's records; unauthorized expenditure; no unauthorized persons are allowed into the laboratory**

unavailable *adjective* not available; **the following items on your order are temporarily unavailable**

◇ **unavailability** *noun* not being available
NOTE: no plural

unavoidable *adjective* which cannot be avoided; **planes are subject to unavoidable delays**

unbalanced *adjective* (budget) which does not balance *or* which is in deficit

uncalled *adjective* (capital) which a company is authorized to raise and has been issued but is not fully paid

uncashed *adjective* which has not been cashed; **uncashed cheques**

unchanged *adjective* which has not changed

QUOTE: the dividend is unchanged at L90 per ordinary share
Financial Times

unchecked *adjective* which has not been checked; **unchecked figures**

unclaimed *adjective* which has not been claimed; **unclaimed baggage** = cases which have been left with someone and have not been claimed by their owners; **unclaimed property** *or* **unclaimed baggage will be sold by auction after six months**

uncollected *adjective* which has not been collected; **uncollected subscriptions; uncollected taxes**

unconditional *adjective* with no conditions; **unconditional acceptance of the offer by the board; the offer went unconditional last Thursday** = the takeover bid was accepted by the majority of the shareholders and therefore the conditions attached to it no longer apply
◇ **unconditionally** *adverb* without imposing any conditions; **the offer was accepted unconditionally by the trade union**

unconfirmed *adjective* which has not been confirmed; **there are unconfirmed reports that our agent has been arrested**

unconstitutional *adjective* not allowed by the rules *or* laws of a country *or* organization; **the chairman ruled that the meeting was unconstitutional**

uncontrollable *adjective* which cannot be controlled; **uncontrollable inflation**

uncrossed cheque *noun* cheque which can be cashed anywhere

undated *adjective* with no date written; **he tried to cash an undated cheque; undated bond** = bond with no maturity date

under *preposition* (a) lower than *or* less than; **the interest rate is under 10%; under half of the shareholders accepted the offer** (b) controlled by *or* according to; **under the terms of the agreement, the goods should be delivered in October; he is acting under rule 23 of the union constitution**
◇ **under-** *prefix* less important than *or* lower than
◇ **underbid** *verb* to bid less than someone
NOTE: **underbidding - underbid**

◇ **underbidder** *noun* person who bids less than the person who buys at an auction
◇ **undercapitalized** *adjective* without enough capital; **the company is severely undercapitalized**
◇ **undercharge** *verb* to ask for too little money; **he undercharged us by £25**
◇ **undercut** *verb* to offer something at a lower price than someone else
◇ **underdeveloped** *adjective* which has not been developed; **Japan is an underdeveloped market for our products; underdeveloped countries** = countries which are not fully industrialized
◇ **underemployed** *adjective* with not enough work; **the staff is underemployed because of the cutback in production; underemployed capital** = capital which is not producing enough interest
◇ **underemployment** *noun* (a) situation where workers in a company do not have enough work to do (b) situation where there is not enough work for all the workers in a country
NOTE: no plural
◇ **underequipped** *adjective* with not enough equipment
◇ **underestimate** 1 *noun* estimate which is less than the actual figure; **the figure of £50,000 in turnover was a considerable underestimate** 2 *verb* to think that something is smaller *or* not as bad as it really is; **they underestimated the effects of the strike on their sales; he underestimated the amount of time needed to finish the work**
◇ **underlease** *noun* lease from a tenant to another tenant
◇ **undermanned** *adjective* with not enough staff to do the work
◇ **undermanning** *noun* having too few workers than are needed to do the company's work; **the company's production is affected by undermanning on the assembly line**
NOTE: no plural
◇ **undermentioned** *adjective* mentioned lower down in a document
◇ **underpaid** *adjective* not paid enough; **our staff say that they are underpaid and overworked**
◇ **underrate** *verb* to value less highly than should be; **do not underrate the strength of the competition in the European market; the power of the yen is underrated**

◇ **undersell** *verb* to sell more cheaply than; **to undersell a competitor; the company is never undersold** = no other company sells goods as cheaply as this one
NOTE: **underselling - undersold**

◇ **undersigned** *noun* person who has signed a letter; **we, the undersigned** = we, the people who have signed below
NOTE: can be followed by a plural verb

◇ **underspend** *verb* to spend less; **he has underspent his budget** = he has spent less than was allowed in the budget
NOTE: **underspending - underspent**

◇ **understaffed** *adjective* with not enough staff to do the company's work

◇ **understand** *verb* to know *or* to see what something means
NOTE: **understanding - understood**

◇ **understanding** *noun* private agreement; **to come to an understanding about the divisions of the market; on the understanding that** = on condition that *or* provided that; **we accept the terms of the contract, on the understanding that it has to be ratified by our main board**

◇ **understate** *verb* to make something seem less than it really is; **the company accounts understate the real profit**

◇ **undertake** *verb* to agree to do something; **to undertake an investigation of the market; they have undertaken not to sell into our territory**
NOTE: **undertaking - undertook - has undertaken**

◇ **undertaking** *noun* **(a)** business; **commercial undertaking (b)** (legally binding) promise; **they have given us a written undertaking not to sell their products in competition with ours**

◇ **underutilized** *adjective* not used enough

◇ **undervalued** *adjective* not valued highly enough; **the properties are undervalued on the balance sheet; the dollar is undervalued on the foreign exchanges**

◇ **undervaluation** *noun* being valued at a lower worth than should be

◇ **underweight** *adjective* **the pack is twenty grams underweight** = the pack weighs twenty grams less than it should

◇ **underworked** *adjective* not given enough work to do; **the directors think our staff are overpaid and underworked**

◇ **underwrite** *verb* **(a)** to accept responsibility for; **to underwrite a share issue** =

to guarantee that a share issue will be sold by agreeing to buy all shares which are not subscribed; **the issue was underwritten by three underwriting companies (b)** to insure *or* to cover (a risk); **to underwrite an insurance policy (c)** to agree to pay for costs; **the government has underwritten the development costs of the project**
NOTE: **underwriting - underwrote - has underwritten**

◇ **underwriter** *noun* person who underwrites a share issue *or* an insurance; **Lloyd's underwriter** = member of an insurance group at Lloyd's who accepts to underwrite insurances; **marine underwriter** = person who insures ships and their cargoes

undischarged bankrupt *noun* person who has been declared bankrupt and has not been released from that state

undistributed profit *noun* profit which has not been distributed as dividends to shareholders

unearned income *noun* money received from interest or dividends, not from salary or profits of one's business

uneconomic *adjective* which does not make a commercial profit; **it is an uneconomic proposition** = it will not be commercially profitable; **uneconomic rent** = rent which is not enough to cover costs

unemployed *adjective* not employed *or* without any work; **unemployed office workers** = office workers with no jobs; **the unemployed** = the people without any jobs

◇ **unemployment** *noun* lack of work; **mass unemployment** = unemployment of large numbers of workers; **unemployment benefit** *or* *US* **unemployment compensation** = payment made to someone who is unemployed
NOTE: no plural

> QUOTE: tax advantages directed toward small businesses will help create jobs and reduce the unemployment rate   *Toronto Star*

unfair *adjective* **unfair competition** = trying to do better than another company by using techniques such as importing foreign goods at very low prices or by wrongly criticizing a competitor's products; **unfair dismissal** = removing someone from a job for reasons which are not fair

unfavourable *adjective* not favourable; **unfavourable balance of trade** = situation where a country imports more than it exports; **unfavourable exchange rate** = exchange rate which gives an amount of foreign currency for the home currency which is not good for trade; **the unfavourable exchange rate hit the country's exports**

unfulfilled *adjective* (order) which has not yet been supplied

ungeared *adjective* with no borrowings

unilateral *adjective* on one side only *or* done by one party only; **they took the unilateral decision to cancel the contract** ◇ **unilaterally** *adverb* by one party only; **they cancelled the contract unilaterally**

uninsured *adjective* not insured

union *noun* (a) **trade union** *or* **trades union** *or* *US* **labor union** = organization which represents workers who are its members in discussions with management about wages and conditions of work; **union agreement** = agreement between a management and a trade union over wages and conditions of work; **union dues** *or* **union subscription** = payment made by workers to belong to a union; **union officials** = paid organizers of a union; **union recognition** = act of agreeing that a union can act on behalf of staff in a company (b) **customs union** = agreement between several countries that goods can go between them without paying duty, while goods from other countries have special duties charged on them
◇ **unionist** *noun* member of a trade union
◇ **unionized** *adjective* (company) where the members of staff belong to a trade union

unique *adjective* special *or* with nothing like it; **unique selling proposition** = special quality of a product which makes it different from other goods and therefore attractive to customers

unissued capital *noun* capital which a company is authorized to issue but has not issued as shares

unit *noun* (a) single product for sale; **unit cost** = the cost of one item (i.e total product costs divided by the number of units produced); **unit price** = the price of one item (b) separate piece of equipment or furniture; **display unit** = special stand for showing goods for sale; **visual display unit** = screen attached to a computer which shows the information stored in the computer (c) **factory unit** = single building on an industrial estate (d) **production unit** = separate small group of workers which produces a certain product; **research unit** = separate small group of research workers (e) **monetary unit** *or* **unit of currency** = main item of currency of a country (a dollar, pound, yen etc.); **unit of account** = currency used for calculating the EEC budget and farm prices (f) single share in a unit trust
◇ **unit trust** *noun* organization which takes money from small investors and invests it in stocks and shares for them under a trust deed, the investment being in the form of shares (or units) in the trust

unite *verb* to join together; **the directors united with the managers to reject the takeover bid; United Nations** = organization which links the countries of the world to promote good relations between them

unladen *adjective* empty *or* without a cargo

unlawful *adjective* against the law *or* not legal

unlimited *adjective* with no limits; **the**

bank offered him unlimited credit; **unlimited liability** = situation where a sole trader or each partner is responsible for all the firm's debts with no limit at the amount each may have to pay

unlined *adjective* **unlined paper** = paper with no lines printed on it

unlisted *adjective* **unlisted securities** = shares which are not listed on the Stock Exchange; **unlisted securities market** = market for buying and selling shares which are not listed on the Stock Exchange

unload *verb* **(a)** to take goods off (a ship, etc.); **the ship is unloading at Hamburg; we need a fork-lift truck to unload the lorry; we unloaded the spare parts at Lagos; there are no unloading facilities for container ships (b)** to sell (shares which do not seem attractive); **we tried to unload our shareholding as soon as the company published its accounts**

unobtainable *adjective* which cannot be obtained

unofficial *adjective* not official; **unofficial strike** = strike by local workers which has not been approved by the main union
◇ **unofficially** *adverb* not officially; **the tax office told the company unofficially that it would be prosecuted**

unpaid *adjective* not paid; **unpaid holiday** = holiday where the worker does not receive any pay; **unpaid invoices** = invoices which have not been paid

unprofitable *adjective* which is not profitable

QUOTE: the airline has already eliminated a number of unprofitable flights
Duns Business Month

unquoted shares *plural noun* shares which have no Stock Exchange quotation

unredeemed pledge *noun* pledge which the borrower has not claimed back by paying back his loan

unregistered *adjective* (company) which has not been registered

unreliable *adjective* which cannot be relied on; **the postal service is very unreliable**

unsealed envelope *noun* envelope where the flap has been pushed into the back of the envelope, not stuck down

unsecured *adjective* **unsecured creditor** = creditor who is owed money, but has no security from the debtor for it; **unsecured debt** = debt which is not guaranteed by assets; **unsecured loan** = loan made with no security

unseen *adverb* not seen; **to buy something sight unseen** = to buy something without having inspected it

unsettled *adjective* which changes often *or* which is upset; **the market was unsettled by the news of the failure of the takeover bid**

unskilled *adjective* without any particular skill; **unskilled labour** *or* **unskilled workforce** *or* **unskilled workers**

unsocial *adjective* **to work unsocial hours** = to work at times (i.e. in the evening *or* at night *or* during public holidays) when most people are not at work

unsold *adjective* not sold; **unsold items will be scrapped**

unsolicited *adjective* which has not been asked for; **an unsolicited gift; unsolicited testimonial** = letter praising someone *or* a product without the writer having been asked to write it

unstable *adjective* not stable *or* changing frequently; **unstable exchange rates**

unsubsidized *adjective* with no subsidy

unsuccessful *adjective* not successful; **an unsuccessful businessman; the project was expensive and unsuccessful**
◇ **unsuccessfully** *adverb* with no success; **the company unsuccessfully tried to break into the South American market**

untrue *adjective* not true

unused *adjective* which has not been used; **we are trying to sell off six unused typewriters**

unwaged *adjective* **the unwaged** = people with no jobs
NOTE: is followed by a plural verb

unwritten *adjective* **unwritten agreement** = agreement which has been reached in speaking (such as in a telephone conversation) but has not been written down

up *adverb & preposition* in a higher position *or* to a higher position; **the inflation rate is going up steadily; shares were up slightly at the end of the day**
◊ **up to** *adverb* as far as *or* as high as; **we will buy at prices up to £25**
◊ **up to date** *adjective & adverb* current *or* recent *or* modern; **an up-to-date computer system; to bring something up to date** = to add the latest information or equipment to something; **to keep something up to date** = to keep adding information to something so that it always has the latest information in it; **we spend a lot of time keeping our mailing list up to date**

update 1 *noun* information added to something to make it up to date **2** *verb* to revise something so that it is always up to date; **the figures are updated annually**

up front *adverb* in advance; **money up front** = payment in advance; **they are asking for £100,000 up front before they will consider the deal; he had to put money up front before he could clinch the deal**

upgrade *verb* to increase the importance of someone *or* of a job; **his job has been upgraded to senior manager level**

upkeep *noun* cost of keeping a building *or* machine in good order
NOTE: no plural

uplift *noun* increase; **the contract provides for an annual uplift of charges**

up market *adverb* more expensive *or* appealing to a wealthy section of the population; **the company has decided to**

move up market = the company has decided to start to produce more luxury items

upset price *noun* lowest price which the buyer will accept at an auction

upturn *noun* movement towards higher sales or profits; **an upturn in the economy; an upturn in the market**

upward *adjective* towards a higher position; **an upward movement**
◊ **upwards** *adverb* towards a higher position; **the market moved upwards after the news of the budget**
NOTE: US English uses **upward** as both adjective and adverb

urgent *adjective* which has to be done quickly
◊ **urgently** *adverb* immediately

usage *noun* how something is used
NOTE: no plural

use 1 *noun* way in which something can be used; **directions for use** = instructions how to run a machine; **to make use of something** = to use something; **in use** = being worked; **the computer is in use twenty-four hours a day; items for personal use** = items which a person will use for himself, not on behalf of the company; **he has the use of a company car** = he has a company car which he uses privately; **land zoned for industrial use** = land where planning permission has been given to build factories **2** *verb* to take a machine, a company, a process, etc., and work with it; **we use airmail for all our overseas correspondence; the photocopier is being used all the time; they use freelancers for most of their work**
◊ **useful** *adjective* which can help
◊ **user** *noun* person who uses something; **end user** = person who actually uses a product; **user's guide** *or* **handbook** = book showing someone how to use something
◊ **user-friendly** *adjective* which a user finds easy to work; **these programs are really user-friendly**

USM = UNLISTED SECURITIES MARKET

USP = UNIQUE SELLING PROPOSITION

usual *adjective* normal *or* ordinary; **our usual terms** *or* **usual conditions are thirty days' credit; the usual practice is to have the contract signed by the MD; the usual hours of work are from 9.30 to 5.30**

usury *noun* lending money at high interest
NOTE: no plural

utilize *verb* to use
◇ **utilization** *noun* making use of something; **capacity utilization** = using something as much as possible
NOTE: no plural

QUOTE: control permits the manufacturer to react to changing conditions on the plant floor and to keep people and machines at a high level of utilization   *Duns Business Month*

Vv

vacancy *noun* empty place *or* room; job which is not filled; **we advertised a vacancy in the local press; we have been unable to fill the vacancy for a skilled machinist; they have a vacancy for a secretary; job vacancies** = jobs which are empty and need people to do them; **vacancy rate** = average number of rooms empty in a hotel over a period of time, shown as a percentage of the total number of rooms
◇ **vacant** *adjective* empty *or* not occupied; **vacant possession** = being able to occupy a property immediately after buying it because it is empty; **the house is for sale with vacant possession; situations vacant** *or* **appointments vacant** = list (in a newspaper) of jobs which are available

vacate *verb* **to vacate the premises** = to leave premises, so that they become empty
◇ **vacation** *noun* (a) *GB* period when the law courts are closed (b) *US* holiday *or* period when people are not working; **the CEO is on vacation in Florida**

valid *adjective* (a) which is acceptable because it is true; **that is not a valid**

argument *or* **excuse (b)** which can be used lawfully; **the contract is not valid if it has not been witnessed; ticket which is valid for three months; he was carrying a valid passport**
◇ **validate** *verb* (a) to check to see if something is correct; **the document was validated by the bank (b)** to make (something) valid
◇ **validation** *noun* act of making something valid
NOTE: no plural
◇ **validity** *noun* being valid; **period of validity** = length of time for which a document is valid
NOTE: no plural

valorem *see* AD VALOREM

valuable *adjective* which is worth a lot of money; **valuable property** *or* **valuables** = personal items which are worth a lot of money
◇ **valuation** *noun* estimate of how much something is worth; **to ask for a valuation of a property before making an offer for it; stock valuation** = estimating the value of stock at the end of an accounting period; **to buy a shop with stock at valuation** = to pay for the stock the same amount as its value as estimated by a valuer
◇ **value** 1 *noun* amount of money which something is worth; **he imported goods to the value of £250; the fall in the value of sterling; the valuer put the value of the stock at £25,000; good value (for money)** = a bargain *or* something which is worth the price paid for it; **that restaurant gives value for money; buy that computer now - it is very good value; holidays in Italy are good value because of the exchange rate; to rise in value** *or* **to fall in value** = to be worth more *or* less; **asset value** = value of a company calculated by adding together all its assets; **book value** = value as recorded in the company's accounts; **"sample only - of no commercial value"** = not worth anything if sold; **declared value** = value of goods entered on a customs declaration form; **discounted value** = difference between the face value of a share and its lower market price; **face value** = value written on a coin *or* banknote *or* share; **market value** = value of an asset *or* of a product *or* of a company, if sold today; **par value** = value written on a share certifi-

cate; **scarcity value** = value of something which is worth a lot because it is rare and there is a large demand for it; **surrender value** = money which an insurer will pay if an insurance policy is given up before maturity date **2** *verb* to estimate how much money something is worth; **he valued the stock at £25,000; we are having the jewellery valued for insurance**

◇ **Value Added Tax** *noun* tax imposed as a percentage of the invoice value of goods and services

◇ **valuer** *noun* person who estimates how much money something is worth

van *noun* small goods vehicle; **delivery van** = van for delivering goods to customers

variable *adjective* which changes; **variable costs** = money paid to produce a product which increases with the quantity made (such as wages, raw materials)

◇ **variability** *noun* being variable
NOTE: no plural

◇ **variance** *noun* difference; **budget variance** = difference between the cost as estimated for the budget, and the actual cost; **at variance with** = which does not agree with; **the actual sales are at variance with the sales reported by the reps**

◇ **variation** *noun* amount by which something changes; **seasonal variations** = changes which take place because of the seasons; **seasonal variations in buying patterns**

variety *noun* different types of things; **the shop stocks a variety of goods; we had a variety of visitors at the office today;** *US* **variety store** = shop selling a wide range of usually cheap items

◇ **vary** *verb* to change *or* to differ; **the gross margin varies from quarter to quarter; we try to prevent the flow of production from varying in the factory**

VAT = VALUE ADDED TAX **the invoice includes VAT at 15%; the government is proposing to increase VAT to 17.5%; some items (such as books) are zero-rated for VAT; he does not charge VAT because he asks for payment in cash; VAT declaration** = statement declaring VAT income to the VAT office; **VAT invoicing** = sending of an invoice including VAT; **VAT invoice** = invoice which shows VAT separately;

VAT inspector = government official who examines VAT returns and checks that VAT is being paid; **VAT office** = government office dealing with the collection of VAT in an area
NOTE: no plural

◇ **VATman** *or* **vatman** *noun* VAT inspector

VDU *or* **VDT** = VISUAL DISPLAY UNIT *or* VISUAL DISPLAY TERMINAL

vehicle *noun* machine with wheels, used to carry goods *or* passengers on a road; **commercial vehicle** *or* **goods vehicle** = van *or* truck used for business purposes; **heavy goods vehicle** = very large lorry; **goods vehicles can park in the loading bay**

vending *noun* selling; **(automatic) vending machine** = machine which provides drinks, cigarettes, etc., when a coin is put in

◇ **vendor** *noun* **(a)** person who sells (a property); **the solicitor acting on behalf of the vendor (b) street vendor** = person who sells food or small items in the street

venture 1 *noun* business *or* commercial deal which involves a risk; **he lost money on several import ventures; she has started a new venture - a computer shop; joint venture** = very large business project where two or more companies, often from different countries, join together; **venture capital** = capital for investment which may easily be lost in risky projects, but can also provide high returns **2** *verb* to risk (money)

venue *noun* place where a meeting is to be held; **we have changed the venue for the conference; what is the venue for the exhibition?**

verbal *adjective* using spoken words, not writing; **verbal agreement** = agreement which is spoken (such as over the telephone)

◇ **verbally** *adverb* using spoken words, not writing; **they agreed to the terms verbally, and then started to draft the contract**

verify *verb* to check to see if something is correct

◇ **verification** *noun* checking if something is correct; **the shipment was allowed into the country after verification of the documents by the customs**

vertical *adjective* upright *or* straight up or down; **vertical communication** = communication between senior managers via the middle management to the workers; **vertical integration** = joining two business together which deal with different stages in the production or sale of a product

vessel *noun* ship; **merchant vessel** = commercial ship which carries a cargo

vested *adjective* **vested interest** = special interest in keeping an existing state of affairs; **she has a vested interest in keeping the business working** = she wants to keep the business working because she will make more money if it does

vet *verb* to examine something carefully; **all candidates have to be vetted by the managing director; the contract has been sent to the legal department for vetting** NOTE: **vetting - vetted**

via *preposition* using (a means *or* a route); **the shipment is going via the Suez Canal; we are sending the cheque via our office in New York; they sent the message via the telex line**

viable *adjective* which can work in practice; **not commercially viable** = not likely to make a profit
◇ **viability** *noun* being viable *or* being able to make a profit NOTE: no plural

vice- *prefix* deputy *or* second in command; **he is the vice-chairman of an industrial group; she was appointed to the vice-chairmanship of the committee**
◇ **vice-president** *noun* *US* one of the executive directors of a company; **senior vice-president** = one of a few main executive directors of a company

view *noun* way of thinking about something; **we asked the sales manager for his views on the reorganization of the reps' territories; the chairman takes the view that** credit should never be longer than thirty days; **to take the long view** = to plan for a long period before your current investment will become profitable; **in view of** = because of; **in view of the falling exchange rate, we have redrafted our sales forecasts**

vigorous *adjective* energetic *or* very active; **we are planning a vigorous publicity campaign**

VIP = VERY IMPORTANT PERSON **VIP lounge** = special room at an airport for important travellers; **we laid on VIP treatment for our visitors** *or* **we gave our visitors a VIP reception** = we arranged for our visitors to be looked after and entertained well

visa *noun* special document *or* special stamp in a passport which allows someone to enter a country; **you will need a visa before you go to the USA; he filled in his visa application form; entry visa** = visa allowing someone to enter a country; **multiple entry visa** = visa allowing someone to enter a country many times; **tourist visa** = visa which allows a person to visit a country for a short time on holiday; **transit visa** = visa which allows someone to spend a short time in one country while travelling to another country

visible *adjective* which can be seen; **visible imports** *or* **exports** = real products which are imported *or* exported

visit **1** *noun* short stay in a place; **we are expecting a visit from our German agents; he is on a business visit to London; we had a visit from the VAT inspector** **2** *verb* to go to a place *or* to see someone for a short time; **he spent a week in Scotland, visiting clients in Edinburgh and Glasgow; the trade delegation visited the Ministry of Commerce**
◇ **visitor** *noun* person who visits; **the chairman showed the Japanese visitors round the factory; visitors' bureau** = office which deals with visitors' questions

visual *adjective* which can be seen; **visual display terminal** *or* **visual display unit** = screen attached to a computer which shows the information stored in the computer

vivos *noun* **gift inter vivos** = present given to another living person

vocation *noun* type of job which you feel you want to do; wanting to be in a certain type of job; **he followed his vocation and became an accountant**

◇ **vocational** *adjective* referring to a choice of job; **vocational guidance** = helping young people to choose a suitable job; **vocational training** = training for a particular job

void 1 *adjective* not legally valid; **the contract was declared null and void** = the contract was said to be no longer valid **2** *verb* **to void a contract** = to make a contract invalid

volume *noun* quantity of items; **volume discount** = discount given to customer who buys a large quantity of goods; **volume of output** = number of items produced; **volume of sales** *or* **sales volume** = number of items sold; **low** *or* **high volume of sales** = small *or* large number of items sold; **volume of trade** *or* **volume of business** = number of items sold *or* number of shares sold on the Stock Exchange during a day's trading; **the company has maintained the same volume of business in spite of the recession**

voluntary *adjective* **(a)** done without being forced; **voluntary liquidation** = situation where a company itself decides it must close and sell its assets; **voluntary redundancy** = situation where a worker asks to be made redundant **(b)** done without being paid; **voluntary organization** = organization which has no paid staff

◇ **voluntarily** *adverb* without being forced or paid

vote 1 *noun* marking a paper, holding up your hand, etc., to show your opinion *or* to show who you want to be elected; **to take a vote on a proposal** *or* **to put a proposal to the vote** = to ask people present at a meeting to say if they do or do not agree with the proposal; **block vote** = casting of a large number of votes (such as of a trade union delegation) all together in the same way; **casting vote** = vote used by the chairman in the case where the votes for

and against a proposal are equal; **the chairman has the casting vote; he used his casting vote to block the motion; postal vote** = election where the voters send in their voting papers by post **2** *verb* to show an opinion by marking a paper *or* by holding up your hand at a meeting; **the meeting voted to close the factory; 52% of the members voted for Mr Smith as chairman; to vote for a proposal** *or* **to vote against a proposal** = to say that you agree *or* do not agree with a proposal; **two directors were voted off the board at the AGM** = the AGM voted to dismiss two directors; **she was voted on to the committee** = she was elected a member of the committee

◇ **voter** *noun* person who votes

◇ **voting** *noun* act of making a vote; **voting paper** = paper on which the voter puts a cross to show for whom he wants to vote; **voting rights** = rights of shareholders to voting at company meetings; **non-voting shares** = shares which do not allow the shareholder to vote at company meetings

NOTE: no plural

voucher *noun* **(a)** paper which is given instead of money; **cash voucher** = paper which can be exchanged for cash; **with every £20 of purchases, the customer gets a cash voucher to the value of £2; gift voucher** = card, bought in a store, which is given as a present and which must be exchanged in that store for goods; **luncheon voucher** = ticket, given by an employer to a worker, which can be exchanged in a restaurant for food **(b)** written document from an auditor to show that the accounts are correct *or* that money has really been paid

voyage *noun* long journey by ship

Ww

wage *noun* money paid (usually in cash each week) to a worker for work done; **she is earning a good wage** *or* **good wages in the supermarket; basic wage** = normal pay

without any extra payments; **the basic wage is £110 a week, but you can expect to earn more than that with overtime; hourly wage** or **wage per hour** = amount of money paid for an hour's work; **minimum wage** = lowest hourly wage which a company can legally pay its workers; **wage adjustments** = changes made to wages; **wage claim** = asking for an increase in wages; **wages clerk** = office worker who deals with the pay of other workers; **wage differentials** = differences in salary between workers in similar types of jobs; **wage freeze** or **freeze on wages** = period when wages are not allowed to increase; **wage levels** = rates of pay for different types of work; **wage negotiations** = discussions between management and workers about pay; **wage packet** = envelope containing money and pay slip; **wages policy** = government policy on what percentage increases should be paid to workers; **wage-price spiral** = situation where price rises encourage higher wage demands which in turn make prices rise; **wage scale** = list of wages, showing different rates of pay for different jobs in the same company
NOTE: **wages** is more usual when referring to money earned, but **wage** is used before other nouns

◇ **wage-earner** noun person who earns money paid weekly in a job

◇ **wage-earning** adjective **the wage-earning population** = people who have jobs and earn money

QUOTE: European economies are being held back by rigid labor markets and wage structures
Duns Business Month
QUOTE: real wages have been held down dramatically: they have risen at an annual rate of only 1% in the last two years
Sunday Times

wagon noun goods truck used on the railway

waive verb to give up (a right); **he waived his claim to the estate; to waive a payment** = to say that payment is not necessary

◇ **waiver** noun giving up (a right) or removing the conditions (of a rule); **if you want to work without a permit, you will have to apply for a waiver; waiver clause** = clause in a contract giving the conditions under which the rights in the contract can be given up

walk verb to go on foot; **he walks to the office every morning; the visitors walked round the factory**

◇ **walk off** verb to go on strike or to stop working and leave an office or factory; **the builders walked off the site because they said it was too dangerous**

◇ **walk out** verb to go on strike or to stop working and leave an office or factory; **the whole workforce walked out in protest**

◇ **walk-out** noun strike or stopping work; **production has been held up by the walk-out of the workers**
NOTE: plural is **walk-outs**

Wall Street noun street in New York where the Stock Exchange is situated; the American financial centre; **a Wall Street analyst; she writes the Wall Street column in the newspaper**

want noun thing which is needed; **want ads** = advertisements listed in a newspaper under special headings (such as "property for sale", or "jobs wanted"); **to draw up a wants list** = to make a list of things which you need

war noun fighting or argument between countries or companies; **price war; tariff war**

warehouse 1 noun large building where goods are stored; **bonded warehouse** = warehouse where goods are stored until excise duty has been paid; **warehouse capacity** = space available in a warehouse; **price ex warehouse** = price for a product which is to be collected from the manufacturer's or agent's warehouse and so does not include delivery 2 verb to store (goods) in a warehouse

◇ **warehousing** noun act of storing goods; **warehousing costs are rising rapidly**
NOTE: no plural

◇ **warehouseman** noun person who works in a warehouse

warn verb to say that there is a possible danger; **he warned the shareholders that the dividend might be cut; the government warned of possible import duties**
NOTE: you warn someone **of** something, or **that** something may happen

◇ **warning** noun notice of possible danger; **to issue a warning; warning notices were put up around the construction site**

warrant 1 *noun* official document which allows someone to do something; **dividend warrant** = cheque which makes payment of a dividend; **share warrant** = document which says that someone has the right to a number of shares in a company 2 *verb* **(a)** to guarantee; **all the spare parts are warranted (b)** to show that something is reasonable; **the company's volume of trade with the USA does not warrant six trips a year to New York by the sales director**
◇ **warrantee** *noun* person who is given a warranty
◇ **warrantor** *noun* person who gives a warranty
◇ **warranty** *noun* **(a)** guarantee *or* legal document which promises that a machine will work properly *or* that an item is of good quality; **the car is sold with a twelve-month warranty; the warranty covers spare parts but not labour costs (b)** promise in a contract; **breach of warranty** = failing to do something which is a part of a contract **(c)** statement made by an insured person which declares that the facts stated by him are true

QUOTE: the rights issue will grant shareholders free warrants to subscribe for further new shares *Financial Times*

wastage *noun* amount lost by being wasted; **allow 10% extra material for wastage; natural wastage** = losing workers because they resign *or* retire, not because they are made redundant or are sacked
NOTE: no plural
◇ **waste** 1 *noun* rubbish *or* things which are not used; **the company was fined for putting industrial waste into the river; it is a waste of time asking the chairman for a rise; that computer is a waste of money - there are plenty of cheaper models which would do the work just as well**
NOTE: no plural
2 *adjective* not used; **waste materials; cardboard is made from recycled waste paper; waste paper basket** = container near an office desk into which pieces of rubbish can be put **3** *verb* to use more than is needed; **to waste money** *or* **paper** *or* **electricity** *or* **time; the MD does not like people wasting his time with minor details;**

we turned off all the heating so as not to waste energy
◇ **wasteful** *adjective* which wastes a lot of something; **this photocopier is very wasteful of paper**

waterproof *adjective* which will not let water through; **the parts are sent in waterproof packing**

waybill *noun* list of goods carried, made out by the carrier

weak *adjective* not strong *or* not active; **weak market** = share market where prices tend to fall because there are no buyers; **share prices remained weak** = share prices did not rise
◇ **weaken** *verb* to become weak; **the market weakened** = share prices fell
◇ **weakness** *noun* being weak

QUOTE: the Fed started to ease monetary policy months ago as the first stories appeared about weakening demand in manufacturing industry *Sunday Times*
QUOTE: indications of weakness in the US economy were contained in figures from the Fed on industrial production *Financial Times*

wealth *noun* large quantity of money owned by someone; **wealth tax** = tax on money *or* property *or* investments owned by someone
NOTE: no plural
◇ **wealthy** *adjective* very rich

wear and tear *noun* **fair wear and tear** = acceptable damage caused by normal use; **the insurance policy covers most damage but not fair wear and tear to the machine**
NOTE: no plural

week *noun* period of seven days (from Monday to Sunday); **to be paid by the week** = to be paid a certain amount of money each week; **he earns £500 a week** *or* **per week; she works thirty-five hours per week** *or* **she works a thirty-five-hour week**
◇ **weekday** *noun* normal working day (not Saturday or Sunday)
◇ **weekly** *adjective* done every week; **the weekly rate for the job is £250; a weekly magazine** *or* **a weekly** = magazine which is published each week

weigh *verb* **(a)** to measure how heavy something is; **he weighed the packet at the post office (b)** to have a certain weight; **the packet weighs twenty-five grams**

◇ **weighbridge** *noun* platform for weighing a lorry and its load

◇ **weighing machine** *noun* machine which measures how heavy a thing *or* a person is

◇ **weight** *noun* measurement of how heavy something is; **to sell fruit by weight** = the price is per pound *or* per kilo of the fruit; **false weight** = weight on a shop scales which is wrong and so cheats customers; **gross weight** = weight of both the container and its contents; **net weight** = weight of goods after deducting the packing material and container; **to give short weight** = to give less than you should; **inspector of weights and measures** = government official who inspects goods sold in shops to see if the quantities and weights are correct

◇ **weighted** *adjective* **weighted average** = average which is calculated taking several factors into account, giving some more value than others; **weighted index** = index where some important items are given more value than less important ones

◇ **weighting** *noun* additional salary *or* wages paid to compensate for living in an expensive part of the country; **salary plus a London weighting**

welfare *noun* **(a)** looking after people; **the chairman is interested in the welfare of the manual workers' families; welfare state** = country which looks after the health, education, etc., of the people **(b)** money paid by the government to people who need it
NOTE: no plural

well-known *adjective* known by many people

◇ **well-paid** *adjective* earning a high salary

wharf *noun* place in a dock where a ship can tie up to load or unload
NOTE: plural is **wharfs** or **wharves**

◇ **wharfage** *noun* charge for tying up at a wharf
NOTE: no plural

◇ **wharfinger** *noun* person who works on a wharf

wheeler-dealer *noun* person who lives on money from a series of profitable business deals

whereof *adverb* (*formal*) **in witness whereof I sign my hand** = I sign as a witness that this is correct

white *adjective & noun* the colour of snow; **white sale** = sale of sheets *or* towels, etc.

◇ **white-collar union** *noun* trade union formed of white-collar workers

◇ **white-collar worker** *noun* worker in an office, not in a factory

◇ **white goods** *plural noun* **(a)** machines (such as refrigerators, washing machines)which are used in the kitchen **(b)** sheets *or* towels, etc.

◇ **white knight** *noun* person *or* company which rescues a firm in financial difficulties, especially which saves a firm from being taken over by an unacceptable purchaser

◇ **White Paper** *noun* *GB* report from the government on a particular problem

whole-life insurance *noun* insurance where the insured person pays a fixed premium each year and the insurance company pays a sum when he dies

wholesale *noun & adverb* buying goods from manufacturers and selling in large quantities to traders who then sell in smaller quantities to the general public; **wholesale discount; wholesale shop; wholesale dealer** = person who buys in bulk from manufacturers and sells to retailers; **wholesale price index** = index showing the rises and falls of prices of manufactured goods as they leave the factory; **he buys wholesale and sells retail** = he buys goods in bulk at a wholesale discount and then sells in small quantities to the public
NOTE: no plural

◇ **wholesaler** *noun* person who buys goods in bulk from manufacturers and sells them to retailers

wholly-owned subsidiary *noun* company which is owned completely by another company

wildcat strike *noun* strike organized suddenly by workers without the main union office knowing about it

will *noun* legal document where someone says what should happen to his property when he dies; **he wrote his will in 1964; according to her will, all her property is left to her children**

win *verb* to be successful; **to win a contract** = to be successful in tendering for a contract; **the company announced that it had won a contract worth £25m to supply buses and trucks**
NOTE: **winning - won**

windfall *noun* sudden winning of money *or* sudden profit which is not expected; **windfall tax** = tax on sudden profits

wind up *verb* **(a)** to end (a meeting); **he wound up the meeting with a vote of thanks to the committee (b)** to wind up a company = to put a company into liquidation; **the court ordered the company to be wound up**
NOTE: **winding - wound**
◇ **winding up** *noun* liquidation *or* closing of a company and selling its assets; **a compulsory winding up order** = order from a court saying that a company must be wound up

window *noun* opening in a wall, with glass in it; **shop window** = large window in a shop front, where customers can see goods displayed; **window display** = display of goods in a shop window; **window envelope** = envelope with a hole in it covered with plastic like a window, so that the address on the letter inside can be seen; **window shopping** = looking at goods in shop windows, without buying anything
◇ **window dressing** *noun* **(a)** putting goods on display in a shop window, so that they attract customers **(b)** putting on a display to make a business seem better *or*

more profitable *or* more efficient than it really is

wire 1 *noun* telegram; **to send someone a wire 2** *verb* to send a telegram to (someone); **he wired the head office to say that the deal had been signed**

withdraw *verb* **(a)** to take (money) out of an account; **to withdraw money from the bank** *or* **from your account; you can withdraw up to £50 from any bank on presentation of a banker's card (b)** to take back (an offer); **one of the company's backers has withdrawn** = he stopped supporting the company financially; **to withdraw a takeover bid; the chairman asked him to withdraw the remarks he has made about the finance director**
NOTE: **withdrawing - withdrew - has withdrawn**
◇ **withdrawal** *noun* removing money from an account; **withdrawal without penalty at seven days' notice** = money can be taken out of a deposit account, without losing any interest, provided that seven days' notice has been given; **to give seven days' notice of withdrawal**

withholding tax *noun* (i) tax which takes money away from interest *or* dividend before it is paid to the investor; (ii) *US* income tax deducted from the paycheck of a worker before he is paid

within *preposition* inside

witness 1 *noun* person who sees something happen; **to act as a witness to a document** *or* **a signature** = to sign a document to show that you have watched the main signatory sign it; **the MD signed as a witness; the contract has to be signed in front of two witnesses 2** *verb* to sign (a document) to show that you guarantee that the other signatures on it are genuine; **to witness an agreement** *or* **a signature**

wording *noun* series of words; **did you read the wording on the contract?**
NOTE: no plural

word-processing *noun* working with words, using a computer to produce, check and change texts, reports, letters, etc.; **load the word-processing program before you start keyboarding; word-processing**

bureau = office which specializes in word-processing for other companies
NOTE: no plural

◊ **word-processor** *noun* small computer *or* typewriter with a computer in it, used for working with words to produce texts, reports, letters, etc.

work 1 *noun* (a) things done using the hands *or* brain; **casual work** = work where the workers are hired for a short period; **clerical work** = work done in an office; **manual work** = heavy work done by hand; **work in progress** = value of goods being manufactured which are not complete at the end of an accounting period (b) job *or* something done to earn money; **he goes to work by bus; she never gets home from work before 8 p.m.; his work involves a lot of travelling; he is still looking for work; she has been out of work for six months; work permit** = official document which allows someone who is not a citizen to work in a country
NOTE: no plural
2 *verb* (a) to do things with your hands *or* brain, for money; **the factory is working hard to complete the order; she works better now that she has been promoted; to work a machine** = to make a machine function; **to work to rule** = to work strictly according to rules agreed between the company and the trade union, and therefore work very slowly (b) to have a paid job; **she works in an office; he works at Smith's; he is working as a cashier in a supermarket**

◊ **worker** *noun* (a) person who is employed; **blue-collar worker** = manual worker in a factory; **casual worker** = worker who can be hired for a short period; **clerical worker** = person who works in an office; **factory worker** = person who works in a factory; **manual worker** = worker who works with his hands; **white-collar worker** = office worker; **worker director** = director of a company who is a representative of the workforce; **worker representation on the board** = having a representative of the workers as a director of the company (b) person who works hard; **she's a real worker**

◊ **working** *adjective* (a) (person) who works; **the working population of a country; working partner** = partner who works in a partnership; **working party** =

group of experts who study a problem; **the government set up a working party to examine the problem of computers in schools** (b) referring to work; **working capital** = capital in cash and stocks needed for a company to be able to work; **working conditions** = general state of the place where people work (if it is hot, noisy, dark, dangerous, etc.); **the normal working week** = the usual number of hours worked per week; **even though he is a freelance, he works a normal working week**

◊ **workforce** *noun* all the workers (in an office *or* factory)

◊ **workload** *noun* amount of work which a person has to do; **he has difficulty in coping with his heavy workload**

◊ **workman** *noun* man who works with his hands
NOTE: plural is **workmen**

◊ **work out** *verb* (a) to calculate; **he worked out the costs on the back of an envelope; he worked out the discount at 15%; she worked out the discount on her calculator** (b) **he is working out his notice** = he is working during the time between resigning and actually leaving the company

◊ **workplace** *noun* place where you work

◊ **works** *noun* factory; **an industrial works; an engineering works; the steel works is expanding; works committee** *or* **works council** = committee of workers and management which discusses the organization of work in a factory; **price ex works** = price not including transport from the manufacturer's factory; **the works manager** = person in charge of a works
NOTE: not plural, and takes a singular verb

◊ **work-sharing** *noun* system where two part-timers share one job

◊ **workshop** *noun* small factory

◊ **workspace** *noun* memory *or* space available on a computer for temporary work

◊ **workstation** *noun* desk with a computer terminal, printer, telephone, etc., where a word-processing operator works

◊ **work-to-rule** *noun* working strictly according to the rules agreed between the union and management and therefore very slowly, as a protest

world *noun* **(a)** the earth; **the world market for steel** = the possible sales of steel in the whole world; **he has world rights to a product** = he has the right to sell the product anywhere in the world **(b)** people in a particular business *or* people with a special interest; **the world of big business; the world of publishing** *or* **the publishing world; the world of lawyers** *or* **the legal world**

◊ **World Bank** *noun* central bank, controlled by the United Nations, whose funds come from the member states of the UN and which lends money to member states

◊ **worldwide** *adjective & adverb* everywhere in the world; **the company has a worldwide network of distributors; worldwide sales** *or* **sales worldwide have topped two million units; this make of computer is available worldwide**

worth **1** *adjective* having a value *or* a price; **do not get it repaired - it is worth only £25; the car is worth £6,000 on the secondhand market; he is worth £10m** = his property *or* investments, etc. would sell for £10m; **what are ten pounds worth in dollars?** = what is the equivalent of £10 in dollars?
NOTE: always follows the verb **to be**
2 *noun* value; **give me ten pounds' worth of petrol** = give me as much petrol as £10 will buy

◊ **worthless** *adjective* having no value; **the cheque is worthless if it is not signed**

wrap (up) *verb* to cover something all over (in paper); **he wrapped (up) the parcel**

in green paper; to gift-wrap a present = to wrap a present in special coloured paper
NOTE: **wrapping - wrapped**

◊ **wrapper** *noun* material which wraps something; **the biscuits are packed in plastic wrappers**

◊ **wrapping** *noun* **wrapping paper** = special coloured paper for wrapping presents; **gift-wrapping** = (i) service in a store for wrapping presents for customers; (ii) coloured paper for wrapping presents

wreck **1** *noun* **(a)** ship which has sunk *or* which has been badly damaged and cannot float; **they saved the cargo from the wreck; oil poured out of the wreck of the tanker (b)** company which has collapsed; **he managed to save some of his investment from the wreck of the company; investors lost thousands of pounds in the wreck of the investment company 2** *verb* to damage badly *or* to ruin; **they are trying to salvage the wrecked tanker; the negotiations were wrecked by the unions**

writ *noun* legal document ordering someone to do something *or* not to do something; **the court issued a writ to prevent the trade union from going on strike; to serve someone with a writ** *or* **to serve a writ on someone** = to give someone a writ officially, so that he has to obey it

write *verb* to put words *or* figures on to paper; **she wrote a letter of complaint to the manager; the telephone number is written at the bottom of the notepaper**
NOTE: **writing - wrote - has written**

◊ **write down** *verb* to note an asset at a lower value than previously; **written down value; the car is written down in the company's books**

◊ **writedown** *noun* noting of an asset at a lower value

◊ **write off** *verb* to cancel (a debt) *or* to remove an asset from the accounts as having no value; **to write off bad debts; two cars were written off after the accident** = the insurance company considered that both cars were a total loss; **the cargo was written off as a total loss** = the cargo was so badly damaged that the insurers said it had no value

◊ **write-off** *noun* total loss *or* cancellation of a bad debt *or* removal of an asset's value in a company's accounts; **the car was a write-off; to allow for write-offs**

in the yearly accounts

◇ **write out** *verb* to write in full; **she wrote out the minutes of the meeting from her notes; to write out a cheque** = to write the words and figures on a cheque and then sign it

◇ **writing** *noun* something which has been written; **to put the agreement in writing; he has difficulty in reading my writing**

NOTE: no plural

> QUOTE: $30 million from usual company borrowings will either be amortized or written off in one sum *Australian Financial Review*
>
> QUOTE: the holding company has seen its earnings suffer from big writedowns in conjunction with its $1 billion loan portfolio *Duns Business Month*

wrong *adjective* not right *or* not correct; **the total in the last column is wrong; the sales director reported the wrong figures to the meeting; I tried to phone, but I got the wrong number**

◇ **wrongful** *adjective* unlawful; **wrongful dismissal** = removing someone from a job for reasons which are wrong

◇ **wrongly** *adverb* not correctly *or* badly; **he wrongly invoiced Smith Ltd for £250, when he should have credited them with the same amount**

Xx

X = EXTENSION

Xerox 1 *noun* (a) trade mark for a type of photocopier; **to make a xerox copy of a letter; we must order some more xerox paper for the copier; we are having a new xerox machine installed tomorrow** (b) photocopy made with a xerox machine; **to send the other party a xerox of the contract; we have sent xeroxes to each of the agents 2** *verb* to make a photocopy with a xerox machine; **to xerox a document; she xeroxed all the file**

Yy

yard *noun* (a) measure of length (= 0.91 metres)

NOTE: can be written **yd** after figures: **10yd** (b) factory which builds ships

yd = YARD

year *noun* period of twelve months; **calendar year** = year from January 1st to December 31st; **financial year** = the twelve month period for a firm's accounts; **fiscal year** = twelve month period on which taxes are calculated (in the UK it is April 6th to April 5th of the following year); **year end** = the end of the financial year, when a company's accounts are prepared; **the accounts department has started work on the year-end accounts**

◇ **yearbook** *noun* reference book which is published each year with updated or new information

◇ **yearly** *adjective* happening once a year; **yearly payment; yearly premium of £250**

yellow pages *plural noun* section of a telephone directory (printed on yellow paper) which lists businesses under various headings (such as computer shops or newsagents, etc.)

yen *noun* money used in Japan

NOTE: usually written as **Y** before a figure: **Y2,700** (say "two thousand seven hundred yen")

yield 1 *noun* money produced as a return on an investment; **current yield** = dividend calculated as a percentage of the price paid per share; **share with a current yield of 5%; dividend yield** = dividend expressed as a percentage of the price of a share; **earnings yield** = money earned in dividends per share as a percentage of the market price of the share; **effective yield** = actual yield shown as a percentage of the price paid; **fixed yield** = fixed percentage return which does not change; **gross yield** = profit from investments before tax is deducted **2** *verb* to produce (as interest *or* dividend, etc.); **government stocks which yield a small interest; shares which yield 10%**

> QUOTE: if you wish to cut your risks you should
> go for shares with yields higher than average
> *Investors Chronicle*

Zz

zero *noun* nought *or* number 0; **the code for international calls is zero one zero (010); zero inflation** = inflation at 0%
NOTE: **nought** is more common in GB English
◇ **zero-rated** *adjective* (item) which has a VAT rate of 0%
◇ **zero-coupon bond** *noun* bond which does not carry any interest *or* where the interest is contained in the capital gain
◇ **zero-rating** *noun* rating of an item at 0% VAT

zip code *noun* *US* letters and numbers used to indicate a town or street in an address on an envelope
NOTE: the GB English for this is **postcode**

zone **1** *noun* area of a town *or* country (for administrative purposes); **development zone** *or* **enterprise zone** = area which has been given special help from the government to encourage businesses and factories to set up there; **free trade zone** = area where there are no customs duties **2** *verb* to divide (a town) into different areas for planning purposes; **land zoned for light industrial use** = land where planning permission has been given to build small factories for light industry

Numbers

you write	you say
0	zero *or* nought *or* oh
0.4[1]	point four *or* nought point four
0.5126[2]	nought point five one two six
¼	one quarter *or* (informal) a quarter
½	one half *or* (informal) a half
¾	three quarters
5/16	five sixteenths
1	one
2	two
3	three
4	four
5	five
6	six
7	seven
8	eight
9	nine
10	ten
12	twelve *or* (informal) one dozen[3] *or* a dozen
15	fifteen *or* one-five[4]
50	fifty *or* five-oh
67	sixty-seven
100	one hundred *or* (informal) a hundred
106	one hundred and six[5] *or* (US) one hundred six
556	five hundred and fifty-six
1000	one thousand *or* (informal) a thousand *or* one K
5001	five thousand and one[6]
10,000	ten thousand
1,000,000 *or* 1m	one million *or* (informal) a million
1000,000,000 *or* 1bn	one billion *or* (informal) a billion
	Telephone
01-608-9940[7]	oh one, six oh eight, double nine four oh
	Year
1987	nineteen eighty-seven
1621	sixteen twenty-one
2000	the year two thousand
1905	nineteen five *or* nineteen hundred and five *or* nineteen oh five
	Date
2.1.70[8]	the second of January nineteen seventy *or*
2/1/70	(US) the first of February nineteen seventy
2 Jan 70	
2 January 1970	the second of January, nineteen seventy
2nd January, 1970	
	Code number
1600	sixteen hundred *or* one six oh oh *or* one six zero zero
45038	four five oh three eight

Note
1. The point (.) is used to show decimals. The comma (,) to show thousands or millions or billions
2. After the decimal point you read number by number
3. The plural is 'two dozen', 'three dozen', etc
4. The difference between numbers like 13 (thirteen) and 30 (thirty) is sometimes difficult to hear so it may be necessary to say 'one-three', 'three-oh' when repeating
5. 'and' is normally said after hundreds; Americans often leave the word out
6. A comma (,) or a space is used to show thousands or millions or billions. There is usually no comma or space in 1000.
7. see also section on *telephone*
8. American dates use the order: month/date/year
   European and British dates use the order: day/month/year

Movement of Numbers

A Graph

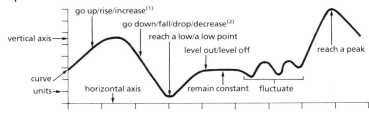

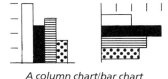
A column chart/bar chart

A pie chart

Note:
1. when describing increase or decrease you can say:

	rose/fell		
"inflation	went up/went down	to	6%"
	increased/decreased		
	went up/went down		
"inflation	increased/decreased	by	4%"
	rose/fell		
"inflation	now stands	at	6%"

2. when describing increase or decrease you can say:

"inflation fell/rose sharply"

"inflation fell/rose gradually"

Measurement

When you describe measurements you say:
"The pipe is five metres (5m) long" *or* "the pipe is five metres in length" *but* "It is a five-metre (5m) pipe".

You can say: "The cable is two hundred feet (200ft) long" *but* "It is a two-hundred-foot (200ft) cable"

The most common measurements are given on the table below:

British and American				Metric	
we say	*we write*			*we say*	*we write*
Length					
inch	in *or* "	0.039	25.40	millimetre	mm
		0.394	2.540	centimetre	cm
foot	ft *or* '	3.218	0.305	metre[1]	m
yard	yd	1.094	0.914		
mile	m *or* mi	0.621	1.609	kilometre	km
Weight					
ounce	oz	0.035	28.350	gram	gm
pound	lb	2.205	0.454	kilogram[2]	kg
hundredweight	cwt	0.196	50.18		
ton		0.984	1.016	metric tonne	tonne
Capacity					
pint	pt	1.70	0.568	litre[1]	l
gallon	gal	0.220	4.546		
Area					
square inch	sq in *or* in^2	0.155	6.452	square centimetre	cm^2
square foot	sq ft *or* ft^2	10.764	0.093	square metre	m^2
square yard	sq yd *or* yd^2	1.196	0.836		
acre		2.471	0.4047	hectare	ha
square mile	sq m *or* mi^2	0.387	2.59	square kilometre	km^2
Volume					
cubic inch	cu in *or* in^3	0.061	16.4	cubic centimetre	cm^3 *or* cc
cubic foot	cu ft *or* ft^3	35.315	0.0283	cubic metre	m^3
cubic yard	cu yd *or* yd^3	1.308	0.765		

Note
1. metre, litre, etc=US: "meter, liter", etc.
2. informal: 'kilo'

Abbreviations

You can find abbreviations of business terms in the body of the dictionary and abbreviations of measurements in the measurement section.
These are commonly used abbreviations[1]. If the abbreviation is marked (*), you can *say* it as well as *write* it[2].

a/c *or* acc *or* acct	account
a.m.* *or* am	in the morning, before midday
approx	approximately
arr	arrival or arrived
cc	copies (on a letter, to show that copies of the letter have been sent
c/o*	care of (on an address to show that the person lives at the address but only as a visitor)
COD* *or* c.o.d.	cash on delivery
cont *or* cont'd	continued
dep *or* dept	department
ditto *or* do	the same (to show that an item, for example in a list, is the same as the previous one)
e.g.* *or* eg	for example
encl *or* enc	enclosure (on a letter, to show that another written paper has been sent in the same envelope)
esp	especially
et al	and others
etc	etcetera, and so on
fig	figure
HQ*[3]	headquarters
i.e.*	that is, in other words
K*	thousand
max	maximum
misc	miscellaneous, mixed and various
NB	note, take special note that...
no	number
ono *or* o.n.o	or near offer (after a price)
p.m.* *or* pm	in the afternoon, in the evening, after 12 midday
ps *or* PS	post script (in a letter, to introduce an added message after the signature)
qty	quantity
recd	received
re* *or* ref	reference, with reference to
RSVP	please reply (on an invitation)
SAE *or* sae	stamped addressed envelope
tel	telephone
v *or* vs	versus, against
wk	week
x *or* ext	extension (after a telephone number)

Note:

1. abbreviations can be written in different ways and sometimes the same letters can have more than one meaning:

m	million *or* mile *or* metre
min	minimum *or* minute
MD	managing director* *or* doctor of medicine
p.a. *or* P.A.	per annum (every year) *or* personal assistant*
pp*	on behalf of (used on letters below a signature when one person signs on behalf of another) or pages

2. in modern English writing, many abbreviations can be written with or without punctuation, in capital letters or small letters:

fmcg *or* FMCG *or* F.M.C.G. fast-moving customer goods

plc *or* p.l.c. *or* PLC *or* P.L.C. public limited company

3. you say *a* headquarters, but *an* HQ

   a managing director, but *an* MD

PUNCTUATION

.	full stop *or* point, US: period	-	dash *or* hyphen
,	comma	/	stroke *or* oblique *or* solidus
:	colon	( )	brackets
;	semi-colon	[ ]	square brackets

SYMBOLS		ROMAN NUMERALS	
%	per cent	I *or* i	1
°	degrees	II *or* ii	2
=	equals	III *or* iii	3
≈	is approximately equal to	IV *or* iv	4
≠	is not equal to	V *or* v	5
<	is less than	VI *or* vi	6
>	is more than	VII *or* vii	7
+	plus	VIII *or* viii	8
−	minus	IX *or* ix	9
÷	divided by	X *or* x	10
×	multiplied by	XI *or* xi	11
∴	therefore	XX *or* xx	20
&	and	L	50
∝	infinity	C	100
√	root	D	500
		M	1000

Business Letters

A letter to a company

printed letterhead
(company name, address,
postcode, telephone and
telex numbers

company name & address

reference codes

"salutation" or opening
phrase[1]

opening sentence

text

closing sentence

"complimentary close"[2]

writer's signature

name and position of writer

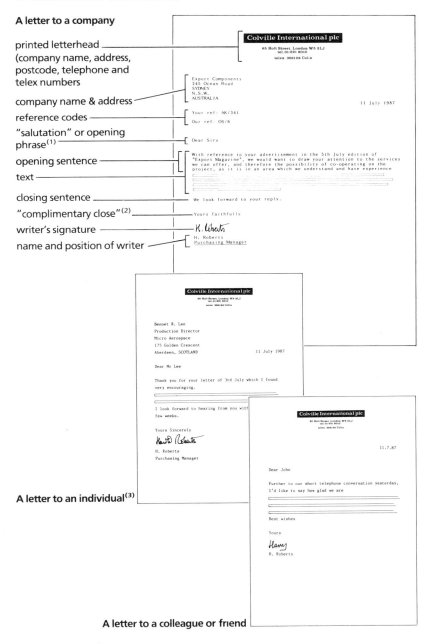

A letter to an individual[3]

A letter to a colleague or friend

Note:
1. In modern business letters punctuation is kept to a minimum. Commas (,) are possible after "Dear Sir", "Yours faithfully", etc, but are not necessary.
2. If you begin a letter "Dear Sir", you must end with "Yours faithfully". If you begin "Dear Mr X", you must end with "Yours sincerely" or "Sincerely yours".
3. If you are writing to a woman, begin the letter "Dear Madam" if you don't know her name. If you know her name, you can begin "Dear Miss X" or "Dear Mrs X", but many women now prefer "Dear Ms X". (Ms is pronounce "Miz")
4. For business and personal letters in English many styles and layouts are acceptable. The examples shown here are probably the most common and widely accepted forms.

The Telephone

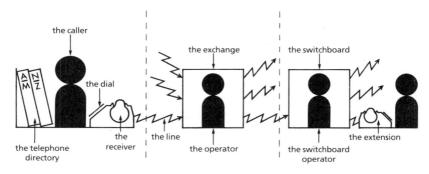

we write: **(44) 01-221 6010 ×142**

we say: "four four, oh one, two two one, six oh one oh, extension one four two"

Certain key phrases are used in most telephone conversations. Opposite are three model telephone calls and five phrases used when there are problems on the line.

Note:
1. American: 'speak *with*'
2. = it is difficult to hear
3. 'You are speaking too quietly'
4. 'You are speaking too quickly'

Financial Documents

British cheque-American check

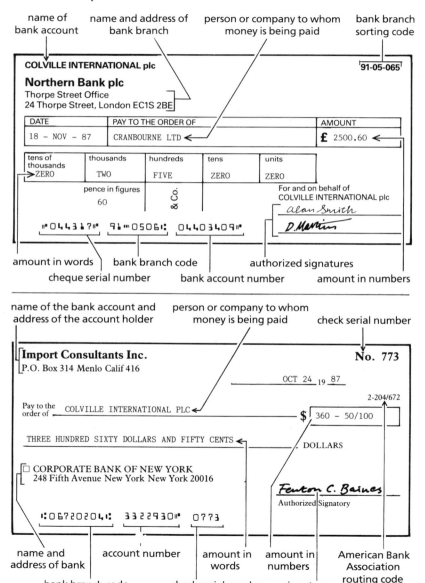

name of bank account

name and address of bank branch

person or company to whom money is being paid

bank branch sorting code

COLVILLE INTERNATIONAL plc

Northern Bank plc
Thorpe Street Office
24 Thorpe Street, London EC1S 2BE

'91-05-065'

DATE	PAY TO THE ORDER OF		AMOUNT
18 – NOV – 87	CRANBOURNE LTD		£ 2500.60

tens of thousands	thousands	hundreds	tens	units
ZERO	TWO	FIVE	ZERO	ZERO

pence in figures
60

& Co.

For and on behalf of
COLVILLE INTERNATIONAL plc

Alan Smith

D. Martin

⑂044317⑂ 91⑂0506⑊ 04403409⑂

amount in words

cheque serial number

bank branch code

bank account number

authorized signatures

amount in numbers

---

name of the bank account and address of the account holder

person or company to whom money is being paid

check serial number

Import Consultants Inc.
P.O. Box 314 Menlo Calif 416

No. 773

OCT 24 19 87

2-204/672

Pay to the order of   COLVILLE INTERNATIONAL PLC

$ 360 – 50/100

THREE HUNDRED SIXTY DOLLARS AND FIFTY CENTS

DOLLARS

☐ CORPORATE BANK OF NEW YORK
248 Fifth Avenue New York New York 20016

Fenton C. Baines

Authorized Signatory

⑊067202044⑊ 3322930⑂ 0773

name and address of bank

account number

amount in words

amount in numbers

American Bank Association routing code

bank branch code

check serial number

signature

The balance sheet

A balance sheet shows the financial position of a company at a particular time, such as the end of a financial year or the end of a quarter:

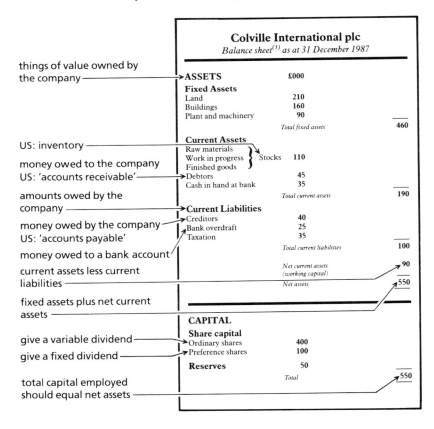

Colville International plc
Balance sheet[1] as at 31 December 1987

things of value owned by the company → **ASSETS** £000

Fixed Assets
Land	210
Buildings	160
Plant and machinery	90
Total fixed assets	460

US: inventory — **Current Assets**

Raw materials
Work in progress } Stocks 110
Finished goods

money owed to the company
US: 'accounts receivable' → Debtors 45
Cash in hand at bank 35
Total current assets 190

amounts owed by the company → **Current Liabilities**

money owed by the company → Creditors 40
Bank overdraft 25
US: 'accounts payable' Taxation 35
money owed to a bank account *Total current liabilities* 100

Net current assets (working capital) 90

current assets less current liabilities — *Net assets* 550

fixed assets plus net current assets —

CAPITAL

Share capital
give a variable dividend → Ordinary shares 400
give a fixed dividend → Preference shares 100

Reserves 50
Total 550

total capital employed should equal net assets —

Note:
1. This is the normal layout of a modern balance sheet. The balance sheet can also be arranged:

CAPITAL LIABILITIES	ASSETS
___	___
Total	Total

or

CAPITAL
___ Total
ASSETS
___ Total

The bank statement

name of bank where
account is held

name of bank branch

number of statement

name and address of
account holder

period covered by
statement

serial number of account

details of deposits and
withdrawals

money out of the account
(debit)

money paid into the
account (credit)

* (or 'C' or 'CR') means the
account is in credit; 'DR' or
('OD') means the account is
overdrawn

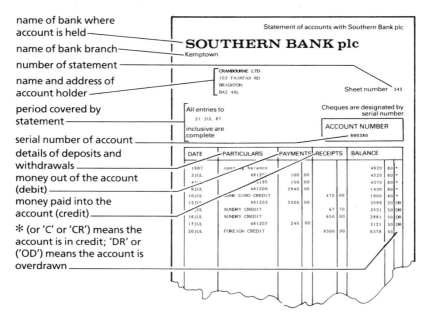

Statement of accounts with Southern Bank plc

SOUTHERN BANK plc
Kemptown

CRANBOURNE LTD
103 FAIRFAX RD
BRIGHTON
BA2 4XL

Sheet number 342

All entries to
21 JUL 87
inclusive are
complete

Cheques are designated by
serial number

ACCOUNT NUMBER
600380

DATE	PARTICULARS	PAYMENTS		RECEIPTS		BALANCE		
1987	opening balance					4620	80	*
3 JUL	481200	100	00			4520	80	*
4 JUL	195	150	00			4370	80	*
6 JUL	481200	2940	00			1430	80	*
10 JUL	BANK GIRO CREDIT			470	00	1900	80	*
12 JUL	481203	5500	00			3599	20	DR
JUL	SUNDRY CREDIT			67	70	3531	50	DR
16 JUL	SUNDRY CREDIT			650	00	2881	50	DR
17 JUL	481207	240	00			3121	50	DR
20 JUL	FOREIGN CREDIT			9500	00	6378	50	*

The profit and loss account

A profit and loss account
shows the income and
expenditure of a company
over a particular period
balanced to show the pre-
tax profit (or loss) made by
the company:

Cranbourne Limited

PROFIT AND LOSS ACCOUNT
Year ending 31 December 1987

	£000	£000	£000
Sales income		853	
Cost of sales			
Materials	340		
Labour	300		
		640	
Gross margin (profit)			213
Expenses			
Salaries	30		
Distribution	30		
Advertising	18		
Administration	25		
Financial charges	15		
Rent and rates			
Heat Overheads	35		
Light			
Depreciation	10		
		163	
Profit before tax			50

Money

British		American	
you write	*you say*	*you write*	*you say*
1p	one penny *or* one pence *or* one p	1¢ $0.1	one cent
56p £0.56	fifty six pence *or* fifty six p	56¢	fifty six cents
£1	a pound *or* one pound	$1	a dollar *or* one dollar
£1.20	one pound twenty *or* one pound and twenty pence	$1.20	one dollar twenty *or* one dollar and twenty cents
£3.75	three pounds seventy five *or* three pounds (and) seventy five pence	$3.75	three dollars seventy five *or* three dollars and seventy five cents
£5m	five million pounds	$3bn	three billion dollars
£5.5m	five point five million pounds *or* five and a half million pounds *or* five million, five hundred thousand pounds		

Note:
1. The letters 'p' and ¢ are written when no pounds or dollars are shown
2. A decimal point is used to divide pounds from pence and dollars from cents. A comma is used after millions and thousands: $15,621,202.75
3. You say: 'The bonus is worth two thousand pounds' but 'it is a two thousand pound bonus'
4. When we write, the symbol or abbreviation ($, DM, F, etc) comes first, when we say the figure, the number comes first

In the list of world currencies that follows, words marked (*) usually have no plural e.g. 1 kyat, 'one kyat', 200 kyat, 'two hundred kyat'

Country	Currency	Divided into	Abbreviation
Afghanistan	Afghani*	puli	Af *or* Afs
Albania	Lek*	qindars	Lk
Algeria	Algerian dinar	centimes	AD *or* DA
Andorra	French Franc	centimes	
Angola	Kwanza*	cents	KW
Antigua	East Caribbean Dollar	cents	ECar$ *or* EC$
Argentina	Austral	centavos	
Australia	Australian Dollar	cents	A$
Austria	Schilling	groschen	Sch *or* ASch
Bahamas	Bahamian Dollar	cents	Ba$
Bahrein	Bahreini Dinar	fils	BD

Country	Currency	Divided into	Abbreviation
Bangladesh	Taka*	poisha	Tk
Barbados	Barbados Dollar	cents	Bds$ BD$
Belgium	Belgian Franc	centimes	BFr or Bf or FB
Belize	Belize Dollar	cents	B$ or $B
Benin	CFA Franc	centimes	CFA Fr
Bermuda	Bermuda Dollar	cents	Bda$
Bhutan	Ngultrum*	tikchung	N
Bolivia	Bolivian peso	centavos	B$ or $b
Botswana	Pula	cents	Pu or P
Brazil	Cruzeiro	centavos	Cr or Cr$
Brunei	Brunei Dollar	cents	Br$ or B$
Bulgaria	Lev*	stotinki	Lv
Burkina Faso	CFA Franc	centimes	CFA Fr
Burma	Kyat*	pyas	Kt
Burundi	Burundi Franc	centimes	Bur Fr or FrBr
Cambodia (see Kampuchea)			
Cameroon	CFA Franc	centimes	CFA Fr
Canada	Canadian Dollar	cents	Can$ or C$
Cape Verde Islands	Escudo Caboverdianos	centavos	CV esc
Cayman Islands	Cayman Island Dollar	cents	CayI$
Central African Republic	CFA Franc	centimes	CFA Fr
Chad	Cfa Franc	centimes	CFA Fr
Chile	Chilean Peso	centavos	Ch$
China	Yuan* or renminbi*	fen	Y
Colombia	Colombian Peso	centavos	Col$
Comoros	CFA Franc	centimes	CFA Fr
Congo	CFA Franc	centimes	CFA Fr
Costa Rica	Colón*	centimos	CR¢ or ¢
Cuba	Cuban Peso	centavos	Cub$
Cyprus	Cyprus Pound	Mils	£C or C£
Czechoslovakia	Crown or Koruna	hellers, halern	Kčs
Dahomey (see Benin)			
Denmark	Krone	örer	DKr or DKK
Djibouti	Djibouti Franc	centimes	Dj Fr
Dominica	East Caribbean Dollar	cents	ECar$ or EC$
Dominican Republic	Dominican Peso	centavos	DR$
Ecuador	Sucre*	centavos	Su
Egypt	Egyptian Pound	piastres	£E or E£
Eire (see Irish Republic)			
El Salvador	Colón*	centavos	ES¢ or ¢
Equatorial Guinea	Ekuele* or ekpwele or peseta Guineana	centimos	E
Ethiopia	Birr* or Ethiopian Dollar	cents	Br
Fiji	Fijian Dollar	cents	$F or F$
Finland	Marakka* or Finnmark	pennia	Fmk
France	French Franc	centimes	Fr or F or FF
French Guiana	French Franc	centimes	Fr or F or FF

Country	Currency	Divided into	Abbreviation
Gabon	CFA Franc	centimes	CFA Fr
Gambia, The	Dalasi*	butut	Di
Germany			
East – Democratic Republic	Ostmark *or* DDR-Mark	pfennig	M
West – Federal Republic	Deutsche Mark	pfennig	DM
Ghana	Cedi*	pesewas	¢
Great Britain (see note above)			
Greece	Drachma	lepta	Dr
Grenada	East Caribbean Dollar	cents	ECar$ *or* EC$
Guatemala	Quetzal	centavos	Q
Guinea	Syli*	cauris	Sy
Guinea – Bissau	Guinea – Bissau Peso	centavos	GB P
Guyana	Guyana Dollar	cents	G$ *or* Guy$
Haiti	Gourde*	centimes	Gde
Holland (see Netherlands)			
Honduras	Lempira*	centavos	La
Hong Kong	Hong Kong Dollar	cents	HK$
Hungary	Forint	filler	Ft
Iceland	Króna	aurar	IKr
India	Rupee	paise	R *or* Re *or* Rs
Indonesia	Rupiah*	sen	Rp
Iran	Rial*	dinars	RI
Iraq	Iraqui Dinar	fils	ID
Irish Republic	Irish Pound *or* Punt	pence	IR£ *or* £
Israel	Shekel	agorot	IS
Italy	Lira	centesimi	L
Ivory Coast	CFA Franc	centimes	CFA Fr
Jamaica	Jamaican Dollar	cents	J$ *or* Jam$
Japan	Yen*	sen	Y *or* ¥
Jordan	Jordanian Dinar	fils	JD
Kampuchea	Riel*	sen	RI
Kenya	Kenyan Shilling	cents	KSh *or* Sh
Korea:			
North Korea	North Korean Won*	jon	NK W
South Korea	South Korean Won*	chon	SK W
Kuwait	Kuwaiti Dinar	fils	KD
Laos	Kip*	at	K *or* Kp
Lebanon	Lebanese Pound	piastres	£Leb *or* L£
Lesotho	Loti*	lisente	L
Liberia	Liberian Dollar	cents	L$
Libya	Libyan dinar	dirhams	LD
Liechtenstein	Swiss Franc	centimes	SFr *or* FS
Luxembourg	Luxembourg Franc	centimes	LFr
Macau	Pataca*	avos	P *or* $
Madeira	Portuguese Escudo	centavos	Esc
Malagasy Republic	Malagasy Franc	centimes	FMG *or* Mal Fr

Country	Currency	Divided into	Abbreviation
Malawi	Kwacha*	tambala	K or MK
Malaysia	Ringgit* or Malaysian Dollar	cents	M$
Maldives	Maldivian Rupee	paise	MvRe
Mali	Mali Franc	centimes	MFr or MF
Malta	Maltese Pound	cents	£M or M£
Mauritania	Ouguiya*	khoums	U
Mauritius	Mauritian Rupee	cents	Mau Rs or R
Mexico	Peso	centavos	Mex$
Monaco	French Franc	centimes	Fr or F or FF
Mongolian Republic	Tugrik*	möngös	Tug
Montserrat	E. Caribbean Dollar	cents	ECar$ or EC$
Morocco	Dirham	centimes	Dh or DH
Mozambique	Metical*	centavos	M
Namibia	South African Rand	cents	R
Nauru	Australian Dollar	cents	A$
Nepal	Nepalese Rupee	Paise	NR or NRe
Netherlands, The	Guilder or Gulden or Florin	cents	HFl or DFl or Gld or Fl
New Hebrides (see Vanuatu)			
New Zealand	New Zealand Dollar	cents	NZ$
Nicaragua	Córdoba	centavos	C$ or C
Niger	CFA Franc	centimes	CFA Fr
Nigeria	Naira*	kobo	N or ₦
Norway	Krone	örer	NKr
Oman	Omani Ryal or Rial	baizas	RO
Pakistan	Pakistan rupee	paise	R or Pak Re
Panama	Balboa	centesimos	Ba
Papua New Guinea	Kina*	toea	Ka or K
Paraguay	Guaraní*	centimos	G
Peru	Sol*	centavos	S
Philippines	Philippine Peso	centavos	P or PP
Poland	Zloty*	groszy	Zl
Portugal	Escudo	centavos	Esc
Puerto Rico	US Dollar	cents	$ or US$
Qatar	Qatar Riyal	dirhams	QR
Reunion	CFA Franc	centimes	CFA Fr
Romania	Leu*	bani	L or l
Rwanda	Rwanda Franc	centimes	Rw Fr
St Lucia	E. Caribbean Dollar	cents	ECar$ or EC$
St Vincent	E. Caribbean Dollar	cents	ECar$ or EC$
Saudi Arabia	Saudi Riyal or Rial	halalah	SA R
Senegal	CFA Franc	centimes	CFA Fr
Seychelles	Seychelles Rupee	cents	SRe or R
Sierra Leone	Leone	cents	Le
Singapore	Singapore Dollar	cents	S$ or Sing$
Solomon Islands	Solomon Island Dollar	cents	SI$
Somalia	Somali Shilling	cents	Som Sh or So Sh

Country	Currency	Divided into	Abbreviation
South Africa	Rand*	cents	R
Spain	Peseta	centimos	Pta
Sri Lanka	Sri Lanka Rupee	cents	SC Re
Sudan	Sudanese Pound	piastres	Sud£ or £S
Surinam	Surinam Guilder	cents	S Gld
Swaziland	Lilangeni*	cents	Li or E
Sweden	Krona	örer	SKr
Switzerland	Swiss Franc	centimes	SFr or FS or SWFr
Syria	Syrian Pound	piastres	£Syr or S£
Taiwan	New Taiwan Dollar	cents	T$ or NT$
Tanzania	Tanzanian Shilling	cents	TSh
Thailand	Baht*	satang	Bt
Tonga	Pa'anga*	senik	
Togo	CFA Franc	centimes	CFA Fr
Trinidad & Tobago	Trinidad & Tobago Dollar	cents	TT$
Tunisia	Tunisian Dinar	millimes	TD
Turkey	Turkish Lira	kurus	TL
Tuvalu	Australian Dollar	cents	$A
Uganda	Uganda Shilling	cents	USh
Union of Soviet Socialist Republics	Rouble	kopecks	Rub
United Arab Emirates	UAE Dirham	fils	UAE Dh or UD
United Kingdom	Pound (Sterling)	pence	£ or £Stg
United States of America	Dollar	cents	$ or US$
Upper Volta (see Burkina Faso)			
Uruguay	Uruguayan New Peso	centesimos	N$
Vanuatu			
Venezuela		vatu	
Vietnam	Bolívar	centimos	B
Virgin Islands	Dong*	xu	D
Western Samoa	US Dollar	cents	$ or US$
	Tala or Dollar or Western Samoan Dollar	cents or sene	WS$ or $WS
Yemen:			
South Yemen	South Yemen Dinar	fils	YD
Northern Yemen	Yemeni Riyal	fils	YR
Yugoslavia	Dinar	paras	Din or DN
Zaire	Zaire	makata	Z
Zambia	Kwacha*	ngwee	K
Zimbabwe	Zimbabwe Dollar	cents	Z$